International Trade and Payments

W. M. Scammell

ST. MARTIN'S PRESS NEW YORK

© W. M. Scammell 1974

All rights reserved. For information, write:
St. Martin's Press, Inc., 175 Fifth Avenue, New York, N.Y. 10010
Printed in Great Britain
Library of Congress Catalog Card Number: 73–87879
First published in the United States of America in 1974

AFFILIATED PUBLISHERS: Macmillan Limited, London—
also at Bombay, Calcutta, Madras and Melbourne

INTERNATIONAL TRADE AND PAYMENTS

By the same author

INTERNATIONAL MONETARY POLICY (1957 and 1961)
THE LONDON DISCOUNT MARKET (1968)

*'The why of the world is an
answerless riddle
Puzzlesome, tiresome, hard to
unriddle.'*
                                JAMES JOYCE

Contents

PREFACE	xi
Abbreviations and Acronyms	xiii
1 Introduction	1

Part One
THE PURE THEORY OF INTERNATIONAL TRADE

2 The Aims and the Tools	13
(i) What the pure theory is about	13
(ii) The basic questions – comparative advantage	15
(iii) Conclusion	27
3 Supply, Demand, and the Gains from Trade	28
(i) Supply with constant costs	28
(ii) Other cost patterns	35
(iii) Transport costs; technological change	44
(iv) Demand	52
(v) Conclusion	64
Appendix: the offer (or reciprocal demand) curve	66
4 Factor Endowments: Commodity and Factor Prices	73
(i) Introduction	73
(ii) Factor endowments	74
(iii) Production functions and box diagrams	78
(iv) The Heckscher–Ohlin theorem	99
(v) Factor-price equalisation	110
5 Putting Theory to the Test: Empirical Studies	113
(i) Introduction	113
(ii) The classical theory and the Heckscher–Ohlin theorem	114
(iii) Empirical testing	120
(iv) The terms of trade	127

Part Two
COMMERCIAL POLICY

6 Tariffs	137
(i) Tariffs: the mechanism	137
(ii) Tariffs: the effects	141
7 Free Trade and Protection	169
(i) Introduction	169
(ii) The free trade versus protection controversy	171
(iii) Getting nearer to free trade: trade liberalisation	179
(iv) The second best	184
8 The Theory of Customs Unions	189
(i) Customs union theory	189
(ii) The effects on trade, production, and consumption	191
(iii) The general equilibrium analysis	203
(iv) The dynamic effects	210
(v) Some practical implications	213
9 Trade and the Nature of the Market	219
(i) Introduction	219
(ii) Monopoly and imperfect competition in international trade	220
(iii) Trade practices and their effect on the market	228
(iv) State trading	234

Part Three
THE ECONOMICS OF THE BALANCE OF PAYMENTS

I The Description and Measurement of Payments

10 The Elements of an International Monetary System	245
(i) The four elements	245
(ii) The forms of international money	247
(iii) The institutional arrangements of international finance	250
(iv) The need for an adjustment mechanism	253
(v) Leadership and control of the international economy	258
(vi) Conclusion	263

Contents ix

11 The Balance of Payments: Cross-section of a Nation's Trade 266
   (i) Surplus and deficit 266
   (ii) Balance-of-payments disequilibrium 279
   (iii) Causes of disequilibrium 286

II Adjustment of a Country's Balance of Payments

12 The Role of the Price Mechanism in Adjustment 291
   (i) The nature of the adjustment problem 291
   (ii) Adjustment: the classical approach 297
   (iii) Summing up 317

13 Adjustment and Income Analysis 319
   (i) A Keynesian approach 319
   (ii) The import and export functions 321
   (iii) National income in a closed and an open economy 324
   (iv) Diagrammatic analysis of the open economy 332
   (v) National income adjustment and the balance of payments 339
   (vi) Monetary factors and income adjustment 340
   (vii) Conclusion 346

14 The Interaction of Price and Income Changes 348
   (i) The need for a synthesis 348
   (ii) Second thoughts on elasticity 349
   (iii) The absorption approach 352
   (iv) The payments approach 357
   (v) The critics of absorption 362
   (vi) Conclusion 369

15 Adjustment and International Capital Movements 370
   (i) Statement of the problem 370
   (ii) The classical theory 372
   (iii) The modern theory 374
   (iv) The terms of trade 380
   (v) Conclusion 385

16 Internal and External Equilibrium 387
   (i) The conflicting aims of economic policy 387
   (ii) Expenditure-switching and expenditure-changing 389
   (iii) The coupling of monetary and fiscal policy 396
   (iv) The distribution between countries of the burden of adjustment 401
   (v) Conclusion 407

III Some Current Account Problems

17 Trade and National Currencies: the Foreign Exchange
   Market   411
   (i) The foreign exchange market   411
   (ii) The *modus operandi* of international payments   426
   (iii) The determination of the foreign exchange rate   428
   (iv) The Euro-dollar market   441

18 Exchange Rate Policy   445
   (i) Introduction   445
   (ii) The equilibrium exchange rate   445
   (iii) The systems of adjustment   455
   (iv) Adjustments in domestic income and prices   457
   (v) Free rates of exchange   460
   (vi) Managed flexibility   473
   (vii) The choice of an adjustment system   482

19 Direct Controls on Trade and Payments   485
   (i) Introduction   485
   (ii) The mechanism of control   488
   (iii) Uses and abuses   504

20 Adjustment and International Liquidity   508
   (i) Introduction   508
   (ii) The nature and need of international liquidity   508
   (iii) The gold standard and the gold exchange standard   525
   (iv) Conclusion   534

21 The Bretton Woods System and the International
   Monetary Fund   536
   (i) Introduction   536
   (ii) The model and operation of the Fund   536
   (iii) Reform of the Fund   550
   (iv) The present position   555

NOTES   557
BIBLIOGRAPHICAL NOTE   574
INDEX   597

Preface

THIS book has been international in the writing as well as the content for it has been written in many places. Begun on the beautiful campus of the University of California at Santa Barbara, completed at my home university of McMaster in southern Ontario and revised while a visitor at the University of Manchester, it reflects, at least to some degree, work and discussion at these universities.

To my hosts at two of these universities and to my colleagues at the other I owe much for their help, tolerance and interest. The only claim to originality which a textbook may have is that at least it reflects the author's evaluation of his subject and of what within it is worthy of particular attention. Even this claim has been conditioned in the present case by the reactions of students during some years of teaching international trade at the graduate and undergraduate levels. I am convinced that here, as elsewhere in economics, relevance to the problems and confusions of our time is the criterion which must be paramount in this exercise in judicious selection.

Apart from the problems of selection, other constraints operate in the writing of a textbook. One of these is to achieve a balance between the rigour of analysis and format and the diffusion of example and illustrative and institutional material. This problem is exacerbated in that institutional and policy discussion quickly shows its age and loses some of its potency even before the book appears. This dilemma I have tried to meet by concentrating on the theoretical rather than descriptive approach to the subject. At the same time I have been mindful of my own oft-declared philosophy: that theory is only useful in so far as it illuminates fact and points to solutions of practical problems.

I am indebted to many friends and colleagues for their views and opinions during the writing of this book. Most of all I am indebted to my wife for help too great and varied to describe.

Hamilton, W. M. S.
Ontario, 1973

Abbreviations and Acronyms

(a) *International Organisations*

AID	Agency for International Development
Basle Club	Group of Central Bank governors meeting in Basle for monthly meetings of BIS
BIS	Bank for International Settlements
CECM	Central American Common Market
CEEC	Committee for European Economic Co-operation
COMECON	Council for Mutual Economic Aid – an Eastern Bloc trade organisation
ECA	European Co-operation Administration
ECAFE	Economic Commission for Asia and the Far East
ECE	Economic Commission for Europe
ECLA	Economic Commission for Latin America
ECM	European Common Market
ECOSOC	Economic and Social Council of the United Nations
ECSC	European Coal and Steel Community
EEC	European Economic Community
EFTA	European Free Trade Association
EPU	European Payments Union
ERP	European Recovery Programme
EXIMBANK	Export–Import Bank of Washington
FAO	Food and Agricultural Organisation
GATT	General Agreement on Tariffs and Trade
IBRD or World Bank	International Bank for Reconstruction and Development
ICA	International Co-operation Administration
IDA	International Development Association
IDB	Inter-American Development Bank
IFC	International Finance Corporation
ILO	International Labour Organisation
IMF	International Monetary Fund
ITO	International Trade Organisation

LAFTA	Latin American Free Trade Association
MSA	Mutual Security Agency
OECD	Organisation for European Co-operation and Development
OEEC	Organisation for European Economic Co-operation
OSA	Overseas Sterling Area
RSA	Rest of the Sterling Area
SA	Sterling Area
SDR	Special Drawing Rights of the IMF
UN	United Nations
UNCTAD	United Nations Committee for Trade and Development

(b) *Bibliographical Abbreviations*

Professional journals are referred to by the following abbreviations:

AER	*American Economic Review*
EJ	*Economic Journal*
Eca	*Economica*
IFS	*International Financial Statistics* (IMF)
JPE	*Journal of Political Economy*
MS	*Manchester School*
OEP	*Oxford Economic Papers*
QJE	*Quarterly Journal of Economics*
RES	*Review of Economic Studies*

Except where it is otherwise indicated the words 'America' or 'American' in this book refer to the United States.

1
Introduction

> '*The man who needs a textbook will never go far. Men of genius read little, practise much and are self-made.*'
>
> DIDEROT

THIS book is not written for men or women of genius but for ordinary mortals who wish to understand the underlying forces which impel, and the institutions which control and facilitate, the trade of nations. No nation exists, none has ever existed, for itself alone. Trade between nations is one of the oldest features of economic life. Its explanation and analysis is one of the most necessary tasks of economics and needs no justification.

It is, however, necessary to justify international economics as a distinct subject – an empire which specialist international economists seem to have established for themselves, separate from, but on friendly terms with, the homeland of general economics. Such a differentiation is only justified if there are qualitative differences between the laws and forces which govern trade when it crosses national boundaries and those which govern exchange within national borders.

We need not make heavy weather of this question. One reason for the distinct study of international economics is that by now the development of the whole science of economics has decreed it so and demands it. We study international economics, as Mallory climbed Everest, because 'it is there'. As economics has grown it has ramified and it demands its sub-divisions like any other science. This propagation by fission in economics began early, and international economics was one of its first new particles. Now, with its own literature, its own subdivisions, its own theory, its own empiricism, its distinct integration is too complete to be ignored.

Still, we may persist, it would even now be possible, without intellectual damage to either general economics or international economics, to reunite them. The pure theory which explains in the latter why trade takes place could be handled within the general theory of exchange; international prices and exchange rates be incorporated in price and market theory; international finance in the theory of money; tariffs as an extension of taxation theory in public finance. It would make a large subject-matter, it is true, but at least it is theoretically possible.

But it is impossible not to feel that, by insisting on such a unity and by treating international economics within the corpus of general economics, something essential would be lost. The division between 'general' and 'international' economics may not be justifiable on purely theoretical grounds but it is amply justified when it is recognised that intra-country transactions are, at least on institutional and pragmatic grounds, qualitatively different from those within a single country. External transactions are in essence a transference between different political and legal systems, between different currency and banking control systems, between different trade union and labour situations, between different climates of business and commercial affairs and between different cultural and ethnic conditions. All these differences impose considerations upon the foreign transaction, be it the sale of goods or services, the transfer of factors or the making of payments, which make such transactions qualitatively different from their purely domestic counterparts and worthy of separate consideration.

If one were to seek a single concept which justifies the distinct study of international economics, it would be the concept of national sovereignty. The classical economists saw one characteristic of a nation: that, within it, factors of production were perfectly mobile; while between it and other nations such factors were immobile. This view was basic to their analysis. But such an assumption is often equally applicable to trade and transactions between geographical regions, or even between cognate and cohesive social groups with internal movement but external immobility — groups such as skilled and unskilled labour, or black and white communities within a country practising racial discrimination. The application of trade theory to interregional and intergroup problems has its place, but in considering trade between nations it is the distinctness of political jurisdictions and national policies, with its institutional consequences, which makes international trade qualitatively different from interregional or intergroup trade. The nation becomes the focus of attention and is the specially significant group in trade theory and policy alike.

Foreign trade has always played a major role in economics, although the motive for studying it has differed from period to period. With the writings of the Mercantilists, as economics moved towards self-conscious existence in the seventeenth and eighteenth centuries, it was the wealth to be derived from trade which formed the central theme.[1] In the

Introduction

vigorous youth of the subject in the early nineteenth century the wish of Smith and Ricardo to establish incontrovertibly the benefits of free trade ensured their lively interest and resulted in their laying the foundation of a theory of foreign trade. Later in the same century it was the growth of trade as the great powers grew, the coming of economic nationalism, the shrinking of the world with the revolution in transport and communication, the growth of foreign lending and international capital markets – in short, the ramifying of the whole problem of international trade relations – which claimed attention. As the international economy emerged and became discernible in the twentieth century, as its institutions proliferated and demanded analysis (and, unhappily, as its problems grew so that all too often international economics became a form of economic pathology) the subject became established as a major part of the science.

International economics has developed and diversified with the international economy and its problems. During the interwar years not only was the pure theory of trade, relying as it did upon the principle of comparative advantage, supplemented and extended by the factor endowment approach but, in the monetary field, growing preoccupation with the balance-of-payments problems of the period led us at first to a detailed study of the gold standard and from there to examination of the whole problem of balance-of-payments adjustment on a broad front. The past twenty years have added greatly to our knowledge of the monetary interplay of trading economies and their management. But, since it is of the essence of international economics that it should reflect the changes of the times, it is of some interest to ask: what changes are now taking place and to what extent are they being reflected in the subject-matter of this branch of economics? It is not our purpose to hold out to the reader the prospect that this book will attempt to force new paths into unknown territory. It is, however, necessary for the reader to form some judgement of how close to reality and change in reality the subject is: to decide whether as a study it is 'up and running' or hobbling painfully in the wake of events. Four features seem to the author useful for the reader to bear in mind.

The first is, regretfully, a major shortcoming in coverage. The international economics which this book describes is applicable basically only to what we may call 'The Bretton Woods system' – to the trading and monetary relationships of those capitalist and mixed economies which rely for economic motivation upon the price system and which have, since the Second World War, been members of the IMF. The motivation of trade between the socialist bloc countries and the institutions through which it functions are absent from this book and from much of what we call international economics in the Western world. We lack universality. That this omission is, in the present state of things, inevitable, makes it no less regrettable.

A second feature of the international economic scene since the Second World War has been the growing power and influence of international organisations. This is new. Before 1914, although some degree of international co-operation appears to have existed through what we may call the international financial community, through the liaison of central bankers, the scene was one of national sovereign states pursuing foreign economic policies more or less in isolation. Although a few international agencies existed, these were of a narrow, functional character, designed to govern international relations in telecommunications, postal services, or similar fields. (The International Telecommunications Union was founded in 1865, the Universal Postal Union in 1874.)[2] The interwar years produced no international agencies of power or standing. – The International Labour Organisation (ILO), established in 1919, and the Bank for International Settlements (BIS), established in 1930, were perhaps the most notable creations of the period. Not until the great upsurge of post-war economic planning in the 1940s did great organisations emerge whose functions were wide enough to bring them into conflict with some of the most cherished prerogatives of national sovereignty. Thus the IMF (1944) brought within its scope such matters as exchange rate changes, exchange controls, and currency policy; GATT (1948) prescribed behaviour patterns in tariff policy, while a proliferation of international and regional commissions were created in the post-war period governing (or seeking to govern) many aspects of trade, payments, and international economic relations.

The essence of these new organisations was not only their size and scope but the fact that the sectors of activity which they sought to control brought them into conflict with national policies and sovereignty so that they became entities in the international power game in fields hitherto sacrosanct to national governments. Such a conflict might, of itself, have caused their extinction but it did not, for organisations of this new type had advantages to confer upon the favoured and sanctions with which to discipline the recalcitrant. They came to be supported, perhaps disliked, often cursed for their intractability but nevertheless a power to be reckoned with – a new force in the political economy of trade management.

This international economy in which the international agency has reached such power and prestige is qualitatively different from the free-for-all which preceded it, just as, in the national field, the mixed economy with its state intervention is qualitatively different from pure *laissez-faire* capitalism. The principles of international economic policy have to take account not only of the economic factors underlying such policies but of

Introduction

the concentrations of national economic power which the international economic agencies constitute. Any reader who doubts this statement should examine the record of the IMF, in particular the power within it of the Group of Ten and the interplay of power politics involved in setting up the new SDR system at Rio de Janeiro in 1967.

A third feature of the international economy of the seventies is the growing unification and drawing together of world banking and finance. Until the Second World War the banking systems of the great countries were separate integral entities. Only in a few great centres such as London and New York were banking institutions of several nations to be found. True, short-term capital moved between centres in response to interest rate inducements or confidence factors, but, while lodged in a given centre, such capital had to rest in national assets of the host country. Now all that has changed. In many financial centres dozens of banks of other countries carry on deposit, investment, and commercial business. Even the domestic commercial banks deal in foreign assets, either themselves directly or through subsidiaries. Great merchant banks regard the world as their theatre of operations. But mere bigness and change of scale would not in itself be remarkable. What is a major innovation is the internationalising of money markets, of which the Euro-dollar market is a leading example. Capital markets, the mobilising of savings, foreign investment, and the movement from centre to centre of short-term funds now have a mechanistically different and more cosmopolitan character. In London alone more than a hundred overseas banks operate. The Euro-dollar market is centred there. The Treasury Bill and the time deposit have yielded to new markets and new assets as the homes of overseas short-term funds. These innovations will be dealt with in their place. It is sufficient here to note their novelty and their importance in a rapidly shrinking world of virtually instant communication. With this has come a revival and growth to greater strength of the nineteenth-century international financial community. The activities of the central bankers of the Basle Club, with their support credits for ailing currencies and their concern for monetary stability, are manifestations of this rejuvenated international financial community.

Finally, in the multinational corporation there has appeared a form of industrial organisation whose significance for international trade and finance is great, although the precise nature of this significance has yet to be investigated. With plants in many countries, sales straddling tariff barriers, vast currency balances to manipulate and outputs which often exceed the GNP of a medium-sized country, it becomes natural to ask whether the laws of international transactions formulated in a world of

Marshall's 'representative firm' apply in a world of such monoliths. The forces which impel their trading, the motivation which moves their funds, may require explanations other than those hitherto given in the textbooks. It will be the task of international economics, once the behaviour patterns of this new world are established, to reassess the relevance of traditional theories.

The breadth of the subject-matter of international economics presents problems of classification and presentation which, in this book, are answered somewhat conventionally – the author believing that, sometimes at least, conventions are established by their utility. Three divisions of the subject are distinguished. In Part One the pure theory of trade examines the motivation of trade, the determination of the pattern of trade, and the gains derived from it. This is the oldest and longest-worked furrow in the trade field. It includes the examination of questions which are 'positive', such as the composition of trade, the precise effects of tariffs, and the effect of trade upon the terms of trade; and questions which are 'normative', such as the effect of free trade upon national welfare and the effect of trade upon world and national income. As theory, this subject-matter is abstract and rigorous and, in its higher flights and more arcane controversies, it can provide some of the most intricate analysis in the business. But it is a cognate and not too extensive subject-matter and its main arguments can be reduced to order by any student acquainted with the conventional tools of micro-economics.

Since pure theory analyses the process of foreign trade under severe classical assumptions, notably free trade and perfect competition, it is appropriate to follow the pure theory analysis with, in Part Two, a theory of commercial policy whose purpose is to examine the implications of policies which impede or seek to control trade flows. Central to this is the study of tariffs; both those for single countries and for internationl groupings in customs unions.

The third division of international economics recognises the existence of different national currencies and monetary systems. Part Three is by far the largest division and it comprises three conceptual subdivisions: the theory of balance-of-payments adjustment, the considerations of policy problems involved in international monetary management, and the description of international financial institutions. These conceptual subdivisions are not directly reflected in the four subsections into which Part Three is divided in this book but they should be apparent in retrospect as the natural divisions into which international monetary economics divides. Although in this division there is a considerable amount of theory, much of it monetary and macro-theory cast in an international setting, it is of

Introduction

lesser abstraction and rigour than that of the pure theory of Part One. The real world is never too far away and much of the analysis comprises an attempt to build a theory of economic policy to fit the international monetary system.

The order in which these divisions of international economics are attacked is important, in the writer's view and experience, only in the coupling of the sections. Pure Theory and Commercial Policy must be studied together and in that order. International Monetary Economics is a subject in itself. In teaching a survey course in trade, such as this text is designed for, the author finds it a matter of indifference whether he starts with money and teaches the theory and commercial policy second or vice versa. In a verbal exposition there is perhaps something to be said for taking money at the outset, since its practicality and application to current problems make it a good opener. Highly formal theory, even when it is easily understood, can be repelling to the newcomer. In any event, whatever order of attack is adopted, the student should recognise from the outset the divisions of the subject and their formal relations. It is essential, from the earliest possible moment, to know one's way around the subject.

In all expository books there comes the problem of striking a balance between theory and applications. It would be quite possible to confine oneself entirely to the theoretical propositions of trade analysis in the various divisions of the subject, presenting the subject-matter in terms of theorems, propositions, and proofs — the whole to form a logical and more or less co-ordinated system.[3] The disadvantage of such a book is that it presents theory in isolation without any demonstration of what it is intended to do or the sorts of practical problems to which it may be applied. Moreover, while in other sciences bodies of theory may often be presented in isolation they form a much more integrated whole than does the theory of international trade, which, by its nature and development, is untidy and imprecise in its formal interrelationships. The pure theory of trade is the most precisely defined sector of trade analysis and may be presented entirely in abstract terms with no relaxation of rigour, but the other divisions of international economics have insisted on developing their own theoretical bases — monetary equilibrium theory, tariff theory, growth theory and so on — each of which must be expounded separately and in relation to the practical and institutional problems which are raised. A balance between theory and practice has to be struck overall and in every distinct division, the balance differing from one to another. Take an example. Originally international monetary equilibrium was concerned with the preservation, through automatic procedures, of payments stability under the gold standard. This monetary theory was extended as institutional changes took place and new problems arose to encompass adjustment under fixed and fluctuating exchange rate systems. Later, with the widespread acceptance by national governments of the responsibility of preserving full employment, monetary theory, in the sense of adjustment theory, grew to include a full theory of balance-of-payments policies, seeking to include such problems as the reconciliation of external and internal equilibrium. Thus the original body of monetary equilibrium theory, justified by the study of a world economy in which different countries have different currencies, has been greatly expanded during the past fifty years. Moreover, it has also been modified by basic changes in economic theory itself, in particular by the application to adjustment theory in the forties and fifties of the new income analysis stemming from Keynesian economics.

From all this it would appear that the theoretical content of international economics is constantly changing as the subject seeks to accommodate itself to the continually changing facts of economic life. New theoretical explanations are being supplied to elucidate economic behaviour patterns. The problem of the expositor is to select from what theory is available just so much (and no more) as will formalise and give meaning to practical issues. Such selection is a personal matter, reflecting the theoretical tastes and predilections of the selector and, in particular, his expository aims. Since this is a general textbook seeking to present to the reader a survey of the subject-matter of international trade, the author has been guided in his selection by two considerations: to include such theory as is generally accepted as being in the mainstream of the development of ideas on each topic; and to make use of such other analytical devices as he himself has found useful in contributing to his own understanding of the subject. These criteria will not have prevented serious sins of omission. It is hoped these are not unforgivable.

We have said that one reason for studying international economics is that 'it is there' and indeed its presence is proclaimed by an imposing literature in which great names of the science—Smith, Ricardo, Mill, Marshall, Keynes, Ohlin, Haberler, Meade and Harrod—appear prominently. Since the Second World War, although the literature in periodicals has been enormous, few books of classic quality have appeared[4] but numerous surveys of earlier literature have helped to extend our knowledge. In international monetary economics numerous works on adjustment theory and balance-of-payments policy have appeared since 1945, while, in commercial policy, customs union theory has broken important new ground. In the welfare applications of this theory the concept of 'the second best' has been a notable innovation, which has wide applications outside the trade field.

Introduction

In the chapters which follow we shall try to signpost this literature effectively. References to source material or to material which has influenced the text will be noted (pp. 557–73) while a bibliography (pp. 574–96) will supply further reference material.

Part One

The Pure Theory of International Trade

2
The Aims and the Tools

(i) What the Pure Theory is About

THE pure theory of international trade is concerned with the basic problems of the exchange of goods in external trade. This is trade at the barter level, excluding the use of money and the problems which it raises. It excludes, too, international capital movements or changes in income. It is simply a study of the forces which move barter exchange between countries.

Like all branches of economic theory the pure theory of international trade seeks answers to fundamental questions. Why does trade take place between countries and, therefore, for the world at large, what determines the structure of trade? What goods are traded abroad and what goods are sold only on the domestic market? In what quantities and at what prices are goods traded? What gains accrue to a country from participating in external trade? These are all questions to which in this and the following three chapters our exposition of trade theory will supply answers.

It is worth noting at this stage that, broadly speaking, the pure theory of international trade seeks answers to two different classes of questions: firstly to questions of positive economics, and secondly to questions which are normative and require answers which fall within the scope of welfare economics. For example, questions such as what goods are traded, in what quantities and at what prices, clearly fall into the category of positive questions, while the question of whether free trade, or some trade, is better than no trade at all is normative in its implications.

To three of these questions—what goods are traded, in what amounts and what are the gains from trade—we are given answers by the theory of comparative costs, a doctrine stemming from Adam Smith, elaborated by Ricardo and developed by Mill and others. The determination of the prices of internationally traded goods requires a rigorous examination of the interaction of supply and demand in order to determine price. Both of these approaches throw light on the determination of the gains from trade. A natural extension of the theory of comparative costs is to enquire what determines differences in the costs of producing goods in various countries, in technical terms why do the transformation curves of countries differ? Ohlin has answered this question by asserting that different goods require for their production different factor inputs and that the basic factor supply of countries, or as we say, their factor endowments, is an important determinant of relative costs of production of traded goods. This opens up a large field of inquiry which has been deeply ploughed in recent years and which we shall survey in Chapter 4.

The foregoing is a very oversimplified classification of the subject-matter of the pure theory of international trade. In the main the theory has been historically developed and augmented in response to the demand for solutions or information concerning particular international policy problems. There are few fields of economics so long established or so worked over by scholars. For a century and a half every aspect of this theory has been explored, concepts have been redefined, tools remodelled. The literature has been enlarged and sometimes enriched by controversies which have raged over issues which no longer excite us. As Tinbergen has said, 'The theory of international trade is a vast body of theorems bearing on situations and problems which show many aspects.'[1] This proliferation has had some interesting consequences. One has been that the pure theory of trade has grown through the refinement and elaboration of techniques taken from the general body of economic theory. Another has been that, until recently, the literature has been somewhat chaotic and its extent and limits have been vague and hard to determine. But every science periodically draws breath and its participants take stock of their positions and of the general situation. There has been a widespread desire in recent years to survey and co-ordinate the theoretical subject-matter.[2] This process has enabled a deeper understanding of it and of the significance of its constituent parts to be obtained. The sheer size and complexity of this great subject-matter makes any classification and selection from it open to question. The one we have outlined is no exception but it has the advantages of simplicity and of providing a firm ground from which the student may move off into less clearly charted waters.

All this pure theory of trade is static, studying the behaviour of trading countries in terms of a static equilibrium and without reference to the processes and upsets of time and change. It is only recently, in the fifties and sixties, that the theories of trade and of economic growth have come into partnership and produced a theory of trade and growth. This theory is not treated in this book. Apart from the fact that its inclusion would lengthen and might encumber this preliminary exposition, it seems to the writer more logical for the student to postpone examination of such theory to a later stage when its significance for the current problems of economic develop-

The Pure Theory of International Trade

ment can be explored. Nevertheless the relevance of trade and growth theory to the pure theory of trade must not be lost sight of through their separation in this formulation. The new growth theory shows how static models can be developed to take account of time and how growth reacts upon the strategic variables of the trade model. It examines changes in the terms of trade, in factor endowments, and technical progress. It illuminates reasons for changes in countries' trading policies.

The pure theory of trade assumes, in its examination of the trading system, that there are no impedances to trade such as tariffs or direct controls and that trade is carried on in conditions of perfect competition. This assumption must not only be removed to allow for such impediments but, since impeded trade is the usual situation rather than the exception, the forces which govern trade in such circumstances and the judgement which must decide the use of this or that form of interference with trade must also be examined. This subject, which is closely related in subject-matter and method to the pure theory of trade, is dealt with in the chapters of Part Two dealing with the Theory of Commercial Policy.

The tools of analysis required for the pure theory of international trade are not peculiar to that subject-matter but are widely used in other branches of economics. Two tool kits are available, at two distinct levels of sophistication. The main concepts may be analysed mathematically with considerable rigour[3] and the use of algebra: alternatively a somewhat loser exposition may be made by the use of geometry. Here the latter method is employed. The geometric tools will already be familiar to most students. They consist of the normal diagrammatic tools of demand and supply analysis with the appropriate accessories of elasticity, consumer, and producers' surplus, indifference curves and the like. For the examination of supply, transformation curves, isoquants, and isocost functions are necessary; while for the study of particular market situations and, later, in the theory of commercial policy, offer curves are widely used. Before embarking on this section, therefore, readers would be well advised to refresh their minds on the properties and manipulation of these tools from any of the numerous textbooks which describe their use.[4]

(ii) The Basic Questions – Comparative Advantage

We face now the first basic questions: why does international trade take place and what gains does it offer for participant countries? This is where the systematic classical theory of international trade began, providing in the theory of comparative advantage one of its best known theorems.

It is necessary to bear in mind, although the significance of the assertion will not be immediately apparent, that classical international trade theory, whose components come to us from Hume, Adam Smith, and Ricardo, is a complete and systematic theory. It has been built in two main stages: the Ricardian theory of comparative advantage and the principle, contributed later by John Stuart Mill, that relative prices of the goods exchanged ensure that the quantities of the goods demanded match the quantities supplied. Our immediate preoccupation is with the first part of this system, the theory of comparative costs. We shall meet with the second aspect of the classical theory when we deal with the theory of balance-of-payments adjustment. The practice in modern discussions of international trade of separating the pure theory of trade from the monetary theory of the balance of payments tends to obscure the unity of the classical system. The fact that we no longer deal with the system entire, but rather meet its surviving parts in a number of contexts should not obscure the fact that a great deal of the original system is still intact and, though flanked with qualifications, alternatives, a changing methodology and a changing institutional environment, it would still be impossible to expound a meaningful and reasonably complete explanation of the whole trade process without it.

Smith and Ricardo were the architects of comparative advantage. They worked, however, within the general structure of classical economics of which they were also innovators. It is, therefore, necessary to examine first the basic characteristics of this system in its relations to trade and to keep them continually in mind as we proceed in this chapter. They may be summarised as follows:

1. The classical economists were concerned with practical issues and their theorising was directed to illuminating these. Viner puts the point well:[5] 'The classical theory of international trade was formulated primarily with a view to its providing guidance on questions of national policy, and although it included considerable descriptive analysis of economic process, the selection of phenomenon to be scrutinised and problems to be examined was almost always made with reference to current issues of public interest.' The overriding problem was to elucidate the superiority and advantages of free trade over protection and autarky and to demonstrate the gains from trade rather than to analyse trade with a formal and determinate model.

2. Classical economics saw international trade as a series of relations between individuals, individuals who bought and sold, loaned and borrowed, paid and received payment. Trade between countries was the reflec-

tion only of trade between individuals and firms within those countries, individually motivated and individually profit-seeking.

3. The principle element of motivation between these micro-entities in trade was perfect competition. This condition characterised the markets in which they bought and sold and the markets in which they hired and obtained factors of production.

4. Within the structure of a theory couched in real terms, goods traded had to be valued for theoretical discussion in terms of some fundamental unit of real cost. This, in accordance with the labour theory of value, was the amount of the labour input used in this production. For example, if with the same expenditure of labour one could make either one coat or two shirts then one coat will exchange always in the market for two shirts. If this exchange ratio were otherwise, say one coat against three shirts, then with existing labour inputs, many would turn to making coats and exchange them in the market for shirts. This would have the effect of increasing the supply of coats and diminishing the supply of shirts so that the original exchange ratio would re-establish itself. The influence of labour costs upon supply and demand determines the exchange ratio.

The simplifications of the labour theory of value are apparent. It assumes that the labour input consists of homogeneous units which of course it does not. Not all labour is equally skilled and competent; not all tasks have the same degree of arduousness, monotony, and involvement. It assumes that labour is an infinitely mobile factor of production, that it is the only mobile factor, and that units of it compete in a perfectly competitive factor market. All these are limiting and unreal assumptions. It is arguable also that, since any productive process takes place over time, the element of interest must be involved. Of this the labour theory takes no cognizance. Nevertheless, despite its simplicity, the labour theory of value was a valuable tool of analysis in the enunciation of the theory of comparative costs. It was a long time before it was possible to replace the device of measuring value in labour terms. Ultimately it became possible for measurement in labour units to be discarded leaving the main structure of the comparative cost argument intact.

5. Classical economists believed that there was a fundamental difference between domestic trade and foreign trade. The difference lay in this: within a country factors of production, labour, and capital moved freely as between places and as between lines of production; across frontiers between countries such mobility was totally lacking. Within countries complete adjustment to wage differences and factor–price disparities would occur as factors moved quickly and easily from sectors of lower return to sectors of high return. Across frontiers no such movements could take

place, and in response to price changes goods, not factors, would flow. Thus the immobility of factors across frontiers was made the very *raison d'être* of international trade.

Two comments must be made upon this reasoning. Firstly, it is of course not true that factors are immobile between countries. The difference between mobility across and mobility within frontiers is merely one of degree. Apart from long-term labour flows in immigration and emigration, there are few frontiers across which labour does not move seasonally. The ebb and flow of Italian labour into Switzerland; the movements of agricultural workers across frontiers at different seasons – Spaniards into France French into Germany and vice versa – are all examples. Capital movements have become more and more international in character. Frontiers are only a minor barrier to capital movements in our own day.

Secondly, this incompatibility of classical theory with the facts would be no more serious than most methodological simplifications in economic theory were it not for a supplementary question which it prompts. If in fact the mobility of factors is not a clear-cut matter of existence or absence but a matter of degree, can it serve as the criterion for the existence of a special status for international trade, which the classicists gave it? Can trade between regions of the same country – between Alberta and Saskatchewan, between California and Pennsylvania – not be qualitatively similar to international trade? The flow of factors between regions, or political subdivisions, may in some cases be as impeded as it is across national frontiers. It has been the thesis of later writers on international trade that the distinction between international and interregional trade is a blurred one, if indeed it exists at all. The best short answer to this question is probably that the distinction is meaningless only if one holds to the classical justification for a special theory of international trade – factor immobility between nations – but that the distinction is meaningful if one adopts other criteria, commonly cited by modern economists – different currency units, different legal systems, different monetary policies, different labour markets with differing labour laws and degrees of unionisation. All these elevate intercountry trade to a different qualitative level than interregional trade.

The assumption that labour is immobile between countries is one which modern trade theorists still make use of. With this and other assumptions they have built an imposing structure including the factor–price equalisation theory. Are they justified in continuing this classical assumption? Probably they are. There is no doubt that although labour does move between countries, such movements are still rather exceptional as compared with the freer movement within countries where mobility involves only inconvenience but is untrammelled by the linguistic, cultural, ethnic, legal,

The Pure Theory of International Trade

and religious differences which inhibit immigration and emigration. Where movements of population have taken place recently they have been between countries in which some of the inhibitions have been mitigated or where the rewards of moving appeared great. Thus much, but not all, of the flow of emigration to the Americas during the past century has been motivated by the draw of exceptional opportunity and has been in time-waves which display a strong ethnic pattern. Latterly the freeing of population movement in western Europe has been aided by the European Economic Community's policies. Between eastern and western Europe there has been very little significant movement.

With these basic characteristics of classical trade theory in mind we may now proceed with our exposition of comparative advantage. Let us first re-pose the question: what determines trade between two countries, whose wages (labour costs) differ and between which no labour movement can take place to equalise these wages?

Adam Smith was aware that a country would gain through trade. To him trade was merely an application, in a wider sphere, of the principle of division of labour. Men made shoes or coats, were carpenters or farmers. Division of labour was based upon skills and aptitudes and not only did it lead to greater and more efficient production but also to an increase in the volume of exchange. With specialisation self-sufficiency became impossible. Countries, like people, might specialise and their specialisation produced and was a determinant of trade. Each country would produce and trade a commodity in whose manufacture it had a cost advantage. Consider a formal example set out in Table 2.1. One unit of the goods A and B will be produced in countries X and Y at the labour cost (say man-hours) shown. Country X is more productive in producing good A; it can produce

Table 2.1

	Good A	Good B
Country X	5	10
Country Y	10	5

it at half the cost of producing good B. Country Y is more productive with good B which it can produce for half the cost of good A. Obviously it would be beneficial to both countries to specialise each in the production of its own good, good A for Country X and good B for Country Y. If the goods were exchanged at a 1-to-1 rate then each country would (assuming no transport costs, selling costs or barriers to trade) save five labour units, Country X exporting good A in exchange for importing good B from Y. Each country now gets its less efficiently produced good in trade for five labour units where it would cost ten units to make that good for itself.

Equally, both countries can obtain, with given labour resources, more goods by trade than by autarky.

This is a simple demonstration of the most elementary form of advantage in trade, where each country has an advantage in one of the commodities traded and mutual specialisation and exchange are obvious advantages. This, in practical terms, is the specialisation of northern Europe in manufactures and the specialisation of the Mediterranean basin in citrus fruits. It is the case of absolute advantage. X has an absolute advantage in the production of A; Y has an absolute advantage in the production of B.

For Adam Smith this was sufficient explanation of trade and its advantages. Indeed, a good deal of trade may be explained in this way. Climatic differences, differences in natural endowments, wide disparities in costs are all explicable in such terms. But another case arises which requires elucidation. Some countries have an across-the-board absolute advantage in the production of all commodities as compared with other countries. Is there then, as the simple model might indicate, to be no trade between them? It is likely that the United States has an across-the-board cost advantage as compared with Venezuela, yet there is trade between them. How may this be explained?

Torrens, Ricardo, and Mill developed a much more general explanation of trade in the theory of comparative advantage.[6] The simple structure of this may be explained also in tabular form and we can do no better than make use of Ricardo's own figures and the time-honoured example of England and Portugal trading in cloth and wine. The cost comparisons in labour units (man-hours) are as shown in Table 2.2. In Ricardo's example

Table 2.2

	Wine (one unit)	Cloth (one unit)
Portugal	80	90
England	120	100

Portugal has an absolute advantage over England in the production of both cloth and wine. A unit of wine costs only 80 labour units in Portugal: in England it is costlier at 120. A unit of cloth is cheaper in Portugal at 90 units than in England at 100 units.

A closer scrutiny of the figures in the table reveals that Portugal is relatively greater in her advantage over England in wine production than she is in cloth production. She produces a unit of wine with 67 per cent of the English labour cost, whereas a unit of cloth costs her 90 per cent of the English labour cost. Portugal has a *comparative advantage* in the production of wine.

The Pure Theory of International Trade

Take the English side of the picture. England has an absolute disadvantage in both wine and cloth as compared with Portugal. But she has a comparative advantage in the production of cloth. This is because the English labour cost is 50 per cent greater than the Portuguese in the making of wine, but only 11 per cent greater in the making of cloth. The English absolute disadvantage is greater in wine-making than in cloth-making. There is a comparative advantage for her in the making of cloth.

Let us generalise these findings. When there are two countries and two goods, and a comparison of the ratios of costs of production of good I in both countries and good II in both countries reveals that these ratios differ, then one country has a comparative advantage in the production of one of the goods and the other country has a comparative advantage in the production of the other good. In this situation both countries will gain by trading the two goods, whether or not one of the countries has an absolute advantage over the other in the production of both goods.

What do the two countries gain from trade as compared with autarky? Consider first the latter condition. In the absence of trade the prices of the two goods, that is to say a unit of each good measured in terms of the other good, will be determined by their costs of production. The following will be the non-trade price situation:

In England: 1 unit of wine exchanges for 1·2 units of cloth;
              1 unit of cloth exchanges for 0·8 unit of wine.

In Portugal: 1 unit of wine exchanges for 0·889 units of cloth;
              1 unit of cloth exchanges for 1·125 unit of wine.

Suppose that trade now begins between the two countries. If England were able to import wine for less than 1·2 units of cloth she would be advantaged, while Portugal would gain if she could obtain more than 0·889 unit of cloth for 1 unit of wine. Both countries would gain if international terms of trade were established such that 1 unit of wine was equal to a value in units of cloth, within the range 1·2 to 0·889. Suppose for simplicity that the rate established after trade is one unit of wine to one unit of cloth. England will then export cloth and import wine. Without trade a unit of wine costs England 120 hours of labour, but after trade 100 hours of labour make one unit of cloth which exchanges in trade for one unit of wine. With the twenty labour hours saved by trade England can either produce more cloth and increase her own consumption or she can take the saved labour time in the form of leisure with the existing consumption. On the Portuguese side, wine is exported and cloth imported, again at 1:1 terms of trade. Portugal now can make a unit of wine at a labour cost of 80 hours and export this unit of wine in exchange for one unit of cloth which would have cost her 90 hours to produce. Ten hours of labour is saved and is available for increased production, for consumption or for leisure.

To sum up, both countries specialise in production of one commodity, reallocating their factors accordingly, exporting that commodity in which they have a comparative advantage, importing that in which they have a comparative disadvantage. By this both countries gain and each can increase its consumption.

Remember that in Ricardo's example we have said nothing about what determines the price under trade conditions. All we have said is that, as long as the price falls within a certain range limited by the two internal cost ratios, trade will be of advantage to both countries. In fact the international terms of trade will be determined like most prices by supply and demand. These forces and their interaction will be the subject of a later chapter.

Thus far the theory of comparative advantage has been presented in a very limited form, with only two countries and two goods. It is possible to extend the argument to include a greater number of goods.[7] To do this we may take the two goods which have been used hitherto each as standing for a whole genus of similar goods. Wine may represent a wide variety of beverages, cloth represent a variety of woven materials. Similarly we may regard the figures of labour costs shown for the two groups as averages of many costs levels each appropriate to a type. With these postulates we may argue that any country engaging in international trade will export those commodities in which it has a comparative advantage — a proposition which must be examined carefully.

The first step in the examination is to rank the goods according to their labour cost. For the sake of simplicity we shall do this only for one of the two countries. We shall stick to England and Portugal for the example, assuming that in Portugal the labour cost of one unit of each of the goods $A-J$ is the same. Table 2.3 shows the situation. Portugal can produce one unit of each of the goods for 10 labour units (man-hours). England can produce one unit of the various goods for the labour costs shown in the ranking. All of the basic Ricardian assumptions for the two-good model still apply.

Table 2.3 **Man-hours required to produce one unit of goods**

	Goods									
	A	*B*	*C*	*D*	*E*	*F*	*G*	*H*	*I*	*J*
Portugal	10	10	10	10	10	10	10	10	10	10
England	20	18	16	14	12	10	8	6	4	2

The Pure Theory of International Trade

Let a_1, b_1, c_1 be the hours of labour required to produce a unit of A, B, and C respectively in Portugal, which country we will denote by the subscript $_1$.

Similarly let a_2, b_2, c_2 be the hours of labour for the equivalent commodities in England denoted by subscript $_2$. Then $a_1 = b_1 = c_1$ to $j_1 = 10$ and $a_2 = 20$, $b_2 = 18$, $c_2 = 16$, etc.

Let $w_1 =$ the hourly wage in Portugal and $w_2 =$ the hourly wage in England; let $p_{1a}, p_{1b}, p_{1c} =$ the prices of goods A, B, C, etc., in Portugal, and p_{2a}, p_{2b}, p_{2c}, etc. = the prices of goods in England. Then, if we assume that labour is the sole cost of production and that there are no selling costs, it follows that

$$p_{1a} = a_1 \times w_1 \quad \text{and} \quad p_{2a} = a_2 \times w_2$$

If, for example, the hourly wage rate in Portugal is 1 escudo and in England £1 we can write for A:

In Portugal $p_{1a} = 10$ escudos and for B: $p_{1b} = 10$ escudos
In England $p_{2a} = £20$ B: $p_{2b} = £18$

Care must be taken in choosing national wage rates for our two countries. By attaching hourly wage rates to labour units we are moving to express comparative costs in money and to think of exchange relations in money prices. It is natural to want to move from the simple and unrealistic expression of comparative differences in labour cost-terms to absolute differences in money prices since it is these which determine the flow of international trade; but it is also necessary fully to understand the significance of the step we are taking. We are in fact perfectly entitled to assume a level of money wages in the two countries provided that the ratio of money wages between the two countries lies within a given range. The limits of this range are fixed. Since it is more convenient now to work in terms of yield than of cost let us make use of Taussig's example[8] rather than try to convert the Ricardian figures. The Taussig example is as follows:

In the United States: 10 days' labour produce 20 units of wheat
10 days' labour produce 20 units of linen

In Germany: 10 days' labour produce 10 units of wheat
10 days' labour produce 15 units of linen

The United States has an absolute advantage in both commodities but a comparative advantage in terms of wheat. She will therefore specialise in wheat while Germany will specialise in linen. Now if we assume that the daily wage in the United States is $1.5 and in Germany $1, the monetary position can be summarised as follows:

Country	Daily wage	Wage for 10 days' labour	Product of 10 days' labour	Money cost = price per unit
United States	1·5	15	20 units of wheat	0·75
	1·5	15	20 units of linen	0·75
Germany	1·0	10	10 units of wheat	1·00
	1·0	10	15 units of linen	0·66

Now in money terms the price of wheat is lower in the United States than in Germany and is exported while linen is imported. If the daily wage in Germany is $1 then the daily wage in the United States cannot exceed $2. The upper limit is fixed by the American real cost advantage in wheat which is 2:1. If the American wage were to exceed $2 then the United States prices for both wheat and linen would be $1; American export of wheat would be no longer worthwhile and would cease. Similarly at the lower end of the range the United States daily wage cannot fall below $1.33. This figure is determined by the American real cost advantage in linen, i.e. 4:3. If the wage in the United States falls below $1.33 then the price per unit of linen would be the same in the two countries and trade would cease. The range of American hourly wages is therefore $2 to $1.33. What would happen if wage rates outside the range were established? If the American wage exceeded $2 an hour America would cease to export wheat but would still import linen; her balance of trade would become adverse, gold would flow out and prices and wages would fall. If the American wage fell below $1.33 the German balance of trade would weaken, gold would flow to America and American prices and wages would rise. Wage rates would be held within the range determined by the real cost ratios by monetary movements between the two countries with resultant changes in wage and price levels. We cannot say where, within the range, the ratio of wages and therefore the ratio of real terms of trade will fall. That can only be determined by relative demands for the two commodities—a matter we have not yet examined.

Return now to our example of England and Portugal. In order to be able to compare the prices between the two countries, in escudos and in pounds, we must know the exchange rate e. e is the number of pounds which exchange for 1 escudo. Assume for simplicity that this exchange rate is 1:1.

Referring again to Table 2.3 we can see that with such an exchange rate the price of producing a unit of A in Portugal will be 10 escudos and in England will be 20 escudos; B will be 10 in Portugal and 18 in England. Now armed with a price comparison we can proceed along the ranked list

The Pure Theory of International Trade

of commodities. Up to (and including) commodity E Portugal has a price advantage and (assuming no transport costs) will export these commodities to England. Commodity F, whose price is the same in both countries, will not be traded. This commodity in the ranking we may refer to as the 'point of neutrality'. Commodities G to J, which are cheaper in England than in Portugal, will be exported by England to Portugal.

It is apparent that for goods A to E Portugal has a comparative advantage while for goods G to J England has a comparative advantage. It is also apparent that under the simple assumptions of this model the comparative advantage is determined by labour cost only. The relative prices as determined by labour costs $p_{1a}:p_{1b}:p_{1c}... = a_1:b_1:c_1...$. The wage rate w_1 is useful only for determining money cost of production but it does not affect the ranking of the goods. However, if wages rose in one of the countries the position of good F would be changed. Suppose wages in England rose by 10 per cent to £1·25 per hour the cost of F in England ($p_{2f} = f_2 \times 1·1$) would at 11 rise above the cost in Portugal and England would import F. If wages in England rose by 50 per cent the cost of G in England would at 12 rise above the price in Portugal, and England would import G. It seems that while a change in the money wage rate in either country will not affect the ranking of the commodity costs it will affect the point at which import gives way to export. The effect of a rise in the wage rate for one country is to increase the imports of that country as it shifts the point on the table where the money costs are equal for commodities to right or left, according to which country increases its wage rate.

The exchange rate e affects the point of neutrality in the same way. It shifts one cost ranking relative to the other so that the non-traded commodity is shifted to left or right. Suppose England devalues the pound by 20 per cent so that 1 escudo now exchanges for £1·2, then the point of neutrality shifts to the left. England gains a comparative advantage in F; E becomes a non-traded good. Further devaluations would push the point of neutrality progressively to the left and England would gain new exports as a result. The effects of changes in the wage rate and the exchange rate are interesting. Both affect exports and imports. The higher the wage rate the less a country will export. Changes in either (or both) of these variables will move the point of neutrality to left or right, according to the direction of the changes, and near to the point of neutrality export goods will become import goods and vice versa. It is apparent, therefore, that the wage level and the exchange rate are both strategic variables for adjusting the balance of trade—a matter which will concern us greatly in Part Three of this book but which we note now in passing.[9]

There is one other matter, however, which should be dealt with here. We have assumed in our reasoning so far that there are no costs of transport for import and export goods. This is a highly unreal assumption not only in practical terms but also because, as long as we maintain it, export goods can be transformed into import goods by any movement to left or right of the point of neutrality on our table.* In other words all goods fall into one of two traded classes. Directly we remove the assumption and allow for the existence of transport goods, a third class of goods appears, namely those which enter only into domestic trade. Export goods do not convert at once into import goods. Rather they pass through the class of domestic goods which are produced in each country only for the domestic market.

Transport costs can be dealt with simply. Refer again to Table 2.3. To the labour costs of goods (a_1, b_1, c_1, etc.) produced in Portugal and goods (a_2, b_2, c_2, etc.) produced in England we may now add transport costs (still in labour units) $_at_{12}$ for good A from Portugal to England, $_bt_{12}, _ct_{12}..._jt_{12}$ and $_at_{21}, _bt_{21}, _ct_{21}..._jt_{21}$ for transport costs in the opposite direction. We will assume that the exporter always pays the transport costs. Applying these transport costs to the commodities in Table 2.3, a good will not now be imported or exported unless the difference in its costs of production between the two countries exceeds the cost of transporting it from one to the other. The application of transport costs in this way changes the order of goods A to J in the table because of the differences in the transport costs. Formerly comparative costs determined that order, now it depends upon these and costs of transport. The schedule of commodities in Table 2.3 which formerly started with goods of the highest comparative advantage and shaded steadily to goods with increasing comparative disadvantage, becomes, after allowing for transport costs, one which starts with goods which are exported, follows with domestic goods, and ends with import goods.

Although the international division of labour is somewhat diluted by the introduction of transport costs from the original simplicity which prevailed in its absence it is still clearly true that division of labour is of advantage to all countries. Transport costs represent a friction which reduces the power of division of labour between countries but does not eliminate it. The fact that trade takes place despite the costs of transport is an illustration of this.

* An almost equally unreal assumption is that goods are produced under conditions of constant cost. The removal of this assumption must wait until the next chapter, when the cost conditions are analysed more fully.

(iii) Conclusion

This brief survey of the theory of comparative costs should be sufficient to explain why trade takes place and why it is advantageous. The chapter which follows is concerned with two developments. It looks more closely at the supply and cost conditions under which goods are produced for trade. We have not as yet examined the implications of various cost patterns but have assumed that the goods discussed are produced under conditions of constant costs. Then there is the question of demand. While we have shown that, between any two countries, goods may be traded at certain terms of trade, of which the range is determined by the supply conditions of the two countries, we have not approached the problem of determining the precise terms of trade at which trade will settle and be carried on. This cannot be determined from the cost data alone but requires the consideration, with these, of the conditions of demand. To make this useful extension of the theory of comparative costs it will be necessary first to repeat some of the material which has been dealt with in this chapter in a diagrammatic setting. This will then be extended to cover a wider range of cost conditions and supply situations. To this will then be added the analysis of trade demand, the whole being then assembled to give a theoretical picture of the gains from trade.

3
Supply, Demand, and the Gains from Trade

(i) Supply with Constant Costs

IN Chapter 2 we asked the questions: what goods will be traded and what will be the gain from trading them? We must now present more formally the answers we gave to these questions and from this develop a more complete picture of the trade process. For this purpose we shall make use of a geometrical analysis employing a number of simple tools: the production possibilities or transformation curve, the offer curve, and later, the community indifference curve.

Before beginning let us reiterate the assumptions under which we are working. They are:

(1) factors are immobile between countries;
(2) factors are completely mobile within countries;
(3) tastes, on the demand side, and technology and factor endowments on the supply side, are unchanging;
(4) trade, when it occurs, is completely free, unimpeded by tariffs or direct state controls; and
(5) there is perfect competition in the markets for final goods and factors.

Some of these assumptions will be relaxed as we proceed.

Take the case of two countries, Britain and the United States, producing two goods, wheat and cloth. Each will, in isolation, produce quantities of the two goods which are determined by the factor endowments of the country. Each country will employ its factors to produce either good so that it minimises its costs, measured in terms of the number of units of the one commodity which it must give up in order to produce the other. An example will demonstrate the principle. In Table 3.1 are shown the production possibilities of the United States and Britain for the two commodities:

The Pure Theory of International Trade

Table 3.1 Production of One Man-Week

Product	In U.S.	In Britain
Wheat	10 bushels	2 bushels
Cloth	6 yards	4 yards

This table shows that the United States is more efficient than Britain in the production of both wheat and cloth. The United States, however, has a comparative advantage in the production of wheat, one bushel of which, in the absence of trade, costs her 0·6 yard of cloth as compared with Britain for whom a bushel costs 2 yards of cloth. For cloth the United States still has an advantage in that she can produce more in one week than Britain, but she can only do so at a higher opportunity cost than Britain. Each additional yard of cloth costs the United States 1·66 bushels of wheat, whereas it costs Britain only 0·5 bushel of wheat. The principle of trade according to comparative advantage then operates. If, in trade, the United States can obtain cloth at less than 1·66 bushels of wheat she is advantaged. This she may do because Britain is advantaged if she obtains for her cloth any price in excess of 0·5 bushel of wheat. If trade begins between the two countries each will be better off if it specialises in that good in which it has a comparative advantage and trades it to the other at a price lower than the cost at which it can itself produce.

There are two features of this example which are new and an advance on the Ricardian example of the previous chapter. The first is that we have implicitly abandoned the Ricardian assumption of the labour theory of value. By saying that the amount of each commodity produced is determined by its factor endowments we mean the amount and quality of all production factors—labour, capital, climatic, and natural advantages and all that goes to determine productivity. The second feature follows from the first. Once we move away from the assumption of a single homogeneous factor to that of many factors used in various mixes we are forced to find another measure of cost for each commodity. Formerly we used man-hours, man-weeks, or some labour–input unit. Now we measure cost not in factor terms but in terms of how much of one commodity we must give up in order to get more of the other. We are now measuring cost in terms of 'opportunity cost'. This advance on labour–input measurement in the theory of comparative cost and its consequent advantage of enabling us to escape from the constricting assumption of the labour theory of value was first suggested by Haberler[1] and was a significant step forward.

The principle of opportunity cost enables us to employ production possibilities curves in the exposition. Fig. 3.1 shows how we may do this:

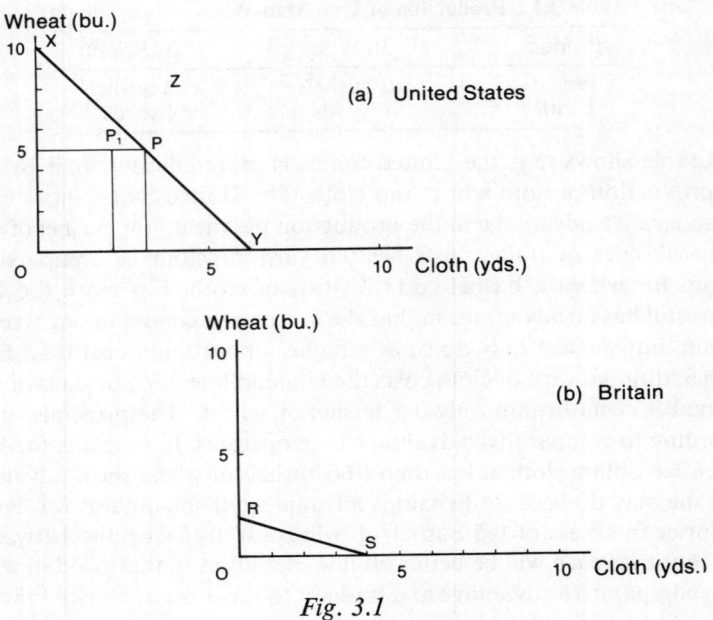

Fig. 3.1

(a) shows the situation for the United States; (b) that for Britain. The vertical axis measures outputs of wheat, the horizontal outputs of cloth. In the United States it is possible with a week's use of the available factors to produce 10 units of wheat at X or six units of cloth at Y. All the possible combinations of wheat and cloth which may be produced in that country are shown by points along XY each measured in terms of the two axes. The production possibilities curve XY thus arrays all the production possibilities for these commodities for the United States in the absence of trade. In a similar way the line RS in Fig. 3.1 (b) shows that 2 bushels of wheat or 4 yards of cloth or many intermediate possibilities are possible for Britain. In both cases the limits of the production of the commodities are shown by the points on the axes, the many intermediate possibilities by the production possibilities curve which joins these points. It should be noted, of course, that such a curve does not tell us what will be produced. It is a mere picture of the supply conditions. Only when these are coupled with demand data can we move to a meaningful picture of what will actually happen.

One thing we do know is that, whatever the demand conditions, the country will, when there is no foreign trade, produce at some point on the production possibilities curve. It would, for example, be impossible for

The Pure Theory of International Trade 31

the United States to produce at a point such as Z outside the curve. Such a point would only be feasible if factor conditions and productivity were so to improve as to give the United States a new production possibilities curve which passed through Z. On the other hand, the United States would be able to produce at P_1, within the production possibilities curve, if it so wished. It would not do so, however, since this point or any other within the curve is less desirable than a point on it. At P_1 5 bushels of wheat and 2 yards of cloth are produced. By moving to P the same amount of wheat and 3 yards of cloth may be produced. If we assume that the United States wishes more of each commodity rather than less it will always move to the more desirable point on the curve XY.

In this example the production possibilities curves are linear. This means that, for the United States, the amount of wheat which must be given up to produce an additional unit of cloth is constant for either small or large shifts of output at 10:6. This ratio is the *marginal rate of transformation* and is constant throughout. Moreover as long as we employ linear production possibilities curves, the marginal rate of transformation between the two commodities is also a price. Wheat will exchange for cloth in the United States at the given ratio of 10:6. Should this price for cloth be exceeded, at say, 11:6, then productive resources would move out of wheat and produce cloth. The supply of wheat would fall as a result and that of cloth would increase, both of these changes tending to restore the former 10:6 price ratio. Any downward shift in the price of cloth would similarly produce resource shifts for the two commodities which would tend to restore the 10:6 price. The fact is that, with existing factor resources, the price will always move to this ratio. Only change in either total factor resources or a move away from a constant marginal rate of transformation will alter it.

To sum up the argument so far: the production possibilities curve pictures the supply conditions and arrays the various combinations of the two commodities which the given country may produce. Moreover, when the curve is linear, representing constant opportunity costs the slope of the curve shows the prices of the two goods. In the example chosen the slopes of the production possibilities curve for the United States and Britain differ when there is no trade between them and therefore the relative prices differ also. Such a difference in exchange ratios indicates that advantage may be reaped by both countries from trade in the two goods.

The gains from trade may be illustrated graphically for the same example. Fig. 3.2 presents the production possibilities curves of the United States and Britain for the same two commodities and with the same marginal rates of transformation — that is, the same exchange ratios. Two adaptations of the previous figures have been made: (i) the curves are superimposed on the same axes and with the same scale; and (ii) the exchange ratios of each have been adjusted so as to have a common value at the cloth axis end. Thus the United States, which formerly exchanged 10 bushels of wheat for 6 yards of cloth, can equally be seen to have an exchange ratio of 20 bushels of wheat for twelve yards of cloth. For Britain the 2:4 ratio becomes 6:12. The marginal rates of transformation, and the exchange ratios, are merely expressed in alternative terms.

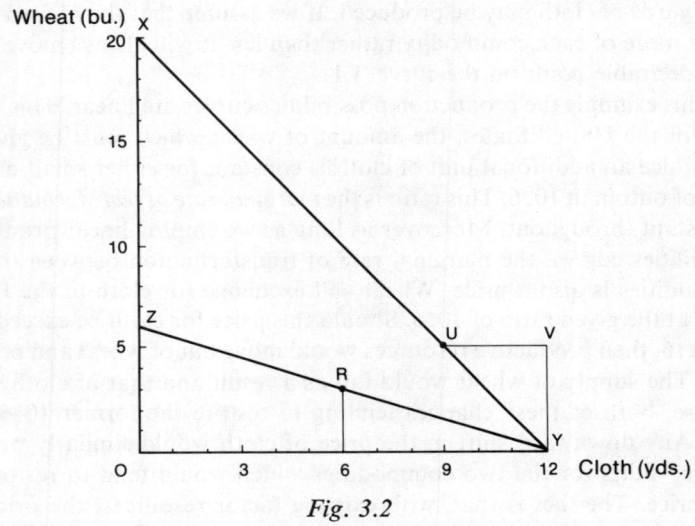

Fig. 3.2

XY and ZY now give convenient representations of the supply possibilities and exchange ratios for cloth and wheat in the United States and Britain respectively. We have no data on demand conditions but let us assume that, before trade, Britain has been consuming the two goods in amounts represented at point R where 6 yards of cloth and 3 bushels of wheat were demanded and supplied. If a more advantageous price than 12:6 were available to Britain by trade then a higher level of consumption could be reached. At the much more advantageous United States price of 12:20 it would be possible for Britain to consume greater quantities of the two goods than at R. At U, for example, it could consume 9 yards of cloth and 5 bushels of wheat. Suppose that Britain specialised entirely in the production of cloth, producing 12 yards. It might then, at the United States exchange ratio, exchange 3 yards of cloth for 5 bushels of wheat; it could achieve the consumption level of U. It retains 9 yards of cloth from home production, exports UV (3) in return for VY (5) of wheat. The terms of

The Pure Theory of International Trade

trade are represented by the slope of UY, i.e. by the price ratio line of the United States. Britain, by moving from R to U and trading at the United States terms of trade, has gained from trade (3 yards more cloth; 2 bushels more wheat); the United States is no better off, exchanging wheat and cloth, before and after trade, at the same exchange ratio. Production has, however, changed in the United States in order to adjust to British trade. Five more bushels of wheat are produced for export and 3 less of cloth are produced, in order to compensate for imports of 3 yards from Britain.

The example chosen is unreal in assuming that, after trade, Britain will be able to exchange its cloth for United States wheat at the exchange ratio prevailing domestically in the United States. However, it is not entirely unreal. With two countries, one very large and one very small, the exchange ratio after trade might behave as in the example. (We may assume that in trade between the United States and Fiji, because the volume of the latter's trade is too small to influence international prices, Fiji will trade at the United States price.) What the example does serve to show, however, is that for Britain there is a gain from specialising in the production of cloth and trading abroad for its wheat at any exchange ratio between the two commodities better than its own domestic exchange ratio before trade. Similarly, it can be shown for the United States that it will improve its position and gain from trade by specialising in the production of wheat and trading wheat for cloth from Britain. In the case of Britain any price for cloth between its domestic price and the American price will improve its position; in the case of the United States any price for wheat between its own and the British price will improve its position. Where will the international price ratio between wheat and cloth be? It may change for one; it may change for both; it cannot remain the same for both.

Let us suppose that the exchange ratio changes for both countries. Such a situation is illustrated in Fig. 3.3. The original exchange ratios are shown as before, XY for the United States and ZY for Britain. The new exchange ratio after trade WY lies between them. With WY 15 bushels of wheat exchange for 12 yards of cloth. With this ratio both countries gain from trade. Britain does not gain as much as she did in Fig. 3.2 but the United States gains this time. The gain from trade, which exists at all exchange ratios between ZY and XY, is shared by the two countries. If we rearranged the diagram to show both exchange ratios with a common point on the wheat axis and the United States production possibilities curve inside the British, the gain to the United States could be demonstrated as it was in the British case. Readers may do this for themselves. Meantime, it is apparent that if the United States can trade wheat for cloth at 15 bushels for 12 yards rather than 20 bushels for 12 yards she has gained from the

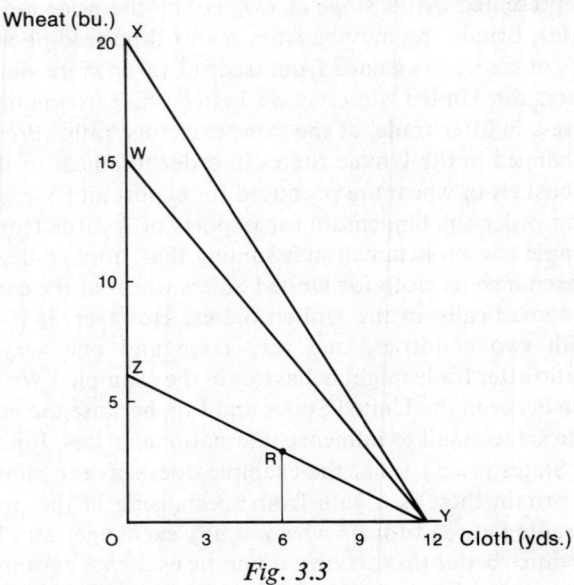

Fig. 3.3

introduction of trade. The British, getting 15 bushels for 12 yards of cloth, also gain as compared with the original 6 bushels for 12 yards.

The question now arises as to whether the specialisation, which is implicit in trade, will be partial or complete. Before trade both countries produced their own combinations of the two commodities. Will the combinations merely change with trade or will the United States end up producing wheat and Britain producing cloth? The answer is that with production possibilities curves which are linear, specialisation between the two countries is likely to be complete. This happens because trade raises the price of one commodity for each of the countries and thus satisfaction is increased by increasing production and sales of the commodity whose price has risen. Britain will increase its production of cloth and the United States its production of wheat and we shall move to the limits of production of the advantaged commodity for each country. In terms of the example in Fig. 3.3, why should Britain produce at home any wheat which costs her 2 yards of cloth per bushel if she can obtain the wheat in foreign trade at 0·8 yard of cloth per bushel?

The phrase 'terms of trade' has now appeared in our discussion. In its context it has been applied to the real exchange ratio under foreign trade between cloth and wheat — the rate at which United States exports of wheat exchange for imports of cloth. In Fig. 3.3 the terms of trade were shown

The Pure Theory of International Trade

by the slope of the line WY. The terms of trade is a much used concept in international trade and we shall meet it at many points along the way in this book. Let us for the present be content with a simple general explanation. A country's terms of trade we define as P_x/P_m where P_x is the price of her export good, P_m the price of her import good. In the pure theory of trade we use the term simply to signify an exchange ratio, in real terms, between two commodities or groups of commodities. An improvement in the terms of trade means that a fixed quantity of exports can now be exchanged for a larger bundle of imports. Later we shall come to more operational applications of the idea in which the terms of trade are represented by indices showing changes over time in the ratios of export to import prices.

(ii) Other Cost Patterns

So far we have assumed a condition of constant opportunity costs expressed by a straight line production possibilities curve. The assumption which underlies constant opportunity costs is that all factors are equally suited to production of the two commodities and that they move easily and painlessly from one activity to another as need arises. This is an unacceptable assumption. All factors have some degree of specificity; some are extremely specific. If we take the two commodities used in our example, cloth and wheat, it is clear that some factors — land, fertilisers, agricultural male labour — are specific to one, and some factors — fibres, machines, female labour — are specific to the other. This degree of specificity, slight though in some cases it may be, gives an inherent tendency to increasing costs. At first and at low outputs of, say, wheat, there is an abundant supply of suitable factors. As output is increased recourse is had to, at first slightly and later to significantly less, suitable factors, so that costs rise accordingly.

This situation reflects itself in a production possibilities curve which is concave to the origin. In Fig. 3.4 we redraw the curve for wheat and cloth in this form. Over the sector XW great increases in cloth output are possible without drawing many factors suitable to wheat production away from that activity and greatly reducing its output. Equally, if the object is to increase wheat production gains in output are dearly bought in cloth terms since cloth workers unsuitable for wheat-growing are being taken away from cloth production in the effort to increase wheat output. Over the sector RY a similar situation prevails. Wheat workers can be taken away from the cloth production at Y with resultant great increases in wheat

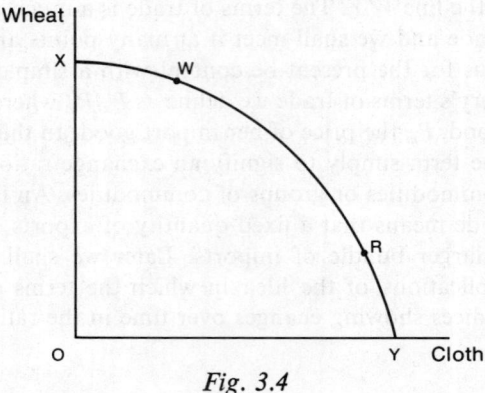

Fig. 3.4

production and little drop in cloth output. If the object is to increase cloth production wheat workers are being taken away from farming, with resultant sharp drops in wheat output, and put to work in cloth production, with not very impressive results. Only over the sector WR are wheat and cloth substitutable for one another without sharply increasing costs.

It seems that the concave production possibilities curve is more realistic than the straight line reflecting constant opportunity costs. It is not so much that abandonment of a single-factor labour theory of value and the acceptance of a multi-factor system moves us to this conclusion but rather that specificity of factors renders the concave curve inevitable and that in a multi-factor world some of the factors are bound to be specific. As we consider systems with more and more factors, specificity is likely to increase rather than diminish and the curve to alter in shape accordingly. Also, as we examine production possibilities curves for different industries the shapes of the curves will alter with the factor mixes which they reflect. A curve showing production possibilities as between potatoes and micro-electronic circuits would (cf. Fig. 3.5 (a)) be an interesting variant of the concave form. Over the sector XW increase of potato output would have almost no effect on the output of circuits since the technicians and workers in this industry are highly specific and probably not inclined to heavy manual labour. Increase in potato output could therefore be carried to W with minimal effect but any increase in such output over W would require perhaps the whole population to take to the fields with immediate and calamitous effect on micro-circuit production. Whatever the production conditions which the production possibilities curve reflects, however, it is likely to be a variant on the basic theme of a curve concave to the origin.

The example just given is not so far-fetched as at first appears. The

The Pure Theory of International Trade

specific factor here is labour, and potato production cannot be increased beyond a certain point without drawing labour into potato production at enormous opportunity cost. One wonders, for example, what the real cost to the Cuban economy of harvesting the sugar crop of 1970 was when Castro virtually ordered all workers, including himself, to take to the fields.

Another feature which affects the shape of the production possibilities curves is the time element and its effect on production conditions. If we are considering a short-run condition we would expect the adaptability of the economy to be lower than in the long run. In the short run the factor endowment must be taken as given and a curve such as XY in Fig. 3.5 (b)

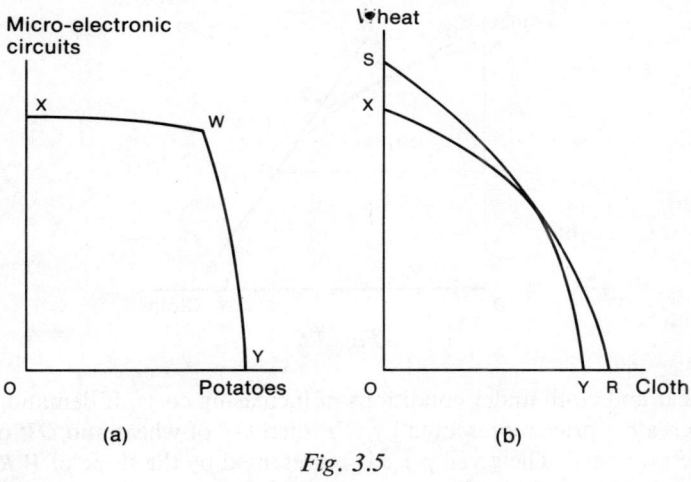

Fig. 3.5

might be expected (we assume now a return to our continuing example of wheat and cloth); in the long-run, factors might be adapted for transfer from one form of production to the other, labour might be retrained, and a smooth curve such as SR might result.

One more observation about the concave production possibilities curve, reflecting increasing costs, is appropriate at this point before we proceed to demonstrate the gains from trade with such a curve. Unlike the constant costs production possibilities curve, the curve of increasing costs is not also a price curve. With the linear curve the slope was constant along its length; it was this quality which enabled it to act as a price line, any point upon it demonstrating the exchange ratio in real terms between the commodities. But with the concave curve the slope differs along its length and the price at any point can only be measured by the slope at that point, that is by the slope of the tangent to the curve at that point. In economic terms, the price ratio and the marginal rate of transformation of the two commodities are equal at that point.

The determination of what particular point on the curve we may choose to consider must wait upon information on demand which, at this stage of the analysis, we do not possess. The price will be, in part, demand-determined and, whatever it may be, it will be represented on the diagram by a straight line from the X to the Y axis whose slope represents that exchange ratio. At the point of tangency of this line to the curve the combination of the two commodities produced will be determined.

Fig. 3.6 demonstrates for one country this determination of the output

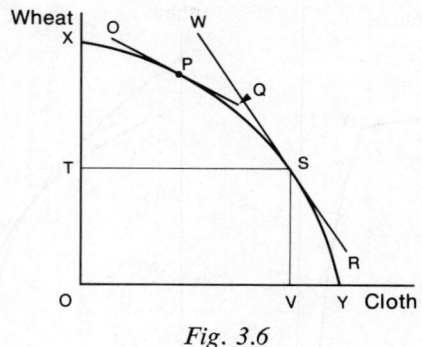

Fig. 3.6

of wheat and cloth under conditions of increasing costs. If demand is such as to create a price represented by WR then OT of wheat and OV of cloth will be produced. The given price is represented by the slope of WR which is the tangent to the production possibilities curve at S, the point determining the combination of quantities produced. With the price represented by the slope of WR (or of XY at S) no other combination of wheat and cloth other than OT and OV could be produced. It would at any other point be possible to earn more by shifting resources out of wheat production and into cloth production or vice versa, thus moving the outputs of each back to OT and OV respectively. The surplus of wheat and shortfall in cloth at P, for example, would require a different price than that represented at S in order to sustain this combination of outputs. The outputs at P could only be sustained by a price represented by the slope of OQ.

We are now in a position to examine the gains from trade in the case of increasing costs. Fig. 3.7 illustrates this case. XY is the production possibilities curve of Britain. In the absence of trade the price of wheat in terms of cloth is represented by SS with production at P. Let us assume that trade, when it begins, increases the price of cloth in terms of wheat to

The Pure Theory of International Trade

$S'S'$. (Once more we must take the price after trade as given because that price is, in part, demand-determined. We must wait until Chapter 4 to explain the forces underlying demand.) $S'S'$ is a higher price for cloth because each unit of cloth now exchanges for more wheat. The steeper the slope of the SS curve the higher the price of cloth in terms of wheat.

With this change in price Britain alters its output combination, now producing at R, OT of cloth and OW of wheat. The shift in production as a result of the opening up of trade depends upon the demand conditions. With demand which produced a higher price for cloth than $S'S'$, the SS price line would be still more steeply sloped. Its point of tangency with XY

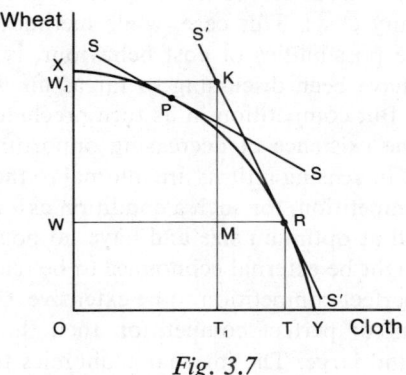

Fig. 3.7

would be to the right of R and Britain would plough still more resources into cloth because of its very high exchange value.

Given that $S'S'$ is the price ratio of the two commodities at whatever level of demand obtains, we may assume that Britain chooses to consume them herself in a combination represented by the point K at which W_1 of wheat and T_1 of cloth are consumed. The difference between what Britain is producing—OT of cloth and OW of wheat, and what she is consuming—OT_1 of cloth and OW_1 of wheat, must be clearly accounted for by foreign trade. The excess production of cloth T_1T is exported in return for WW_1 of wheat. T_1T is equal to MR and WW_1 to KM. The ratio of exports to imports, MR to KM is the slope of KR and of $S'S'$, the price line or terms of trade. As a result of trade Britain is able to consume more of both commodities than would be possible at P, the before-trade position.

As we saw above, under conditions of constant costs, comparative advantage leads to complete specialization, each country producing to full capacity the commodity in which it has advantage and importing the other. Such is not the case under conditions of increasing costs. The reason for this is fairly obvious. The implication of increasing costs is that diminishing returns will set in in both countries before full specialisation is reached. As Britain steps up her output of cloth the factors which produce cloth become scarcer. Machinery has to be used more intensively, less efficient labour is pressed into service, overtime is worked, the cost per unit of cloth rises. In each country diminishing returns will probably cause the cost ratios to move towards each other. They will be equalised and trade will be curtailed before the position of complete specialisation is reached.

We have discussed the cases of constant and of increasing costs. It is logical to expect some discussion of the only other possible case, that of decreasing opportunity costs. This case, while methodologically respectable to complete the possibilities of cost behaviour, is suspect on other grounds. What we have been discussing so far assumes the existence of perfect competition. But competition in its turn precludes in its definition and by its nature the existence of decreasing opportunity costs, i.e., of increasing returns. If increasing returns are internal to the firms, then there cannot be perfect competition, for such a condition assumes that the firms in an industry are all at optimum size and have no potential for internal economies. There might be external economies to be reaped but these are not thought under perfect competition to be extensive. Once, however, we drop the assumption of perfect competition then the picture changes. Firms may be few and large. The internal economies to be reaped from further increases in size may be considerable. A whole prospect of increasing returns is opened up.

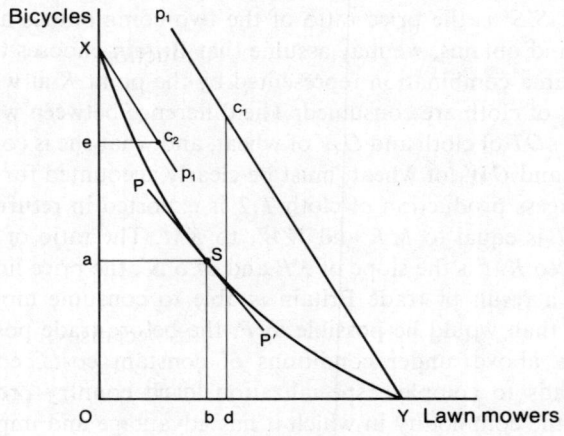

Fig. 3.8

The Pure Theory of International Trade

There is a great incentive to relax the perfect competition assumption and to discuss the implications of decreasing opportunity costs; for in international trade it is impossible to escape the impression that participation in trade in industrial products is much conditioned by the size, efficiency, high productivity and potential for technological change of imperfectly competitive industries in the great countries—in the United States, Britain, Japan and the countries of western Europe. Decreasing opportunity costs may be outside the purview of a model based on perfect competition, but there can be little doubt that in the real trading world they exist in many forms. This is our justification for including a brief discussion of them here.

A number of possible cases of decreasing opportunity costs may be distinguished and we shall take them one by one. In Fig. 3.8 the production possibilities curve is convex to the origin. XY is a production possibilities curve for bicycles and lawn mowers* produced in a country before trade and under conditions of increasing returns. As we substitute lawn mowers in production for bicycles we do so at a diminishing cost in terms of bicycles, that is to say, as we move from bicycles to lawn mowers we get increasing returns of the latter from additional factor applications. Suppose the price ratio is at S on the apex of the curve and is represented by the slope of PP'. This position cannot be maintained. Any increase of the price of lawn mowers in terms of bicycles (represented by a steepening of PP') will make producers shift out of bicycles and into lawn mowers. But there will be no equilibrium set of outputs at which they can settle, and factors will continue to be switched to lawn mowers until output settles at Y with complete specialisation in lawn mowers. If, on the other hand, the price-ratio line moves to become flatter than PP', thus increasing the price of bicycles in terms of lawn mowers, then production will be impelled to shift to X. Once trade is established, therefore, complete specialisation of each country in one commodity with exchange of appropriate amounts by trade will be established. Both countries will be better off after trade than before.

The last point can easily be demonstrated on the diagram. Suppose that before trade the price ratio in Britain is PP', with Oa of bicycles and Ob of lawn mowers being consumed and produced. When trade begins production becomes specialised and moves either to X or to Y, no matter what the terms of trade may be. Suppose Britain specialises in lawn mowers

---

* Our much-used example of wheat and cloth would not be very appropriate here. It could hardly be expected that factors could move between such contrasting industries as wheat and cloth, with decreasing costs. Factor mobility is conceivable between production lines which are similar technically.

and the terms of trade become such as are represented by the slope of Yp_1 then consumption at c_1 becomes possible with dY of lawn mowers being exported in exchange for dc_1 of bicycles. If Britain specialises in bicycles, however, with the given terms of trade she could only consume on Xp_1 (which is parallel to Yp_1) say at c_2, at which she exported Xe of bicycles for ec_2 of lawn mowers. It can be seen that both c_2 and c_1 are better consumption positions than S, the pre-trade position, but that, of the two, c_1 is the better. With the post-trade price ratio as shown it will be more advantageous for Britain to specialise in lawn mowers. This will give her a superior range of consumption positions along Yp_1. The determinant of which commodity a country should specialise in, under the conditions specified in the diagram, is clearly the terms of trade as indicated by the slope of the lines Yp_1 and Xp_1. Different slopes will change the relative positions of c_1 and c_2. Whatever the terms of trade may be, however, specialisation will still be complete and any post-trade consumption position on Xp_1 or Yp_1 will be preferable to a pre-trade consumption position on PP'.

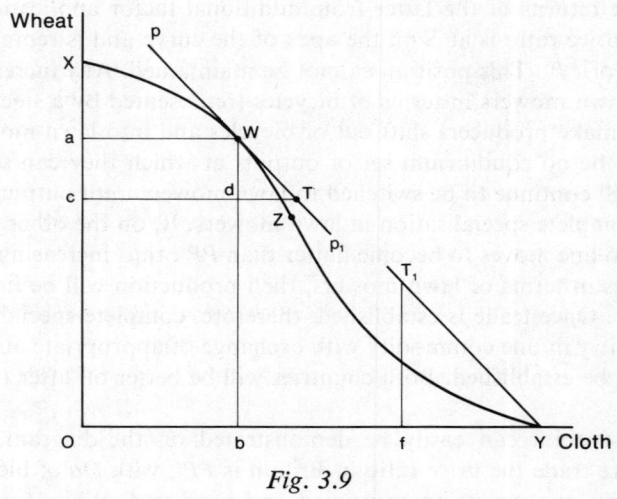

Fig. 3.9

A second case of increasing returns is that where, in our two-commodity world, one commodity is produced under increasing returns and one under diminishing returns. Fig. 3.9 illustrates this case. XY represents the British production possibilities curve between wheat and cloth. Wheat is produced under conditions of increasing costs so that up to the point of

The Pure Theory of International Trade

inflection the curve is the traditional one of an increasing marginal rate of transformation. Beyond the point of inflection Z, XY becomes convex to the origin reflecting the fact that in cloth manufacture increasing returns to scale are to be reaped. These returns to scale may be large enough to dominate all the factors which tend to increase opportunity costs and result in net decreasing opportunity costs in the cloth sector.

The case just given is clearly not an outlandish one. Wheat production may be the work of a competitive agricultural sector; cloth production the work of a few great firms in which considerable economies of scale may be realised.

Suppose that trade is already taking place and that terms of trade of pp_1 have been established with production at point W, at which Oa of wheat and Ob of cloth are being produced. Consumption may be at point T where Wd of wheat is exported in return for dT of cloth. There are advantages from trade, since T falls outside the production possibilities curve. But what happens if output is disturbed and moves beyond Z into the sector of decreasing opportunity costs for cloth? It would quickly be realised that progressive increases in cloth production at diminishing cost would be available. As we move towards Y less and less wheat would have to be sacrificed in order to produce more cloth. Production would move quickly to Y and complete specialisation in cloth. Assuming that the terms of trade remained as before at pp_1 then it would be possible for Britain to consume T_1, exchanging fY of cloth for fT_1 of wheat. Since T_1 is still further outside the production possibilities curve than T, T_1 is a preferred position made possible by complete specialisation. The case is thus established theoretically that countries with significant industrial sectors yielding economies to scale would do well to specialise in output from those sectors for trade purposes.

It is a necessary condition for the conclusion arrived at above that the curve XZT must be such that Y lies on the horizontal axis so that YT_1 is to the right of pp_1. If the sector of increasing returns is not strongly accented or if the exchange ratio between wheat and cloth is not strongly in favour of cloth then YT_1 will lie to the left of pp_1 and the country concerned would do better not to move to full specialisation but to remain at some consumption point on pp_1.

The production possibilities curve has proved to be a useful device for analysis is of a number of cases of the supply side in international trade. We have now dealt with the standard cases in production by its aid. There are, however, two special topics which must be discussed before we pass to the analysis of demand: transportation costs and technological change. To these we turn in the next section.

(iii) Transport Costs; Technological Change

It is obviously desirable that we should take account of transport costs in international trade. We need not make heavy weather of defining these costs. They constitute the difference (in the absence of tariffs or taxes) between the value of a good at its point of production and its value at the point of final use. They include items such as freight, insurance, financial charges, lost interest for the value of the goods for the period of transit, port charges, loading, unloading and forwarding charges. In practical terms they are important; in theoretical terms it is desirable that any model should approach reality as nearly as possible. The chief effect of introducing transport costs is to destroy one beloved assertion of trade theory: that trade equalises the prices of traded goods in all countries. This is true only if one takes no account of transport costs. As soon as one does so it is possible to see that they have an effect upon relative prices, alter the gains from trade, reduce the volume of trade, modify economic structure and in fact influence the whole structure of comparative costs upon which trade is based.

We can easily demonstrate how transport costs influence international trade by reverting to the basic diagrams used in the previous section of this chapter. Fig. 3.10 is an elaboration of Fig. 3.7 and shows the trading position of both Britain and the United States in terms of the earlier example, but now makes allowance for transport costs. With the given production possibilities curves WX and YZ for Britain and the United States respectively, and with S_1 as the terms of trade line, Britain produced at R and consumed at T; the United States produced at V and consumed at Q. The United States exported je of wheat, Britain imported ac of wheat, Britain exported bd of cloth, the United States imported fh of cloth. Both countries benefited from trade with consumption points outside their transformation curves.

Consider the effect upon all this of transport costs. We shall assume that transport costs are f.o.b., that is that the buying country pays the transport costs. In this case, the price of cloth rises to United States and the price of wheat rises to Britain. For both, in other words, the commodity terms of trade worsen. The effect of this is to shift S_1 to S_2 for Britain and S_1 to S_3 for the United States. Britain must consume at a point on S_2, the United States at some point on S_3. Suppose that Britain moves to T_1 and the United States to Q_1. There is no reason, other than simplicity, why we

The Pure Theory of International Trade

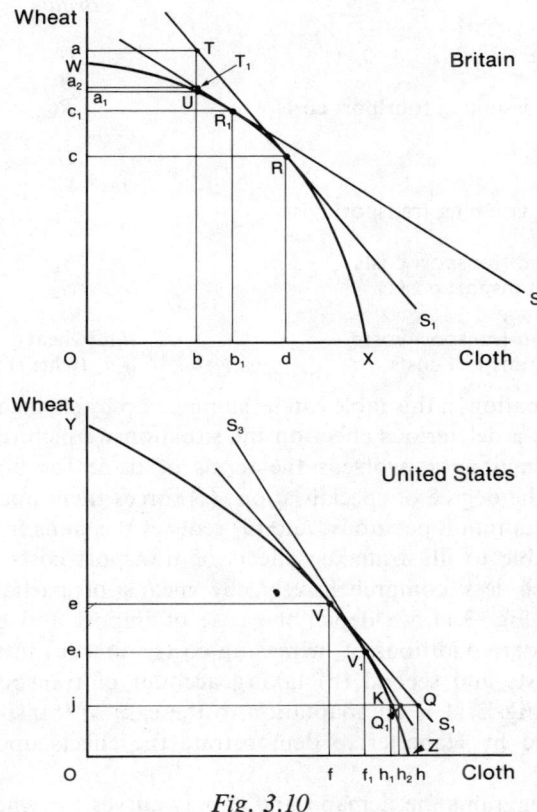

Fig. 3.10

should assume that consumption should locate at these points. If they do locate at T_1 and Q_1 it means that, for each country, there is no change in home consumption of the good exported. This is in fact unlikely for transport costs will have changed the relative prices of export and import goods lowering the former and thus encouraging a rise in its consumption. It is thus more likely that T_1 will be to the right of its assumed position (but on S_2) and that Q_1 will be to the left of its assumed position, but on S_3. In any event, it is clear that there is a loss in consumption relative to the consumption points T and Q which existed before transport costs were taken into account.

The shifts in the major elements of the trade situation which have taken place as a result of the introduction of transport costs are so numerous that it is perhaps easier to present them in tabular form. They are as follows:

	Britain	U.S.A.
Output		
Before trade	U	K
With trade	R	V
With trade assuming transport costs	R_1	V_1
Consumption		
Before trade	U	K
With trade	T	Q
With trade assuming transport costs	T_1	Q_1
Terms of Trade		
Assuming no transport costs	S_1	S_1
Assuming transport costs	S_2	S_3
Gains from Trade		
Assuming no transport costs	a_1a (wheat)	h_1h (cloth)
Assuming transport costs	a_1a_2 (wheat)	h_1h_2 (cloth)

The information in this table can be summed up by saying that transport charges have a deleterious effect on the situation we pictured in Fig. 3.7. Their introduction (a) worsens the terms of trade for both countries; (b) reduces the degree of specialisation; (c) forces them upon less advantageous consumption positions; and (d) reduces the gains from trade.

It is possible to illustrate the effects of transport costs more simply, though much less comprehensively, by means of partial equilibrium analysis. In Fig. 3.11 we depict the case of import and export in two countries under conditions of increasing costs—first (a) in the absence of transport costs and second (b) taking account of transport costs. The diagram in Fig. 3.11 is an adaptation to the case of transport costs of a diagram used by Haberler to demonstrate the effects upon trade of a tariff.[2]

In these diagrams the demand and supply curves for wheat are placed back-to-back for the two countries, the importing country on the right, the exporting country on the left. Price and cost are measured vertically on a common axis. Amounts of wheat produced and demanded read from O to the right and to the left for the importing country (m) and exporting country (x) respectively. In the absence of trade in part (a) of the diagram each country would produce to a price and amount appropriate to the intersection of its demand and supply curves, at E_m and E_x. Once trade begins, however, price will be reduced for the m country and increased for the x country; x_1x_2 will be exported by x and an equal amount m_1m_2 will be imported by m at the price OP. The price of wheat is higher in the exporting country x because with increasing costs price must rise to supply the additional output for export.

When we come to part (b) of the diagram we must add to the production costs of wheat a uniform charge for freight, etc., so that the export part of

The Pure Theory of International Trade

the diagram may be raised by this amount. OO_1 is the cost of transport to the importing country. The price of wheat in m (OP_1) is now higher than the price in x (O_1P_1) by the amount of the transport cost OO_1. Of course, the actual price of wheat in m may not rise by as much as OO_1, for

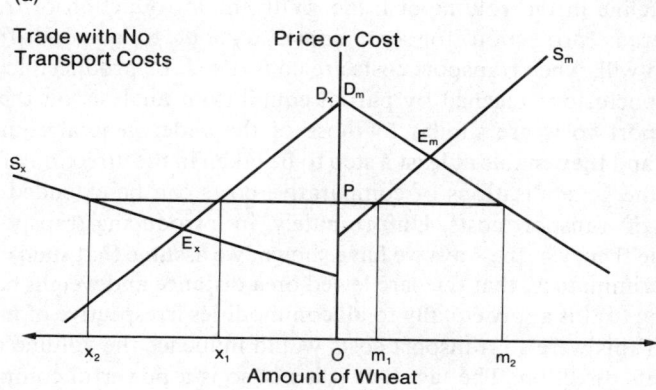

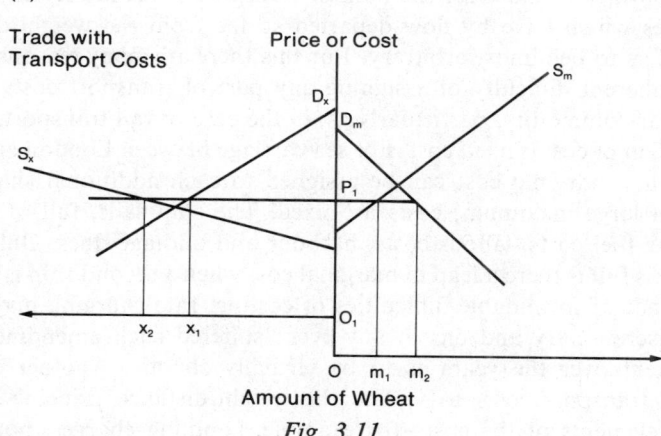

Fig. 3.11

demand in that country falls with the price rise. Om_2 the total amount bought in m is now smaller than in part (a). This fall in demand reduces production in x. O_1x_2 is less than Ox_2 in part (a) because we have come to a lower point on the supply curve S_x. The transport cost is added to a supply price which is lower than before so that the price in m, the importing country, rises by less than the full transport cost. The effects should now be clear from the diagram. Price has been reduced in x and domestic consumption O_1x_1 has as a result been increased. In m price has increased. Domestic output has expanded. Om_1 is larger in part (b) than in part (a), and since demand in m has also diminished with the price rise, imports m_1m_2 are smaller. The result of the transport costs has been a loss in specialisation and a decline in the volume of trade. With the introduction of transport costs there is 'protection' for some domestic goods. Some goods formerly imported will, when transport costs are considered, be produced locally.

The conclusions reached by partial equilibrium analysis on the effects of transport costs are similar to those of the wider general equilibrium analysis and they enable at least a step to be taken in the direction of reality, so that the generalisations of comparative costs can be extended to take account of transport costs. Unfortunately, in introducing transport costs into trade theory in the ways we have shown, we assume that such costs are non-discriminatory, that they are levied on a distance and weight basis and according to this apply equally to all commodities irrespective of nature or origin. If this were so transport costs would influence the volume of trade but not its direction. The fact that it is not so is a powerful complication which makes the generalisations of theory very approximate indeed. Freight charges, which account for the bulk of transport costs, are levied on rate schedules which have by now departed so far from the weight/distance formula as to be almost arbitrary. For this there are many reasons. There is the inherent difficulty of assigning any part of transport costs to any particular commodity, particularly as, in the case of rail transport, a high proportion of cost is fixed cost. For sea carriage between London and New York what marginal cost can be assigned to each additional shipment? Up to a large maximum, costs are fixed. The ship sails, full or empty, incurring fuel costs, labour costs, harbour and pilotage dues. Only when the ship is full is there a leap in marginal cost when a second ship is put on. In the face of formidable difficulties of costing, rate charging may be almost discretionary and has in any event suffered such amendment and adjustment over the years as to be virtually chaotic. Another element causing transport costs to violate the weight/distance principle is that certain elements of the cost—for example, handling charges, port dues, financial costs, and commissions—are fixed and are incurred on shipments regardless of distance, so that they are in effect a regressive element in the total so far as distance is concerned. For these reasons we can take it that transport costs are highly differential and conform to no reliable pattern which can be built into a theoretical framework. Other reasons contributing to this view include: the practice of allowing lower rates for the long-haul, of charging low-rates for return journeys so as to avoid returning in

The Pure Theory of International Trade

ballast, and of charging risk premiums on certain volatile or explosive cargoes.

A second special topic which requires attention at this stage of our exposition is that of technological change. We have discussed the motivation of trade in terms of very simple static models. The production possibilities curves which we have used were assumed to be unchanging and to define the supply conditions under which countries produced. To produce within the curve was to waste resources; to produce outside it was impossible with the given factor supply and technology. We must try to modify this simplicity a little. What follows is not intended to be a foray into growth theory, but merely a step towards removing some of the naïveté of the simple supply theory. We can do this with no more than the simple tools we have already used.

Advances in technology cause the production possibilities curve to move to the right. In the case of two goods, technical advance will enable more of one or both of the goods to be produced and will thus alter not only the position but the shape of the curve. We can distinguish three types of technological change, each of which will have its particular effect on the production possibilities curve: labour-saving technological change, capital-saving change and neutral change. This can be illustrated in Fig. 3.12.

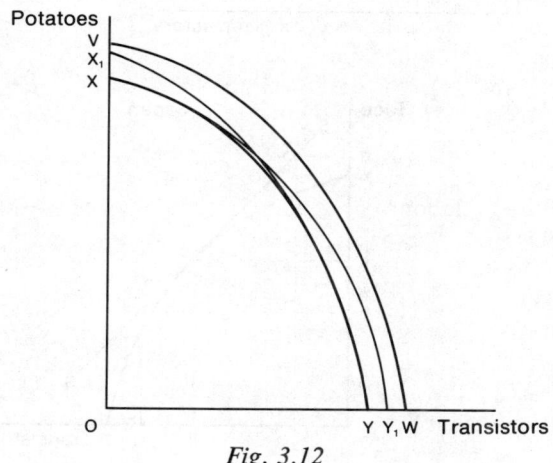

Fig. 3.12

Suppose XY is the production possibilities curve for a given country between potatoes, a labour-intensive good, and transistors, a capital-intensive good. Neutral technological change, being both labour- and capital-saving moves the country to a new and parallel transformation curve at *VW*. Any new technical application which was markedly labour-saving would be likely to shift *XY* to X_1Y, increasing the potential output of the labour-intensive good; one which was capital-saving would shift *XY* to XY_1.

Improvements in factor efficiency through technical change will alter the curve of any given country in our model in these basic ways. What effects upon the model of comparative costs will such movements have? Let us explore this question through a formal example. Suppose that Thailand and Japan produce rice and transistors respectively. This situation would then be depicted in the diagrams of Fig. 3.13.

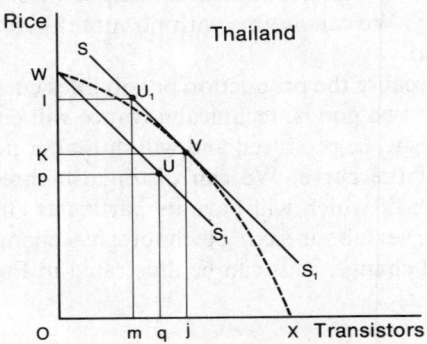

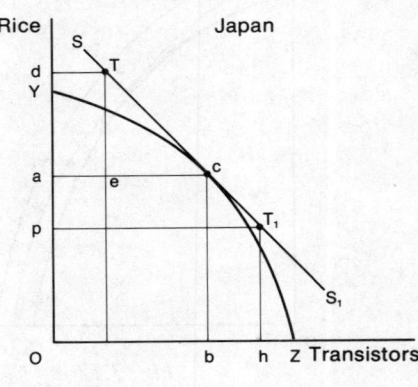

Fig. 3.13

For the two commodities the production possibilities curves would, theoretically, be *WX* and *YZ*. *YZ* shows a practical series of possibilities for Japan, which can produce a supply of both the commodities along that curve. WX for Thailand is, however, no more than hypothetical, for that country can in fact only produce OW of rice, transistors, for the moment, being beyond her technical competence. Thailand's production possibilities limit is therefore the point W, the maximum amount of rice which she can produce. The two countries trade at the terms of trade SS_1. This trade consists of Japanese rice imports of ad in return for ec of transistors and Thailand exports of Wp of rice for ec of transistors. (Since da is equal to Te, it follows that at terms of trade SS_1, da of rice will buy ec of transistors.) Thailand, under these conditions, must consume at U. Both countries are advantaged by this trade which is based essentially on technological attributes. Suppose now that the highly intelligent and talented Thai people decide to produce transistors and that they are able to overcome the technical problems inherent in establishing an industry for that purpose. As soon as they do so, their production possibilities curve expands from W to WX. If we assume that the terms of trade remain the same then Thai output shifts to V, at which oj of transistors and ok of rice are being produced. The new consumption point is U_1, at which lk of rice is being imported in return for exports of mj transistors. The technological advance has changed not only the quantities but the content of Thai trade. She has become an importer of rice and an exporter of transistors. Since U_1 lies outside her transformation curve WX, she has benefited from the change.

As for Japan, if the terms of trade are unchanged, she will continue to produce at C. There will be no change in the structure of the economy. But there will be a change in trade. Consumption shifts from T to T_1. Japan thus becomes a rice exporter where before she was an importer and a transistor importer where before she was an exporter. At the new consumption point T_1, ap of rice is exported for imports of bh of transistors. The change in technology has changed the Japanese comparative advantage in transistors to a comparative advantage in rice. She may still consume at T_1 and be better off from trade although now, due to the change in comparative advantage, the trade is differently structured. The most striking improvement as a result of the technological advance is in Thailand's improved consumption by the move from U to U_1. The technological advance has enhanced welfare in one country and has not diminished it in the other. The theoretical argument derived in this example would appear to support popular belief and the demonstration of history that the more a country can invest in capital improvement through technology and basic research the greater the benefit to it through trade. The example of Japan who, in twenty years, has established a technology which has become the basis of industries as diverse as shipbuilding and micro-electronics and grown to be one of the largest trading nations of the world, is an obvious one to quote in this regard. Patterns of world trade have changed greatly since the Second World War.[3] It would be possible to point to major changes in the trading structure of older commercial nations like the United States, Britain, and Germany and to point to the upsurge of new nations like Japan. We became accustomed in the earlier twentieth century to regard changes in the world trading pattern as being gradual – almost processes of evolution. It is clear from recent experience that the pace of technical change is quickening rather than slowing and that we must expect this to transform trade structures, relative economic strengths of nations and the social and political environment in an unprecedented way.

(iv) Demand

We come now to the subject of the second stage of development of the theory of comparative advantage and the gains from trade: the relation between the quantities demanded in international trade and the quantities supplied. Hitherto, we have assumed that particular levels of consumption and demand exist. We must now inquire what determines these.

First, let us re-pose the problem in terms of our standard example, the data of which was as follows:

Table 3.2 Production of One Man-Week

Product	In U.S.	In Britain
Wheat	10 bushels	2 bushels
Cloth	6 yards	4 yards

With autarky wheat and cloth exchange in the United States at 10:6 and in Britain at 2:4. These without-trade ratios set limits within which the after-trade terms of trade must lie. Britain will not pay more than 20 yards of cloth for 10 bushels of wheat; the United States will not accept less than 6 yards of cloth for 10 bushels of wheat. Britain trading at 10:6 would be greatly advantaged by trade although the United States would be indifferent. In trade with Britain at 10:20 (i.e. 2:4) the United States would command better terms for its wheat in cloth than by autarky while Britain would be indifferent to trade. Within these two limits lie many possible terms of trade which would advantage both countries. We are tacitly assuming here that both countries are of approximately equal size. If one country is very small it will almost certainly find itself able to trade with the large country on that country's terms of trade. Bali can buy

The Pure Theory of International Trade

transistors from Japan at the Japanese price and sell rice at the price determined by Japan and Thailand. The case for trading at one of the limits may be a common one in international trade. In this chapter, however, we assume countries to be of equal size. Only by knowing the demand of each country for the good exported by the other can we know what will be the final terms of trade.

Two main tools and two approaches may be used in the simple analysis of trade demand to answer this question: the offer curve approach and the indifference curve analysis. We shall deal with these in turn.

The first attempt to extend the theory of comparative advantage and to analyse the determinants of demand was made by John Stuart Mill.[4] It was further developed by Marshall, who evolved the offer curve (or reciprocal demand curve) as a diagrammatic device to handle this problem.[5]

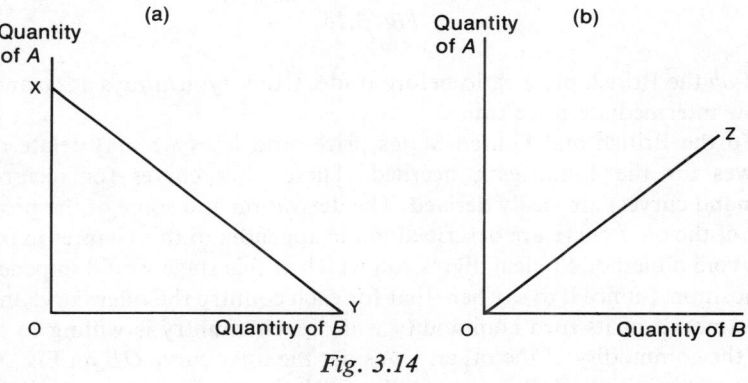

Fig. 3.14

Assuming constant opportunity costs, the production possibilities curve between two countries and two commodities is as portrayed in Fig. 3.14 (a). This shows the cost, in terms of units of either commodity, of increasing production of the other. It is also a price line showing the price ratio between A and B. As such it shows the quantity of A which is of the same value as a quantity of B. At any point on XY it is its slope which is the price ratio. We can reproduce the slope of XY more conveniently in Fig. 3.14 (b) by changing it from a negative slope in XY to a positive slope in OZ. The sign is of no significance. OZ still shows us the price ratio of A and B but it is now in a form which enables it to be used conveniently in combination with other elements in a diagram. We can now draw, as in Fig. 3.15, a whole series of rays which are price-ratio lines representing terms of trade between two commodities. Those shown in the diagram are taken from our continuing example, oa being the United States price ratio

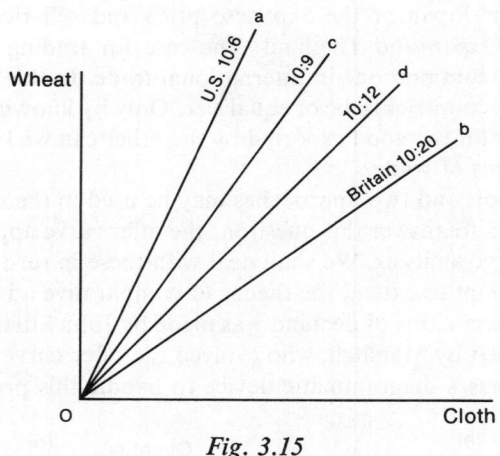

Fig. 3.15

and *ob* the British price ratio before trade. Other typical rays at *oc* and *od* show intermediate price ratios.

To the British and United States price-ratio lines we may relate offer curves for the countries concerned. These offer curves (or reciprocal demand curves) are easily derived. The derivation and some of the properties of the offer curve are described in the appendix to this chapter in order to avoid a methodological digression which at this stage would impede the exposition. Suffice it to say here that for each country the offer curve shows the amount of its own commodity which each country is willing to offer for the commodity of the other. Consider the offer curve *OB* on Fig. 3.16. This curve initially follows the path of *Ob* the British price-ratio line (a) because *Ob* is a price limit below which the country will not export cloth because it can get wheat at home on *Ob* in greater amount than at any point below *Ob*; and (b) because for small amounts of wheat it may not be worth while to go to the trouble of exporting but be easier to exchange cloth at the domestic rate of *Ob*. Sooner or later, however, the offer curve *OB* will diverge from the domestic price-ratio line, rising in the way shown and showing the amounts of cloth Britain will offer for various amounts of wheat at various prices. Initially its slow divergence from *Ob* indicates British anxiety to get as much wheat as possible for the sacrifice of only a little more cloth; later the curve rises more steeply, reflecting increasing British unwillingness to give up further cloth, even for considerable gains in wheat. At *B* Britain's offer curve, judged as a demand curve for wheat, has become unit elastic, since it offers only the same amount of cloth for increasing amounts of wheat. Judged as a supply curve of cloth it has zero elasticity,

The Pure Theory of International Trade

since the amount of cloth offered is now impervious to the blandishments of increasing amounts of wheat. The curve reflects Britain's trading offer of cloth; but it also reflects her trading demand for wheat. Every point on the curve may be connected by a ray to the origin which represents the price ratio of the two commodities at that point.

Turn now to the United States offer curve as shown on Fig. 3.16 by OA.

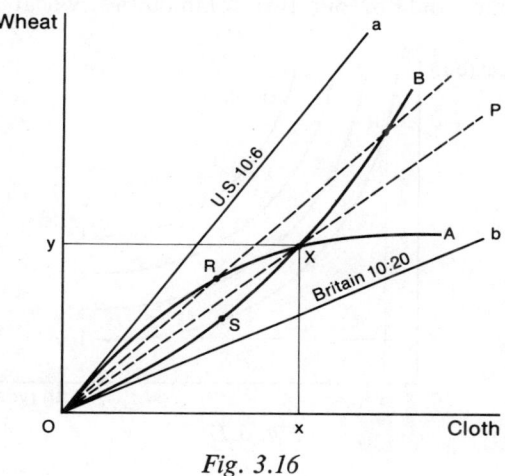

Fig. 3.16

This exhibits similar behaviour to the British curve OB. Starting on the domestic price-ratio line Oa it follows this for a short time and then bends below it as the United States seeks trade at lower prices for cloth or higher prices for wheat. With curves of this form for Britain and the United States they will intersect at X. This point indicates the position at which trade will take place. Here the prices of wheat and cloth in each country are equal and, assuming no transport costs, both countries are prepared to trade. The ray OP joining X to the origin represents the terms of trade, while Ox and Oy represent the amounts of the commodities traded, i.e., the volume of trade.

The equilibrium nature of the point X can be demonstrated by examining other points on the offer curves. At R, for example, the United States would be offering only a little less wheat than at X for somewhat less cloth. But for this amount of cloth Britain will, at S, accept much less wheat. At neither R nor S will the offers of the two countries clear the market. At OR the relatively high price of cloth in terms of wheat causes the Americans to offer only R of wheat where the British want much more at T.

We now turn to the indifference curve method of defining the trade equilibrium. This presents little difficulty since most readers will be familiar with the indifference curve as a standard tool of analysis in demand theory. We content ourselves with a very brief account of it here.[6]

An indifference curve is a contour line which, for two commodities, shows all possible combinations of the two commodities which provide a given level of utility for the individual consumer. Curve I in Fig. 3.17 shows for one consumer and for our two commodities, wheat and cloth, all

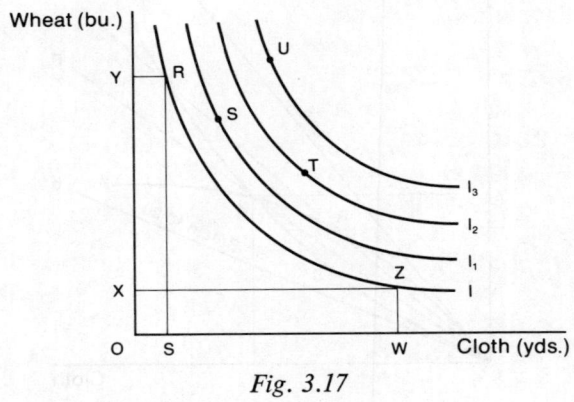

Fig. 3.17

possible combinations which will yield the same satisfaction. With OY of wheat and OS of cloth at R the same utility is obtained as with OX of wheat and OW of cloth at Z. The consumer is indifferent as to whether he consumes R or Z. Only by moving to a new indifference curve such as I_1, can he increase his utility. I_1 has the same characteristics as I, save that it represents combinations of wheat and cloth which yield to the single consumer a higher degree of utility. Further indifference curves I_2 and I_3 would, in their turn, show progressively higher yields of utility. The further the indifference curve from the origin, the higher the level of utility it represents. Here we might remind readers that indifference curves are generally convex to the origin. As the consumer obtains more and more cloth, he is prepared to give up less and less wheat to obtain an additional unit of cloth. If we define *the marginal rate of substitution* as the amount of wheat that a consumer is prepared to give up in order to obtain an additional unit of cloth, without, as a result, sustaining a loss of utility then we may say that the marginal rate of substitution of one good for the other diminishes along the curve. Fig. 3.17 is referred to as an indifference map. The parallel curves, I, I_1, I_2, I_3, may be taken to indicate degrees of satisfaction (or levels of utility) for the consumer. Thus we may conceive

The Pure Theory of International Trade

of an infinite number of parallel indifference curves as we proceed outward from the origin, any one of which represents greater satisfaction than those nearer the origin and less satisfaction than those further from the origin. Thus while R and Z yield similar degrees of satisfaction S is superior to either. T is superior to S and U to T. Thus if we take U, the highest level of utility shown, a move from T to U would involve an increase in the amount of wheat consumed and a decrease in the amount of cloth. Since U has a higher utility than T, the increase in wheat has more than compensated for the decrease in cloth.

We can also deal with the concept of price on this diagram. Each curve can be interpreted to stand for a given level of real income in terms of wheat and cloth and at any given price the consumer will consume the quantities of wheat and cloth which are determined by the point of tangency of the price line as depicted in Fig. 3.14 (a) to the indifference curve.

All this is simple demand theory relating to the behaviour of a single very rational consumer. In international trade, however, we are concerned with the demand of a whole community or nation. What we are after for trade analysis is a *community indifference curve*. But there are daunting difficulties about proceeding smoothly from an indifference curve for an individual to one for a community. The choices and utility evaluations involved in an individual decision to give up x units of cloth for y units of wheat are subjective but, assuming a rational consumer, are acceptable enough to establish his indifference curve at least as a conceptual device. For a community of many persons and groups even this simple choice of x cloth for y wheat looks very different. Some will want to make the choice, some will not. How will the utility of those who support the choice compare with the disutility of those who oppose it. Not only 'yes' and 'no' groups but the preference scales of many groups in between complicate the issue. It is difficult to measure satisfaction for an individual; it is impossible to measure it for a large aggregation of people. It is upon a constant level of satisfaction that the whole concept of an indifference curve depends.

As is so often the case in economics, this difficulty is not met frontally. The obstacle is not removed — it is by-passed. The methodological advantages of a community indifference curve are too great to be foregone. We admit the difficulties inherent in the concept but mitigate them somewhat by certain assumptions. We assume that the tastes, evaluations and preferences of the individual are a prototype for those of the group; we assume that these subjective characteristics are constant over time; and we assume that there are no changes in income distribution. These assumptions are unrealistic but, for the present, they enable us to turn an awkward corner.

Later in the theory of commercial policy when the merits and demerits of particular tariff policies and their welfare effects have to be judged we face the problem of community evaluation more directly, and the community indifference curve ceases to help. For the moment we keep it, proceeding with caution.

Once we accept the community indifference curve as a device we can proceed easily. With it we can demonstrate in Fig. 3.18 the way in which

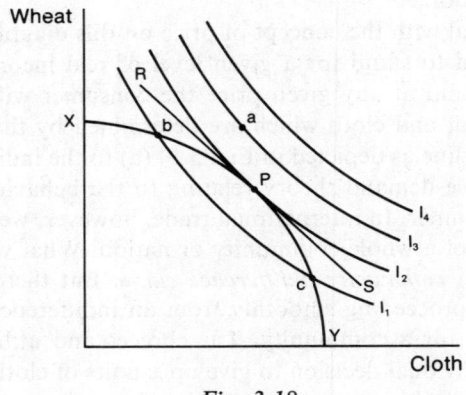

Fig. 3.18

equilibrium is established in each of the countries concerned, in the absence of trade. We assume a production possibilities curve showing decreasing returns as in XY. I_1, I_2, I_3 and I_4 are community indifference curves. The equilibrium point is P at which XY is tangent to I_2. RS the straight line tangent to I_2 at P is the price line showing the terms in which the two commodities will, under optimum conditions, be traded in that country. At any point such as a we are outside XY and therefore beyond the country's production capacity; at points such as b and c it would be possible to increase satisfaction by moving to a higher indifference curve than I_1. At P satisfaction is maximised and the marginal rate of substitution in consumption equals both the opportunity cost in production and the price ratio between the two goods. Given the shape of the indifference and transformation curves P is a unique optimum point.

When international trade begins it becomes possible for a country to produce and consume at prices which are impossible in isolation. Without trade and with a price line RS the country would produce at P, as in Fig. 3.18. The trade situation is shown in Fig. 3.19. The international terms of trade are given by the slope of the line R_1S_1. Such a price-ratio line may

The Pure Theory of International Trade

be drawn in a form which is tangent to XY at Q and would also be tangent to an indifference curve I_3 at T. With production at Q and consumption at T, the marginal rate of substitution in production equals the terms of trade and equals the marginal rate of substitution in consumption. LQ of cloth would be exported in return for TL of wheat. The point T is then an optimum point for the country in trade. All the salient variables are equal at that point and T is also on a higher indifference curve than was P, the equilibrium position before trade.

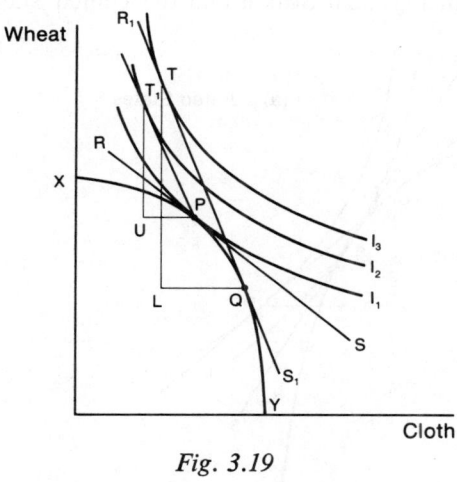

Fig. 3.19

It is possible to demonstrate also with the aid of this diagram that the gain from trade is composed of two elements; the gain from exchange and the gain from specialisation in production. Note that in the diagram, consumption moved to T and production to Q after trade. Suppose that in fact the country was incapable of adapting its productive facilities and was forced after trade to continue production at P. Its gain from trade would then be limited to the gain from exchanging at the new price ratio. This gain could be had by moving from P to T_1, that is along the price-ratio slope to a point of tangency T_1 with indifference curve I_2. At this point $T_1 U$ of wheat would be imported and UP of cloth exported. The volume of trade would be less, and although the point T_1 would be on a higher indifference curve I_2, it would not be as satisfactory a point as T on I_3. In fact, T_1 is not an optimum point because the marginal rate of substitution in production at P is not equal to the marginal rate of substitution in consumption at T_1. It is a better position than P but an inferior position to T, which flexible production would make possible.

60 *International Trade and Payments*

The foregoing deals with the case of one country's gain from trade, given its factor endowments, its demand pattern and the world terms of trade when trade begins. We must now extend the analysis to examine the case of two countries, the quantities of two goods which will be traded and at what terms of trade. We can do this first by assuming tastes and the demand side to be identical in the two countries but the factor endowments and productive structure to differ, and second by assuming changes in taste and demand with identical supply conditions.

Assume that in Fig. 3.20 Britain and the United States have different

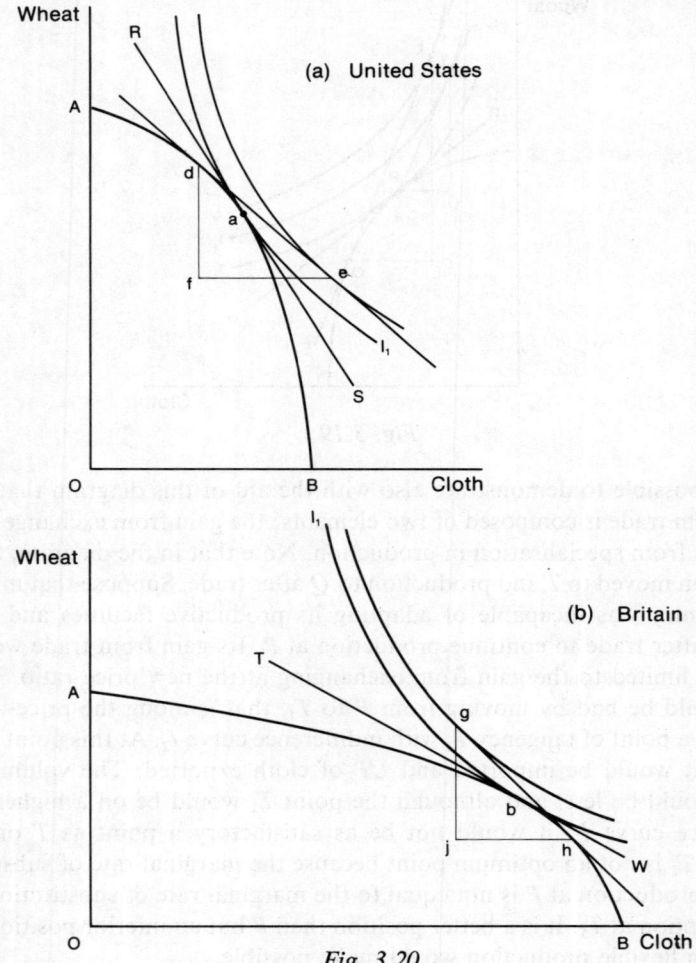

Fig. 3.20

The Pure Theory of International Trade

factor endowments, depicted in different production possibilities curves, but face an identical demand pattern reflected in similar indifference curves. On the supply side the United States has, as before, an advantage in wheat production while Britain has an advantage in cloth production. Both production possibilities curves AB reflect increasing opportunity costs. In a condition of autarky, output and consumption in both countries would be determined by the points of tangency a and b of the production possibilities curves AB to the highest possible indifference curves. The domestic terms of trade are indicated by the slope of the tangents RS for the United States and TW for Britain.

The situation after trade is represented by the lines de and gh. These lines are parallel since both represent the terms of trade between the two countries. They are equal in length since the exports of each country must equal the imports of the other. They are each tangent to the production possibilities curve and to a higher indifference curve than I_1. Their slope is at some value lying between the slopes of the two price-ratio lines under autarky. With these lines the United States consumes e of cloth of which fe is imported. It consumes e of wheat and produces d, exporting df. Britain consumes g of wheat of which gj is imported and produces h of cloth of which jh is exported.

It will be noted that with the production possibilities and indifference curves as drawn, trade results in greater specialisation in production, the tangency points moving along towards each extremity of the curve and less specialisation in consumption, the tangency points tending to move in along the indifference curves towards a similar consumption level for each country. This occurs because in each country there is, after trade, substitution of consumption in favour of the commodity which was scarce and expensive before trade but which has now fallen in price as a result of trade.

Turn now to the case in which two countries have identical supply conditions (i.e. factor endowments and technologies) but different demand conditions (tastes and preferences) and hence differently shaped community indifference curves. This case is illustrated in Fig. 3.21. Once more we take the example of the United States and Britain, but this time we do not specify particular commodities, being content with A good and B good. The production possibilities curves, AB in each case, are identical for the two countries. Demand conditions differ. The United States prefers to consume a lot of the A good at point T; Britain prefers to consume a lot of B at point U. This is the result of the differences between the indifference curves of the two countries which reflect their different tastes and preferences. Note also that the price ratio of the two goods in each country before trade is different, represented by the different slopes of p_1p_1 and

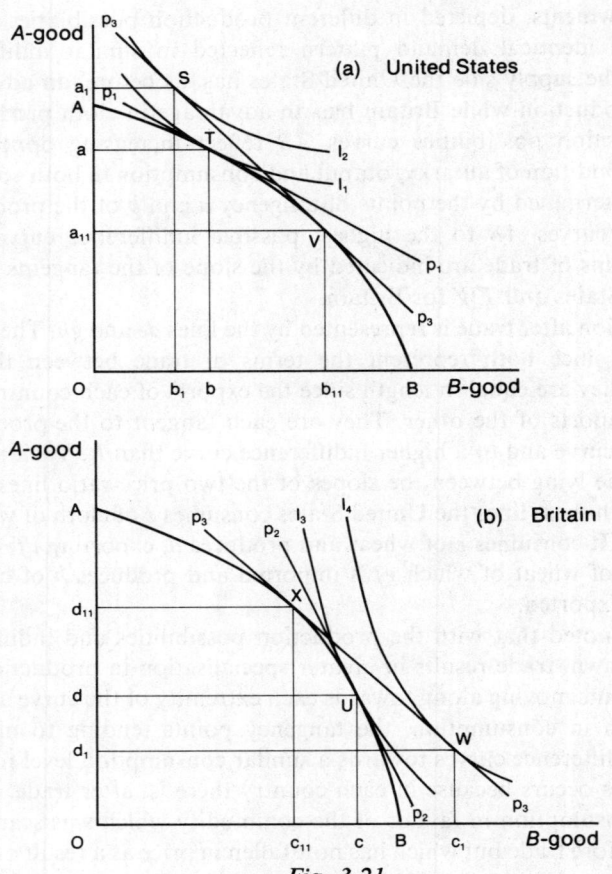

Fig. 3.21

p_2p_2. This price difference, created by the difference in demand conditions, is the justification for trade between the two countries.

Once trade begins the price ratio moves to p_3p_3. These price-ratio lines are determined for each country as in Fig. 3.20, that is they will be: (a) lines of equal length between their points of tangency to the production possibilities curve and the points of tangency to a higher indifference curve — i.e., $SV = WX$; (b) lines which are parallel to one another — as in p_3p_3 in (a) and (b); and (c) lines which run in opposite directions from the production possibilities curve in order to reach, in each case, a higher indifference curve. With these new price-ratio lines production and consumption shift in both countries: the United States produces at V and

The Pure Theory of International Trade

consumes at S; $a_1 a_{11}$ of A being imported and $b_1 b_{11}$ of B being exported; Britain produces at X and consumes at W, $d_1 d_{11}$ of A being exported and $c_1 c_{11}$ of B being imported. Imports and exports are in equilibrium for both countries at the new price ratio. It will be noted from the diagram that in this case (in contrast to the case of Fig. 3.20) trade results in both countries specialising more in consumption but less in production. At a practical level a country which before trade had a preference for bread rather than fruit and which grew bread grains on land more suited to fruit would, after trade, grow fruit on the land suited to it with a good yield and trade the fruit for bread grains.

We may, for logical completeness, deal briefly with the final case, that of identical factor endowments and identical tastes under increasing returns. Clearly this case is only conceivable under the assumption of increasing returns. With either constant or diminishing returns, that is with a straight line or concave to the origin transformation curve, the price ratios would be identical in both countries and no trade would take place. With increasing returns, however, there are, as we saw earlier in this chapter, trade possibilities. Fig. 3.22 demonstrates the case for both countries. Suppose the United States and Britain both produce bicycles and lawn mowers with a transformation curve XY and output in each at p with the same price ratio. Once the producers in both countries become aware of the economies of scale which may be reaped by specialisation the United States may move to X and specialise in bicycles and Britain to Y specialising in lawn mowers. Trade between the two countries may now take place at p_1, allowing both to move to a higher indifference curve.

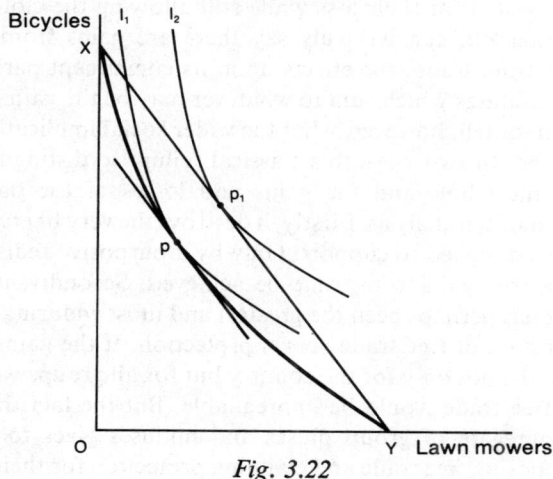

Fig. 3.22

(v) Conclusion

We have tried to show in this chapter how the Ricardian theory of comparative advantage has been extended and ramified by later economists until it is now a comprehensive system purporting to explain the *raison d'être* of international trade, the goods which will be produced and traded, the terms of trade or real prices at which trade will take place, and the gains to be derived from trade as compared with autarky. It is an impressive system which has provided a continuous basis of intellectual development for more than a century and which, in its essentials, has survived as the centrepiece of trade theory. It is appropriate to end this chapter with some general comments upon it.

The first comment is that, in terms of its original intention, the classical doctrine leads directly to a paradox. Its original purpose was to support and justify the liberal trade conception — a world-based division of labour buttressed, for distribution of its bounty, by free trade. Under free trade each country would necessarily be better off. This, at least, the preceding pages have shown. Unfortunately there is a difficulty. There is no necessary identity of gain between the individual, the group, and the nation. Certainly we showed in Fig. 3.19 that the country depicted would improve its consumption position by trade at T. By so doing it has slightly increased its cloth output and greatly diminished its wheat output. But then changes in production will involve a redistribution of income, in favour of cloth producers and away from wheat producers. Only if the wheat producers can be compensated for their loss while still allowing the cloth producers to remain better off, can we truly say there are gains from trade. The country gains from trade: the effects upon its constituent parts is a series of pluses and minuses which sum to whatever may be the gain in economic terms. We cannot tell, however, what the wider social implications of these changes may be. In two ways this classical failure to distinguish between the gains of the whole and the gains and losses of the parts detracts from the power of the analysis. Firstly, it destroys the very liberal idea which the theory was designed to support. Only by a purposive redistribution of income can a true gain from trade be achieved. Secondly, it clouds the issue, in what has perhaps been the greatest and most enduring controversy in economics, that of free trade versus protection. If the gains from trade were shown to be not only for the country but for all groups within it, then the case for free trade would be impregnable. But the fact that the trade gain is an aggregate of group pluses and minuses gives to the latter a reason for opposing free trade and claiming protection for their group. The free trade argument may, if the groups to be disadvantaged are numerous and socially or strategically important, become a very qualified one. We shall take up this question again in greater detail when we come to consider commercial policy in Part Two

A second comment on the classical theory is that by confining itself to a two-country and two-goods model it is so restrictive as to limit its usefulness. We have shown on p. 22 a very simple attempt to ease this restrictiveness by introducing for each of the two countries more commodities and arraying them in order of comparative advantage so that, for each country, a ranking in exports and imports may be obtained. This, and the device of nominating one of the countries to the role of the rest of the world, does something to increase generality, albeit still only slightly. We are not here, however, in a position where we have been seeking to establish a theory of full operational standing. It is doubtful if, in this huge context, that will ever be possible. But a theory, which answers with as much generality as possible the questions which we posed at the opening of Chapter 2 and which arrayed for inspection the strategic variables in the trade model, was a necessary starting point to any serious study of international trade. This the classical and neo-classical theory has done. We pass in the next chapter to newer and more detailed approaches and developments.

Appendix: The Offer (or Reciprocal Demand) Curve

The *reciprocal demand curve* (now more frequently called the *offer curve*) was first introduced as an analytical device by F. Y. Edgeworth. Marshall made extensive use of such curves in his *Money, Credit and Commerce*.[7] By their use he was able to carry a stage further Mill's theory of international values which had extended into the field of demand the original Ricardian theory of comparative advantage. The geometry of these curves was brought to a high degree of sophistication by James Meade in his *Geometry of International Trade*.[8] We shall consider in this appendix two aspects of such curves: how to derive them and what are their properties once they are derived.

Derivation of the Offer Curve

Meade has employed a simple geometric device to construct the offer curve from the production possibilities curve and the consumption indifference map. We proceed in two stages: first, we derive a trade indifference map from the consumption indifference map for each of the two countries; second we derive an offer curve for each country from its trade indifference map. What follows is based upon Meade's derivation.

In Fig. 3.23 we set out upon a system of co-ordinates the trade of two countries A and B. The horizontal axis measures A's exportables (B's importables) and the vertical B's exportables (A's importables). We shall combine, upon these coordinates, the demand and supply conditions which lead to a general equilibrium solution for two economies in international trade. The demand conditions are shown by consumption indifference maps, the supply conditions by production possibilities curves, or as we shall here call them, production blocks. First of all let us be clear what we can show on the diagram. The north-east quadrant is capable of describing conditions of trade. Along A_x we may measure exports of country A to country B and along B_x we may measure exports of country B to country A. The north-west quadrant describes the consumption of country A the amounts of the two goods being measured from O along the two axes. In

The Pure Theory of International Trade

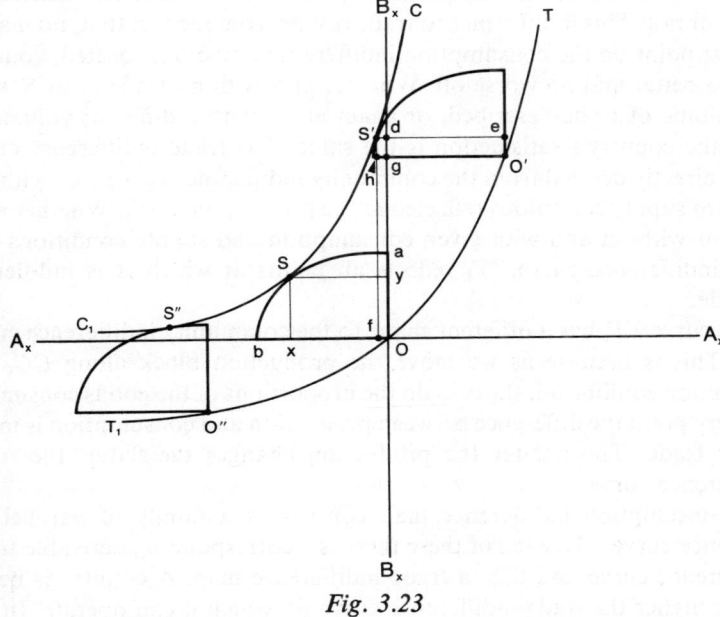

Fig. 3.23

the two southern quadrants the roles are reversed. The south-east measures consumption of country B and the south-west measures the trade conditions but in the opposite direction to those depicted in the north-east quadrant.

Take country A. In the north-west quadrant is shown its production block abO. Under conditions of no-trade this is tangential to a consumption indifference curve* at S at which country A consumes and produces Oy of B_x and Ox of A_x. Now take the production block of A and slide it up the consumption indifference curve CC_1, keeping the corresponding axes parallel and with the curved sector facing westward, to a new equilibrium point at S'. At the new equilibrium, consumption in A is now Od of good B_x and Of of good A_x. A's production is $O'e$ of B_x and $O'h$ of A_x. The quantity of $O'g$ of A_x is exported in trade for imports of fh of B_x.

If we continue to slide A's production block along the indifference curve CC_1 the origin of the block O will trace out a trade indifference curve TT_1.

* Let us clarify the terminology. We have been dealing in these examples with community indifference curves. These are also consumption indifference curves. They are to be distinguished from what we are now seeking to derive, namely, trade indifference curves which are each the loci of particular volumes of trade.

This curve is the loci of all points at which A is indifferent whether it trades or not. This indifference to trade results from the fact that, no matter at what point on the consumption indifference curve S is located, country A is no better and no worse off. Whether at S with no trade or at S' with the volume of trade described, or again at S'' with a different volume of trade the country's satisfaction is the same. The trade indifference curve TT_1 is directly derived from the community indifference curve CC_1 with the constant supply conditions reflected in the production block. Whether with trade or without and with given consumption and supply conditions this trade indifference curve TT_1 reflects all points at which A is indifferent to trade.

The curve TT_1 has a different shape to the community indifference curve CC_1. This is because as we move the production block along CC_1 the production equilibrium shifts as do the proportions of the goods consumed. At every point the difference between production and consumption is made up by trade. The greater the production changes the flatter the trade indifference curve.

A consumption indifference map consists of a family of parallel indifference curves. To each of these there is a corresponding derivable trade indifference curve and thus a trade indifference map. A country is better off the higher the trade indifference curve on which it can operate. In the example, A improves its position by moving to higher indifference curves — higher being judged by a movement south-east to north-west.

We can construct A's offer curve from its trade indifference map. This process is shown in Fig. 3.24. TI_{1-6} are trade indifference curves derived in the way which we have described. Rays drawn through the origin — as $p_1...p_6$ — represent price ratios in trade between the two commodities. The slope of Op_1 shows in the absence of trade the domestic price ratio in A for the two goods. That is to say, below Op_1 A would not be prepared to offer any A goods in return for imports from B. Such goods are obtainable more cheaply at home. At Op_1 trade might just commence, home and foreign prices being equal. Progressively as the international price rises to Op_2, Op_3, etc., A would be prepared to offer more A goods for goods from B. The improvement in the terms of trade would allow A to move to higher trade indifference curves and hence to preferred positions. In each case the amount of A's goods offered at each price ratio is determined by the point of tangency $(t_1, t_2...t_6)$ of the price-ratio line to a trade indifference curve.

As the terms of trade for A improve, A is prepared to offer more A goods for the increasing amounts of B goods available. Beyond t_3, however, and at price ratios better than Op_3, the amount of A goods offered begins to decline, partly because a scarcity of these goods is beginning to manifest

The Pure Theory of International Trade

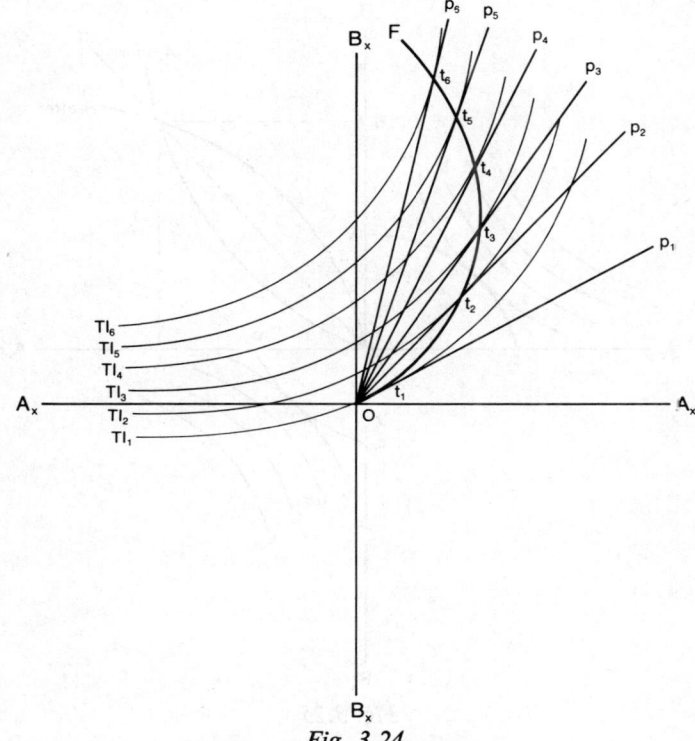

Fig. 3.24

itself in A and raise their value, and partly because the A market is now becoming glutted with B goods. From t_3 onwards A is only willing to accept more B goods if they are at a lower price in A goods terms. The offer of A goods at first becomes zero and then negative.

The curve OF is the desired offer curve of country A. It is the locus of all points of tangency of all possible price-ratio lines with all possible trade indifference curves. It shows how much of its exports a country is prepared to offer for imports at various terms of trade.

B's offer curve could be derived by the same procedure by which we obtained A's. A B production block moved on the B consumption indifference curve in the south-east quadrant would produce a trade indifference map from which, in the north-east quadrant, B's offer curve might be derived. Such an offer curve would slope upward from left to right intersecting the A offer curve. Fig. 3.25 illustrates the final situation with both offer curves in the north-east quadrant. The point X is the position of

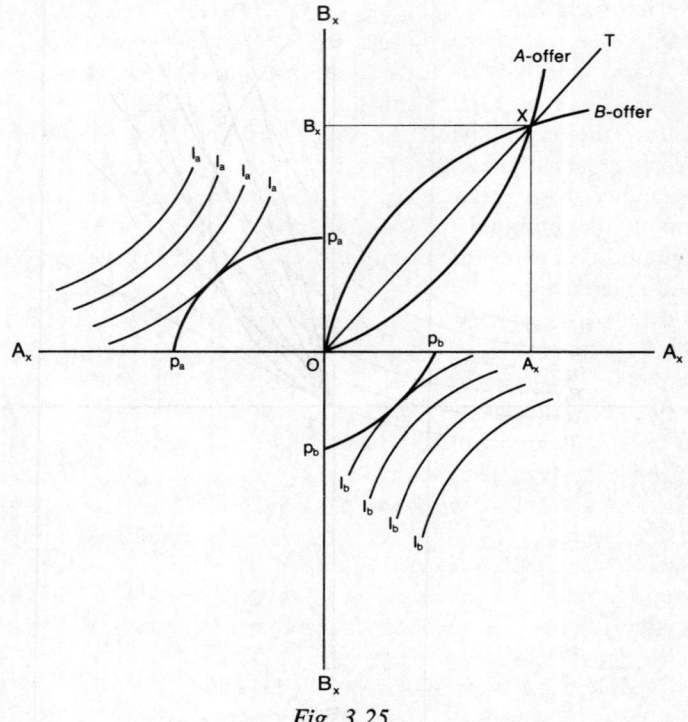

Fig. 3.25

balanced trade and the slope of *OT* is the terms of trade at which trade takes place.

Properties of the Offer Curve

So much for the derivation of the offer curve. We need also to know something of its properties and characteristics.

The reciprocal demand curve, offer curve, or international demand curve is a widely used tool in international trade. Useful for demonstrating the relations of demand to international price ratios, it has applications in the gains-from-trade analysis, in tariff theory and in exchange rate theory.

Although an offer curve resembles a demand curve in some respects, it is unwise to couple the two conceptually since they differ in what they show and in certain aspects of their geometry. For one thing it can, by

The Pure Theory of International Trade

virtue of its 'reciprocal' nature, be viewed either as a demand curve or a supply curve. It shows simultaneously amounts of, say, wheat which Britain is anxious to obtain for cotton, but it also shows the amounts of cotton which will be forthcoming in return for wheat. Then again, if viewed from the demand side, the offer curve has these important differences from the demand curve. The latter measures changes in the demand for commodity A with changes in unit money price. An offer curve measures demand for commodity A with changes in total amount of commodity B. If commodity B is regarded as money, then an offer curve approximates to a total revenue curve.

Important to the economist is the shape and slope of the offer curve, for these show its elasticity. We must, however, take care of how we apply the concept of elasticity to this curve, for the term may be interpreted in three ways, according to the aspect of the offer curve we have in mind. It may be viewed as an export elasticity relating a given change in exports with a change in the price of the other commodity; or it may be viewed as a total elasticity relating a percentage change in imports to a percentage change in exports at any point on the curve. Since understanding of the elasticity of offer curves is relevant in many pieces of analysis, it is worth brief attention here. We shall confine our attention to the case of demand elasticity for imports, leaving the reader to examine the other aspects of offer curve elasticity as an exercise.

Fig. 3.26 divides a typical foreign offer curve OF (of the United States) into sectors, each of which has a different elasticity (ϵ). The United States is demanding imports of cloth in exchange for exports of wheat, its

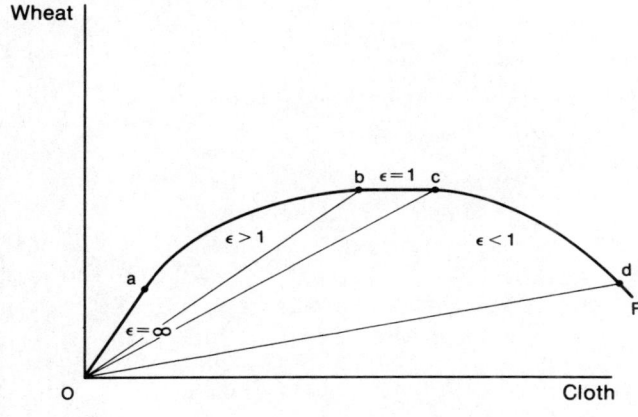

Fig. 3.26

terms of trade improving from Oa, to Ob, Oc and Od. Over sector Oa the offer curve is a straight line coinciding with the terms-of-trade line and is infinitely elastic, since the total wheat offered for cloth is increasing at a constant rate. Over sector ab the elasticity of the curve is greater than unity, since the total wheat offered for cloth is increasing with improved terms of trade up to point b. Over sector bc elasticity is unity, since the total amount of wheat offered for cloth is constant despite further improvement in the terms of trade. Over sector cd elasticity is less than unity, since the total offer of wheat for cloth is now falling. For the home offer curve with opposed curvature the relevant sectors of elasticity along the curve are easy to distinguish.

In the model demonstrated in Fig. 3.26 we have, for simplicity, made the bc sector of the offer curve a horizontal straight line. In most cases, however, unit elasticity would occur only at one point; that is, at the point of tangency of a horizontal straight line to such an offer curve or, in the case of the home offer curve, the point of tangency of a vertical straight line to the offer curve.

4
Factor Endowments: Commodity and Factor Prices

(i) Introduction

IN Chapter 3 we set out briefly the central arguments of the primary theory of international trade. The supply of goods in trade was based on comparative costs. The classical economists in the Ricardian tradition measured these costs in labour units following the labour theory of value. Later Haberler dispensed with this simplication, measuring cost not in input units but in opportunity cost terms. However measured, the supply side of the model remained based upon comparative costs. This has so far been accepted, but it is now necessary to inquire what may be the determinants of comparative costs themselves and further, what effect does trade have upon the cost differences which create it? This chapter is, therefore, an elaboration of the theory of supply in international trade. It starts by examining a phrase which has already crept into the discussion – the phrase 'factor endowments'. It is here that we may amplify the theory of comparative costs into a theory of relative prices. It ends by demonstrating that, under the assumptions of the trade model, trade causes cost differences themselves to disappear. The first part is concerned with the Heckscher–Ohlin theorem, the second with the factor-price equalisation theorem.

In this chapter it must not be taken that 'factor endowments' is a new approach to the supply side of international trade which supersedes and nullifies comparative advantage; it can more truly be appreciated in terms of Romney Robinson's phrase 'the factor proportions account of comparative advantage'. The reader should, also, be continually comparing the Heckscher–Ohlin theory of factor endowments with the classical theory of comparative advantage in order to appreciate their true relationship.[1]

(ii) Factor Endowments

First, let us backtrack a little. Classical value theory (for a closed economy) relied originally for its explanation of values, and ultimately relative prices, upon measurement in terms of labour. It relied upon the assumption of a single factor of production, labour, mixed in fixed combination with capital. The development of modern price theory has been, in one sense, an emancipation from this early simplification and its replacement by a progressively sophisticated general equilibrium theory, in which supply is seen as the result of a combination of several production factors used in variable proportions, while demand is seen as an aggregate of individual consumer choices, conditioned by individual incomes and tastes. Supply and demand in the market determine, by their relationship, the prices for all commodities. It follows, too, that since the demand for commodities implies a secondary (or derived) demand for production factors, any discrepancy between actual factor prices and those that should obtain, in order to balance their supply and the demand for them inherent in the demand for commodities, will be adjusted by changes interacting throughout the system.

This simple equilibrium system applies to any single homogeneous market — such a market implying perfect competition among goods and factors and perfect mobility of the latter. It is a system reflecting a closed economy but it is not applicable to international trade, if only because there is not perfect mobility of factors between the national markets which an international trade system implies. Only to some hypothetical country of miniscule size — a uni-market entity — does such a system truly apply. We may regard a large modern economy such as the United States, Canada or Britain as a series of markets, properly comparable to a series of countries in international trade. A multi-market economy is comparable in this sense, theoretically, to a multi-countried trade system. Put in another way, and from a theoretical point of view, there is no apparent difference between inter-country (or international trade as we know it) and inter-regional trade between numerous uni-market regions.

This logic has had its effect on the theory of international trade, and Ohlin, in a major book,[2] treats interregional and international trade as similar. While it is arguable that different units of account and different banking systems, frictions to goods movement such as tariffs, import controls and the like, and different legal systems and institutions, all differentiate countries more clearly than they do regions, yet, withal, these special characteristics are more germane to other aspects of international trade than they are to its pure theory. They are relevant to such matters as the balance of payments, exchange rate policy and commercial policy. As one writer puts it 'the fundamental theorems of international trade theory apply to the relations among both kinds of market'.[3] This conception of interrelated market systems – whether regional or international – is central to modern trade theory. By its use we are able to use identical value theories in our analysis of the interrelations of such markets, passing beyond the comparative costs approach of the classicals with its reliance on labour value and even beyond the later opportunity cost approach which succeeded, to a fuller consideration of the determination of the relative prices which impel trade.

The classical economists said: comparative costs are the basis of trade. We now move forward and say: relative price differences are the basis of trade. If countries have identical price structures no trade exists between them; if they differ in their price structures, relatively cheap goods will be exported in return for the relatively cheap goods of other countries. But if price differences generate trade we may further ask: what in turn causes price differences? Clearly we can answer this question by reciting a considerable list of price-determining forces – the nature of production functions, the power of consumer demand as determined by tastes and incomes – but among such forces two may be singled out as specially important, the endowment of the given country with factors of production, and the use of these production factors with differing degrees of intensity. From mere casual observation it is apparent that these characteristics do much to determine a country's import and export list. Canada, the United States and Australia are well supplied with land and moderately well with capital. The United States, Germany and Britain each have an industrial complex in which capital, technical expertise and a great infrastructure contribute to low-cost industrial production. In some countries, for example Japan, labour is an abundant factor. If we use the term factor endowment to stand for the peculiar and variegated mix of factors which each country displays, we mean by it not only the quantities of factors but their quality and inherent characteristics, their relative strengths and weaknesses, their flexibility in face of changing techniques, and their degree of scarcity or uniqueness to each country. Few things are so unique and individual to a country as its own factor endowment.

An important difference between the classical and the Heckscher–Ohlin theory should be noted at this point. The Ricardians base trade on differing production systems *including differing factor productivities*. The Heckscher–Ohlin approach assumes the productivity of like factors to be uniform, but bases trade on differences in (a) their quantities and (b) the intensity of their use.

The country-to-country variation of factor endowments as the basis of trade was embodied in the modern theory of international trade during the interwar period by two Swedish economists. Eli Heckscher, well known for his work on mercantilism, published an article in 1919 which provided the foundation for a 'factor proportions' theory of international trade.[4] (Heckscher in a note to the 1949 English translation of his article acknowledges a debt to Wicksell.) This was developed and reshaped by Heckscher's pupil Bertil Ohlin, first in his doctoral dissertation in 1924 and then more fully in his *Interregional and International Trade*, first published in 1933. The resulting Heckscher–Ohlin theorem is now an established part of the general structure of trade theory. It is not a refutation or even a qualification to the classical comparative cost doctrine. Indeed, it lends powerful support to classical doctrine. But it probes deeper, seeking the roots of comparative cost and purports to explain why costs of production differ between countries – what are the reasons for international differences in commodity values. It may be claimed that the Heckscher–Ohlin approach has done two things for trade theory: it has developed and deepened the study of comparative costs, and it has brought the supply side of the trade equation to a stage in which empirical investigation can be (and has been) brought to bear. The scepticism which these empirical studies has induced has produced in the fifties and sixties an immense renewed interest in trade theory and a questioning of many of the fundamental propositions. For these reasons we must examine the Heckscher–Ohlin approach in some detail.

In order to explain trade we must lay bare the reasons for differences in commodity prices. In part, such differences may be explained by differences in factor prices which are themselves largely explained by the relative scarcity or abundance of factors. Thus agricultural products tend to be cheapest where land is most plentiful; products with a large labour input are cheapest where labour is most abundant. The influence of the factor price on commodity price is easily seen in some cases but, in many cases where the factor combination for production of a commodity is variable and where the same good can be produced at similar cost with different factor groupings, the connection between factor scarcity and final commodity price may be very tenuous. Take some examples. The influence of factor price on commodity price is greatest where production is intensive for that factor. Many industries are intensive in this way. Wheat growing in Canada is land intensive. For each the price of the commodity produced is dominantly influenced by the price (and therefore in great part by the supply) of the intensive factor. But by contrast wool, although always

The Pure Theory of International Trade

dependent upon natural fibres as main factor, may be produced from sheep allowed to roam the hills by upland farmers, or by sheep kept to fields which are rotated with other crops, or by sheep which serve the alternative use of providing meat. The factor mix here is variable and it is more difficult to connect factor prices accurately with final wool prices. It is here the factor proportion, the substitutability of factors, that makes the relation between factor price and commodity price more complex. Once trade takes place, however, the relative factor–price situation as between countries is changed. Imports to the high-price countries, exports from the low-price countries equalise commodity prices in the trading countries. As long as price differences exist it is advantageous to expand trade, and this incentive remains until all price differences are eliminated. Later in this chapter we shall also demonstrate, what is now not as readily apparent, that trade will equalise factor prices as between the trading countries.

It would appear then that, if relative goods prices are the basis of trade and if factor endowments determine the supply side of goods traded, two aspects of factor endowment are important: the relative supplies of factors in the nation, and the factor proportions required by commodities. To put the argument in another way, trade takes place because nations are differently endowed with factors of production and because commodities can be produced by different factor combinations. Countries will tend to export products which reflect their factor endowments, land-rich countries exporting agricultural products, capital-rich countries exporting sophisticated mechanical products.

It may be helpful now, at the risk of repetition, to sum up the argument so far in a series of propositions:

1. The pattern of factor prices in each country is different. Assuming a neutrality of demand, factors which are plentiful are cheap, those which are scarce are dear.
2. The price of a commodity will be low when the factor most essential to its production is cheap and plentiful and vice versa.
3. Since differences in relative prices are the main cause of trade, a country will export commodities which require large quantities of plentiful factors of production. It will import goods in which factors scarce to it are dominant in production.
4. Differences in relative costs and prices will disappear as a result of trade.

It is apparent immediately from all this that any serious theory of trade must concern itself with the detailed aspects of production, in particular with factor quantities and factor proportions. It is appropriate to describe the modern theory of international trade as a factor proportions theory. Differences in factor proportions and variances in production functions have extended the theory of comparative advantage so as to provide an important extension to the classical theory. As before, the aim is to determine for any country what goods are exported and what are imported and what are the gains to be derived from trade participation. In the section which follows we shall examine in more detail the factor proportions approach to the supply side of international trade. Readers must then compare this more modern approach to the simple explanation of supply already provided.

(iii) Production Functions and Box Diagrams

Our need is now for tools of analysis which will enable us to handle the two basic variables of the Heckscher–Ohlin theorem — relative factor abundance and factor intensities. These tools are available from production analysis and, by the use of production functions, isoquants and the Edgeworth–Bowley box diagram, it is possible to carry the analysis of factor endowments and the supply side of international trade a significant stage further. What follows now is a detailed examination, by the tools of production analysis, of the forces which determine the production possibilities curve, whose role in the theory of trade we have already examined in Chapter 3.

Let us look first at the production function. This function defines the relation between inputs of factors and the output of a final commodity. In practice there are many factors, but the constraint of two dimensions must limit us to the consideration of two, capital and labour. Thus, given the production function for cloth, we can determine the amounts of labour and capital which will be required to produce one unit of cloth. This production function is a stable one. In any short period it is a reflection of the technical nature of the production process for making the product. It will only change in the longer period in which technological innovations may alter the relation between quantities of factor inputs and output. Apart from this, production functions may be of various types. For example, a production process may be such that labour and capital are substitutes over a wide range, or again it may be that labour and capital can be used only in fixed proportions. The fixed proportion, or Leontief type of production function, is a case which is important in production theory and we will make some use of it later in this chapter, but, for the present, we will confine our discussion to production functions of the first type.

The Pure Theory of International Trade

One way of demonstrating the production function is by the use of isoquants or equal-product contour lines. Fig. 4.1 illustrates by isoquants the case of a production function for an industry in which capital and labour are substitutable, so that a given quantity of output can be produced by using either much capital and little labour or much labour and little capital. Each isoquant, Q_1, Q_2, Q_3, shows all combinations of capital and labour for increasing discreet levels of output, each appropriate to one of these isoquants. Note the shape of the isoquants. They are convex to the origin

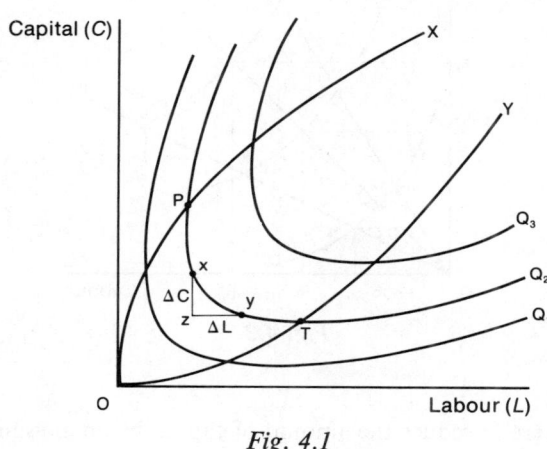

Fig. 4.1

because, as one input is increased, it becomes progressively difficult to substitute it for the other—this reflecting a diminishing marginal rate of substitution for each input. Only part of each isoquant is relevant to the analysis. For example, outside the points P and T on Q_2 the slope of the isoquant is such that an increasing amount of both inputs are required to produce Q_2. A producer would not in these circumstances operate outside the sector PT of the Q_2 isoquant. For a number of isoquants (Q_1, Q_2, Q_3) representing progressively higher levels of output, the effective sectors would be limited by the 'ridge lines' OX and OY joining the origin and the points on the isoquants at which the curves begin to bend back upon themselves.

After this brief digression on the geometry of isoquants we can redraw Fig. 4.1, simplifying it in Fig. 4.2 by showing only the effective sectors of the isoquants contained within the ridge lines. Q_1, Q_2 and Q_3 are now isoquants each appropriate to a progressively higher level of output.

From any isoquant we may establish an interesting relationship of which we shall later make some use. On Fig. 4.1 let us take Q_2 to represent any isoquant, i.e. a curve along which the quantities of product produced are constant. In terms of the diagram: by moving from x to y along Q_2 the change in output $dQ = 0$.

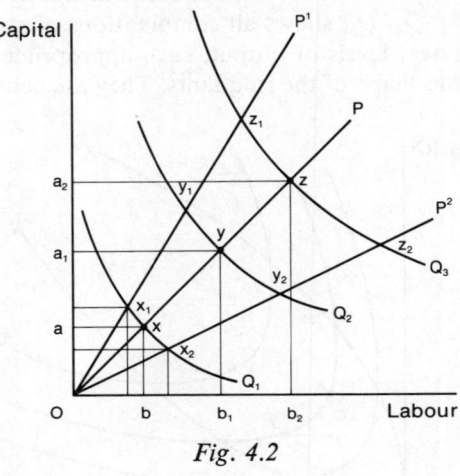

Fig. 4.2

If at x we were to reduce the amount of capital by an amount ΔC, while at the same time we hold the amount of labour constant, we would be obliged to accept a lower output on some new isoquant passing through z. The only way to restore the output appropriate to Q_2 would be by increasing the amount of labour by ΔL, thus getting back to Q_2 at y. (When the distance between x and y is small, it is customary to adopt the notation dL for ΔL and dC for ΔC.) For the reduction in capital there would be a substitution of an appropriate amount of labour. The reduction which occurred in output by reducing C would be approximately the reduction in the amount of capital multiplied by its marginal product at x, that is $dC \cdot (\partial Q/\partial C)$; while the increase in the amount of output which occurred through increasing L would be the increase in labour L multiplied by its marginal product, that is $dL \cdot (\partial Q/\partial L)$. The substitution puts us back on Q_2 with no change in output.

It may be shown by calculus that, for sufficiently small values of ΔC and ΔL we may write:

$$dQ = dC \cdot \frac{\partial Q}{\partial C} + dL \cdot \frac{\partial Q}{\partial L} = 0 \tag{1}$$

If we assume that we are remaining on the same isoquant $dQ = 0$ and thus

$$dC \cdot \frac{\partial Q}{\partial C} + dL \cdot \frac{\partial Q}{\partial L} = 0 \qquad (2)$$

Subtract $dL \cdot (\partial Q/\partial L)$ from both sides of the equation and we get:

$$dC \cdot \frac{\partial Q}{\partial C} = -dL \cdot \frac{\partial Q}{\partial L} \qquad (3)$$

Divide both sides of (3) by $-dL$ and we get:

$$-\frac{dC}{dL} \cdot \frac{\partial Q}{\partial C} = \frac{\partial Q}{\partial L} \qquad (4)$$

Finally divide both sides of (4) by $\partial Q/\partial C$ and we get:

$$+\frac{dC}{dL} = -\frac{\partial Q/\partial L}{\partial Q/\partial C} \qquad (5)$$

This equation now furnishes us with significant relationships. dC/dL is in mathematical terms the slope of the isoquant at x (or more precisely the slope of the tangent to the isoquant at x) and in economic terms is the marginal rate of substitution of the factors, that is the rate at which the factors must be substituted in order to keep output constant at the level Q. On the right-hand side of the equation $\partial Q/\partial L$ is the marginal product of labour while $\partial Q/\partial C$ is the marginal product of capital. Thus in economic terms we may write (5) in the following form:

$$\text{Marginal Rate of Factor Substitution} = \frac{\text{Marginal product of Labour}}{\text{Marginal product of Capital}}$$

Let us return to the production function, the basic relationship between factor inputs and product output for a good. Under our assumption of two factors, labour and capital, this may be expressed in the form

$$Q = f(L, C)$$

where Q stands for total product output, L for labour and C for capital. What may we assume about this function?

Initially we might wish to assume merely that the relationship between output and factor inputs exists but to leave any more precise relationship unspecified. In fact it is customary in trade theory to be more specific, assuming the production function to be such that any proportionate change in inputs results in an exactly equal proportionate change in output. If L and C are both doubled, Q is doubled; if L and C are both reduced by 5 per cent then Q is also reduced by 5 per cent. (In more technical parlance we assume that the production function is homogeneous of the first degree or that the production function is linearly homogeneous.) From this assumption of a linear homogeneous production function two important relations follow.

The first of these can be illustrated by total differentiation of the basic equation

$$Q = f(L, C)$$

in order to get

$$dQ = \frac{\partial Q}{\partial L} \cdot dL + \frac{\partial Q}{\partial C} \cdot dC$$

In this equation $\partial Q/\partial L$ is the expression for the marginal productivity of labour while $\partial Q/\partial C$ is the expression for the marginal productivity of capital.

We may assume that both of these expressions are positive. This means that with a given capital stock an increase in the labour force will increase output. Equally, if with a given labour force we increase capital (say, by installing more machines) we must increase output.

If we go on to derive second partial derivatives, the expressions

$$\frac{\partial^2 Q}{\partial L^2} \quad \text{and} \quad \frac{\partial^2 Q}{\partial C^2}$$

will show how the marginal productivities of labour and capital each change as labour and capital are increased with a fixed amount on the other factor. It is likely that the value of these expressions will be negative. As labour is progressively increased relative to capital an increasing number of workers will come to lack capital; similarly as capital is increased relative to labour a point will be reached beyond which capital remains idle for lack of workers to use it.

It is possible to proceed further by taking mixed second partial derivatives

$$\frac{\partial^2 Q}{\partial L \partial C} \quad \text{and} \quad \frac{\partial^2 Q}{\partial C \partial L}$$

The first of these shows how the marginal productivity of labour varies as we alter the amount of capital, the second shows the pattern of the marginal productivity of capital as we increase the labour factor. If the production function is homogeneous these second partial derivatives will be positive. In practical terms increasing capital relative to labour will certainly increase the marginal productivity of labour, since labourers will be better

The Pure Theory of International Trade

equipped; and increasing labour relative to capital will increase the productivity of capital, since capital equipment will be more fully utilised and better maintained.

A final, but important, property of the linear homogeneous production function must be examined. It is this: when two factors of production are employed, and when changes in the amounts of these factors are such as to preserve their combination in the same proportion, then the marginal productivities of both factors remain constant. Alternatively, we may say: the marginal productivities of both factors depend solely upon the proportion in which they are employed in the productive process.

This proposition may be illustrated geometrically from Fig. 4.2. Any straight line through the origin, such as OP, shows labour and capital combined in the same proportion. At points x, y, and z along OP,

$$\frac{Oa \text{ of capital}}{Ob \text{ of labour}} = \frac{Oa_1 \text{ of capital}}{Ob_1 \text{ of labour}} = \frac{Oa_2 \text{ of capital}}{Ob_2 \text{ of labour}}$$

and similarly for all points on OP. This is so because the ratios of the factors at each of these points also measure the slope of OP. Moreover if the production function is linearly homogeneous the tangents at x, y and z will be parallel. In economic terms the marginal productivities of labour and capital are the same at all points along OP.

If we draw other rays OP^1 and OP^2 from the origin they have the same properties. Each ray, according to its slope, represents a different marginal productivity of the factors; but along each ray the marginal productivity is constant. We can now relate the marginal productivity along the rays to the marginal productivity along the isoquants Q_1, Q_2, and Q_3. Take Q_1. At x_1 where OP^1 cuts Q_1 the marginal productivity of labour is higher at x_1 than at x, while that at x is higher than at x_2. This is so because at x_1 the capital–labour ratio is higher than at x, so that workers are better equipped at x_1 than at x or at x than at x_2. The more capital intensive the production the higher the marginal productivity. As we move north of OP and for any further isoquants such as Q_2 or Q_3 marginal productivities of labour rise with high capital intensity. As we move south of OP marginal productivities of capital rise as more labour is used.

All this tells us something about various factor combinations or methods of production. The isoquant gives us for any product the various factor mixes which will sustain a given level of output. It is, of itself, a reflection of the technology of the product. We are, however, interested as economists in the most efficient economic combination of these factors. To determine the precise way in which they will be combined, however, we require further data, the nature of relative factor prices.

Let us start from the three isoquants Q_1, Q_2, Q_3 which we now transfer to a new diagram in Fig. 4.3. These isoquants show the factor combinations for progressively higher levels of output of a given good. A producer with a given amount available to buy inputs may distribute that sum between purchases of capital and labour, his available options being represented by the line XY. He may devote all of his monetary resources to purchasing OX of capital or to purchasing OY of labour, or he may purchase a mix of these factors represented by any point along XY – providing, of course, the prices of capital and labour remain constant. This line we may refer to as the 'factor expenditure' or 'factor budget' line. Its slope measures the relative prices of the two factors being considered.

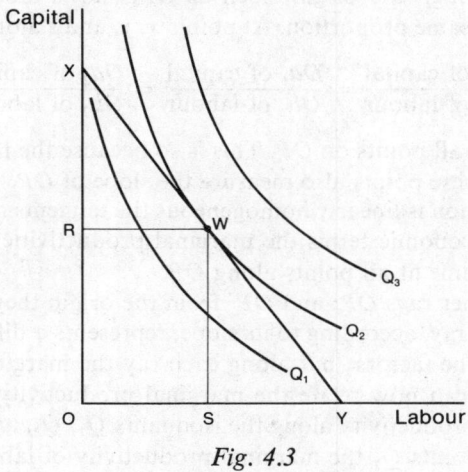

Fig. 4.3

Any producer will wish to allocate his factor expenditure to the best result – that is, he will wish to maximise his output with his given resources. This will occur when the expenditure line is tangent to the highest possible isoquant, as at W on the diagram. At W the producer is producing the highest possible output consistent with his factor expenditure and involving him in a productive process using OR units of capital and OS units of labour. No other level of production than Q_2 is feasible under the circumstances. Q_1 would not satisfy the profit maximiser, since it leaves part of his factor budget unused and would condemn him to a lower output than he is obliged to have; Q_3 is an impossibly high output for which the production process is beyond his factor budget. We can also say that W represents the point of maximum output at minimum cost. That W represents minimum cost for output Q_2 can easily be seen from the diagram since to produce Q_1

The Pure Theory of International Trade

with any combination of factors other than OR and OS would involve movement to a new budget line to the right of XY. To sum up, W is an equilibrium position providing maximum output of the product at minimum cost and with an optimal combination of factors.

Earlier in this section we examined some of the properties of an isoquant (see p. 79 above). One of these was that the slope of a tangent to an isoquant, representing the marginal rate of factor substitution, was equal to the inverse ratio of the factors' marginal productivities. Now we see that at W, the equilibrium position of production, we are on a tangent to the isoquant whose slope represents the factor–price ratio. This tells us that, at W, the ratio of factor–prices, the marginal rate of substitution between the factors and the inverse ratio of the productivities of the factors are all equal. In symbolic terms at W:

$$\frac{OX}{OY} = \frac{MP_L}{MP_C} = MRS \text{ of capital for labour}$$

If we wish to convert OX/OY, the physical ratio of exchange between capital and labour into a ratio of money prices of factors we may do so by taking the reciprocal of the physical exchange ratio and calling it P_L/P_C.* Then we have:

$$\frac{OX}{OY} = \frac{P_L}{P_C} = \frac{MP_L}{MP_C} = MRS$$

In a situation where capital is costing twice as much per unit as labour it is only worth using capital if its marginal product is at least twice that of labour. As long as it is less than this it is better to substitute labour for capital, causing labour's marginal product to fall and capital's marginal product to rise until the ratio of the marginal products equals the price ratio of the factors.

Let us shift the focus of attention, remembering still that our purpose is to give greater precision to the rather vague-sounding term 'factor intensiveness'. Let us ask now: what will be the relative amounts of two factors used in a production process? Will a process be dominated by the use of one factor or other or will there be a moderate utilisation of both factors? What, in short, will be the 'factor intensity' of the process? An industry such as atomic power production is capital intensive; wood carving is unavoidably labour intensive.

* This can readily be seen if we assign prices and amounts to OX and OY on Fig. 4.3. If a producer has $1000 to spend on labour and capital and the prices of these factors are $50 per unit of capital and $25 per unit of labour he may acquire 20 units of capital (i.e. OX) or 40 units of labour (i.e. OY) so that $OX/OY = \frac{1}{2}$. But the factor price ratio in money terms is $50/$25 or 2.

We may illustrate the concept of factor intensity by the use of isoquants. Remember that any technological production process is reflected in a production function for which, in turn, there is an isoquant. Factor intensity is implicit in the relative amounts in which two factors (capital and labour to continue the example) combine at any point on the isoquant. We may illustrate the point with Lerner's diagram in Fig. 4.4.[6] First, take the simple case where two commodities are produced under the same technological conditions. For the same amounts of labour and capital the two commodities will have identical isoquants and relative factor amounts will be the same point for point upon such isoquants. Commodities x and y

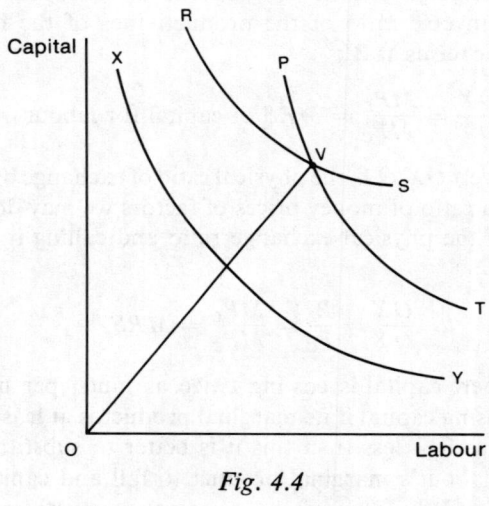

Fig. 4.4

might both be reflected in the isoquant XY. It is more likely, however, that two commodities will have different production functions so that for the same factor inputs the isoquants will be of different shapes. They reflect different factor proportions or different factor intensities. RS and PT are such isoquants. Since they intersect at V, at this point but at this point only, are factor proportions the same, the capital–labour ratio being shown by OV. For the rest, the commodity represented by PT is labour intensive and the commodity represented by RS is capital intensive. This can readily be seen from the fact that both isoquants to the left of the intersection point are relatively capital intensive as compared to the right of V at which both isoquants are relatively labour intensive. But RS is more capital intensive than PT because at any point to the left of V, RS requires for any given amount of capital less labour than does PT. Similarly, to the right of

V, in the more labour-intensive sectors of the isoquants, PT requires a smaller amount of capital at each level of labour input than does RS.

Factor intensity is, however, only a meaningful term when we consider it in conjunction with factor prices. This can be seen clearly by extending the scope of Fig. 4.4. In Fig. 4.5 (a) we show two production functions which are assumed to be linearly homogeneous, one for steel and one for wheat, facing a given producer for whom XY is the factor budget line. The producer can either combine labour and capital by producing steel at R with Oa of capital and Ob of labour, or wheat at S with Oa_1 of capital and Ob_1 of labour. R and S are the points of tangency of the steel and wheat iso-

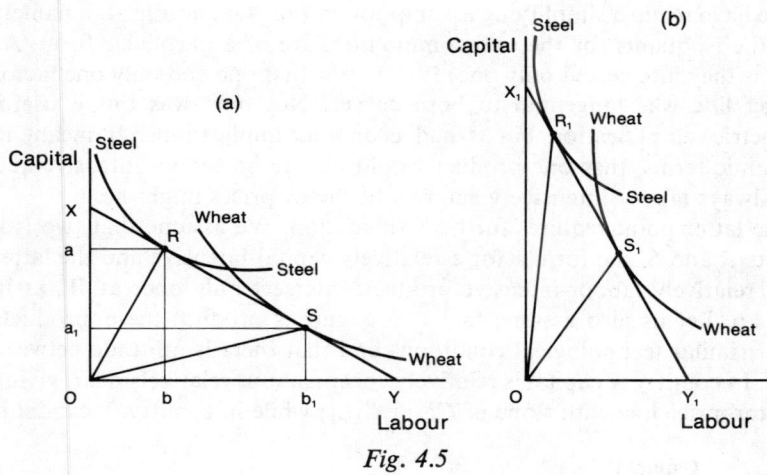

Fig. 4.5

quants with XY, the factor budget line. The rays OR and OS show the capital–labour ratio for steel and wheat respectively and at the points R and S the ratios between the marginal productivities of capital and labour are equal to the factor–price ratio.

Suppose now that factor prices change and that the price of labour increases compared to that of capital, giving, on Fig. 4.5 (b) a new and steeper factor budget line X_1Y_1. To accommodate the price change, production becomes more capital intensive in both processes, capital being substituted for labour as the latter becomes more expensive. Because of the assumption of linear homogeneity the steel and wheat isoquants take the same form but the minimum cost production points are located on the isoquant upward and to the left, reflecting the greater capital intensity in production. The capital–labour ratios are now steeper at OR_1 and OS_1. It is unnecessary to demonstrate the effects of a rise in the price of capital relative to labour. In this case the factor budget line XY would have become less steeply sloped than in Fig. 4.5 (a); the cost-minimising points would lie on isoquants located to the right and downward and the slopes of OR and OS would have been less than in the first position.

The reader should note that it is a necessary assumption in this analysis that perfect competition prevails. The production functions and factor prices are given, the latter being determined by demand and supply in the market. If a single producer, such as that whose behaviour is depicted above, were able to influence prices in the factor market, the order and nature of events would be different from that shown.

We have made a simplifying assumption in Fig. 4.4 and Fig. 4.5, namely that the isoquants for the two commodities are of a particular form. As long as they intersected only once it was clear that one and only one factor budget line was tangential to both curves. Not only was this a useful geometric simplification but it had economic implications. It meant, in economic terms, that one product would always be capital intensive and one always labour intensive whatever the factor prices might be.

The latter point requires further explanation. We assume that two isoquants R and S, the former for a relatively capital-intensive and the latter for a relatively labour-intensive product, intersect only once at W, as in Fig. 4.6. Let us also assume that two countries produce these products under similar technological conditions and that there is no trade between them. In country X capital is relatively cheap, labour relatively dear, giving a factor–price line with slope of CL or C_1L_1; while in country Y capital is

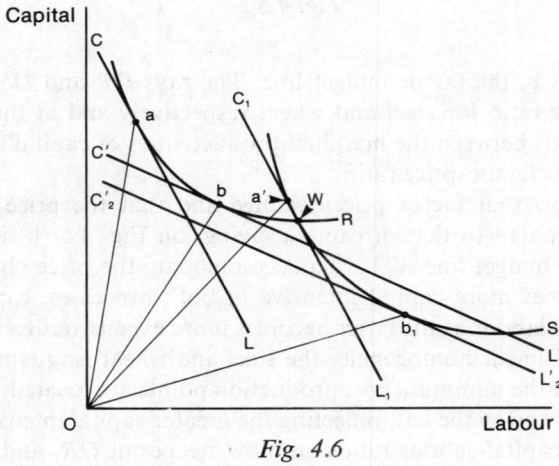

Fig. 4.6

relatively dear and labour relatively cheap, giving a factor–price line with slope of $C'L'$ or $C'_2L'_2$. In these conditions in country X, commodity R is more capital intensive than commodity S because the slope of Oa is greater than that of Oa'. In country Y commodity S is, despite the different factor–price relationship, also more capital intensive than is commodity R because Ob is steeper than Ob_1. What we are in fact saying is that if, assuming isoquants of this type, two commodities are compared, the one which was capital intensive would remain so irrespective of whether the countries compared had low capital costs and high wages or high capital costs and low wages. In other words the relative factor intensity exists at any set of factor prices. This assumption (usually referred to as the 'strong factor intensity requirement') as to the nature of the production functions reflected in the shape of the isoquants is important. It reflects a condition whose fuller implications will be explored later in this chapter.

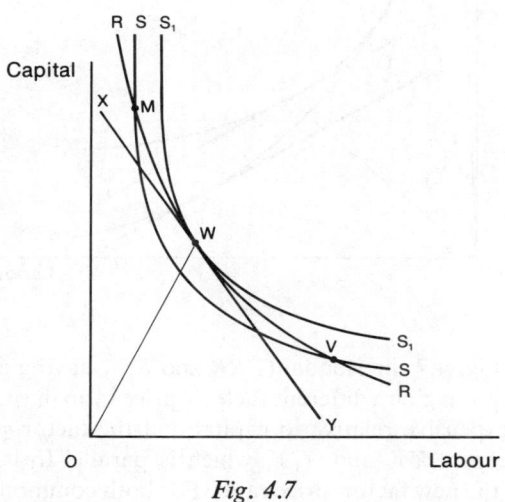

Fig. 4.7

In the meanwhile let us consider what happens if we remove this assumption and allow the isoquants for our two commodities to cut twice. In Fig. 4.7 this condition is illustrated. Suppose that RR and SS are the isoquants of two commodities and that their shapes are such that they intersect at M and V. Both isoquants are, however, members of an infinite series so that it is possible to find a parallel curve for say SS at S_1S_1 which is tangential to the RR curve at W. At this point the factor–price ratio is shown by the slope of the straight line XY which is tangential to both curves at W while OW, a ray from the origin shows the proportion in which the two factors are combined, i.e. the factor intensity, for both products. This situation would, however, hold good for only one unique factor–price ratio. A change in the relative prices of the two factors would change the whole situation.

Let us suppose that this happens. In Fig. 4.8 we have the same basic

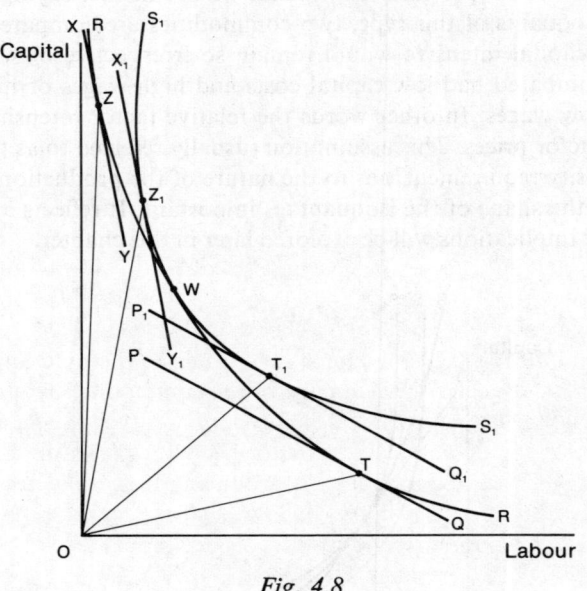

Fig. 4.8

situation as in Fig. 4.7 the isoquants RR and S_1S_1 having a point of tangency at W. Now imagine a different factor – price ratio in which labour has become more expensive relative to capital and the factor–price-ratio line has become steeper. XY, and X_1Y_1 which is parallel to it, would by its slope represent the new factor–price ratio. For both commodities (R and S) the production would become more capital intensive as the price of labour rose. For R the factor intensity would be represented by OZ and for S_1S_1 by OZ_1. The more the price of labour rose relative to capital the further Z and Z_1 would move to the left and the steeper OZ and OZ_1 would become. R would, for all factor–price ratios in which labour is more expensive than at W, be more capital intensive than S_1S_1.

What happens if the factor ratio changes in the other direction and capital is relatively more expensive than labour? The factor–price ratio may now be represented by the slope of PQ (or P_1Q_1) and the factor intensities for R and S_1S_1 would be OT and OT_1 respectively. The more the price of capital rises relatively to labour the more labour intensive would become the production of both commodities. R, which was the more capital intensive of the two goods when labour was dear, now becomes the more labour intensive when capital becomes dear.

To generalise the results apparent from Fig. 4.8, the degree of factor intensity in different lines of production depends on the factor–price ratio between capital and labour. In contrast to the case of strong factor intensity, in which the relative factor intensities of two commodities remain the same whatever the relative money costs of the two factors, the case we have now examined is one in which the factor intensity depends upon the ruling factor–price ratio. In terms of Fig. 4.8, RR is only more capital intensive than $S_1 S_1$ for factor–price ratios in which labour is dear. $S_1 S_1$ is more capital intensive than R for factor–price ratios in which labour is cheap. The relative factor intensities of the two products reverse themselves on either side of W. There has been a reversal of factor intensities as between the two products.

Before we proceed further with the analysis, let us look briefly at the economic implications of the factor reversal case. It would appear that, if two countries are each producing one of the commodities, country A, with a plentiful supply of capital, could export commodity R which, at its factor–price ratio, is capital intensive. Country B, with plentiful labour might, however, also export commodity R, producing it at its factor–price ratio by a different productive process which was labour intensive. Alternatively the capital-rich country might produce and export its labour-intensive product. It would seem that to predict the specialisation of international trade on a basis of factor endowments alone becomes impossible. As one writer puts it, unless we know more than the bald facts of factor endowments we can explain only some trade but not all trade.[7]

By returning to the diagrams we can throw more light on the case of factor reversal. Remember that it occurs when the isoquants of the two commodities cut twice. In terms of Fig. 4.7 the double intersection basic to the reversal case occurs because SS is more convex to the origin than RR. What does this difference in the shape of the curves reflect?

It reflects the different possibilities for substitution of capital and labour in the productive process of each product. Even intuitively it can be seen that in RR the two factors of production are closer substitutes one for another than they are in SS. In technical jargon the differences in slope of the production functions reflects the difference in the elasticity of substitution of their factor inputs. As a final tax upon the reader's tolerance let us briefly try to formalise this elasticity concept.

First let us recall some of the basic aspects of the geometry of isoquants.

Two variables are important. First, there is the marginal rate of substitution of one factor for the other, the rate at which, along the isoquant, labour must substitute for capital (or vice versa) in order to maintain the constant output which the isoquant represents. This *MRS* (marginal rate of substitution) is denoted by $-dC/dL$ The second important variable is the factor ratio. Any point on the isoquant represents a particular capital–labour ratio (C/L). As we move along the isoquant both the *MRS* and the factor ratio change at every point. The elasticity of substitution is the proportional relationship between changes in C/L and $-dC/dL$.* If we denote the elasticity of substitution by $\mathscr{E}_s$ we can express this concept of the proportional change of the two variables by the expression:

$$\mathscr{E}_s = \frac{d\left(\frac{dC}{dL}\right)}{\frac{dC}{dL}}$$

Translate this back into diagrammatic terms for the benefit of the visualists. The value of $\mathscr{E}_s$ at any point on a given isoquant is shown by the curvature of the isoquant at that point. The greater the curvature the smaller the value of $\mathscr{E}_s$. If the curvature of the isoquant is great any given change in the *MRS* (dC/dL) will produce only a small change in the factor ratio $d(C/L)/(C/L)$ – the numerator of the expression will be reduced. If the isoquant has a low curvature the value of $\mathscr{E}_s$ will be greater, the numerator changing by a greater amount.

It would be possible to carry this digression on elasticities of substitution a good deal further distinguishing the limiting cases of infinite and zero elasticity of substitution, but such matters belong properly to the theory of production and for our present purpose we have sufficient criteria to view isoquants used in trade analysis critically. Readers should, however, refresh their memories on this type of analysis from the appropriate textbooks.[8]

Let us now return to the main theme of this section. This was to elucidate, with the aid of tools from production analysis, the forces shaping the production possibilities curve of a country engaged in international trade. Thus far in discussing these tools we have talked in terms of the decisions and optimal production positions of firms. The prices of factors

---

* As in other elasticities, it is conventional to discard the minus sign. In price elasticities price change and quantity demanded have different signs but it is usual to multiply the true elasticity by -1. The same convention is followed here. As in other elasticities the changes in the variables are expressed in proportional terms thus avoiding problems arising from the choice of measurement units.

The Pure Theory of International Trade

have been given and this has enabled us to determine optimal production positions. When, however, we turn to whole economies, it is not factor prices but factor supplies which are given. The problem is now to derive optimal factor inputs and outputs for a whole economy, given production functions and given total amounts of factors. For this problem we turn to the box diagram.

The box diagram enables us to construct a two-factor/two-commodity model. Assume that in a given economy there are two factors, labour and capital, and two types of commodities, X goods and Y goods. The factor endowments of the economy must be fully employed in producing these goods in order for it to maximise its economic welfare.

Consider Fig. 4.9, which is encompassed within a rectangle the vertical

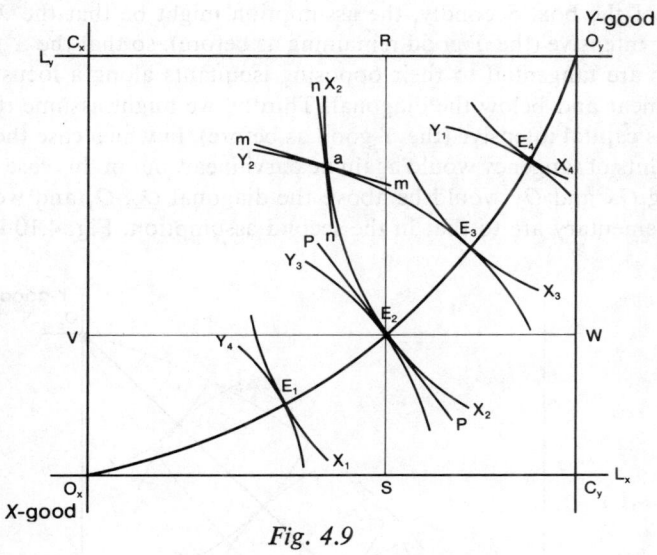

Fig. 4.9

sides of which measure the total capital resources available in the economy while the horizontal sides measure the total labour resources. We then have two sets of equal ordinates, $O_x C_x$ and $O_x L_x$ measuring the possible capital and labour inputs for the X good and $O_y C_y$ and $O_y L_y$ the same factor inputs for the Y good.

In the case of the X good the use of factors is represented by an infinite series of isoquants of which X_1, X_2, X_3, etc., are examples, convex to the O_x origin. For the Y good there is a similar set of isoquants with Y_1, Y_2, Y_3, etc., convex to O_y origin. Because of the opposite curvature of these two sets of isoquants each isoquant of each set will have one opposing isoquant of the other set which is tangential to it. These points of tangency, E_1, E_2, E_3, E_4, etc., are points at which the two productive factors are employed with maximum efficiency and the line joining them $O_x E O_y$ is the so-called optimum-efficiency locus describing a set of output alternatives.

Before developing the argument further we must make some sort of assumptions about the form of these opposing sets of isoquants, for according to the shape of each set so will their points of tangency alter and trace out a distinct locus or efficiency path within the box. Let us look at three possibilities, only one of which is illustrated in Fig. 4.9.

The first possible assumption is that both factors are used in the production of both X and Y goods in equal proportions. In this case the points of tangency will lie along the linear locus represented by the diagonal $O_x O_y$ of the box. Secondly, the assumption might be that the X good is labour intensive (the Y good remaining as before), so that the X good isoquants are tangential to their opposing isoquants along a locus which is curvilinear and below the diagonal. Thirdly, we might assume that the C good is capital intensive (the Y good as before), in which case the locus of the points of tangency would again be curvilinear, but in this case the curve joining Ox and Oy would be above the diagonal O_x, O_y and would be a complementary arc to that in the second assumption. Fig. 4.10 illustrates

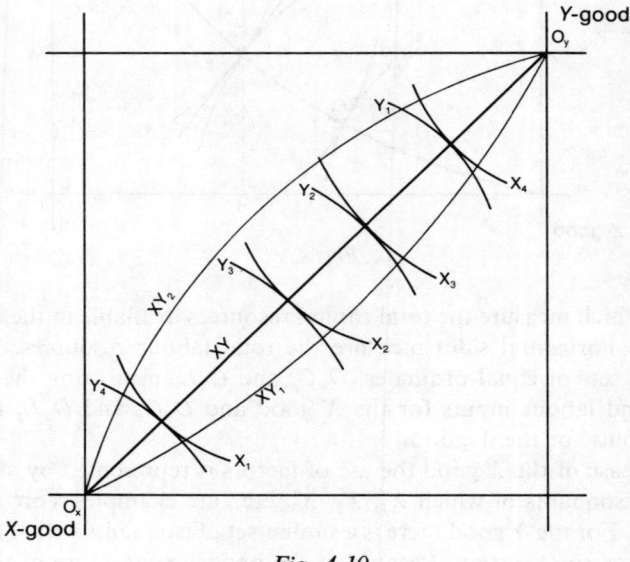

Fig. 4.10

The Pure Theory of International Trade

the three possible locii appropriate to these three possible conditions of factor intensity for X. XY represents the assumption of equal proportions of both factors for both goods; XY_1 assumes that the X good is labour intensive, XY_2 assumes that the X good is capital intensive. (Clearly when Y's factor intensity changes simultaneously the picture becomes more complex.)

Let us return to Fig. 4.9 in which it is assumed that X is a labour-intensive commodity. The *optimum-efficiency locus* or (*contract curve*) $E_1E_2E_3E_4$ traces the positions at which factor use will be optimised for production of the two goods. This is a proposition which requires further demonstration.

Allocation of the country's factor resources could be denoted by any point within the box. Suppose we take the point E_2 in Fig. 4.9. At this point an amount of X (appropriate to the isoquant X_2) is produced with O_xV of capital and O_xS of labour; an amount of Y (appropriate to the isoquant Y_3) is produced with O_yR of labour and O_yW of capital. These allocations of capital and labour for the two goods together make up the total capital and labour available in the economy. Both factors are fully employed at E_2 and it is impossible to increase the production of one good without at the same time reducing the output of the other. Moreover at E_2 the line PP is a common tangent to both the isoquant X_2 and Y_3. The slope of the tangent is therefore equal to the inverse ratio of marginal productivities in the production of both X and Y – that is,

$$\left(\frac{dC}{dL}\right)_x = \left(\frac{MP_L}{MP_c}\right)_x = \left(\frac{MP_L}{MP_c}\right)_y = \left(\frac{dC}{dL}\right)_y$$

This means in economic terms that, at E_2, labour and capital are equally productive in making X and Y. If, however, we take such a point as a at the intersection of X_2 and Y_2, here, as at E_2, both factors would be fully employed. a would not, however, be an equilibrium point. If we take the two isoquants at this point they have different slopes designated by the slopes of the two tangents mm and nn. The slope of nn, the tangent to the isoquant X_2, is equal to the inverse ratio of marginal productivities in the production of X goods:

$$\left(\frac{dC}{dL}\right)_x = \left(\frac{MP_L}{MP_c}\right)_x$$

Similarly, the slope of the tangent mm is equal to the inverse ratio of the marginal productivities of the factors in the production of Y goods,

$$\left(\frac{dC}{dL}\right)_y = \left(\frac{MP_L}{MP_c}\right)_y$$

But the slope of *nn* is much greater than that of *mm* so that

$$\left(\frac{MP_L}{MP_c}\right)_x > \left(\frac{MP_L}{MP_c}\right)_y$$

In economic terms this means that at *a* labour is relatively more productive in the production of X goods than in the production of Y goods and vice versa for capital. Labour should be deployed from producing Y goods to producing X goods and capital deployed from X goods to Y goods. This deployment could be achieved by moving along Y_2 to E_3, reducing the capital content and increasing the labour content of X, and increasing the capital content and reducing the labour content of Y. Moreover, it would be possible by moving along Y_2 from *a* to E_3 to obtain the same output of Y good at E_3 as at *a* (because we move along the same isoquant) but to obtain a higher output of X good, since at E_3 we are on a higher X isoquant than at *a*. Only at some E point where tangency of the isoquants for the two products occurs are the outputs of the two products maximised by efficient factor combinations and all the conditions of production equilibrium satisfied. Any point within the box, but not on the optimum-efficiency locus, can be shown to represent an inferior output position to points along the locus. We cannot, however, determine precisely where on the efficiency locus production will take place. This can be determined only when we know the demand conditions.

We are now almost back to the point at which we began, in Chapter 3, our simple model of supply in a trading economy. We can derive from the box diagram of Fig. 4.9 the production frontier or production possibilities curve. This done, we are in a more commanding position to analyse the whole supply side of an economy engaged in trade.

In Fig. 4.9 we may read off from the efficiency locus the respective outputs of X and Y which, at full employment of the available factors, may be obtained at the points of tangency of the isoquants for the commodities. These data can then be used to plot a new curve on different axes which show the amounts of X good and Y good which may be produced at full employment. This curve, which is the production possibilities curve (or transformation curve or production frontier), shows all possible alternative couplings of production in the given economy, given the factor situation which was reflected in the box diagram. This curve is illustrated in Fig. 4.11. Using the sort of data which might be taken from such an optimum-efficiency locus as that in Fig. 4.9 a production frontier such as YX might result. Points such as *a* within the curve are not conceivable production points. As long as there is full employment of the available factors it would be possible to increase production by moving up to YX. Points such as *b*

The Pure Theory of International Trade

are also inconceivable, since they would represent combinations of outputs beyond the capacity of the available factors.

The form of the production possibilities curve depends upon what assumptions underlie the isoquants from which, in the box diagram, we have derived it. We may classify the possible assumptions as:

(i) continuous production functions with constant returns to scale (linear homogeneous) allowing continuous variation in the factor mix. Such production functions may be (a) different as to factor intensity for each commodity, or (b) the same for each commodity; and

(ii) production functions reflecting fixed proportion combinations of the two factors and constant returns to scale.

It is necessary to glance at the implications for the production frontier of these assumptions.

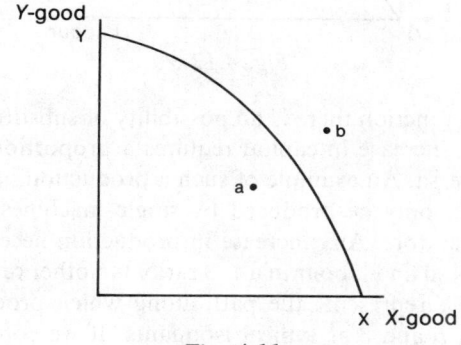

Fig. 4.11

Assumption (i) (a) yields a production possibilities curve of the form in Fig. 4.11. It is negatively sloped—since X and Y are alternatives—and concave to the origin. The marginal rate of substitution of the commodities varies along the curve and is represented by the slope of the tangent to the curve at any point. The implications of different production possibilities curves of this type have been explored in Chapter 3 above.

Assumption (i) (b) assumes an identical factor mix. In this case the tangency points of such identical but opposed isoquants would lie along the diagonal of the box (as in XY of Fig. 4.10) and the outputs measured for the two commodities upon the diagonal would yield a straight-line production frontier. To the extent that the production functions of the two commodities differ the production function will show curvature.

Assumption (ii), that is one of production functions reflecting fixed proportion factor combinations, has not so far been illustrated. Such a production function is shown in Fig. 4.12. Because of the technological nature

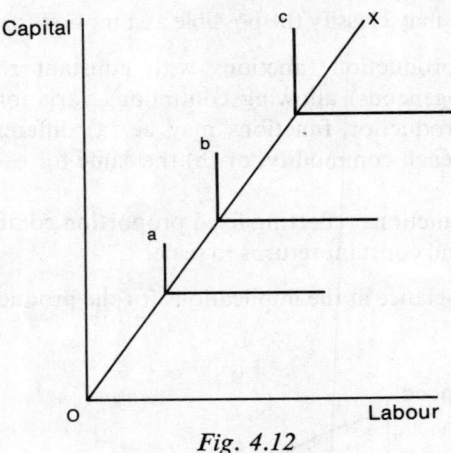

Fig. 4.12

of the production function there is no possibility of substituting one factor for the other. An increase in capital requires a proportionate increase in labour and vice versa. An example of such a production process would be where a good can only be produced by single machines each of which requires three operators. Any increase in production necessitates discreet increments of capital and labour in a 1:3 ratio. No other ratio is feasible.

In Fig. 4.12 OX represents the path along which production can be expanded with a, b and c as typical isoquants. If we combine two commodities, each with fixed factor proportions, but with the proportions different for the two commodities, in a box diagram we would get the situation depicted in Fig. 4.13. X is a capital-intensive good with isoquants

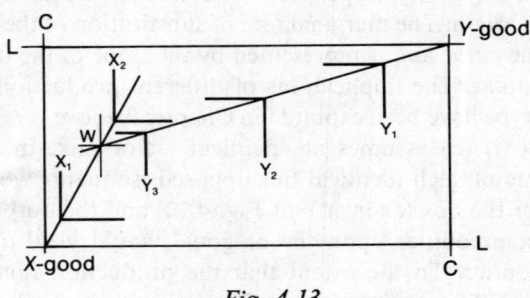

Fig. 4.13

The Pure Theory of International Trade

X_1, X_2, etc.; Y is a labour-intensive good with isoquants Y_1, Y_2, Y_3, etc., and for these two commodities there is only one possible combination at W, the intersection point of the two expansion paths. Only at this point is there full employment of the factors. The production frontier for this case is of the form shown in Fig. 4.14 in which W is the only point of full employment.

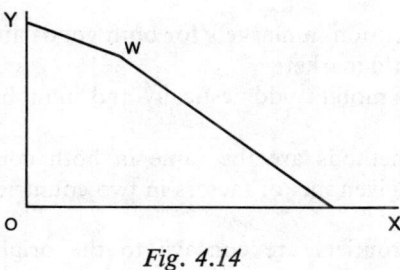

Fig. 4.14

A special case of the fixed factor proportion example is that where the fixed proportion is the same for both commodities. In this case the expansion paths for the two commodities would, as in the case of identical continuous production functions, coincide along the diagonal, giving a straight line transformation curve as case (i) (b) above. Identical production functions, whether continuous or of the fixed factor type, yield a straight-line production frontier.

(iv) The Heckscher – Ohlin Theorem

We will return now to the simple verbal exposition of the Heckscher–Ohlin theorem with which we ended section (ii) of this chapter. A more detailed analysis is now possible in the light of section (iii).

Let us summarise in a number of short propositions the position we have reached.

(a) Trade between countries is the result of particular relations between the amount of their factor supplies. These determine the pattern of national specialisation and of trade.

(b) An abundant factor is much used in production, yielding comparative advantage and a basis for trade — products of the abundant factors being exported and products of relatively scarce factors imported.

(c) Comparative advantage is the result of differing factor endowments in countries and differing factor groupings, or factor intensities, in the production processes of different commodities.

(d) The Heckscher–Ohlin approach to trade theory does not supersede the classical approach. The latter ascribes trade between countries to comparative cost differences, the former goes further in explaining why cost differences exist.

In its most rigorous form the Heckscher–Ohlin model is a two-factor, two-commodity, two-country model. It imposes certain assumptions. These are:

1. perfect competition in markets for both goods and factors, internally and in the world market;
2. perfect factor mobility domestically and immobility across national frontiers;
3. production methods are the same in both countries for identical goods, i.e. a given mix of factors in two countries provides the same output;
4. production frontiers are concave to the origin, i.e. they reflect increasing cost industries;
5. for both commodities there are constant returns to scale for progressive application of inputs;
6. factor intensity is a basic characteristic of production functions by reference to which they may be classified;
7. factors are of the same quality in both countries;
8. the supply of factors is given;
9. there is full employment; and
10. there are identical preferences and unitary income elasticity for all products.

Let there be two countries A and B, two factors C (capital) and L (labour) and two commodities X and Y. In Country A labour is the relatively abundant factor; in Country B capital is relatively more abundant. For the commodities, X is more labour intensive than Y.

The total factor endowments of the two countries (F_a and F_b) can then be given as:

$$\text{Country } A \quad F_a = C_x + C_y + L_x + L_y$$
$$\text{Country } B \quad F_b = C_x + C_y + L_x + L_y$$

It is impossible under existing assumptions to determine the value of F for either country. To do so would require a common unit in which factor endowments could be measured or some simplifying assumption of one homogeneous factor such as the labour theory of value. It is necessary then to think in terms of relative, rather than absolute, factor endowments. The relative factor endowments may be expressed as

The Pure Theory of International Trade

$$\left(\frac{L}{C}\right)_A > \left(\frac{L}{C}\right)_B \quad \text{or} \quad \frac{L_A}{L_B} > \frac{C_A}{C_B}$$

where $C = C_x + C_y$ and $L = L_x + L_y$ in the two countries. Either of these expressions shows that A has relatively more labour than B. From this statement the other significant statements about relative factor endowments follow:

(i) B has relatively more capital than A;
(ii) B has relatively less labour than A; and
(iii) A has relatively less capital than B.

Given one such statement about relative factor endowments the others are immediately implied.

The two commodities X and Y have the same production functions in both countries, since they represent identical technological conditions. These production functions are:

$$Q_x = f(C_x, L_x)$$
$$Q_y = f(C_y, L_y)$$

With full employment in both countries, which is assumed, there is competition for the two factors.

Turning to the commodities, either commodity can be described as relatively labour (capital) intensive if, with the same relative factor prices in both the industries producing X and Y, it requires more $L(C)$ than $C(L)$ to produce each output unit of the good, as compared with the other good. For example if good Y is capital intensive relative to X then,

$$\frac{C_y}{L_y} > \frac{C_x}{L_x} \quad \text{or} \quad \frac{C_y}{C_x} > \frac{L_y}{L_x}$$

Again, as with the statements on relative factor endowments above, one statement as to one of the commodities' proportionate use of the factors enables three other statements concerning relative factor intensity to be derived.

Let us apply now some of the tools which we derived in section (iii) of this chapter. Each commodity has an identical production function in both countries A and B. From these production functions we could derive two sets of isoquants showing various levels of output for X and Y. A series for X would be identical in both countries as would a different series for Y. If we assume that there is continuous factor substitution between C and L, the isoquants in each series for X and Y would be curved. If they were identical, that is to say if X and Y had an identical production process, then in a diagram such as Fig. 4.10 above, their points of tangency would lie along XY. If the production processes were not identical then the optimum-efficiency locus (contract curve) would be of the form XY_1 or XY_2 according to the relative capital intensities of the two processes. Let us for the moment assume that there is no factor substitution between C and L in producing either X or Y, we then have isoquants of the form shown in Fig. 4.12. If this is the case there are two possibilities: either (i) that factor intensities are the same in both the industries producing X and Y, implying identical production processes; or (ii) that factor intensities differ implying different production processes. We will take these cases in turn. In case (i), with constant returns to scale and one production process, the production frontier for X and Y would show constant opportunity costs over its whole length and no trade in the two commodities would be possible between the two countries: this follows from the fact that, with a set of identical production functions for the two commodities in the two countries, the contract curve and the production possibilities curve would be straight lines. (The domestic terms of trade between the commodities for both countries would be the same.) In case (ii) the production frontier for each country has two segments of constant opportunity costs and a single point at which the opportunity costs changed and at which there was full employment of labour and capital — the production frontier shown in Fig. 4.14.

We can now illustrate case (ii) diagrammatically. Fig. 4.15 takes the production frontiers of a single country, producing two commodities by different productive processes similar only in the fact that in each process factor proportions are fixed, and applies it to our example of two commodities produced in two countries. Country A's constant cost possibilities are represented by the straight line VT, country B's by the line VU. These two lines, moved in parallel, UV to BS and VT to SA, give a world production frontier for X and Y or BSA. The triangle BTS shows B's production possibilities with the origin at T rather than at O. The slope of UV is equal to the slope of BS. Also the slope of SA is equal to the slope of TV, which represents A's production possibilities. Thus, of the two sectors of the world production frontier for X and Y, BSA, the slope of BS gives the marginal rate of substitution of one commodity for the other in country B (MRS_B), while the slope of SA gives the marginal rate of substitution for the commodities in country A (MRS_A).

Turning to examine the original production possibility curves — VT for A and UV for B — it is clear that A has an advantage in the production of Y and B in the production of X. If the countries are of like size and factor endowment this sets the trade pattern, A specialising in Y and B in X. It may well be, however, that one country is much greater in size and factor endowment than the other. For example, A may be so large that even if B specialises in X it cannot meet A's demand and A must still produce X. In this case the MRS_A will be the preponderant rate of substitution in determining world prices. Similarly, if B is the larger country and A cannot supply it with enough of Y then the marginal rate of substitution between the two commodities in B, MRS_B, will be preponderant. Consider this point in terms of the diagram.

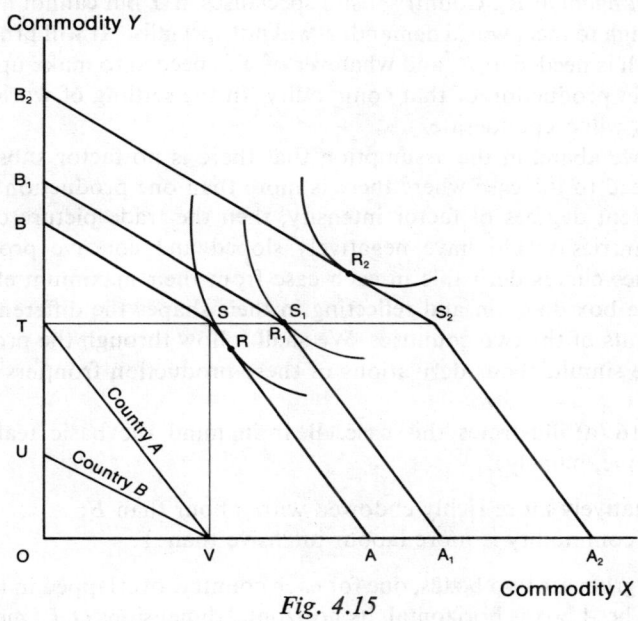

Fig. 4.15

BSA is the production possibility curve of the two-country world. Suppose that, on the demand side, both countries A and B have identical preference schedules, then we can suppose a world consumer indifference curve, one example of which will be tangential to BSA at R. Since the point of tangency occurs on A's production possibilities curve (SA is parallel to VT) world prices are in accordance with MRS_A. As for specialisation, B with a maximum production of X at OV cannot supply the world demand at R. She will, however, specialise completely and leave the shortfall to be provided by A which, if she specialised fully in Y, would produce more of that commodity than the world was demanding at R. A would deploy some resources to producing the shortfall in X. Suppose B were able to grow, so as to expand its factor supply and output, so that the world production possibilities curve became $B_1S_1A_1$, touching another of the family of world indifference curves at R_1, a point which is also S_1 the junction of the A and B sectors of the possibility curve. In this case the indifference curve is not tangential to either the MRS of A or B. Both countries will specialise, A in commodity Y and B in commodity X. Suppose B expands still further to make possible a further world production possibilities curve in $B_2S_2A_2$, to which one of the same family of world indifference curves is tangent at R_2. Country A still specialises in Y but cannot now produce enough to meet world demand. B will not specialise. It will produce all of X which is needed at R_2 and whatever of Y is needed to make up for A's shortfall in production of that commodity. In the settling of world prices the MRS_B will preponderate.

When we abandon the assumption that there is no factor substitution and proceed to the case where there is more than one production process and different degrees of factor intensity, then the trade picture changes. Both countries would have negatively sloped and concave production possibilities curves derivable in each case from their maximum efficiency loci in the box diagram and reflecting in their shapes the different factor endowments of the two countries. We shall follow through the process by which the simultaneous derivations of these production frontiers may be achieved.

Fig. 4.16 (a) illustrates this case. Bear in mind the basic features of our example, namely:

A is relatively more richly endowed with labour than B;
X as a commodity is more labour intensive than Y.

In the diagram are two boxes, one for each country, overlapped in the form of an L. The A box is horizontal, its horizontal dimensions O_xL_A measuring A's total available units of labour and O_xC_A measuring vertically its available units of capital. The B box is vertical with its origin at O'_y. O'_yL_B measures B's available labour and O'_yC_B its available units of capital. Equal units are used in measuring factor-inputs for both countries. The dimensions of the two boxes reflect their relative factor endowments: A has more labour relative to capital than has $B - O_xL_A/O_xC_A > O'_yL_B/O'_yC_B$. The partial coinciding of the boxes, so as to have one common origin at O_x, is for geometric convenience in the development of the diagram.

We now place in the diagram the isoquants which depict the production functions for the two commodities. The outputs for X are measured from the common origin O_x for each country. They are denoted by xx. The outputs for Y have to be measured from both of the Y origins O_y for country A outputs and O'_y for country B outputs. This necessitates two sets of isoquants for commodity Y but, assuming that the production function for each commodity is the same in both countries, the two sets of isoquants for Y still represent the same production function. The Y isoquants are denoted by yy.

From the two sets of isoquants for each country it is possible to derive maximum-efficiency locii, or contract curves. For A the locus is the curve $O_x O_y$; for B the curve $O_x O'_y$. Both curves are of course derived by drawing through the points of tangency of the x and y isoquants and are the locii of the equilibrium combinations of the production factors for the two commodities. At each of the points of tangency the marginal rates of substitution of the factors for both commodities are equal. So too are the ratios of the marginal products of the factors (see p. 95 above). Under conditions of perfect competition the ratio of the factor prices in the industries producing the commodities is identical at these points.

From the contract curves it is a straightforward matter to derive the production possibilities curves for the two commodities X and Y in the two countries. Fig. 4.16 (b) shows this derivation. On the usual axes showing amounts of commodities of X and Y we can, from data obtainable from Fig. 4.16 (a) plot curves $P_a P_a$ and $P_b P_b$, the production possibilities curves for countries A and B respectively. For each curve the points are obtainable by reading off the quantities of the isoquants X and Y on the contract curve. Thus for country A the points p and p' give amounts of X and Y which can be transferred to the axes of the lower diagram at points p_{ta} and p'_{ta} respectively. A similar process for country B transfers the output values at p to p_{tb} and so on for all points along $O_x O'_y$.

In this somewhat simplified diagram the production possibilities curves reflect the factor endowments of the two countries. A has a comparative advantage in the production of Y — a situation in which a potential gain from trade exists.[9]

It is possible to demonstrate the advantages of trade by two simple diagrammatic methods which we shall now show in turn. The first method uses the production possibilities curves for countries A and B which were derived in Fig. 4.16 (b). These are shown once more in Fig. 4.17, $P_A P_A$ for country A, $P_B P_B$ for country B. On the same axes we can place a set of indifference curves showing the consumption pattern for X and Y in the two countries. (It is necessary in this context to assume that consumer tastes in both countries are identical and unchanging. Without this assumption difficulties would occur as income distribution changed with changes in factor prices due to trade.) From the two sets of curves it is then possible to derive equilibrium positions for consumption and production both

(a)

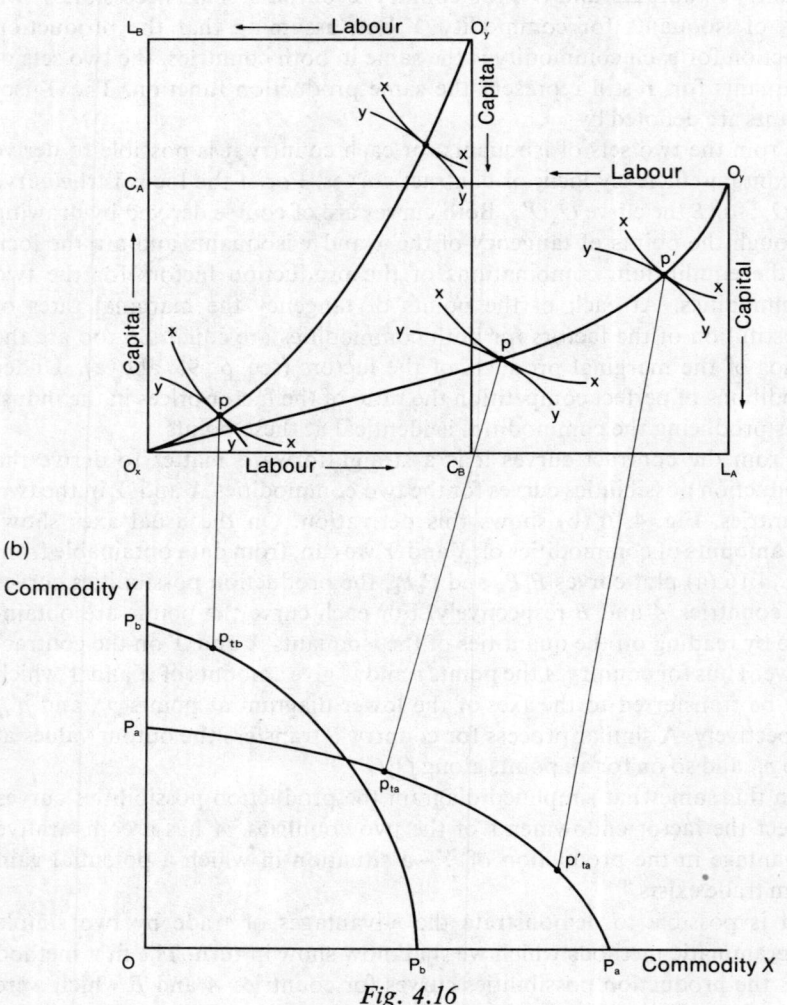

Fig. 4.16

before and after trade. First, however, remember the requirements of the equilibrium condition. These are:

$$MRS_c = P_x/P_y = MRS_p$$

In verbal economic terms this means that in equilibrium the marginal rate of substitution of the goods in consumption is equal to the price ratio of the

The Pure Theory of International Trade

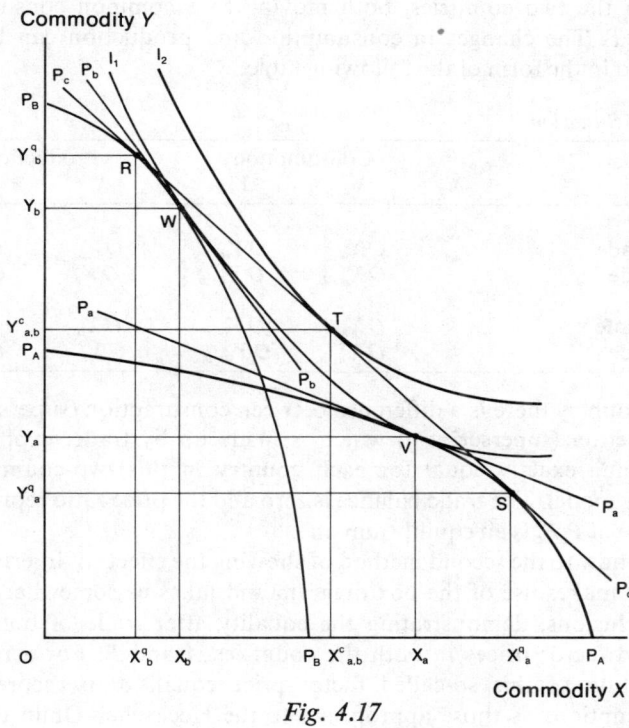

Fig. 4.17

goods and to their marginal rate of substitution in production (or marginal rate of transformation). These conditions are satisfied for goods X and Y before trade at the points W and V. In country A, OX_a of commodity X and OY_a of commodity Y are consumed and produced at a price ratio shown by the slope of P_a; in country B, OX_b of commodity X and OY_b of commodity Y are consumed and produced at a price ratio shown by the slope of P_b. It is evident that $(P_x/P_y)_A > (P_x/P_y)_B$, and that in the differences of the price ratios in the two countries there is an incentive for trade to take place. Once trade begins, A will specialise in X and B will specialise in Y and, assuming that there are no barriers to trade or transport costs, X and Y will exchange at the same price ratio in both countries. This new common price ratio is shown on the diagram by P_cP_c which is tangential to a higher indifference curve I_2 at T and to the A and B transformation curves at S and R respectively. It is apparent that the new price ratio after trade is between the two pre-trade price ratios, greater than that for A, less than that for B. It will be seen also that consumption of the two commodities is changed in the two countries, both moving to a common consumption pattern at T. The changes in consumption and production can best be summarised in the form of the following table.

Equilibrium Situation

	Consumption		Production	
	X	Y	X	Y
Country A:				
Before trade	OX_a	OY_a	OX_a	OY_a
After trade	$OX^c_{a,b}$	$OY^c_{a,b}$	OX^q_a	OY^q_a
Country B:				
Before trade	OX_b	OY_b	OX_b	OY_b
After trade	$OX^c_{a,b}$	$OY^c_{a,b}$	OX^q_b	OY^q_b

For each country there is a difference between consumption (superscript c) and production (superscript q) which is made up by trade, exports and imports being exactly equal for each country in this two-country/two-commodity model. The trade balance is zero and the price ratio represented by the slope of $P_c P_c$ is an equilibrium one.

We pass now to the second method of showing the effects of international trade. This makes use of the box diagram and takes us somewhat further in its conclusions, demonstrating the equality after trade of both commodity and factor prices in both the countries A and B. For a rigorous demonstration of this so-called factor–price equalisation theorem, the same assumptions as those appropriate to the Heckscher–Ohlin theorem are required if we adopt, as we have earlier, the two-commodity, two-factor, two-countries model.

In Fig. 4.18 we return to the construction used in Fig. 4.16 (a), that of two superimposed box diagrams. Once more country A, which is labour abundant, is represented by the horizontal box; country B, which is capital abundant, by the vertical box. Both countries produce both commodities X and Y which are labour intensive and capital intensive respectively. Their optimum-efficiency loci are $O_x O_y$ for X and $O_x O'_y$ for Y.

Let us assume that, before trade, country A produces at R, a point dictated by its domestic demand conditions. Country B produces at T. For each country the factor returns are shown by the slopes of the lines p and p_1. These factor returns differ for the two countries. Remember that the slope of the common tangent to the isoquants at any production point represents the relative marginal product of the factors and thus their relative returns (see p. 95 above). In this diagram the isoquants are, for simplicity, omitted.

In country A (labour abundant) the returns to labour are low relative to

The Pure Theory of International Trade

capital. The opposite is the case in B, the capital abundant country. With the beginning of trade A begins to specialise in the labour-intensive X good and B to specialise in the capital-intensive Y good, so that the production equilibrium for each country moves along its optimum-efficiency locus, for A to S and for B to U. The lines p_2 and p_3 show by their slopes the factor returns at S and U respectively. If we assume that there are no transport

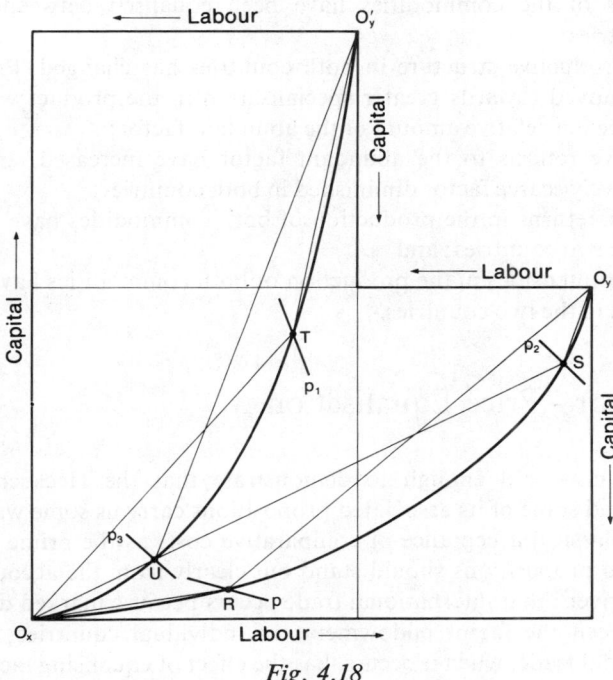

Fig. 4.18

costs and that trade expands until the prices of X and Y are equal in the two countries at S and U, then p_2 and p_3 will have the same slope – that is, with similar technologies and conditions of production the factor proportions used in producing X and Y will be equal in A and B after trade as will also the ratio of the factor returns.

The factor proportions employed at each equilibrium point are shown by the slope of the rays from the origin to the equilibrium point for each good. Thus O_xR shows by its slope the factor proportions in producing X in A before trade, O_xS shows the same factor proportions after trade. Note that, after trade, the factor proportions used in production of commodity X in country A (the slope of O_xS) is the same as the factor proportions used in production of commodity X in country B, i.e. O_xU. Similarly the factor proportions used in both countries' production of Y after trade are equal. The slope of O'_yU equals the slope of O_yS.

This is an important conclusion. Let us restate it even more clearly. As a result of trade between the two countries and subject to the stated assumptions, the following changes have occurred:

1. prices of the commodities have been equalised between the two countries;
2. the productive structure in both countries has changed. Production has moved towards greater specialisation in the product which uses the greater relative amount of the abundant factor;
3. relative returns to the abundant factor have increased, and to the relatively scarce factor diminished in both countries;
4. factor returns in the production of both commodities have equalised in the two countries; and
5. factor intensities in the production of both commodities have become equal in the two countries.

(v) Factor – Price Equalisation

We have now said enough to demonstrate that the Heckscher–Ohlin theorem and some of its associated propositions carry us some way further than the classical acceptance of comparative costs as the prime mover of trade. Two propositions should stand out clearly from the account which has been given: that international trade occurs because marked differences exist between the factor endowments of individual countries; and that international trade, when it occurs, has the effect of equalising factor prices between countries, serving as a substitute for mobility of factors.[10] Such theoretical conclusions as these, following as they do upon a vigorous period of innovative writing and critical examination, require some qualification. They have been subjected to this in a large literature which can only be noticed briefly here, but it is at least possible to codify some of the qualifications.

The first relaxation of the general truth of the statements results from a realisation that they depend for their validity upon assumptions – some general, like those of perfect competition, the non-existence of barriers to trade, the absence of transport costs and the like which apply equally to classical trade theory and to the Heckscher–Ohlin theorem; and some factual, concerning the technical processes of production and variation of

The Pure Theory of International Trade

factor endowments. Moreover, the assumptions increase in number and become more restrictive as we proceed from the Heckscher–Ohlin theorem itself to the associated factor–price equalisation theorem. Finally, the whole argument is radically simplified by considering only the case of two countries, two goods and two factors of production.

The constraints which these assumptions impose take us far from reality and reduce the factor–price equalisation theorem to a mere statement of tendency. So far as prices are concerned it is easy to accept the general practical proposition that trade promotes equality of commodity prices between countries. When there are price differences between countries it clearly pays to expand trade and to continue to do so until the price differences reduce to a level commensurate with transport costs and tariffs. It is harder to accept the proposition that factor prices also equalise themselves as the model indicates. Are wages, relative to other factor prices, the same in the United States, India and Japan; is the return to capital the same, in relative terms, in Canada as in Mexico or Indonesia? The model takes us far from reality here.

Another spectre looms to destroy our satisfaction in the security of the factor–price equalisation theorem – the possibility that the whole applicability of the theorem may be greatly reduced by the widespread existence in modern productive systems, with their great diversity of factor combinations, of the phenomenon of factor reversal. Discussed as a special and interesting case in the literature, there is the possibility, indeed perhaps probability, that this situation is in the real world quite ubiquitous. To the extent that it is, the theorem is seriously qualified.[11]

It seems probable that the reduction of factor–price equalisation from theorem to statement of tendency is the result of the non-fulfilment of assumptions and the restrictions imposed by the simplicity of the model. Among the assumptions an important one is that of identical production techniques in both countries. This is far from reality. True, advanced and sophisticated productive techniques tend to equalise in all trading countries. Steel is, broadly speaking, manufactured by similar processes in the United States, Britain and Germany. Electronics techniques are copied quickly and improved from country to country. But many similar products are produced by different processes in different countries, either by reason of different factor endowments or because of lags in process changes and technical innovation. Moreover, the background conditions of production functions differ widely, influenced by climate and natural conditions, and can never be identical. Nor are labour units, as is assumed in the model, homogeneous in all countries. These assumptions carry us far from reality and are not even approximated to in practice.

What can be done to extend the range of the model? Attempts have been made to extend the analysis to more than two factors, two countries and two products. Some writers, notably Meade and Land, extended it first to three products[12] and later to three commodities and factors.[13] Once the extension progressed beyond three dimensions, however, to a world of many countries, many products and many factors it became unmanageable without recourse to systems of simultaneous equations and mathematics at a fairly advanced level. Not only is the method of analysis more complex but the opinions of what takes place became less unanimous. Some writers argue that in a multi-country model complete specialisation and factor–price equalisation will be achieved, others that factor–price equalisation will in this case occur among groups of countries within the larger world group. It is difficult to extract from this literature as yet any distinct threads of development and any account of it would require a seriatim account of the contributions of individual scholars. We leave it, therefore, noticing it as a profitable byway in which the interested reader can pursue his own interests.[14]

While much of what has been said in qualification of the factor–price equalisation theorem in this final section may appear to deprive the generalisation of worth and reduce the labour of its evolution to the level of an analytic exercise, much may still be said in its support. Its innovators made no sweeping claims for its validity[15] or practical significance but they encouraged a body of theoretical writing which has carried our knowledge of the comparative cost principle far beyond the point at which the classical economists and their successors left it. This section of the pure theory of trade is a very different affair now than it was when, at the outbreak of the Second World War, Haberler's *Theory of International Trade* (the English edition appeared first in 1936) was the last word. There is something still to be said, and the movement of the theorising into methods of greater complexity and mathematical abstraction may be as much, or more, a pursuit of greater reality than a love of rigour and abstraction. The *leitmotif* of much pure trade theory in recent years has been the necessity to effect a junction between such theory and empirical observations, much of which, at first sight, lent little support to the abstract analysis. To a brief examination of the role which empirical observation has played in directing the recent efforts of theorists, we turn in the next chapter.

5
Putting Theory to the Test: Empirical Studies

(i) Introduction

ANY final chapter of a theory section must assess the value of theory but, at the risk of becoming a rag-bag or a last-minute assortment of odds and ends, it must include such topics as have not fitted happily into the general arrangement of the material which has preceded it. Three largely unrelated matters are included in this chapter. We have dealt with two broad lines of development in trade theory: the classical theory, based on comparative costs, and the development of factor endowment analysis, summed up and suggested by the Heckscher–Ohlin theorem. Some further but brief discussion of the relation of these two strands is appropriate. This is our first task.

The second is that of examining the light thrown upon theory by attempts at empirical verification. One of the many changes which has taken place in economics in the last quarter-century has been the determination of scholars to submit their hypotheses to the test of factual investigation. International trade has shared this tendency. As a recent writer aptly put it: 'The truth is that we have tried to do too much on the basis of *a priori* reasoning alone. Too little effort has been put into fact-finding, measurement and sophisticated analysis of observed data.'[1] Probably few branches of economics are so unrelievedly abstract and divorced from reality as the pure theory of trade with its rigidly constrained models and its special 'half-world' of mythical behaviour patterns and contrived situations. What is the predictive value of these theories and how are they likely to fare as the supply of data from the trading world is collected and analysed? In this chapter we shall glance at some of the findings of empirical studies and the extent to which they corroborate the generalisations of theory. As might be expected, it is from the studies which breed scepticism that most is to be learned.

The third task is that of extending into the practical field a concept of which we have made use in these chapters, namely the terms of trade.

Thus far this term has implied the real exchange ratio of goods for goods in trade between countries, of exports relative to imports in real terms. This relationship in the real world must be expressed in money-value terms, with all the attendant complications of changing price levels and their measurement by index numbers. When we speak of the terms of trade outside the purely theoretical context, it is money terms of trade to which we refer. Their importance will appear in many discussions as we proceed. It is, therefore, necessary to be explicit as to the nature and measurement of the terms of trade. This necessary clarification is our final task.

(ii) The Classical Theory and the Heckscher – Ohlin Theorem

The Ricardian model of comparative advantage and the rigorous two-factor/two-country model of Heckscher–Ohlin invite comparison. Although separated by a century in time, both are examinations of comparative advantage; one simple and self-contained, the other more searching, more ambitious but, perhaps, less logically consistent. The Ricardian model was incapable of elaborate development because it was based on a primitive theory of value which assumed only one factor, and not until comparative advantage, judged in terms of the productivity of that factor, was replaced by comparative costs, based upon the principle of opportunity cost, could the Ricardian system be extended in scope and application. It served, however, from the outset to imply that trade theory has inherently two roles to fulfil, the positive and the normative. Its positive role was to explain the structure or pattern of trade, of what goods are exported and imported and on what terms. Its normative role was to show the advantage of free trade by showing that in such a condition the gains from trade are maximised. In the original Ricardian exposition the latter role was probably the dominant one. Although modern trade theory does have a normative aspect, it is less stressed. The assumption of free trade is basic to the Heckscher–Ohlin theorem but the theorem itself could not be described as a demonstration of the advantages of free trade. It is rather a widening of generality and an extension of the study of comparative costs to an increasing number of situations. The Heckscher–Ohlin model, allowing two factors of production and drawing upon tools used in the theory of production, has at its disposal a wider range of problems for examination.

It is perhaps wise to stress first the similarities of the two approaches. Both examine comparative advantage; both are concerned with the supply side of trade; both are concerned with production; both stress the gains to be derived from trade (higher consumption, better terms of trade, increased specialisation); both have to assume demand conditions in order to do this. In the Ricardian model we were able to rank goods according to their labour content and thus their comparative advantage. In the Heckscher–Ohlin model we can rank them according to their factor intensities. With these the similarities end.

The autonomy of the Heckscher–Ohlin model, as an account of comparative advantage in production terms, is broken by the fact that factor abundance, the basis of comparative advantage, may be defined in two different ways, each having its own particular implications. It may be defined in terms of factor prices, which are themselves the result of a complex of forces, including demand itself, which is, for the moment, not the subject of investigation. Such a definition, however, tells us that country A is more capital rich than country B if capital is relatively cheaper in country A than in B. It is a fairly simple matter to show from this that if we compare production costs in A and B of two goods, a capital-intensive X and a labour-intensive Y, we find that it is relatively cheap to produce X in country A and Y in country B; and that country A will export X and country B will export Y. Thus the Heckscher–Ohlin theorem that the capital-rich country exports the capital-intensive good and the labour-rich country exports the labour-intensive good is demonstrated.[2]

A second definition of factor abundance is in terms of physical quantities. In this sense we may say that country A is capital rich if $C_a/L_a > C_b/L_b$ where C and L stand for capital and labour and the subscripts $_a$ and $_b$ denote the two countries. If this is so then country A will probably produce the capital-intensive good and country B the labour-intensive good. This can be shown diagrammatically in Fig. 5.1. Assume that good X is capital intensive and good Y labour intensive, then the production possibility curve of A for the two goods will be of the form aa_1 and that of B will be of the form bb_1. The proportion in which X and Y are produced can be shown by a ray from the origin. Suppose that both countries produce the two goods in the same proportion as shown by the ray OR. Then country A would produce at S_a and country B at S_b. Since the slopes of the production possibilities curves at S_a and S_b differ, that at S_a being much steeper than at S_b, it follows that in country A good X would be cheaper than in country B and that good Y would be cheaper in country B than in country A. For country A the cost of expanding output of X is less than for country B and for country B the cost of expanding the output of Y is less than for country A. Country A, being rich in capital, will produce the capital-intensive good; country B, being rich in labour, will produce the labour-intensive good.

We have been talking thus far of production. Will each country export the good which it can produce most cheaply? The answer is that it will all depend upon the nature of demand and whether its influence will or will not offset the tendency imparted by cheapness. This can be seen from Fig. 5.1. If we assume that demand in country A takes the form represented by the set of indifference curves I_aI_a, and in B by the set of indifference curves I_bI_b; that is that demand in A is concentrated mainly upon the capital-intensive good and demand in B mainly upon the labour-intensive good. In this event it is the case that, before trade, good X is relatively

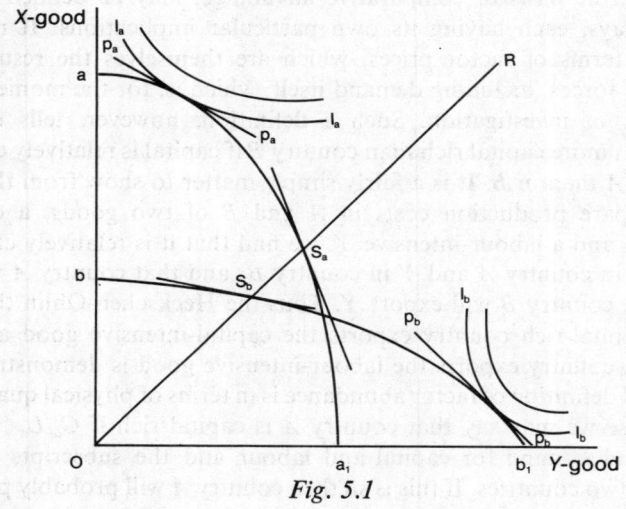

Fig. 5.1

more expensive in country A than in country B. This is shown by the greater steepness of p_bp_b, the line representing relative prices in B, than p_ap_a which represents relative prices in A. When trade between the two countries begins, country A will export the relatively cheap and labour-intensive commodity Y and country B will export commodity X. The effect of demand has been to change the trade situation from that which would have been expected from the relative production costs of the two commodities. The capital-intensive country exports the labour-intensive good; the labour-intensive country exports the capital-intensive good.

Thus it can be seen that it is only partially true to say that, given a country's factor endowments, we can tell precisely what will be the structure of its trade. It depends upon how the factor endowment for the country is defined. If it is defined in factor/price terms, then the Heckscher–Ohlin theorem is a reliable guide. If factor endowment is defined in terms of physical quantities, then, in the absence of precise data on demand, the structure of trade is indeterminate.

Returning to the differences between classical trade theory and the Heckscher–Ohlin theorem, there is one difference which is fundamental, namely the assumptions which the two theories make about the nature of the production process. The classical theory of comparative advantage assumes that in differences in the productivity of labour lies the reason for trade pattern. Thus, in country A, more labour is required for a given output of a commodity than in country B. That is, more labour is required in conjunction with other factors in A than in B. There is an implied difference in the mix of production factors between countries, that is, their production functions differ. By contrast the Heckscher–Ohlin theorem, while it assumes two factors, assumes also that, between countries, production functions are identical. In both countries A and B the same mix of factors is required to produce the given commodity. What differs between the two countries is the relative endowment of a given factor or factors.

What claims are there that the Heckscher–Ohlin theorem enhanced the value of trade theory? The writer would distinguish three such claims. The first has already been amply made and, it is hoped, amply demonstrated. It is that the new approach made possible a far more searching examination of the principle of comparative advantage. It enabled the principle of opportunity cost, by means of which Haberler had led the classical theory out of the blind alley in which the labour theory of value had placed it, to be fully and creatively exploited. The second claim is that the Heckscher–Ohlin theorem made possible a far more searching analysis of the classical proposition that trade equalised goods and factor prices in the participant countries. However qualified the factor-price equalisation theorem may be and however much its necessary assumptions appear to constrain its practical applicability, its systematic investigation has been, and may be still more in the future, a great gain for trade theory.

The third claim has not yet been investigated in this book and its brief description will close this section. It is this. The Heckscher–Ohlin theorem claims in essence that the pattern of trade is a function of the factor endowments of countries. The reverse may also be true: trade may affect the domestic economic structure of the trading countries. In particular it poses the question: what is the effect of trade upon income distribution in a trading country? The focusing of attention upon this relation may be one of the most interesting contributions of the new approach.

In our description of the factor endowments approach we have seen the effect of trade upon commodity prices, upon factor intensities and upon the composition of output. To consider the effects of trade upon the distribution of income we must look more closely at the relative returns of the factors of production under trading conditions.

Trade, we are told, increases the relative scarcity of the factor which is in short supply. With this there is an increase in the relative return to the abundant factor and a decrease in that to the scarce factor. In the case of a country rich in capital and short of labour, the result would then be to reduce wages relative to the return on capital. This, if true, is an alarming statement. Its implication is that, in such a country, organised labour should, in its own interests, lobby for restriction of trade. Protectionism would have some justification.

Let us examine the proposition.[3] It can be most easily demonstrated by the diagram in Fig. 5.2. In this diagram we depict the situation of a

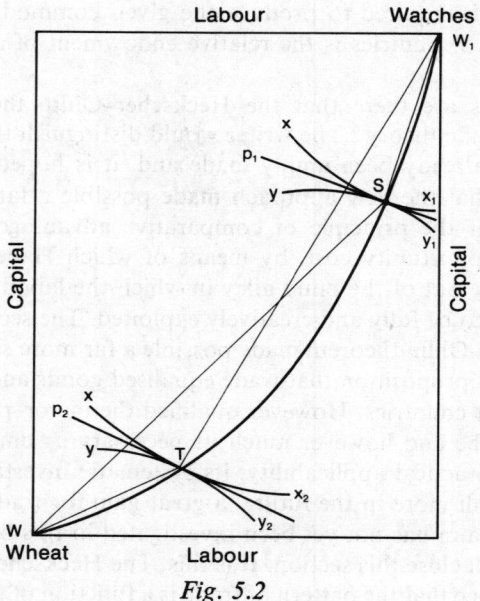

Fig. 5.2

relatively capital-rich, labour-scarce country producing two commodities, one of which, watches, is capital intensive and one of which, wheat, is labour intensive. (The example chosen is taken from the Stolper–Samuelson article.) WW_1 is the optimum-efficiency locus (contract curve) for production of these two commodities. Two situations are shown for comparison. The first situation at S shows the production situation before trade. The slope of the common tangent to the isoquants represents the ratio of the return to labour to the return to capital. When trade takes place, the capital-rich country increases its specialisation in the capital-intensive product and production shifts from S to T. The effects of this shift are as follows:

(a) At point T the methods of production in both industries are more labour intensive than they were at S, as indicated by the slope of the new rays WT and W_1T, as compared with the old rays WS and W_1S. This occurs because as the capital-intensive watch industry expands, it will bid factors of production away from the wheat industry. But the declining wheat industry will release a lot of labour and only a little capital compared to what the watch industry demands. Thus substitution will occur in *both* industries towards using relatively more labour and less capital. Returning to the diagram, because of the assumptions made about production functions, any movement along the contract curve shows a drop in the marginal productivity of one factor and an increase in its relative importance in the production of both goods. This last feature is consistent with fixed total quantities of both factors because the 'weights', i.e. the relative outputs of the two commodities, are changing.[4]

(b) Marginal productivities of labour are lower and marginal productivities of capital higher at T than at S.

(c) Given that factor prices reflect marginal productivities, the marginal productivity of capital at T, as indicated by the slope of p_2, is greater than the marginal productivity of capital at S, as represented by the slope of p_1.

(d) Because marginal productivity determines the wage, wages are lower and returns to capital higher at T, the trade position, than at S, the before-trade position.

The plain economics of the Stolper–Samuelson theorem are somewhat alarming. As a result of trade, workers in both industries have less capital with which to work and their marginal productivity falls, causing the individual wage to fall. Because both the before- and after-trade situations assume full employment, the total wage bill falls. It would appear that the proportion of the national income going to labour falls as a result of the opening of trade. Equally, if we apply protection and move from trade back to autarky, the position of labour will be improved again. Here is a powerful argument with which organised labour might oppose free trade. This is an argument running completely contrary to the central normative claim of Ricardian trade theory; the superiority of free trade.[5] Its implications will be further explored in the section of the book dealing with Commercial Policy.

(iii) Empirical Testing

There have been attempts to test statistically some of the trade models we have been discussing. Large-scale empirical exercises testing the two major models have been few, but numerous attempts have been made to assess the force of various component elements such as elasticities. In this section we shall give attention only to the major exercises, dealing (a) with those which have been made to test the classical theory of comparative costs, and (b) the Heckscher–Ohlin theorem. We shall confine ourselves to the major issues which these studies raise. Readers interested in the statistical minutiae must go directly to the articles themselves.

(a) The major statistical study of the classical theory of comparative costs was made by G. D. A. MacDougall.[6] Earlier work[7] on the productivity of British and American industries made the test possible.

MacDougall first states his working version of the classical theory. It is 'that when based on a labour theory of value and assuming two countries, each will export those goods for which the ratio of its output per worker to that of the other exceeds the ratio of its money wage rate to that of the other.'[8] Applying this model to late interwar period (1937) data, MacDougall found that, where American productivity was more than twice that of the British, the United States had the bulk of the export market; for products where it was less than twice as high, the bulk of the market was held by Britain. A complication arose in that, unlike the two-country textbook examples, the exports of each country did not, in the main, go to the other but largely to third countries. The large differences in productivity between the two countries enabled Britain to dominate in some third markets, the United States to dominate in others. But, even when Britain with a comparative advantage could undersell the Americans in third markets, she still was only able to secure a small fraction (less than 1 per cent) of the American market. In the opposite direction, when America had the comparative advantage, her exports to Britain were a little larger but were still only 'a few per cent of total British consumption'. The reason for this small 'mutual' trade, apart from the mere existence of the large third market, was attributed by MacDougall to the tariff barriers of the two countries and a long central section of the first article is concerned with the offsets to comparative advantage which the tariffs constituted.

In examining the possible effects on his data of removing the classical assumption of perfect competition and measuring performance in imperfect markets, MacDougall makes one observation[9] for which he has been taken to task by an American economist. He draws attention to the fact that, even in industries in which American productivity (output per worker) was double the British and thus exceeded the British by as much as her wage level, America tended to export less than the British. America exported as much as the British only when her productivity was $2\frac{1}{2}$ times that of Britain. This greater British propensity to export and greater penetrating power in foreign markets MacDougall seems to attribute to certain imponderable British advantages in world markets — imperial preference, export-oriented industry, commercial leadership and the like. However this may be, it is true, as Richard Caves points out,[10] that there is nothing in the theory to justify MacDougall's surprise. There is no reason to expect any parity between productivity and export performance measured in quantities. There are too many other variables in the relationship to expect close parity between the two variables to which MacDougall draws attention.

Apart from the core argument recounted above, MacDougall's two articles examine a number of important aspects of the Anglo-American trade relationship in the period. Section B of the first article takes up the question of exports and prices and in its conclusions supplements the earlier section on comparative costs. It was found that a fairly clear inverse relation existed between the relative prices of British and American exports and the relative quantities exported. Another section of the work (Section C of the second article), deals with the statistical problem of estimating the elasticity of substitution between the exports of two countries.

MacDougall claims in his conclusion that the crude labour theory of value does provide an explanation of British and American export trade in manufactures and that it demonstrates the constraint placed upon this trade by tariffs. It shows also, he argues, that a country can compete in trade in certain commodities with a country whose productivity is much higher.

A small number of other economists have done work which has strengthened the classical hypothesis that labour productivity does much to determine comparative advantage.[11] Studies by Balassa and Stern, using data for the post-war period, corroborate the conclusions of MacDougall that there is a high correlation between labour productivity and a country's share in the export market. Forcheimer's investigation of the importance of relative wage differences on the composition of foreign trade, since it is based upon a deduction from the comparative cost model, falls into this category of empirical testing. Forcheimer concludes that relative wages are of considerable importance and that this is most marked in industries in which costs other than that of labour are approximately equal, as when transport costs are low and raw materials are bought in world markets at international prices. An example of such an industry is textiles, and here the influence of low relative wages is fairly discernible, but the author suggests that availability of data and closer study would reveal similar characteristics in a wide range of light industries. Another case in which low relative wages might occur, with considerable advantage, is when they arise by the employment of 'cheap-labour groups' whose retention is often sought in order to reap trade advantage.

This raises the question as to whether wages tend to be higher or lower in export industries. Given that relative wage differences underlie trade patterns, it might be expected that relatively lower wage rates would obtain in export industries than in domestic industries. For an industry to rank low in the scale of comparative advantage when costs are measured in labour unit inputs and still be an exporting industry, would require that it should have extraordinarily low relative wages. This is one theoretical possibility. Another might be that, as some economists have expected, export industries, particularly in times of expanding trade, might have relatively higher wages reflecting their higher levels of productivity. Kravis's work on wage levels in United States industries supports the latter view. Export industries, it appears, pay higher wages. Kravis doubts, for two reasons, whether differences in wages are a cause of comparative advantage. Firstly, hourly earnings of workers rank almost the same in different countries, as demonstrated by him from United States and Japanese data. Secondly, competition in the labour market causes industrial wage levels to cluster closely around the national average wage as determined by productivity. Moreover productivity ratios differ between countries more than do relative wages from industry to industry.

In general the classical theory of trade is more sustained than harmed by the statistical work to which it has been subjected. The fairly positive support given by MacDougall, Balassa, Kravis and others is only broken by the doubts of Bhagwati, who, after using more elaborate statistical methods than the others, finds that linear regressions of export–price ratios on labour-productivity ratios for the United Kingdom and the United States give no significant regression coefficients. The regressions for unit–labour costs on export–price ratios likewise yield no significant results. Bhagwati concludes that his results, 'limited as they are, cast sufficient doubt on the usefulness of the Ricardian approach (as generally understood). Contrary therefore to the general impression (based on the MacDougall, Balassa and Stern results) there is as yet no evidence in favour of the Ricardian hypotheses.'[12] Empirical support for classical theory is therefore considerable but not unanimous.

(b) Empirical investigation of the Heckscher–Ohlin theorem has led to

The Pure Theory of International Trade

interesting results and to some useful speculation as to the reasons why statistical studies have failed to validate the theory. MacDougall, in the article cited above, using Rostas's figures on comparative industrial productivities in Britain and the United States, failed to confirm the theory that each of the countries would export products whose manufacture would require relatively large amounts of the factors with which they are well endowed. Britain, for example, displayed no tendency to outstrip the United States in exporting more of the products requiring a low ratio of capital to labour.[13] Kravis, who used book value of capital as an index of capital endowment, also failed to find any relation between this variable and the foreign trade commitments of United States industries.

One memorable attempt has been made to put the Heckscher–Ohlin model to the test: Wassily Leontief's work on the capital structure and trade of the United States. This famous series of articles,[14] which unveiled what has come to be called the 'Leontief paradox', sparked off a literature of comment and explanation which it is impossible to do justice to in short compass. We must be content to describe Leontief's main conclusions and to summarise some of the more important comments which have been made upon them by his critics.

Leontief's argument runs as follows. A country exports goods in whose production factors dominate which are plentiful in that country relative to other countries. It will import goods in whose production factors dominate which are relatively scarce. The United States is a very capital-intensive country. Therefore the United States might be expected to export goods requiring relatively large amounts of capital in production in exchange for import goods requiring relatively large amounts of labour. This is the hypothesis which Leontief sets out to test.

In sections II and III of his first article Leontief arrays his data in terms of an input–output table which describes the 'actual flow of commodities and services among all the different parts of the American economy'.[15] On the basis of such a table it is possible to determine the effects of changes in any given sector of the economy upon production rates in the other sectors. A given increase in automobile production in the United States would require, the table tells us, given increases in the outputs of steel, non-ferrous metals, components and ancillary services. It is possible ultimately to summarise from the table the total amounts of capital and labour necessary for the domestic production of each of the multifarious commodities on the American export and import list. In section IV the author applies this data to the hypothesis 'that the United States exports commodities the domestic production of which absorb relatively large amounts of capital and little labour and imports foreign goods and services which —

if . . . produced at home—would employ a great quantity of indigenous labour but a small amount of domestic capital'.[16] The test is applied by assuming that by some restrictive device (revenue tariff or embargo) the United States reduces both its imports and exports by an identical amount. The cut on the export side is such that exports of each commodity are cut by the same percentage amount so as to leave the proportional commodity content of exports unchanged. On the import side the cut is applied proportionally only to imports which compete with domestic industries and not to so-called non-competitive imports. In order to replace the cut in imports, the factors released from the contraction in exports must be transferred to the production of the domestic goods which are required to replace the frustrated imports. The export contraction must release relatively larger amounts of capital and lesser amounts of labour than will be absorbed by the industries expanding to replace imports.

The results of the statistical test of this proposition proved to be directly contrary to the proposition. A marginal reduction of American exports would free *more* labour and less capital than import-competing industries would require for their marginal expansion. It would appear, in Leontief's words, that 'America's participation in the international division of labour is based on its specialisation on labour-intensive, rather than capital-intensive lines of production. In other words, this country resorts to foreign trade in order to economise its capital and dispose of its surplus labour rather than vice versa'.[17] If this thesis was correct (and Leontief made several statistical re-examinations of the conclusions), then not only was the basic Heckscher–Ohlin theorem wrong for the American case but several surprising corollaries also came into view.[18] Firstly, invoking the Stolper–Samuelson theorem, which was the theme of section (ii) of this chapter, it would seem from Leontief's findings that tariff protection is detrimental rather than favourable to American labour. A rise in the United States tariff would result in a decrement in the volume of competitive imports which, after adjustment of the balance of trade, would curtail American exports by a like amount. Since trade serves as a means to relieve the pressure of the now-revealed labour surplus, a reduction in trade increases such pressure. Thus protection is likely to weaken the bargaining position of American labour. Secondly, and perhaps less obviously, it appears that further accumulation of capital by the United States tends to reduce the advantage of international trade to that country by making the before-trade cost ratios of America and other countries nearer to each other.

The perverse implications of his investigations clearly worried Leontief and his first reaction was to cast around for simple explanations. His first such explanation was to argue that the truth of the hypothesis, that rela-

The Pure Theory of International Trade

tively plentiful capital and relatively scarce labour compelled export of capital-intensive and import of labour-intensive goods, depended upon an assumption which was not fulfilled in practice — namely that 'the *relative* productivity of capital and labour, if compared industry by industry, is the same here and abroad'.[19] If, instead, one assumed that American labour was, say, three times as productive as labour in other trading countries, then the American labour force would require to be weighted for its productivity, in this case being multiplied by three and the relative sizes of the capital stock and the labour force would be reversed. This argument is supported by some speculative reasons — better entrepreneurship, superior education, a work-oriented society — for the superior productivity of American labour. This does not mean that the American worker is more productive than the non-American because he is equipped with more capital but that he is x times more efficient when working with the same amount of capital as a non-American worker.

There were many comments and reactions to Leontief's results. One later empirical exercise designed to test the Heckscher–Ohlin theorem by reference to the capital structure and trade of India in 1951 reached the same conclusion as had Leontief — that the facts were the opposite of the theorem. Indian exports were not, as might have been expected, labour intensive but capital intensive.[20] We can only present a brief summary of this literature.[21] We shall do so in the form of a seriatim list of critical points, footnoting each with the names of the main authors listed in note 21.

1. A country may produce the good requiring more of its plentiful factor but may not export it, simply because its consumer taste is even more biased towards consuming the good than its factor endowment is towards producing it.[22] Similarly, a country well supplied with capital may still import capital-intensive goods if it has a level of real income such that the income elasticity of demand for such goods is high. In the same way a labour-rich country may export a capital-intensive product if the level of its income is such that it chooses to use the labour-intensive product at home. We must, it appears, look closely at the consumption patterns which emerge from changes at the income margin.[23]

2. Leontief may have over-simplified his classification of factors of production by too readily gathering them into the convenient categories of capital and labour and neglecting the factor of natural resources, a factor in which Vanek has argued the United States is relatively lacking.[24] Capital and natural resources are complementary in many forms of production. The productivity of even a relatively abundant capital in the United States might be impaired by a relative scarcity of natural resources.

3. Some of the content of United States' imports is accounted for by the products of American subsidiaries abroad. These may be more American in character, that is, in this context, more capital intensive than the products of the countries from which the imports come. Some writers[25] have suggested that if such imports be disregarded in the American import bill, then production in the import-competing industries in the United States which compete with the remaining imports, might well be more labour intensive than American export production.

4. Ellsworth has been a pungent critic of the Leontief paradox.[26] Two features are chosen for attack. The first is that Ellsworth asserts that the basic hypothesis stated at the opening of Leontief's analysis is incorrect. The degree of capital intensity of American import-competing industries is not relevant to the comparison. What must be compared are the capital intensities of American exports and the exports of other countries to America. If the United States is a capital-rich country, then naturally the American goods made to replace imports are capital intensive. Import replacements simply conform to American productive practices. The proper object of Leontief's investigation should have been to investigate the factor content of American goods in their countries of origin.

Ellsworth has been accused of himself misunderstanding the basic significance of the Heckscher–Ohlin theorem, the testing of which is the overriding purpose of the whole exercise. It is an assumption of the theorem that production functions are identical in all countries. Ellsworth, in his criticism, however, seems to assume that they may differ from country to country. This is implicit in the view that there is no necessary similarity of factor intensities for American imports in their countries of origin and in the United States. Leontief, sticking as he does to the Heckscher–Ohlin assumptions, is quite entitled to proceed as he does and assume that production functions for these goods are the same whether they are imports produced abroad or import-competing goods produced in the United States.

Ellsworth's second objection is to Leontief's attempt to reconcile his findings with the Heckscher–Ohlin theorem by pointing to the greater productivity of American workers as compared with their foreign counterparts. In particular, Leontief's anxiety to divorce the superiority of American labour from the high capital–labour ratio and attribute it to externalities such as superior entrepreneurship comes in for attack. This 'conceptual awkwardness' would be avoided, Ellsworth argues, if Leontief would regard labour as of inherently the same quality in every country and to explain its higher productivity in terms of plentiful supplies of the other factors *including* capital. For himself, he regards the higher productivity of American labour to superior 'social overhead facilities'. There is, in the end, not a great deal at variance between Ellsworth and Leontief on this point but, as Caves points out, Leontief's original point still holds, namely that 'one cannot in the short run claim that part of the United States labour productivity is due to collaborating capital, unless one assumes factor market imperfections . . ., that is to say, that American labour generally earns more, and American capital less, than its marginal product'.[27]

5. Leontief has been criticised on statistical and methodological grounds. W. P. Travis has argued[28] that tariffs and direct trade impediments may distort trade and certainly do so in the case of the United States. To the extent that they do so, they rank, along with factor endowments, as a factor determining trade structure. Swerling criticised Leontief for including in his industrial list a number of industries with low capital–labour ratios which tended to bias his results. Leontief, apparently impressed by this point, re-worked his study, taking a wider range of industries, but with the same result as before.[29] Valavanis-Vail made a sweeping criticism by asserting that input–output models are not suited for examining a foreign trade case. In particular, fixed-input coefficients are not compatible with world trade equilibrium, in which every country gains from trade, there is full employment and the output of commodities has been altered by the existence of trade itself. Controversy has centred around the weight (but not the validity) of this criticism.

The conclusion at the end of a scrutiny of the large literature on the Leontief paradox must be that the Heckscher–Ohlin theorem, in the purity of its original statement, survives the ordeal. It is neither proved nor disproved. All that has emerged is the proven difficulty of testing it.

(iv) The Terms of Trade

The phrase 'terms of trade' has been frequent in these theory chapters. In the Richardian model they signified comparative cost-ratios marking, for any country, the limits between which goods might be exchanged. A country would offer in trade a given quantity of x in exchange for y, so long as the amount of y to be had from trade was greater than the amount of it which could be obtained domestically from giving up production of x and producing y instead. In the trading-partner country a given quantity of y would be exported only if the amount of x to be had in exchange by trade exceeded the amount which might be produced at home by switching from y to production of commodity x. The domestic comparative cost ratios of the two countries defined the limits between which trade would profitably take place for each country. Ricardo was not himself concerned to demonstrate either the magnitude of the gains from trade nor to which country they accrued.

It was left to J. S. Mill, over thirty years later, to demonstrate how the gains from trade were to be divided between the participant countries.[30] To do so, it was necessary to determine at which precise ratio, within the Ricardian limits, trade would take place. For this it was necessary to take account of the demand of each country for the product of the other and Mill evolved what he described as the 'Equation of International Demand'. Much of the process whereby the terms of trade between the two countries were settled has already been dealt with in Chapter 3. We shall summarise Mill's contribution in his own words: 'When two countries trade together in two commodities, the exchange value of these commodities . . . will adjust itself . . . in such a manner that the quantities required by each country, of the articles which it imports from its neighbour, shall be exactly sufficient to pay for one another.'[31] Mill thus evolved a view of an equilibrium level of barter exchange between two trading countries which was the first account of the terms of trade. Thereafter, the terms of trade and the forces which played upon them were the subject of a developing literature, through Marshall and others, to our own day. But in 1848 Mill certainly gave the term 'life' and elementary meaning. To him the terms of trade illustrated an exchange relationship — the terms upon which a country exchanges exports for imports. The terms of trade would 'improve' or become more 'favourable' when exports commanded a greater volume of imports in exchange, 'deteriorate' in the converse situation. These were 'real', 'barter' or 'commodity' terms of trade, uncomplicated by any reference to money values or changing price levels.

Nowadays, for discussion outside the classroom, and in the policy rather than the theoretical field, we are confronted with various statistical indicators of the terms of trade. In the light of this we must frame our definition in price terms, defining now the terms of trade of a nation as being indicated by the prices of its export goods, relative to the prices of the goods which it imports.

Before we proceed further let us be quite sure of the elements which are involved in the measurement of the terms of trade. Firstly, there are 'real' quantities. We started with these in the classical theory — the amount of good exchanged for good in factor terms. Secondly, there are ratios of money prices for the two goods, the price of each representing its factor value embodiment. Thirdly, there is the ratio of *all* export prices to *all* import prices, embodying an averaging problem for each category; and fourthly, there is the element of time which introduces an index number

The Pure Theory of International Trade

problem, in that changes in the average of export and import prices must be measured relative to some base date or period. It should be noted that operationally the terms of trade are only meaningful when compared over time — a characteristic which they share with certain other economic concepts, for example, the value of money. At a given moment of time one can only say that a given value of exports commands in return a given value of imports — that $x of exports buys $m of imports. When one says, however, that today $x of exports buys $m of imports where last year it bought $(m+q) of imports, it is a significant statement implying that the buying power of exports has fallen for the country concerned — that is, that the terms of commodity trade have moved unfavourably for that country. Taking any chosen year as base, we can always compute the amount and direction by which the terms of trade have changed over a period.

With these elements in mind, let us now examine the various terms of trade measurements. They are of three broad types: the barter terms of trade; the factoral terms of trade; and the income terms of trade. We shall deal with each in turn.

Changes in the barter (or commodity) terms of trade over time are measured by comparison of a country's changing import prices with its changing export prices. If import prices fall, export prices remaining unchanged, it means that more imports may be obtained for a given amount of exports — that is, that the terms of trade have moved favourably. If in the same circumstances import prices rise, they have moved unfavourably. To generalise the relationship, if

T is the terms of trade,
PX_0 is the average price of exports in year 0,
PX_1 is the average price of exports in some later year,
PM_0 is the average price of imports in year 0, and,
PM_1 is the average price of imports in the same later year,

then

$$T = \frac{PX_1/PX_0}{PM_1/PM_0}$$

Alternatively, and for everyday manipulation more simply, the terms of trade T is simply the index of export prices P_x divided by the index of import prices P_m and expressed as a percentage. That is

$$T = \frac{P_x}{P_m} \times 100$$

where both export and import indices have the same base year. Suppose that with 1970 as base year (100), that by the end of 1971 export prices have risen by 5 per cent, the export price index now standing at 105; and that import prices have fallen by 3 per cent, the import price index now being 97; then the terms of trade have improved by 8·25 per cent and the terms of trade may be given as 108·25. The higher the terms of trade index goes above 100 in this case, the greater the improvement in the terms of trade.

There is lack of uniformity in the way the ratios of export and import prices are expressed. The change in the price may be expressed as the ratio of the export price index to the import price index or vice versa. In the former case a 'favourable' movement in the terms of trade is indicated by the rise of the terms of trade index; in the latter by its fall. It is of no great importance which method is used, so long as the method is clearly understood. Uniformity is perhaps desirable and, as Viner says it might be 'more convenient to represent favourable movements of the indices by rising indices'.[32]

The barter terms of trade is the most practical of the terms of trade concepts and indices of this measure find their place in the official statistical manuals of the trading nations. The indicator must, however, be used with some circumspection. Its prevalent use reflects the fact that it is the most easily calculable of the terms of trade measures rather than the most satisfactory. A number of defects should be kept in mind. Firstly, the index number problem, with all that that implies in terms of coverage, base year and method of calculation, must be accepted. Secondly, the period over which the terms of trade are studied and compared must be carefully chosen. If it is too short, no meaningful change may register between the base date and the present; if it is too long, the structure of the country's trade is likely to have altered and the import and export commodity content may be non-comparable between the two dates. Thirdly, no account can be taken of quality of imports and exports. It has been argued that long-term changes in the terms of trade between primary-producing and industrial countries are influenced by this. Primary products have changed little in quality over the years, whereas the quality of manufactured products has improved. Some writing up of their value above the price index level would therefore be appropriate if the rise in quality were quantifiable, which, of course, it is not.

A final and more fundamental difficulty with the barter terms of trade lies in the fact that it takes account only of changes in export and import prices but not of how such price changes have come about. Clearly there is a great qualitative difference between a change in the terms of trade index caused by a rise in export prices relative to import prices (a) when export prices have risen by reason of strong demand for exports abroad, and (b)

The Pure Theory of International Trade

when export prices have risen as a result of wage inflation at home. Conversely there is a great difference between the cases (a) where export prices have fallen due to a contraction of demand abroad for these exports, and (b) where export prices have fallen due to rises in productivity at home. This difficulty can only be met by constructing a terms of trade measure which takes account of changes in productivity and changes in the level of demand consequent upon price.

The latter element was the concern of Taussig, who advocated the use of an index showing the time change in ratio of physical export quantities to physical import quantities.[33] This *gross* barter terms of trade can be summarised simply as $T_{gba} = Q_{ax}/Q_{am}$ where T_{gba} is the gross barter terms of trade of country A, Q_{ax} is the volume of A's exports, and Q_{am} is the volume of its imports. The higher the ratio, the better the gross barter terms of trade. A greater quantity of imports can be had for the same volume of exports.

It may be objected that there is no satisfactory way in which the quantities of imports and exports may be measured, no units applying equally to wheat and to platinum, to butter and to electrical energy. Taussig's method is, however, to relate the total *money* value of imports and exports and to correct the crude figures for each by a relevant price index. Once more objections arise. If the barter terms of trade may be faulted for giving us only an uncritical ratio of export/import price changes, the gross barter terms give us only an uncritical ratio of quantities. All exports are included in the quantity index whether they be normal trading exports or unilateral transfers such as the transfer of goods associated with a reparations payment. (A form of transfer much to the fore at the time when Taussig wrote in 1925–7.) Exports of capital are equally a complication but are also lumped in the general figures for exports. It clearly will not do to take a single annual figure for exports and imports without examination of the items subsumed in each. The concept of the gross barter terms of trade was used by Taussig in an attempt to evaluate the true British gains from trade during the period of British trading greatness, and although many interesting aspects of the terms of trade concept arose in the discussion, it has been dismissed by later writers as 'unreal' and the concept as impracticable as a statistical indicator.[34]

It is appropriate here to comment on a point of terminology. Taussig (and others) referred to the commodity terms of trade (i.e. ratio of import and export prices) as the *net* barter terms of trade and to his export/import quantity ratio as the *gross* barter terms of trade. Viner continues to use the term *net* as do a few more modern writers. More often, nowadays, both *net* and *gross*, as adjectives for the two concepts of the commodity terms of trade, have been allowed to lapse and we refer to the survivor, i.e. the export/import price ratio as the commodity terms of trade.

Let us return to the question of how productivity may be embodied in the terms of trade measure. An attempt to do this is the so-called *factoral* terms of trade. These purport to show us changes in the amount of resources (factors) required by a country to purchase a given amount of imports. The single factoral terms of trade are computed by multiplying the commodity terms of trade index for that country by an index measuring changes in productivity in the country's export industries. It can be expressed as

$$S_a = T_a \cdot P_a$$

where S_a is the single factoral terms of trade for country A,

T_a is the commodity terms of trade for country A, and

P_a is an index of productivity in A's export industries.

The expression clearly shows that a country's factoral terms of trade improve as productivity in its export industries improves.

The term 'single', applied to the factoral terms of trade, denotes that we take account only of productivity in the country whose terms of trade we are measuring and not in the countries with which it is trading. We may extend the measure to take account, not only of productivity in the home country's exporting industries but also of productivity of the exporting industries of its trading partners and therefore in its imports. In this case the extended measure is described as the *double factoral* terms of trade. In effect it seeks to adjust the price ratio of exports and imports to take account of the changing factor content of both. The double factoral terms of trade may be summarised in the expression

$$D_a = T_a \cdot \frac{P_a}{P_b}$$

where D_a is the double factoral terms of trade in country A,

P_a is an index of productivity in A's exporting industries, and

P_b is an index of productivity in the export industries of A's trading partners.

It is hard to escape the feeling that the double factoral terms of trade can exist only conceptually, indeed that it is merely an extension to logical completeness by including the productivity of both trade parties. In practice it could never be a feasible indicator, since it would require a measure of productivity in many export industries of many countries. Indices of productivity are notoriously difficult to construct and even for the single

The Pure Theory of International Trade

factoral terms of trade there are very few series and, to this writer's knowledge, none in the manuals of official statistics.[35] Apart from practicability, it is arguable that the double factoral terms of trade, if calculable, would give us data in which we are scarcely interested. We do want to know what our domestic production factors can earn in foreign goods; we are not too concerned with what our factors can demand in terms of the services of foreign factors.

The last item of this list of terms of trade measures, impressive for its length rather than for its usefulness, is that of the *income* terms of trade. This index embraces changes in export and import prices (that is, the commodity terms of trade) and the volume of exports. Its aim is to show a country's changing import capacity in relation to changes in its exports. Its construction is denoted by the expression

$$I_a = T_a \cdot Q_a \tag{1}$$

where I_a is the income terms of trade for country A,
T_a is A's net barter terms of trade, and
Q_a is A's export volume index.

If we re-write (1) as

$$I_a = \frac{\text{Index of export prices} \times \text{Export quantity}}{\text{Index of import prices}}$$

we can summarise the income terms of trade as the ratio of the index of export values to an index of import prices.[36] A rise in I_a indicates that country A can import a greater quantity of imports for the sale of exports. It should be observed, however, that it does not really measure import capacity precisely. Such a capacity is a function of a country's total foreign currency earnings and not solely of the earnings from its commodity exports. For a developing country with negligible invisible earnings, however, the income terms of trade is a useful indicator of the country's ability to sustain a given import level.

Part Two

Commercial Policy

*'... don't suppose that everything that you won't
be able to understand is a piece of stupidity.'*

WITTGENSTEIN – in a letter to
Bertrand Russell

Part Two

Commercial Policy

... I don't suppose that everything you say won't
be taken today as a piece of stupidity.

WITTGENSTEIN—in a letter to
Bertrand Russell

6
Tariffs

(i) Tariffs: the Mechanism

THE tariff is the standard instrument of commercial policy. Any serious discussion of commercial policy depends upon a knowledge of it and its effects. We therefore preface the consideration of the broader issues of commercial policy by an examination of the tariff.

However, the tariff is not the only instrument of protection. Import quotas, embargoes and import restrictions are also widely used, but these are more often employed as instruments of balance-of-payments policy and we discuss them, in that context, in Chapter 19.

A tariff is essentially a tax levied by the state on goods which enter a country. Much less common are two other forms of duty: the export tax, which is levied on goods leaving a country, and the transit duty, levied on goods passing through *en route* to another. We deal here only with tariffs.

Export duties are rare, largely because most countries wish to maximise exports for balance-of-payments reasons and do not wish to impede them by duties. In the United States export duties are unconstitutional, presumably because it was deemed undesirable that the federal government, which imposes external tariffs, should have any power to tax articles exported by individual states.[1]

Internationally the most common type of import duty is the *ad valorem* tariff levied on the total value of the commodity as a percentage. (The levy is on the total value of the commodity at the custom frontier, i.e., on its c.i.f. (cost, insurance and freight) value.) Thus we may speak of a country as having a 20 per cent general tariff, meaning that all imports are subjected at the frontier to a tax determined by 20 per cent of their c.i.f. value. Slightly less common is the *specific* tariff, levied either on individual units of the imported commodity, as $\$X$ per automobile, or on unit measurement as $\$Y$ per ton of coal or t cents per litre of wine. Occasionally there are *compound* duties, which are a combination of the *specific* and the *ad valorem* tariff. Here, units of a commodity are subject to a specified duty on each unit plus a percentage *ad valorem* duty.

All duties levied on imports by a country are listed in its tariff schedule. Those commodities on which there is no duty are said to be on the 'free' list. Within the tariff schedule there may be relative simplicity where a country has a so-called 'single column' schedule, listing commodities and the single duty, specific or *ad valorem*, applicable to them; or there may be greater complexity where, in a 'multi-column' schedule, different rates are imposed on a single commodity according to the country of its origin. When we add to these complexities the fact that commodities are defined in the lists with varying detail and are continually redefined, that goods are moved from tariff schedule to free list and back again, that rates are frequently altered or adjusted, the final product, the country's tariff structure, is complex and sometimes baffling. Indeed, the very complexity of a tariff schedule may be used as a protective weapon, the uncertainty as to tariff liability deterring the potential importer from bringing in the goods at all. The accumulation of tariff rates and procedures has given rise in most advanced countries to a great army of officials which 'lives off the tariff' and whose livelihood depends on its continuance. Whether free trade, were it to come, would lead to the economy of their disbandment is unlikely. Even within the European Common Market, where the internal tariff has been eliminated, border checks and examinations are retained on various pretexts.

One immediate practical difficulty which arises from the complexity of tariff structures is that of comparing them. We make frequent references to a country as being 'protectionist' or as having a 'high tariff wall', implicitly or explicitly comparing it to other countries, less protectionist or more so. How in fact can we gauge the height of a country's tariff wall? The complexity of its tariff schedule is no guide, nor is it very helpful to know whether its tariffs are imposed for protection or for revenue purposes, since these aims are frequently both present although one may be paramount. Despite the difficulties of comparing tariff walls in different countries[2] many attempts have been made to do so. The very necessity of arguing about the relative heights of tariffs in international negotiations leads politicians and bureaucrats to demand measurement which economists have not been slow to undertake.[3]

Two imperfect methods of tariff comparison, either between countries or of the same country over time, are employed. The first is to calculate the expression $R/M \times 100$, where R is the total revenue from duties, M the total value of imports, and the ratio is expressed as a percentage. Implicit in the expression is the assumption that the higher the ratio the higher the tariff wall. This need not be so. It is a serious flaw in this ratio that a very high tariff wall which excludes dutiable imports may reduce R to near zero, leaving the country's imports to consist almost entirely of free list commodities. With a zero or negligible value for R and some value for M the ratio would be low. A high protective tariff might not reflect well, or even at all, in such a ratio.

A second measurement is made by converting all duties into terms of an *ad valorem* rate and then taking the average of all such rates. The resulting average tariff may then be used either for inter-temporal or inter-country comparisons. This method also must be used with caution. Almost always it will be appropriate to use a weighted average. What then decides the weights to be used? Even if weights are well chosen and applied the results of intra-country comparisons may be misleading, for the degree of protection afforded depends not only on the average tariff rates but on demand conditions in the countries compared and the supply conditions in the supplying country. For example, a lower average rate in country B than in country A may still afford more protection to B if demand for import goods in B is highly elastic while that in A is inelastic. The supply conditions, altering as they do the supply price of imports with changes in the amount demanded, have to be considered and may have various effects on the final price after duty and on the degree of protection. Clearly the comparison of tariff levels statistically even by this, the more satisfactory method, is a tricky business, and indicators must be used with caution.

Still further problems await us when we seek to gauge the 'protective effect' of tariffs, that is, the precise extent to which they shield domestic supplies from foreign competition. To do this we must delve further than the tariff rate on the commodity itself, taking account also of the tariff rates on the component inputs which go to the manufacture of the commodity. An example will clarify the argument.

If country X imposes a 10 per cent *ad valorem* tariff on cameras we have some information about the degree of protection thus provided to domestic producers of cameras. But our information is incomplete. We must know also what changes, if any, have occurred in the import tariffs on components such as lenses and shutters. If we find that country X has lowered its tariff on lenses from 5 per cent to zero and on shutters by the same amount we may assume that the protective effect of the tariff on cameras for country X is greater by reason of the lowered taxes on these inputs. This can be seen from the fact that with the reduction in the input prices, resulting from the lower tariffs, the production cost of camera producers will fall, their product will become more competitive with foreign camera imports and imports of foreign cameras will decline by more than they would have done had the only tariff change been the 10 per cent tariff on complete cameras. To put the argument in general terms: a tariff on a final product will have a greater protective effect when the tariffs on its component inputs are low than it would if the tariffs on those inputs were high. The opposite applies: the protective effect of a given tariff on a final product will be lower the higher are the tariffs on its component inputs. We cannot then equate the tariff on an imported final good with the protective effect. The latter is compounded of (a) the tariff on the finished good and (b) the whole range of tariff rates on its inputs. Real protection is a matter of tariff structure rather than of individual tariffs.

It is possible to demonstrate algebraically the factors which determine the effective rate of protection for a given final product.[4]

For any given final product its total value is the total value of all the component inputs *plus* the value added by the manufacturer. Thus, per dollar of output, the value added in an industry $X(V_x)$ plus the proportion of each dollar of final output represented by imported components (r) gives us

$$V_x + r = 1 \qquad (1)$$

Suppose that a tariff is imposed on an imported commodity competing with X, then the domestic selling price of X rises by the amount of the tariff t_x. If we assume that the supply of component inputs is perfectly elastic then the value added by domestic producers will increase to V'_x and the post-tariff situation is shown by

$$V'_x + r = 1 + t_x \qquad (2)$$

and if tariffs are imposed on the inputs themselves and the value of each input becomes $1 + t_i$ then equation (2) becomes

$$V'_x + r(1 + t_i) = 1 + t_x \qquad (3)$$

The effective rate of protection (f_i) we may define as the total increase in value added as a result of tariffs. This, expressed as a percentage gives us

$$f_i = \frac{V'_x - V_x}{V_x} \qquad (4)$$

Transposing terms in equation (1) we get

$$V_x = 1 - r \qquad (5)$$

reflecting the pre-tariff situation, and transposing terms in equation (3) we get

$$V'_x = 1 + t_x - r(1 + t_i) \qquad (6)$$

reflecting the post-tariff situation.

Now substitute the values for V_x and V'_x given in equations (5) and (6) in the numerator of equation (4) and we get

$$f_i = \frac{1 + t_x - r(1 + t_i) - (1 - r)}{V_x} \qquad (7)$$

which reduces to

$$f_i = \frac{t_x - rt_i}{V_x} \qquad (8)$$

But from equation (1) $V_x + r = 1$ or $V_x = 1 - r$
Therefore we can rewrite equation (8), substituting in the denominator, as

$$f_i = \frac{t_x - rt_i}{1 - r} \qquad (9)$$

This gives us a formula for the effective rate of tariff. It shows clearly that f_i the effective rate is higher the lower is t_i the tariff on components and the higher is r. If components are duty free the formula becomes $f_i = t_x/(1 - r)$ and if the tariff rate on finished goods is the same as that on components (i.e. where $t_x = t_i$, then $f_i = t_x$, and the effective rate is equal to the nominal rate).

This distinction between the 'nominal' and 'effective' rates of protection is a very real one with considerable practical significance. In particular, until this distinction was realised, tariff negotiations were conducted in terms of nominal levels of protection. It is now possible to form clearer pictures of the protective effects of countries' tariff structures. Countries claiming low tariff walls on the basis of low nominal rates are likely to have their claims questioned. A well-known recent case has been that of the tariff protection of the developed countries *vis-à-vis* the developing countries in which the effective protection of the former is very much higher than might be indicated by the nominal tariff rates.

(ii) Tariffs: the Effects

While tariffs have a variety of effects which we shall shortly review, these are attained predominantly by their power to reduce imports. This fundamental characteristic is easily demonstrated. If we assume two countries X and Y both producing butter, selling in X for 80 cents and in Y for 60 cents per pound, then, assuming there is free trade and that there are no transport costs or transport costs less than 20 cents per pound, butter producers in Y would export their product to X. The price of butter would fall in X and rise in Y, settling at some level between 80 and 60 cents per pound. The import of butter into X could, however, be prevented by the imposition by X of an *ad valorem* tariff on butter imports from Y, equal to the difference between the new trading price and the original price in X. With no transport costs and assuming that butter is of identical quality in X and Y, the import of Y's butter into X would cease. Thus, assuming no transfer costs, the imposition of a tariff equal to the difference between the home price before trade and the price of the imported substitute eliminates trade. If we allow transport costs a lower tariff suffices.

We must be careful here about the size of the tariff V. If V is considered as a tariff on imports from Y at Y's price before trade then a $33\frac{1}{3}$ per cent tariff will exclude all imports from Y and no trade will take place. The necessary tariff to exclude Y's products from X is, however, less than $33\frac{1}{3}$ per cent, for if trade is free between X and Y the resulting price is an XY-world price higher than Y's supply price before trade. The necessary tariff for exclusion of Y imports from X is therefore V as shown on Fig. 6.1, V being less than $33\frac{1}{3}$ per cent. As an approximation it is true to say that a tariff calculated on the difference of the pre-trade prices will prevent trade, but it is unnecessarily high and a tariff based on the XY-world price will be sufficient.

The example may be demonstrated graphically (Fig. 6.1) by using simple demand and supply curves. Before trade OM lb of butter are being sold in X at Op_x per pound; in Y, ON lb are sold at a price of Op_y. Once free trade is achieved a common price $O^1p_x = O^1p_y$ establishes itself in both countries. At this price in Y there is a surplus of supply over demand of ab which is exportable to X and is equal to the amount cd at which, at the price O^1p_x,

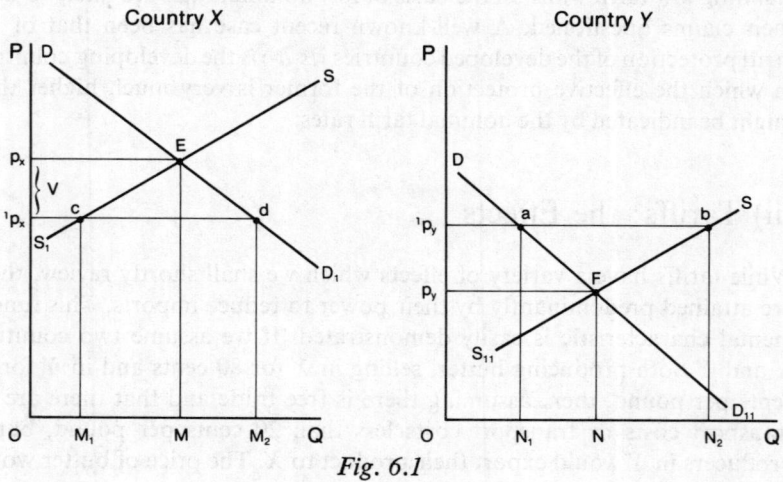

Fig. 6.1

Commercial Policy

demand in X exceeds supply. The volume of trade is then $M_1 M_2$ imports to X, or $N_1 N_2$ exports from Y.

The equality of excess supply in Y and excess demand in X follows from the fact that, with free trade, no transport costs and a two-country world, the total world demand and supply of butter establishes the new price $^1 p_x = {}^1 p_y$. Therefore if supply exceeds demand in one country at that price, it must fall short of it in the other country by a like amount.

Suppose the importing country X imposes a tariff. All it needs do to exclude all imports is to impose a tariff of V. Such a tariff will expand domestic supply from c to E and reduce domestic demand from d to E. In X the demand fall to E reduces the demand for Y's surplus at the free trade price ($^1 p_y$). Supply in Y contracts from b to F and at the lower price demands expands from a to F. Thus, in the absence of transport costs, a tariff in the importing country equal to the difference between the pre-trade price and the free trade price will eliminate all trade between the two countries. To the extent that there are transport costs, a lower tariff will suffice.

The protective effect of a tariff can always be obtained if the tariff duty is high enough. It may be that a government wishes to protect a home industry by totally excluding competing imports of the product. If so, the tariff must be high enough to constitute a virtual embargo of that import. It may, however, be sufficient merely to give a measure of protection to the home industry and a tariff duty high enough to raise the price and to reduce, but not to eliminate, the quantity of the good imported. In this case revenue accrues to the state from the imports.

Apart from reducing imports, tariffs yield revenue and may be imposed for that purpose alone, in which event they are described as revenue tariffs. Such a tariff must be at a duty rate low enough not to exclude trade altogether. The ideal revenue tariff is one levied upon a good for which the domestic demand is inelastic, which has no close domestically produced substitute and whose higher price, as a result of the tariff, does not have adverse domestic economic effects—as, for example, by unduly raising the costs of an industry using the good as a raw material or by raising the price of an essential food stuff to the public in general. Few tariffs are imposed solely for revenue—although tariffs on imported luxuries come close to this—and most tariffs are imposed with an admixture of effects while at the same time the government has one major purpose in mind. The effects of a tariff are in fact likely to be much wider than the single aim or group of aims for which it is imposed and it is necessary to review fairly fully all of these effects.

Kindleberger distinguishes[5] eight tariff effects. To these we shall add a ninth. This list forms a convenient agenda for discussion and we shall use it. The nine effects are:

1. the protective (or production) effect,
2. the consumption effect,
3. the revenue effect,
4. the redistribution effect,
5. the terms of trade effect,
6. the competitive effect,
7. the income effect,
8. the balance-of-payments effect, and
9. the cost effect.

We shall deal with these effects in turn.

(1)–(4) The protective effect can be simply illustrated in partial equilibrium terms, from the figure depicting the market situation for butter in country X (Fig. 6.1). cd represents the amount of imports at the price $O^1 p_x$, with free trade. To this amount must be added OM_1, which is produced at home. When the tariff V is imposed in X, imports drop to zero and home production increases by $M_1 M$. This increase in home production measures the protective effect. It is clear from the diagram that the size of the protective effect is decided by the elasticity of the supply curve SS_1. If this curve is highly elastic, $M_1 M$ will be large. If it is inelastic, the protective effect will be small. In the case illustrated by the diagram the tariff is prohibitive, the protective effect being sufficient to expand domestic production to that level at which it meets domestic demand without any imports. There is, of course, no reason why this 'total' protection should take place. Smaller tariffs than V would give smaller protective effects.

To illustrate certain of the other tariff effects, a new diagram (Fig. 6.2) will be useful. Suppose that this shows the trade situation in butter between Britain and Denmark. Without trade the price of butter would be determined by the intersection of the demand and supply curves in each country, the price in Britain being higher than that in Denmark. With the opening of trade (and assuming no transport costs), a world price establishes itself at O_{p_1}, which lies somewhere between the Danish and British before-trade prices. As in Fig. 6.1 the excess supply fg in Denmark is exported and equals de imports in Britain. (This assumes that it is a necessary condition for the new world price that trade between Britain and Denmark should be in balance. This assumption is a continuing one for all cases covered by this diagram.)

Britain now imposes a tariff of t to protect her dairy farmers. This tariff will raise the price in Britain (but not by the full amount of the tariff) and

Commercial Policy

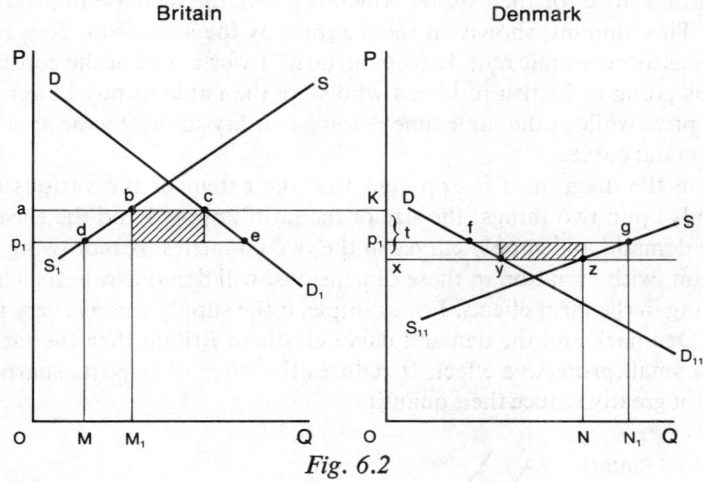

Fig. 6.2

lower the price in Denmark until the difference between the two prices is equal to the tariff t. This distribution of the tariff's effect on the two countries' prices occurs because, as the price rises in Britain with the tariff, the demand for butter imports falls and, with anything less than an infinitely elastic supply curve in Denmark, the supply price in that country falls with the decline in the export demand. The tariff affects prices in both countries. Eventually in the new equilibrium the price effect of the tariff will be distributed in the manner shown on the diagram, Britain importing bc and Denmark exporting yz. The more elastic the Danish supply curve the greater the effect of the tariff on the British price and the less on the Danish. If the Danish curve was infinitely elastic the full rise in the British rise would be equal to the tariff.[6]

The protective, consumption, revenue and redistribution effects can all be illustrated on this diagram. The protective effect – or, because it is shown in total output terms, what is sometimes called the 'production effect' – of the tariff in Britain is to increase domestic butter production from OM to OM_1 and reduce domestic production in Denmark by N_1N. The consumption effect will be to lower consumption of butter in Britain from p_1e to ac, and raise it in Denmark from p_1f to xy. The revenue effect is shown by the change in government receipts as a result of the tariff. Since the tariff was initially zero the revenue must consist of the amount of the tariff t multiplied by either bc or yz. Geometrically it will be represented on the diagram by the sum of the area of the rectangles which are shaded on the two figures. The redistribution effect results from producers in Britain receiving after the tariff a price for their butter which is above the increase in production costs. This amount, shown on the diagram by the area $abdp_1$ goes to producers as an economic rent. Before the tariff it was a part of the consumers' surplus going to British residents who were then able to buy butter at the lower price while at the same time reaping a utility shown by the area under the demand curve.

From the diagram it is apparent that the extent of the various effects depends upon two things: the size of the tariff imposed and the elasticities of the demand and supply curves in the two countries. A redrawing of the diagram, with variation in these dimensions, will demonstrate the changes resulting in the tariff effects. For example, if the supply curve is very inelastic in Denmark and the demand curve elastic in Britain then the tariff has only a small protective effect. It reduces the price of imports sharply but does not greatly reduce their quantity.

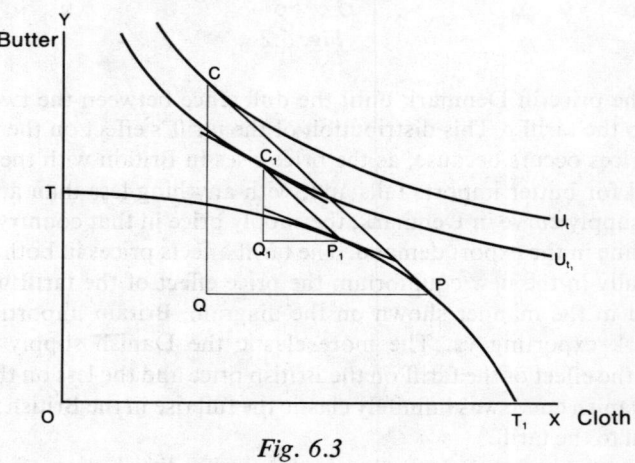

Fig. 6.3

The protective and consumption effects can also be illustrated in general equilibrium terms and as the diagrammatic analysis for this has a later application we shall include it here. Fig. 6.3 shows the standard two-country/two-commodity case, the x axis measuring exports of cloth, the y axis exports of butter. TT_1 is the transformation curve between butter and cloth and U_t is the indifference curve reached under free trade. C and P are the free trade consumption and production points respectively. PQ of cloth is traded for QC of butter and the slope of PC represents the terms of trade. The size of the tariff is indirectly inferred from the difference of the slopes of the tangents at P_1 and C_1, the new production and consumption positions after the imposition of the tariff. This is readily understandable

Commercial Policy

when we bear in mind that internal equilibrium of producers and consumers demands that price should be equal to the marginal cost of transformation between the two goods (i.e. the slope of the tangent at P_1) and the marginal rate of substitution in consumption (the slope of the tangent at C_1). Under free trade PC the line joining P and C has a constant slope, but with the tariff the tangents at P_1 and C_1 have different slopes because the tariff raises the domestic price of the import good above its price in international trade. The greater the tariff the more the slopes of the tangents will differ. If P_1 and C_1 are the new production and consumption points after the tariff, then the protective effect is the change in production from P to P_1 and the consumption effect is the change in consumption from C to C_1. It is assumed, for simplicity in the diagram, that the terms of trade are unchanged as a result of the tariff, i.e. that P_1C_1 is parallel to PC. This ensures that as a result of the tariff the country moves to a lower indifference curve U_{t_1}.

(5) When we turn to examine the effects of a tariff upon the terms of trade of the country which imposes it, we may illustrate the argument either in partial equilibrium terms with Fig. 6.2 or by the use of Marshallian offer curves for a general equilibrium analysis. We start with knowledge gained already from Fig. 6.2. There it was shown that the price effects of a tariff imposed by Britain against Denmark were distributed between the two countries. The full tariff t increased the British domestic price by ap_1 and lowered the Danish price by p_1x. The British buying price for the imports of butter after the tariff was Ox but this was raised (in Britain) by the tariff to Oa. As long as the supply curve in the exporting country is less than perfectly elastic, the importing country gets the product cheaper. The fact that the consumer in the importing country pays more for it is offset by the revenue effect of the tariff, part of which falls on producers in Denmark, the exporting country.

The terms of trade effect is then that a country imposing a tariff improves its terms of trade by getting its imports more cheaply (save in the case where the supply curve in the exporting country is perfectly elastic), the foreign exporter being forced to pay some part of the duty.

The analysis through offer curves demonstrates the argument in general equilibrium terms and is a more complete and widely applicable demonstration of the effects of a tariff on the terms of trade. Fig. 6.4 shows offer curves of Britain and Denmark for trade in the two commodities butter and cloth. OX is the offer curve of the foreign country, Denmark, for cloth; OY is the offer curve of the home country Britain, for butter.

Under conditions of free trade the slope of the line OR indicates the terms of trade. Any tariff imposed by Britain on Danish butter results in a new offer curve between OY and the vertical axis, its precise location being determined by the amount of the tariff. Suppose that the British tariff on butter is a 100 per cent *ad valorem* tariff levied in terms of cloth by the British government, then the new offer curve OY_1 will result. (The tariff rate $t = R_1C/R_1b$.). It should be noted that the curve OY_1 may represent an import tax on butter or an export tax on cloth. If it is the latter Britain now offers less cloth for any given amount of butter and collects the export tax in units of cloth. For Ob of butter it formerly offered bC of

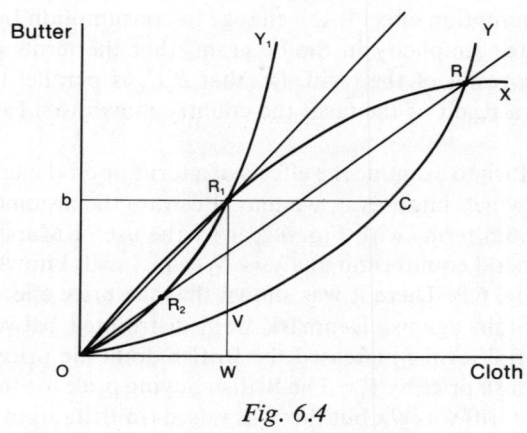

Fig. 6.4

cloth but now offers only bR_1, R_1C being, in cloth terms, the amount of tax collected. If it is the former, it formerly offered OW of cloth for VW of butter whereas it now requires R_1W of butter and collects a tariff R_1V.

In either event the shift of the offer curve to OY_1 improves the terms of trade for Britain from OR to OR_1. This improvement in the British terms of trade does not, however, apply to the individual British consumer, whose terms of trade have worsened because of the tariff. To him the price of butter is now compounded of the world market price for butter plus the tariff. For the British domestic consumer a greater amount in exports is now required in order to acquire the same amount of imports as before the tariff.

It will be noted, from the geometry, that the extent of the improvement in the British terms of trade depends on two factors: the size of the tariff and therefore the extent of the movement of the British offer curve (OY) to the left; and the elasticity of the Danish offer curve OX. In the extreme case where the Danish offer curve was perfectly elastic and took the form of a straight line through the origin with slope OR, then a tariff would never

Commercial Policy

improve the terms of trade for Britain but would merely curtail the volume of trade, as at R_2.

It appears that the imposition of a tariff by one country, providing it does not induce retaliation by the other, will improve the terms of trade for the tariff-imposing country but will reduce the volume of trade. At this stage we cannot say whether the tariff is beneficial for the country which imposes it or not. It may be that the terms of trade improvement more than offsets the effects of the drop in trade volume; it may be, however, that the drop in volume, even with better terms of trade, results in a deterioration of the tariff country's trading position. This is a matter we shall investigate shortly.

The simple changes in the terms of trade of a tariff-imposing country as compared with those under free trade will be complicated by the uses to which the revenue proceeds of the tariff may be put. As long as the tariff proceeds are consumed by the goverment itself all is well, but if the government wants to consume the other commodity it can only obtain it in the world market so that its own demand for the commodity must be added to private demand thus producing a revised trade offer curve and new terms of trade. These in turn will react upon the private sector to cause a further change in the offer curve in accordance with the revision in relative prices. Similar problems arise if the government decides to distribute the tariff proceeds as a subsidy to the private sector to recompense them for the worsening in their domestic terms of trade as a result of the tariff. If they do not wish to consume the subsidies but rather to trade them for other commodities, they invoke a change in the whole demand pattern which leads to new offer curves and a revision of the terms of trade yet again. To explore these possibilities in short compass is impossible. The student should, however, be aware of their existence and realise the simplicity and limitations of the picture we have presented.

One interesting feature is the effect which the elasticity of the offer curve of the foreign country has upon the extent to which the home country can improve its terms of trade by a tariff. Fig. 6.5 illustrates this point. OC_1, OC_2, OC_3 and OC_4 are foreign offer curves of varying elasticity. OC_1 is perfectly elastic and is the same as the free trade terms of trade line. This means that the foreign country offers its exports at a fixed real exchange rate with imports, whatever the volume of trade. If OB_1 is the offer curve of the home country, then OR represents the terms of trade and any change in the offer curve as a result of a tariff, as to OB_2, leaves the terms of trade unchanged at OF. As foreign offer curves become less and less elastic, as OC_2, OC_3 and OC_4, so the terms of trade of a tariff-imposing country improve. In the diagram they move progressively from OF to OG to OH and OJ. The less elastic the foreign offer curve the more advantageous the terms of trade procurable to the home country by the imposition of a tariff. This point has some practical significance. A very small country, which is confronted by an offer curve for the rest of the world which is almost perfectly elastic, will be powerless to effect any change by a tariff in its terms of trade. A large country, e.g., the United States, may make considerable improvement in its terms, although the possibility of retaliation against a tariff, which is small for a small country, will here be considerable.

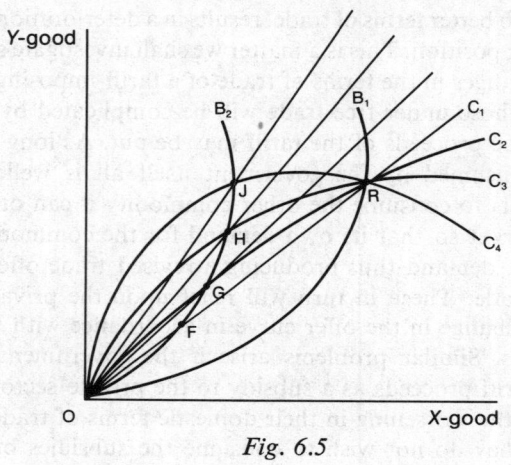

Fig. 6.5

Two questions of substantial importance are raised by the terms of trade question. Both are really qualifications of the proposition that a tariff may result in improvement in the terms of trade of the country which imposes it. The first is what happens when country B retaliates to the tariff imposed by country A; and the second, what is the optimum tariff which a country may impose? To these questions we now turn.

It is unlikely that, if a country may so easily improve its terms of trade as by imposing a tariff, it will be allowed to do so by other countries. More likely is it that they will in turn impose retaliatory tariffs. The effect of such counter-action is illustrated in Fig. 6.6. The original offer curves of Britain and Denmark are shown by OY and OX respectively, with the terms of trade at OR. Britain imposes a tariff on Danish butter such that her offer curve moves to OY_1. This is promptly countered by a Danish tariff on cloth such that the Danish offer curve moves to OX_1. The new terms of trade would be shown by OR_1 and there would be a substantial reduction in trade in both commodities at R_1. Further offer curves OY_2 and OX_2 show how a further tariff and further retaliation reduce the trade volume still further at

Commercial Policy

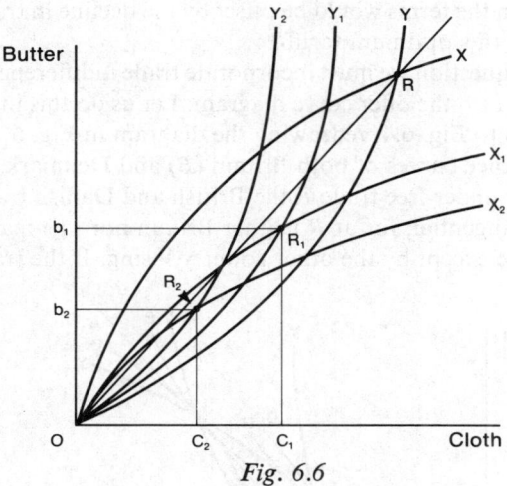

Fig. 6.6

OR_2 terms of trade. The effect, then, of a succession of tariffs and counter tariffs by the two countries is to reduce progressively the volume of trade with only small differences in the terms of trade and, in the limit, no change in the terms of trade at all as we converge on O. At R_2 and R_1 both countries would have been willing to trade much more at OR_2 and OR_1 terms of trade, if the domestic price relationship were the same as these terms of trade. In both countries, however, the tariffs have produced high prices of the imported commodities with resultant shrinkage of consumption at such prices. Both countries have lost by the tariff impositions; their progressive removal on a reciprocal basis benefits both countries. Whether or not the process of tariff and counter-tariff will continue until finally the volume of trade is reduced to zero is a question to which we recur when we have dealt with the next case – that of the optimum tariff.

We return to the basic effect of a tariff on the terms of trade. From the analysis of Fig. 6.4 it was apparent that, providing there were no retaliation, a country might expect to improve its terms of trade as compared with the free trade position by imposing a tariff, but must expect a contraction of the volume of trade. Whether this improvement in the terms of trade is likely to improve the country's trade position it is, however, impossible without further investigation, to say. The profit from trade has risen on each transaction as a result of the improvement in the commodity terms of trade, but if the volume of trade declines sharply this improvement in the terms may be more than offset. There must clearly be some optimum tariff which pushes the improvement in the terms of trade only to the point at which any further gain in the terms would be offset by the decline in trade volume. What determines this optimum tariff?

To answer this question we must incorporate trade indifference curves for the two countries into the offer curve diagram. Let us do this in two stages. First let us return to Fig. 6.4, redrawing the diagram in Fig. 6.7 to include the trade indifference curves of both Britain (B) and Denmark (D). At the equilibrium point under free trade R the British and Danish trade indifference curves are tangential, for at R neither Britain nor Denmark can gain further from trade except by the other country losing. If the trade point R

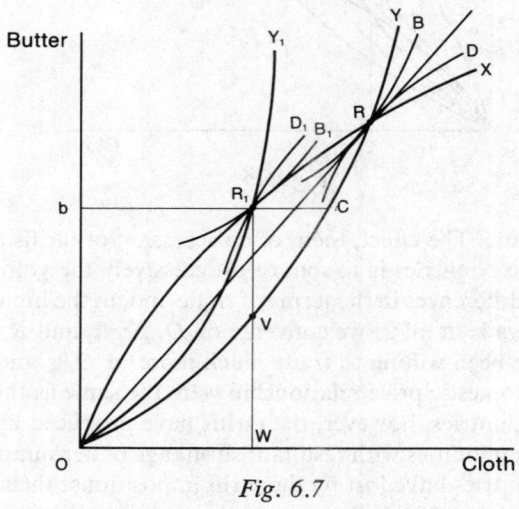

Fig. 6.7

shifts to the left, this means a movement to higher trade indifference curves for Britain but lower for Denmark. The opposite is true for a movement of R to the right. Thus, at R_1 we find that with the imposition of the tariff on butter represented by the movement of the British trade offer curve to Y_1 Britain is on a higher trade indifference curve B_1 but Denmark is on a lower one at D_1.

Let us now use these tools in a new diagram, Fig. 6.8, to illustrate the determination of the optimum tariff. The problem, in diagrammatic terms is: at what point to the left of R must the new British offer curve OY_1, reflecting the new tariff, be drawn in order to optimise the level of the tariff? On the diagram, free trade equilibrium is at R where the terms of trade are represented by the slope of OR and the volume of trade is Oa of butter and OV of cloth. Britain is, at R on the trade indifference curve B_1 and Denmark on D_1. With these conditions Britain wishes to impose a

Commercial Policy

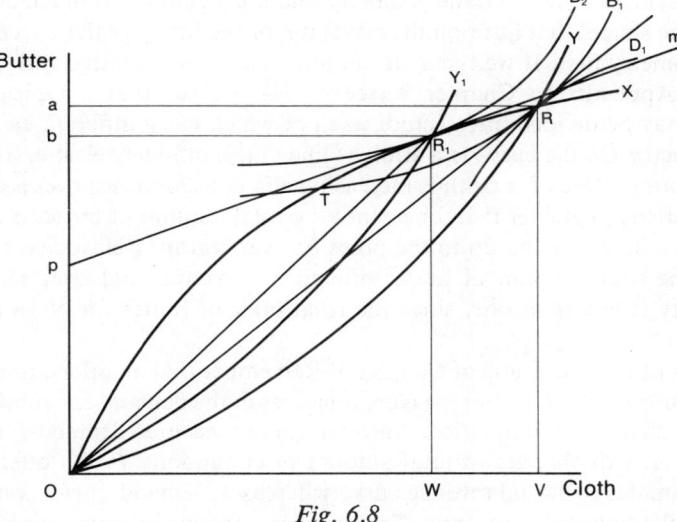

Fig. 6.8

tariff of such magnitude as will place her on the highest possible trade indifference curve.

With free trade Britain is on the trade indifference curve B_1. This intersects the Danish offer curve at R and at T. It is evident that any indifference curve which intersects the offer curve within the sector TR will be a superior trade indifference curve. Therefore any movement of the original British offer curve OY to reflect a tariff, such that its intersection points with the trade indifference curve lie within the sector TR, will ensure a higher British indifference curve. The highest possible such curve will be at that point where the sector TR is minimised, namely, where it comes to a point at R_1, the point of tangency of the indifference curve B_2 with OX. If Britain can impose a tariff such that her new offer curve OY_1 can intersect the Danish offer curve at this point of tangency R_1, then she optimises her trade position. Given that there is no retaliation from Denmark and given the Danish offer curve, there is no tariff that will produce a better trade situation for Britain than that at R_1. At that point Britain trades Ow of cloth for Ob of butter, and the domestic price ratio, i.e. the price ratio of the two commodities in Britain, is shown by the slope of the line pm which is tangential to the trade indifference curve B_2 at R_1. The world price ratio which will obtain after the British have imposed the tariff will be shown by the line OR_1 and the difference between the world price ratio, bR_1/bO, and the domestic price ratio, bR_1/bp, must be equal to the revenue collected by Britain from the tariff.

It is evident both from the geometry and the algebra that much depends upon the shape, that is, upon the elasticity, of the foreign offer curve. Take the geometry first. If we recur to the principles demonstrated in Fig. 3.26 in the Appendix to Chapter 3 (see p. 71), we see that a typical offer curve may be divided into sectors, each of which has a different elasticity. Over sector Oa the curve is a straight line and is infinitely elastic, since the total butter offered for cloth is increasing at a constant rate; over sector ab the elasticity is greater than one, since the total amount of butter given for cloth is still increasing up to the point b; over sector bc elasticity is unity, since the total amount of butter offered is constant; and over sector cd elasticity is less than one, since the total offer of butter for cloth is now falling.

We repeat the warning of Chapter 3. Remember that an offer curve is not a demand curve. The latter measures changes in the demand for commodity A with changes in unit price. An offer curve measures demand for commodity A with changes in total amount of commodity B. An offer curve approximates to a total revenue curve whereas a demand curve compares quantity and average revenue. The principles for measuring ϵ for an offer curve are therefore those of the total revenue curve.

Apply the sectors of the offer curve to the problem of the optimum tariff as revealed in Fig. 6.8. In order to move R_1 as far to the left of R as possible, the foreign offer curve requires to be unit elastic. With a trade indifference curve sloping downward to the left, the point of tangency is then pushed further and further to the left and the optimum tariff is thus raised. If the elasticity of the foreign offer curve is greater than one, the movement of R_1 to the left will be smaller the more ϵ exceeds unity. When $\epsilon = \infty$, that is, when the foreign offer curve is a straight line, then the offer curve implies constant terms of trade and the country (probably a small country) facing such terms of trade cannot improve these by a tariff. A tariff, if levied, would only reduce the volume of trade. Finally, in the case where the elasticity of the foreign offer curve is less than unity and the curve slopes downward to the right, it is clearly impossible for such a curve to be tangential to an indifference curve as drawn in Fig. 6.8.

We can easily derive a formula for the optimum tariff algebraically. If t is the rate of the tariff, and remembering that the domestic price ratio in the home country and the world price ratio differ by the revenue collected from the tariff, then the tariff rate which equalises the two ratios is determined by the equation

$$(1 + t)\frac{bR_1}{R_1 W} = \frac{R_1 b}{bp} \tag{1}$$

Commercial Policy

We can reconstruct this equation to isolate t by rearranging the terms

$$t = \frac{R_1 W}{bp} - 1$$

$$= \frac{bO}{bp} - 1 \quad (2)$$

Divide both numerator and denominator of bO/bp by Op and we get

$$\frac{bO/Op}{bp/Op}$$

and also (from Fig. 6.8) $bp = bO - Op$; so then

$$\frac{bO}{bp} = \frac{bO/Op}{bp/Op} = \frac{bO/Op}{(bO - Op)/Op} = \frac{bO/Op}{(bO/Op) - 1} \quad (3)$$

But bO/Op is a measure of the price elasticity of the foreign offer curve[7] so that

$$\frac{bO}{Op} = \epsilon$$

Thus equation (3) reduces to

$$\frac{bO}{bp} = \frac{\epsilon}{\epsilon - 1}$$

and substituting this in equation (2) we get

$$t = \frac{\epsilon}{\epsilon - 1} - 1$$

$$= \frac{1}{\epsilon - 1}$$

This gives us the formula for t the optimum tariff where ϵ is the elasticity of the foreign offer curve.

When we apply the optimum tariff formula $t = 1/(\epsilon - 1)$ to the problem of selecting the tariff it is evident that a country applying a tariff will be in the position of maximum advantage when it trades at a point as far as possible to the left on the unit-elastic sector of the foreign offer curve. In terms of the formula, when a country faces a foreign offer curve of unit elasticity, then the optimum tariff is infinity. When ϵ rises above unity the value of t falls; when ϵ is less than unity t has a negative value – thus indicating that no optimum tariff exists on the inelastic sector of the foreign offer curve.

The theoretical conclusion that the most advantageous position for a country, and one exploitable by a tariff, is that where it finds a foreign offer curve of unit elasticity, is verified in the real world. If a country finds that a foreign country gives up a fixed amount of exports for any quantity of imports, that country will naturally seek to exploit this situation by applying a very high tariff so as to obtain that fixed amount of imports at the best terms of trade to itself. This it may do by imposing a tariff pushed to a limit determined by the length of the elastic sector of the foreign offer curve.

We have, thus far, dealt with five of Kindleberger's eight tariff effects. There remain: the competitive, income, and balance-of-payments effects. We shall now deal with these in turn.

(6) The competitive effect of a tariff is to protect the domestic industries producing the product, upon which the tariff is imposed, from foreign competition. Theoretically, if an industry cannot compete with imports it may be assumed that the country has a comparative disadvantage in the production of its product and it would be better to allow that industry to disappear and its present factors to move to industries in whose products the country has a comparative advantage. Overall welfare will be served if this is done. Narrower conceptions of welfare may, however, prevail. For example, the industry may be protected by an import tariff because it is regarded as a strategic defence industry, because it is an employment-yielding industry and is important in regional planning, or because the industry commands a powerful political lobby willing to support its protection—as the agricultural lobby in the British parliament of the 1840s was for long able to frustrate the repeal of the Corn Laws. The arguments for protection may vary from the plausible through the selfish to the downright perverse. In essence, however, all imply a choice—a choice between the welfare of the industry, its components and surroundings, and the welfare of the economy as a whole. Overall welfare gains by the elimination of the tariff and the untrammelled working of comparative costs.

The 'infant industry argument' is the agreed exception and has long been accepted by economists as a valid argument for protection. The argument runs thus. To operate most efficiently, and therefore most competitively, industries must attain optimum size. Until this size is attained tariff protection may be justified, since foreign competition may inhibit growth. The inference is that an industry once nurtured to optimum size should no longer be protected, since it can now hold its own in the international market. It is arguable that tariffs to protect infant industries ultimately increase the volume of world trade by helping industries with potential comparative advantage to realise their potential.

Essentially, the infant industry argument rests therefore on an historical view, the view that comparative advantage does not spring like Pallas Athene from the head of Zeus but is built up slowly and is the product of economic, social and cultural change. The nascent advantages of a country's production must be nurtured and protected. Typically the agricultural country which aspires to industrial strength requires protection.[8] Mill put the argument succinctly: 'The only case in which, on mere principles of political economy, protecting duties can be defensible, is when they are imposed temporarily (especially in a young and rising nation) in hopes of naturalising a foreign industry, in itself perfectly suitable to the circumstances of the country.[9]

The record of the infant industry argument in practice is a mixed one. The potential misuse of the argument is obvious and needs no documentation. The infant industry which is protected may stagnate behind its tariff wall until infancy is hard to distinguish from senility. Alternatively it may indeed grow but having attained size be unwilling to relinquish its advantage. Often in practice the infant industry has been born during the autarky of war and seeks tariff protection to allow it to live and grow in the peace which follows. The British economy, cut off from supplies of German lenses and optical instruments during the Second World War, nurtured a barely adequate domestic optical industry into the post-war period using both a protective tariff and import controls to exclude German cameras, lenses and binoculars. The industry languished, and after 1959, when the protective policy was abandoned, it was quickly swept away by the import of German and Japanese optical products.

It must be asked whether all industries are of a type which will benefit from protection during the growth period. It is not enough to say that during this period an industry cannot compete at world prices without increasing losses. Initial losses are often a feature of new industries and must be budgeted for in the investment calculation and provided for in the initial capitalisation of the firm. (Insufficient capital or lack of access to capital markets is a frequent problem for the developing country and strengthens the infant industry argument in application to this case.) When the industry yields returns to scale, however, there is a case for protecting it until it acquires a domestic market large enough for these returns to be reaped. The real argument for infant protection is that it allows the protected firm(s) to reach optimum size.

To apply infant industry protection in the way implicit in the term is difficult and requires a degree of detachment and impartiality rarely found in governments. It is easy to use the argument to justify protective tariffs for a new industry in a mature country – a case to which it is not applicable.

Finally, it must be asked whether, even for the new industry in a developing country, a tariff is the correct form of assistance. It is arguable that a direct subsidy, which absorbs initial losses without constricting trade, is a preferable policy tool.

An interesting and sophisticated twist has been given to the infant industry argument by Lewis, Hagen, Myint, Corden and others — the so-called Manoilesco argument.[10] This argument starts from the observable fact that in developing countries (and in some developed countries) average income in the advanced sector is higher than in the rural subsistence sector. This has been advanced as an argument for a movement of labour out of agriculture and into industry. Whether this argument is justified is a matter for debate. There is much dispute as to whether the facts indeed justify the argument. Only if the marginal product of labour in the advanced sector were higher than in the subsistence sector would the argument be valid.[11] Assuming, however, that the facts justify it and that this is the case, we may then ask is there a further argument for indirect subsidisation of the advanced sector by protection? The answer is a qualified one and varies with those who give it. Johnson regards this as a 'second best argument since protection affects relative commodity prices and the source of the welfare loss is a discrepancy in factor prices'.[12] Corden points out that since the cost of capital may be higher in the subsistence than in the advanced sector, this may offset the higher costs in the industrial sector coming from the higher wage. With capital expensive in the subsistence sector and labour expensive in the industrial sector it may be appropriate to subsidise the supply of capital to the former and the supply of labour to the latter. It may be that protection, appropriately applied, would help here and if so a special case of the infant-industry argument is justifiable. It may be, however, that output in the industrial sector is dominantly determined by the availability of capital and management skill, and would not increase either with a rise in the price or in the real wage. If so, protection would simply result in subsidised profits in that sector and, at the worst, result in domestic industrial output being available to the subsistence sector only at higher prices. It would appear that a general case for protection based on the Manoilesco effect is somewhat dubious, and that an examination of individual cases must precede policy action.

If the infant-industry argument is perhaps the oldest argument for tariffs acceptable to economists and concerns itself with the temporary elimination of the competitive effect, there is another and more modern view which sees in tariff removal and an intensified competitive effect a vitalising industrial influence which may restructure and revive an industry. There is no paradox in these two arguments: they might be regarded as the tariff policies for youth and age. The latter view is still unformed and may die as empirical evidence of the effects of new customs unions accumulates, but it is worth recording. Many exponents of the customs union principle, who initially claimed that industries in member countries would benefit by the widening of the market which the union makes possible, now see a further advantage through the so-called growth effects of the elimination of the internal tariffs between member countries. This dropping of trade barriers, particularly when undertaken progressively, exposes domestic industries to foreign competition. This results in the elimination of marginal firms, the concentration of output in the most efficient units, and the development of managerial efficiency both for cost reduction and for market penetration. Such competition, it is arguable, may be very beneficial for long-established industries, driving them to an earnest examination of their structure, position and prospects. Two examples of this view come readily to mind. A first is the observed break-up of inefficient monopoly units in the French iron and steel industry after the coming of the European Economic Community. Formerly a price was maintained for relatively small and inefficient units by the few companies which, under protection, controlled the industry, but with the elimination of the tariff the smaller units were forced to combine and modernise in order to survive. A second example of belief in the virtue of the competitive effect is the argument put forward consistently by both Conservative and Labour governments in Britain during the controversy over British entry into the EEC, that exposure to full competition, especially from Germany, would stimulate British industry to new and more efficient efforts and launch the British economy into growth. Since nearly the same effect could have been procured without joining the EEC by simply abolishing the British import tariff and negotiating a reciprocal agreement with the Six, it must be supposed that British entry into the EEC was regarded by the parties as a politically easier way to achieve this revitalisation or that they were not really convinced enough of the merits of free trade to embark upon it unilaterally.

(7) We come now to consider the effect of a tariff upon national income. There are two aspects of this effect: the impact of a tariff upon the income of the country imposing the tariff; and the effects of the tariff upon the distribution of national income. We shall deal with these in turn.

In the tariff-levying country, if the tariff fulfils its primary purpose of reducing imports, and assuming that it invokes no retaliation, it will increase the value of $(X - M)$, the injection to the country's income stream coming from the foreign-trade sector. Providing that the income diverted from imports is spent, or even in part spent, and that the country is not fully employed, income and employment will be raised. If the country is already at full employment, real income will not be raised (but will probably be lowered by malallocation of resources) while money income will be raised by a rise in prices. Meanwhile in the country (or countries) whose exports are reduced by the tariff, income and employment will fall as, for it, $(X - M)$ decreases. If the tariff-imposing country has raised its level of income and employment, it has done so at the expense of its trading partner(s). This beggar-my-neighbour policy is rightly ostracised as an exporting of unemployment. The interwar period with its intense economic nationalism furnishes many examples of it.

Another tariff effect demonstrated by elementary income theory is that of the beneficial result of reduction of a tariff for a country in a state of inflation due to a high rate of absorption (i.e. $C + I + G$) at home. Reduction of an existing tariff here leads to a diversion of demand from home absorption to imports and, at the cost of a reduction in $(X - M)$, the inflationary pressure is eased. These income changes through tariffs are familiar enough processes and were understood at least in their policy implications long before modern income adjustment relationships were formulated. It is worthwhile, however, restating these tariff-income effects as 'expenditure switching' policies, so that we may recognise them as such at a later stage. The phrase 'expenditure switching' is much used in recent absorption theory and was first used by H. G. Johnson (see p. 360 below).

It is perhaps worth demonstrating the arguments of the last few para-

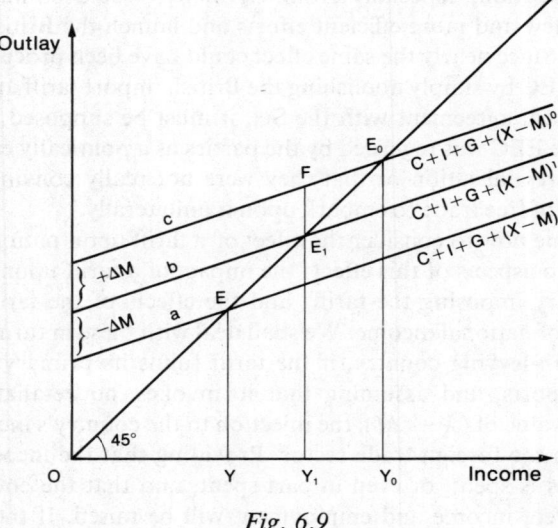

Fig. 6.9

Commercial Policy

graphs diagrammatically. Fig. 6.9 shows the two effects on income of raising and lowering tariffs. With a total outlay line a the given country has an equilibrium level of income of OY. If a tariff is imposed so as to lower imports by $-\Delta M$ then a new outlay line b gives equilibrium at E_1. If we may suppose the resulting level of income Y_1 to be that which is appropriate to full employment, then the country by imposing the tariff has raised itself to the full employment level. If, on the other hand, we suppose that the country was, in the first place, at a level of outlay c such that there was an inflationary gap E_1F which gave an equilibrium money income of Y_0 exceeding real income Y_1 by Y_1Y_0, then a reduction of tariff would reduce outlay towards b. Demand in c would be switched away from $C + I + G$ to $(X - M)^0$ and decrease that expression towards $(X - M)^1$, at which level of outlay the inflationary gap would be eliminated.

As we have already shown (see pp. 145–6 above), a tariff has certain redistribution effects. Because of its imposition domestic producers of the protected product are likely to enjoy higher profits. In terms of the exposition based on Fig. 6.2, there is a transfer of consumers' surplus to the producers of the protected commodity. Apart from these 'micro' redistribution effects, however, it is possible to distinguish more far-reaching macro effects, as the tariff redistributes income among factors of production. A re-reading of Chapter 4 will remind the reader that free trade has the effect of increasing the price of the factor which is plentiful and reducing the price of the factor which is scarce. By inference the opposite applies. A restriction of trade raises the price of the scarce factor, reduces that of the abundant. Thus a tariff, in a country rich in capital and short of labour, would have the effect of raising the wages of labour. This argument, the theoretical details of which are discussed in Chapter 5 (see pp. 118–19 above), appears to provide organised labour with an argument for restriction of trade. Since the Stolper–Samuelson argument is perhaps somewhat recondite for use in a political lobby, labour unions might alternatively argue that as a scarce factor labour's monopolistic position in wage bargaining is strengthened by resisting the free trade which reduces the power of the monopoly, while employers might argue for free trade on grounds that the removal of tariffs enhances the return to capital in a capital-rich economy.

Some may find it surprising that here, when orthodox economics apparently provides a clear-cut argument in the free trade versus protection controversy, it has not been made use of. But the fact is that in tariff controversy at policy level, argument is *ad hoc* and opportunistic rather than theoretical. Labour unions and those who advise them are reasonably well informed on current economic thinking but would be likely to ignore the Stolper–Samuelson thesis, if only on the ground that it is too sophisticated to provide a slogan or a rallying call. Perhaps, too, they realise that the theorem is based on rigorous assumptions governing a two-good, two-factor model and that to argue its general applicability would create more heat than light in discussion. The labour argument for protection, when it has been made, has been for the protection of highly paid workers in older countries from the competition of low-paid workers in developing countries. Even this argument, popular in the thirties, has been less heard in the expanding trade and full employment world economy which we have had since the Second World War.

(8) The balance-of-payments effect of a tariff will not be explored in this chapter. The initial impact of the tariff will be to reduce imports in the tariff imposing country and reduce exports in the rest of the world. Even if the rest of the world does not retaliate against the protectionist country, the ultimate balance-of-payments effect must depend upon the total income effects of these changes in imports and exports and their balance of payments repercussions. These relationships will be explored in Chapter 13.

(9) The cost effect of protection is a matter of comparatively recent discussion. Because of its attempt to open up new vistas of inquiry and in particular to imbue tariff policy with greater precision through measurement of the economic gain or loss of particular policies we include it here, although space allows only very cursory treatment.[13]

Exploration of the cost effect of protection in precise quantitative terms is important for any protectionist country but especially so for those countries which have developed to richness and maturity on a basis of resource industries but which nurture their manufacturing industries by protection. Australia and Canada are obvious examples. The work of the Brigden Committee, which calculated the cost of the Australian tariff in 1929 by measuring the excess costs of protected production, was an early attempt to grapple with this problem. Canadian economists before and including Johnson have bent to it and there have been signs of interest by students of the United States tariff.[14] As new mathematical and statistical techniques make it possible to quantify important aspects of economic relationships, the choices of commercial policy acquire a greater precision. The nature of the choices appears more clearly and a field in which judgements have tended more than in most to be value judgements is given some element of scientific method. Johnson's contribution is twofold: he examines how it may be possible to calculate the cost of protection and, given this cost, how it may be possible to set it against the claimed beneficial results of the tariff which achieves such results at minimum cost to the economy. In a more general sense it makes an interesting contribution to the old free trade versus protection controversy.

Commercial Policy

The first task is to define the cost of the tariff. The Brigden Committee defined what is called the 'excess cost' of the tariff as the excess of the market value of the output which is protected over the cost of the imports which would replace this output under free trade. This concept to be operational depends upon identifying that part of domestic industrial output which is dependent upon protection, calculating its output value at constant prices and deducting from that value the money cost of replacing the protected output by exactly substitutable and cheaper imports. John Young, in his much later work on the cost of the tariff in Canada, adopted a similar definition, defining the 'cash cost' of the tariff as the difference in the amount paid for protected goods and the amount which would have been paid if these goods had been purchased at the lowest available prices on the world market. Although accepting this as a practical concept Young also pointed out that the 'real cost' of protection was almost certainly greater than the 'cash cost'. To the latter it was necessary to add the loss in export income which is almost always incurred by a tariff-imposing country as foreigners retaliate by imposing their own tariffs. Nevertheless, while the difference between real cost and cash cost might be considerable, Young accepted the latter as a working basis because of the non-quantifiable element in the former.

Corden and Johnson have slight reservations about the Brigden–Young definitions of the cost of the tariff. The latter sees the cost of a tariff as comprising two elements: first there must be some gain in real income which could be reaped by abandoning the tariff for free trade; second there must be reciprocal tariff remissions to be had by bargaining with other protectionist countries once the decision to end the tariff has been taken. Both of these advantages are foregone by maintaining the tariff and may be regarded as its cost. The second advantage cannot be measured in any scientific way and is left out of the discussion, but, as Johnson says, it might well be of considerable value, particularly if a country's trade is narrowly concentrated with another country, as is the case with Canada and the United States.

To remit tariffs and adopt free trade would reallocate factors in industries and realign the consumption of goods with concomitant effects on the prices of both and with new patterns in international trade itself. The result would be nothing short of a new general equilibrium in the world economy. To any country remitting a tariff the cost can 'be measured in terms of the goods that could be extracted from the economy in the free-trade situation without making the country worse off than it was under protection'.[15] Two diagrams illustrate the cost of the tariff. The first (Fig. 6. 10), used by Corden,[16] does so in simple partial equilibrium terms. A more complex two-good general equilibrium model illustrates the effects upon a tariff

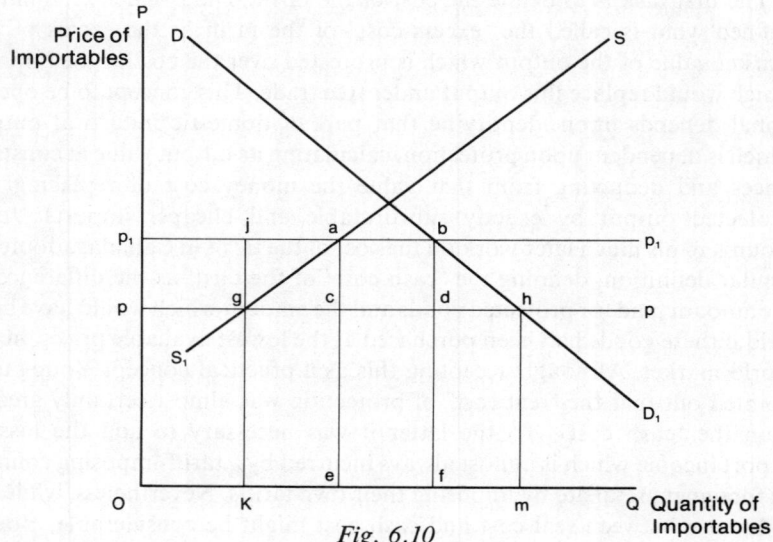

Fig. 6.10

country of adopting free trade and the problem of measuring the gain from it. We proceed to this later.

In Fig. 6.10 *pp* is the free-trade price in the tariff-imposing country. *OK* is produced, *om* consumed and *Km* is imported. A tariff of pp_1 is then imposed. As a result, production rises to *Oe*, consumption falls to *Of* and *ab* (or *ef*) is imported. Revenue of *abcd* is collected, consumers' surplus falls by pp_1bh, and producers' surplus rises by pp_1ag. If we disregard the terms of trade effects, which are not demonstrable on this diagram, then: cost of protection = cost of tariff in consumers' surplus − (revenue from the tariff + increase in producers' surplus), which in geometric terms is

$$pp_1bh - (abcd + pp_1ag)$$

or

$$agc + bdh$$

Implicit in this calculation is a redistribution of income from consumers to producers.

If we apply the Brigden–Young definition of the cost of protection to the diagram then the excess of the market value of the protected output (*jaeK*) over the cost of the equivalent imports at world prices (*gceK*) is *jacg*. This differs from the formula of the preceding paragraph in which the cost of protection was demonstrated as $agc + bdh$. Only if *jga* were equal

Commercial Policy

to *bdh* would the two formulations agree. They differ, Corden tells us, because the Brigden–Young formulation exaggerates production cost and neglects consumption cost. He points out that the Brigden Committee overestimated the volume of protected output by failing to appreciate that raw materials being protected may raise the costs of home producers. If the tariff was removed the production costs of raw material-importing industries would then fall and their exports might well increase as they became more competitive. In spite of these qualifications, however, Corden's approach to the cost of protection is close to that of Brigden and Young. His conclusion is that when all factors have been considered the approach of the latter slightly overestimates the excess cost of the tariff.

The terms of trade gain from the tariff cannot be shown on the partial equilibrium diagram, but Corden discusses it briefly in verbal terms. From optimum tariff theory he argues that, providing the tariff imposed is small and providing the elasticity of the foreign offer curve is appropriate, a gain in the terms of trade as a result of the tariff will more than offset the loss from diminution in the volume of trade. This net gain must then be deducted from the cost of protection as calculated on his own or the Brigden–Young formula.

It is possible to illustrate graphically for a standard two-good general equilibrium model the effects of the adoption of free trade and the problem of measuring the gain from it. In Fig. 6.11 the transformation curve between Y and X is TT^1. U_t is the community indifference curve reached with the tariff. With C as the country's initial consumption point and P its level of production, its imports of Y are shown by CQ and its exports of X by PQ. The terms of trade are indicated by the slope of CP, while the tangents at C and P (not drawn) indicate the internal (tariff included) price ratio between the goods. The national income of the country, as measured in terms of its exportable good, is OR. If consumers were allowed to buy goods at the CP terms of trade they could obtain the same level of satisfaction at C'', i.e., where the most leftward terms of trade line $C''S$ (parallel to CP) just touches the community indifference curve at C''. This would be at the lower level of national income OS. The difference SR indicates the *consumption cost* of the tariff. This is the loss imposed by distorting consumption away from the optimal position appropriate to the international price ratio.

Turning to production, if producers were allowed to produce and trade at the international terms of trade, then production would be at P^1 – the highest point on the transformation curve to which a line of the slope CP can be tangent. Here the international value of the product in X terms would be OV which exceeds OR by RV. RV indicates the *production cost* of the

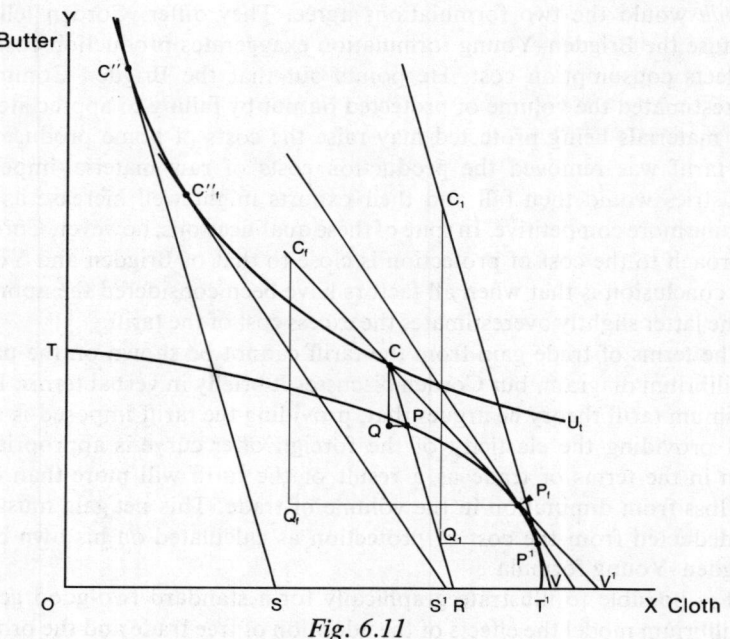

Fig. 6.11

tariff. This is the loss imposed (in foregoing production) by the distortion of production by the tariff. SV (i.e. $SR + RV$) represents the total of consumption and production costs of the tariff.

These are the costs of the tariff but, as we have seen (see pp. 147–9 above), a tariff improves the terms of trade of the tariff-imposing country, and only if the foreign offer curve were perfectly elastic, that is, if the country's terms of trade were independent of the volume of trade, would the adoption of free trade not change the terms of trade adversely to the country. The net cost of a tariff must then be the sum of the consumption and production costs of the tariff *less* the gain from the improved terms of trade.

We must examine the terms of trade gain from the tariff more closely to judge what its dimensions might be. At the protection terms of trade the country would want to export P^1Q_1 of X for C_1Q_1 of Y. The foreign country, on the other hand would only want to trade CQ of Y for PQ of X as before. As soon as free trade is established, the tariff-remitting country's consumption and production equilibrium points would not be at C_1 and P^1 but at points appropriate to less favourable equilibrium terms of trade. Such points might be C_f and P_f. With these, the gain from trade would not be SV but the smaller quantity S^1V^1. Indeed, S^1V^1 could even be negative.

This would occur where the reduction in production from P_1 to P_f was so great as to so slope $C_f V^1$ that a parallel terms of trade line $C'_f S^1$, tangent to U_t, would cut the X axis to the right of V^1. The difference, positive or negative, between SV and $S^1 V^1$ represents the favourable effect of the tariff on the country's terms of trade.

There is a further complication. If we accept that $S^1 V^1$ is the net cost of protection with improved terms of trade, it should follow that $S^1 V^1$ represents a quantity of goods that could be taken from the economy to leave it as well off with free trade as it was with the tariff. This is not in fact the case. If the gain is to be taken entirely in exportable goods then it will not be $S^1 V^1$ but a larger amount whose extraction would involve better equilibrium terms of trade. If the gain is to be taken entirely in importable goods then it will not be the quantity of such goods for which $S^1 V^1$ exchanges in equilibrium but a lesser amount the extraction of which would be at worse terms of trade. As Johnson sums up: 'The gain must be conceived of as a set of combinations of quantities of exportables and importables which could be extracted from the economy while leaving it in free trade equilibrium at the level of satisfaction achieved under the tariff.'[17] As can be seen, Johnson brings the terms of trade effect under closer scrutiny than does Corden.

The interesting points emerging so far from the analysis are these: the cost of protection is the sum of the consumption and production costs *less* the terms of trade gain; in some cases the terms of trade gain might (at least conceptually) be so large as to more than offset the consumption and production costs of protection and yield a negative cost, i.e. a net benefit; and the net cost (or benefit) must be measured in terms of a quantity of each good and not of only one of them.

Having arrayed the elements and properties of tariff cost in general equilibrium terms, the next stage is to move towards a general case in which many goods are considered, a necessary preliminary to practical estimation of such costs. To achieve this Johnson temporarily sets aside the terms of trade gain from protection and, as a preliminary, deals with the consumption and production costs of protection at constant terms of trade. By so doing it becomes possible to translate the argument into partial equilibrium terms and so evolve first a formula for the cost of protection assuming only one export good, one import good and a single tariff rate, and then an extension of the formula to the case of a country producing many goods. The algebraic derivation and refinement of these formulae are too lengthy to follow here and must be pursued in the original literature. Some of the conclusions are, however, interesting and have practical significance. Johnson's view is that the consumption cost of protection is likely to be a

168   *International Trade and Payments*

small percentage of national expenditure, and although the production cost may be somewhat larger, the total, particularly when reduced by the terms of trade benefit, is 'a small proportion of the level of national income at any point of time'. Thus, if protectionists are right in their assertion that protection increases an economy's rate of growth, such growth might in a short time easily raise national income by much more than its reduction from the cost of protection. In these terms the free trade versus protection argument is presented in a new light and two magnitudes become important: the cost of protection expressed in national income terms, and the effect of protection on the growth of national income. If the latter quantity were high enough to more than offset the former the great historical debate takes a new and interesting turn.

7
Free Trade and Protection

(i) Introduction

THE pure theory of international trade demonstrates convincingly that world production of goods and services is maximised by freedom of trade between countries and that specialisation of function according to natural and factoral endowments is, in the long run, in the interests alike of individual countries and of the world economy. Turning from theory to practice we bow to the fact that, in the real world, such freedom of trade nowhere exists between sovereign states but that nations, in accordance with what we call commercial policy, impede, divert, reduce or eliminate this optimal free movement. In the theory of commercial policy it becomes our task to examine the effects of barriers to trade and exchange, to explain why they are imposed, and to seek criteria by which their operation may be judged. In doing so we find ourselves concerned not only with the macro aspects of the problem—that is, with the effects of trade restriction on the national incomes, terms of trade and balances of payments of countries as a whole—but with its micro aspects—that is, with its significance for the many components of the economy, regions, firms, industries and individuals.

The free trade versus protection controversy is perhaps the oldest argument in economics. We shall in this chapter briefly review the elements of this argument, not with the aim of establishing a case for one or the other but to provide the reader with a reference basis which he may use in evaluating the various effects of tariffs, the aims which motivate their imposition, and the conditions in which they are used.

During the whole of the modern period the issue of free trade and protection has been hot controversy—the balance swaying to and fro. From the commercial revolution of the sixteenth century and for over two centuries the mercantilist view prevailed and shaped commercial policy. By this view foreign trade was to be manipulated and controlled to enhance the power and wealth of the state. The last years of the eighteenth century saw the decline of mercantilism and, with the liberal experiment in politics, a growing movement for free trade which gained momentum in the nineteenth century and reached its zenith in the 1860s. The First World War ended this movement. Britain was the only major power which opened her economy completely, and from the 1850s to the 1920s she was virtually a free-trade country. In the interwar years, economic depression, market rivalry and economic nationalism destroyed any chance which the world economy had had of establishing complete trade freedom. Moreover, in this period the significance of the balance of payments came to be realised and a new motive for direct regulation of trade appeared. From 1931 until the outbreak of war in 1939 a new wave of economic authoritarianism, a mercantilism of a new sort, gathered force, and during the war exchange control and constricted trade reached a level which had no precedent.

The post-war period brought a new movement for trade freedom. This formed part of the wave of international economic co-operation which followed the Atlantic Charter and produced the Bretton Woods Agreement of 1944. But the effort to bring commercial policy under the control of an international agency proved too much and the original intention to establish an International Trade Organisation was not fulfilled. Meanwhile the balance-of-payments problems of the post-war period caused direct controls and impediments to trade to proliferate. But the drive for a more liberal economy did not fail entirely. A twofold policy emerged, pressed by the Americans and supported by the Western nations with varying enthusiasm. The first aim was to reduce direct controls on trade and, in particular, their discriminatory effects; the second was to maintain some impetus in the movement for the lowering of tariffs themselves — a continuance of the old free-trade movement. The first aim proved partially successful. By 1959 the Western nations had reduced to a low level their direct balance-of-payments controls and trade was once more pursued (outside the Soviet bloc) on a more or less multilateral basis. The second aim, pursued through the GATT and the Kennedy Round, has had only qualified success.

The journey from 'mercantilism to free trade and back again'[1] might well lead the student to the belief that free trade, like the elimination of sin, is a desirable but unattainable condition. The writer holds this view. The existence of a world of nation states with discordant economic policies renders this inevitable. It is best to recognise that restrictions on trade are a manifestation of economic nationalism and the nation state and that, as long as such political conditions obtain, commercial policy or the purposive manipulation of trade restrictions will remain. True, restrictions alter, the balance between freedom and protection sways this way and that. Nineteenth-century trade arguments were carried on in terms of the case for and against the tariff; today that is but a part of the discussion, and

Commercial Policy 171

other restrictive mechanisms designed for more specific purposes than revenue or general restriction of imports have become a subject of attention.

The forms of interference with the free flow of goods between countries are now many, but at this stage a dual classification may be made which is not too arbitrary. We must distinguish between tariffs, or taxes on imports, and what we have come to call direct trade controls imposed primarily for balance-of-payments reasons — for the reduction of imports in order to reduce foreign payments for monetary rather than industrial purposes. The distinction between these two groups is reasonably clear cut. The motivational dichotomy is clear and, while tariffs may be maintained or raised for balance-of-payments reasons and import quotas, having the side effect of protecting domestic industry may be maintained with this end in view, the prime purposes of the two groups of measures are distinct. Moreover they are historically separated; for while tariffs and taxes on trade are as old as trade itself, direct controls are a comparatively new genus, spawned in the interwar period to protect the balances of payments of countries caught in the dilemma of choosing between internal and external equilibrium in their economies. Since the thirties direct controls have been used by many countries. By their use trade flows have been dammed or diverted into desired channels, usually those dictated by exchange-rate policy, convenience in payments or other balance-of-payments considerations. Trade is thus made bilateral or is restricted within currency areas, imports only being taken by a given country from countries whose currencies are in adequate supply.

It is our purpose in this chapter to examine the case for free trade — not because this controversy has hope of a final and liberal outcome but because the argument enables us to establish norms by which commercial policy may be judged.

(ii) The Free Trade versus Protection Controversy

As Haberler says: 'The arguments for free trade are clear cut and their application to trade policy is simple.'[2] Perhaps the first part of his sentence is truer than the second, for while classical trade theory demonstrates convincingly the case for international free trade, trade policy presents a confusion of aim and scant unanimity of view. This section examines briefly the 'clear cut' theoretical case for free trade and seeks to bring a little order into the motivation of trade policy.

Maximum national product is the criterion by which we measure the effect of trade. If we assume perfect competition and high factor mobility, unrestrained international trade increases the real income of the world economy and of its participant countries, while the gains from trade are distributed among countries in accordance with reciprocal demand.

As we narrow the focus, the gains from trade become more problematic. Given our assumption, the gain at world level and for each country is assured but as we move downward to the region, the group and the individual within a country the gain is more problematic. Even here, if we maintain the argument in terms of abstract efficiency, gain is assured. If international price ratios differ from those within the country, and if we accept the validity of a community indifference curve for the population as a whole, then free trade allows the population to move to a higher indifference level. But we move here too far from reality. The assumptions necessary to a community indifference curve are unreal and it is clear that in practice, while a country gains from free trade, some sections of the community gain more than others. Some may even lose. The argument for free trade is aggregative. It asserts the advantage for the world and for countries as a whole. It does not prove conclusively that all groups, all persons, all regions are advantaged. We must not therefore expect support for free trade to be unanimous.

The argument that international division of labour, as dictated by comparative costs, is to the benefit (in national product terms) of all trading countries, is the basis of the free-trade argument. This argument assumes not only a competitive price system but a high mobility of factors, including labour, within the participant countries. If free trade is suddenly established and specialisation in accordance with comparative costs dictates concentration upon production of a particular good in country A and its export to country B, in which the good has hitherto also been produced but under higher cost conditions, then the industry producing the good in B must be contracted or eliminated and its factors must move into production of a good or goods in which B has a cost advantage and in which the factors will be more highly rewarded. Put in another way, if a tariff is imposed by B to protect producers of the good from A's imports, then there is a clear opportunity cost involved in retaining factors in B in the production of the good, when they might have higher marginal productivity in other industries which would be expandable if trade were free. This is the 'cost of the tariff' which we examined in Chapter 6.

Let us extend the argument to the more realistic case where only some factors are mobile, while others are specific to the industry and have either no value, or only very limited value, in other uses. This is the case with

Commercial Policy

many manufacturing plants in which labour is relatively mobile while the plant itself has value only for manufacture of one product. A steel rolling mill, an oil refinery, an atomic reactor are examples. In this case when such an industry becomes exposed under free trade to the competition of a lower priced substitute import, the price of the specific factor will fall rapidly, and if import is sustained the plants in this industry will be forced out of business as soon as they become unable to pay the market price of the mobile factor. But other industries in the country are expanding as a result of trade. The mobile factors will move to these expanding industries and the specific factors in the declining industries will be abandoned. True there is loss of capital, but this loss is still quite compatible with a *net* rise in the country's national product. Income in the exporting industries has risen, while income in the import-competing industries has fallen. In output terms the country's position has improved. There has been with the rise in national product a redistribution of the product. This redistribution tends to be greater in countries in which factors are less mobile. If all factors were perfectly mobile there would be an increase in national product without the redistributive effect.

In terms of an abstract argument, and reckoning in national product terms only (and not in terms of welfare), there is therefore a theoretical case for free trade. It is an argument which is subject to certain assumptions, the non-fulfilment of which in practice must reduce the generality of the argument, but upon the argument, however restricted, rests the scientific case of liberals for free trade.

To this general argument the free trader will add a number of other claims which we will briefly note in passing. He will argue that the absence of tariffs ensures a lower price for imported goods, that it facilitates the price system and impedes the formation of protected monopolies, and that it provides wider markets for exporting industries, enabling productive units to attain optimum size and unit costs to be reduced. These are, however, partial arguments, each one of which requires close scrutiny and some of which may be subject to qualification. They form no part of the established scientific case for free trade. They are rather a supplement to it.[3]

The first factor weakening the free trade case is that the case itself is argued in terms of efficiency and real output and not in terms of social welfare. Given its assumptions it is unassailable in these terms. But commercial policy—the imposition and manipulation of impediments to trade—is justified not in terms of output but in terms of welfare and in terms of divergent views on where welfare lies. Once this becomes the objective, a number of aims other than maximising output appear. It becomes indeed rationally possible to accept the assertion that output is higher under free trade but at the same time to advocate protection because it supports policies which appear to lead in the direction perhaps of lower total output but of higher social welfare. Free trade involves the expansion of some industries and the curtailment or elimination of others. This involves social costs and benefits, the net result of which becomes hard to determine. Who will adjudicate, for example, on the far-reaching social and non-economic implications of allowing agriculture to decline in a country simply because its diminution is dictated by the principle of comparative costs? Even if there is high mobility of all production factors in a country and factors released from contracting industries can be absorbed by expanding ones, the effect of trade on general social welfare will still be in doubt. Indeed, the pursuit of output on the one hand and what is deemed social welfare on the other produces an instant division of opinion. Within the ranks of those who seek to maximise welfare there will inevitably be wide division, each identifying a different policy route to achieve this.

A second factor engendering support for tariffs in face of the logic of the free-trade argument is naked self-interest. The scientific argument for free trade and international specialisation is aggregative. It asserts the advantage in real terms for the world as a whole and for countries. Within this encompassing increase, however, there are, as we have explained, many pluses and minuses. The incomes of exporters will rise while the incomes of producers of import-competing goods will fall. While the net level of world and country income will rise, in each country some groups will be better off, some will be worse off. Presumably the gaining exporters will be enthusiastic for free trade, while the losing domestic import competitors will be protectionist. The unequal distribution of the income gains from trade partially explains the lack of unanimous support for a condition which might initially have seemed to promise general advantage.

If, as it seems, the redistribution of income resulting from free trade seriously qualifies the advantages which might be claimed for that system, might it not be possible to offset this redistributive income effect by taxing the income gains of the winning exporters and transferring the proceeds to the import-competing losers? If this could be done (without distortions resulting from the tax system) there would be clear and universal gain from trade. Some would have gained; none would have lost. While the practical and political difficulties of such a redistribution operation would be great, probably so great as to make it impractical, the assumption of such a possibility at least demonstrates one important fact: that it is *possible* to increase total welfare by free trade as compared with that obtaining when trade is restricted. The extent to which the social welfare gain is realised

Commercial Policy

depends on the ability of government to achieve the necessary income redistribution to compensate disadvantaged groups. We cannot assume, however, that there is a perfect division of function between price system and tax system, one maximising income by creating an output and efficiency optimum, one redistributing the income gain in order to optimise welfare. In fact the price system itself has far-reaching effects on the distribution of income. Monopoly, monopsony, cartels, imperfect labour markets all influence the distribution of income and in diverse ways. It is no more than a conceptual argument that the redistribution problem can be solved by fiscal means.

A third feature which dilutes support for free trade is the extent to which, in the real world, the assumptions underlying the free-trade argument are not fulfilled — notably the assumption of factor mobility. While the theoretical argument for free trade does not require factor mobility as a necessary condition, it is clear that, in practice, immobility of factors and a large number of specific factors greatly enhances the difficulty of adjustment and reallocation resulting from free trade. It is assumed in the theoretical argument that factors in declining industries can move smoothly and quickly into expanding industries. In practice they do not. It may not be easy to judge whether an industry's decline is temporary or long-lasting. Firms do not retire from a declining industry immediately they become extra-marginal. Often they hang on for a long period, living off reserves and hoping for better times, their output resulting in over-supply in the market and further falls in price. The adjustment of an import-competing industry to foreign competition can be a long, painful and socially distressing experience which leaves its victims in no mood for a dispassionate discussion of the merits of free trade. The decline, for whatever reason, of an industrial group is almost always accompanied by demands for its protection or subsidy.

Before concluding this section it might, in the interests of completeness, be appropriate to list briefly some of the conventional arguments which are advanced,[4] for tariffs. The infant-industry argument, the only argument which economists are prepared to consider, and usually to concede, has already been considered (see pp. 156–9 above). We shall mention here only a few of the arguments most commonly used.

1. *Tariff protection sustains industries which are socially important as agriculture is claimed to be, or strategically important as iron and steel, machine-tool making and aviation are claimed to be.*

This argument takes the discussion out of the economic field. It can only be sustained by social, political or strategic value judgements. If a nation wishes to nurture hill farming in order to preserve a sturdy peasantry or electronics to support 'rocketry' and an arms race in ballistic missiles, it may do so. The social or strategic aims may override the criterion of economic efficiency.

2. *Tariffs protect domestic workers from the competition of low-paid foreign workers.*

Typically it is argued that American goods produced by workers with high real wages cannot compete with goods from countries like Taiwan where real wages are still relatively low. Taiwanese goods should therefore be excluded by tariff.

This is one of the oldest pro-tariff arguments and is now heard less than formerly, probably because of its economic naïveté. It is easily met. The argument has two implications: that the price of a finished article is determined by wage rates, and that labour is the sole factor of production. In fact, products are made by a combination of factors, varying in their proportionate mix from product to product. In one type of product only, that of labour-intensive goods, can low-paid labour have a cost advantage over labour paid higher wages. Even here the advantage of the low-wage country is questionable. The level of productivity is a determinant of unit cost and if high wages spring from high productivity, unit costs may well be lower in high-wage countries than they are in low-wage countries with low productivity. Productivity in the highly capitalised mature countries is usually such that unit costs and therefore prices can sustain a great deal of competition from low-wage producing countries.

There is one qualification favourable to the 'low-wage competition' argument for tariffs — that which comes from the Stolper–Samuelson theorem (see pp. 118–19 above). As we have seen, in a labour-scarce country free trade will enable labour-intensive imports to enter, thus reducing labour scarcity and reducing the wages of labour relative to the return to capital. This is, however, a somewhat more sophisticated argument than that which we are discussing here. Moreover the Stolper–Samuelson argument, resting as it does on exacting assumptions, has proved to be of little use to protectionists.

3. *Tariffs reduce imports. By this domestic production is stimulated and employment and income increased.*

This argument for tariffs was widely canvassed in the industrial countries in the depression period of the thirties. Certainly, if imports are reduced, the balance of trade injection ($X-M$) to the income circulation is increased, providing there is not a corresponding reduction in exports. Unfortunately

Commercial Policy

such a reduction is all too likely, since countries adversely affected by the import tariff will probably retaliate by imposing a similar tariff, thus reducing the exports of the country which first imposed the tariff. The most likely result of a tariff imposed by one country to increase its employment is to invoke a series of retaliatory tariff measures in which all countries are likely to suffer a loss of income from trade contraction.

4. *Tariffs may be used to diversify the industrial structure of a country.*

If tariffs are to be used as a policy tool to secure 'balanced growth', then presumably they must nurture growing industries and allow them to grow to strength to take their place beside industries which have grown under the stimulus of cost advantage. This is but a special case of the infant-industry argument considered above (see pp. 156–9 above) and is subject to the qualities and defects of that argument. If, however, the country's policy is to base its growth not on a broad and balanced industrial advance but on the growth of a few great industries which will spread their expansionary influence through the economy, then we may assume that such industries are at least initially competitive. If so there is no case for protection.

5. *Tariffs are necessary in a protectionist world to give bargaining power in trade negotiations.*

Undeniably tariffs are useful as bargaining levers. It is true that large protectionist countries hold a strong bargaining position at the negotiating table because of the attraction to other countries of penetrating the now protected market. This is, however, quite a different argument to saying that a country should build a tariff wall merely for this purpose. Once tariffs are imposed, vested interests are created to maintain them, and these may become so powerful that to remove them again, in a reciprocal bargaining situation, may become impossible. Moreover, if tariffs are imposed for future bargaining purposes they are likely to induce retaliation in the form of new tariffs by other countries. Reciprocal concessions may then serve only to move both countries towards, but perhaps not even entirely to, the original position.

6. *Tariffs are necessary in order to counter discriminatory practices by foreign suppliers.*

This, like (5), is a frequent argument of commercial policy tacticians. The practice of 'dumping', that is, of exporting a product which is heavily subsidised so that it may be sold at a lower price than is justified by its normal cost and transport elements, is one which may be countered by a tariff by the importing country. Such a tariff would certainly be demanded by the import-competing firms. While dumping has an unpleasant history, it is arguable that it is better controlled by an import quota on the subsidised product than by a tariff. Such a limitation on the quantity of the import will raise its price in the importing country and frustrate the market penetration which is the original aim of the dumping. If the dumping country subsequently removes its discrimination it is somewhat easier to remove a quota than to reduce or eliminate a tariff.

7. *Tariffs improve a country's terms of trade.*

This argument has been considered at length (see p. 147 above). The short comment which may be made at this stage is that tariffs do improve a country's terms of trade but at the cost of diminishing its trade volume. The balance of these positive and negative influences must be sought through the theory of the optimum tariff.

It should by now be clear that there is no paradox in the fact that, while free trade is a necessary condition for maximisation of world production and a sufficient condition for increase of social welfare in individual countries, every country can find reason to impede trade by a complex web of regulations and impositions. These impediments exist for three reasons: firstly, because within any state there are vested interests, often powerful, wishing for their own benefit to limit trade either generally or in particular fields; secondly, because it is possible for individual countries to obtain for themselves at the expense of trading partners a larger share of the gains from trade by impeding the flow of imports; and thirdly, because national governments devise commercial policies to serve unilateral national aims. Thus commercial policy becomes a matter of tangled and complex motivation not focusing upon the aggregative aims of maximum world and national production and gain through trade, but reflecting many divergent group interests, often in conflict, so that now one now another, determines commercial policy. Protection is a tool, perhaps the major tool, of foreign economic policy. We have gone to some trouble to explain its existence in the light of traditional trade theory. In fact, commercial policy consists of assessing impediments to trade and their economic effects in the light of a theory which tells us that, while their existence is inevitable, it imposes upon us a 'second best' situation.

(iii) Getting Nearer to Free Trade: Trade Liberalisation

Let us summarise the argument so far. It would appear that there is a qualified case for free trade. Such a condition is efficient, that is, it maximises output, although it has redistributive effects which cloud the issue as to whether it maximises welfare. But free trade depends for its efficiency on the working of the price system. Only under certain assumptions about the price system will it become the optimum condition. If these are met there will, under free trade, be optimum allocation of trade between countries, of goods among consumers, of resources among activities. When free trade has had its way, goods prices are (apart from transport costs) equal in all countries. Production is everywhere in equilibrium, with prices equal to marginal costs and factors distributed in such a way that their earnings, adjusted for productivity, are the same in all industries. This is the condition of Pareto optimality. It is now undesirable to make changes. A move for betterment in one place will only result in a worsened position somewhere else in the system. As one writer has said the case for free trade is that, in its pure sense, it takes us closest to the position of Pareto optimality.[5]

Three things, in essence, cause the case for free trade to be a qualified case. The first is the dependence of the efficient working of the price system upon certain unattainable conditions. Perfect competition and mobility of factors are nowhere to be found. Rigidities, monopoly and monopsony, state interference — all these condition the case when we turn from the theory to the real world. The second qualification to the free-trade case is that the optimum is one of efficiency measured by output: it is not an optimum of welfare. We may have to modify the case for free trade because we prefer to evaluate its effects on grounds of equity or social value rather than of output alone. The third qualification arises from the fact that we make our judgement of free trade too broadly. We compare the effects of two extremes: those of free trade and those of no trade at all, using pure theory to prove the superiority in income terms of the former. Yet most often in the theory of commercial policy we are not primarily interested in so broad a comparison but rather in whether free trade is superior in income terms to particular levels of trade with varying degrees of restriction. We are interested most often not in a world of no tariffs but in a world with more or less tariffs. To get down to cases, we must in the real world take a view on trade liberalisation. We must have criteria by which to judge whether a tariff remission improves the position or disimproves it.

This third qualification of the free trade case is our immediate concern. The first two are dealt with elsewhere. In the remainder of this chapter we shall examine briefly what tools are available to the economist to judge the effects of tariff remissions and to evaluate constrained trade situations in the spectrum between free trade and no trade.

Consider the case of a country whose trade has, by tariffs, been reduced below the level it would attain under free trade. Will such a country be advantaged by unilateral reduction of its tariff or is tariff remission only advantageous when carried out step by step with the other country on a basis of reciprocally negotiated remissions? We shall take these questions in turn using the two-country offer curve analysis used in Chapter 6 for the analysis of the optimum tariff.

First, the simple case where one country (B) only has imposed a tariff. This might be a small country whose tariff invokes no retaliation from its larger trading partners. Fig. 7.1 illustrates such a case. Offer curves OA

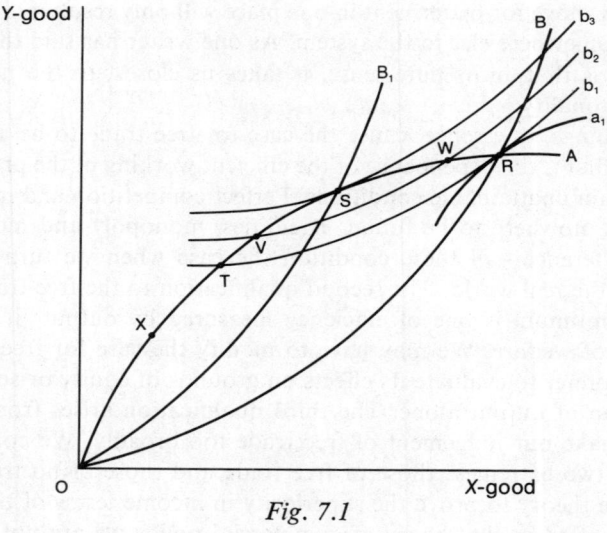

Fig. 7.1

and OB, for foreign and home countries respectively, intersect under free trade at the point R. At that point the welfare conditions are represented by the trade indifference curve b_1 which passes through R and also intersects the foreign offer curve OA at T.

Let us suppose that the home country has imposed the optimum tariff

Commercial Policy

which is such that the tariff-distorted offer curve OB_1 intersects the foreign offer curve OA at the point of tangency of OA to the highest trade indifference curve b_3. A reduction of the tariff represented by OB_1 cannot in these circumstances improve B's welfare. The new tariff offer curve would intersect OA between S and R and any such intersection point would mean that B would be on a lower trade indifference curve than b_3. The reduction in the tariff would reduce welfare for B. This would occur because the increase in trade volume would be more than offset by a deterioration of the terms of trade.

If country B has *initially* imposed a tariff higher than the optimum tariff, so that the tariff distorted offer curve cuts OA at, say, T, then a unilateral remission of tariff, up to the level represented by OB_1, would move B on to a higher trade indifference curve and increase B's welfare. Suppose the tariff distorted offer curve of B passed through V then any lower tariff represented by an offer curve cutting OA between V and W would mean an increase of welfare. One cutting OA between W and R, however, would mean a loss of welfare.

Finally, suppose that the tariff-distorted offer curve of B cuts OA to the left of T, for example at X, then complete removal of the tariff will result in the higher indifference curve b_1 and will thus increase welfare. In this case, however, complete elimination of the tariff will yield a lesser gain in welfare than a partial remission. Greater gain in welfare will accrue from holding the remission within the sector TR of OA and the greatest gain will come by remitting to the optimum tariff at S.

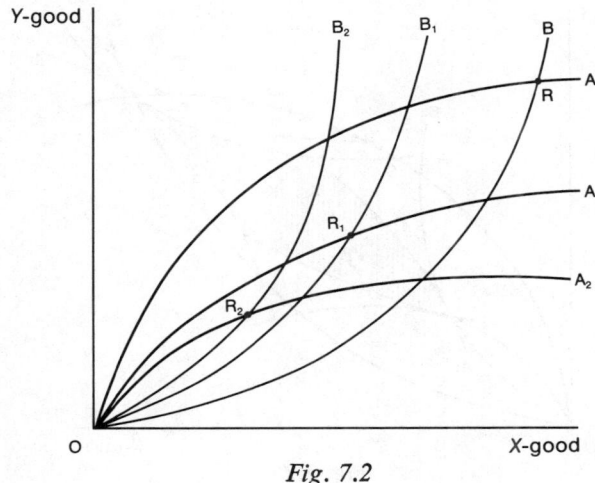

Fig. 7.2

Take now the case where both countries in the two-country model impose tariffs on imports. Diagrammatically this means (see Fig. 7.2) that whatever the size of the tariffs, and therefore whatever the position of the tariff-distorted offer curves of both countries, the trade points marked by their intersection, R_1, R_2 . . ., etc., must lie within the area ORO encompassed by the two original free-trade offer curves OA and OB. The exact location of the trade points depends upon the size of the two countries' tariffs.

All the arguments applied to Fig. 7.1 apply to the two-country/two-tariff case. If country B contemplates reducing its tariff unilaterally it will increase welfare by so doing only if its new tariff-distorted offer curve cuts the other country's tariff-distorted offer curve so that the new trade point is on a higher trade indifference curve. The geometric argument is the same as in the single tariff case except that here the reduction of B's tariff produces the new trade point by intersecting a foreign offer curve already distorted by a tariff.

It is impossible to encumber the diagram by drawing upon it all the relevant trade indifference curves, but it should be apparent that there is a better chance of either country improving its welfare position, if it can induce the other to make a negotiated reciprocal tariff reduction. Assuming that such negotiations take place and are successful, there are two possible outcomes: either both countries agree to remove tariffs entirely or each country agrees to reduce its tariff against the other. Consider both cases from the standpoint of the home country, B.

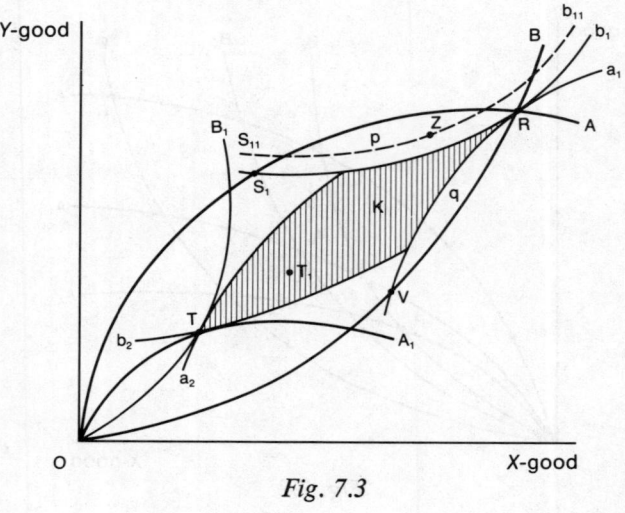

Fig. 7.3

Commercial Policy

Once more in Fig. 7.3 we have the two offer curves, OA for the foreign country, OB for the home country. They intersect at the trade point R. The home country is on the trade indifference curve b_1 the foreign country on the trade indifference curve a_1.

If A and B each levy a tariff against the other the new trade point must lie somewhere within the area ORO bounded by the two free-trade offer curves. Wherever within this area the new tariff-distorted trade point may be, any movement from it and back towards the free-trade point R will mean a movement to a higher trade indifference curve. If the trade point after the imposition of tariffs is T then it is clear that removal of the tariffs will benefit both countries since it will lift them from the lower indifference curves a_2 and b_2 to the higher free trade indifference curves, a_1 and b_2.

Consider the implications when the trade point with tariffs falls within the area p. Within this sector a removal of tariffs will mean a return to a lower indifference curve, e.g. if the trade point with tariffs were Z then a total neutral remission of tariffs would return the home country from the relatively high trade indifference curve $b_{11}S_{11}$ to the lower free-trade indifference curve b_1S_1. If the trade point with tariffs falls in the area p, i.e., between the foreign free-trade offer curve and the trade indifference curve of the home country applicable to free trade, then it is inimical for the home country to engage in bargaining for tariff removal. If, however, the tariff-distorted trade point falls anywhere in the area ORO except the sector p then B, the home country, will gain from a return to free trade by both countries.

Let us turn from the case of complete removal to that of partial removal, or reciprocal negotiation of tariff reductions. In terms of Fig. 7.3 the tariff-distorted trade point (before negotiations) will move not back to R but to some other point within ORO. When then will it be advantageous for country B to engage in negotiated tariff reductions?

Return to the starting point for such negotiations, namely the tariff-distorted trade point T. Country B is there on the trade indifference curve b_2 and country A is on a_2. Country B will gain by any change in the tariff-distorted trade point which carries it from b_2 to b_1; country A will gain by any change in the point which carries it from a_2 to a_1. The shaded area K is then an area of mutual benefit. Any tariff changes which carry the new tariff-distorted trade point from T into this area K will improve the welfare position of both countries.

If the first set of negotiations carried the new tariff-distorted trade point to T_1, then the area K would shrink accordingly, being limited at its south-west extremity by the new point T_1. Further tariff negotiations would be beneficial for both countries as long as the new trade points $T_2 \ldots T_n$ were located within the shrinking area of K. The ultimate in this process of negotiation is, of course, the coincidence of T_n with R and the re-establishment thereby of free trade. Only if a new trade point fell outside K, in p for country B and q for country A would it not be advantageous for the countries to negotiate their way to free trade. If either country manages to negotiate itself into the peripheral areas p and q, it should refuse to negotiate further and the bargaining process is at an end.

(iv) The Second Best

In the preceding section we examined the case of an approach to free trade in a two-country, tariff-protected world. The general conclusion was that, although both countries might well progressively lower their tariffs by negotiation until their welfare was maximised at free trade, it might also be that one or other country might under certain conditions achieve a position in which, still with a tariff, its welfare position was superior to that of free trade and it refused further negotiation, the tariff being retained at that value. Even with two countries and two goods, optima were possible for individual countries well short of free trade.

Once one departs from the simplicity of two-country/two-commodity models the agony of uncertainty increases. There is now no more than a presumptive case in favour of free trade. Moreover, when we proceed to three or more countries, another aspect of trade interference other than tariffs, appears — the aspect of convertibility. It is not enough merely to have free trade; it is necessary to have free and multilateral trade. The processes of comparative advantage and gainful trade which may be impeded by tariffs are impeded also if a country may buy only from such other countries as will accept its currency and not from others. Trade, when convertibility is limited, is diverted into channels determined by monetary availability and administration and not by comparative advantage. We are not concerned here with the special problems posed by convertibility and non-convertibility of currencies and of the extent to which trade may be bilateral or multilateral. It is sufficient at this stage to note that multilateral trade is a necessary condition for free trade itself.

We must now approach on a wider front the question which we examined for two countries and two commodities. What happens as we move towards free trade? As we reduce tariffs and apparently reduce protection do we move progressively to ever preferable welfare situations?

Not necessarily. One example culled from the previous chapter demonstrates that the removal of some tariffs does not necessarily improve even the existing protective situation. If in a given country we maintain a tariff on its imported inputs we increase the effective rate of protection (see p. 139 above). The remission of these tariffs does not lead to an improvement in the situation. Equally, reduction of a tariff on commodity A may give rise to increased imports of commodity B (particularly if A and B are complements). If the divergence of marginal revenue and social cost on commodity B is greater than on commodity A, the welfare situation is not improved but worsened.

It is therefore necessary to set up criteria in terms of which we may use the terms 'improve' and 'worsen' with greater precision. This would be a long task if we were to do it fully. Much of the basic theory lies in the field of welfare economics and we must leave the reader to fill this in for himself,[6] contenting ourselves here with a very brief summary.

Under a free-price system—which includes free trade—marginal social net product equals marginal social net cost. As Meade puts it, 'Common sense suggests that such free agents are more likely to decide to do what is in the interests of society if the rewards which they are offered in each activity correspond to the value to society of the additional product which they would produce in each line of activity'.[7] Certain forces work in a competitive situation to equate these values of marginal social net product and marginal cost. In particular, the very nature of perfect competition, under which no single factor can influence its own return (which is determined by its marginal product), no single employer can affect the price of factors, and no single consumer can affect the price of the product, tends to achieve this equality of the marginal variables.

When we turn from theory to the real world, however, there are certain to be divergences between the marginal cost of a factor and the marginal value of its social net product. These divergences spring from the discarding of the simplifying assumptions which we make in the theoretical model. They may be classified under four causes of divergence: the absence of price competition; the existence of external economies and diseconomies; the existence of government intervention; and the existence of taxes and subsidies.

We are then faced with (a) an optimal situation which fulfils certain marginal conditions and which we describe as a condition of utopian efficiency, and (b) real world divergences from this utopian norm. Before we examine this comparative situation let us look a little more closely at the utopian optimal situation. This is the norm from which we shall measure divergences. This is the condition of maximum efficiency. It is the situation in which 'it is impossible to alter the use of (those) resources in such a way as to make one citizen better off without making any other citizen worse off'.[8] It has four aspects according to which it may be analysed. Here we are interested dominantly in one of these: the condition of optimum trade. The other three aspects cited by Meade are: the condition of maximum production; the condition of optimum production; and the condition of optimum effort.

Trade will be optimised when prices at which commodities can be bought by consumers are in the same ratio to each other for all consumers. This assumes that consumers have no monopsonistic powers and that each consumer in the free market buys a commodity until its marginal value to him equals the marginal outlay required to obtain one more unit. This can be illustrated for the simple case of two consumers and two commodities by Table 7.1. As long as both x and y have the ratios shown in the table no further trade between them, of shirt for coat or vice versa, can increase their welfare. The figures in brackets, however, demonstrate that, as soon as there are two commodities the ratio between whose marginal values

Table 7.1 Trade Optimisation

	Marginal value to		Change in amounts consumed by		Change in welfare of	
	x	y	x	y	x	y
Shirt	$5	$4 (4)	−1	+1	−5	+4 (4)
Coat	$5	$4 (2)	+1	−1	+5	−4 (2)

differ for two consumers, trade will not be optimised. This is so because in the second case if x gets one more coat it will add to his welfare the same amount as he will lose by giving up a shirt, whereas if y gains a shirt his increase in welfare is more than his loss by giving up a coat.

It would be possible to examine each of the other three aspects of the utopian efficiency optima and establish that all have in common the feature we have just established for the trade optimum, namely, a marginal condition must be fulfilled. If it is not fulfilled, it is then possible to make one citizen better off without making another worse off. Any economic policy which can do this we may regard as desirable.

We may now restate in general terms the question which we asked above concerning removal of a single tariff. There our concern was whether such a single remission was preferable, in welfare terms, to no remission at all. But the question can be placed in a wider setting as a welfare problem of which our tariff question is but a special case. Confining ourselves for simplicity in the above analysis only to what Meade calls 'utopian efficiency', ignoring certain other optima such as 'utopian equity' which he distinguishes,[9] and starting from a position in which the marginal conditions for utopian efficiency are not fulfilled, but where there are divergences between marginal values and costs in the economy due to such features as taxation, or monopoly, there may be one particular divergence which, by an act of policy, might be reduced. The question is: will the reduction of one divergence between marginal values and costs in one sector of the economy lead to increased welfare even if all other divergences remain as before? More specifically, under 'what conditions will the reduction of one particular divergence raise and in what conditions will it lower economic welfare'?[10]

The theory which emerges is one which analyses the conditions for the improvement of welfare, 'for making things better rather than achieving the best possible, for maximising welfare subject to arbitrary constraints which preclude the technically possible maximum conditions'.[11] This so-called 'theory of the second best' and its special significance for international economics was suggested by Jacob Viner in his early work on customs union theory. An article by Marcus Fleming in 1951 prepared the way for a full statement of the theory by Meade in 1955. Since that time there has been further elaboration by a number of economists[12] and a fair amount of application particularly in the field of customs union theory.

Meade's procedure is in essence simple enough, although applications would become unbearably intricate. Any tariff reduction or remission improves welfare if it reduces the total divergence of marginal social value from marginal social cost and vice versa. The tariff reduction will create a number of changes in the divergences not only for the commodity covered by the tariff, but for a number of other commodities related to it through the market, as by complementarity or substitutability, through the production process, or in some other way. The net effect of all these changes in divergences is the gauge of welfare improvement. If the net effect is to narrow the total divergences for the economy, then the effect of tariff remission is beneficial; if the net effect is to increase it, the effect of the remission is inimical. Meade's method is to use a theoretical system whereby the weighted divergences of marginal social value from marginal social cost are added algebraically. Net reduction is beneficial, net increase detrimental.

An example may be useful. Let us suppose that Britain lowers its tariff on imported butter. By this the divergence between marginal social cost and marginal social value of butter in Britain will be lessened – a social welfare gain. Other changes follow upon the initial tariff reduction. There is likely to be a fall in the consumption of margarine as the consumption of butter rises. There may be only slight divergence between marginal social value and cost in the making and sale of this commodity. Other induced changes may occur, some with a narrowing of divergence, some with a widening. These changes must be weighted. Take, for example, a change of tariff, the weight is determined by the *ad valorem* rate of incidence of the trade barrier to which that particular type of trade is subject. 'If the sum of all such changes so valued and weighted is greater than zero, then there is an increase in economic efficiency as a result of the partial move to free trade',[13] which the reduction in Britain's tariff on butter represents.

It will be noted from the example that we can distinguish in a typical tariff change primary, secondary and tertiary effects, to all of which may be assigned observed divergence changes, appropriately weighted. The resulting calculation of net gain or loss is conceptual rather than practicable and one may question its usefulness and turn in search of some useful presumptive conclusion. Meade himself supplies one. He argues that there is, indeed, in deciding whether reduction of a tariff is beneficial to welfare or otherwise, a presumption in favour of reducing a particular tariff. The primary effect of such a reduction is always beneficial; the secondary and tertiary, while diverse in effect, are often unimportant. He argues further than this: favourable presumption is stronger in the case of reductions in such duties as have a specially high *ad valorem* incidence. In this case the high primary expansion of trade as a result of the tariff reduction will have a 'high welfare weight relatively to the welfare weights to be applied to any possible secondary or tertiary trade destruction. Finally, the presumption in favour of the cut is increased if it applies to a whole class of similar goods rather than to a particular good in a general class.'[14]

There we must leave the free trade versus protection controversy. It is like a long war, exhausting, confused and, at the end, inconclusive. But perhaps, after all, free trade wins in the end. Its opponents argue that there is a case for tariffs. But they argue it as a realist may argue that even in a moral world there is a case for sin, but that also in a well-ordered world there is a need to keep sin in bounds. There seems little prospect that anyone who reads this book will ever live in a free-trade world. That is not to say that such a world would not be a better world to live in, and that the progression towards that condition is not worth all the time and effort that is lavished upon it.

8
The Theory of Customs Unions

(i) Customs Union Theory

CUSTOMS union theory is a new sector of the theory of tariffs. Born in 1950, it is now a lusty, if somewhat untidy, child. One book gave it life, Viner's *The Customs Union Issue*. It has received later stimulus from the writings of Meade, Lipsey and others.[1]

All this occurred while the establishment and growth of the European Common Market, the European Free Trade Association, and other customs unions were a centre of attention. Yet the theory has wider practical significance than to these new groupings. It provides a framework by which any discriminatory trading system and its impact on the rest of the world may be judged.

The regional trading group is the typical case. Such a group of countries agrees to reduce or eliminate tariffs on goods imported by any country in the group from any other such country while maintaining either a common tariff, or each country its own tariff, against goods from the rest of the world. This constitutes, of course, a trading preference for other members of the group and discrimination against the import of goods from non-member countries. The theory of customs unions is concerned with the changes in economic relationships which result from this discrimination, with, for example, changes in production and consumption patterns, the terms of trade, the balance of payments, and the rate of growth.

There are two types of discrimination in tariff theory: commodity discrimination where different tariff rates are applied to different commodities and country discrimination where different tariff rates are applied to the same commodity according to its country of origin. Customs union theory deals with problems raised by the latter type of discrimination. It is defined by Lipsey as 'that branch of tariff theory which deals with the effects of geographically discriminatory changes in trade barriers'.[2]

Before proceeding to the main task of examining the theory of customs unions we must tidy up the institutional nomenclature. There are four types of discriminatory trade and regional economic groupings: they are in ascending order of cohesion, the free-trade area, the customs union, the common market, and the economic union. The free-trade area is a loose grouping of countries between which tariffs and other barriers to trade are dismantled while each country retains its own tariff and/or trade restrictions and its own commercial policies and bargaining positions with countries outside the free-trade area. The main emphasis of the grouping is on intra-area trade and it will probably not extend beyond this. There is no reason why the countries concerned should have a common frontier. The second type of grouping, the customs union, differs from the free-trade area in at least one important respect. While eliminating intra-country tariffs and trade barriers within the union it has a concerted commercial policy and a common tariff. In trade negotiations the customs union acts as a unit, and some degree of similarity in the economic policies of members is implicit in the arrangement.

The common market carries the customs union principle a stage further than commercial policy into the fields of international resource allocation, tax harmonisation and labour migration. Implicit in the arrangement is the concept of a unified market area in which there is free movement of products, services and factors of production within what is probably also a geographically integrated regional grouping of nation states. In the fourth type of grouping, cooperation is pushed to the point where fusion of the constituent economies is the ultimate aim. The economic union, or economic community, implies a common tariff, a harmonisation of industrial and social policies, concerted monetary and exchange-rate policies, a progression towards a common currency and banking system, and agreed policies on transportation facilities and operation.

The theoretical considerations with which we are concerned in this chapter apply to customs unions, a grouping which we have defined in terms of its tariff policy. They are, however, applicable in principle to all the above groupings. The free-trade area is somewhat exceptional because, lacking a common tariff, it presents to the exports of the rest of the world a tariff wall of uneven height — a feature which poses difficulty to the analysis. This difficulty can be partially overcome by assuming that the lowest national tariff of the free-trade area is equivalent to the common tariff of a customs union and that goods enter the area over the lowest part of the tariff wall that surrounds it. This is not a satisfactory assumption, particularly in a free-trade area which is geographically dispersed, but it enables much of the formal analysis of customs unions to be applied to free-trade areas.

(ii) The Effects on Trade, Production, and Consumption

In spite of the long list of customs unions which economic history provides, serious analysis of them did not begin until comparatively recently. (It would appear from a United Nations report that some twenty customs unions had been formed up to the date of its publication in 1947.)[3] Early discussions favoured them. They were seen as constituting 'a step toward freer trade'[4] and favoured because, in the context of the 1930s, they appeared to be nearer to free trade than were the preferential tariff systems of the time (such as that established by the Ottawa Agreement of 1932). Haberler, writing in 1943 saw the economic case for customs unions as 'identical with the old classical arguments for free trade.'[5] However beneficial customs unions might have appeared in that economic climate it should still have been possible to see — even, as it were, by inspection — that the case for them was far from clear cut and that they carried potentialities both for good and evil. On the one hand they were an advance upon national separation, obtaining, at least for the region they encompassed, some of the advantages of free trade — opportunities for specialisation and economies of scale. These advantages are, however, limited. For example, country A within a customs union of A, B and C would be more limited in its comparative-costs choice than if it were operating in a free trade world of countries $A-X$. On the other hand, by substituting a common tariff wall for the individual tariffs of constituent countries, a union implemented high discrimination against the rest of the world. Where, it might at any time have been asked, lay the balance between these beneficial and baneful effects? Only fairly minute analysis would reveal it.

In the book which opened the serious literature on customs union theory,[6] Viner posed these questions. He examined the production effects of customs unions. Such a union would both create trade and divert trade and reorient the production pattern of a number of commodities. If the shift is from a high-cost to a low-cost source, it creates trade and inclines to the free-trade position. If, on the other hand, production is concentrated on a high-cost source this diverts trade and the move is away from the free-trade position. Thus a customs union affects the efficiency with which resources are used. Viner saw the production effects of customs unions as being both beneficial and detrimental, the net effect depending upon which of the two opposing effects is the stronger. His analysis of this problem rests on two basic concepts of customs union theory which have become familiar: those of *trade creation* and *trade diversion*.[7] These can be illustrated by a numerical example.

The following table shows the prices at current exchange rates of commodity X in three countries:

	Money Prices of X		
Country	I	II	III
Price	$40	$30	$25

It is assumed that the costs of producing X in all three countries are constant, i.e. supply curves are infinitely elastic. Country I is the home country. Country II is partnered with country I in a customs union, and country III is the rest of the world. In this situation country I can protect her domestic industry by a tariff of 100 per cent on imports from either II or III. But if country I forms a customs union with either of the other two countries she will improve her position. If the union is with country II she will get one unit of the product by trade with II at an opportunity cost of $30 worth of exports as compared with a cost of $40 through domestic production. Thus, a customs union of countries I and II will be trade-creating.

Suppose that the tariff levied by country I before the formation of a customs union had been lower than 100 per cent. At 50 per cent country I would have been buying X from country III because of the cost advantage offered by such trade. What happens if countries I and II now form a customs union? Country I will now import X from country II, from where X, at $30, can now come in free of the tariff. She will do this instead of buying X from III at $25, as she did before the formation of the union. Trade has in this case been diverted as a result of the union and since the trade diversion has been from a low-cost source of supply to a higher cost source of supply it results in a less efficient allocation of resources.

From Viner's analysis it is possible to array the trade possibilities that arise from a customs union between countries I and II. They are:

1. If a commodity is not produced in either I or II then both countries will import this commodity from III. The elimination of tariffs can cause no trade diversion. Both countries will import from the cheapest source outside the union. However, because the commodity is now entering over the common tariff there may be a reduction in trade volume, if that tariff is higher than the tariff on the commodity in either country before the union.

2. If country I produces a given commodity at high cost under tariff protection while country II is a non-producer then the effect on trade will

Commercial Policy

depend upon country I's tariff level before the formation of the union. If I's tariff is high enough to eliminate competition from the lowest cost source in III and if the common tariff of the union is not less than this, then country I with her relatively inefficient industry will secure II's market for the product. The change in this case will be trade-diverting.

3. Both countries I and II may be producing the commodity inefficiently under tariff protection before the union. In this case, since the union removes tariffs between them then the least inefficient will capture the total union market. The change will be trade-creating.

From these trade possibilities it is apparent that formation of a customs union will probably cause both trade creation and trade diversion. Even for a single commodity it is likely to do this, but when many commodities are traded both effects are certain. In order to assess the production effects of establishing a customs union one must 'predict the relative strengths of the forces causing trade creation and trade diversion'.[8]

If we assume that these effects are measurable then efficiency in the use of resources is improved if the positive influence of trade creation exceeds the negative influence of trade diversion — efficiency being defined as the ability to produce more with given resources.

An increase in efficiency does not imply an increase in welfare. Since changes in production are localised some individuals, groups and countries will benefit, and others will be affected detrimentally. The increase in total production which comes with greater efficiency does imply, however, that some groups and countries can be better off without making some worse off if there is a compensating transfer to the disadvantaged. To say that increased efficiency means necessarily increased welfare is to ignore the distributional problem.[9]

It might be helpful at this stage to demonstrate the principles of *trade creation* and *trade diversion* diagrammatically. Fig. 8.1 does this in partial equilibrium terms for a single commodity.

Let us assume that DD and SS are the demand and supply curves of commodity X in country I and that X can be produced (under constant costs) both in country II and in III, the rest of the world. There is at first no customs union but country I imports JK of X from III with a tariff WH. OW is the world price at which III can supply any amount of X. OP is the price in II at which that country can supply any amount of X. S_{II} and S_{III} are then the infinitely elastic supply curves of countries II and III respectively.

The trade situation before the customs union is then as follows: in the absence of imports the price of X in I would be OF but with a tariff of WH country I can import JK from III; country II is out of the market since its

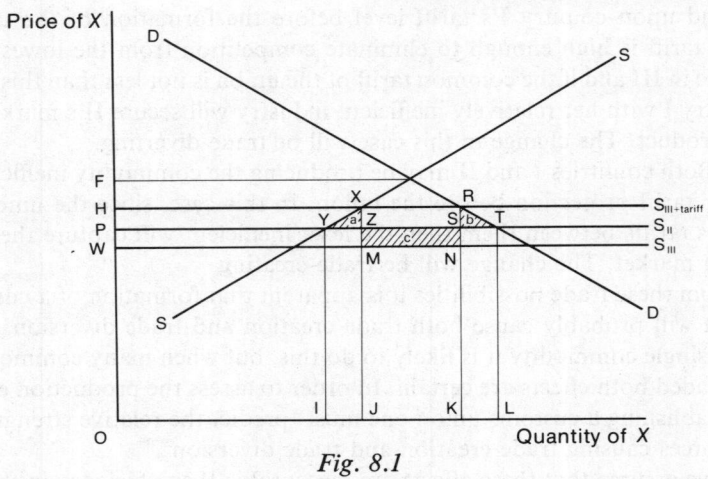

Fig. 8.1

pre-tariff price is higher than in III. If a union between countries I and II is formed there are both trade-creating and trade-diverting effects.

Let us assume that a customs union is now formed between countries I and II between which there are no tariffs but that the tariff WH now applies to imports from III. All imports now come from II at a price of OP; none from III. Imports to country I expand to IL. Country I's production will have fallen from OJ to OI. As a result of the fall in the home price in country I from OH to OP consumption will have risen by KL. Thus the increase in imports or *trade creating effect* can be divided into an effect coming from a fall in production and a rise in consumption in country I.

There is a gain in welfare to country I as a result of the union. If country I had itself to produce the addition IJ coming from the union, then the cost in resources would be equivalent to the area under the I supply curve for this quantity, namely the area $XJIY$. When this quantity is imported rather than produced the cost to country I is, at price OP, $YZJI$. The difference between the cost to I's producers and the import cost is therefore a net saving to I's residents. It is measured by the area of the triangle XYZ. This saving constitutes a welfare gain accruing from the trade-creating effect of the union.

It can readily be seen that there is a welfare gain on the consumption side coming from the same source. As consumption of X in I expands by KL due to the price fall resulting from the union, we can measure the total utility accruing to country I residents by the area under the demand curve, $RKLT$. But this additional consumption costs I residents only $TLKS$. There is, therefore, a welfare gain measured by the triangle RST.

Commercial Policy

If we examine the size of these welfare effects of the customs union they can be seen to depend on the following factors:

1. the amount of the tariff obtaining in country I before the union, i.e. on the size of WH — the higher WH, the higher the welfare gains from abolition of the tariff;
2. the slope of I's supply curve SS; and
3. the slope of I's demand curve DD. The welfare gains will be large, the greater is the elasticity of the supply and demand curves. This is so because, with given values for RS and XZ, the flatter the demand and supply curves the greater YZ and ST become and the greater is the area of the triangles a and b.

So far in this example we have been concerned with trade creation; what of trade diversion? Trade diversion exists in the example. Before the union, country I buys from the most efficient producer, country III, while country II is excluded. After the union, country II, because it is within the union, secures the union market. Country I no longer buys from the most efficient producer in the world but from the most efficient producer in the union. There is trade diversion from the low-cost to the high-cost producer. Instead of importing JK of X from III, country I now imports IL of X from II.

Of this increase in imports, IJ and KL are due to trade creation. Consider only JK of the imports, diverted from III to II. The cost, before the union, of importing JK from country III was twofold: at the price OW, $MNKJ$ was paid to exporters in III, while $XRNM$ was paid by importers to the customs officials in country I. The total cost to country I consumers was $XRKJ$. But of the two cost components the customs cost $XRNM$ was really a transfer within country I. The amount to be paid out abroad was $MNKJ$.

After formation of the union, country I, for the same quantity of X (JK) has to pay $ZSKJ$ to country II. Thus external payments for the product have increased as a result of the trade diversion by $ZSNM$. This is the result of switching trade to a less efficient producer. Such trade diversion results in welfare losses measurable in this case by the area of the rectangle $ZSNM$.

The net welfare effect of the formation of the union is thus the difference between the welfare gains of trade creation and the welfare losses of trade diversion, in terms of the diagram $(a + b - c)$.

The analysis of this diagram can be extended to cover the case of union and trade among countries whose supply curves are not infinitely elastic.[10] The geometry in this case becomes much more intricate and the assessment of welfare gains and losses more problematic.

Viner's analysis concludes that customs unions will lead to losses in efficiency when the countries forming the union produce complementary commodities and will lead to gains when the commodities produced by them are substitutes or near substitutes. In the former case, where the range of commodities produced in the two countries does not overlap, the protected industry in one country will, after the formation of the union, take over the whole of the market for its product with a less efficient reallocation of resources. In the latter case, where there is a large overlap in the commodities produced, the more efficient of the two countries will capture the whole market within the union and the reallocation of resources will lead to an increase in efficiency.

The precise measurement of the gains and losses arising from trade creation and trade diversion are elusive. For the constant costs case described above, Meade suggests[11] a rough method of estimation. The gain from trade creation may be calculated by multiplying the difference in unit costs between the old and new sources of supply by the number of additional units of trade created: losses from trade diversion can similarly be estimated by multiplying the difference in costs by the number of units of trade diverted. The net result of the two effects is then calculable. If, however, costs are not constant, or if consumption of the good varies, this method is not applicable.

Once we drop the assumption of constant costs, assessment of gains and losses becomes more difficult. Let us now assume that three countries, I, II, and III produce product X under increasing costs, and that country I gets its supply of X, partly from producers at home and partly from imports from countries II and III. If countries I and II now form a customs union, then country I will no longer levy a tariff on imports from II. The supply of X in the union situation will be altered. Assuming that I's consumption of X is constant country I will import more of X from II, will reduce its imports from III and will reduce its domestic demand. A part of the increased imports from II will replace high-cost domestic production and part will replace supply from III, that is, it will be a trade diversion.

The computation of gains and losses is, in this case, impossible. It is compounded of a rise in costs in II as output rises to meet I's demand, and falls in costs in countries I and III with the declines in their output. Nevertheless certain useful conclusions can be drawn. Firstly, the higher is the elasticity of supply in country I the more favourable will be the effect of trade creation as the high-cost domestic producers reduce output in face of the competition of low-cost producers abroad. Secondly, the higher the elasticity of home supply in III the greater will be the amount of trade diversion and the greater the detrimental effect on productive efficiency. This is because as III's exports to country I decline the price will fall and, with this, the greater the elasticity of supply the greater the fall in output and the greater the trade diversion as III's exports are replaced within the union market.

To which countries do the benefits of trade creation accrue? In the case of constant costs the gains accrue only to members of the union. Unless there is trade diversion, trade with non-union members does not change. If there is trade diversion, productive efficiency within the union and most likely in other countries will be reduced. In the union, resources are shifted to industries that have a comparative disadvantage as compared to industries in the non-union countries. At the same time the lower exports of non-union countries may cause a shift of resources in those countries to goods in which the comparative advantage is less than those formerly exported.

In the increasing costs case, trade creation will still benefit union-member countries and if there is trade creation and no trade diversion non-union countries will not be affected. Trade diversion will be detrimental both for union and non-union countries.

Thus far we have been concerned predominantly, as Viner was, with production effects. Fig. 8.1 revealed, however, the existence of certain consumption effects the more precise nature of which should now be explored. The most apparent consumption effect is that, when a price of a product falls in a country newly within a union because, in the absence of a tariff on goods from other union members, that product may be imported more cheaply than formerly, then consumption of that product will increase — unless the demand for that product is of zero elasticity. In the case depicted in Fig. 8.1 the fall in price of X from OH to OP caused trade creation out of which KL was taken in increased consumption.

Apart from the positive consumption effect which is demonstrated in the diagram there are more general positive consumption effects. Consumers, after the formation of the union, are not limited to highly priced domestic products but may switch to lower-priced versions of such products obtainable elsewhere in the union. Their real incomes are increased. The range of consumer choice is widened.

There are negative consumption effects as well as positive. Before the union consumers in countries I or II were able to buy many commodities from the world at large at world market prices — these prices being the lowest available. After the union has been formed, these products will be subject to the common tariff, and union countries will have to obtain such products from each other at higher cost or import them over the tariff.

The higher prices which consumers must pay result in a decline in their real income, and the range of their consumption is thereby reduced.

Viner implicitly assumed that goods were consumed in a fixed proportion which took no account of relative prices—an assumption which implied an elasticity of demand for individual products of zero. As soon as this assumption is relaxed, the forming of a customs union is sure to change consumption: to the extent that it makes consumption more efficient, that it directs it to lower-priced goods, it increases welfare. It would appear that, as with production, the forming of a union presents the problem of weighing positive and negative consumption effects.

The leading analyst of consumption effects is Meade,[12] who provides a model which is an interesting contrast to that of Viner. Meade assumes that the structure of production remains constant, each country producing a fixed amount of a single product, so that the supply elasticities for these products is zero. The pattern of consumption changes after a customs union is formed because the union changes relative prices and hence changes demand both within countries and in trade between countries. Meade then analyses the changes in the trade content of the countries concerned through a comparison of their domestic price ratios. It is worth following through his example.

Assume three countries I, II and III producing goods X, Y and Z respectively. Country I has an import tariff of 10 per cent, country II one of 20 per cent and country III one of 30 per cent. Countries I and II form a customs union. The situation is then summarised by the following table:

Country	Product produced	Unilateral tariff	
I	X	10	Customs union formed
II	Y	20	
III	Z	30	

The ratio of the marginal utility of products within each country is taken as indicated by their home price ratios.

Before the formation of the customs union the ratio of the prices of goods X and Y in country I was greater than the same ratio in country II. In country I product Y was subject to a 10 per cent tariff which raised its price; in II product X was subject to a 20 per cent tariff which had the same effect for X. The ratio of the prices of X and Y, and hence of their marginal utilities, was greater in country I than in II by 30 per cent. This, Meade argues, is a measure of the gain to be had from an increase in trade between them if, as with the union, tariffs are lowered. This gain only

Commercial Policy

accrues initially, since the growth of trade ultimately reduces the margin between the ratios of marginal utilities in the two countries.

What happens with the formation of the union? In country I more of Y will be imported with the removal of the tariff. Since no change has taken place in the price of either X or Z the demand for both of these will in all likelihood fall as the demand for Y rises. In country II the demand for imports of X will rise with the elimination of the tariff and will be accompanied by a reduction in demand for Y and Z. In country III, extra-union exports of Z decline as do imports of both X and Y. There is increased trade between countries I and II which increases income in those countries but diminishes trade between III and the union which adversely affects the incomes of all three.

According to Meade the net effect upon income (and welfare) is dependent upon the structure of tariffs before the union and upon the elasticities of demand for the products X, Y and Z. The higher were the pre-union tariffs between countries I and II the greater will be the trade creation resulting from their removal, and the greater the gains in consumption resulting from increased trade. If the pre-union tariffs between countries I and II were very high and the tariff of III was very low, then the formation of the union would have the maximum beneficial effect because there would then be maximum trade creation from the elimination of the tariffs between countries I and II by the formation of the union and the minimum loss on the contraction of trade between III and other countries. So far as elasticities are concerned, the best condition will be that in which the elasticities of demand of countries I and II for each other's goods is high and, at the same time, low for goods of III. This will maximise the trade creation as the prices of goods in I and II fall with the removal of the tariff and minimise the trade diversion as a result of the tariff between III and the union.

We have now moved beyond the Viner world in which customs unions were analysed only in terms of production effects. Lipsey and others,[13] using an analysis based on a three-country/three-commodity model distinguished between production and consumption effects of unions. Lipsey sees this development in terms of a wider view of substitution. Viner's analysis, he argues[14] sees the cause of changes in welfare in customs unions as rooted in shifts in the location of production. The Lipsey analysis (and that above) emphasises the effect of substitution in consumption. Lipsey, indeed, suggests that the distinction between production effects and consumption effects commonly made in customs union theory is somewhat misleading, since consumption effects and production effects are to some degree interdependent. A more satisfactory distinction, he argues, would be one between *inter-country substitution* and *inter-commodity substitution*. The former would encompass Viner's trade creation and trade diversion. The latter occurs when one commodity substitutes for another at the margin following a shift in relative prices. Either form of substitution leads to changes in the patterns of both consumption and production.

Before proceeding to further analysis of the effects of a customs union there is one practical question which may conveniently be asked, and perhaps answered, at this juncture. It is this. It appears that the establishment of a customs union has both net production and net consumption effects which determine by their magnitude the net effect upon welfare in a member country. We can assess the impact of the customs union upon the economy of that country. Given that a country has derived net benefit from the union, might it not have done as well or better by adopting some other commercial policy, in particular, by reducing or eliminating tariffs from all other countries? It is arguable that such a policy would result in a greater welfare gain for an individual country than would membership of a customs union. For example, in the long controversy as to whether Britain should or should not join the EEC there was a significant body of opinion which asserted that she would do better to remain apart from the Community but should reduce unilaterally the level of her tariffs. This and other questions can be explored by using a simple partial equilibrium diagram such as the analysis which follows; it is the work of Cooper and Massell.[15]

Fig. 8.2 shows the domestic demand and supply curves for a given

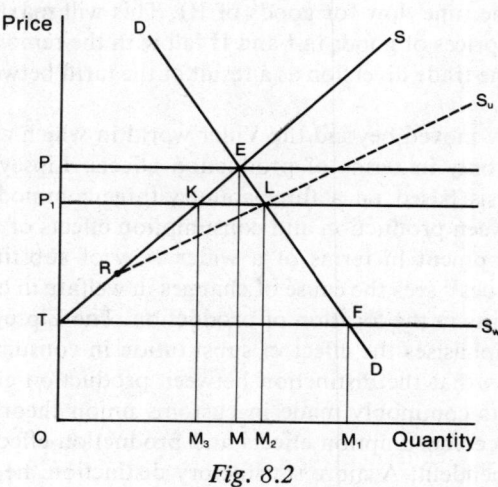

Fig. 8.2

country's market for a commodity produced under conditions of increasing cost. In the absence of trade, equilibrium would be at E for a quantity OM at a price OP at which output exactly equals home demand.

If we assume that the country and its production of this commodity form an unimportant part of total world trade, then the line S_w shows the supply conditions in the world at large for this commodity. Since the country concerned, cannot, by varying its own demand for imports, influence its own terms of trade, S_w must be a horizontal straight line.

With complete free trade, equilibrium would be at F and quantity would be OM_1 at a world price of OT. There is no domestic production.

Suppose that the commodity is imported but that a tariff of TP_1 per unit is levied. Domestic consumers demand OM_2 for which they pay a unit price of OP_1. Of this amount OM_3 is supplied by domestic suppliers and M_3M_2 is imported at the world price OT. Now, if the country decides to form a customs union with a number of other countries, the customs union might have a supply curve for the commodity such as S_u, i.e. a curve of less than infinite elasticity, compounded of domestic supply plus the supply of the other union countries. With this the price for domestic consumers will still be OP_1. The effects of the union will be: OM_2 will still be demanded but it will now be supplied entirely from within the customs union; the former imports from the rest of the world M_3M_2 will be eliminated, as will be the customs revenue from the tariff. There are no detrimental consumption effects.

It is otherwise with the production effects. The elimination of M_3M_2 imports at price OT (plus the tariff TP_1) has resulted in their replacement by imports from partner countries at price OP_1. This involves a shift from a low to a high-cost supplier – a case of trade diversion with adverse productive effects. It would appear, therefore, that, since there are zero consumption effects but negative production effects, the net effect of the customs union is detrimental.

Suppose the initial tariff was greater than TP_1, say at TP or above. In this case domestic demand would have been satisfied, or more than satisfied, by domestic production without imports. If a customs union is formed then high-cost domestic production is replaced by imports from other union members, and the price to the domestic consumer is reduced to P_1. Moreover, the consumer's choice is broadened. In this case the effects of the union are entirely beneficial. Production has shifted from high to low-cost suppliers. Consumption has been improved.

There is a third case remaining: the initial tariff might have been between TP_1 and TP. Here the customs union lowers the price to consumers to OP_1. Although their choice is somewhat curtailed the consumption effect is, on balance, probably positive. On the production side, however, things are otherwise. Before the union domestic demand was satisfied partly from domestic production and partly by imports from the lowest-cost source. After union domestic output reduces to OM_3 while the source of foreign supply is no longer the low cost S_w but the higher cost union supplies at S_u. The real cost of supply has been increased. The net production effect is both positive and negative, reduced production and increased reliance on high cost supply: the consumption effect is beneficial, the net effect is probably beneficial.

We can now summarise the three cases above:

1. If the country's initial tariff was TP_1 or less than TP_1, the effects of a customs union will always be detrimental.
2. If the initial tariff was TP or greater, the effects of a union would be beneficial.
3. If the initial tariff was between TP_1 and TP the effect is, on balance, beneficial.

The last case may be pursued further. If the initial tariff was greater than TP_1 could the benefit not have been increased by lowering the tariff to all comers to TP_1 rather than by forming a union? The consumption effect would be the same in either case. But with the unilateral tariff reduction the high cost union supplies at S_u would be replaced by low cost world supplies at S_w, while the country (by retaining a tariff at TP_1) would collect customs revenues of $TP_1 \times M_3M_2$.

We cannot conclude from this that unilateral tariff reduction profits a country more than joining a customs union. On the import side it would appear that the arguments on balance point that way. But there remains the export side. Once a customs union is formed the home country's exports have free access to the markets of other members of the union. The resultant expansion of exports and the shifts in production and consumption which it occasions in the home country and in the entire union have to be taken into consideration. These do not accrue to unilateral tariff reduction. If we also concede that, in terms of practical politics, it is often easier for a government to carry a country into a customs union than to secure a general reduction in its tariff, the customs union may yet be the preferred second best, in welfare terms, to free trade.

Commercial Policy

(iii) The General Equilibrium Analysis

The discussion so far in this chapter has been carried on in terms of partial equilibrium analysis. In this section we shall set out some of the analysis of the effects of customs unions in general equilibrium terms. We shall confine our attention to a limited number of cases. These may serve the reader as a launching pad for further exploration in the literature. We shall deal seriatim with the effects on a union member (a) when consumption is fixed, (b) when the pattern of consumption is variable, and (c) in more wide-ranging circumstances when both consumption and production vary and when the effects are studied in three countries, two in the union and one symbolising the world at large.[16]

1. The case of trade diversion when the consumption pattern is constant has been demonstrated in a model by Lipsey.[17] Lipsey began by demonstrating graphically the elements of the Viner assertion that trade diversion necessarily lowers welfare. This, Lipsey shows, depends upon the implicit assumption that commodities are consumed in some fixed proportion which has nothing to do with the structure of relative prices. This is illustrated in Fig. 8.3.

Assume a small country, A, specialising in production of a single commodity Y and importing commodity X from country C, the low-cost producer. The fixed proportion in which X and Y are consumed is shown by the slope of OZ, the income and price consumption line for all prices and

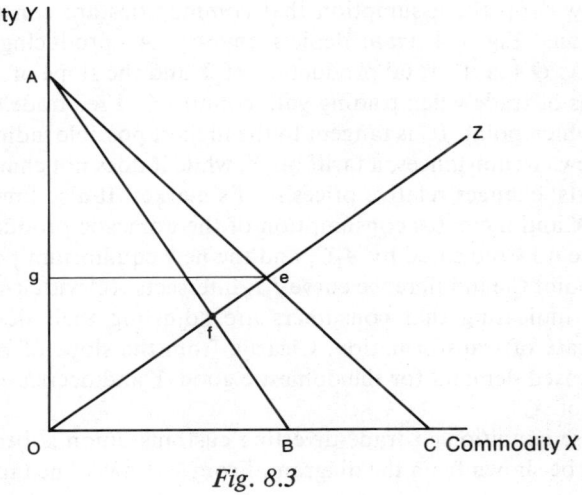

Fig. 8.3

incomes. OA is the amount of A's production of Y and the slope of AC shows the terms of trade offered by C, which is the lowest-cost producer of X. Under free trade, country A will be in equilibrium at e. A's consumption of Y will be Og and it will export Ag of Y in return for ge of X. If a tariff were imposed which did not affect A's terms of trade with C and was not high enough to protect an industry in A producing Y, the equilibrium position at e would be unaffected by the tariff. Relative prices would be changed but consumers would not react to this change, and as long as foreign trade continued at terms of trade shown by AC, the equilibrium at e would be maintained. Assume, now, however, that A forms a customs union with B, so that A must now import X from a higher-cost producer. The price of X in terms of Y is now higher and the new terms of trade are shown by the line AB. With this change the equilibrium has moved to f. Less of both commodities is now consumed and the effect of the union on A's welfare has been detrimental. Trade diversion, under the demand conditions which were assumed, has reduced A's welfare.

Lipsey claims that Viner's assumption that changes in relative prices have no effect upon the proportions in which goods are consumed obscures the real effects of a customs union. One might expect *a priori* that a union would change relative prices; that the pattern of consumption would change with this; that imports from the rest of the union would be increased and imports from the rest of the world diminished; and that consumption of domestically produced goods might decline. The results of substitution in consumption are, it would seem, important, and they have been explored by a number of economists.[18]

2. Now drop the assumption that commodities are consumed in fixed proportions. Fig. 8.4 again depicts country A, producing Y and importing X. OA is A's total production of Y and the slope of AC represents A's terms of trade when trading with country C. Free trade equilibrium is at e, at which point AC is tangent to the highest possible indifference curve. In the new circumstances, a tariff on X, while it does not change the source of imports, changes relative prices in A's market. It also lowers consumption of X and increases consumption of the domestic product Y. Relative prices are now indicated by A_1C_1 and the new equilibrium position is at h. At this point the indifference curve I_1I_1 intersects AC with a slope the same as A_1C_1 indicating that consumers are adjusting their demands to the market rate of transformation. Clearly, from the slope of A_1C_1 the tariff has increased demand for the domestic good Y and decreased demand for imports of X.

In these conditions a trade-diverting customs union is beneficial for A. This can be shown from the diagram. From A draw a line tangential to the

Commercial Policy

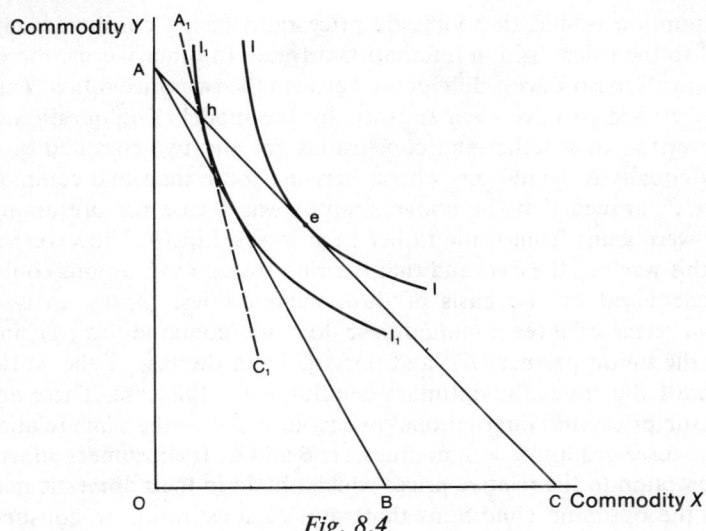

Fig. 8.4

indifference curve I_1I_1 to cut the X-axis at B. If A should form a customs union with B and buy her imports of X from B at terms of trade represented by the slope of AB, her welfare (still being on I_1I_1) will be unchanged. Should the new terms of trade be worse than the pre-union terms AC, but better than the terms of trade shown by the slope of AB, A's welfare will be increased by the customs union's trade diversion. This follows from the fact that there is on the diagram an area in which indifference curves higher than I_1I_1 still lie below the international price line, that is the area above I_1I_1 and below AC. As long as the final equilibrium falls within this area, trade carried on without tariffs and within a union, at terms of trade inferior to those of AC, will increase welfare.[19] Therefore consumers in A obtain X at a lower relative price after the union is formed than they formerly did by importing from C and paying a tariff. The effect of the customs union on A's welfare will be detrimental only if the terms of trade after trade diversion are worse than AB.

There is a favourable consumption effect in A because consumers in that country can adapt their consumption to the same price ratio as that which enables country A to exchange commodity Y for commodity X by trade with country B. Before the union consumers in B adjusted consumption to a price ratio which included the tariff and so represented a higher price for X than the rate at which Y could be changed for X by trade with C.

3. In the conditions of the model—where there are two commodities, complete specialisation and constant costs—the condition for optimum

consumption is that the domestic price ratio facing consumers must be equal to the price ratio in international trade. In other words, there must be no tariff to produce a differential between the two price ratios. This condition we see to have been satisfied by the model. The question arises, however, as to whether the conclusions for the two-commodity model apply equally to conditions where there are more than two commodities. Gehrels[20] argued that the above analysis was a case for presuming that there were gains from trade rather than losses. Lipsey,[21] however, argued that this was not the case and that the case for customs unions could only be generalised on the basis of three commodities. Lipsey analyses the case in terms of three commodities: domestic commodities (A); imports from the union partner (B); and imports from the rest of the world (C). Table 8.1 illustrates the optimum conditions for this case. These are that domestic prices and international prices should have the same relationship for the three groups of commodities, A, B and C. If consumers adjust their consumption to the relative prices which obtain in their domestic markets, 'then the optimum conditions that rates of substitution in consumption should equal rates of transformation in trade can be stated in terms of equality between relative prices ruling in the domestic markets and those ruling in the international market.'[22]

Table 8.1

Free trade (i)	Uniform tariff on all imports (ii)	Customs union between A and B (iii)
$\dfrac{P_{Ad}}{P_{Bd}} = \dfrac{P_{Ai}}{P_{Bi}}$	$\dfrac{P_{Ad}}{P_{Bd}} < \dfrac{P_{Ai}}{P_{Bi}}$	$\dfrac{P_{Ad}}{P_{Bd}} = \dfrac{P_{Ai}}{P_{Bi}}$
$\dfrac{P_{Ad}}{P_{Cd}} = \dfrac{P_{Ai}}{P_{Ci}}$	$\dfrac{P_{Ad}}{P_{Cd}} < \dfrac{P_{Ai}}{P_{Ci}}$	$\dfrac{P_{Ad}}{P_{Cd}} < \dfrac{P_{Ai}}{P_{Ci}}$
$\dfrac{P_{Bd}}{P_{Cd}} = \dfrac{P_{Bi}}{P_{Ci}}$	$\dfrac{P_{Bd}}{P_{Cd}} = \dfrac{P_{Bi}}{P_{Ci}}$	$\dfrac{P_{Bd}}{P_{Cd}} < \dfrac{P_{Bi}}{P_{Ci}}$

Subscripts A, B and C refer to the countries of origin, d to prices in the domestic market of A, and i to prices in the international market.

Under free trade all three optimum conditions are satisfied. In the absence of a union, with a uniform tariff on both imports, the optimum conditions will be met in one case only, that for imports to A of both B and C goods, which are both subject to the same tariff so that the ratio of their prices is unchanged. The price of goods from B and C will, however, be higher in A's domestic market than in the international market thus increasing the denominator on the left-hand side in both the relevant ratios.

Commercial Policy

After formation of a customs union the price of imports from B, the union partner, is reduced so that the first optimum condition is met, but in both ratios involving goods from C the tariff raises the domestic price and prevents satisfaction of the optimum conditions. Formation of the customs union, as an alternative to a general tariff, simply moves A from one non-optimal position to another and it is not possible to make any comment as to the effect on welfare. The case for a customs union is, Lipsey argues, inconclusive.

A final model, the work of Jaroslav Vanek,[23] which employs offer curves to examine the case of equilibrium between three countries with two traded goods must be considered.

Two countries, A and B, form a customs union. A third country, C, symbolises the rest of the world. Commodities X and Y represent the exportable commodities of A and B respectively. C, the rest of the world, can export Y. Before the union between A and B is formed, we may assume there is trade between them and that such trade is shown by the offer curves OA and OB in Fig. 8.5.

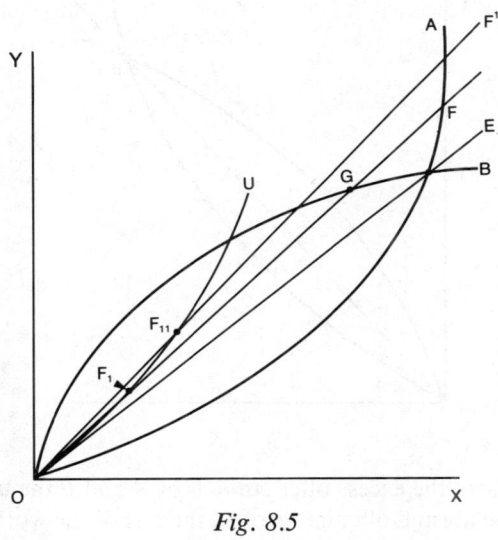

Fig. 8.5

Once the union is formed the quantities which A and B, the union members, are prepared to exchange with C can be shown by an *excess offer curve*. This shows the different XY combinations which the union is willing to trade with C under different terms of trade. At the terms of trade OE trade between A and B is balanced and the union will not wish to trade with

C. The first point on the excess trade offer curve is therefore O, the origin. Now draw a further terms of trade line OF. With this, country B will want to trade quantities of X and Y shown by OG while A will want to trade amounts shown by the larger quantities at OF. There is an excess offer of X by A as compared with B's demand for it or alternatively A's demand for Y exceeds B's offer of Y. In either case GF measures the excess offer of X for Y. Measure GF from the origin along OF and we get F_I. This is the second point on the excess offer curve of the union $(A + B)$. (The first point is the origin.) Further points, such as F_II, may be obtained by the use of additional possible price lines (on the model of OF) and the measurement upon them of the excess offer. Let us be clear what this new curve shows: it depicts the excess offer of X for Y by A and B, the union members, in their trade with C. For terms of trade with a steeper slope than OE, the excess offer curve will be convex to the x axis; for lines with a lesser slope than OE, the excess offer curve will be concave to the x axis; the latter type of curve indicates that the union would offer Y in return for X.

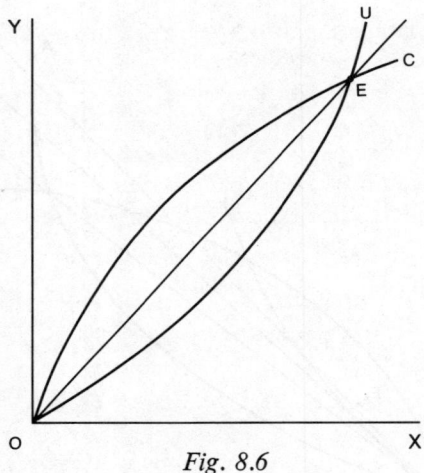

Fig. 8.6

Figure 8.6 places the excess offer curve U of A and B the union countries in relation to the normal offer curve of C, the rest of the world. The point E is that at which the markets for both X and Y are cleared in all three countries. OE is the price ratio at which this is achieved.

The analysis may be carried further. Suppose that A and B before the union imposed tariffs on each other. Figure 8.7 shows the offer curves of these two countries, A_f and B_f being those for free trade (within the union) and A_t and B_t being those with tariffs.

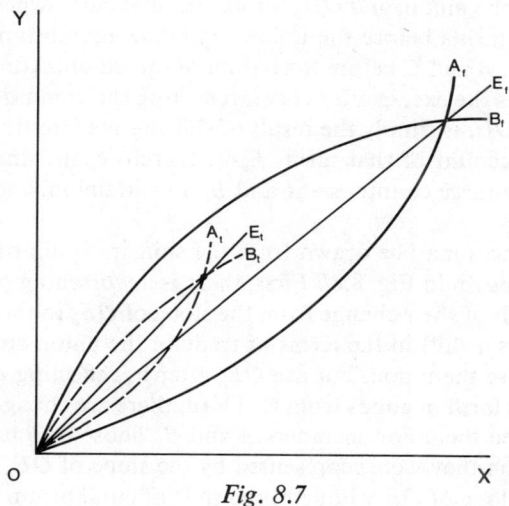

Fig. 8.7

As soon as the customs union between A and B is formed, the tariffs between them disappear, but the common tariff applies on all goods imported from C. In order to examine the effects of forming a union it is necessary to construct the excess offer curves of A and B, both for the free-trade situation and for the situation obtaining before the union when there were tariffs between A and B. Figure 8.8 shows the offer curve OC for C, the rest of the world, OU_f the excess offer curve with free trade between

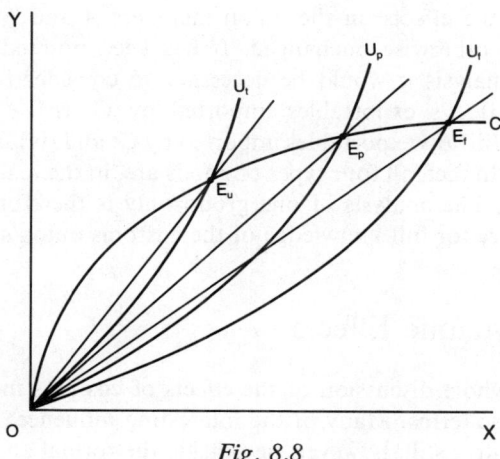

Fig. 8.8

A and B under the union, and OU_p the excess offer curve when A and B still had their own tariffs before the union. E_p is the equilibrium position for trade among A, B and C before formation of the union. After the union of A and B, OU_t is the excess offer curve, reflecting the common tariff on imports from C. OU_t is simply the result of shifting the free-trade offer curve OU_f to take account of that tariff. E_u is, therefore, the final equilibrium position for the three countries — A and B, now in union, and C the rest of the world.

What inferences may be drawn from the shift in equilibrium as a result of the union, shown in Fig. 8.8? First, there is a worsening of C's terms of trade, as a result of their change from the slope of OE_p to the slope of OE_u. Second, there is a shift in the terms of trade of the union countries. These were OE_f before the union, but are OE_u after it, reflecting the magnitude of the common tariff in goods from C. Third, there are changes in the terms of trade between the union members A and B. Those of B have improved. Before the union they were represented by the slope of OE_p and, after the union, by the slope of OE_f. Fourth, the shift of equilibrium from E_p to E_u shows the discrimination in trade against C and the reduction in the trade of union countries with C. This discrimination will be the greater, the greater is the common tariff against C. Fifth, A's terms of trade worsen, but this is somewhat mitigated because A exports more of X to B.

Vanek's model, although interesting for the elegant way in which it deals with the variables, is incomplete. It deals with the case in which C, the rest of the world, imports A's export good, that is when the union has excess supply of X. It would be perfectly possible to treat the case in which Y was the commodity in excess supply to the union. This would merely reverse the effects on the union members A and B but leave the general picture otherwise unchanged. It has been pointed out[24] that to complete the analysis it would be necessary to consider four groups of commodities: (i) A's exportables imported by C; (ii) A's exportables exported by C; (iii) B's exportables imported by C; and (iv) B's exportables exported by C. In fact, all four types of goods are, in the real world, traded simultaneously. The analysis of one group only is therefore far short of what is necessary for full knowledge of the customs union's effects.

(iv) The Dynamic Effects

Thus far, the whole discussion of the effects of customs unions has been couched in static terms. Many of the interesting influences around which controversy centres still, however, lie outside the formal analysis; for they are concerned with the effects of customs unions both upon constituent countries and upon the world at large, over time. These dynamic effects are not amenable to rigorous analysis and theory is not of much help in discussing them, but they are important — perhaps in the final issue more important than the static concepts of trade creation and trade diversion. There is widespread disagreement about the significance and strengths of dynamic influences. We shall review them briefly to direct readers towards the controversy.

Four dynamic effects come up for attention in the literature.[25] They are: the stimulus imparted to countries in the union by competition; the probable acceleration of technological change; the stimulus given to investment; and the economies of scale which union makes possible for industries in participant countries.

The galvanic effect of competition within a customs union has already been touched upon. This influence has strong *a priori* support. As tariffs fall away between union members, monopolies and cartels within individual countries become exposed to pressure in their domestic markets from firms elsewhere in the union. Inefficient or unenterprising firms and firms below optimum size are similarly exposed. The result, it is arguable, will be a restructuring of industry for survival or for wider market penetration with beneficial effects on costs and prices. Scitovsky has argued[26] that this competitive effect has been an important one in the European Economic Community.

A second view which favours customs unions is that they will speed economic growth, since the enlargement of the market will encourage innovation and technological change.[27] As the market grows so the optimum size of firms will increase and additional resources be deployed into research and development. Whether this will result in a faster rate of innovation is of course problematic. There is scant empirical evidence to show that the rate of technical innovation in large firms exceeds that in small firms. The most we can say is that the potential for innovation is there and that wide markets and keen competition provide a favourable climate for it.

It may be expected that, within the union, investment will be stimulated by wider market opportunities, by changes in prices, and by the increase of competition. The total impact upon investment is hard to estimate, however, since it will be compounded of a number of influences, some favourable, some less so. We may expect, firstly, some gain in net investment for the reasons cited above. Against this must be offset a probable measure of disinvestment from the run-down of domestic industries now displaced by imports from other members of the union. Finally, there is a pull to locate new investment in 'union' countries near to the frontier with other union members. The already strong forces which make for the decay of remote fringe areas—Calabria in Italy, Newfoundland in Canada—may be greatly exacerbated. Exactly what is the total effect on net investment in a union country may be determined by how near to full-capacity working the industry of that country was before the union. If it was considerably under-employed, then the stimulus imparted by the union might serve to lift it towards full employment but with the same capital structure. If it was already at full capacity there would be some element of inflation led by the twin thrusts to demand coming from trade creation and investment to raise capacity.

Apart from domestic investment, union countries may experience a growth of investment from abroad. Foreign firms with plants already within the union may expand or regroup these to meet the new circumstances created by the union. In addition, firms which formerly exported to union countries may anticipate the common tariff by setting up plants within union countries. This form of investment was an observable feature in the EEC. After 1955 American investment in Western Europe increased strongly. One may be sure that some part of this was in anticipation of the growth in the market which would take place within the Community.

It was widely argued during the period preceding the Treaty of Rome that the growth of industry in the United States and the high per capita income of that country sprang in great part from the huge market which American industry has served and the economies of scale which this has made possible. Great would be the advantages for European industry when a market of 250 million people was provided within the Community. It is an enticing prospect—if the argument is well founded. It is certainly arguable, in terms of the economics textbook, that, within the union, industrial specialisation will take place; that as a result unit costs will fall with full utilisation of plant, long production runs and growing expertise of labour and management; and that further economies will be made possible by scientifically planning and locating such costly basic industries as steel, base metals and power supply. To developing countries with an industrial structure still to build, these economies seem particularly attractive; and indeed they are more likely to be true economies in this case than for mature countries, where the industrial structure and location must be taken as given and be moulded by the union only over a long period of time. Perhaps the textbook quality of the economies of scale argument in itself makes one suspicious of it. There are great and efficient industries which are not large and do not enjoy large markets. Sweden makes excellent cars of world reputation and the world's greatest still camera.

Switzerland has an economy of great wealth based on tourism, banking and small but highly efficient industries. For these countries, and others, the road to affluence has not been through mass markets.

(v) Some Practical Implications

This chapter must conclude with some discussion of the practical aspects of customs unions. Let us first summarise very briefly the main lessons which emerge from the theory. They are:

1. When a union is formed both trade creation and trade diversion will take place. The higher the elasticities of demand and supply for goods that will come into trade between union members after elimination of the tariff, the more will be the trade creation.
2. The more the foreign trade of union members was with other union members before the union was formed, the more likely it is that the union will raise welfare.
3. The higher the pre-union tariffs between members of the union, the greater will be the trade creation once the union is formed and the tariffs are removed.
4. The lower the level of the common tariff of a union the less trade diversion the union will cause.
5. Trade creation and greater efficiency in resource use will result from a customs union between countries which are rivals in trade than between countries whose goods are complementary.[28]

Most of the foregoing arguments are straightforward and have already been demonstrated in earlier sections of the chapter. Some may be examined for their applicability to concrete cases, such as that of the ECM. Point (5) requires some further examination. Consider the alternative possibilities of trade rivalry and complementarity. Let us assume two types of commodities which, prior to union, are subject to tariffs by the countries later forming the union. The first type of good is produced under varying cost conditions in all countries forming the union; the second type is produced in one country only. Once the union is formed, and the tariffs removed, the most efficient firms producing the first type of good will capture the whole union market in their product. The shifts in production are the result of trade creation and they reflect an improvement in the use of resources. In the second group the one country producing each product will capture the union market but it will also by so doing replace imports by other members from other countries outside the union. This is trade diversion, and by it efficiency in the use of resources is impaired. Because the union is one of trade rivals, however, there are likely to be more products of the first type than of the second, and there is a net trade creation as a result of the union. There is argument as to whether the ECM fits fairly closely into this pattern. Much of the pre-union trade of members was with each other and there was much industrial rivalry. *A priori*, the Common Market should lead to considerable trade creation. Empirical evidence of the growth of trade between the Six since the Treaty of Rome seems to bear this out.[29] Scitovsky argues,[30] however, that the scope for trade creation is small because there are only miniscule differences between costs of production in the member countries. Here there are differences between writers on the magnitudes, and some do not share Scitovsky's view and assert that the cost differences are great. There have been inconclusive attempts at statistical analysis.[31] Some trade diversion in industrial goods is likely because of the extent to which ECM countries formed a market for products from elsewhere. In raw materials, trade diversion is likely to be much less, since ECM countries have long imported the bulk of their raw materials from outside the Six. In agriculture, in contrast to manufactures, trade diversion may well occur as ECM countries divert their demand for non-European fruits and agricultural products to the colonies and dependencies of the Six, particularly to French dependencies in Africa. (Such dependencies are associate members of the Community and have preferential tariff treatment.) Some temperate zone agricultural products from North America may also suffer from diversion.

It is possible to summarise these influences only by the most intuitive judgements. For what it is worth, it might appear that customs unions such as ECM are economically advantageous to the participants. The trade creation probably outweighs the trade diversion, and there is a probable gain in resource efficiency.

The European Free Trade Association was different in its pre-union structure from the ECM and has had different results from its development. The group was complementary in trade. Britain, the main manufacturing country of the group, occupied a dominant position in trading magnitude and contrasted in this respect with smaller members, such as Austria and Switzerland. While four countries – Britain, Sweden, Switzerland and Austria – were all exporters of manufacturers, other members – Denmark, Norway and Portugal, Finland was an associate member – were exporters of food and primary products. The amount of pre-union trade carried on between members was lower for EFTA than for ECM.

Commercial Policy

It is probable that, as a result of the union, the elimination of intra-country tariffs created some trade diversion, occurring in all types of goods — food, primary and industrial products.

A number of other customs unions — such as the Latin American Free Trade Association (LAFTA) and the Central American Common Market (CACM) — exist among developing countries and thus exhibit a yet different structure. Such groups of countries do not generally trade greatly with each other but rather tend to export food and primary commodities to the developing countries in return for manufactures. There is little scope for trade creation by increased trading with other group members. Only where there are small manufacturing industries in each can these be protected by the common tariff and some trade creation take place. Even then, it is doubtful if a developing country will be prepared to expose its new and delicate industries to competition within the union — still less to allow its less efficient industries to give way to others more efficient in other union countries. A likely effect of union among developing countries is the substitution of home-produced and protected manufactures for imports from the developed countries. Such trade diversion is detrimental. It is hard to find much theoretical argument to support the establishment of customs unions among developing countries. Such countries need maximum trade creation, whereas unions, for them, seem to lead inexorably to trade diversion.

Two related matters require attention before closing this theoretical discussion of customs unions; their size and the distance between members. We shall deal with these in turn.

On the question of size we may start by stating a generalisation to which there are subsequent qualifications: the bigger the union, size being measured in GNP, the greater is the chance of the reallocation of production to low-cost producers and for trade creation within the union.[32] Moreover, a large union will provide a large market for union producers with possible economies of scale and favourable conditions for growth. In practical terms, we might argue that the ECM fulfils more satisfactorily the criteria of customs union success than do the customs unions formed by developing countries in Latin America.

The qualifications do not erode this generalisation but make us approach it with caution. First, what do we mean by size? From size we look for trade creation, competition, and the possibility of a large market for manufactured products. Clearly size is only vaguely measured by geographical area or even crude population. The real test of size is aggregate national income, and population with a high per capita income and consuming potential and mature production methods. Within this frame-work, the switches of consumption and production, the potential for specialisation, may have maximum effect.

But, apart from size, homogeneity is required in the market. A large market may still have diversity, individual national consumer tastes and preferences which will inhibit the effect of its size. This is a factor which may ultimately cause the large consumer market of the ECM to have less effect on trade creation and industrial growth within the Community than was expected, and less than the large mass market of the United States is alleged to have had in the growth of the economy of that country. Tastes and individual idiosyncracies of three such mature and long-formed nations as the French, the German and the Italians — to say nothing of the Dutch, the Belgians, the Luxembourgers and the British — may alone serve to partition the gross market to some extent. It may be many years, even without tariffs, before that market is comparable to the coast-to-coast market which exists in the United States.

A second qualification to the argument for sheer size in customs unions is that large unions will probably include large nations which enter the union with foreign economic policies of their own, perhaps with traditions as protectionist countries. A union may give to such countries merely a vehicle for exclusive and exploiting policies inimical to all countries outside the union and perhaps to some within. France, although a member of the Common Market, has contributed nothing to its growth as a liberal, outward-looking community. She has seen in it a vehicle for the pursuit of her own unilateral advantage and, as a group, for the building up of an economic force to rival the United States.

We turn now from the size of customs unions to the question of how their members may be dispersed. Is it necessary for the union to form a territorial bloc with common frontiers and internal lines of communication or is it feasible for member countries to be dotted here and there as separate national entities?

One thing is immediately apparent: it is impossible to achieve trade creation if mere location — distance and the intervention of other countries — precludes it. If trade would not easily take place under tariff freedom between countries A and C because distance and high transport cost prevented it, it is unlikely that the trade creating forces of union would overcome these obstacles. Viner argues,[33] that growth of trade and specialisation within a union will be greater, the smaller the gap which divides the member states. This is so not only because of the growing transport costs which are a function of distance but also because geographical remoteness implies often differences in the tastes, cultures and social conditions of peoples which are detrimental to the shifts of trade upon which a customs union relies for success. The influence of transport costs is self-evident from the simplest trade theory. We argue the case for specialisation in international trade in the absence of transport costs. Once such costs are taken into account it is unlikely that production will be concentrated with the suppliers who produce at lowest cost. The higher are transport costs the less likely that production will be allocated by trade to the lowest cost sources. Once transport costs become prohibitive between alternative sources of supply then competition between the suppliers (except in third markets) will be eliminated and trade will be restricted. This applies between members of a customs union. In a geographically cohesive group the most efficient supplier will dominate the union and concentration in a cheap source of supply results; where the union countries are scattered this may not be the case at all. We must measure distance here in terms of real cost of transport and not in miles. Contiguity may be deceptive. Two countries with a common frontier may have markets less accessible to each other (particularly for bulk materials) than two which are separated by an ocean. Transport costs between, say, a number of countries on the Pacific Rim might be much less than transport costs between China and Tibet, which have a common frontier.

It is fairly evident that transport cost in monetary terms is the yardstick of distance for the purpose of this discussion. A simple method is to define distance in terms of transport costs, i.e. the difference between the export value of goods shipped by country A and their value c.i.f. as imports at the ports of country B. This simple method when applied to actual cases shows high correlation between the high trade volumes and the low transport costs between the contiguous countries of Western Europe. It demonstrates that the most advantageous union in Western Europe on the spatial criteria, would be between Belgium, the Netherlands, Luxembourg, France and Germany, and that advantage declines significantly when Italy, a peripheral member of ECM, is included.[34]

It would appear on theoretical grounds that the ECM, tightly integrated geographically as it is in the centre of the trading world, has a much stronger potential for reaping the advantages of union than have the other free-trade areas, particularly those in the developing world.* It might be tempting to argue also that these latter may suffer from the disparity of customs and culture observable among their members. This is likely, but as the degree of industrialisation in countries increases the argument that cultural differences impede specialisation may have less

---

* Readers will note the fact that the case for the Latin American unions and those in the developing world has appeared to diminish through this chapter, while that for ECM has steadily gained.

force. It is arguable that the industrial 'culture', once attained, is uniform and that its values are generally pervasive, so that uniform consumption patterns develop once disposable per capita income is available. This may well be the case, but for many of the countries in the developing world, which look to customs unions for trade creation, this state of affairs is still some way off.

9
Trade and the Nature of the Market

(i) Introduction

THE classical model of international trade assumes that there are no artificial impediments to trade flows and that perfect competition exists in international markets. The discussion of commercial policy is, in great part, the consideration of aberrations to this free-market structure. In the last two chapters the significance and effects of the main impediment to trade flows, namely, tariffs, have been explored. It is now appropriate to consider the implications of removing the assumption of perfect competition. In international trade, as in domestic trade, competition is the exception rather than the rule and we must accommodate our thinking to the evident existence, in the markets for both goods and factors, of varying degrees of imperfection. It is unnecessary in these days of the conglomerate, the multi-product firm and the multinational corporation to stress the practical importance of this qualification to the theory.

Other features than the size and nature of firms in international trade exist to vitiate the classic assumption. Two call for attention: the first encompasses certain market practices such as dumping and the influencing of prices and market sharing through commodity agreements; the second is the intrusion into the trading sphere of the state itself. This latter aspect raises in turn the peculiar problems of trade (a) between socialist states where all transactions between countries are between state buying and selling agencies, and (b) between socialist countries operating through state agencies and non-socialist countries trading through private traders.

The chapter which follows will discuss these matters. We shall deal first with the consequences for trade of monopoly and imperfect competition; second, with the effects of practices such as dumping; and third, with the implications of state trading.

(ii) Monopoly and Imperfect Competition in International Trade

Let us begin by reminding the knowledgeable, but possibly forgetful, reader of some elementary facts about perfect competition.

The perfectly competitive market requires rigorous conditions. There are many sellers, freedom to enter the market and withdraw, and a homogeneous product. With such conditions no single seller can influence the market by his output policy. As for price, he must accept that which prevails in the market. For sellers, in the aggregate, price is determined by the equating of supply and demand, but for each individual seller the price is represented by an infinitely elastic demand curve; indicating that, at that price he may sell all he produces, at a higher price he will not be able to sell at all, while at a lower price he will needlessly sacrifice profit. Figure 9.1 demonstrates these facts. At a price P a firm in a competitive industry is in

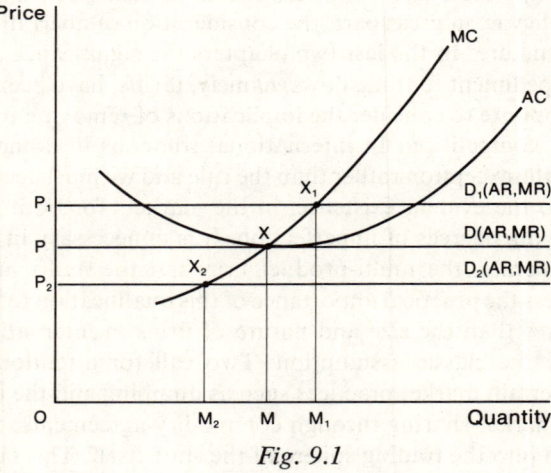

Fig. 9.1

full equilibrium. The price OP also fixes the infinitely elastic demand curve of the firm and represents both average and marginal revenue. At X the firm's marginal cost not only equals its marginal revenue but the price equals average cost (including normal profit) and the firm does not incur losses or earn abnormal profits. Moreover since PX is tangential to the average cost curve at its lowest point the equilibrium level of output OM is the most efficient for the firm since it minimises average cost. OP_1 and OP_2

Commercial Policy

are not prices at which a firm with such cost curves could sustain its position. At OP_1 such a firm would be earning abnormal profits which would attract new firms to the industry until such profits were eliminated. At OP_2 the firm is incurring losses, since price is now lower than average cost. The firm may have to cease production. If it has large reserves it may remain producing at a loss at OM_2 until other sub-marginal firms have been forced out of production and price has risen again to OP.

With perfect competition in factor markets and in goods markets the allocation of resources and the level of output are determined by demand. At the long-term equilibrium output at minimum average cost, factors are combined with optimal efficiency. Since, in the long run, there are only normal profits, then the total price of the commodity (average revenue) is the same as the sum of all the factor costs. Moreover if there is perfect competition in the factor market, factor costs must be the same in all of the possible factor uses in industry. They must equal the marginal revenue. All this follows from the nature of perfect competition and the working of the price system.

Let us turn to the vastly different conditions which in fact prevail. Goods are not homogeneous but highly differentiated. Entry to industry is impeded by patent rights, capital requirements, restrictions as to location and membership of conferences or producers' associations. Individual firms are of a size to influence or come near to controlling the price. Firms and markets are not located either at the limiting points of perfect competition or pure monopoly on the market spectrum but at points between, while in the markets for factors the same imperfections exist.

The main feature of the firm under imperfect competition is that it can influence price by varying the amount of the product offered for sale. The factor limiting the seller's influence over price is the elasticity of demand of the consumer. To achieve a higher price he must expect to sacrifice some measure of demand; to achieve increased sales he must reduce the price. This follows from the shape of the relevant curves in Fig. 9.2. Now, under imperfect competition, the demand curve is no longer horizontal nor is it coincidental with the marginal revenue curve. The demand (average revenue) curve slopes downwards and the marginal revenue curve is below it at all levels of output. As the price is reduced marginal revenue falls more quickly than price. The firm's cost curves are, as under perfect competition, U-shaped and the firm maximises profits at W, where marginal cost is equal to marginal revenue. At this level of output OQ, average cost is QV, average revenue (or price) QR and the profit per unit of output is RV. The total profit is shown by the shaded area $PRVT$. At the equilibrium output OQ the firm is operating at less than its optimum size which would

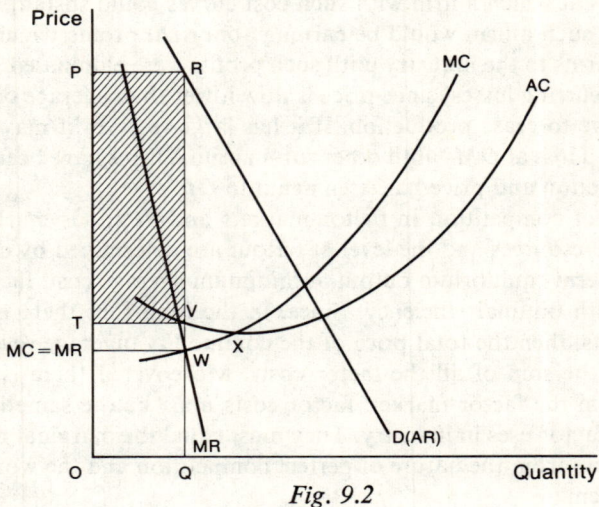

Fig. 9.2

be at X the point of minimum average cost. Clearly if marginal cost and marginal revenue were to be equated at X they could only be so in the case of perfect competition where average and marginal revenue curves are coincident and are tangent to the average cost curve at its lowest point. Under imperfect competition prices are higher and outputs lower than under perfect competition and monopoly profits accrue which are greater, the less is the freedom of entry for new firms into the industry.

In factor markets imperfect competition has a similar effect. Changes in demand do not result in flexible changes in factor utilisation and this inflexibility in the face of changes of international demand vitiates the principle of comparative cost as a determinant of trade flows. Economies of scale, which are a feature of the large corporation operating in an imperfectly competitive market, also bear upon comparative costs.

The whole outlook for the application of the principle of comparative advantage begins to look different in a non-competitive world. Nor is it wholly certain that a diminution of competition has deleterious effects upon trade. While on the supply side imperfect competition results in a less than optimal efficiency in the use of resources, on the demand side it has a considerable stimulating effect. With imperfect competition there is a great amount of product differentiation as each firm seeks by advertising to establish a monopolistically competitive position for its branded products. If all cars were homogeneous a few centres (or Detroit alone) could supply the world. But they are not homogeneous and car manufacturers spend much time, money and resources in persuading us that they are not. As a result all car-producing countries export their own product and import the cars of others. With a vast range of manufactured products it is a similar story. Product differentiation has a powerful trade-creating effect. It is hard to be persuaded that the classical analysis is here of much help in assisting us to judge the extent of the forces which cause trade to flow. The assumption of perfect competition in trade is useful as a conceptual datum but little else. It is impossible to evaluate the net effect of the several effects upon trade which imperfect competition may have. It is, however, possible to examine the trade implications of some forms of market imperfection. The most interesting case is that of price discrimination.

In one market there is one price: this was basic in the above analysis, whether the market was perfect or imperfect. Institutionally, however, it is often possible for a large monopoly producer to break up an apparently unified market for a homogeneous product and sell that product at different prices to different buyers. This sectorising of the market may occur within a country or even within a city. A good may be higher priced in the fashionable shops of the city centre than in the suburban supermarket. Professional services are bought at different fees by different income and social groups. In these cases the market differentiation arises because buyers are either apathetic in exercising their choices or because they lack knowledge of supply prices. In foreign trade, differentiation occurs because markets are separated geographically. Not only are they separated by space but also they are distinguished by cultural and linguistic differences which influence demand conditions in each market sector and enable different price policies to be followed. In more technical terms, if the elasticities of demand in the market sectors are different then the discriminating seller will improve his position by selling at different prices in the various sectors. But the general rule for profit maximisation still holds: profit for the whole selling operation is highest when marginal cost, which is the same for all sectors of the market, is equal to marginal revenue in the individual sectors. The differences in marginal revenue in the market sectors are the important determinants of price and selling policies in the sectors.

The seller, who for convenience we personify as 'he' but who in practice will be a multinational corporation or an international cartel, has two possible courses: he may disregard the difference in the marginal revenue curve of the two markets selling in both at the same price; or he may charge different prices in each, that is discriminate between the two markets. It is easy to show that in the second case he increases his profits by moving sales from the market where demand is less elastic to that in which it is more elastic.

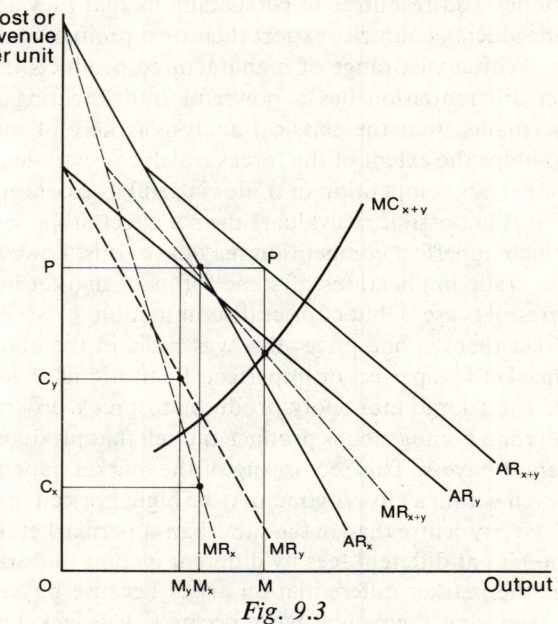

Fig. 9.3

The first case is illustrated in Fig. 9.3. Average revenue curves for two markets X and Y are added to give an average revenue curve for both markets AR_{x+y}. Similarly marginal revenue curves are added to give an aggregate MR_{x+y} curve for the whole market. With an aggregate marginal cost curve, MC_{x+y}, OM units will be produced at a price OP. This output OM will be made up of OM_x in market X and OM_y in market Y. The sale of OM_x in market X yields a marginal revenue of OC_x, while the sale of OM_y in market Y yields the much higher marginal revenue of OC_y in market Y. The charging of the flat price OP in both markets means a much higher marginal return in Y than in X. The seller could increase his profit by shifting sales from market X to market Y, that is from the less elastic to the more elastic.

This leads us to the second case, which is illustrated in Fig. 9.4. Here we can simplify the diagram by putting the curves for each market on each side of the vertical axis. The average and marginal revenue curves only are shown. At the price OP (taken from Fig. 9.3) OM is produced in each market and MM is sold in the aggregate. MM is the same as OM in Fig. 9.3. M_1M_1 is equal to MM but represents a different distribution between the two markets such that the marginal revenues in each, M_1V in X and M_1W in Y, are equal. In other words a shift of MM_1 from X to Y will pro-

Commercial Policy

vide a better output distribution between the markets, reflected in the equal marginal return obtained from each. But this involves price discrimination. In market X the price rises, as a result of the switch, from P to P_x; while in market Y the price falls from P to P_y. The higher price is now in the market with the less elastic demand curve and the lower price in the market with the more elastic demand curve.

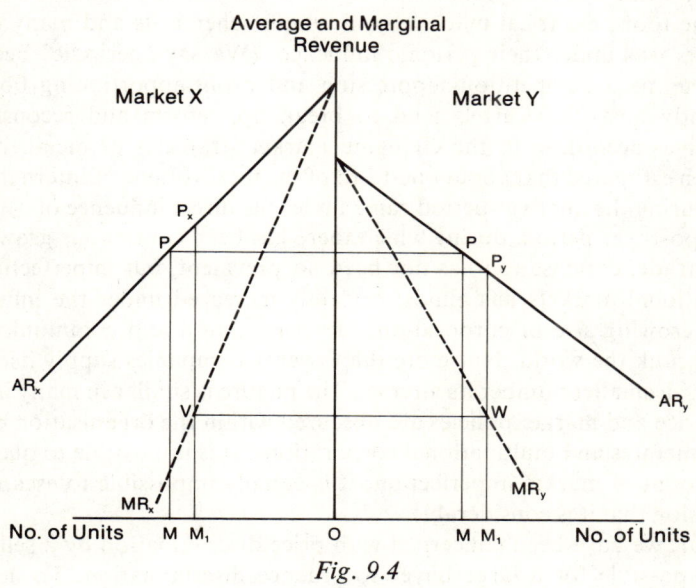

Fig. 9.4

Such price discrimination as this can only take place where the seller is in a monopolistic or imperfectly competitive position. Such is, however, the typical condition in foreign trade in consumer goods (or consumer durables) where large corporations producing goods sold under brand names have vigorously and painstakingly created a monopolistically competitive market. Alternatively the formation of an international cartel may confer monopoly power on the seller. Such a cartel is most easily created where the total world supply of a particular commodity is in the hands of two or, at most, a few sellers. Instead of competing in all countries (including each other) the suppliers may form a cartel to apportion the world market between them. Each seller may then, within the group of countries allotted to him as market by the cartel, pursue a discriminatory price policy such as we have described.

The forms of cartel are many and varied. Their formation, life-cycle and degree of cohesion have been the subject of a considerable literature.[1] This is not our present concern. Suffice it to say here that it is the purpose of a cartel to obtain profits for the constituent firms in excess of what they might obtain under conditions of perfect competition and that this motivation has led to their repeated creation, particularly in international markets. The interwar period with its intense competition for a contracting volume of world trade was the 'golden' age of the cartel, and international trade in machine tools, electrical machinery, dyestuffs, chemicals and many other products was under their periodic influence. (We say 'periodic' because the cartel as a competition-suppressing and profit-apportioning body is inherently unstable. Cartels tend to break up, reform and reconstitute themselves according to the changing market strategies of members.) It has been estimated that about one-third of the total volume of international trade during the interwar period came under the direct influence of cartels.[2] In the post-war period, during which there has been continuous growth of world trade, cartelisation has not been so prevalent, but imperfection of international markets has almost certainly increased under the influence of the growing size of corporations. Transportation and communication have shrunk the world. Not more than twenty companies supply its automobiles, a smaller number its aircraft. The picture is similar in many industries. Price and market policies are obscured within the organisation of the conglomerates and multinational corporations. It is impossible to quantify the amount of market imperfection: it is equally impossible to escape the conclusion that it is considerable.

So far, we have been concerned with price discrimination by a seller. It is also possible for a large buyer to practice discrimination. To do this the buyer must be a monopsonist – that is, he must be a buyer (such as a giant corporation, or a state purchasing agency) whose demand is so large that by withdrawing it or switching it he influences price in the market. A large manufacturing corporation may buy its raw materials from only two or three suppliers, or in two or three markets. It will then as a monopsonist allocate its demand among these markets in order to minimise the cost. A diagram used by Kindleberger[3] demonstrates in Fig. 9.5 the principles which govern this allocation. Here it is the cost curves in each market, reflecting as they do the elasticity of supply, which are relevant to the choice. If the buyer shifts his demand from the market with the less elastic source of supply to that with the more elastic and pays a lower price in the former market then the total cost is reduced. The aim is to equalise the marginal cost in both markets. Fig. 9.5 illustrates this.

Noting that for the international monopsonist, who is a buyer, the marginal cost of obtaining his supplies must include transport cost we see

Commercial Policy

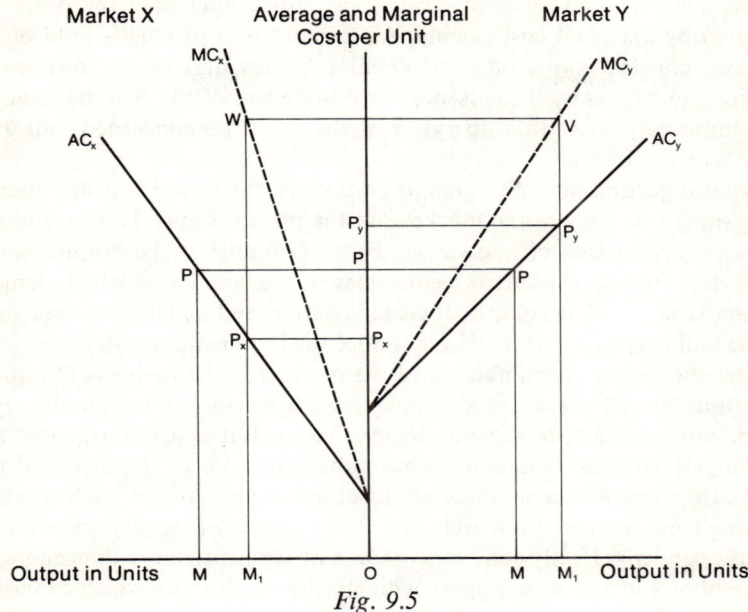

Fig. 9.5

that in Market X supply is less elastic than in market Y. At a constant price P in both markets, a demand of MM is allocated between the two markets with OM in each. By equalising marginal cost in the two markets which occurs at WV the same total demand is allocated differently between the two markets with OM_1 in each. Now, however, the price in market X is lower at P_x, while in market Y it is higher at P_y. The discriminating monopsonist, by shifting his demand from the less elastic to the more elastic source of supply, has improved his position.

The power of buyers and sellers, under imperfect competition, to fix their own price and the fact that the principle of profit maximisation indicates that they should fix it differently in different markets are of great significance for international trade. Many individual instances point to widespread discriminatory pricing policies. As might be expected when the export and home markets are of similar size there is a tendency for across-the-board pricing to occur. When the two markets differ in size, irrespective of which is the larger, discrimination appears. That there is considerable disparity in the price policies of exporting firms has been demonstrated by experience in both of the British devaluations, in 1949 and 1967. Some firms immediately reduced the foreign prices by the full percentage of the devaluation: others raised the domestic price and left the foreign price unchanged. No doubt many criteria influence pricing decisions other than the profit one dictated by marginal cost pricing. Assessment of a product's hold on the market, considerations of commercial relations and of the scrutiny of foreign governments, the closeness or remoteness of the two markets, the anti-monopoly legislation operative in the countries concerned—all these must play a role.

What objection may we make to price discrimination? Is it not after all a legitimate strategy of the market and the price system? To this question there can, for a lack of knowledge, be no firm answer. Discrimination of this type certainly exploits the consumer in the country in which demand for the product is least elastic. It curtails output and malallocates resources in the selling country. It may even induce the importing country to embark on the uneconomic manufacture of the product in the interests of import-substitution. All these are the standard objections to monopoly, upon which governments, in varying degree, frown. But is it not arguable that the imperfection of competition has come with size of the firm and that with size there are economies of scale and other savings such as those coming from increased research and development? It is very questionable whether under perfectly competitive trade we would do more than eliminate the textbook losses of monopoly while losing much more which cannot be evaluated. Discriminatory pricing, where and when it is practised, forms part of the behaviour pattern of large corporations, a pattern which is very inadequately analysed by the criteria of conventional marginal analysis and the theory of the firm.

(iii) Trade Practices and Their Effect on the Market

We now leave the more general implications of price discrimination, which arise from the size and number of firms and their market power and turn to an important particular case of international price discrimination—the practice of dumping. This term denotes the practice of selling on foreign markets at prices different from those charged to domestic consumers.

Let us clear up some ambiguities in nomenclature. The term dumping, originally used to denote the sending of goods abroad, at any price, in order to support the home price, came to be used, particularly in the twenties and thirties, as a blanket term covering every type of trading abuse, real or imaginary, associated with foreign competition. To some extent this aura of uncertainty and odium still surrounds it. Jacob Viner, author of the seminal work on the topic,[4] is firm in his definition: 'Dumping is price-discrimination between two markets.' It would appear from the Viner definition that the practice so defined subdivides. Dumping, pure and simple, occurs when goods are sold abroad at a price below that of the home market: 'reverse' dumping occurs when the foreign price is above that of the home market. For the sake of completeness there is a third form of price discrimination, which is that described in section (i), in which the seller discriminates not between home and abroad but between two or more foreign markets. This dual pricing policy has been discussed above and we will not pursue it further.

For dumping to take place certain conditions must be satisfied. The first of these is that goods sold abroad at a price below the domestic price cannot be shipped back to the home market for resale. If the price differential is narrow transport costs will, in all probability, prevent this, but if they do not, other devices may be employed. If the support of government is to be had, and if the dumping is a long-term policy, then a tariff may be imposed to prevent re-entry. In default of this the selling agents abroad may be bound by agreement not to return their unsold stocks to the source. The second necessary condition is that the seller should have a monopoly or monopolistically competitive position on the home market. If he has not such a position then he is unable to influence the price for the product but is forced rather to accept the price determined by the market. How the imperfection of competition is created is theoretically unimportant – whether by size, product differentiation or the creation of a cartel. The ability to control price is the strategic factor.

Dumping may take various forms. We adopt a threefold classification.[5]

Sporadic dumping takes place when the 'leftovers' from the home market are exported at the close of a selling period. This is usually indulged in by firms which have no great interest or commitment in foreign markets but who realise that the greater elasticity of foreign demand may relieve them of excess stocks.

Intermittent dumping is the periodic sale abroad of goods at a price below the home price. Its purposes may be various: to gain a foothold in a foreign market (sometimes referred to as 'predatory' dumping), to retain a long-held position in face of new competition, to eliminate or discipline a competitor, or simply to maintain a monopoly by preventing the entry of new suppliers. Such belligerent selling policies have implications which deter their use. The importing country may impose a tariff to end the dumping, and in these days of consumer vigilance the practice may soon draw such adverse publicity as to make it unprofitable. During the interwar years, however, such dumping was common.

Long-period dumping may have beneficial results for the seller when it enables his plant to be continuously used to full capacity, or even for new plant to be used, which lowers average cost and thus increases profit on the home market. In this case the home price must remain above marginal cost and the price in the foreign market at least must equal marginal cost. Such dumping is most often found in the expansion phase of industries in which great economies are to be had from size. It may also occur when the selling firm regards prices in the home and foreign markets as a means of allocating the two main elements of cost. If average variable costs are low relative to average total costs, and if average fixed costs can be covered by home market sales, then further sales in the foreign market, so long as they are above marginal costs, will increase the profits of the firm. Long-period dumping may be greatly encouraged when the state itself takes a hand and grants an export subsidy to the seller, thus enabling him to support what would otherwise be a loss on foreign market sales.

Attitudes towards dumping are confused. The term has too many overtones in the public mind and value judgements upon it come thick and fast. Moreover, it overlaps two other areas of controversy in which there is often more heat than light: the free trade versus protection argument, and the problem of monopoly versus competition. The view of the latter necessarily conditions the whole approach to dumping. If one takes the view that monopoly and imperfection of competition are undesirable, one regards dumping as one more obnoxious manifestation of market imperfection. If one takes the perhaps more realistic view that imperfect competition is a fact of life, must be lived with and has mixed results, then dumping becomes a phenomena in itself to be judged and dealt with separately.

It is most severely judged by free traders who claim, quite rightly, that, the country with a liberal trade policy leaves its nationals open to dumping while in a protectionist world, they themselves cannot dump on any significant scale. Britain, which remained a virtually free-trade country until 1932, claimed that she suffered much from the dumping of her competitors, particularly Germany. What is not said, however, is that a country is not necessarily adversely affected by cheap imports. Her nationals may in fact be advantaged provided the flow of imports continues. As Haberler points out, 'it makes not the slightest difference from the standpoint of the importing country whether the goods come in cheaply because the exporting country enjoys a natural comparative advantage or because they are dumped, nor does it matter in the least whether the dumping is due to monopoly abroad or to export bounties given by the foreign government or by some other body. Not one of these circumstances disturbs the fundamental free trade argument. They are significant only in so far as they indicate whether or not the cheap imports are likely to continue.'[6]

Commercial Policy

The adverse effects of dumping seem to lie most in the structural stresses it can create in the importing country's industry when it is discontinuous. Production is altered one way to accommodate the imports when they begin; another way when they cease. Industries may be established to use or market the cheap imports, and may be left high and dry if they cease. When the dumped goods are consumer goods, the structure of demand may be induced to alter when they first appear and later have to reverse itself when the supply ceases.

Some of the deleterious effects of dumping are more hypothetical than real. It is arguable whether, if prolonged dumping is practised by a monopoly or cartel to eliminate competition within the importing country in order to bring it within the monopoly, the ultimate effect on the importer is disadvantageous. The argument is true but the circumstances are unlikely. A prolonged price war of this type would be expensive to the attacker, who might in any event be robbed of the fruits of victory in the end by the imposition of a tariff by the government of the importing country.

What are the implications of dumping for the exporting country? The immediate answer is that it is advantageous only if it reduces the price of the dumped goods to the domestic buyer. But this is unlikely, for this will occur only if the supplier is operating under conditions of falling marginal cost. If, as is more likely, the supplier is producing under increasing marginal costs, the dumping will raise the producer's domestic selling price and increase the spread between the home and the foreign price.

It is not necessarily a condemnation of dumping, even if it does raise the home price. Most exports can be said to raise the home price in that if they were directed to the home market the price there would fall. The real comparison lies between the effects of the rise in price to consumers on the one hand (measured by a loss of consumers' surplus) and the rise in the profits of the producer on the other — a comparison which cannot be easily made.

The case for or against dumping is indecisive on purely theoretical grounds. In its essence it is the case for or against discriminating monopoly practised by a firm in international trade. To achieve its equilibrium position the firm dumps its product, that is, it discriminates between home and foreign buyers. A protective tariff does this too. But a tariff is government imposed and lofty-sounding reasons will be forthcoming to defend it. The motivation of a firm (or group of firms) pursuing the practice for profit appears to be judged somewhat differently. That dumping is frowned upon by governments is apparent from the anti-dumping tariffs, quotas, domestic subsidies — devices employed by governments against goods said to be dumped from abroad. It is perhaps worth asking whether the impediments to trade which these anti-dumping measures undoubtedly constitute are not more deleterious in the long run than the practice they seek to eliminate.

There is a further infringement of international price competition to be examined – the subsidising of exports by the government. Export subsidies are diverse in form but they have a common purpose: to assist firms operating in the export market, strengthening their competitive position both at home and abroad by enabling them to sell abroad at prices lower than cost conditions would, in the absence of subsidy, permit. The theoretical implications are clearly shown by Haberler in his back-to-back import–export diagram which he uses to illustrate the effects of a tariff and of an export subsidy.[8] It is a useful exercise to compare the two diagrams, since an export subsidy and a tariff are exactly opposite in their effects. Fig. 9.6 demonstrates the effect of a subsidy on the home and foreign prices.

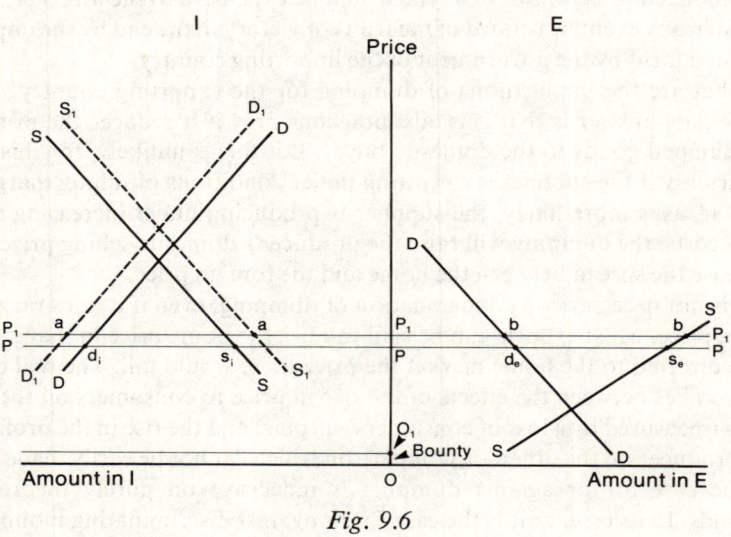

Fig. 9.6

Country E is the exporter, country I the importer. The supply and demand situation in I, is, for demonstration purposes, turned around and placed back-to-back with the diagram for E. When trade takes place E will be the exporting country since the price in E is lower than in I. With trade the price will rise in E and fall in I. If we assume that there are no transport costs and that there is free trade between the two countries, they will form one market within which there is one price. This price will be that at which the total demand and supply of the two countries taken together is equal. At the new price P supply in E exceeds demand by $d_e s_e$ and this excess supply

Commercial Policy

exactly equals the amount, $d_i s_i$ by which demand exceeds supply in I. $d_e s_e$ is, therefore, exported by E and imported by I.

Suppose now that a bounty is paid by E to exporters. Producers in E look upon the bounty as being an increase in the price to be had by selling in I. The whole curve system in I is raised by the amount of the bounty OO_1 and new demand and supply curves DD_1 and SS_1 parallel to the pre-bounty curves result. A new price line such that the sector of it between the two E curves equals that between the two new I curves must result. Such a price line is P_1P_1 on which aa imports in I are equal to bb exports from E.

The results of the bounty are evident. In E production and exports have been increased, while in I output has been reduced and imports increased. Abroad the price has fallen, at home it has risen; the difference between the two prices is equal to the amount of the bounty. More of the product is sold abroad, less is sold at home.

It should be remembered that such a bounty on exports must be accompanied by a duty (or some form of direct embargo) on re-entry. If it is not, and if the bounty exceeds the 'there-and-back' cost of transport, the commodity will simply return to the home market and the export bounty acts as a bounty on production. In this case the home supply curve would be lowered, the home price would fall and home sales increase. Abroad the effects on price and on sales would be similar to those of an export bounty.

Turning to practical aspects of export subsidies, two matters claim attention: the forms which such subsidies may take and their appraisal as a device of commercial policy. As to form, a preliminary distinction must be made between pure and compensatory export subsidies. The former are subsidies designed to encourage commodities in the export market although these commodities are in no way uncompetitive with their foreign competitors. The latter are designed to compensate an exporting industry for burdens it may bear, through domestic taxation or other impositions.

Apart from this basic distinction, there are four common ways by which exports may be subsidised. The simplest is that whereby the exporter receives a direct payment by the government on completion of an export sale. Such a payment may be based on the volume of sales or it may be *pro rata* to the difference between the export price and the exporter's average cost. A second and indirect form of subsidisation occurs when the government or a state agency buys commodities from domestic producers at fixed prices and then 'dumps' these in foreign markets at prices below those in the domestic. A third and common form of subsidy comes through artificially low freight rates made possible by government subsidy of the shipping (or shipbuilding) industry. Finally exporters may receive tax concessions. They may be exempted from or reimbursed for certain business taxes. Such taxes raise the selling prices of finished commodities but since they are remitted only on export sales, subsidies in this form discriminate against the domestic consumer to whom prices are not reduced. Indeed, it is arguable that the domestic consumer is doubly penalised: he is discriminated against pricewise, and, as a taxpayer, he has to bear the burden of the subsidy as well.

Although export subsidies may present an immediate appeal to the economic politician seeking a strong balance of payments, it must be remembered that they should be judged, as tariffs are, as a force which diverts trade from its optimum comparative cost channels. Their immediate appeal is to the neo-mercantilist: exports are encouraged, the balance of payments strengthened, the subsidies accrue at home and increase domestic income. These are immediately attractive and vote-catching attributes. But against them must be set the diversion of trade from the pattern appropriate to comparative costs. Either they lead the economy to produce products which, in the absence of a subsidy, could be obtained more cheaply abroad, or they induce firms producing for export to expand output into the spectrum of increasing average costs: both undesirable distortions. A further powerful argument against subsidies is that, like tariffs, they spawn intervention with the normal flows of trade. The subsidising country, in order to prevent re-entry, must impose a tariff. The foreigner, to protect himself against subsidised low-price goods, may also resort to protection. Since export subsidies are often used for balance-of-payments purposes, they may in turn induce direct balance-of-payments controls in the countries which have to prevent artificially stimulated imports.

We may conclude this appraisal of export subsidies on a note of guarded censure. The general free-trade argument condemns them as detrimental to general welfare. Like sin, they are undesirable in a well-ordered world. But sin is tolerated to some degree and may even be justified. In accordance with second-best arguments and in view of their wide variety and manifold application it is hard to condemn export subsidies right out of hand. Individual instances have to be examined on their merits.

(iv) State Trading

The basic characteristic of state trading is that the normal forces of the price system in international trade are replaced by a pattern in which prices are fixed by state decision in accordance with a wide variety of motives. Instead of the trade pattern being determined by prices, costs and the relative strengths of demands, decisions on the desirable volumes, directions

Commercial Policy

and content of trade are taken by governments, and prices are used actively or passively, in accordance with these overall aims.

Perhaps this assertion rather over-intellectualises and indeed over-stresses the place of trade in a collectivist environment. In the great spread of state trading which has taken place since the Second World War, both in the Communist world and elsewhere, the formation of trade policies has been largely *ad hoc*. Governments have been preoccupied with the domestic aspects of collectivisation, with the planning problems, the sectoral balance and the rate of industrial growth, and to these trade has had to accommodate itself. At first the Soviet Union regarded economic autarky as the aim of its trade policy. Later, after the Second World War, when the Eastern European countries became collectivist, this policy had to be revised. There is, however, a strong element of opportunism about socialist trade policies and generalisations have to be treated with reserve.

Complete state trading means that there is a monopoly of both the import and export trade of a country. Even if the state trading is on one side only there is some element of monopoly: if the exporting is done by a state agency then there is monopoly on the supply side; if the importing is a state preserve there is monopsony, in that, for that country, there is one buyer only. In any event, state trading produces many of the monopolistic features outlined earlier in this chapter. It may be, of course, that state trading extends to only a few commodities and that the bulk of trade remains free and under the influence of the price system. Even in the mixed economies state-trading agencies are common.

State trading works through a variety of devices, but two are almost universal: the bulk purchase agreement and the bilateral trade agreement. Under the bulk purchase agreement the importer agrees to purchase a certain quantity of a commodity annually from the supplier. It is claimed for such agreements that they provide an element of assurance for both producer and consumer, that they enable long runs in production, and that they reduce price fluctuation. Against these advantages (which do not always materialise in practice) must be set the losses of foregoing trade according to the pattern of comparative advantage.

Bilateral trading agreements are another vehicle of state trading. They provide for the mutual exchange of stipulated quantities (by value or volume) of products. The Soviet Union may agree to supply to Roumania x tractors in return for y tons of fertilisers. Prices will probably be stipulated or the value of imports and exports will be defined in terms of the foreign currency outlay in each case.

It would appear then that there are various facets or levels of state trading which we would do well to distinguish at the outset. These are:

1. trade involving state agencies in mixed economies, e.g. the importing of wines by the provincial liquor control boards in Canada, and the export sales of grain by the Wheat Board;
2. trade between a fully collectivised state, buying and selling through state agencies, and private enterprise units in a mixed economy; and
3. trade between two fully collectivised states.

1. The first of these forms of state trading goes back a long way. In many countries state monopolies for certain commodities — tobacco and alcohol — were established in the nineteenth century, and in some they persist to the present. The provincial governments of Canada, while deploring sin in all forms, have long institutionalised for their profit the healthy thirst of Canadians by selling alcohol only through outlets owned and controlled by the liquor boards, which thus become the operators of a great state-trading chain, the buying side of which makes them large (but not always well-informed) importers. Whatever may have been the original reasons for the creation of such state-trading monopolies they have become profit maximisers, buying in the cheapest market and selling in the dearest. In the Havana Charter, drawn up (but never ratified) in 1948 to establish the International Trade Organisation, a rule was included to enshrine the principle that state buying organisations should buy at the lowest price available, regardless of source, and sell at the highest or at the going market price. They should not protect home industry by buying, where possible, at home, even at a higher price than substitute goods are available abroad.

State buying agencies became numerous and were the typical agency of international trade in wartime Britain. Then, and for some years after the war, importing was carried on in terms of bulk purchase on long-term contract. Theory had it that such contracts would lead to long runs in production, or to assured markets for suppliers, which would reduce unit costs and prices. Unfortunately, there is also a theory of monopsony which enabled the state buying agency to use its power as sole (or dominant) buyer and each re-negotiation of contract became a tough bargaining session with a trial of strength between buyer and seller. In fact, there was probably more uncertainty about prices than would have occurred under normal trading by private buyers and sellers. In 1951, when a Conservative government came to power in Britain, there was a reversion to private trading and a sharp reduction in trade participation by public agencies, although state trading remained a considerable feature — if only because of the size of the public sector.

Apart from state agencies, permanently engaged in particular forms of business, governments are themselves major purchasers for their own use.

No code governs their operations in this sphere. They often buy at home rather than abroad and in the past their policies in this respect have varied with time and circumstance. The 'Buy British' campaign in the thirties was presented to the public as an anti-depression programme and reflected the same protectionist sentiment which made the Ottawa Agreement and the Empire Preference system of 1932. The United States has long had a 'Buy American' motif in its official purchasing programmes in which a specific percentage is laid down for home purchases. This has varied over the years, averaging 25 per cent in the protectionist thirties, falling to 10 per cent in the fifties and rocketing to 50 per cent in the face of balance-of-payments deficit in the sixties. There is here the application of a double standard in the matter of protection as between the public and private sectors. The former by its buy-at-home policy practises a form of covert protection; the latter is subject to a protective policy which is open for universal inspection and must conform to the standards of GATT and the IMF.

2. Trade between private enterprise economies with their many buying and selling units in a private sector on the one side and fully collectivist economies operating through state-trading agencies on the other, presents a variety of problems, most of which have been exhibited since the Second World War in the record of East-West trade. One fundamental problem in such a trading relationship as this is that on the one side there are profit-maximisers, motivated accordingly: on the other we have large buying and selling agencies motivated by many things, some political, some economic. There are inevitable difficulties of practice, understanding, and communication between them. Perhaps the fundamental problem to the private enterprise seller is that he is unaware, in such circumstances, of what advantages his product possesses because the buyer's motivation is not revealed to him. He cannot have choices or bargains because he does not know the elements of choice. So far as trade with that country is concerned, the state buyer is an enigmatic monopsonist, prepared to exploit that position. In East-West trade, Western nations have experienced such difficulties in varying degree. The United States, with its total restriction on trade with Communist China and Cuba and its restricted lists of products for trade with the Soviet Union, has been on the fringe of these problems, but Western European countries, both in trade with the Soviet Union and with satellites like Poland and Czechoslovakia, have experienced them to the full. It is true to say that here the limitation on East-West trade has not been entirely on political grounds but has encountered other impediments to growth. One of the greatest of these is uncertainty. The future policies of the Eastern buying and selling agencies are unknown. Sales of a given commodity may be

curtailed or stopped without warning, with dire consequences to the Western buyers. This is particularly a danger in that Eastern selling is often 'distress selling' of surpluses which may cease when the surpluses have been exhausted. Equally, Eastern purchases, upon which a Western seller has come to rely, may suddenly cease, leaving no prospect of an alternative market.

On the Eastern side the impediments to trade with the West have been strong. First among them has been procurement. Eastern countries have not had much in the way of disposable surpluses for foreign sale except in product lines in which the West were marginal buyers. The surpluses available, mainly of primary products, have often not been acceptable in exchange for technical capital goods, particularly when Western countries have been well aware that Eastern bloc technology conserves its sparse exportable surpluses of machinery, machine tools and electronics for military aid to selected developing and Soviet satellite countries. A second problem for Eastern buyers has been credit. With debts to be settled in Western currencies, the burden of borrowing the foreign exchange falls on the East, while Western sellers have often been uncertain of the credit risk involved.

3. The last case of state trading, that of trade between socialist countries, must be dealt with briefly. It falls in part in the field of international economics, in part in the field of economic strategy and its relations to national political aims. We abstract from the latter.

In examining the problem of trade within a group of socialist states we must ask ourselves similar questions to those which we ask (and which for better or worse the pure theory of international trade answers) concerning trade among states trading within the price system, namely:

 (i) What goods should be traded?
 (ii) In what quantities should they be traded?
 (iii) At what prices should trade take place?
 (iv) How may the value of goods exported equal the value of those imported for each country on a multilateral group basis?

To these we should, in the case of socialist states, add a further question,

 (v) How may these states reconcile whatever answers they may give to (i), (ii) and (iii) with the trade motivation of their political policies?

It is worth glancing briefly at the answers which seem to be made to these questions.

At the outset, and in approaching the first three questions, it must be remembered that trade in a socialist economy tends to be subsidiary in importance. It is perhaps surprising that, despite their area, population and industrial magnitude, UN statistics reported that, in the period 1960–5, only about 12 per cent of world trade was directly with the Communist world. From UN data it appears also that, for Communist countries, foreign trade is less significant relative to GNP than it is in Western countries. The overall economic plan in socialist countries is defined in terms of output targets and stocks and flows of materials. In this matrix trade must necessarily take its place. The absolute natural advantages of individual countries will of themselves assure this. But, for the most part imports will be regarded as desirable in order to achieve output and comply with the plan, and exports will be a matter of products which are surplus to it. This may determine the trade content of individual countries but how does it produce a viable trade structure in a group of several socialist countries each similarly trade motivated? A group of ten socialist countries each striving mightily to import vital foodstuffs, materials and products and to pay for them with an offer of unwanted surpluses is hardly likely to produce more than a tangle of *ad hoc* agreements representing a very partial satisfaction and a trade structure with no durability, subject to continual revision.

This is the picture which in fact seems to emerge from the trade of the Soviet Union and the Eastern European countries in the post-war period. In the interwar period, when the Soviet Union was the sole collectivist power, its limited participation in trade was clearly aimed at achieving an eventual condition of self-sufficiency. Primary products were offered in return for capital equipment for Soviet industrial development. Despite shortages of some commodities in the Soviet Union the system appears to have worked. But in the post-war period there emerged, in addition to the Soviet Union, a sizable group of collectivist powers – the Eastern European countries, the Chinese People's Republic and later Cuba. Within this enlarged group trade was now regarded as desirable.

It was progressively realised among Eastern European countries that autarky and unco-ordinated economic growth produced many problems. Prominent among these was shortage of raw materials, with which Eastern Europe is not richly endowed. The necessity to produce a co-ordinated plan for the raw-materials base to serve industrial expansion pointed to trade, not to autarky. In promoting this trade the difficulties we have described above at once appeared. COMECON (The Council for Mutual Economic Aid), the trade organisation of the Eastern Bloc, founded in January 1949, has sought in vain to provide a stable pattern for Eastern trade. The choice of what to export and import, pricing and multilateral clearing within the group – all oppress this organisation.

Pricing has been a major problem. The Soviet Union had established the practice in the interwar period of trading at world prices, and the

Eastern bloc sought to adopt this method. But what had been workable with a narrow range of goods proved much more difficult for the much wider range of commodities and products which were now involved. Problems of definition and comparison arose as trade in differentiated products began. For example, how should an Eastern bloc automobile traded between Russia and Poland be priced? If the world price method was to be adopted, with what automobile on the world market was the Russian product to be compared? In the case of bulk goods in Eastern trade, little help was to be had from the world price which was certain to contain a large transport cost and probably a price-support element. With such difficulties to meet it is not surprising that Eastern bloc prices have given an appearance of considerable disarray. Often it is apparent that higher intra-bloc prices rule for goods than those at which they are exported outside the group. What causes this is obscure and many possibilities come to mind. What is certain is that it leaves the Eastern bloc countries as open to charges of price discrimination, dumping and other universally decried practices as their capitalist neighbours.

Another aspect of the pricing problem is that it bemuses the choice of what goods to trade. Trade and the choice of traded goods in Western countries depend upon the comparisons of real economic values that come to us through the price system. But in Eastern bloc countries these are lacking, or are at best obscured. Prices in these countries include a large taxation element which has to be adjusted for foreign trade, that is added to imports and subtracted from exports, so that it may take place even at nominal exchange rates. Another difficulty in price determination lies in deciding the prices of factors. If, for example, capital is underpriced, as it usually is as a factor, then capital-intensive goods would be low priced and would tend to be exported, while labour-intensive goods would tend to be overpriced and be imported — a trade structure which would be undesirable to almost all the Eastern countries. Meanwhile, in default of a satisfactory price structure reflecting real values, the choice of goods for trade is made arbitrarily and is constantly changing. Surpluses and shortages, political and economic strategy, foreign demand and willingness to meet it — all these exist and alternate in deciding the pattern of Eastern bloc trade.

Part Three

The Economics of the Balance of Payments

'Sometimes we need repetition of the obvious rather than elaboration of the obscure.'
ADLAI STEVENSON

Part Three

The Economics of the Balance of Payments

I The Description and Measurement of Payments

10
The Elements of an International Monetary System

(i) The Four Elements

IT is the purpose of this and subsequent chapters to lay bare and examine the working of the international monetary system. In setting out the general principles of its operation there is a great and constantly growing body of theory, much of which is of recent vintage, for theory in this field has tended to follow and seek solutions to the great international monetary problems of the interwar and post-war periods. Some of this theory, such as the theory of the gold standard, is a carry-over from the classical economics of the nineteenth century; some of it, as, for example, absorption theory, is an application in an international setting of the newer income theory of macro-economics which came to us from the Keynesian model of the domestic economy. Finally, some theory has been distilled from observation and a deepening understanding of international monetary institutions and currency systems. To approach this formidable array is a daunting task in which the only consolation is that probably no attempt to classify, codify, or simplify can be wholly adequate. The one which is followed in this and later chapters makes no effort to be encyclopaedic. It is pragmatic and aims at a wide view of the country. With a map of reasonable accuracy the student's knowledge can be deepened by progressive exploration.

First a warning. Any attempt to present an overall view of the international monetary system has the drawback that it presents it primarily as a system, as a structure of interlocking parts, a mechanism whose operation can be understood and, at least in some measure, anticipated. This is the cost of oversimplification. But in fact, the international economy and its monetary system are conglomerates, the results of diverse systems of growth and development in which the participants are for the most part unaware of any behaviour conditioned by a system as such. We talk of an international monetary system, yet this is an aggregate of many national monetary systems whose relationships have, at least until very recently, been conditioned mainly by a few institutional contacts and practices operating under conditions of trial and error. Only since the Second World War has the concept of an international economy crept into the mental consciousness of bankers, economists, politicians and international civil servants. It gains strength daily in their thinking, planning and ideas, but probably they imbue it with a greater integration, cohesion and self-consciousness than is in fact its due. With the conscious risk that we shall continue this error, we proceed.

The international monetary system is an integral part of what we have come to call 'the international economy', that is, of the total economic relations between the participant countries of the world — commercial flows of goods and services between countries, movements of factors between them, and the institutions, both national and international, which exist to service these flows and interrelationships. Within this structure of relationships the international monetary system is concerned with flows of current and capital funds, and with the relationships between national currencies, monetary systems and central banks. This system has a certain loose cohesion through the relations of monetary institutions in different countries, through a community of interest such as that which exists among central bankers and through a consciousness of the existence of common problems. It is not unrealistic to speak of an 'international monetary community' and to regard it as part of the framework through which the international monetary mechanism works.

The existence of such an international monetary community can be seen from about 1870 onwards. From then until the present its nature, sense of community and cohesion have varied from period to period. In the years 1870 to 1914, in the period of the international gold standard, the standard functioned through procedures and operations tacitly agreed upon among the central bankers of a few leading countries. In the interwar period cohesion was shattered and the community disrupted by a variety of forces, predominantly the intrusion into the monetary sphere of the operations and policies of national governments. During this period of collapse of the gold standard it is hard to see more than vestigial traces of the old pre-1914 financial community. In the post-war period the community has had a great resurgence, partly in the work of international organisations, but perhaps more powerfully in the central bank co-operation which has, through organisations like the Basle Club, sought to strengthen key currencies.

An international monetary system must have four elements. These are:

The Economics of the Balance of Payments

firstly, a form of international money which may be used by countries within the system for clearing residual balances with other countries and in which reserves against this contingency may also be held; secondly, institutional arrangements in the form of interrelated banking systems, money markets, foreign exchange markets and the like, through which flows of international money may pass throughout the system; thirdly, a method whereby the distribution of international money can be adjusted by action upon the balances of payments of participant countries; and finally, some power to control the working of international monetary arrangements. These elements have their parallel in domestic monetary systems where a money form, a banking system, a credit policy to control flows of funds, and a central bank to implement monetary policy form the essential structure of the system. In the international economy, however, the elements function differently and have only a remote family resemblance to those of the domestic system.

The four elements of the international monetary system will be considered in their many facets in Part Three of this book. Around some of them imposing bodies of theory have already developed. This theory is, broadly, of two types: theory which generalises the relations of the working elements of the system and which within a rigorous framework provides a model of the working components of the system; and a theory of economic policy, which examines how the components may be manipulated in order to achieve various policy aims. In this chapter we will do no more than provide some introduction to the elements themselves and their interrelationships, and let the reader become familiar with the characters who later will dominate the stage. We shall deal with each in turn.

(ii) The Forms of International Money

As forms of international money there have been historically, and now are in coexistence, three: gold; the currencies of certain important trading countries; and the liabilities of international monetary organisations, at present the International Monetary Fund. These are used between monetary authorities of countries for the clearing of final balances in international payments because they possess the widest acceptability and are the recognised forms of what we have come to call 'international liquidity'. Since the demand for international liquidity is for the clearing only of residual balances, the amount of required international liquidity in the system is not primarily determined by the volume of international transactions but rather by the degree of balance or imbalance as between countries in international payments. The need for international liquidity is minimal when balances of payments between countries are in balance, and at its greatest when they require large flows of funds to preserve their balance. This point will be developed in Chapter 20. For the present, residual balances are those remaining in balances of payments after all unregulated current and capital transactions have taken place and which are required to maintain equality of supply and demand for currencies in the exchange markets if existing exchange rates are to be preserved. If $(E - M) + (FB - FL) + AF \equiv O$ in the balance-of-payments identity, then AF will be large or small according to the extent that $(E - M)$ and $(FB - FL)$ are equal but of opposite sign. (Where $E =$ value of exports of goods and services, M the value of imports of goods and services, FB the value of foreign borrowing, FL the value of foreign lending and AF the value of accommodating flows.) Alternatively, we may follow Robert Mundell and say that if B_i denotes the balance of regular transactions of country i and B_t the balance of settling transactions then the balance of payments identity is $B_i + B_t \equiv O$. Mundell's B_i is the same as our $(E - M) + (FB - FL)$, which spells out the elements of regular balance; his B_t is the same as our AF.[1] The demand for international liquidity in the international monetary system is therefore determined by two forces: the total volume of international payments, and the degree of imbalance in international payments.

Historically, three forms of international money have been used. Gold (and to a much smaller extent silver) was the dominant form until 1914. Used as domestic money in many economies, it was fully convertible into most of the leading trading currencies and served, therefore, between countries as a common denominator whose possession was a prerequisite to a transfer into all gold-based currencies. Even in the high summer of the international gold standard (between 1870 and 1914), however, it was common for international trading balances to be held for convenience in currencies whose gold value was regarded as certain and which were the currencies of great trading countries, balances of which were earned and accepted as payment in foreign trade transactions. Before the First World War sterling was the main example of such key currencies but, in the interwar period, it was joined by the United States dollar. Moreover the great growth in the value of world trade relative to the world supply of gold (in the interwar period this growth was, of course, in price terms and resulted mainly from the great inflation of prices during the 1914–1918 war) had produced fears of a gold shortage which led to the adoption in the twenties of a gold-exchange standard under which gold-backed currencies as well as gold itself served as international media. This system, with certain variants, was re-established after the Second World War. The arrangements embodied in the Bretton Woods Agreement of 1944 ensured the continuance of the role of gold and the use of international currencies, of which the U.S. dollar has been, in the post-war period, the most important.

The third form of international money did not appear until after the Second World War when, with the establishment of the IMF, currency balances of that organisation were, under certain limiting conditions, usable by member countries to supplement their own reserves of gold and key currencies. Such balances are severely restricted in scope as compared with gold or key currencies (a) because they are only available to members of the Fund; (b) because they are, apart from an initial drawing right, available to members only on progressively stringent conditions; and (c) because the Fund's ability to supply particular currencies is limited to its holdings of those currencies. It is therefore arguable that Fund drawing rights are dubiously inclusive in the list of international money forms; but on the other side, it may be argued that *de facto* countries do so include them and that their use in practice as a means of meeting balance of payments deficits entitles them to inclusion as a constituent part of international liquidity.

More recently, in April 1968, the purposive creation of a new form of international money under the Special Drawing Rights provision has greatly augmented the IMF's contribution to total international liquidity, making this third category of international money more important both in quantity and status than was formerly the case. Moreover, the acceptance in the Special Drawing Rights provisions of the principle that international money can be created by the IMF in amounts sufficient to meet the growth of world trade was a significant innovation in the international liquidity field. Earlier forms of international money, gold and key currencies, are cash forms, actual bullion or currency balances earned in international transactions. In contrast, SDRs as a creation of the IMF represent for the first time a banking-credit element in international final settlements. Up to 1968 the Fund's balances were amounts deposited by its members, but they now include an element of credit creation by which the international organisation can add to international liquidity by the purposive creation of internationally acceptable drawing rights. With this innovation, the international monetary system has taken a sizeable step forward, moving from the primitive nineteenth-century practice of using only cash money to the more sophisticated modern banking principle of creating deposits *pari passu* with the expanding needs of the international economy.

(iii) The Institutional Arrangement of International Finance

The second element of the international monetary system which claims attention is the set of institutional arrangements through which it functions. Many countries form the international economy, each country with its currency, its centralised banking system and its financial markets. Some rank high in importance playing a formative role; others are of minimal significance and must take the international monetary system as they find it.

In a world of many national currencies, it is essential both for current trade and for capital transactions to be able to move balances from one currency into another, buying the desired currency with another currency which, for the moment and for the purpose in hand, is less desired. The purchase or sale of a national money unit of one country against that of another is a foreign exchange transaction: the price of one currency unit in terms of another is referred to as an exchange rate. It is in effect, the price of a national currency unit in the international foreign exchange market.

Not all currencies are thus traded. The currencies of minor countries whose stake in international trade is small are little in demand, since their use for clearing debts owed to that country or for holding assets in it is limited. Many small countries are obliged to pay for their imports in the currency of the larger country from which they import; therefore, they will, in their turn, look for payment for their own exports in a currency which they can use to discharge their own debts. In practice a group of about twenty currencies has come to comprise the foreign exchange market, while the many other national currencies have domestic significance only.

The point can be carried further. Among the twenty or so leading world currencies there is a much smaller number which, for purposes of convenience, dominate the foreign exchange market. The transactions motive for holding such currencies rests on the volume of trade of the countries concerned; on the size, skill and probity of the banking systems and ancillary financial services which service them; on the degree of stability of the price level and the exchange rate for the currency; on the suitability of the currency as a vehicle for the holding of international reserves and on other less important factors. Such international currencies are not only great trading currencies but also are central in the making of international loans, the clearing of residual balances in countries' balances of payments, and the holding of national currency reserves. We may therefore loosely rank currencies as falling into one of three classes: first, national

The Economics of the Balance of Payments

currencies of limited international use, the currency being bought and sold in the exchange market only for purposes of travel within the country; second, currencies used in international trade predominantly for transactions purposes in clearing import and export payments, for travel, tourism and other such purposes; and third, international currencies used not only for transactions purposes but held also for speculative reasons and used as reserves by individual countries.

Moving from currency to currency involves a transaction in the foreign exchange market, an offer of one currency and a demand for another. An examination of what forces determine the currency prices, or exchange rates, must wait until Chapter 17. It is sufficient here to note the importance of the foreign exchange market in the international monetary system and some of the simpler aspects of its construction.

The foreign exchange market is a world market in titles to national monies. Formerly, it was a market in credit titles — bills of exchange of various tenor; nowadays, it is predominantly a market in demand deposits. This market is located in a number of world financial centres (New York, London, Zurich, Paris and Frankfurt are examples), in each of which currencies are bought and sold. In any given centre, say, New York, the buyers and sellers consist of foreign exchange dealers, the large commercial banks, the merchant banks, and probably the central bank of the country itself, operating in the market for various reasons but predominantly to influence the price of its own currency through its own buying and selling. Demands for and supply of foreign currencies from within the country concentrate in these institutions in main financial centres. In any given centre there is no necessity for the demand and supply of foreign exchange to be equal. If in New York there is a surplus of pounds, this surplus may be saleable in Paris or Amsterdam. It is the equality of aggregate demand and supply in all foreign exchange centres which is important and which is secured by the setting of such a price for a currency as will always clear demand and supply in this world market. The prices for a currency in the various centres of the exchange market will be equalised by the swift movement of balances from one centre to another in response to any price differentials. Telegraph and telephone make communication almost instantaneous between the centres.

Within each country engaging in international trade and finance, the banking system or at least some part of it must participate in the international monetary system. Even in small countries with minimal world trading interests whose currencies are not quoted in the exchange rate tables of the world, the commercial banking system will be engaged in remittance business with other banks abroad and will handle foreign exchange business for tourists and for those with debts to settle outside the country. The central bank for its part will hold and administer whatever national reserves the country may possess. Elsewhere, in larger trading countries, whole sections of the banking system will be engaged in foreign exchange, remittance, and agency functions, while in great financial centres the domestic banking system is augmented by specialist banking and quasi-banking institutions, by merchant banks specialising in overseas business, and by branches of overseas banks carrying on banking, foreign exchange and financial activities within the financial centre for their own nationals. The existence within financial centres of this large group of international banking institutions holding large balances may influence and itself be influenced by the existence within the financial centre of money markets where surplus balances may be invested. Funds moving in and out of the centre may find temporary and highly liquid investment in bill markets, inter-bank loans markets or other outlets available in the centre. However, not all financial centres are well-endowed with such markets: London, with its short-loan call-money market, its inter-bank loan market and its local authority loan market is the best equipped. Finally, the largest financial houses of the centre will handle long-term investment capital either entering the country to the bond market or being sought within the country by foreigners in its new issues market.

Little has been said so far of the place in the international economy of central banks. For some countries with a small stake in international trade this is not surprising. The central bank of Chile, whatever it may be to the Chilean economy, is certainly not a powerful force in the international monetary scene. Yet size is clearly not the determining factor in every case; Switzerland's central bank, for example, is of great significance. Wherein lies the difference? The first factor is that whatever may be the country's foreign trade commitment, whatever may be the degree of simplicity or sophistication of its financial institutions, the central bank sets for the country the tone, stability and, for foreigners the degree of financial security, which are the *sine qua non* of deep participation in international finance. The dominance of London as a financial centre between 1870 and 1914 was greatly aided by the high standing of the Bank of England among the central banks of that period. In more recent times, the conservative policies of the Swiss National Bank and the apparent sureness of its touch in monetary matters have made Switzerland and its banks a leading repository for a great share of the world's liquid funds. True, in both these cases a great financial infrastructure lies behind the central bank, in the absence of which international financial activity would be small. Nevertheless by conditioning the climate, by itself operating with skill and

awareness of international needs, the central bank is an important factor.*
In a more practical sense the central bank has two functions of international significance. The first of these is the control of interest-rate policy, through its own bank rate, within its own country. Changes in interest rates and relative interest-rate levels have a great influence on flows of international funds and, in countries whose international stake is great, one of the skills of the central bank must be the manipulation of interest rates within the country so that both domestic and international monetary policy may be in accord.

The second practical task of the central bank which is of international significance is the control it exercises over the national currency reserves of its country and, through this, over its exchange rate. It is true to say that, while decisions as to the level of the exchange rate — whether to devalue or to revalue — are now semi-political decisions taken by the government with the monetary authorities as advisers, the day-to-day maintenance of the agreed rate is a central bank responsibility, the implementing of which implicates it in the banking system and the foreign exchange market.

It is not appropriate at this point to provide a detailed description of the central bank's administration of national currency reserves. It is sufficient for present purposes to say that the reserves of foreign currencies (and gold) are used by the central bank in the foreign exchange market to support the rate, i.e. to buy the home currency with the foreign currencies held in the reserve when there is an excess supply of the home currency on offer in the market. This will, of course, be when the balance of payments of the home country is in deficit or when for speculative reasons balances are being withdrawn from the currency.

(vi) The Need for an Adjustment Mechanism

The third necessity of an international monetary system is an 'adjustment mechanism'. While an international money serves to settle deficits and surpluses in the balance of payments when they arise, the adjustment mechanism is designed to minimise these movements, to check and correct them, and to invoke correctionary forces as disequilibrium arises. When a balance of payments moves into deficit, the ideal adjustment mechanism

---

* An example of this was the fostering and preservation by the Bank of England of the London discount market during the thirties. This was motivated by Montague Norman's belief in the market as one of the international aspects of the city of London.

retards that movement, checks it and restores it to balance. Needless to say, in an imperfect world such precision and swiftness is not attainable. If it were, it would not be necessary to provide international money at all, since such perfect adjustment would hold all balances of payments perpetually in balance with no residuals to clear. Yet, on the other hand, adjustment must be and is present in the international economy, for if it were not all international money would flow persistently to a few surplus countries and away from deficit countries, and thus ultimately the mechanism of payments would break down. So in fact, reality does approximate to the ideal. The adjustment in the system prevents this extreme maldistribution of international money on the one hand, but is, on the other, not so perfect as to render international liquidity dispensable.

The analysis of adjustment must wait until Chapters 12–16, but it is appropriate at this stage to glance briefly at the systems which have served the international economy during the past century. It is a short list of three: the international gold standard, free exchange markets and the hybrid system of 'managed flexibility'.

The gold standard was neither invented nor consciously planned. It grew steadily during the eighteenth and early nineteenth centuries, as countries from a choice of different metallic standards—silver, gold or bimetallic—adopted gold as the basis of their coinage and monetary system.

The gold standard was an English development. Following an uneasy period of bimetallism with silver between 1663 and 1798, when the coinage of silver was suspended, the Coinage Act of 1816 definitely established the gold standard, with the pound as the unit of account and a fixed value for gold in terms of sterling. After 1850 the French franc became a gold unit, so that the two great financial centres of London and Paris were from then on gold-based. In 1871 the German Empire made gold its standard and Switzerland and Belgium followed in 1878, virtually completing the gold standard in Western Europe. In the United States monometallism based on gold did not come until the Gold Standard Act of 1900. Thereafter gold was the basis of international payments among the leading countries until the First World War transformed the international economy which the standard had served.

The gold standard up to 1914 was a gold *coinage* standard which was in contrast to the gold *bullion* standard of the interwar period under which gold was no longer freely coined and did not serve as a national currency. Under the bullion standard only gold bullion was freely importable and exportable and a fixed price between this and the notes which circulated domestically secured a fixed exchange rate with the currencies of all countries operating a similar system. Under the coinage standard, however, gold coins circulated domestically and were interchangeable with notes at the central bank which held a gold reserve to maintain and safeguard convertibility. Whenever this reserve was threatened by an unduly heavy demand for gold to replace notes (for example, to make foreign payments) or whenever the reserve was increased by gold sold to the central bank in return for notes (e.g. gold received from abroad), then certain monetary techniques were available to the central bank to redress the undesired movement. When gold flowed out to meet a deficit in the country's balance of payments it reduced the monetary base within the country, and this would happen whether the standard was a coinage standard or a bullion standard. If under the former coins were exported, the monetary supply was *de facto* reduced by the amount of the export, if the system was a bullion standard where gold reserves bore a stated relation to note supply then reduction of the reserves would force a reduction of the money supply (the amount being determined by the ratio of reserves to note circulation). Directionally, the effect was the same, but the amount of the reduction of home money for the same export of gold would differ as between gold coinage and gold bullion standards.

According to the quantity theory of money an outflow of gold would tend to reduce prices relative to prices in other countries. This reduction of prices would reduce the price of exports and import-competing goods, improve the competitive position of the country, improve its balance of trade and adjust the original deficit. Put in another way, the principle of the gold standard was that differences between foreign receipts and payments for any country would be counterbalanced by such gold flows as would, by enlarging or depleting the monetary stock, produce appropriate price changes as to alter demand for the imports and exports of the countries concerned and thus correct the imbalance. In brief, the theory of adjustment which underlay the gold standard was one of the equalisation of prices internationally, gold movements preserving the distribution of the world's monetary supply in a way appropriate to this.

In the last years of the nineteenth century, the model of national price changes induced by gold flows in and out of central banks was supplemented by the argument that, for short-term balance of payments imbalance, changes in interest rates would produce an adjustment effect. When, for example, the Bank of England lost gold as a result of a British payments deficit, a rise in bank rate would draw short-term funds to London and give relief to the balance of payments. By 1914, the Bank of England had devised a bank-rate policy geared to such balance-of-payments control, and there was universal confidence that central banks by their interest rate policies could go far to control world movements of gold.

The First World War shattered the international economy within which the gold standard was the device for balance-of-payments adjustment. When, after 1918, the painful task of reconstruction began, it gradually became apparent that changes so fundamental as to make rehabilitation of the gold standard impossible had taken place. In particular the price inflation of the war years had so increased the value of world trade as to cause fear that the world's gold supply would be inadequate for a gold standard of the pre-war type. The attempts which were made in the 1920s to re-establish a gold standard aimed, therefore, at a so-called gold exchange standard, under which currencies held their central reserves, either in gold or in certain key currencies (in practice the pound or the United States dollar) which were convertible into gold. This system, advocated by the Genoa Conference of 1922, became the basis for the attempts by the leading powers to return to gold in the twenties. (The return to gold was made in April 1925 in the case of Britain; December 1926 by France; by Germany under the Dawes Plan in 1924; Norway in May 1928; Denmark in January 1927; and Italy in December 1927.) Britain restored the standard in 1925 and, after a struggle to maintain it, abandoned it in 1931. The United States, which had suspended the standard only during the war years, remained on it until 1934. Other leading countries of Western Europe, having returned to gold at various dates during the twenties, left it on the break-up of the Gold Bloc in 1936. In effect one manifestation of the economic malaise of the interwar period was this failure and eclipse of the gold standard as an international adjustment system.

It was replaced by what then seemed the only viable alternative, a free market for currencies in which exchange rates were allowed to fluctuate in accordance with supply and demand. From 1918 until the restoration of the gold standard and again after the collapse of gold, fluctuating exchange rates served as the adjustment system within the international economy. In the period from 1932 to 1939 progressively (and especially after 1936), the monetary authorities of individual countries operated in the foreign exchange market, their declared aim being to reduce the degree of fluctuations of their currencies by ironing out day-to-day fluctuations but allowing long-term influences to operate upon the exchange rate.

The link between a fluctuating exchange rate and the balance of payments is direct. A deficit in the balance of payments indicates that there is an excess demand for foreign currencies in the foreign exchange markets in terms of the home currency: the price of foreign currencies rises in terms of the home currencies, that is, the value of the home currency depreciates. Such a depreciation has the effect of cheapening exports of the home country and of increasing the price of its imports. For example, if the dollar were to depreciate from $3 = £1 to $5 = £1, then after the depreciation, American exports to Britain would be cheaper in that £1 now buys $5 worth of American goods, where previously it bought only $3. To Americans, a British import worth £1 which formerly cost $3 would now cost $5. American exports would be cheapened by 40 per cent; American imports from Britain would become dearer by 66 per cent. Assuming that demand for both imports and exports is sensitive to price changes the effect of the depreciation will be to increase exports and reduce imports, both of which changes have a beneficial effect on the balance of payments and tend to adjust the original deficit.

Thus far we have been talking about true mechanisms of adjustment, that is, sets of institutions or procedures built into the institutional framework of the international economy which act progressively on the elements of the balance of payments — in particular on the flows of imports and exports — so as to correct deficits or surpluses when they arise. It remains to mention that there is a third form of adjustment somewhat different to the two already described, namely, direct controls on the flows which comprise the balance of payments — either direct control by tariff, embargoes or quota restrictions on the goods flows, or direct monetary control of the financial flows.

The obvious fact about direct controls as an adjustment mechanism is that they do not provide adjustment at all, in the sense in which we have hitherto used the term. They merely contain the balance-of-payments deficit by reducing, by direct intervention, the effect of the elements which cause it. Since deficits springing from an excess of imports over exports are common, the most common form of control is that which reduces imports directly by limiting or prohibiting their entry.

Apart from their balance-of-payments effect, direct controls raise many questions which it is not our business to explore at this stage. In one aspect they are a part of the great controversy on tariffs and free trade, in another, of the problem of multilateral versus bilateral trade. In their theoretical aspects they cut across the monetary, pure theory, and welfare aspects of international trade. Some of these aspects have already been considered in earlier chapters. Perhaps the important thing to realise is that they are a legitimate feature of the international economy and not a species of authoritarian aberration on the face of an otherwise liberal and automatic equilibrium system.

(v) Leadership and Control of the International Economy

One final element of the international monetary system remains to be discussed, its leadership. Those elements we have described already have been functional and operational aspects of the working mechanism. Is there any feature, however, which gives the system cohesion, which welds it together and distinguishes it from a mere congeries of institutions or series of attributes unworthy of being described as a system at all? An affirmative answer to this question is important, because if it were negative not only would the very *raison d'être* of our concept of an international monetary system collapse, but the hopes of planning the future development of the international monetary system, which have, since 1944, occupied so much time and attention, would be unfounded.

The answer to the question must be rephrased and sought in the history of the international economy over the past hundred years, that is, since the improvements in transport and communications which took place in the 1870s made of the world one market for goods, established lines of movement and points of concentration for world monetary flows, and in greater or lesser degree changed the economic and monetary values of all countries of the world. From 1870 to 1914 the international gold standard dominated the international monetary scene, 1918 to 1939 was a period of swift change, improvisation and, at times, chaos; while the post-war period has seen co-operation among governments to solve *ad hoc* monetary problems, producing a pattern which is giving to the international economy control and management institutions of its own.

The control of the gold standard era was loose, undefined and unselfconscious. It consisted of two elements: in the broadest sense, the international fraternity of central bankers, who increasingly through common interests and policies evolved the rules of the gold standard game; and in a narrower sense, and at operational level, the Bank of England, which as a central bank, controlling the monetary policy of the strongest and most widely used gold-backed currency, was at least *primus inter pares* within this fraternity, the manager of the technical operation and evolution of the system. For the stage of development and the economic conditions of the times, this system of control was adequate. The strength of sterling and of the Bank of England was such that it possessed not only the power but the sanctions against defaulters which were necessary to make it effective.

In the interwar years these features were lacking. The gold standard had to be restored after the intermission of the First World War. Not only was there doubt as to who would control the system, there was doubt even as to what the system was to be. Moreover, the international financial fraternity which had administered the old gold standard had been wellnigh annihilated by the war and was to take long to recover. It was sovereign governments acting through international conferences such as that at Genoa in 1922 which sought to establish and to run the new gold standard. When the new standard came, it failed for many reasons, but one was the lack of any cohesive controlling force within itself. The Bank of England no longer possessed the power. Sterling was not strong enough, no longer the dominant and unassailable currency of the old days, to give the Bank the power to direct or sanction. No longer did central banks operate the system. Now it was 'monetary authorities', amorphous groups encompassing for each country much else than the central bank, in particular treasuries, ministries of finance and government forces in various admixtures, all bent on preserving national monetary policies and, in crises, national monetary survival. Thus, in one sense, the interwar monetary chaos reflected an absence of any effective form of direction in the international monetary system. Even after the breakdown of the gold standard in 1931, the period of flexible exchange rates which followed, until 1939, was characterised by such intense rivalry and efforts by Britain and the United States to manipulate and influence the exchange market for their own ends, as to underline even more heavily the lack of central control in the international monetary sphere.

Even though international monetary co-operation, the growth of international organisations and the return of cohesion to the international monetary scene belongs to the post-war years, it had its beginnings in the anarchy of the thirties. The Gold Bloc, consisting of eight countries — France, Belgium, Italy, Holland, Switzerland, Luxembourg, Poland and the Free City of Danzig — which remained on a gold standard in 1931 when sterling and the sterling bloc countries left gold, came to an end in 1936. It was apparent that, to the already individualistic actions of Britain and the United States in foreign exchange dealings were to be added the actions of several powerful countries, each now with a floating exchange rate, and each intent on manipulating the market for its own ends. The need for order in exchange rate policies was obvious. The Tripartite Monetary Agreement of 1936, laying down principles to guide countries in their exchange rate policies was the immediate result of this realisation. It was also the base from which more serious planning for monetary control was to begin in 1944.

Authority in the international monetary system in the postwar period has had two developments. The first is the establishment by international agreement of a number of functional international organisations, each designed to influence some control over a particular field. The most notable, the IMF, is charged with certain functions in the fields of international liquidity, exchange rates and the establishment and preservation of multilateral trade; the IBRD sponsors and finances projects in the development field; GATT is concerned with tariff reforms and the drive for freer trade; while a number of regional organisations, some within the United Nations — ECE, ECLA, ECAFE — and some outside it — OECD — are concerned with monetary and general economic aspects of trade within regions.

The second development of the post-war period has been the resurgence of central bank co-operation. The sense of financial community, so apparent in the late nineteenth century and so rudely shattered by the First World War, reappeared in the fifties. The Basle Group of central bankers, meeting frequently and informally to discuss technical problems of mutual interest, has made frequent and timely interventions in such matters as the support of currencies under speculative pressure and the reorganisation of the gold market, and has developed known views on the international economy which gives the group, in spite of its informality, the power and influence of international authority.

It is tempting, in the light of the development in the post-war period of this proliferation of international organisations and forces, to see a shift in the control of the international economy away from individual nations (and particularly from great nations operating key currencies) in the direction of international control. It may be that the beginnings of such a shift have indeed taken place. No single nation dare now take action in the fields of exchange rates, exchange controls or the level of its economic activity without taking some thought for the effects and the political implications of its actions. But whether this is a result of the existence and increasing power of international organisations, or results merely from a shrinkage and drawing together of the international economy in the jet age, is a moot point.

It might be appropriate to end this section, therefore, by inquiring very briefly what conditions must be satisfied in order that international co-operation in the monetary, or for that matter in any other economic field, can move appreciably towards international control of the international system. The pre-conditions of co-operation are already met. The monetary chaos of the thirties has demonstrated the need for some centrally planned direction of the international economy. The point has been taken by politicians, economists and bankers that in great part the difficulties of that period were the result of a fragmentation, an uncertainty of purpose and a clash of divergent policies which must not be repeated. There is a general recognition among those who make the financial policies of countries, particularly in the key currency countries, that the solution of international monetary problems must be sought co-operatively. Coupled with this is a far deeper knowledge of the working of the international economy than we possessed fifty years ago. Meagre though economists' understanding of the dynamics of economic processes may be, it is yet much greater than in 1931. Income analysis has laid bare the forces determining the levels of income and employment; the business cycle is better understood; the relation of the balance of payments to domestic income and prices has been established and the alternative processes of international adjustment have been, and are, subjected to constant scrutiny. In all these sectors empirical and econometric work has deepened our knowledge. We know more, albeit only a little more, about international economic processes and this must influence our policy. Its most immediate and apparent influence has been to point the need for international co-operation and control.

Between 'co-operation' and 'control' there is, however, a qualitative difference: here liberals, planners, idealists and pragmatists hitherto in step would part company and march off in different directions. Any viable international system must inevitably be a compromise between the extremes of a single world currency, centrally administered and with surrender of control by national governments, and an unco-ordinated congeries of separate currencies and unrelated monetary systems on the other. One of these extremes (the latter) has been experienced and the world has, rightly, shrunk back appalled from what it saw. The question still remains, however: how far towards the other extreme are we prepared to go? How far beyond 'co-operation' is 'control'? This brings us to the conditions we set out to find. To move beyond international co-operation and towards international control these conditions must be satisfied. There are three.

Firstly, a controlled international monetary system must involve some loss of national sovereignty, as national monetary authorities submit to external authority. To be complete, this authority would have to encompass decisions as to exchange rates, policies to be followed by countries for balance-of-payments adjustment, even decisions affecting the domestic level of prices and income. These are big pills for national governments to swallow. Exchange rate changes, for example, have in all international negotiations so far been held to be the prerogative of the country concerned. Control of the right to inflate or deflate, with all that the decision connotes in employment, industrial and social policies, is likely to be the most jealously guarded right of individual governments. We are a long way from the surrender of sovereignty which makes a transfer of such decisions as these possible. If the international planner hopes for this dawn, there is as yet no lightening of the sky.

Secondly, international control must involve sanctions which can be brought to bear against countries which abrogate agreed procedures or pursue unilateral policies. In the absence of such sanctions any international body or co-operative agency is foredoomed to failure at the first confrontation with a member or members. Such sanctions may vary in type and stringency. They may consist merely in publicising and reporting the actions of a recalcitrant member, or they may be more extreme and consist of the withdrawal of rights, benefits and privileges conferred by the membership of the organisation. In this latter case the sanction becomes stronger, the greater is the potential benefit to be derived from the organisation. This point may be illustrated from recent history. During the period 1947–56, when the IMF was supplying currencies to member countries on a very limited scale, when no automatic right to use of the Fund's resources existed and when the benefits to be derived from Fund membership were meagre, member countries were prepared to flaunt the Fund's wishes with impunity. France devalued in 1948 without the Fund's consent; Canada adopted a floating exchange rate in 1951 with little thought of the Fund's views. But from 1957 onwards when the Fund has supplied currencies to members to the limit of its power, when 'stand-by' arrangements have been made available, and when there is virtually automatic access to foreign currencies up to a stipulated amount (25 per cent of the member's quota, the so-called 'first tranche'), the Fund has been courted by members; its views have carried weight; it has had moral if not *de jure* authority. Other instances could be quoted, notably that of the European Payments Union in the fifties, whose utility to its members gained for it the respect which enabled it to surmount several crises.

This is the point in the evolution of international monetary control at which we now stand. A number of functional organisations – the IMF, IBRD, OECD – have established themselves over the past twenty years with a mild authority which can be flaunted but at the cost of foregoing certain tangible benefits which the agencies have in their gift. This is as far as we are likely to go towards international control for some time. Individual governments show no sign of readiness to relinquish their sovereign power over the key decisions of international finance. Nevertheless the gain accomplished is not small. Its extent can be measured by a glance at the international economy as it was in 1934 after Roosevelt's death-blow to the London Economic Conference, and by a comparison with the international monetary history of the fifties and early sixties, where solutions to currency and payments problems were sought in some spirit of co-operation.

The Economics of the Balance of Payments 263

Finally, and to achieve the ultimate in international economic control, it is necessary to recognise that such control is but a part of the wider problem of general international economic planning. It is not something which is likely to be achieved in isolation. 'The money flows of which a payments system consists are but the results of flows of goods and services which reflect the international specialisation which is the motivating force of all international trade. If the structure of trade is stunted or malformed, it is of little use replanning the payments system which is its reflection. Only with a broad advance along the whole front of economic co-operation can we tackle monetary problems with any confidence that our efforts will be successful.'[2]

(vi) Conclusion

It is appropriate in ending this chapter to note some of the simplicities and shortcomings into which this exercise in classification of the international economy has led us. In particular we have seen the system thus far as an economic one, neglecting the powerful political forces to which it is subject. Once we regard the international system in a political as well as an economic way, at least two considerations arise. The first is that in speaking of the 'international monetary system' in this chapter, we have regarded the system as that which prevails 'among the nations of what is commonly described — with some degree of euphemism — as the "free world" and not of the countries of the Communist bloc.'[3] Immediately, therefore, we have for practical purposes abandoned any idea of a world system in a geographical sense. Great powers, great in an economic as well as in a political sense, lie outside it, embodying in themselves great trading systems which touch the system we have described at only a few points. Russia and the Warsaw Pact powers in Europe form one such system, China and certain states of South-East Asia form another. Although these groups, through individual countries within themselves, do trade with 'the West', this trade is limited, and to each of the groups, both East and West ('East' is taken to mean the Soviet bloc of countries; 'West' the countries which form the Bretton Woods system and are members of the IMF), trade and payments with the other form a sizable anomaly to which they resort only for expediency and convenience. It is not only political cleavages which determine this grouping but differences in the means of conducting trade and payments. In the East, these are conducted both within the countries of the group and between the group and the West as part of a controlled and planned economy. In the West, the principles of multilateral trade and freedom of trade within an international economy such as we have described in this chapter, receive wide support and are regarded as characteristic of the system. Much of the writing in international economics of the past quarter-century ignores this cleavage or is content, as we must be in this book, to note it in passing and return to the 'world' of exchange rates, balances of payments and international liquidity—to the familiar benchmarks of the Bretton Woods system.

The developing countries form the largest dissentient group within the international economy of the Western world. Their discontent is with several things. They regard the great functional agencies such as the Fund and World Bank as part of a grand Western design to circumvent their economic development. The Fund, in particular, which through its drive for convertibility and multilateral trade has often tried to force monetary orthodoxy on countries seeking to protect balances of payments by unorthodox exchange controls and currency devices, has seemed a disciplinary rather than a helpful institution. The Bank, through its insistence on financial soundness and economic viability, has also come in for its share of criticism. GATT with its bargaining for reciprocal tariff reductions has seemed an unsatisfactory institution to poor countries and weak bargainers. Finally, the developing countries regard it as being the responsibility of the mature industrial countries to aid them on a massive scale, not only by grants of development aid, untied general purpose loans and technical assistance, but by special advantages in the trade field to enable them to advance with an expansion which is, partly at least, trade-led. These are formidable demands and the political drive behind them is great and increasing. In the functional agencies the vast voting power of the mature countries protects them from any disruptive effects of this drive, but in the United Nations, where the voting power of the developing countries is dominant, they are exposed to a constant blast of criticism.

Politics is not the only complication which must be admitted to disturb the simplicity of the international monetary system as we have described it. There is also the element of time. The system as we have described it, with its simple elements, is a static one – one in which the interrelationships are appropriate to a given stock of productive resources at a given moment of time, in which changes in trade strength redistribute wealth among nations but do not increase it as a whole. What, we may ask, happens to all this when we think of the international system in its dynamic reality with some countries growing, some stagnating, some growing at different rates? The answer to this would require a complete re-examination, in a dynamic context of the elements we have discussed. It is better that this should take place elsewhere, in the more detailed discussion of these elements which

The Economics of the Balance of Payments

follows in subsequent chapters. Suffice it to say at this stage that there is one obvious and important relation of the international monetary system to economic growth in the world at large: it is that one essential condition for such growth is the existence of an efficient international monetary system. If growth in the advanced countries can continue steadily, through the existence of adequate stocks of world liquidity and quick-acting adjustment systems, unimpeded by balance-of-payments crises, or by checks to full employment and to growth itself, then that growth in the advanced countries will be transmitted to less developed countries through the normal growth-transmitting mechanisms and growth will be widened. If through an inefficient international monetary system the growth in advanced countries has to be checked by deflationary policies for monetary reasons, then growth is constricted and not diffused. Whatever the effect upon individual elements of the international monetary system of moving from a static system to one which is dynamic, it is certainly true that an efficient international monetary system made up of the components we have discussed is a *sine qua non* of a growing international economy.

From the preceding sections of this chapter the reader will, let us hope, have become aware of the main features of the international monetary system. This gives him the landmarks for the exploration that is to follow. Although most of the features of the international monetary system which have been briefly introduced in this chapter will receive detailed attention in later chapters, it is as well to notice that there are constraints upon this development. To some features, like the adjustment system, development of our ideas means the exploration of a considerable and still growing body of economic theory, while to evaluate some of its forms means an excursion into economic history which we must forego. Any account must be selective and the record of the international economy is going to be one of our omissions. From that it is not to be inferred that this record is unimportant. It is of primary importance. The history of the international monetary system over the past century is the test bench of the international economist. If he aspires to sophistication he must know it thoroughly. Its acquisition from history, report, biography, and memoir forms a necessary background to more rigorous efforts elsewhere.

11
The Balance of Payments: Cross-section of a Nation's Trade

(i) Surplus and Deficit

THE balance of payments is one of the most important statistical statements for any country. It shows the variations in its foreign earnings, capital and current, and in the international transfers which affect it. From it may be inferred the effect of foreign transactions on its national income and on its capital position in relation to other countries. On the changing picture which it reveals must be based the manifold decisions which we collectively refer to as 'international economic policy'.

The balance of payments of any country is 'a systematic record of all economic transactions during a unit period between residents of the reporting country and residents of other countries'.[1] As such, it has, initially, a certain spurious simplicity which, on closer acquaintance, should be replaced for the reader by an attentive scepticism. The mechanism of the account is ill-understood; its terminology is unscientific and inconsistent, while even the interpretation of its most meaningful and final categories is in dispute. Moreover, the leading countries, despite the efforts of international organisations to secure uniformity of classification, are prone to a disconcerting individuality in the presentation and format of this important set of accounts.

As far as terminology is concerned one immediate obscurity to which Yeager draws attention is the use of the word 'payments' in the term. This infers that the individual items record payments. They do not: they record 'flows', some real, some monetary. For example, the item 'exports' does not record payments for exports but the value of goods exported. Some of these goods are subsequently paid for, the money flows being recorded in other items in 'the balance of payments'; some, however, may be gifts, some may be traded goods on which payment is defaulted. It is, as Yeager says, far better to regard the balance of payments as a 'balance of international transactions'.[2]

Before embarking on a detailed description and analysis of the balance of payments it is as well to set out succinctly what we want it to do. First, it must explain quantitatively and, of course, *ex post*, what has been happening in a country's external transactions during a given period. (The period is always a calendar year. Balances of payments for quarterly periods are also prepared by most countries, but the reduction in period entails a sacrifice of accuracy.) Secondly, it must identify the main elements in a country's foreign transactions, grouping these meaningfully to suit a variety of needs: the needs of the national income economist who is interested in the balance's national income effects; the needs of the monetary economist, interested in the source, direction and volume of flows of funds; and the needs of those interested in real flows of imports, exports, etc. All these, the balance of payments should reveal. It should enable behaviour patterns to be established for the main categories and for individual items. As far as possible it should, in doing this, distinguish between the transactions which stem from the public and the private sectors. Finally, the balance of payments should in its compilation and format be so arranged as to allow intra-country comparisons of the main payment flows: exports, imports and flows of capital. Such criteria as these the ideal balance of payments must satisfy. They should be borne in mind during the description which follows.

All transactions of a country which involve a demand for foreign money in terms of the home currency or a demand by foreigners for domestic currency in terms of foreign currency are included in the balance of payments. Those transactions which involve a demand for the home currency by foreigners are described as credit items and bear a plus sign; those which involve a domestic demand for foreign currencies are described as debit items and bear a minus sign. Transactions are listed under debit and credit headings according to normal accounting principles.

The word 'balance' as used in the term 'balance of payments' requires comment. There is confusion because it is used in two different senses. In one sense the balance of payments as a schedule of debit and credit transactions must always balance. It is, after all, merely a schedule of the sources of total foreign exchange earned in the period by the reporting country and of how that foreign exchange has been used. If all sources and all uses are included the debits and credits must necessarily be equal. This point is obvious if one compiles a balance of payments for an individual in his transactions with the rest of the economy. The following table demonstrates the automatic balance in the sense of equality of credits and debits if all outlays and all sources of funds are included:

To cover calendar year

Sources	$	Outlays	$
(i) Personal income from job	10,000	Living expenses	5,000
(ii) Investment income	2,000	Rent	1,000
(iii) Sundry receipts, gifts, etc.	500	Travel	1,500
(iv) Maturing of bonds	1,000	Purchase of bonds	3,000
		Loan interest	500
		Loan to bank	2,500
	13,500		13,500

In this example the individual concerned has had income from various sources in the year which exceeded his outlays by $2500. This $2500 he has left in his bank account as a working balance into the next year. This shows in the account as 'loan to bank'. Had his outlays exceeded his income he would have had to: (a) borrow from his bank, his friends or his suppliers or (b) accept charity. In any event the source would have been shown on the credit side. In this form of account equality of debit and credit sides is automatic and inevitable.

But there is another feature which makes balance, in this sense of equality of debits and credits, inevitable. It lies in the fact that every external transaction is reflected in two items in the schedule, one debit and one credit. The transactions recorded are not all money transfers as in a Receipts and Payments account. Instead, they are 'directional' debits and credits showing sources of foreign earnings and their use. Take an example. The export of goods is a trade transaction which takes place because a firm sells goods to a foreign buyer. It is an 'initiating', or, as we say, an 'autonomous' transaction and its value, since it eventually results in a payment by foreigners to the home country, is a credit item. The item showing the use to which this earning of foreign exchange is put may appear in several ways. It may typically be in an item such as short-term lending, when the foreign purchaser of the exported goods pays for them by a bank deposit in favour of the exporter in the importing country or by a three-month bill accepted by the importer for payment ninety-one days hence. It may be reflected in an item such as Foreign Aid, which shows, elsewhere in the balance of payments and on the opposite side, the value of goods given abroad for aid purposes. Whatever example of a foreign transaction, whether current and deriving from trade or from transfer of capital, whether deriving from the public or the private sector, it will result in some like item of opposite sign on the other side of the account. The two sides of the whole balance-of-payments schedule will, therefore, add to the same

The Economics of the Balance of Payments

figure simply because of the way the whole schedule is constructed, each transaction being recorded twice; once on the debit, once on the credit side. Balance, in this accounting sense, is a necessary structural feature.

The word balance is also used in balance-of-payments analysis in the sense of balance being a difference between two totals. This occurs in the individual sections into which the balance of payments is divided where the terms 'balance of trade', 'balance of invisibles', and so on have this meaning. This is an untidiness of nomenclature which is so built in to balance-of-payments accounting that there is now no getting rid of it, and we must tolerate it. We must also, however, be aware of it. The significance of this distinction lies in the fact that while individual sections (or groups of items) in the balance of payments may have balances, with either (+) or (−) signs, the balance as a whole must be zero. In fact, this total balance is also the sum of the balances of the individual sections.

The automatic equality of the debit and credit items of the balance of payments as a whole will take place of itself without the intervention of monetary authorities, but the accomplishment of this equality unaided may involve features which the monetary authority of the reporting country wishes to avoid, features such as depreciation of the currency unit or disturbing adjustments of the country's level of domestic income, prices and costs. Anticipating an excess of total foreign payments over total foreign receipts which would involve such adjustments, a country may negotiate a loan abroad or it may draw upon its foreign currency reserves. Such transactions we refer to as 'accommodating payments'. They are made to meet the surplus or deficit on the other items which would occur and have to be adjusted in their absence. They are deliberate payments to reduce or prevent the gap which would otherwise exist and whose consequences are regarded as undesirable by the monetary authorities. They must be distinguished from the 'autonomous' items which 'take place regardless of the size of the other items in the balance of payments'.[3] Understanding of the relation between autonomous and accommodating payments and the motivation of the latter lies at the heart of balance-of-payments analysis, and we shall return to it later in this chapter.

When we turn to the many and diverse transactions which compose the balance of payments, we are faced with two problems: that of distinguishing them as credit or debit items, and that of classifying them into meaningful categories and sections. The first distinction is quickly disposed of. All international transactions which give rise to foreigners' money claims on the home country are debit transactions and are given a minus sign in the account; all those giving rise to domestic money claims on foreigners are credit transactions and are given a plus sign. Thus commodity imports, which the home country must pay for and which give rise to a foreign claim upon it, or service charges on a loan from another country, or a loan to a foreign country, direct or through portfolio investment — all these are debit items and bear a minus sign in the schedule. Exports, expenditure within the home country by foreign tourists, and grants in aid from foreign countries are examples of credit items. Demand in the foreign exchange market for the home currency is the touchstone of a balance-of-payments credit; demand for foreign currencies and offer of the home currency is the touchstone of a debit. An alternative distinction of debit and credit which readers may find useful is that of Robert Mundell: 'Transactions are either *debit* items which arise from *purchases*, or credit items which arise from *sales*. Sales of goods, of claims, and of gold and foreign exchange are credit items, and purchases of goods, of claims and of gold and foreign exchange are debit items.'[4]

The individual transactions, apart from their division between debit or credit, must fall into homogeneous groups. Some such groups are fairly obvious, as for example, the export and import groups which head the trade section: many, particularly those which are capital transactions, are not easily classified and their assignment to particular groups may be somewhat arbitrary. Some groups, for example, unilateral transfers, may be large and contain fairly diverse transactions ranging from migrants' remittances, to foreign aid from the public sector given in the form of gifts to underdeveloped countries. To set out these diverse items separately means a large and cumbrous account with many groups of transactions; to group them together may mean a compression which defeats some of the purposes of the account. A common practice of many balance-of-payments returns is to divide transactions into fairly large groups which, although involving a sacrifice of clarity, give a simple and unencumbered structure to the whole account. These groups may be further broken down into their diverse constituents in abstracts shown separately from the main account.

When we turn to the division of the whole balance of payments into sections alternatives present themselves. In spite of the efforts of international monetary agencies to standardise balance-of-payments presentation by all countries there still persist a number of alternative divisions favoured by particular countries.

The simplest approach to the problem of dividing the whole balance of payments into sections which individually constitute meaningful transaction categories and money flows whose behaviour we wish to examine is to follow Meade's example[5] and divide the whole account into five groups of transactions marshalled in two sections. An examination of this

The Economics of the Balance of Payments 271

division demonstrates the principle underlying the relations of groups and sections. This format is shown in Table 11.1.

Table 11.1 Pro Forma Balance of Payments

(a) Trade items

Credits (+)		Debits (−)	
1. Visible exports (i.e. export of goods)	1000	6. Visible imports (i.e. import of goods)	1200

Balance of Merchandise Trade (1−6) −200

2. Invisible exports (i.e. payments to the home country for services rendered to foreigners)	600	7. Invisible imports (i.e. payments by the home country for services rendered by foreigners)	300

Balance of Invisibles (2−7) +300

Trade Credits−Trade Debits = Balance of Trade *or* Balance of Payments on Current Account $(1+2)-(6+7) = +100$.

(b) Transfer items

3. Gold exports (i.e. physical export of the metal or reduction of the amount of gold held on earmark abroad)	250	8. Gold imports (i.e. physical import of the metal or increase in the amount of gold held on earmark abroad)	0
4. Unrequited receipts (gifts, etc., received from foreigners)	300	9. Unrequited payments (gifts, etc., paid to foreigners)	450
5. Capital receipts (i.e. loans from, capital repaid by, or assets sold to, foreign nationals)	1200	10. Capital payments (i.e. loans to, capital repaid to, or assets purchased from, foreign nationals)	1400

Balance of Transfer $(3+4+5)-(8+9+10) = -100$

Total Receipts	Total Payments
(1, 2, 3, 4, 5)	(6, 7, 8, 9, 10)

Table 11.1 is the theme of any balance of payments. On this theme there are numerous variations.

The full statement is divided into two sections: section (a) the Trade Items and section (b) the Transfer Items. Section (a), the Trade Items, falls into two sub-sections: the first shows the sales and purchases of commodities, the second the sales and purchases of services. Items 1 and 6 show the value of goods imported and exported during the period. (Note that these items denote commodity flows in value terms. The payment flows which result from commodity sales and purchases are shown elsewhere, in the Transfer Account.) The difference between these two items is known as the 'balance of merchandise trade' or, less frequently, the 'balance of visible trade'. In items 2 and 7 are grouped the sources of inward and outward payments in respect of services — shipping freights, tourist expenditures, payments for financial and insurance services, and interest payments in respect of outstanding loans. Once more, as with the commodity trade items, we are recording money payments from nationals of one country to those of another made in respect of flows of goods and services in the opposite direction. The difference between the value of invisible exports and invisible imports, is referred to as the 'balance of invisibles'.

For the Trade Section as a whole, total credits minus total debits is called the 'balance of trade' or the 'balance of payments on current account'. Alternatively, we may say that the balance of trade is the difference between the value of goods and services sold to foreigners by residents of the reporting country and the value of goods and services purchased from foreigners by them. Care must be used here with the terminology. Some writers define the balance of trade as the difference between the value of merchandise imports and the value of merchandise exports, making it the same as the 'balance of merchandise trade'. The present writer prefers to follow the example of Meade.[6] Unlike the merchandise trade balance, which is of minor economic significance, the balance of trade is probably the most significant single variable in the whole balance of payments, for it includes all transactions which give rise to or consume national income. (In the familiar equation $Y = C + I + G + (X - M)$, the expression $(X - M)$ denotes the balance of trade.) It is not possible from this balance alone to draw meaningful inferences as to whether the reporting country is or is not in monetary equilibrium with the rest of the world. In certain circumstances, and since the balance of trade is a national income injection, it is appropriate to regard an active balance (i.e. an excess of credits over debits) as a desirable state of affairs. In other circumstances, as with a developing economy, to which large import of capital is appropriate, the balance of trade may for long periods be passive. In fact, it is only by relating the balance of trade to the transfer items that we can obtain a complete picture of a country's international payments position.

Turning to the Transfer Items, 3 and 8 record movements of gold from and to the reporting country. The movements reflected in these items are monetary movements, that is, they show the movements of monetary gold which take place as final balancing transfers between the reserves of the reporting country and the rest of the world. Gold exports represent in

The Economics of the Balance of Payments

this part of the account a loss to the international reserves of the reporting country, gold imports a gain to the reserves.* Where gold is exported as a commodity, as may be the case with gold-producing countries such as South Africa, it is appropriate to record such movements under commodity exports in the Trade Account and not under item 3 in Table 11.1.

In items 4 and 9, unrequited receipts and payments, are shown such receipts and payments as are not matched by simultaneous flows of goods and services in the opposite direction. Private transfers of funds, such as migrants' remittances, government grants in aid, or reparations payments fall into this category. Here the double entry aspect of the item is not immediately obvious. Examples may make it so. We will confine ourselves to unrequited receipts, since all that is said of this item applies in reverse to unrequited payments. In the unrequited receipts item is recorded (as a credit) the fact that foreigners are making unilateral transfers of this value to the recording country. Since these transfers are of various types they are recorded in different ways on the debit side and are reflected in various items on that side of the account. Suppose that a Canadian remits a $100 cheque as a Christmas gift to a relative in Britain. To Britain, this is an unrequited receipt and is thus included as a credit item in the British balance of payments (item 4). The British bank into which the Canadian cheque is deposited then holds a Canadian bank deposit which is technically a British short-term loan to Canada. This short-term loan constitutes the debit item (item 10) matching the credit of the unrequited receipt in the British balance of payments. As a second example, let us suppose that Britain sends a gift of medical supplies to Greece to be used in a disaster area. Here there is no money payment at all. In this case the Greek balance of payments shows the value of the supplies as an import (item 6) on the debit side while the same value is shown as an unrequited receipt (item 4) on the credit side. The item unrequited receipts (and payments) is variously treated in the balances of payments of different countries. Some (U.K. and U.S.A.) treat unrequited receipts and payments as current account items: others show them as transfer items. In fact, they are neither

---

* It is sometimes a source of worry to students as to why a loss of gold should bear a plus sign and be classed as a receipt. There is nevertheless logic in this, if one remembers the criterion mentioned above, namely, that all transactions which involve a demand for the home currency class as plus and all that involve an offer of the home currency class as minus. When an excess of total external payments over receipts takes place, there is an excess amount of the home country's currency on offer in the exchange market. In order to preserve the IMF parity (i.e. the exchange rate), the monetary authority of the home country must enter the exchange market to buy its own currency. This it can only do with gold and/or foreign currencies from its reserve holdings. A drop in reserves always results therefore in a demand for the country's currency, and the reserve loss shows as a positive item in the balance of payments.

true current nor capital items but constitute a distinct category in themselves.

The remaining items, 5 and 10, in the table show the movements of capital funds into and out of the country. Such movements may take many forms. The government, companies and individuals in one country may borrow money from government, companies or individuals in another country. The borrowing may be direct, as between government and government; it may be through the intermediary of a capital market as with portfolio investment in shares, bonds or debentures; or it may be through the banking system or money market where documents of credit are held against eventual payment for traded goods or against short-term funds. Looked at from the point of view of time, capital transactions may be of long duration, such as where a government-to-government loan is made for repayment at some distant date, or where there is investment by a firm in one country in a subsidiary in another; or they may be of short duration, as in a shift of funds from bank deposits (or other liquid asset) in one country to bank deposits in another. Loans, acquisition across borders of capital assets or money claims, loan repayments, delayed payments for commodity trade, cross-border movements of funds in response to the differentials which may exist between national interest rate levels, some representing autonomous items and some accommodating — the forms of international capital movements are so many and so diversified that a complete list at this stage would be an impediment rather than an aid to understanding. Such items are best understood and fall naturally into place in the examination of actual balances of payments for particular countries.

So much for a brief description of the items included in Table 11.1. It is necessary next to pass on to the interrelation of these items. This is the heart of balance-of-payments analysis.

It has already been established that, from its method of construction, the total debits and total credits of the table must be equal. Within this equality, however, exists a relation of the various sectional balances which make up the whole schedule. Each of these sectional balances represents by its amount and sign, that is, by whether it is positive or negative, the volume and direction of the flows of external transactions which are recorded within its group. How large these flows are and how they relate to one another enables us to form qualitative judgements about the whole balance of payments. In order to illustrate this let us, in Table 11.2, break down Table 11.1 into its constituent balances as a means of illustration.

Scrutiny of these constituent balances carries us a step forward in our understanding of the reporting country's external position. The picture which emerges from Table 11.2 is that of a country whose deficit on mer-

The Economics of the Balance of Payments

chandise trade (-200) is offset by a favourable balance of invisible trade to give a slightly active balance of payments on current account. This is the most significant balance so far distinguished. It tells us: (a) that the country's current earnings abroad exceed its outgoings; (b) that there is an injection to its national income which will have the usual multiplier effects; and (c) that the country has, to the extent of the positive balance, funds available for overseas investment or capital transfer.

It is necessary at this point to come to terms with the somewhat mystifying jargon of adjectives which economists apply to these balances. A balance of trade may be described as either 'favourable', 'active' or 'positive' when it has a plus sign; 'unfavourable', 'passive' or 'negative'

Table 11.2 Balances Within the Balance of Payments

	\$mn		
1. Balance of merchandise trade (items 1—6)	$1000 −	$1200 =	−200
2. Balance of invisibles (items 2—7)	600 −	300 =	+300
3. Balance of trade or balance on current account	1600 −	1500 =	+100
4. Balance of gold transfers	250 −	0 =	+250
5. Balance of other transfers	1500 −	1850 =	−350
Balance of transfer	1750 −	1850 =	−100

when it has a minus sign. Favourable and unfavourable are the most popular terms but are the least scientific because of their qualitative significance which is often misplaced. Favourable or unfavourable are words which should only be applied to the whole balance of payments after searching analysis.

The balance of transfer in Table 11.2 tells us nothing in itself. It is, as we know from our existing knowledge of balance-of-payments accounting, the same in amount, but of opposite sign, to the balance on current account. It is to the constituent balances of the transfer section that we must look for enlightenment. Of these items, 5 and 10 show us that the country has a net outflow of capital of -200, that is that it was a net lender abroad but to an amount in excess of its balance on current account. Items 4 and 9 show that the country had *net* unrequited payments of -150 which further increase its negative transfers to -350. Items 3 and 8, however, show us that an outflow of gold of $+250$ closed the gap between transfer outflow and current balance. Taken in this order, the sectional balances infer a certain pattern for this balance of payments. This country, which was a net earner on current account, transferred abroad by capital outflow and unilateral payments an amount greater than the surplus on current account, thereby running down its gold holdings by the required amount to balance the whole account.

This example oversimplifies the structure of a balance of payments, and impatient and well-informed readers, anxious to get on, may argue that it sufficiently illustrates the point that if a country overspends abroad, currently and on capital account, that overspending must be offset by an export of gold. True. But for this we must assume a gold standard, we must neglect the accommodating quality which lurks within certain of the other items and we must accept a number of implications of Table 11.2 which require qualification and development. However, the example does show clearly the importance within the whole balance of payments of the constituent balances and how necessarily these combine to bring about the equality of total debits and credits. What it does not show, and what is of the essence in understanding a balance of payments, is which among these balances arise of themselves as the aggregate of many and manifold decisions to buy and sell, borrow and lend, transfer and invest, and which items arise as consciously made offsets to these; which items, in short, are autonomous items and which accommodating. This distinction we have already made; it is necessary, however, to develop it further and examine its complete significance.

Let us first return to basic principles. Our aim in examining a country's balance of payments is to form a quantitative and qualitative assessment of that country's external payments position. In common terms we want to know whether it is in 'deficit' or 'surplus' and where in the table the deficit or surplus appears.

Let us suppose that in Table 11.1 there is an unforeseen increase in imports of 200. This change of imports might induce the economic authorities to take action to offset the effect upon the balance of payments of the rise in the import bill. They might, for example, allow the increase in traders' demands for foreign currencies to pay for the additional imports, to bid up the price of foreign currencies in terms of their own, thus depreciating the value of their currency. They might alternatively check the amount of imports directly by instituting import embargoes or quotas, or they might prevent payment for additional imports by operating monetary exchange control. They might even pursue deflationary policies in order to reduce the level of domestic income and demand and thereby reduce imports. We will, however, suppose that they do none of these things. Instead they allow the import expansion to take place and importers to pay for their purchases abroad. This they do by going to the exchange market and purchasing from dealers the necessary foreign currencies to discharge their debts. Foreign exchange dealers, who hold working balances of foreign

The Economics of the Balance of Payments

currencies, will find these balances of foreign currencies reduced and their balance of the home currency augmented. This switch of exchange dealers' balances, from foreign to home currency, represents a capital receipt for the home country and will be reflected in item 5 in Table 11.1. If the whole of the additional demand of 200 for foreign currency can be absorbed by this switch of dealers' currency balances then the credit increase of 200 in capital receipts will completely offset the original debit increase of 200. Suppose, however, that it does not do this but that only 100 is absorbed by switches in dealers' balances, still leaving 100 in demands for foreign currencies to be absorbed in some other way. In this situation the monetary authority, if it is maintaining a fixed exchange rate, will be prepared to sell foreign currencies (or gold at a price which reflects the price of foreign currencies) at a fixed price from its central bank reserves and importers will obtain their 100 of foreign currency in this way to discharge their debts. As far as the monetary reserve of the central bank is concerned, the transaction means a switching of balances from foreign currencies to the home currency, that is, a capital receipt from the point of view of the balance of payments. All such capital receipts (or payments) which are centred in the central bank exchange reserves are shown in a distinct item in the balance of payments. In our simplistic example in Table 11.1 they would appear in items 3 and 8; in the more sophisticated balance-of-payments tables of everyday usage they bear various titles of which 'change in reserve holdings' would be typical.

A third type of offsetting item occurs where a foreign country agrees to lend its currency up to an agreed total (or annual) amount to cover the foreign exchange cost of imports from it by another country. This form of government loan would appear in the balance of payments of the recipient country as a capital receipt under item 5.

The feature which characterises all these offsetting items is that none would have occurred but for the initial item reflecting the rise in imports. Two of these items are unplanned and incidental, arising as pure adjustments to the original increase in demand for foreign means of payment; the third is discretionary, the result of conscious and planned government action to meet the anticipated deficiency in foreign payments. These three payments are all accommodating payments. Meade describes them well by saying that 'they have taken place only because the other items in the balance of payments are such as to leave a gap of this size to be filled'.[7] In contrast, autonomous payments take place 'regardless of the other items in the balance of payments'.

It is possible now to rewrite our balance of payments of Table 11.1 in a new form, showing the items grouped according to this new classification of autonomous and accommodating items. Table 11.3 does this. No figures will be assigned to the items. It would be possible to rearrange the figures of Tables 11.1 and 11.2 but this would lengthen the description and would involve us in making assumptions about how these figures are made up. The principle involved in Table 11.3 emerges clearly enough without figures.

Table 11.3 Autonomous and Accommodating Items of the Balance of Payments

Credits	Debits
Autonomous items	
1. Autonomous exports (visible and invisible)	7. Autonomous imports (visible and invisible)
2. Autonomous unrequited receipts from abroad	8. Autonomous unrequited payments to rest of world
3. Autonomous capital receipts	9. Autonomous capital payments
Balance of autonomous items = + $x mn.	
Accommodating items	
4. Accommodating exports (visible and invisible)	10. Accommodating imports (visible and invisible)
5. Accommodating unrequited receipts from abroad	11. Accommodating unrequited payments to rest of world
6. Accommodating capital receipts	12. Accommodating capital payments
Balance of accommodating items = − $x mn.	

The external situation reflected in Table 11.3 is one in which a country's external receipts and payments made without regard to the state of the balance of payments produced a surplus of $x million. This surplus was consciously adjusted by manipulation of the discretionary accommodating items so as to produce an overall accommodating balance of like amount.

It is apparent from Table 11.3 that some items, e.g. exports and imports, may be either autonomous or accommodating; for example, a government may make a grant to a foreign government which is in turn offset by imports from the donor country. A short-term loan by a country may be accommodating, as when it offsets an export transaction, or autonomous, as when money moves to a foreign country in response to a rise in interest rates abroad.

We are now, after this rearrangement of the balance of payments, in a position to define and identify a deficit or surplus in the balance of payments. A deficit is measured by the actual amount of discretionary accommodating finance required over a given period of time (as credits); a surplus is the amount of discretionary accommodating finance which must be disbursed (as debits). To put the point another way round: the surplus or deficit in the balance of payments is really the balance of autonomous trade and transfers less the amount of automatic accommodating finance. It is this balance which must be equalled and offset by a like amount of discretionary accommodating finance. This discretionary accommodating finance is often referred to as 'compensatory finance'. This explanation of the deficit defines its nature, locates it in general accounting terms within the balance of payments and highlights the importance in policy terms of reserves of international payments.

(ii) Balance-of-Payment Disequilibrium

Let us examine more carefully some of the implications of the definition of surplus and deficit at which we have arrived. Our object is to arrive at a judgement of the nature of balance-of-payments disequilibrium.

Clearly to say that imbalance in a country's balance of payments is measurable by its outflow or inflow of discretionary accommodating finance is only a starting point. Such a condition may arise and be temporarily tolerated by one country, while in another it may create conditions of crisis. Under some international monetary conditions wide swings in the balance of payments can be accommodated; under other conditions such swings would endanger the whole system. A full understanding of such problems must wait until the chapters dealing with balance-of-payments adjustment, but at the present stage some examination of balance-of-payments 'pathology' is appropriate.

It is essential at the outset to realise that a balance-of-payments disequilibrium is not a national problem only but one shared by a number of countries, perhaps by the international economy as a whole. The balance-of-payments surplus of country A is but the obverse of the balance-of-payments deficits of countries B, C and D; the deficit of R but the obverse of the surpluses of X, Y and Z. If the country in imbalance is a small and relatively unimportant one, the disequilibrium may be no great matter save to itself and to the small group of countries concerned. If, however, the country in disequilibrium is a major economic and financial power the problem is one of significance, and its solution may lie perforce not with one country but with many. Nor does the direction of the imbalance matter in this wider sense. A balance-of-payments deficit has a more hostile aspect to the country experiencing it than does a surplus and there are sanctions operating on the deficit country to correct the deficit; a surplus, involving as it does the accumulation of inflows of compensatory finance, lacks such immediate incentive to correction. But one country's surplus is another country's deficit, and some onus lies on the surplus country to aid in the adjustment process.

When we turn to the balance-of-payments disequilibrium of a particular country two aspects call for attention: its location, and its duration. The source of imbalance in a country's external payments may be in either the current account or the capital account of the balance of payments, or even in both. The possible cases for these interrelationships of current and capital account autonomous items may be set out as follows in Table 11.4:

Table 11.4 Possible Relationships of Current and Capital Accounts

	(1)	(2)	(3)	(4)
	Surplus +,	Deficit −		
Current account	(a) +100	(a) −100		
Autonomous balance	(b) +120	(b) −120	+	−
	(c) +80	(c) −100		
Capital account	(a) −100	(a) +100		
Autonomous balance	(b) −100	(b) +100	+	−
	(c) −100	(c) +120		
	Inflow −,	Outflow +		
Necessary accommodation	(a) 0	(a) 0		
	(b) −20	(b) +20	−	+
	(c) +20	(c) −20		

There are four possible directional combinations of deficit and surplus in the current and capital accounts. In case (1) a current account surplus is coupled with a capital account deficit. If, as in (a), the surplus is equal to the deficit then no accommodation is necessary; if, as in (b), the surplus on current account exceeds by $20 mn the deficit on capital account, then there will be an accommodating inflow of $20 mn. If, as in (c), the surplus on current account is not large enough to match the deficit on capital account, there will be an accommodating outflow. In case (2) a deficit on current account is coupled with a surplus on capital account and, according to the magnitudes of the surplus and deficit, there is a zero, a positive or a negative necessary accommodation. In case (3) surpluses on both current and capital account necessitate an inflow of accommodation equal to the sum of the surpluses; in case (4) deficits on both current and capital account require an outflow of accommodation equal to the sum of the deficits.

It would be tedious and unnecessary to spell out the practical aspects each of these eight cases. Taxonomy has its uses and its limitations. Here it serves to highlight certain principles. Firstly, current and capital accounts with similar signs are both undesirable; they tend to maximise the amount of necessary accommodation. Secondly, the correct behaviour for a country with a surplus on current account is to lend abroad, and the necessary condition for a country with capital and development responsibilities abroad is to cultivate a surplus on current account. Thirdly, a country with a persistent current deficit may mitigate that deficit by long-term borrowing. The orders of magnitude attached to cases (1) and (2) provide interesting variations on which the reader may test his ingenuity.

It is interesting to test the realism of the principles implicit in the table by applying them to the recent history of particular countries. The United Kingdom, which fulfilled in the nineteenth century the role of a surplus lender, has come in many post-war years to be a lender to an extent greater than its surplus on current account warrants. The United States is now in a similar position. Her outward capital flow in the sixties more than counterbalanced her current account surplus. Canada provides consistently the case of a country whose deficit on current account (recently small current surplus) is swamped by her huge inflow of capital, while Germany, in the 1950s, accumulated huge reserves from the inflow caused by a very large current account surplus unmatched by any sizeable foreign lending.

Turn now to the second aspect of a balance-of-payments deficit (or surplus): its duration. Time is an essential element in judging the nature and importance of imbalance. For example, a country may suffer a deficit in a given year because of some fortuitous and non-repeatable event which influences its trade and, for the time being, its economic relations with the rest of the world as reflected in its balance of payments. It may suffer a natural disaster which brings a one-season crop failure or there may be political events which spark off a temporary withdrawal of foreign funds from the country's money market. Such temporary conditions have only a transient effect on the balance of payments, which may be offset by a variety of devices. Such a deficit does not deserve to be treated as more than a passing phase. In contrast to this is the deficit which is repeated year after year and which reflects some structural change in the trade or the international payments position of the country concerned. Such a deficit is a fundamental or structural disequilibrium in a country's balance of payments. Its correction is likely to be difficult and prolonged while the flows of funds required to accommodate the persistent deficit will be large and difficult to sustain.

Time is important, too, when related to the nature of the accommodation which offsets a deficit. There is clearly a great difference between a country whose trade deficit is offset by long-term foreign borrowing and whose external account is technically in balance, and a country whose trade deficit is for the moment fortuitously covered by a simultaneous inflow of short-term funds perhaps drawn from abroad by interest rate margins or seeking asylum from less secure financial centres abroad. Such short-term funds are highly mobile and their sudden removal would reveal the deficit and demand immediate remedial action. For a complete picture of a country's balance of payments, the items, particularly the accommodating items, should be viewed critically as well as quantitatively and in relation to their variations over a period long enough to eliminate random and seasonal variations.

A second time-influence on the balance of payments lies in the short-term and seasonal fluctuations which take place in most such balances. Short-term, day-to-day fluctuations are detectable only by the ebb and flow of demand for currency in the foreign exchange markets; they may sometimes be detected also in the quarterly figures for the balance of payments issued by most countries. They may be due to changes in short-term inflows and outflows of capital for speculative and other purposes, or to grouping of payments for commercial transactions. Seasonal fluctuations are detectable in the quarterly balance-of-payments figures of most countries. They often reflect the heavy payments that are made at certain seasons for crop imports (or exports), the payments of tourists in the summer months, and similar causes. Over the year as a whole and in inter-year comparisons such seasonal variations need not be considered but for any period shorter than a year balance-of-payments figures (unless seasonally adjusted) will present a deceptive picture. Moreover seasonal variations will reflect themselves in movements of accommodating finance, with reserves ebbing out during a seasonal deficit and returning in the period of seasonal surplus. Over the year any change in the country's reserve holding may be attributed to long-term forces acting on the balance of payments.

There is one final qualification resulting from considering the balance of payments over a period of time which must be discussed here. It relates to the time element implicit in the forms of accommodating finance. If any of the forms of such finance should be so mercurial, so ready to dry up or to reverse the direction of flow, then the above-the-line items would quickly be left unbalanced and some other form of accommodating finance would be required to fill the gap. Such a form of accommodating finance is short-term capital. Before deciding whether or not we should include it in the accommodating finance group below the line, its nature should be examined more carefully.

Short-term capital movements reflect changes in the flow of at least two distinct types of funds. First is that of short-term loans for the finance and ultimate settlement of commercial transactions. These may involve several types of institution and several credit instruments. The second is that of balances of funds which move quickly across frontiers from financial centre to financial centre under the stimuli of differences of interest rates and changes in the international view of the safety and prospects of different assets and different money markets. At first sight, the nature and motivation of these two groups appears to be different. On closer inspection, however, there is a similarity at least in the forces that act upon and make for change, and certainly in their effect on the balance of payments. Short-term loans which arise from trade transactions may be held by the creditor country in the form of bank deposits or short-term paper, such as trade bills. If, for example, Britain exports to Canada, payment for the exports may be made by a bank deposit or by the acceptance of a bill of exchange drawn by the British exporter on the Canadian importer. In either event, the effect is one of a short-term loan by Britain to Canada by, in fact, a short-term capital outflow from Britain. The use or repatriation of the bank deposit or the payment of the bill cancels the debt by a contrary flow. Even such commercial payments as these may be transformed, however, by the risk assessment and speculative view of the parties involved. Let us suppose that this view is that Britain's balance-of-payments position is so weak as to make it likely that the pound will shortly be devalued. In this case, importers in Canada will do all in their power to delay payments for British exports, that is, to increase their borrowing from the United Kingdom in the hope that devaluation will take place and that the cost of the exports from Britain in Canadian currency will be reduced.* British importers, on the other hand, will accelerate their payments for their imports from Canada, since the devaluation would have the effect of raising the foreign currency price of these. This would have the effect of reducing Canadian short-term lending to Britain. Both of these influences, which constitute a movement of short-term capital against Britain, would have an adverse effect on the British balance of payments. The short-term capital movement implied here is in fact the 'leads and lags' effect which has been detrimental during the speculative attacks on sterling in the sixties. Short-term loans which arise from transfers to a country of mobile risk capital require little explanation. A Swiss bank holding funds in United States Treasury bills when the New York Treasury bill rate is 6 per cent and the British rate $5\frac{1}{2}$ per cent will move to Britain if the British rate is moved to $6\frac{1}{2}$ per cent, but may move out again if the short-term rate in Paris is raised to 7 per cent. (This is, of course, an oversimplified example which dodges all the complexities of forward-cover and the non-economic aspects of the

---

* A devaluation of sterling such as that of November 1967, in which the sterling exchange rate in terms of the Canadian dollar was reduced from £1 = $3 to £1 = $2.6 means, in effect, that after the devaluation $2.6 buys the same amount of goods as formerly cost $3, a reduction of approximately 14 per cent. On the British side £1 after the devaluation brought only $2.6 worth of Canadian goods; before it brought $3.

risks involved. It is near enough to reality, however, and suffices to make the point.) Clearly enough, the effects of such capital movements may be highly destabilising and are similar to the movements implicit in the leads and lags effect for commercial movements. Indeed, movements are likely often to be co-ordinated, leads and lags speculation and outward risk-covering movements taking place together, when there is lack of confidence in a currency.

Since all movements of short-term capital are made without thought for their effect on the balance of payments they should be excluded from the list of accommodating payments and have their place above the line in the balance of payments. Short-term capital movements are not taking place, so that there may be funds to finance a surplus or deficit in other items of a country's balance of payments. They are temporary and reversible movements. A country whose deficit on other autonomous items is covered by an inflow of short-term capital is in the precarious position that any reverse of the flow will necessitate an increase in the balance of the accommodating items. There is, however, lack of unanimity as between reporting countries as to the classification of this item. With some, it is included among the monetary movements which are regarded as being accommodating items; with others, it is not. Be that as it may, there are unassailable theoretical arguments and strong practical ones for regarding it as an autonomous item.

One obvious practical implication is that if we regard short-term capital movements as accommodating there is logically no distinction between the balance-of-payments position of a country whose deficit on current account is offset by long-term development loans and one whose deficit is, for the time being, offset by short-term capital imports. The practical difference between the two cases is surely obvious.

One final point, unrelated to time, which must be made about balance-of-payments equilibrium, remains. A distinction must be made between a disequilibrium in a country's balance of payments with the whole of the rest of the world and disequilibrium with a particular country or group of countries. In a world economy where there are free exchange markets for all currencies unimpeded by exchange controls of any kind, this distinction has little significance. Balances earned by a surplus with countries A, B and C may be used in payment of debts resulting from a deficit with countries D, E and F. As long as the overall balance of payments is in equilibrium the country will have no difficulty in meeting its external obligations. If, however, there is not freedom to move balances from currency to currency, if countries are willing to accept some currencies in settlement but not others — if, in short, there is not a multilateral payments system but one with regional payments arrangements where groups of countries specify their acceptable currencies or bilateral payments and where total transactions between two countries must be cleared on a quantitative barter basis – in these circumstances sectional balances with groups of countries or with individual countries become important. This distinction between multilateral balances of payments and regional or bilateral balances of payments became of great importance between 1945 and 1958 when the great surplus of the United States created a chronic shortage of dollar currency. Countries in deficit with the United States were not able to use their surpluses with other countries to clear their debts with the United States because these other countries in their turn were short of dollars, required them for payments to the United States, and were unwilling to use them save for that purpose. The sectional balances of payments of countries with the United States became in these circumstances more significant than their overall balances of payments. It became important not only to have a surplus but to have a surplus with particular countries in order to have balances of their currencies. Since December 1958, when the Western European currencies were made convertible and a multilateral payments system was restored, and in the absence of a U.S. payments surplus, the above distinction has not been important. If, however, some breakdown in the payments system were again to drive individual countries or groups of countries to solve their balance-of-payments problems by resort to exchange control, it would be a distinction of very real meaning.

We are now in a position to define with greater accuracy the nature of imbalance, that is, of a deficit or surplus in the balance of payments; and in so doing, we can make some generalisations about the nature of a balance-of-payments disequilibrium.

First, and at the risk of being repetitive, we may define a deficit in the balance of payments as being 'measured by the actual amount of accommodating finance required over a given period of time (as credits); a surplus as the amount of accommodating finance which must be disbursed (as debits)'.[8] Second, a deficit which persists so long as to cause a dangerous depletion of reserves and other accommodating finance for the country concerned, or a surplus which causes reserves to accumulate, we may describe as a balance-of-payments disequilibrium. Constancy of the level of reserves is the criterion of balance-of-payments equilibrium. The period of time over which constancy of reserves becomes the criterion should be long enough to cover all seasonal and short-term fluctuations in the balance of payments.

Short-term capital movements should not be included in the category of accommodating finance, but should be regarded as items within the autonomous sector of the account.

From the picture of the balance of payments which we have given, one clear idea must emerge. The balance of payments shows an *ex post* equality of the demand for and supply of the reporting country's currency—an equality ensured by the structural principles of the account. But *ex ante* there was no such equality of demand, for these were the result of dispersed and divergent desires and motives acting upon the autonomous items of the account. The means of reconciliation of the *ex ante* divergence and the *ex post* equality lies in four methods of adjustment:

1. The excess of demand for the country's currency over its supply may be met by drawings upon the reserves of those countries which experience the scarcity, or by the voluntary loan or gift of its currency by the surplus country or countries.

2. The divergence of demand and supply of the country's currency may cause its price to alter, that is, the exchange rate will change.

3. Prices and income in the country may alter and so bring shifts of demand for imports and exports which will tend towards balance.

4. Direct controls over foreign currency transactions may seek to establish equality of supply and demand for the currency.

These four methods of achieving *ex post* equality of foreign receipts and payments exhaust the possibilities of adjustment.

(iii) Causes of Disequilibrium

Disequilibrium in a country's balance of payments may arise from many causes. Three main groups of disturbance are, however, clearly discernible. First, there are many random, unavoidable and unforeseeable shocks which may have a once-over impact on a country's external situation. Natural disaster may cause the failure of a harvest on whose export the country depends, a sudden shift in demand resulting from changing consumer taste, technological innovation, or political changes abroad may alter a country's export prospects. The income derived from foreign investments may dry up or change. Such random sources of balance-of-payments instability are inevitable and any process of adjustment should be capable of dealing with them. In general, such 'acts of God' are more important for small countries than for large. Single-crop exporters are obviously more vulnerable than multi-trading giants like the United States. But for this very reason these random shocks to balance-of-payments equilibrium are limited in their effects and are capable of being contained. A common source of external instability which we must place in this category but which may be less amenable to correction, arises as a result of changes in the policies of governments, as when one country imposes an import tariff, an export subsidy or a restriction by quota or embargo upon imports or exports. Such measures not only affect the balance of payments of the reporting country but probably invoke retaliatory action by that country, so that interference with international trade and payments tends to become widespread. This group of shocks to payments equilibrium is so various in type and magnitude as to defy meaningful classification. In fact, its sole common distinguishing feature is that each such shock demands its own peculiar treatment for correction. It may be such as to be correctable by the built-in forces for the restoration of stability which we call the adjustment mechanism. It may be that it calls for elaborate *ad hoc* measures.

Secondly, instability of the foreign balance can result from cyclical fluctuations in the domestic economy of the reporting country. Whether the deficit occurs as a result of the cycle and its effect on the country or whether it occurs because, as in the case of the United Kingdom in the fifties and sixties, domestic policies to control the balance of payments were applied in a cyclical pattern is not, in this context, important. The significant factor here is the ebb and flow of reserves which mark the repeated and successive phases of change in the balance of payments.

The third form of balance-of-payments disequilibrium is somewhat different to the first two forms which we have described. Both of these disequilibria constituted relatively short-term fluctuations of the balance of payments. They were of such a character and duration that, in seeking their adjustment, we might take the structure of the world economy, the nature of production, the character of demand, the world distribution of population and such other aspects of the economic environment as fixed and given, so that such counter-measures as may be used for their adjustment are chosen only in relation to the short-term problem which they must meet. But international equilibrium is subject also to long-period forces whose working may extend over decades and which, while inextricably intermingled and overlaid with short-term events and problems, work out their own inexorable will. These we may describe as 'structural' changes, using the word to imply that such changes are large, fundamental and usually irreversible. These structural problems provide not only changes in themselves but an ever-changing background to short-term problems. They ensure, moreover, that no two problems of short-term adjustment are ever quite the same, being cast against a different background. This makes it dangerous for the makers of international economic policy to place great reliance on theoretical models. Our model-building in international economics necessarily deals with short-term situations and has little light to shed on the working of long-term forces. Even short-run adjustment problems, complicated as they inevitably are by the setting in which they occur, tend to become fit subjects for individual case studies rather than for straightforward applications of theory to policy.

The international economic problems of our own time serve to demonstrate this dilemma. We established in the post-war period in the Bretton Woods mechanism an elaborate system to facilitate short-period international adjustment but the functioning of that system has been continually confused and undermined by structural changes in the world economy, some of which had their origins before the war (for example, the secular change in the world trading position of the United Kingdom), some of which arose as a result of it and the realignment of economic strengths which it produced. At least four structural problems have bemused the post-war period: the so-called dollar problem of the immediate post-war period, when the manufacturing dominance of the United States and the devastation (and some thought also the senility)[9] of Western Europe, produced a chronic surplus in the United States balance of payments, a shortage of dollar currency and a defence by the European countries of their own balances of payments which involved exchange and import controls and a retreat into bilateral and discriminatory trading which set the working of the Bretton Woods system in abeyance for more than ten years. The dollar problem of the forties and early fifties was replaced in the later fifties and sixties by a dollar problem of a different type. Now the outflow of dollars on capital account, to furnish aid to the needy and the politically uncommitted, to maintain United States forces abroad, and to invest in the now booming and growing industries of Western Europe, has been unmatched by the necessary surplus on current account and has been financed by a steady outflow from the once-considered impregnable American official gold stocks. This brought us to the confidence crises of 1967, 1969 and 1971, in which the whole Bretton Woods system was shaken and threatened.

A third structural imbalance has been that of the United Kingdom, whose recurrent balance-of-payments crises since the Second World War indicate basic changes in the British economy and its place in the world, to which British policies have been unable to accommodate themselves. Finally, West Germany, once set on the road to economic recovery in 1950, quickly developed through its thriving export trade a current account unmatched by any comparable outflow on capital account, resulting in a great and sustained inflow of reserves and a threat through its chronic surplus to Western European multilateral trade.

II Adjustment of a Country's Balance of Payments

12
The Role of the Price Mechanism in Adjustment

(i) The Nature of the Adjustment Problem

ANY investigation of the problem of adjustment falls naturally into two parts: an examination in theoretical terms of the forces which may be harnessed to adjust a balance-of-payments disequilibrium; and the policies which countries adopt in seeking adjustment. It is tempting to say or imply that the policies adopted act in accordance with the principles, embodying them in working systems, but this is not always the case. It is only since the First World War that the discussion of what we now call adjustment theory has been taken up by economists — and it was only after the Second World War that, with the wider understanding of national income behaviour made possible by Keynesian economics, adjustment theory came to be widely discussed and related to the practical policy problem of choosing and working an actual adjustment system. Up to that time, policies to secure adjustment of balance-of-payments disequilibria were a hotchpotch of *ad hoc* measures pursued by monetary authorities. Sometimes, as in the late nineteenth century and the period up to 1914, these measures followed a discernible pattern, as they did under the international gold standard; sometimes, as in the interwar period, they were diverse, contrary to theory as we now know it, and often chaotic.

The problem appears fundamentally at two levels: at the level of the individual country pursuing its own policies to protect itself from the effects of balance-of-payments disequilibrium, and at the world level where some system of adjustment is clearly necessary if national adjustment policies are to be co-ordinated. We shall have both these aspects in mind in this chapter.

Correction of a balance-of-payments disequilibrium is a prime necessity for the country which experiences it. In the case of a deficit, the country can only sustain the deficit, without changing its exchange rate or resorting to controls on its imports, as long as its stock of international liquidity holds out. In the case of a surplus, the forces impelling correction are less strong. The surplus country will accumulate international liquidity and will continue to do so as long as the surplus persists. Such an accumulation of international liquidity may have repercussions upon the price-level of the surplus country. If the growth of reserve holdings is persistent and large enough it will, despite the efforts of the monetary authorities to neutralise it, force up the domestic money supply with stimulating effects upon the price level. Deficit countries losing reserves to the surplus country will no doubt bring pressure upon it to correct the surplus and they may discriminate against the surplus country by imposing restrictive tariffs, import quotas, embargoes and the like against its exports. But in the absence of discriminatory action by deficit countries, the sanctions operating against a surplus country to correct its surplus are not as strong as those operating against a deficit country to correct its deficit. Eventually, a limit is set to the tolerance of the latter by the size of its reserve holdings. It is always more pleasant to accumulate international money than it is to see it flow out to other countries. In the last resort the sanctions against the deficit country are real and compelling; those against the surplus country are moral and persuasive only. There are numerous examples in monetary history of surplus countries whose resistance to the moral suasion of their neighbours has been great and prolonged. Nevertheless and despite the inequality of the sanctions operating against surplus and deficit countries, we must regard both as balance-of-payments disequilibria requiring correction. This we must do if only because the surplus of one country (or of several countries) is the deficit of another (or of others). Finally when discussing balance-of-payments disequilibrium it is usual to think in terms of a deficit. Appropriate changes are easy to make when considering the case of a surplus country.

Clearly the size of a country's reserve holding determines, in great part, the urgency of the need for adjustment if a deficit develops in its balance of payments. A country with large reserves may be able to tolerate a deficit for a long time, using its reserves to maintain its exchange rate by equalising the demand and supply of its currency in the foreign exchange market. Yet ultimately and however large the country's reserve holdings may be, action to adjust the deficit will have to be taken. 'The function of international liquidity is to finance deficits that are in process of being corrected, not to remove the need for correction.'[1]

The argument may be put in another way. We have seen that the greater the reserves held by a country the less is the pressure upon it to adjust a deficit in its balance of payments. Only when the reserves approach depletion is the country compelled to take action for adjustment. Equally, it

The Economics of the Balance of Payments

is true that the more efficient the adjustment mechanism is, that is, the more quickly the balance of payments is brought back to equilibrium by it, the smaller the stock of international liquidity needs to be. Where countries in the international system have the means of correcting balance-of-payments disequilibria quickly and where they resort to these means immediately disequilibrium occurs, there is need only for small stocks of international liquidity for settlement of residual balances between these countries. The demand for international liquidity becomes greater the less efficient the adjustment mechanism. This point has great significance for policy and we will recur to it in Chapter 20 when considering international liquidity.

It is a necessary preliminary to classifying the types of adjustment mechanism required to consider the problem of adjustment as it presents itself to a country with a deficit in its balance of payments. Such a country is faced with the following choices:

1. it may allow the deficit to continue, financing it from its own reserves of gold or other acceptable international money;
2. it may impose controls on its trade in such a way as to suppress the deficit – usually by limiting imports and/or by controlling payments on current and capital account to other countries;
3. it may seek to improve the trade balance by reducing, by deflationary monetary and fiscal policies, the level of its domestic prices and costs relative to other countries;
4. it may change its price/cost relationship with other countries by changing its exchange rate* – either by a series of discrete changes or by allowing the rate to change freely with supply and demand for the currency in the exchange market; or
5. it may make *ad hoc* interventions in trade and payments designed to influence its own balance of payments and avoid the more drastic measures of domestic deflation or exchange rate change.

This list of choices for a deficit country is an exhaustive one. If it does not follow options (2), (3) or (4), if it lacks the reserves to follow option (1) and if its *ad hoc* measures under (5) are mischosen, then the excessive supply of its currency in the foreign exchange market arising from the deficit will cause the rate for its currency in that market to fall and settle at whatever level will equalise supply and demand in the market.

---

* In the vast majority of cases this means 'by devaluing its exchange rate'. However, as we shall see, it is at least theoretically possible that in certain rare circumstances a country in deficit might improve its balance-of-payments position by revaluing its exchange rate, i.e. by raising the value of its currency in terms of other currencies.

From this list of possible actions to meet a balance-of-payments deficit we may arrive at a shorter list of adjustment policies. In doing so we must remember that the criterion of an adjustment mechanism, as distinct from a balance-of-payments policy to meet a deficit, is that the former implies not only that the country protects itself from the deficit and its effects but that the measures correct the deficit itself. Moreover adjustment implies something more than the mere unilateral actions of this list. It implies a recognition on the part of the deficit country that balances of payments are many sided and that policies designed to influence them touch many countries. A balance-of-payments policy is a national policy; adjustment assumes membership of an international system with which individual countries conform. By this criterion options (1) and (2) must be eliminated. Option (1) implies simply a decision to tolerate the deficit as long as reserves last. There is no question of correcting the deficit. Option (1) may of course be quite an acceptable policy in certain circumstances — for example, if it is clear that the deficit is the result of some transient cause and will be short-lived. It contains, however, no provisions for dealing with and ending the deficit. Option (2) perishes in the same way. Direct controls do not imply any mechanism for permanently changing strategic items in the balance of payments so as to correct the deficit. They have no effect other than to dam up and restrict the flow of imports or the magnitude of external payments. They bring the balance of payments to temporary balance by frustrating external payments; and if nothing else, either the exchange rate or the level of prices, is altered, imbalance will remain and reappear directly the controls are removed. Controls do not bring about adjustment in the true sense but rather avoid the consequences of adjustment. Nevertheless, while it does not satisfy the conditions of a true adjustment system, the direct controls method has been so widely used and so confused as an alternative with true adjustment systems that one might be tempted to treat it as such. It might be argued, for example, that a country which imposes and maintains direct controls on its balance of payments for years may expect that if it removes or modifies these controls, it may find the balance of payments so altered as to be qualitatively different from that on which the controls were originally imposed. True, but there is no reason to suppose that the original deficit will now be corrected. The balance of payments may now be different; that is all we can say. Controls imply no device for bringing the balance of payments back to balance with their removal. The widespread use of controls, the frequency with which they have been resorted to and, as we shall later show, their appropriateness to certain balance-of-payments policies entitle us to consider their merits and demerits as an element in balance-of-payments policy. This we shall do in a later chapter. Controls, however, have no place in a theory of true adjustment mechanisms.

Option (5) we must also set aside as a method of adjustment. Indeed, it is not a method at all but a Micawberish approach to balance-of-payments policy by governments which, while recognising the need for adjustment in an international system, shy away from their responsibilities hoping that by rolling adjustments to the domestic economy, timely changes in interest rates to attract short-term capital and a multitude of stop-gap measures, they may keep national price levels in such approximate relationship to one another as will minimise reserve transfers. This 'systematic ad-hoccery' (a name given to this blinkered approach by Mr Robert Roosa, former Under-Secretary for Monetary Affairs in the United States Treasury) cannot replace an adjustment system except under conditions in which the stock of international money and its distribution were other than at present. Under this system — or lack of it — realignment of prices and costs in main countries takes place so slowly that deficits are too large to be met by transfers of reserves. The system is characterised by repeated strains and crises, which could be avoided by the existence of a proper adjustment system. The endless stratagems and measures of the British to protect the pound from devaluation in the early sixties and the measures taken by the United States to maintain the gold value of the dollar are obvious examples of this 'ad-hoccery'.

We are left, therefore, with options (3) and (4) on our list. These when used by countries in their balance-of-payments policies imply adjustment as well as containment of the deficit. Both of these methods work in the same way but by a different route. The first (option (3)) is to alter the relation of prices and costs within the adjusting country as compared with those in the rest of the world by deflationary policies which reduce prices and costs within the country. The second (option (4)) is by altering the exchange rate for the country's currency in terms of other currencies, so that international prices of the country's goods to the foreigner are thereby reduced. Once this alteration in relative prices, by whichever method achieved, takes place there is alteration in the demand for exports and imports of the country concerned. The demand for its exports rises as their prices fall, the demand for its imports falls as their prices rise relative to home-produced goods. The balance of merchandise trade is improved and ultimately, if relative prices are altered sufficiently, the improvement in the merchandise trade balance brings about the required adjustment. It is the change in relative prices *implicit* in both these methods which brings about the adjustment effect.

There is an important side effect of changing relative prices which has an independent effect upon adjustment, although it operates in the same direction. It is this: it is usually not possible to alter the price level of a country without at the same time altering its national income. Any reduction in prices achieved by deflationary domestic policies in the deficit country will almost certainly involve a reduction in that country's income relative to other countries; a rise in prices will involve an increase in income. (This we know either from observation, observing that rising prices are correlated with expanding activity, or from elementary macro-theory.) These income changes, which accompany the price adjustments, must be examined separately for the effect they have upon the trade balance. In this and subsequent chapters we shall consider changes in relative prices and costs and changes in national income and the means by which these changes achieve adjustment in the balance of payments. Our method of approach will be first to deal theoretically with the processes by which adjustment may be achieved through price and income changes in countries participating in the international monetary system. At a later stage we shall examine the consequences of achieving price changes via changes in the exchange rate. In all this we must try to draw a distinction between the theoretical foundations of adjustment and the institutional framework within which, in the last resort, it must operate. The 'eternal verities' of adjustment theory cannot be escaped; they dominate the problem and condition the policies which countries may follow to achieve adjustment. Yet it is within the institutional framework that the world as a whole and countries individually have choices. The criteria according to which such choices are made – whether to adjust via the exchange rate or via domestic price changes, whether to adjust via a freely fluctuating exchange rate or one which is changed at discrete intervals – must be examined. Once the eternal verities have been established we must try to illuminate these and many other choices which face governments and the international monetary system.

This brings us back to a point made early in this chapter. Adjustment must be a force, or set of forces, built into the international monetary system. Indeed, it is a *sine qua non* of any such system which is to survive and deal with the strains to which an international monetary system is subject. This means that the choice which apparently lies before countries as to how they will adjust their balances of payments is a very constrained choice indeed, constrained predominantly by the choices of other countries in the international monetary system. Ideally, an adjustment system is something which should be built into a consciously planned international monetary system and should indeed be its operational centre. There is growing evidence of the realisation of this in the great flurry of thinking,

The Economics of the Balance of Payments

writing and discussion which has surrounded the efforts since 1963 to remould the world's monetary system. But the dictation from above, from some international monetary organisation, of the method of adjustment to be followed by individual countries implies a surrender of national control of economic and monetary policies which countries are not yet willing to accept. For the present the best that can be hoped is that countries will mould their balance-of-payments policies in conformity with some conscious view of how adjustment may best work in the modern world. The harmonising of national balance-of-payments policies to produce a viable international adjustment mechanism is probably the greatest problem in international monetary economics. Table 12.1. shows the extent to which at various times this harmonisation has been so matched.

(ii) Adjustment: the Classical Approach

The central problem of adjustment analysis is to show the impact, to an individual country and to the world economy, of any disturbance to equilibrium in the balance of payments of that country, and to examine the nature and strength of whatever forces may be invoked to restore equilibrium. Any discussion of the adjustment process must examine the relation between national economies in a world system—each economy with its

Table 12.1

Individual countries: Balance-of-Payments policies	World economy: Adjustment system
1. Finance deficits from reserves	—
2. Direct controls	—
3. Changes in domestic prices and costs	Gold standard; gold exchange standard
4. Changes in exchange rates:	
(a) Floating rates	1918–25*
	1931–9
(b) Changes in fixed rates when needed	IMF system, in theory
5. *Ad hoc* interventions in the external field to achieve temporary balance-of-payments improvement	IMF system, in practice, since 1959

* Dates are those for the U.K.

own currency unit, price level, exchange rate, domestic interest rate, real and money wage level, employment level, income and income distribution, productivity, monetary and fiscal policy, all variables whose absolute and relative dimension changes constantly with time. The usual method of procedure is to assume a number of countries in a state of balance-of-payments equilibrium, assume some autonomous disturbance to this equilibrium, and observe the process by which equilibrium is restored. In doing this it is impossible even with a complex model to take account of the changes involved during this process in more than a very few of the variables set out above. The variables upon whose variation we shall concentrate initially are those of price level and national income. The behaviour of some of the other variables can often be inferred from these – for example, we may assume that national income and the level of employment are positively correlated and are likely to move together – but clearly certain of these variables are strategic prime movers and the aim is to focus attention on those variables which, in the policy field, are the most important and whose control may provide us with the means to initiate adjustment policies.

Since, fundamentally, adjustment analysis is concerned with the way in which a country reacts to external imbalance and with the way in which the balance of payments returns to equilibrium, it is necessary to be clear about what we mean in this context by (a) imbalance and (b) equilibrium in the balance of payments. Changes in either of these may present serious methodological difficulties which, at this stage, are best avoided. For example, if in a given case of imbalance the cause is a monetary one in that the deficit country has developed for the moment a higher rate of inflation than its neighbours, then the very cause dictates the method of adjustment (a check to the rate of inflation of the deficit country) and even the definition of external equilibrium – one in which balances of payments are held unchanged by constant relative rates of growth of income, productivity and prices. We shall define balance-of-payments equilibrium as a condition in which the foreign demand for the home country's currency is equal to the supply of that currency coming from home nationals' demand to make foreign payments. From this it follows that disequilibrium is a condition in which discrepancies between this demand and supply are covered by inflows or outflows of reserves, to the country concerned. Imbalance we shall be content to define as any autonomous force causing a change in this balance-of-payments equilibrium which, if it is not adjusted, will persist in its effects. In this, time is a factor. Clearly many influences act upon a country's balance of payments which, given time, are self-adjusting. The seasonal movements in demand and supply of a country's currency in the exchange market are an example. These must be excluded by making our time-focus wide enough to encompass such ebbs and flows but not so wide as to introduce the movements of secular change to which all countries and the relations of countries are subject.

The Economics of the Balance of Payments 299

Economic theory provides us with two explanations of the adjustment process: the classical approach which points to changes in the price levels of countries as the force which restores equilibrium; and the more modern approach which sees in the changes of income wrought by changes in the balance of payments a process which reacts upon the balance of payments in turn and tends to restore the balance. These approaches are not alternative theories, mutually exclusive through the correctness and modernity of one and the obsolescence of the other. They are rather complementary ways of regarding the adjustment process. Each applies to the problem the theoretical tools of the economic theory current at the time of its inception; the classical approach reflecting the Ricardian system with its emphasis on price changes, the quantity theory of money, and flexibility of costs and prices; the income approach reflecting the Keynesian theory of income determination with its emphasis on injections and leakages and their influence through multiplier effects upon the income stream. Each approach concentrates upon different variables and in turn implies a different emphasis for policy, the classical approach implying price adjustment through monetary policy, the income approach reflecting the use of fiscal policy for income adjustment. The synthesis of these two views into a complete adjustment policy is still proceeding. The classical approach has yielded little ground to the newer ideas which have supplemented it. In the adjustment process price and income changes work in the same direction. The power of both within the whole process has, however, been enormously illuminated. Once it was thought that price changes alone wrought the necessary changes in the flows of trade to restore balance. Now it is seen that the process is much more complex and that price changes are but a part of it. In this chapter we shall examine the part played by price changes in the adjustment process. In the next chapter we shall look at the effect of income changes. Some of the implications of their interaction will then be explored.

The price mechanism can operate in two ways to produce balance-of-payments adjustment. It is as well for clarity to separate them. The first and most obvious way is for prices to act directly, through changes in the price levels of countries; the second is indirect and occurs where changes in relative prices are brought about by changes in the exchange rate between two currencies. Consider first the simpler case of direct changes in the price levels. This is the classical approach *par excellence.*

The classical approach to the adjustment problem as it was developed from David Hume to Alfred Marshall was an application to international trade of the well-known concept of static equilibrium. The flow of goods in international trade is considered to be the result of differences in national price levels. The upward or downward movement of an individual country's price level changes the direction and volume in which goods flow and therefore, since earlier writers assumed away the existence of international capital transactions, changes the balance of payments of the country concerned. If, therefore, disequilibrium is the result of a change in relative price levels, in its turn it can be adjusted by a further change. In the last resort it might then be possible to describe a country's external equilibrum position as a unique one, reflecting its own price/cost relationship relative to that in the other countries within the world system.

At the heart of the classical approach lay the quantity theory of money which dominated ideas on general price-level determination. According to Ricardo, for equilibrium to obtain, the world's supply of money must be distributed among nations in the same ratio as their national products, such a monetary distribution ensuring price ratios appropriate to general equilibrium.[2] An increase in a country's national product would result in a favourable trade balance, an inflow of gold and so a redistribution of the monetary supply in such a way as to restore a pattern of prices appropriate to equilibrium.

The institutional expression of this approach to adjustment was the international gold standard. With such a standard in operation differences between foreign receipts and payments would be offset by such gold flows as would, by enlarging or depleting the national monetary stock, produce appropriate price changes to alter the demand for the imports and exports of the country concerned and thus correct the balance. In brief, the classical theory was one of the equalisation of prices internationally, adjustment of prices as a result of gold movements being the means of establishing the normal relation of equality.

Underlying this classical account of the adjustment process were a number of implicit assumptions: the validity of the quantity theory of money; the efficiency of the banking arrangements whereby an increase in the money supply had an immediate impact on the domestic monetary situation; complete mobility of factors within the country concerned; completely flexible prices; and, in the country and the world at large, a quick and considerable reaction of both demand and supply to price changes. Some of these assumptions were, at least in the free economy of the nineteenth century, quite justifiable. In the early days, when the gold standard was a gold bullion standard, movements of gold in and out of an economy did directly augment or deplete the money supply; later when gold was held as a reserve to a domestic money supply which bore to it some specified ratio and when the whole paraphernalia of credit control and interest rates became involved, the connection between gold movements and the domestic money supply became more tenuous. So far as factor mobility was concerned, movements in and out of export industries as the trade balance varied were certainly freer in Ricardo's day than they were even later in the century, still less in modern times. In the case of flexible prices the validity of the assumption diminished with the passing of the century. The progressive unwillingness of prices – and in particular that most important of prices, money wages – to fall as easily as to rise was, from a comparatively early stage, a serious discrepancy between gold standard theory and practice. The stickiness of money wages, which made it difficult for wages to adjust downward with other prices in response to a gold outflow, meant that deflation worked itself out by a drop in employment rather than a fall in the wage level. The non-fulfilment of these assumptions tended in the latter-day gold standard of the nineteenth century to build into the system a more deflationary bias than was intended. Employment fell rather than wages, producing (or exacerbating) an unemployment problem. Export industries became subject to recurrent booms and slumps, the immobility of factors resulting in serious surplus capacity in the trough periods. The classical assumptions of flexibility of supply and distribution were, in this field, as in so many other fields of economics, getting more and more out of touch with the facts. But the most sweeping assumption inherent in the classical theory of adjustment was that, when prices fell in a deficit country (following its loss of gold), demand for its exports would rise by such an amount as would not only offset the fall in export prices but would actually raise total export revenue. On the import side it was assumed that since goods from abroad would become relatively dearer as home prices fell, domestic goods would be substituted for imported goods. This assumption of high elasticity of demand for exports and imports in international trade was a vital one for the classical theory of price adjustment. Its non-fulfilment would abrogate the whole system. This is a theoretical and practical difficulty of some importance. To nineteenth-century economists, who usually assumed that elasticities of demand were high, it did not appear so. Now it requires closer scrutiny.

Before we proceed to this problem let us be quite sure of the wideness of its applicability. Classical economics assumed that a balance-of-payments deficit could be adjusted by a change in relative price levels as between the deficit and surplus countries, however this price-level change was brought about. Thus far in our discussion we have been thinking in terms of a gold standard whose chain reaction produced the desired changes in the actual price levels themselves. But equally applicable, and equally a manifestation of the price system, is the change in relative price levels brought about by devaluation of an exchange rate. Since this method of varying price relationships is more topical than that of the gold standard, we shall conduct our discussion of the elasticity condition in these terms.

The exchange rate for a currency is the price in foreign currency terms of a unit of the home country's money. Thus the price of the pound sterling in dollar terms is $2.4 and the exchange rate is said to be $2.4 = £1. Clearly any change in the exchange rate alters the price to the foreigner of all exports of the country concerned. In the example quoted, if the exchange rate were devalued to £1 = $1.2 then the prices of British goods would be halved to United States buyers; if the sterling/dollar exchange rate were revalued to £1 = $4.8, all British prices would be doubled for United States buyers. Thus a condition in which the price level is constant and the exchange rate varies is the same conceptually as one in which the exchange rate is fixed and the price level alters. In what follows we shall assume that domestic prices are constant and that when the balance of payments moves into deficit the exchange rate depreciates on the foreign exchange market until the relation between home and foreign prices has altered sufficiently, exports cheapening and imports becoming dearer to the home country, to adjust the balance-of-payments deficit. Such a system of adjustment finds institutional expression in a floating exchange rate system such as that which succeeded the First World War and lasted until the restoration of the gold standard in the middle twenties, or later between 1931 and 1939.

The immediate task is to consider how exports and imports are affected by changes in the exchange rate and in particular how far the balance of payments is improved by them. Any precise answer to this question involves us in considering the sensitivity of both exports and imports to price changes, not only with regard to the way in which demand for them varies with price but also how supply reacts to it. We are concerned, in short, with the elasticities of demand and supply in foreign trade. These elasticities are relevant in deciding whether and how far depreciation improves the quantity:

value of exports minus value of imports.

To be precise this expression represents the balance of trade (balance of payments on current account), the $(X - M)$ of the simple national income model. To the extent that this expression is improved by a depreciation we are tending towards adjustment of the balance of payments, when it is in deficit.

When depreciation of an exchange rate takes place (in response to a deficit) the immediate price effects are:

The Economics of the Balance of Payments

(a) in terms of home currency — the price of exports is unchanged but the price of imports rises more than in proportion to the depreciation; and

(b) in terms of the foreign currency — the price of exports falls proportionately to the depreciation, while the price of imports remains unchanged.*

In examining how these price changes react upon the trade balance, four elasticities are relevant and will be used in this exposition. For the depreciating country these are:

(i) the foreign demand-elasticity for exports,
(ii) the domestic supply-elasticity of exports,
(iii) the home demand-elasticity for imports, and
(iv) the foreign supply-elasticity of imports.

Consider first the case of one good which is traded internationally between two countries. In the absence of international trade the market

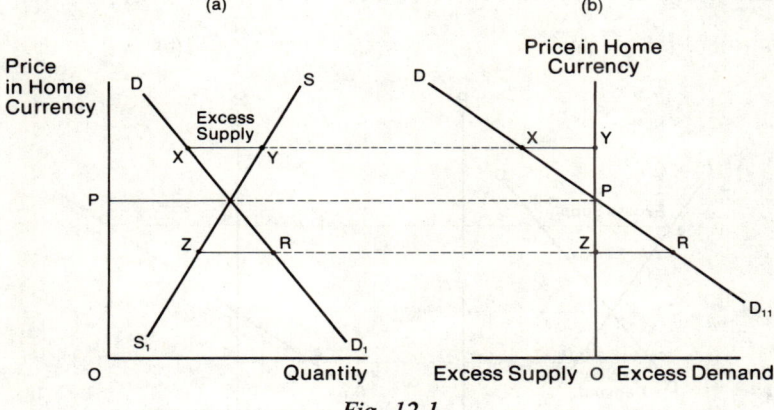

Fig. 12.1

situation in the importing country is shown in Fig. 12.1 (a) in which the ordinary domestic demand and supply are shown in terms of the currency of that country. In this case the market would be in equilibrium at price P which equates supply and demand. At prices greater than P supply exceeds demand, the excess supply increasing the farther the price rises above P; at prices less than P there is excess demand, the amount of which increases

---

* In September 1949, when the pound was devalued from £1 = $4 to £1 = $2·8, a reduction of 30 per cent, the rise in the price of imports in home currency terms was 43 per cent.

the further the price falls below P. The way in which excess supply and excess demand vary with price can be shown on the diagram in Fig. 12.1 (b) which is directly derivable from Fig. 12.1 (a). It is this excess-demand curve DD_{11}, which is relevant to the foreign trade situation of the good, since it shows the additional demand for the good which will be generated should the price in international trade fall below the domestic price in the absence of trade. It will be seen that the properties of this excess demand curve, as far as elasticity is concerned, are derived from the elasticities of the domestic demand and supply curves which are, of course, shown by their slope. The elasticity of the derived excess demand curve is greater than the domestic demand curve simply because there is some home elasticity of supply. If home elasticity of supply were zero (that is, if SS_1 were vertical) then DD_{11} would have the same elasticity as DD_1. The greater the elasticity of SS_1, the more the elasticity of DD_{11} exceeds that of DD_1. If domestic supply were infinitely elastic at P (that is, if SS_1 was a horizontal line at that price), then DD_{11} would be infinitely elastic at the same price.

We can apply this method to the market situation of the exporting country. Fig. 12.2 (a) shows the domestic demand and supply situation

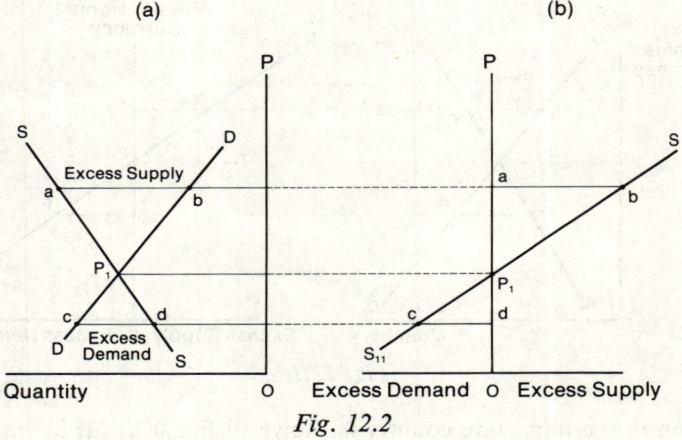

Fig. 12.2

in the exporting country. This time the supply and demand curves must be reversed and shown, as it were back to back, in order that in Fig. 12.2 (b) we can derive an excess supply curve of appropriate slope. The scale of the price axis is shown in the currency of the importing country since it is necessary at the next step to combine the excess demand and excess supply curves on one diagram. The excess supply curve SS_{11} shows the amount of excess supply available to the importing country at various levels of price.

The Economics of the Balance of Payments

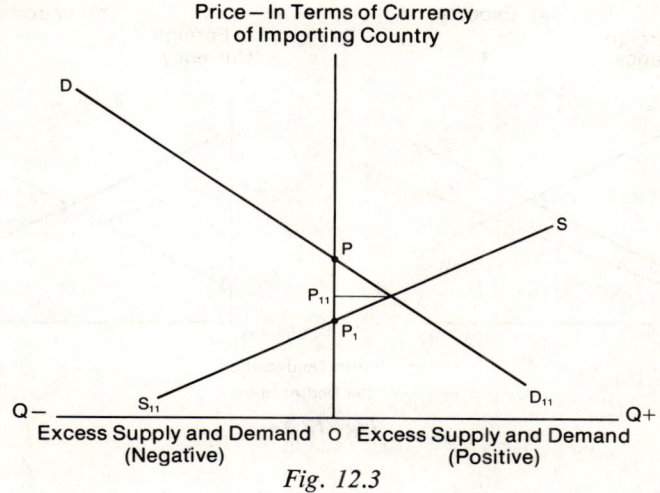

Fig. 12.3

Fig. 12.3 then combines DD_{11} and SS_{11} on one diagram to show the equilibrium position in the international market for this commodity, expressed in prices in terms of the currency of the importing country. This simple partial-equilibrium diagram shows the price in the international market at P_{11}, which is lower than the original domestic price in the importing country without trade and higher than the price in the exporting country in the absence of trade. Both countries are advantaged by the trade.

We can use diagrams of this type depicting excess demand in one country and excess supply in another to show what occurs when a foreign exchange

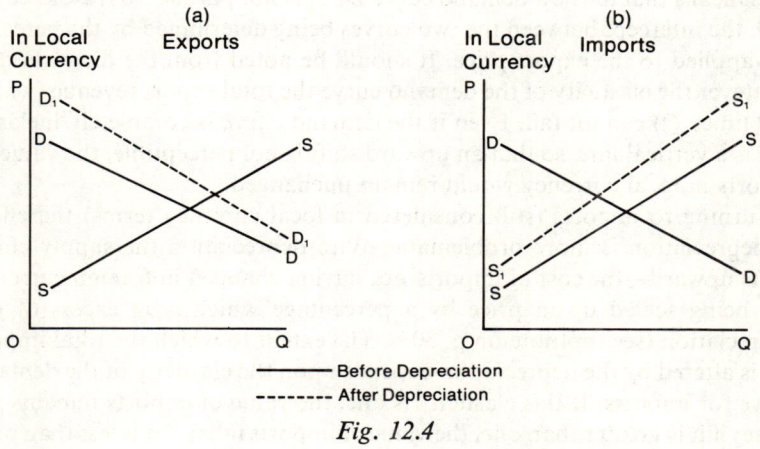

Fig. 12.4

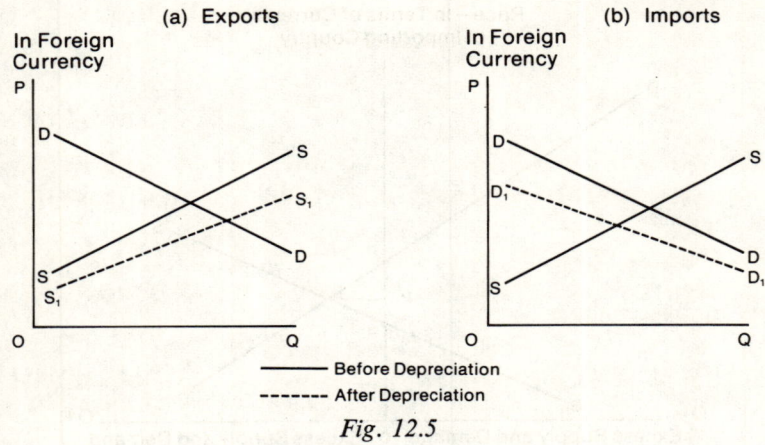

Fig. 12.5

rate is devalued and why the elasticities of demand and supply influence the impact of the depreciation. This can be done by showing four diagrams: Fig. 12.4 (a) (for exports for the given country) and Fig. 12.4 (b) (for imports), showing the effect in local currency; and Figs. 12.5 (a) and 12.5 (b) showing the effect in foreign exchange. We must still assume that there is only one traded commodity.

First, look at the local currency effects (see Fig. 12.4 (a) and (b)). The effect upon exports of a depreciation is to shift upward the demand curve for exports. Since this is fixed in foreign exchange, the effect in local currency is to raise the demand curve by the percentage of the depreciation. This means that the new demand curve $D_1 D_1$ is not parallel to the old curve DD, the intercept between the two curves being determined by the percentage applied to the export price. It should be noted from the diagram that whatever the elasticity of the demand curve the total export revenue (which is P times Q) cannot fall. Even if the demand curve is completely inelastic and is a vertical line, so that an upward shift is not perceptible, the value of exports in local currency would remain unchanged.

Turning to imports (still considered in local currency terms) the effect of depreciation is more problematic. With depreciation the supply curve shifts upward — the cost of imports not having changed in foreign currency but being scaled up in price by a percentage which is in excess of the depreciation (see footnote on p. 303). The extent to which the total import bill is altered by the depreciation depends upon the elasticity of the demand curve for imports. If this elasticity is one, the value of imports remains the same; if it is greater than one, the value of imports falls; if it is less than one,

The Economics of the Balance of Payments

the value of imports will rise. In terms of the diagram the effect of a depreciation on the value of exports in local currency depends on the slope of *DD* in Fig. 12.4 (b).

The effects of a depreciation on total exports and total imports in terms of foreign exchange can be traced on a further pair of diagrams, Fig. 12.5 (a) and (b), on which the demand and supply curves for each are shown, this time in terms of foreign exchange. Only when there is a foreign exchange rate of one are the pre-depreciation demand and supply curves for local currency and for foreign exchange identical. In this case depreciation shifts the supply curve downward in the case of exports and the demand curve downward in the case of imports; but in each case the value of the change in exports and in imports depends upon the elasticity of the intersecting curve. The lesson once more is that the elasticities of demand for imports at home and for exports abroad are strategic in influencing the export bill and the export revenue.

Let us summarise the findings so far:

1. If the elasticity of demand for imports is greater than one, a depreciation must improve the trade balance, for the value of imports (in home currency) will fall while, even if the foreign demand for exports is zero elastic, the value of exports (in home currency) will be unchanged.

2. If the elasticity of demand for imports is less than one, the balance of trade will improve, if the foreign elasticity of demand for exports is such that exports increase more than sufficient to offset the rise in the import bill. To the extent that the elasticity of demand for imports is less than unity the foreign elasticity of demand for exports must compensate for this.

3. From the foregoing it follows that a balance of trade may improve with a depreciation even when elasticities of home and foreign demand are each less than one, provided that together these elasticies are greater than one. If the sum of the elasticities is unity then the balance of trade remains unchanged; if it is less than unity then the balance of trade will deteriorate.

This famous condition, the so-called Marshall–Lerner* condition, is a

---

* The name Marshall–Lerner condition arises from the historical derivation of this theoretical proviso. Marshall (in *Pure Theory of Foreign Trade*, 1879) noted the problem but, believing elasticities to be high in the real world, regarded it as an intellectual exercise having little significance for policy. It is clear from his other writing (e.g. *Money, Credit and Commerce*, p. 171) that Marshall's view was that the elasticities relevant to the condition were much higher than unity. The correct conditions of exchange stability were first stated by C. F. Bickerdike in a note, 'The Instability of Foreign Exchange' in the *EJ* (March 1920). Joan Robinson, in her essay on the foreign exchanges published in 1937, developed Bickerdike's ideas and pointed to the influence of low elasticities of supply as a force weakening the rigour of the condition. Abba Lerner, in his *Economics of Control* (New York: The Macmillan Co., 1944) p. 377, stated the condition fully and revived interest in it, an interest which was shared by the statisticians

necessary condition for improvement of the balance of trade by a depreciation, provided that the elasticities of supply of exports and imports are large. If, however, these supply elasticities are relatively low the force of the condition is weakened. If, for example, the elasticity of supply of exports is low the price of exports will tend to rise (in home currency terms — not fall so far in foreign currency terms) as demand for them expands with the depreciation, and thus foreign exchange earnings will not decline to the same extent as they would have done with a high or infinite supply elasticity. This reduces the power of the Marshall–Lerner condition to one where it is a sufficient but not necessary condition for balance-of-payments improvement. The sum of demand elasticities can be less than unity and still improve the trade balance if supply elasticities are low.

This last point is well illustrated by Kindleberger in a single diagram (Fig. 12.6). If DD, the demand curve for exports in foreign exchange, has an elasticity of less than one, it can be seen that with low elasticity of supply (SS and $S_{11}S_{11}$), the price of exports in foreign exchange will not fall so low in foreign exchange, and foreign exchange earnings will not decline as much as when the elasticity of supply is infinite (SS and $S'S'$). The price fall with low supply inelasticity is Oa, and with infinite supply elasticity Ob. The higher price at a more than makes up for the decline in volume. This follows from the fact that ab is part of DD which has an elasticity of less than one.

A further limitation on the Marshall–Lerner condition is that the imbalance which must be corrected is not too large, i.e., that imports must not greatly exceed exports. If the condition is met and the sum of the elasticities exceeds unity, the *percentage* increase in exports will always be greater than the percentage increase in imports. But if imports are much larger than exports in the first place, then the absolute increase in imports may be larger in home currency or the absolute decrease in imports may be smaller in foreign exchange terms. If the initial deficit is large, much higher elasticities will be required in order to eliminate this deficit and secure adjustment.

The Marshall–Lerner condition has important theoretical implications. If it operates rigorously not only does it imply that price reductions, either directly or through exchange rate depreciations, are ineffective in adjusting a balance of payments, but it points to the possibility that depreciation may even worsen the balance and that, in certain circumstances, any movement away from exchange equilibrium will produce forces which serve to increase

---

and advocates of free exchange rate policies. For a good formal presentation of the theoretical implications of the condition see G. Stuvel, *The Exchange Stability Problem* (Leiden: Stenfert Kruese, 1950).

The Economics of the Balance of Payments 309

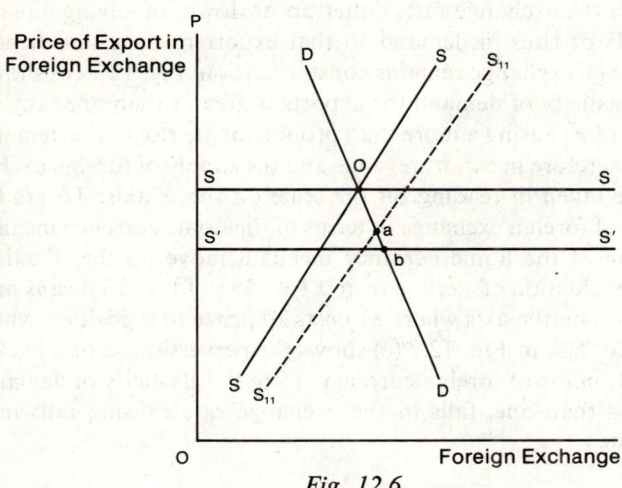

Fig. 12.6

the disequilibrium rather than correct it. This point can be shown diagrammatically.

In the following series of diagrams, the demand and supply curves for foreign currency are shown. For the moment these curves will be drawn as straight lines, as it is assumed they are immediately around the points of intersection. Take the supply curve first.

The supply of foreign currency comes from the sale of exports and can be reflected in supply curves of the type shown in Fig. 12.7. Fig. 12.7 (a) illustrates the case where foreign elasticity of demand for exports is one,

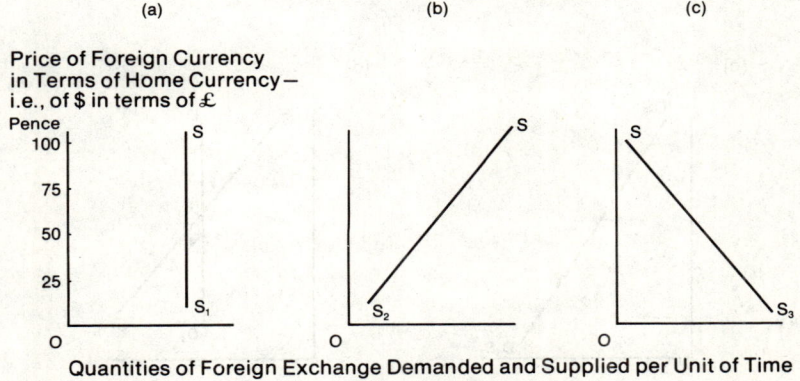

Fig. 12.7

any change in the exchange rate, either up or down, involving equal proportional falls or rises in demand so that export revenue and hence the supply of foreign exchange remains constant. SS_2 in Fig. 12.7 (b) shows the case where elasticity of demand for exports is greater than one, any fall in the exchange rate causing a more than proportionate rise in the demand for exports and therefore in export revenue and the supply of foreign exchange. Care must be taken in reading off the scale on the Y axis. To grade this axis for price of foreign exchange in terms of the home currency means that a depreciation of the home currency means a move up the Y axis. For example, a devaluation of sterling from £1 = \$5 to £1 = \$3 means moving from a position on the axis where \$1 costs 20 pence to a position where \$1 costs 33 pence. SS_3 in Fig. 12.7 (c) shows the perverse case of a backward sloping supply curve of foreign currency. Here the elasticity of demand for exports is less than one, falls in the exchange rate causing falls in total export revenue.

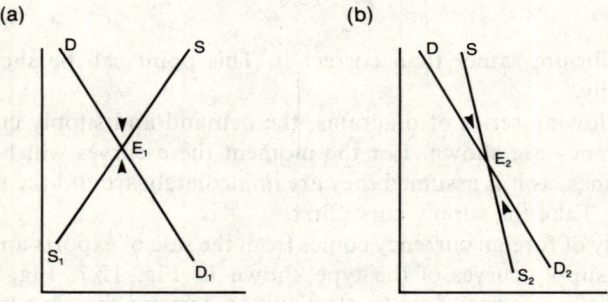

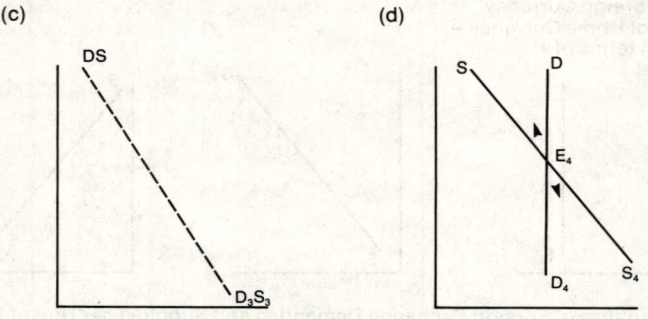

Fig. 12.8

The demand curve for foreign exchange is more uniform. In all diagrams it is shown sloping downward to the right. A fall in the price of imports (as the price of foreign exchange diminishes in the home currency) will, in varying degree, cause the quantity of foreign exchange demanded to rise. It is inconceivable that a rise in the price of foreign exchange would make domestic buyers increase their demand for foreign exchange. The limiting case for the demand curve would be that of a vertical position denoting an elasticity of demand of zero.

Combining the supply and demand for foreign exchange in the following set of diagrams, therefore, gives us four cases — as shown in Fig. 12.8 (a), (b), (c) and (d). We assume in (a), (b) and (c) that the demand curve is of unit elasticity. (Remember still that the curves as drawn represent only the sectors around the intersection points of much longer curves.)

The first two cases are those of stable equilibrium. Any movement of the exchange rate away from E_1 or E_2 sets up forces which tend immediately to restore the equilibrium. In Fig. 12.8 (a) the elasticity of demand for foreign currencies reflects an elasticity of demand for imports of one, the elasticity of the supply curve reflects an elasticity of demand for the country's exports of more than one. In Fig. 12.8 (b), although the elasticity of demand for exports (reflected in the slope of the supply curve for foreign exchange) is less than one, the demand curve still has an elasticity sufficient to give a stable equilibrium at E_2. Fig. 12.8 (c) shows the case where the sum of the elasticities for imports and exports, reflected in the supply and demand curves for foreign currency, are just equal to one and the equilibrium is indeterminate. Fig. 12.8 (d) shows the case where equilibrium is unstable. The supply curve SS_4 now represents an elasticity much less than one for the country's exports. For convenience DD_4 shows the extreme case of zero elasticity of demand for imports, so that the elasticities now sum to less than unity. Here any movement of the exchange rate away from the level appropriate to E_4 sets up forces which only increase the disequilibrium — for example, a reduction of the rate making supply of the currency exceed demand, thus forcing a further reduction. If we assume a demand curve for foreign exchange and for imports which is vertical and has, therefore, an elasticity of zero and if we allow it as in Fig. 12.9 to be intersected by supply curves of foreign exchange reflecting different elasticities of demand for exports, then we can see intuitively how the case where $\epsilon_{di} + \epsilon_{de} = 1$ is the dividing case between stability and instability in the exchange equilibrium.

If DD has ϵ of 0, and SS_1 has $\epsilon > 1$ then $\epsilon_{DD} + \epsilon_{SS_1} > 1$ but if SS_2 has $\epsilon < 1$ then $\epsilon_{DD} + \epsilon_{SS_2} < 1$ and the equilibrium is unstable. As long as SS_2 is to the left of DD (as it is in the condition of instability) the amount by which the elasticity of SS_2 is below unity is greater than the amount

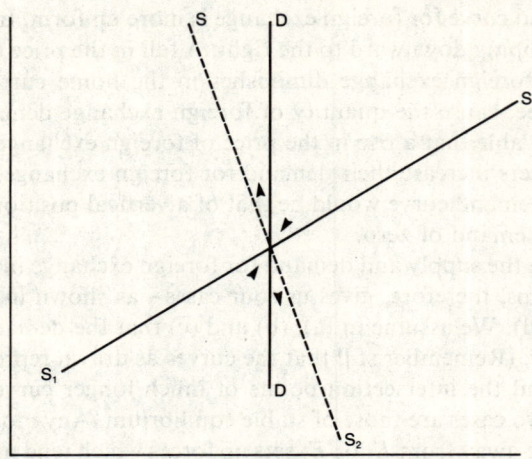

Fig. 12.9

by which DD is above zero, and the sum of the elasticities is less than unity.

So far this diagrammatic analysis of foreign exchange equilibrium has assumed the demand and supply curves to be straight lines and has been concerned only with their relationships just around the intersection point in each case. Once one broadens the view, however, to examine what happens to these curves over a greater length, new possibilities appear. Consider Fig. 12.10. There are now three intersection points. The interesting case is that of the unstable equilibrium. If we take the demand

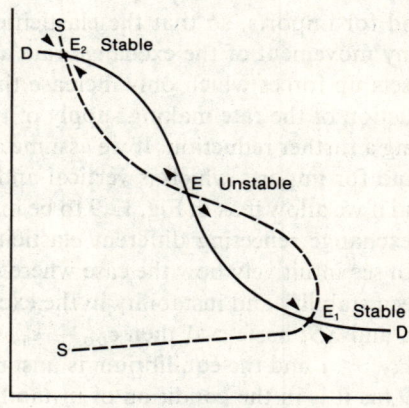

Fig. 12.10

The Economics of the Balance of Payments

curve for foreign exchange (and for imports), repeated depreciations would eventually lead to an elastic sector of the curve at which very small amounts of foreign currency would be bought, DD would bend back towards the Y axis and cut the SS curve at E_2. Similarly, south of E the SS curve would swing back to the vertical and then incline towards the origin, intersecting DD at E_1 in so doing. This backward and downward swing of SS reflects the likelihood that at very high exchange rates for the home currency the elasticity of demand for its exports would become high, rising to unity and beyond. The SS curve would reflect only some minimal demand for the country's exports at this high exchange rate. If these extrapolations of the demand and supply curves are correct an unstable equilibrium exchange rate would be flanked above and below by stable equilibrium rates. We cannot offer proof that these two stable equilibria must exist with the curves as drawn. We can only say that it is highly likely. For example, E_2 must exist as an intersection point, if only because at some value, however high, DD must touch the price axis, whereas the limit of SS's slope in this sector is a rectangular hyperbola. South of E is more problematic, but it is likely that there is some price of the home currency at which foreigners would buy no exports and so the SS curve would curve round to touch the price axis, while in the same sector the DD curve would be moving to the right reflecting high demand for imports at the low cost of foreign exchange.[3]

Which of the stable equilibria would be achieved is problematical. E_1 reflects the better terms of trade for the home country, and in practice the monetary authorities would try to move the rate towards E_1, there to allow the equilibrium forces to operate. With a perfectly free exchange rate, i.e. with no interference from monetary authorities, the rate would be repelled from E, but whether to E_1 or E_2 would be a matter of chance, depending upon the direction of the initial movement away from equilibrium. If the shapes of the supply and demand curves are as we postulate them, however, escape from the Marshall–Lerner condition (from what we may call the 'perverse elasticities case'), would be possible for a deficit country. Moreover the existence of one position of instability in the market would not necessarily render a free exchange market unworkable.

How powerful a constraint upon balance-of-payments adjustment by price change is the Marshall–Lerner condition? We have shown that, with high elasticities of supply of imports and exports, it would appear at least to impose a necessary condition, that of high demand elasticities, upon the success of exchange rate changes. What evidence have we that such a condition is formidable, and that it imposes itself upon a country seeking to correct imbalance by an alteration of its exchange rate?

It must be remembered that the condition is a necessary one only if elasticities of supply are infinite. In practice they are not likely to be so. There are few products for which elasticity of supply is of this order, and still fewer of them enter into international trade. Moreover, in these days of full employment policies, labour shortage in the great industrial economies together with an increasing specificity of technical factors are influences which tend to impose inelasticity of supply. Thus, at the very outset the force of the Marshall–Lerner condition is weakened, turning it from a necessary to a sufficient condition.

What of the elasticities themselves? What light have the statisticians and economic historians to throw upon their likely values? Opinions have varied. Before the Second World War the consensus was that low elasticities placed at least a considerable impediment to price adjustment methods. Statistical estimates made after the war – by Chang, Neisser, Polak, Tinbergen and others – indicated probable values for elasticities so low as to make it wellnigh certain that exchange rate changes would be ineffectual. Theory and empirical work both caused scepticism to surround price or exchange rate changes as means of adjustment. The view of the statisticians was altered, however, by the publication in 1950 of Guy Orcutt's survey of the estimates of elasticities which had theretofore been made.[4] Orcutt alleged that the estimates were, for a number of reasons, too low. They had been made on the basis of too narrow a range of experience and they assumed important variables, such as income, to be constant. Errors and bias in the available data of quantities and prices of imports and exports had been overlooked. The estimates had been based on historical price and quantity indices which reflected price changes of commodities with very different price elasticities; but since one might expect price to change most where demand was inelastic, such indices might well reflect unduly the price changes of commodities with inelastic demands. Estimates were for short-run instead of long-run elasticities. All these defects led Orcutt to call in question past estimates and leave the door open for new work. In Orcutt's view, statistical findings gave no reason to suppose that depreciation would prove an ineffective corrector of a deficit in the balance of payments.

On the historical side, the evidence all points to high long-run elasticities. Britain in 1931, 1949 and 1967, France in 1958 achieved striking improvements in their trade balances by devaluation. The history of the British economy between the wars – its relative depression between 1925 and 1931 as a result of overvaluation of sterling, its relatively swift recovery from the depression after the 1931 depreciation of sterling, its trade improvement in the 1950s after the devaluation of 1949, its strong trading recovery after the 1967 sterling devaluation (and subsequent Deutschmark revaluation), all point to changes in the exchange rate for sterling as having considerable influence on the fortunes of the British economy.

Depreciation has also been practised with advantage by primary producing countries. Here, although the demand for the product may be inelastic, elasticity of supply is low, thus mitigating the force of the elasticity condition. Moreover, primary products of some large countries are often sold under highly competitive world market conditions (e.g. butter and dairy products in which competition among Australia, New Zealand, Holland, Denmark and other countries is severe) in which the elasticity of demand for one country's product will be much greater than the elasticity of demand for the product as a whole. On the import side, depreciation is likely to achieve at least some curtailment for primary producers, particularly of the developed type such as Australia and New Zealand. Moreover, the fact that primary producing countries (with certain notable exceptions) are often of small size and of peripheral importance makes it unlikely that depreciation will be followed by retaliatory action on the part of other countries.

Time is a factor having great influence on the elasticity condition. There must surely be some difference between elasticities in the long and short run. Foreign trade is conducted through many media of selling and forwarding agents, financial and banking contacts, transport and insurance groups at home and abroad. For price changes of short duration, buyers in foreign trade will not switch their demands and break established lines of contact. But price changes which are of long duration, and a devaluation, indicating a move into a new climate of prices and relative prices, will induce merchants to switch their demands to alternative products. Certainly, in the long run, adjustments to a price change will be made and it is therefore likely that long-run price elasticity of demand for goods in foreign trade is greater than for that in the short run.

Another factor in the elasticity of demand for goods in foreign trade is the size of the price change involved. For small price changes a switch of demand may not be worthwhile, but for a large price change the elasticity of demand may be much greater. That for small price changes a switch of demand may even be virtually impossible may be seen from the following example of where a country imports a given fuel or raw material commodity a switch to another type may involve insupportable money costs if capital equipment has to be altered. A country importing fuel oil is not likely to switch to natural gas because the latter has a small price advantage. In the long run or with a large price advantage the switch may be worth while.

All of these considerations tend to weaken rather than strengthen fears that the Marshall–Lerner condition negates the power of a depreciation to improve the balance of payments. There is still a presumptive case for the use of the price mechanism. Of the extent of the improvement in the balance of payments and how long it takes to act there is no exact guide; countries must fall back on experience or, in default of this, on the shaky forecasts which our knowledge allows.

One final factor which must serve to weaken somewhat the long-run effect of a depreciation on a country's foreign balance is that of the income effects of the initial change in the balance of payments. Even if we assume that all conditions for the success of a depreciation are met, the improvement in the balance of payments when it takes place will raise national income in the adjusting country and lower it in the rest of the world. This will have the effect of increasing imports into the home country while its exports to the rest of the world will be reduced. This secondary, income-generated, worsening of the balance of trade must be set against the primary improvement brought about by the price effects. The stimulus to exports and check to imports resulting from depreciation will be progressively reduced by income effects, and the final favourable result of depreciation, taking into account both price and income effects, is smaller than it would be in the absence of the latter.

There is, it seems, a formidable list of qualifications to the force of the Marshall–Lerner condition. Yet another must be added. It should be remembered that the whole analysis on which the condition was evolved is a partial equilibrium one only, that is, it examines the effects of depreciation on trade flows, with all other variables regarded as constant. The defects of this method for an analysis of the changes wrought by such an important variable as the exchange rate should be obvious. We may be content with 'other things being equal' when we are considering the market for golf balls; we can hardly be so content, still less prepared to formulate judgements and policy prescriptions, when we are considering the impact of changes in the most important single price in an economy, the exchange rate. As Kindleberger says: 'a change in this price produces changes which reverberate throughout the economy, altering incomes and goods prices over a wide range so that other things cannot be taken as equal.'[5] This leaves us with the uneasy question: what will the total elasticities be if all possible effects of depreciation, including income, be taken into account? What the answer to this question might be is very problematic, and in the last resort can be little better than a guess. All we can say is that the record of depreciation in recent times seems to indicate that 'total elasticities' must have values high enough to have significant effect upon trade balances.

The Economics of the Balance of Payments

There is nothing in modern currency history to throw serious doubt upon the efficacy of depreciation.

(iii) Summing Up

It is time to sum up. The following facts seem to emerge from this discussion of the adjustment process by price changes.

1. Only under certain conditions will a change in a country's price level be an effective means of adjusting a deficit in a country's balance of payments. These conditions can be summarised in the condition that demand for imports and exports of the depreciating country should be sensitive to changes in their price. To the extent that variations in the supply of such goods invoke changes in their prices, the force of this condition is weakened.
2. If accepted in its most rigid form, the elasticity condition would have detrimental implications not only for the price adjustment mechanism as a policy device but for the whole classical theory of balance-of-payments adjustment. Such a view is, however, based on too narrow an interpretation of the condition. Not only is the condition reduced in rigour by a more searching analysis, which reduces it virtually to the status of a special case, but discussion of the empirical evidence might lead one to the conclusion that it is a special case not often met with.
3. Currency history strengthens rather than weakens the case for price and exchange rate variations.
4. The fact that demand reactions to price changes are greater in the long run than in the short, and greater for large price changes than for small, tends to strengthen the view that periodic changes in the exchange rate may have a considerable effect on the long-run balance of payments.
5. Apart from the economic aspects of price change, political aspects are important. Depreciation is likely to be more successful, the smaller is the country depreciating, the less its currency is in general use for world-wide payments settlement, and the less its products are in direct competition in world markets with those of the great powers.
6. The secondary effects of changes in the trade flows brought about by a change in relative prices will to some extent retard the adjustment effect of such a change on the balance of payments. This retarding effect will be the greater, the greater is the marginal propensity to import of the country concerned.

However one interprets the balance of advantage of this summary, it is certainly true that the case for adjusting a balance of payments by changing the relation of national price levels is a qualified one, qualified in two respects: firstly, by the existence of another force, namely, income changes, which works and interacts with price changes; secondly, in that even if it is admitted that price changes have a role to play in adjustment, we are still left with the question of how price changes are to be brought about, by exchange rate variations or by domestically engineered changes in the level of home prices. This is followed by the contingent question that, if the medium of exchange variations is the chosen one, how should the exchange rate variations be made—continuously, through the movements of floating exchange rates in a free exchange market; or periodically, by discrete changes made from time to time in the light of reserve flows and changes in balances of payments? These questions will be taken up in subsequent chapters. The first task is to examine the other great force operating for balance-of-payments adjustment, namely, changes in the level of national income.

13
Adjustment and Income Analysis

(i) A Keynesian Approach

ALTHOUGH the part played by income changes in balance-of-payments adjustment is Keynesian in approach and method, Keynes himself took no direct part in its formulation or development. Uneasiness as to the explanation given by classical economists dates from the early twenties. Keynes in his controversy with Ohlin argued on conventional classical lines that the transfer of German reparations payments could only be made by a reduction of the German price level relative to those countries to which transfer was to be made. Scepticism of the older approach came first from other writers. Although a number of empirical studies of the working of the price adjustment mechanism[1] appeared to confirm the working of the classical process, they revealed at the same time so swift and complete an adjustment as made observers sceptical that it could have been affected by price changes alone. Some other equilibrating mechanism might be at work to speed up and augment the changes made by price movements. At the same time (in the 1920s and early 1930s), the efforts of statisticians to measure elasticities of demand in international trade seemed to show that such elasticities were so low that the Marshall–Lerner condition must surely impose some constraint upon adjustment by price movements alone.

The new approach to income determination theory marked by the appearance of Keynes' *General Theory of Employment, Interest and Money* in 1936 made possible the formulation of a new approach to the adjustment process by Mrs Robinson, R. F. Harrod, Fritz Machlup and others.[2] This new approach showed that an imbalance in international payments involved an adjustment in income, employment and output irrespective of what changes took place in prices and of how the deficit was financed. It showed an interaction between the balance of payments and national income which was a dual one: the 'adjustment process', by which a balance of payments is adjusted by changes in the income levels of the home country and the rest of the world; and the 'transmission process', which shows how variations in the national income of one country may through their balances of payments cause variations in the national incomes of other countries. Moreover, it enabled certain powerful analytic tools of income analysis, such as the national income multiplier, to be applied to the adjustment process.

A second important feature of the income approach lay in the light which it threw upon disequilibrium as well as upon the adjustment process itself. It showed, for example, that since deficits were adjustable by relative movements of national income, by reduction of income in the deficit country and increase of income in the surplus country, correction of a deficit must, under static productivity conditions, necessarily involve a reduction in national income. It showed sharply the contrast which might arise between external and domestic equilibrium in the case where the former was possible only under income conditions which gave balance-of-payments equilibrium to the adjusting country at a level of national income well below that of full employment. It showed that a deficit country might well be unwilling to allow adjustment of its balance of payments to take place if such adjustment involved for it a serious loss of national income. The full condition of equilibrium for a country had now to be redefined as one in which total external receipts equalled total external payments *at full employment*. This linkage of external equilibrium for a country with its level of income and employment by the new approach enabled a much clearer and more realistic view to be taken of balance-of-payments policy in the post-war period. It is now clear that there may be serious conflict between the domestic policies of a country with respect to its income, employment and growth, and its external policy for preservation of a satisfactory balance of payments. For example, the United Kingdom has been unsuccessfully pursuing policies for a higher rate of economic growth at the same time as she has been seeking a recurrent surplus on her balance of payments. Neither policy has been successful. When the balance of payments has gone into deficit the United Kingdom has purposefully checked the growth of her income; when she has allowed her income once more to grow her balance of payments has gone into deficit. It would appear that the national income desired by the United Kingdom is incompatible with a payments surplus, indeed even with a bare equilibrium.

In this chapter we shall set out fairly fully the mechanism by which the balance of payments and national income are connected. First, we shall examine some of the simpler relations between imports, exports and national income. Thus armed, we shall examine the process of income change and the national income multiplier in a closed economy, and in an open

The Economics of the Balance of Payments

system. Finally, we shall demonstrate the media through which adjustment is partially achieved by income changes.

(ii) The Import and Export Functions

In this chapter, we shall make the following assumptions:

1. all prices are constant so that changes in income are changes in real income;
2. there are some idle resources, since expansion and contraction of output can take place without changes in prices;
3. time and its effects are not taken into account; there are no lags between receiving income and spending it; the multipliers evolved are simultaneous multipliers;[3]
4. balance-of-payments deficits are financeable by transfers of international liquidity;
5. exports are sold from current production and not from inventories;
6. imports are for immediate domestic use and not for re-export;
7. all functions are linear and constant.

Since imports and exports, the items comprising the merchandise trade balance, are basic to the balance of payments and its adjustment, our first task is to examine their relations with income. We start with imports.

For this relationship we make use of the method, familiar in domestic income analysis, of stating an income constituent or changes in an income constituent as a fraction of income itself. (Imports are of course only an income constituent when considered in relation to exports. $(X - M)$ is the constituent we are interested in. It forms part of the simple equation $Y = C + I + (X - M)$.) Thus we think of consumption as C/Y, the average propensity to consume and $\Delta C/\Delta Y$, the marginal propensity to consume; the former signifying the proportion of income spent on consumption, the latter the proportion of any increment of income which is consumed. Imports and national income have a similar relationship and it is convenient to use the same formulation. Thus, M/Y is the average propensity to import, which shows simply the money value of imports as a percentage of total national income. The average propensity to import is only mildly interesting as a statistic. It may be very low (4 to 5 per cent) for a self-sufficient country and very high (40 to 50 per cent) for a highly specialised small country. It tells us, merely, whether the country is or is not a large importing country. As is usual in economics, it is change which is important, and the marginal propensity to import shows change. Specifically, it shows the change (ΔM) in imports which occurs with a given change in income (ΔY). The marginal propensity to import ($\Delta M/\Delta Y$) tells us that when income rises by $100 million and imports rise by $20 million, then the marginal propensity to import is one-fifth or 0·2. However, the marginal propensity to import should not be confused with the income elasticity of imports. The former is the ratio of the increment of imports to the increment of income; the latter is the percentage change in imports associated with a given percentage change in national income, i.e. $(\Delta M/M)/(\Delta Y/Y)$. A 3 per cent increase in imports coming from a 9 per cent increase in national income implies an income elasticity to import of 0·3.

For any given country it is unlikely that the average and marginal propensities to import will be the same. An underdeveloped country, living near to subsistence level, may have a low average propensity to import, but since a rise in national income and an increase in living standards will probably induce a sharp rise in imports, its marginal propensity to import is almost certainly high. A mature country, on the other hand, may be a large trading country with a high average propensity to import; but since domestic output is more diversified, a rise in income may well induce only a small increase in imports and the marginal propensity to import will be less than the average propensity.

Imports are positively related to national income. In algebraic terms $M = f(Y)$ where M is the level of imports and Y the level of national income. Fig. 13.1 shows the function diagrammatically. When national income

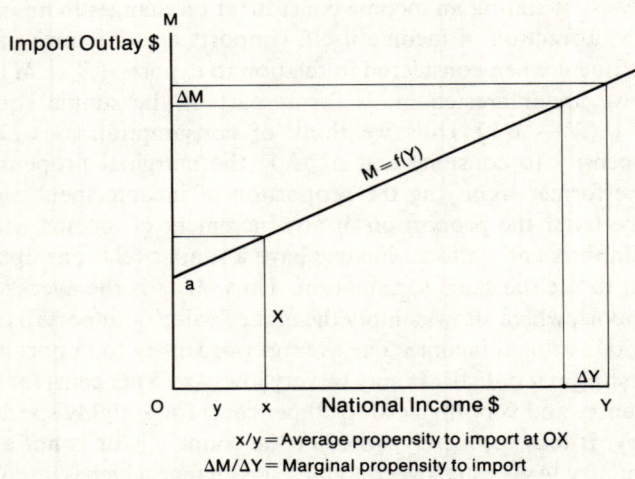

x/y = Average propensity to import at OX
$\Delta M/\Delta Y$ = Marginal propensity to import

Fig. 13.1

The Economics of the Balance of Payments

increases there will be an additional demand for imports, so that the marginal propensity to import will be shown by the slope of the import function. The import function will not pass through the origin, since even at zero national income some minimal amount of imports (Oa) will be bought, presumably out of reserves or by borrowing from abroad.

Although we have assumed that the import function is linear, implying a constant marginal propensity to import over a wide range of income, we must remember that in practice this is certain to be otherwise. For example, a given increase in income may emanate from the industrial sector and draw in large imports of raw material; an equal increase in income coming from the agricultural sector may draw in practically nothing in imports. Or again, at very low levels of income the marginal propensity to import may be high; at high levels of income it may be considerably less. Yet again, a rise in incomes when inventories are low may cause imports to rise sharply; a rise in income when inventories are high may cause only a modest rise in imports. In short, the marginal propensity to import of a country may differ with time, the phase of the business cycle, how the increase in income is generated, and many other factors.

When we turn to exports the relation with income is quite different. Firstly, since exports are produced from current income they represent an increase in income itself. They are, like investment in the domestic economy, income creating. Secondly, unlike imports they have no marked functional relationship with income. Indeed, we might assume that exports are constant for all levels of income. On the same axes as were used in Fig. 13.1, they would then be represented by a horizontal line whose height above the lower axis would be determined by their value as in Fig. 13.2 (a).

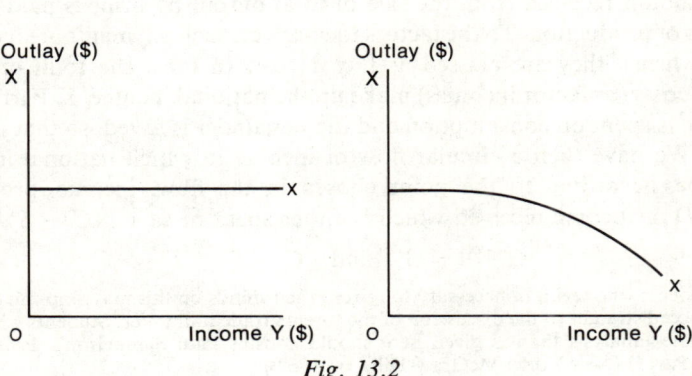

Fig. 13.2

The situation depicted in the diagram implies that either what is exported is not wanted or not consumed at all in the home country, or that if it is consumed the demand for it is income-inelastic. Clearly this assumption has great limitations. It may be applicable enough to a primary-producing country supplying some basic primary raw material for a manufacturing process which is only carried on outside the country. It is not, however, applicable to diverse manufacturing economies in which exports and investment and exports and consumption are competitive activities and not, as in the former case, independent. In the latter case, it is possible that as income increases exports might fall, giving a negative relation with income as in Fig. 13.2 (b). The shape of this function is not, however, important for what follows, and for simplicity we shall assume it to be as in Fig. 13.2 (a).

(iii) National Income in a Closed and an Open Economy

Having completed these necessary preliminaries, we can now proceed to describe the process of income-creation and the national income multiplier in a closed economy. This we shall do in both algebraic and diagrammatic terms.* We shall then apply the same process to an open economy to describe the foreign trade multiplier.

In a closed economy with some idle resources and constant prices, the level of national income Y is shown by the level of aggregate demand $(C + I)$ where C is the demand for consumption goods and I the demand for investment goods. In the analysis which follows we shall assume, for simplicity, that G, the level of government expenditure, is included in C and I, according to whether it is upon consumer goods or investment goods. The amount received from the sale of total output by firms is paid to the factors of production. To the factors themselves, such payments are income; to the firms, they are classed as factor cost. In turn, the total of these factor costs (or factor incomes) make up the national income Y. Part of the income is spent on consumption and the remainder is saved, so that $C + S = Y$. We have then a circular flow of income in which national income may be, according to the point chosen in the flow, income produced $(C + I)$ or income received which is either spent or saved $(C + S)$. Since

$$C + I = Y \quad \text{and} \quad C + S = Y$$

* Students who feel it unnecessary to refresh their minds on this may skip this section and proceed straight to the discussion of the foreign trade multiplier. Students who wish for a fuller analysis than is given here should consult Paul Samuelson's *Economics*, 7th ed., Part II (New York: McGraw-Hill Co., 1967).

The Economics of the Balance of Payments

then
$$C + I = C + S$$

and, by taking C from both sides,
$$I = S$$

This equality of saving and investment becomes an identity under the very limiting assumptions of this model. Later in the diagrammatic analysis we shall see that equality of S and I is a necessary condition of equilibrium.

Any autonomous increase of demand constitutes an injection into the income flow and will increase income not only by the amount of the original injection but by a multiple of it — this multiplier effect being the result of the primary, secondary and tertiary effects of the initial increase in demand. Let us suppose that there is an autonomous increase in I; that is, that additional capital goods, valued at ΔI, are added to the country's capital stock. The expenditures represented by ΔI are new and will result in an increase in factor incomes in the capital goods industries. For each recipient of the additional income, part of the increment will be spent and part saved. If we call the proportion of the part of the total increment which is spent $\Delta C/\Delta Y$ the 'marginal propensity to consume' and the part saved $\Delta S/\Delta Y$, the 'marginal propensity to save', then clearly $(\Delta C/\Delta Y) + (\Delta S/\Delta Y) = 1$. From the initial injection of demand (ΔI) there is generated an increase in consumption of $\Delta C/\Delta Y . \Delta I$ by the initial recipients of ΔI. This amount is passed on to a new group of income recipients who in turn spend $\Delta C/\Delta Y$ of their additional incomes. From them $(\Delta C/\Delta Y)^2 . \Delta I$ is passed on to yet another group. Assuming that, at each round of spending, the marginal propensity to consume $\Delta C/\Delta Y$ is constant (which is not an unreasonable assumption, spending–saving patterns being fairly uniform for small changes of income), then at the nth round the increase in consumption will be $(\Delta C/\Delta Y)^n . \Delta I$ and the total increase in income for the n rounds will be the sum of this geometric progression to n terms. n is assumed to be large. In practice, it will be so, for many rounds of expenditure will be required for the process to work itself out fully.

The formula for the sum of a geometric progression to n terms is

$$S = \frac{a(r^n - 1)}{r - 1}$$

where S is the sum required, a, the first term, r, the common ratio and n, the number of terms. Applying this formula with ΔI as the first term and $\Delta C/\Delta Y$ as the common ratio, the equation becomes

$$S = \frac{\Delta I[(\Delta C/\Delta Y)^n - 1]}{(\Delta C/\Delta Y) - 1}$$

and since we are interested economically in the sum as n approaches ∞, and as n approximates to ∞, so $(\Delta C/\Delta Y)^n$ may be discarded leaving

$$S = \Delta I \left[\frac{1}{1 - (\Delta C/\Delta Y)} \right]$$

or

$$S = \Delta I \cdot \frac{1}{(\Delta S/\Delta Y)}$$

Thus, by applying the simple formula for the sum of a geometric progression to n term $(\Delta C/\Delta Y)^n \cdot \Delta I$ reduces to

$$\Delta Y = \Delta I \left[\frac{1}{1 - (\Delta C/\Delta Y)} \right]$$

or

$$\Delta Y = K \cdot \Delta I$$

where the multiplier

$$K = \frac{1}{1 - (\Delta C/\Delta Y)}$$

or since

$$1 - \frac{\Delta C}{\Delta Y} = \frac{\Delta S}{\Delta Y}$$

$$K = \frac{1}{\Delta S/\Delta Y}$$

It is useful to see the above process in numerical terms. If the primary income recipients spend three-quarters of the increase of their incomes then an amount equal to $\frac{3}{4} \cdot \Delta I$ is passed on to the second group, who, in turn, spend three-quarters of their additional income so that $(\frac{3}{4})^2 \cdot \Delta I$ is passed on to the third group. If at each round of spending three-quarters is spent $(\Delta C/\Delta Y)$ and one-quarter is saved $(\Delta S/\Delta Y)$, then at the nth round the increase in income will be $(\frac{3}{4})^n \cdot \Delta I$ and the total increase in income for the n rounds will be 4. The multiplier K is determined by how much is passed on in further consumption at each round of expenditure, that is on the marginal propensity to consume. Alternatively, we may say that the multiplier is the reciprocal of the marginal propensity to save. Or, in verbal terms, an increase in investment will increase income by K times the increment of investment, where K is the reciprocal of the marginal propensity to save. To put the same argument in terms which will be more suitable for our later argument

$$\Delta Y = K \cdot \Delta I$$

where

$$K = \frac{1}{\Delta S/\Delta Y}$$

Therefore
$$\Delta Y = \frac{1}{\Delta S / \Delta Y} \cdot \Delta I$$

In verbal terms, the increase in income resulting from an autonomous injection is found by dividing the injection by the marginal propensity to save.

In the process of income circulation described, the marginal propensity to save is best regarded as a 'leakage', since at each stage of the circulation money saved is withdrawn from the income stream. Were it not for this leakage, the original increment of investment would lead to an infinite increase in income. The multiplier may then be spoken of as the reciprocal of the value for the leakage.

The same result may be achieved by diagrammatic method.

The equilibrium level of national income is the level at which investment and savings are equal, where $I = S$. If we show the savings schedule for changes in national income on a diagram we get a savings function SS of the form shown in Fig. 13.3 (a). This shows that savings rise with national income, that they are zero at some positive level of income OY and that there is dissaving of OX at zero income. Fig. 13.3 (b) shows on the same

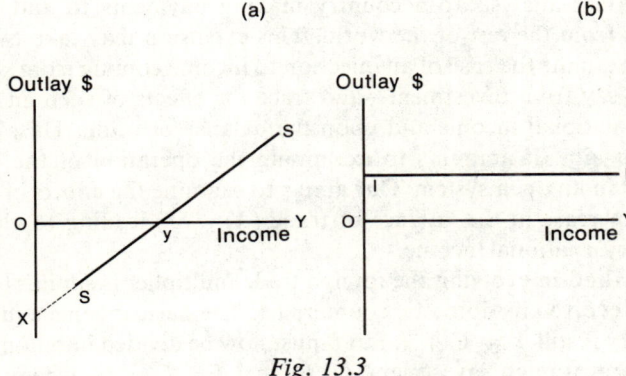

Fig. 13.3

axes, the level of investment II, which is assumed here to be constant for all levels of income. Figure 13.4 shows these functions combined on a single diagram. E, the point where these functions intersect, is the equilibrium position where $I = S$ at OY level of income.

If an autonomous increase takes place in the level of investment, the investment function moves to II_1. There is a new equilibrium at E_1 and an increase in national income by YY_1 to OY_1. The multiplier is shown on the

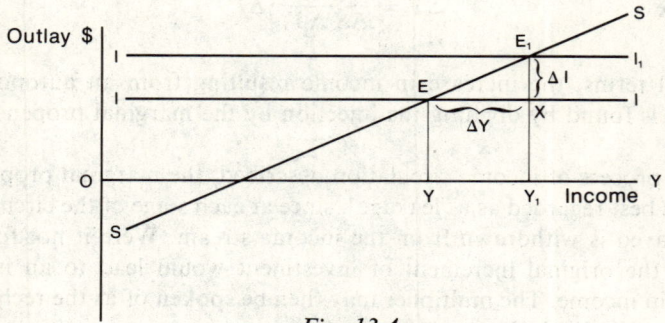

Fig. 13.4

diagram by the ratio of ΔI to ΔY. If we take the triangle $E_1 XE$ we can see that $\Delta I/\Delta Y$ is also the slope of the savings function $\Delta S/\Delta Y$, so that $\Delta I/\Delta Y = \Delta S/\Delta Y$ and therefore $\Delta Y/\Delta I$, which is K the multiplier, is the reciprocal of $\Delta S/\Delta Y$, i.e. $1/(\Delta S/\Delta Y)$. Once more, as in the algebraic version, $K = 1/(\Delta S/\Delta Y)$, where $\Delta S/\Delta Y$ is the leakage, the marginal propensity to save.

We may now abandon the assumption of a closed economy and extend the multiplier analysis to a country making payments to and receiving payments from the rest of the world. This extension may take two forms. We may examine the case of an injection to income coming from within the country—say from investment—and trace the effects of such an injection upon the national income and upon the balance of trade. This, however, is not our aim. It amounts to examining the operation of the domestic multiplier in an open system. Our aim is to examine the effects of an autonomous increase in the balance of trade $(X - M)$ leading to changes in the country's national income.

The method in evolving the foreign trade multiplier is similar to that by which we evolved its domestic counterpart. The basic income equation for the country is still $Y = C + I$. But I must now be divided into home investment I_d and foreign investment I_f, so that $I = I_d + I_f$, where I_d represents net addition to the country's capital stock, and where I_f the amount of foreign investment is equal to the change (positive or negative) in the country's total foreign investment as a result of lending and borrowing. Such foreign investment is, however, equal to the difference between exports and imports of goods and services, in other words to the balance of trade. Thus, if X is the value of all exports of goods and services and M the value of all imports, then the basic income equation for an open economy becomes $Y = C + I_d + (X - M)$. A favourable balance of trade is, like

The Economics of the Balance of Payments

domestic investment, an income creating injection for the country concerned and is subject to a multiplier effect in the same way as is an increase in domestic investment. An increase in the balance of trade will cause income in the country concerned to rise by a multiplied amount.

The basic income-multiplier relationship evolved for the closed economy should be borne in mind as we develop that for the foreign trade multiplier. That relationship in the most general terms was

$$\text{Increase in money income} = \frac{\text{Autonomous injection}}{\text{Leakage}}$$

where an autonomous injection may be any autonomous increase in demand and the multiplier is the reciprocal of the leakage. (An 'autonomous' increase is one which is not brought about by changes in the home country's income.)

Let us now apply this formula to several cases which arise under international trade.

Case 1: Domestic Saving

Assume that there is an autonomous increase (E) in the exports of country X to the rest of the world W. Sellers of exports in X find their incomes augmented by E_x. Part of this increased income they use for further outlay and part they save, the part saved being S_x (the subscript denotes the country concerned). The increase in X's income is then shown by the formula

$$\Delta Y_x = \frac{E_x}{S_x}$$

In this simple case saving is the only leakage taken into account.

Case II: Domestic Saving Plus Induced Domestic Imports

Next, assume the same autonomous increase in X's exports and the same rate of domestic saving as in Case I. As national income in X rises with the stimulus of the rise in demand for its exports, a part of the increased income at each successive stage of its circulation besides being saved, is spent on imports. This import expenditure passes out of X's income stream and thus constitutes a second leakage M_x. The basic formula can now be rewritten to take account of both leakages, saving and induced imports. It now reads

$$\Delta Y_x = \frac{E_x}{S_x + M_x}$$

Here the marginal propensity to save and the marginal propensity to import have been added in the denominator to give the total leakage from the income stream.

These two major leakages do not, however, exhaust the possibilities.

Case III: Case II Plus Induced Reduction of Foreign Purchases

Consider once more the situation as in Case II. The initial autonomous increase in exports creates new income in X, but if it is a true autonomous increase in exports, it will have reduced incomes abroad by E_x, the amount of the increment. (If X's income has been augmented by a switch of demand to its exports, some countries in W must have in aggregate lost E_x demand for their exports.) This fall in income in the rest of the world W reduces W's demand for X's exports. This 'foreign repercussion' we call ^xR_w. For X this repercussion is really a third leakage which must be added to the other two to make the formula still more comprehensive. It now becomes

$$\Delta Y_x = \frac{E_x}{S_x + M_x + {}^xR_w}$$

This account of the foreign repercussion is highly simplified. We can refine it a little.

Consider the home country X as its income rises as a result of the original injection coming from the rise in exports E_x. As X's income rises its marginal propensity to save is likely to increase; while in W, the rest of the world, the marginal propensity to save is likely to fall. This follows from the generally accepted shape of the consumption function whose slope diminishes with rising income (as in Fig. 13.5). That is, the marginal propensity to consume falls and the marginal propensity to save rises and conversely with falling income.

Thus, in X, the increased saving tends to curtail X's induced imports from W, thus reducing the stimulus which these imports by X have been giving to W. For W, the fall in saving tends to offset the decline in imports from X. Thus, the ultimate repercussion effect is one in which ^xR_w above is corrected to make allowance for these changed rates of saving and the term for trade repercussion becomes $M_w(S_x/S_w)$ where M_w is the induced change in W's imports, S_w is the induced change in W's savings, both expressed in terms of W incomes.

It should be noted that the smaller X is, as a country, the less important the foreign repercussion items will be. If the country is very small, clearly an

The Economics of the Balance of Payments

increase in its imports will not stimulate income abroad by any very marked amount.

We are now in a position to state a more refined formula for the general case of the national income multiplier where there are trade and income reactions in both countries. The increment (or decrement) of income ΔY

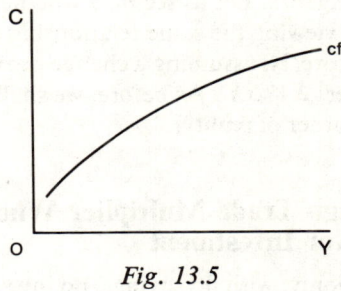

Fig. 13.5

brought about by an autonomous increase (or decrease) in the balance of trade E is always E times the multiplier k, k being the reciprocal of the aggregate value of all the leakages. The formulae for income changes in X and in the rest of the world W are as follows

$$\Delta Y_x = E_x \cdot \frac{1}{S_x + M_x + M_w(S_x/S_w)}$$

and

$$\Delta Y_w = E_w \cdot \frac{1}{S_w + M_w + M_x(S_w/S_x)}$$

The effect of income changes on the balance of payments should now be apparent. An active balance of payments, either by additional exports or by additions to income from foreign borrowing, will create additional income. This addition to income will be some multiple of the original increase in the balance of trade. How large the multiple is depends upon the amount of domestic saving, the marginal propensity to import, and the trade and income reaction of the rest of the world to the changes in the home country.

(iv) Diagrammatic Analysis of the Open Economy

We have thus far described the working of the foreign trade multiplier in terms of very simple algebra. Let us see now whether anything is added to our understanding by viewing the same relationship in terms of diagrams.[4]

Our question, as before, is: assuming a change in exports, ΔX, what is the foreign trade multiplier, $\Delta Y/\Delta X$? As before, we shall distinguish a number of cases of increasing order of reality.

Case I: The Foreign Trade Multiplier Where There is Neither Savings Nor Investment

Assume an open economy, with no savings, no investment and no government to tax or make public sector outlays. Then the goods produced Y plus imports M must be equal to goods bought C plus exports X, and

$$Y + M = C + X$$

But
$$Y = C$$

Therefore
$$M = X$$

In other words, exports are equal to imports at the equilibrium level of income. Fig. 13.6 then shows the equilibrium position of income with given export and import schedules. Here, with a given import schedule M

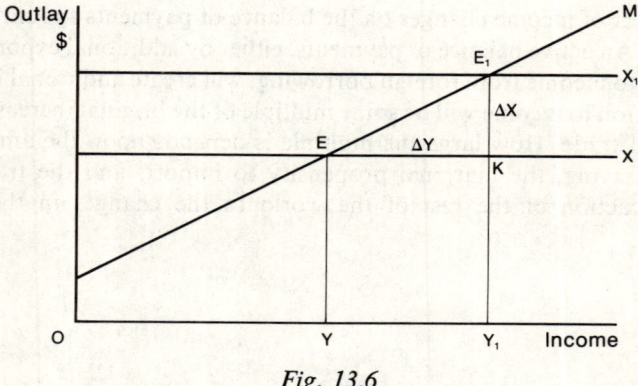

Fig. 13.6

The Economics of the Balance of Payments

and a given export schedule X, equilibrium will be at E for a level of national income OY. An increase in the export schedule to X_1 shifts the equilibrium to E_1 for a new level of national income OY_1. The increase in exports is shown within the triangle EE_1K as ΔX, the increase in income (within the same triangle) as ΔY. $\Delta Y/\Delta X$ is our foreign trade multiplier. The slope of M is shown by $\Delta X/\Delta Y$ or by the marginal propensity to import $\Delta M/\Delta Y$. Therefore, $\Delta X/\Delta Y = \Delta M/\Delta Y$ which can be written

$$\Delta Y/\Delta X = \frac{1}{\Delta M/\Delta Y} = \frac{1}{\text{Marginal propensity to import}}$$

The lesson from this picture of a highly simplified economy is that any increase in exports produces such an increase in income as will increase imports and completely adjust the balance of payments.

It should be noted in passing (see Fig. 13.7) that a shift in the import

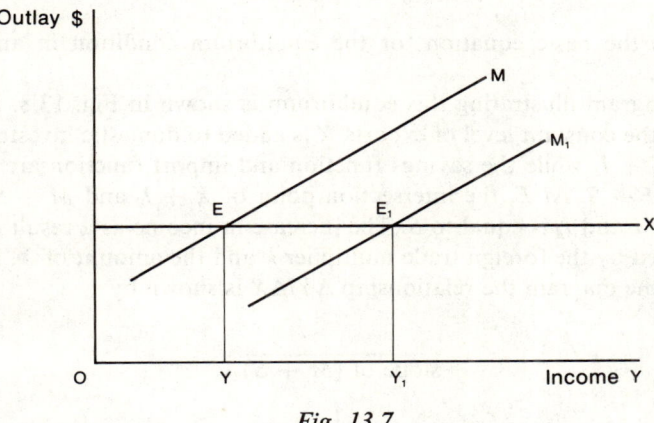

Fig. 13.7

schedule will also change national income in this case. If exports are shown on X and remain unchanged but the import function moves to M_1 so that at each level of income imports are less, the national income increases from OY to OY_1. Such a shift of the import schedule might occur as a result of a change of tastes, or a redistribution of income away from a group formerly buying luxury imports. Note that, although there is a downward shift in the import function, there is no diminution of actual imports, for the shift of the function has generated a higher level of national income out of which increased imports are generated, the addition being such as to bring imports once more to equality with exports, which are in this case constant.

Case II: The Foreign Trade Multiplier with Savings and Investment

Once we relax the rigorous assumptions of Case I (save for that of no government outlay, which remains), we return to a state in which $I = S$, but I must now be divided into two parts I_d, home investment and I_f foreign investment, so that

$$I_d + I_f = I = S$$

But $$I_f = X - M$$

so that we may write $$I_d + (X - M) = S$$

or $$I_d + X = S + M$$

This is the basic equation for the equilibrium condition in an open economy.

The diagram illustrating this equilibrium is shown in Fig. 13.8. In this diagram the constant level of exports X is added to domestic investment I_d to give $X + I_d$ while the savings function and import function are added to give $M + S$. At E, the intersection point of $X + I_d$ and $M + S$, X is equal to M and I_d is equal to S. The increase in income as a result of X is determined by the foreign trade multiplier k and the amount of X. In this case, on the diagram the relationship $\Delta Y/\Delta X$ is shown by

$$\frac{1}{\text{slope of } (M + S)}$$

that is $$k = \frac{1}{\Delta S/\Delta Y + \Delta M/\Delta Y}$$

The relationship of the main variables in Fig. 13.8 has been simplified by drawing the figure so that $X = M$ and I_d equals S, the intersection point of S and I_d being on the same vertical axis as that of $M + S$ and $X + I_d$. It is perfectly possible, however, to take account of the cases where these variables are not equal individually, although the basic equilibrium condition that $M + S = X + I_d$ is still satisfied. Fig. 13.9 (a) and (b) shows the other two possible cases.

In (a) exports X_1 are shown by Eq while imports are shown by Ep; exports exceed imports by pq. But saving also exceeds investment by pq

The Economics of the Balance of Payments

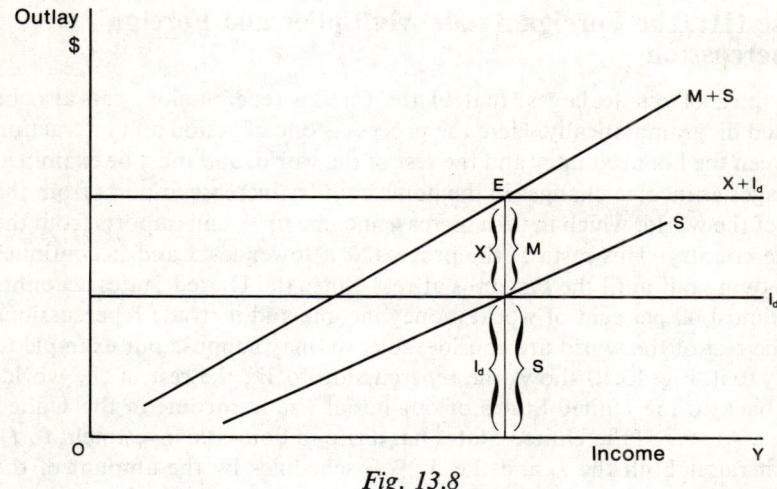

Fig. 13.8

and the basic equilibrium is still satisfied. In this case the surplus of exports over imports pq can be looked on as foreign investment against which the excess of saving over domestic investment (py over qy) is offset.

In (b) exports are shown by Ep_1, while imports are shown by Eq_1, imports exceeding exports by q_1p_1. Once more, however, saving and domestic investment show a divergence p_1q_1, exactly equal, but of opposite sign to the divergence of imports and exports. The excess of imports over exports in this case can be regarded either as supplementary savings or as disinvestment to be subtracted from I_d.

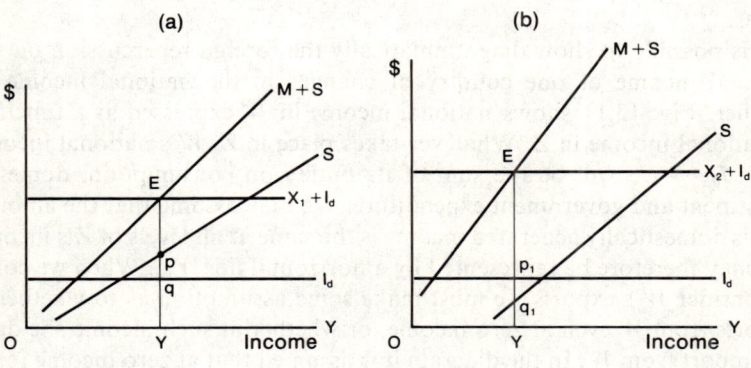

Fig. 13.9

Case III: The Foreign Trade Multiplier and Foreign Repercussion

The third of our leakages, that of the foreign repercussion, can also be treated diagrammatically. Here the process is one of action and interaction between the home country and the rest of the world, and must be examined in stages as income changes in the home country increase imports from the rest of the world, which in turn increase income in W and imports from the home country. This restarts the process at a lower level and it continues on a dying fall until the system is at rest. Since the United States accounts for almost 40 per cent of world money income and its trade repercussions on the rest of the world are considerable, we may suppose our example to apply to it. Fig. 13.10 shows the repercussion to W, the rest of the world, and back to the United States of our initial rise in income in the United States. At stage I the United States has a rise in domestic investment to I_d^1 which raises both the I_d and the $X + I_d$ schedules by the amount of the increase. Equilibrium income in the United States is moved to Y_1, and imports rise by the difference between ab and a_1b_1. The amount by which they rise is dependent on the differences of the slopes of S and $M + S$, that is, on the slope of M, which is, of course, the marginal propensity to import.

The rise in United States imports which ended stage 1 reappears at stage 2 as an increase in the export schedule to $X^1 + I_d$. This raises national income in W to Y_1 and increases imports. At stage 3 we move back to the United States where the rise in W's imports of stage 2 appears as a rise in exports which reduces the original import surplus. Given patience we could pursue this process back to W and then once more to the United States. The point is, however, made sufficiently by looking at only three stages.

It is possible to show diagrammatically the foreign repercussion on the national income of one country of changes in the national income of another. Fig. 13.11 shows national income in W expressed as a function of national income in Z. Whatever takes place in Z, W's national income $C_w + I_{dw} + G_w$ will be the sum of its outlay on consumption, domestic investment and government expenditure. We may assume that the amount of this domestically generated income is the same at all levels of Z's income and may therefore be represented by a horizontal line Y_{dw}. When we come to consider W's exports we must make some assumption as to whether Z imports from W even at zero income, or whether at such income she does not import from W. In the diagram it is assumed that at zero income for Z that country imports X_w. These exports increase as Z's income increases,

The Economics of the Balance of Payments

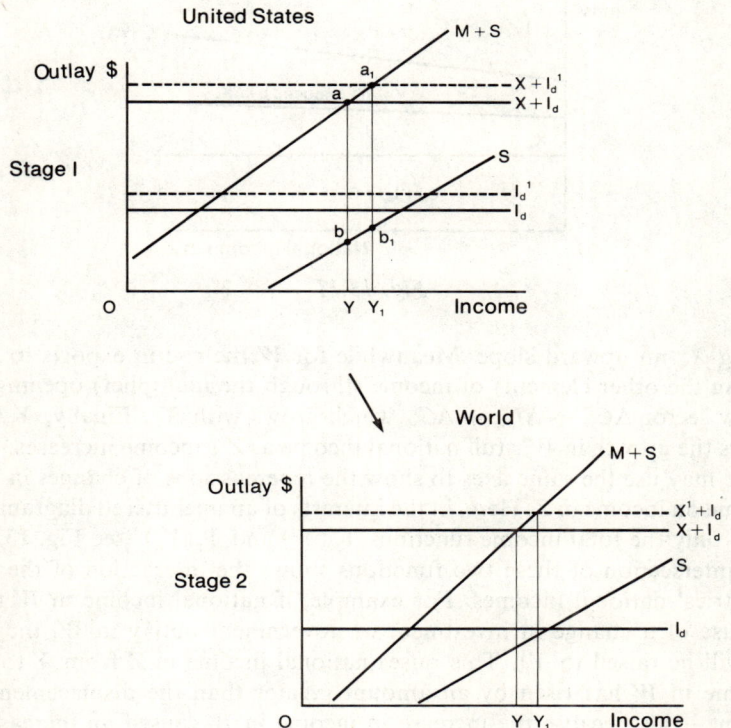

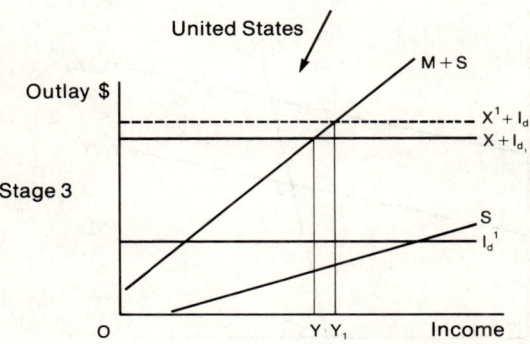

Fig. 13.10

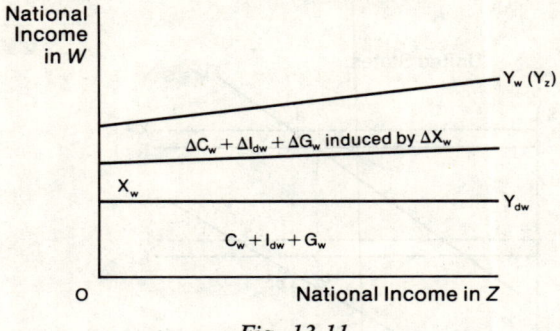

Fig. 13.11

giving X_w an upward slope. Meanwhile for W the rise in exports to Z is raising the other elements of income (through the multiplier) opening up a new sector $\Delta C_w + \Delta I_{dw} + \Delta G_w$ which grows with X_w. Finally, $Y_w(Y_z)$ shows the growth in W's full national income as Z's income increases.

We may use the same axes to show the repercussions of changes in W's income on income in Z. Here, in the interests of an uncluttered diagram, we show only the total income functions $Y_w(Y_z)$ and $Y_z(Y_w)$ (see Fig. 13.12). The intersection of these two functions shows the interaction of the two countries' national incomes. For example, if national income in W rises because of a change in investment or government outlay in W, the line Y_w will be raised to Y_w^1. This raises national income in Z from Y to Y_1. Income in W has risen by an amount greater than the displacement of income — this because the increase in income in W caused an increase in imports from Z, in income in Z, and hence in imports from W, so raising W's exports and national income again.

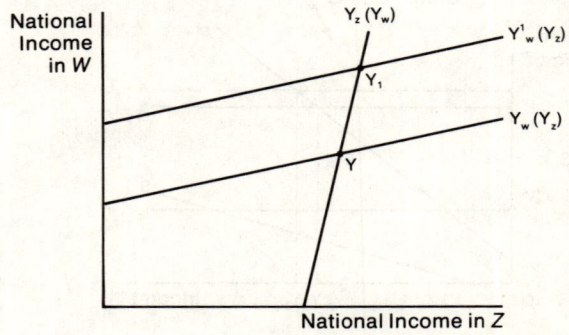

Fig. 13.12

The Economics of the Balance of Payments

It is clear from this diagram that the magnitude of any change in national income for two countries through the interaction of their trade balances depends upon the slope of their respective income functions, that is, upon the propensities which underlie these, the marginal propensities to save and to import.

(v) National Income Adjustment and the Balance of Payments

We must now recur to the twin formulae for national income changes and the foreign trade multiplier which we evolved in section (iii) (and set out on p. 331) and inquire what is the nature and magnitude of the adjustment effect of these relationships upon the balance of payments. A necessary preliminary to this is to call to mind the basic identity which has been with us throughout this discussion of national income multipliers: that *ex post* any new injection into the income stream, whether domestic investment or an autonomous increase in exports, equals the sum of the leakages, or withdrawals, from the income stream. In the case we have been examining, the injection has been an improvement in the trade balance achieved through a rise in exports. To assess the adjustment effect of the foreign trade multiplier, we have but to examine the nature of the leakages which offset the original injection.

Let us assume that X's balance of payments was originally in equilibrium: an autonomous increase of exports of $100 million then takes place, giving rise to a favourable current account balance of this amount. If we also assume that the marginal propensity to save was 0·25, the marginal propensity to import 0·2 and the foreign repercussion 0·02, then the resultant rise in income:

$$\Delta Y_x = \frac{100}{0·25 + 0·2 + 0·02} = \$212.77 \text{ million, and}$$

the multiplier is 2·12. Moreover, the leakages from the income flow have been as follows:

Injection (millions)	Offsets to Injection	As part of X's income	As % of total leakage	As money value (millions)
$100	Induced imports M_x	0·2	43	$43
	Foreign repercussion ^xR_w	0·02	4	4
	Domestic saving S_x	0·25	53	53

This table tells how adjustment is made to X's balance of payments in order to offset the original increase in exports of $100 million. There are three offsets. First, as income rises in X, that country increases its imports by $43 million. Second, foreigners, with their incomes falling, cut $4 million off their imports from X. Third, the remaining $53 million is then left to be settled by loan or transfer abroad and for these purposes $53 million in domestic savings is available out of the increase in income. Thus, by these adjustments, all of which are brought about by the income change resultant upon the original increase in X's exports, the balance of payments may be restored to equilibrium. But it is apparent from the example that adjustment is likely to be incomplete. Only a part ($47 million) of the original increment of $100 million in X's balance of payments is offset within the balance of payments itself. The remainder ($53 million) is available for offsetting but only if we assume a willingness on the part of X's citizens to export the capital available from savings will it be so applied. It can be seen from the formulae which have been evolved and from the table showing the means of adjustment that complete adjustment of the balance of payments by income effects and solely through the export–import relationship in fact depends upon such values of the marginal propensity to import and the foreign repercussion as will produce the appropriate changes in imports and exports as between the two countries. One of two conditions must be satisfied: either S_x, the propensity to save in X, must be zero or if S_x has some value, then all of the resulting savings must be invested abroad. If, as is likely, there is some positive value for S_x and some part of saving is retained in the economy, then for full adjustment the income effect upon imports and exports in the balance of payments will have to be supplemented, either by price effects or by the export of all the savings made from the surplus to the deficit country. These are conditions whose satisfaction is unlikely in practice, and we must tentatively regard the mechanism through which income changes affect the balance of payments as incomplete for adjustment purposes. It would appear that a more comprehensive model is necessary. To an examination of what factors may supplement the forces of income adjustment we shall proceed in the next section.

(vi) Monetary Factors and Income Adjustment

It is necessary to look more closely at the conclusion reached with regard to the limits of income adjustment in section (v). The conclusion was that, except in certain limited and specified circumstances – namely, when there are no savings in the adjusting economy, or in the existence of savings, that they are all exported – income forces would of themselves be insufficient to restore a balance of payments to equilibrium. This conclusion was shared by other writers[5] and Metzler summarised the matter by saying[6] that 'the conclusion of most economists seems to be that, except under unusual conditions, the adjustment of a country's balance of payments by means of income movements is likely to be incomplete'. Another fact which has practical bearing on this condition is that major economies are now irrevocably committed to domestic policies of full employment and price stability the effect of which is to offset, at least to some extent, the working of the income adjustment process. If we recur to the simple equations used earlier in this chapter to define employment and income equilibrium in an open economy, namely

$$I - S = M - X$$

this point becomes clear. In order for full domestic and external equilibrium to obtain, both sides of the equation must equal zero. If the two sides exceed zero, the situation implied is one of balance of payments disequilibrium but of income and employment equilibrium. Further it is a situation in which no income effects can diminish or eliminate the balance-of-payments disequilibrium.

From all this it should be clear that, if there is a strong tendency for balances of payments to adjust themselves completely, we must look to forces other than income changes whose effects are powerful but apparently partial; their effects, under realistic assumptions, falling short of full adjustment. Price effects are obvious candidates for inspection, since these are the forces suggested by classical adjustment theory. But let us leave them aside for the moment and seek other candidates. One line of approach suggests itself when we recall that the whole of the income-adjustment model, as we have presented it, rests upon the simple Keynesian macroeconomic model of the economy, taking no cognisance of the monetary mechanism, or of the relationship between the money supply and spending which has been the subject of so much monetary theorising since Keynes. It is this gap we must now repair by considering, albeit somewhat briefly, the effects of such factors as the money supply, the rate of interest, and short-term capital movements upon spending and the balance-of-payments adjustment process.

Let us begin with the equation used above. If $I - S = M - X$ then domestic employment equilibrium will be secured by the fact that any excess of home investment over saving will be equalled by an import surplus. There is no satisfactory way, through income effects alone, in which this external imbalance can be corrected. If income rises, the import surplus is increased; if it falls, the domestic employment equilibrium is impaired. If, however, we turn to monetary forces, the picture is less black. The excess of domestic investment over saving $(I - S)$ is likely to lead to an increase in interest rates in the home capital market. Such an increase in turn will lead to an inflow of capital, which, through the capital account, may re-establish the balance of payments in equilibrium. This is a simple statement of how adjustment might be achieved. It is, however, a good deal too simple and we will spell it out a little.

The rate of interest we may regard as determined in a market in which supply consists of an accumulated stock of loanable funds and demand consists of the accumulated stock of securities as well as the stock of money which the community in the aggregate wishes to hold. Current saving adds to the stock of loanable funds; current investment to the stock of securities. Movements by the community in or out of money may augment the demand for securities from a given level of savings or, if liquidity preference is high, reduce it, the savers preferring to hold money balances. In fact current saving and investment do add to the stock of loanable funds and the stock of securities respectively, so that any divergence between them may be expected to influence the rate of interest. The first examination might lead to the conclusion that this influence will only work gradually for two reasons: firstly, because the additions of current saving and investment to the supply and demand sides are small compared to the total stocks of loanable funds and current securities; and secondly, because in a closed economy divergences between savings and investment are adjusted quickly through changes in the level of income. In a closed economy the equilibrium equation is $I = S$, since by inference there are neither exports nor imports. If I in this case exceeds savings there is a rise in income out of which the additional savings are forthcoming to restore equality. If I exceeds S in the equation for an open economy, the divergence is matched by an import surplus, i.e. $I - X$. Any effect on the interest rate would necessarily be the result only of a long-lasting and persistent difference between I and S; assuming a closed economy, it is arguable that we may almost ignore divergences between current savings and current investment as determinants of the market rate of interest.

In an open economy it is different. Current investment is not necessarily equal to current savings, and the stock of securities and the stock of accumulated savings may now grow at different rates. Where investment exceeds savings, the stock of securities grows faster than the savings flow adds to loanable funds. The prices of securities will tend to drift downward and their yields to rise, as long as the excess of investment over saving persists. As Scitovsky[7] points out, the same argument holds good for a liquidity preference theory of the rate of interest. Here, a loss of reserves by the deficit country depletes the quantity of money and will, if liquidity preference remains unchanged, raise interest rates.[8] Thus, in the deficit country there is a rise in interest rates. This is accompanied by a fall in interest rates in the other countries in which an export surplus and matching savings surplus create a growing stock of loanable funds relative to securities. The prices of these are bid up while their yields fall. This creation of an 'interest-rate-gradient' between deficit and surplus countries makes for a flow of funds to the former, which will adjust the balance of payments and will only cease when adjustment has been accomplished. It is true that other forces may be at work which may obscure and overlay this change in interest rate levels. Speculative movements of funds in or out of securities in either country, temporary changes in liquidity preference and the like, may be temporary influences accenting or diminishing, for the moment, the effect of unequal investment and saving. But this effect, while gradual, is persistent and cumulative and will exert its long-run effect, unless it is deliberately offset by monetary policy.

It would appear, then, that in the case postulated, where income effects cannot completely adjust a balance-of-payments deficit, that changes in relative interest rates as between the deficit and surplus countries can supply a residual equilibrating factor. It might be useful to apply this argument to the example which we used earlier in discussing income adjustment, namely, that where an autonomous increase in exports occurs which raises the income of the country concerned, it raises imports but fails, because of some positive level of domestic saving, to offset the original rise in exports.

It will be remembered that with a postulated autonomous rise in exports of E in country X the rise in income in X will be

$$\Delta Y_x = E \cdot \frac{1}{S_x + M_x + {}^xR_w}$$

where S_x is the marginal propensity to save, M_x the marginal propensity to import and ${}^xR_w$ the foreign repercussion. This rise in income will not with savings of S_x be sufficient to generate in active leakages an amount equal to E the original injection. To this extent adjustment will be incomplete.

Returning to our argument it will be seen that in the case just mentioned there has been no change in investment, the basic equation $I - S = M - X$ (or $S - I = X - M$) being maintained after the autonomous increase in X by the increase of S out of the now higher level of income. S now exceeds I (as X exceeds M) and, in accordance with the process described above, interest rates in X fall while those in other countries tend to rise. The result will be an adjusting outflow of capital from X to other countries which have a higher return on capital. This adjustment should continue until, with the income adjustment already postulated, it brings the balance of payments back to equilibrium.

It will be observed that adjustment of interregional balances of payments as between regions of the same country are subject to the same adjustment effect from interest rate differentials and equilibrating capital flows as are different countries in a world system. Between regions of the same country differences in security yields may draw capital powerfully, since there are no institutional impediments such as exchange rates or differences in banking systems when capital moves within the same country. If there is a well organised capital market, capital flows within a country may be very smoothly and easily accomplished. Indeed, Scitovsky argues that 'equilibrating capital flows among regions of the same country are probably the main reason why one never hears of balance of payments difficulties in interregional relations'.[9]

A second and less direct way in which interest rate changes can exert an adjustment influence on the balance of payments is through their induced effects on investment and income. Continuing with our example, if interest rates fall in X because of the excess of its savings, then this fall in interest rates will induce a rise in investment which will have stimulating effects on income. To the extent that this happens imports will be increased and a further adjustment effect on the balance of payments will be invoked. It may be that the increase in investment will reduce exports but the net effect will still be to cause a rise in imports greater than any fall in exports which may result from a substitution of productive resources to domestic investment and away from exports.

Clearly the freedom with which funds may flow from country to country unimpeded by exchange controls or other barriers and the efficiency of capital markets in facilitating such flows and enabling funds to follow, as it were, the 'interest rate contours' have an important influence on the extent to which interest rates and capital movements are allowed to exercise their adjustment function. If capital movements are impeded there will still be an adjustment effect working through the second of the two routes described above. Interest rates will still change according to the savings–investment relation within countries and adjustment will be achieved by changes in income induced by changes in investment in response to the interest rate changes. The adjustment in this case will be through the trade balance and not through induced capital flows.

So far we have assumed that monetary policy is neutral and that these changes in interest rate levels are allowed to take place and to invoke their adjustment effects. But monetary policies are unlikely to be neutral. Will they in fact retard or accentuate the adjustment? Take first the case of a country with an import surplus and an excess of domestic investment over saving. The influences operating on the monetary authority here would be two: (1), to raise domestic interest rates with the object of attracting short-term funds so as to ease the pressure on the balance of payments and the exchange reserves; (2), since the excess of investment over saving would be stimulating income and employment in the economy, the authority might wish to check the expansion by monetary restriction, including a rise in interest rates. The latter influence might not be strong if the economy were well below the full-employment level, but at least there should be no tendency for interest rates to be reduced. They would be either raised or held steady. In the case of a country with an export surplus, the impelling forces to change interest rates are less strong. If it is conscious of a moral pressure to adjust its trade balance for the convenience of its neighbours it may lower interest rates and allow migratory funds to move out. To the extent that its export surplus is due to a falling level of income, it may seek to raise this by trying to stimulate investment through cheaper money. The impelling forces in either case may be weak but at least they are in the right direction.

It would appear, then, that the probable effects of monetary policy on interest rates lie in the same direction as the underlying forces we have described above and that no neutralising of these forces by the conscious action of the monetary authorities is likely. When one diverts one's attention from interest rates to other factors such as income changes and induced price changes, however, the picture alters. While there are reasons for believing that capital flows resulting from interest rate changes have strong equilibrating effects on the balance of payments, it is obvious that changes in national income and price levels are subject to continual interference, to modification and intervention by governments whose economic policies aim at domestic stability, construed as high levels of employment and stable price levels. This conflict between the forces making for adjustment and equilibrium in the balance of payments, and policies designed by governments to secure domestic stability of prices and employment, is an old and fundamental one, and once more it is to adjustment of the balances of payments of regions within the same political entity that we should turn to observe the unimpeded classical working of adjustment forces. Here where income changes and money flows are unimpeded and where governmental policies for domestic stability are aimed at the whole state rather than the region the adjustment forces work themselves out in a way not now possible between national states. Unfortunately they must do so unseen. Lack of regional balances of payments, regional income statistics or money and credit flows statistics, makes observation or measurement impossible.

The working of adjustment forces is a subject which deserves a chapter to itself, and we will return to it in due course. For the moment, we are concerned with establishing as fully and clearly as possible the means whereby adjustment of the balance of payments which we saw to be incomplete through income changes, may be completed. Changes in interest rates brought about through monetary forces are, we have seen, a powerful force in this respect and with income changes may yield complete adjustment.

(vii) Conclusion

It is appropriate to end this chapter by reiterating briefly and succinctly some of the main points of its rather wide-ranging theoretical discussion; and perhaps, in so doing, add to it some glosses and reflections.

First, it must be remembered that a macro-analysis like that which we have followed gives a spurious air of simplicity and exactness to a set of conditions which in the real world are far more intricate and grandiose than our poor two-country model can adequately reflect. Moreover, we have evolved our model behind a formidable set of simplifying assumptions. The validity of these assumptions and the consequences of removing even some of them are matters which the reader should ponder. In the following chapter some of the consequences of relaxing the assumption of stable prices and of allowing both income and price levels to move together will be briefly explored. Time, once allowed into the picture, brings with it a host of complexities — lagged responses of consumption and investment to income, induced changes in investment brought on by changes in consumption, complications in the multiplier process itself. Some of these can, of course, be dealt with by more elaborate mathematical models, but it remains doubtful if the result moves us much nearer to reality. The assumptions that functions such as those for consumption, and imports and exports, are linear and constant is one whose limitations need no underscoring for the student of anything beyond the most elementary macro-economics, while the assumption that balance-of-payments deficits are financeable by transfers of international liquidity is heroic in the present state of the international economy. Moreoever the assumption of general underemployment (idle resources) restricts the analysis in its applicability to most of the foreign balance problems of our day, which must be seen against a background of full employment and incipient inflation.

Finally, the whole model as originally conceived is Keynesian in spirit and approach, dealing with income changes only and ignoring the money supply and its influence on spending. This shortcoming we have already tried to meet in section (vi).

Yet withal, very positive gains do accrue from income-adjustment analysis. The most obvious gain is the way in which the income approach supplements the older classical view of adjustment. Both theories envisage a more or less automatic process for restoring equilibrium to balances of payments: they differ only in the causal factors which they stress. But the income approach compensates, at least to some extent, for what was surely the major defect of the classical approach: its lack of realism. Relying as it did on a simple chain of cause and effect the classical approach made no allowance for the conditions under which the adjustment process had to operate. In particular it did not explain domestic equilibrium of countries in the world system, because it took no account of the level of employment. Certainly income theory does not take account of all extraneous factors, but it gives us a tool with which a far wider range of conditions and problems may be analysed and it identifies for scrutiny the significant variables for policy.

14
The Interaction of Price and Income Changes

(i) The Need for a Synthesis

WE have presented two approaches to the adjustment process. The first, with classical insistence on the flexibility of the system, stressed the adjusting role of price or exchange rate movements. In this price-elasticities were important, their magnitude conditioning the adjustability of the system. The second and later Keynesian theory focused attention on the adjusting role of income changes. In this the important tool was the foreign trade multiplier. It was, however, apparent that, only under very restricting assumptions, would changes in income completely adjust external imbalance. Complete adjustment required the supplementation of income changes by other forces. Development of adjustment theory in recent years has taken a number of routes. We discern two. These are not always clearly marked, and they have tended at times to look depressingly parallel routes, but more recently they have moved towards each other and merged. The first distinguishable movement was in the direction of saving, more or less intact, the old elasticity approach, partly by re-examining it and partly by seeking new empirical evidence to assess the effect of price changes. These second thoughts on the elasticities approach we shall glance at in section (ii) of this chapter. Secondly, attempts have been made to combine the income and price models of adjustment into a single theory and to effect a synthesis of the two approaches. Such attempts have followed one or other of two routes: either dropping the assumption of constant prices and constant incomes and, with both free-moving in aid of adjustment achieving a theory of much greater generality; or seeking generality at a lower level of abstraction by posing the questions of balance-of-payments adjustment so as to focus upon policy implications, and in particular examining these implications in a world of full employment and creeping inflation.

In the field of pure theoretical synthesis, formidable difficulties attend a move into a world of freely moving prices and incomes. It is a much less determined system. Only a few valiant attempts have been made to achieve this type of pure theoretical synthesis of the price and income approaches, and these are so tentative that we will leave the interested reader to pursue them for himself.[1] A general exposition of them would not be useful here. It would rather involve the separate examination of individual contributions which are tentative and undeveloped. Moreover, the mainstream of development in adjustment analysis has flowed in another direction and we must follow it.

When we move to the discussion of balance-of-payments adjustment in terms of policy, the problem of exposition is only slightly easier; for here too, little generality has been achieved and advance has been made by the examination of a number of distinct problems, each studying some particular facet of the relations between income, prices (and the policy tools which influence these), and the balance of payments. We have no alternative but to follow this procedure and select the most significant of these developments — the so-called 'absorption approach'[2] which has opened up the most interesting approach to adjustment in recent years. In sections (iii) and (iv) we shall describe the elements of this approach and in section (v) some of the criticisms which have been made of it.

(ii) Second Thoughts on Elasticity

Much of the adjustment theory of recent years has sprung from examination of a particular problem of balance-of-payments policy: what are the effects of devaluation upon the trade balance? This preoccupation with devaluation problems has sprung from two sources, one practical and one theoretical. In a practical sense devaluation in the postwar period was looked upon as a viable policy for control of the economy. Of all the main variables of an economic system — price level, wage level, money quantity — the exchange rate was the easiest to alter. Why should policy be denied this regulator? In a practical sense devaluation appeared to have worked well for the British in 1931. True there were often disquieting political side effects, but it was at least a policy to be considered, and the IMF, by its permission (from 1946) of the policy in the case of a fundamental disequilibrium, tacitly invited some examination of its method and consequences. But the theoretical view of devaluation was disquieting. The theoretical proposition existed that devaluation, far from improving the trade balance, in some cases might result in its deterioration. The mechanism whereby devaluation acts upon the trade balance had only partly been explored. The accepted model of devaluation (in 1945), under which it was thought of as altering certain basic price relationships which, given adequate elasticities of supply and demand, would so alter goods flows as to improve the trade balance, was clearly, and in the light of the new Keynesian macro-economics, oversimplified. The probability—nay, certainty—that devaluation would alter income levels had been virtually ignored. Clearly some fairly drastic revision of the traditional model was necessary. This revision took two forms: a revision of the elasticities approach and a more searching empirical scrutiny to support it; and a new exposition of the effects of devaluation based upon simple Keynesian income analysis and leading towards a working (as distinct from a theoretical) synthesis of price and income effects, the so-called absorption approach. This latter course has in recent years been developed to examine systematically in monetary and income terms the formal implications of balance-of-payments policies in economies operating at and near the full employment level. Not surprisingly, strong rearguard actions have been fought by those still favouring the old elasticities approach. A large literature couched in terms of the effects of a devaluation upon the trade balance has grown up from which the wider conflict of absorption versus elasticity approach to the balance of payments stems. In the present section we shall consider very briefly the later variants of the elasticities approach.

We have already outlined the elements of the elasticities approach. It is unnecessary to do more than call it to mind. It was a partial equilibrium approach in which the success of the devaluation—here interpreted as meaning an improvement of the trade balance—depended upon the reaction of demand for imports and exports to the changes in their prices (and certain other relative prices) attendant upon devaluation. For devaluation to improve the trade balance, the sum of the elasticities of demand for imports in the devaluing country and for its exports in the rest of the world would have to be greater than some ascertainable value. If the elasticities of supply of imports and exports were assumed to be infinite so that their quantities might be freely varied without a change in price, then the significant value for the sum of the elasticities was unity. This condition represented not only a requirement for the success of a devaluation but also a condition of stability for the exchange market.

Defects in the straightforward application of this condition were soon realised and laid bare by several writers in the fifties. (Notably, Meade, Balogh, Streeten and Machlup.) Clearly to use the elasticities approach to examine the effects of a devaluation abstracting from income changes, when devaluation was itself a known cause of income change, was to depart too far from the facts. The result was the inclusion in the analysis of changes in income and prices which had been induced by the devaluation.

An example of this approach was the work of Sohmen,[3] who restated the supply and demand curves in 'total' terms. This meant that the price elasticities, upon which the effectiveness of the devaluation depended, were calculated as though all the adjustments attendant upon devaluation were already complete. While this saved the theory, it added nothing to the solution of the practical problem of 'to devalue or not to devalue?' Such an answer could only be given if such total elasticities were ascertainable by empirical investigation and they were not.

A second development of the traditional elasticities approach lay, not in changing the theoretical measurement of the elasticities themselves but in redefining the stability condition. This approach, pioneered by Tinbergen and Brown[4] and refined by several other writers[5] continued to define the elasticities in partial equilibrium terms but incorporated a number of other variables, such as income elasticities and the propensities to import and save, in order to arrive at stability formulae of growing sophistication and complexity. Nor was much comfort to be derived from these by the practical devaluationists, for it now appeared that the conditions to be satisfied before a devaluation could be successful were far more exacting than the simple Marshall–Lerner condition formula had implied. The inclusion in the formula of income effects, including those coming from changes in the terms of trade, tended to offset the beneficial effects of price movements upon the balance of trade. One writer[6] stated that the strength of the income effects was such that, with infinite supply elasticities, the significant value of the sum of the demand elasticities for imports and exports was not one, as in the older condition, but considerably in excess of one. The quietus which this conclusion might have given to devaluation as a policy, however, was avoided by the empirical work being done in the fifties on the statistical computation of demand elasticities in foreign trade. These, it was argued (see the reference on p. 314 above to Orcutt's criticism of statistical estimates of elasticities), were subject to a downward bias and all erred on the low side. Harberger, whose work had helped to establish one of the more stringent stability formulae, was nonetheless optimistic of the power of the price mechanism to work 'powerfully and pervasively in international trade'.[7] Not only were elasticities low because of a downward bias in the method of their calculation; but if long-run rather than short-run elasticities were applied, the effectiveness of price changes would be still greater. The stringency of the new stability condition evaporated in the glow of the new empirical evidence. Harberger argued that, for the typical country, the short-run import demand elasticity lay between 0·5 and 1, and the short-run export demand elasticity in the region of 2,[8] long-run elasticities of export demand he felt 'are substantially greater than 2'.

Both the belief that import and export demand elasticities in the long run were high, and the practical success of the British devaluation of sterling in September 1949, in improving the balance of payments, engendered a more optimistic approach to devaluation as a policy weapon in the fifties.

The more advanced versions of the stability condition which we have described were, perhaps, more intellectually satisfying than the older, simpler elasticity model, but they attained realism only in that they incorporated income in the model. The problems of really differentiating and defining the magnitudes of income and price effects remained. Instead of drawing nearer, the new models departed farther from the world of policy in which, inevitably, devaluation analysis belongs. It seemed in the later fifties that the discussion of devaluation from the elasticities viewpoint had been talked out but that the problem remained. Some new approach was necessary and this Alexander endeavoured to supply in his absorption approach.

(iii) The Absorption Approach

The novelty of the absorption approach lies in seeing the balance of payments, not as a relation between the country's debits and credits on international account, but rather as an element in the relation between aggregate receipts and expenditures of the economy. It concentrates 'on the relationships of real expenditure to real income and on the relationships of both of these to the price levels'.[9] To Alexander, the foreign balance B, is the difference between total output of goods and services Y, and total absorption A of these goods and services by the home economy. Absorption here is the name given to the aggregate of domestic demand $C + I_d + G$, that is to the amount of goods and services taken off the market domestically. Thus, $B = Y - (C + I_d + G) = Y - A$. Upon the trade balance, so defined, what, it is asked, are the effects of a devaluation?

A devaluation can affect B in two ways only: first, it can lead to a change in the output of goods and services within the country: this in its turn will induce a change in A, so that the change in B will be compounded of a change in income Y and the income-induced change in absorption A; and second, devaluation may change A for any given level of real income. Changes in the foreign balance (B), income (Y), or absorption (A) are denoted by b, y, and a respectively, so that

$$b = y - a \tag{1}$$

This shows that any change in the foreign balance must be equal to the difference between the change in income and the change in the amount of goods and services absorbed by the domestic economy.

Now let us examine y and a separately; first, a. Absorption of goods and services depends on a number of factors: on the amount of real income, on the price level, and on any other changes wrought by the devaluation. If c is the propensity to absorb (which we may define briefly as the propensity to consume plus the propensity to invest) and d a term denoting the direct effect of devaluation on absorption, then

$$a = cy - d \qquad (2)$$

This equation tells us that the change in absorption ($C + I_d + G$) in real terms as a result of devaluation is compounded of cy, which is the change in real consumption plus real investment caused by the change in income brought about by the devaluation; and d, changes in absorption coming from any other cause than the change in income.

If we combine equations (1) and (2) we get:

$$b = y - (cy - d)$$

or
$$b = (1 - c)y + d \qquad (3)$$

This equation arrays the variables which seem to be strategic and directs attention to three basic questions: how does devaluation affect income; how does absorption change with income, or more specifically what is the value of c, the marginal propensity to absorb; and how large are the non-income effects of devaluation? Look at these questions in turn.

The extent to which income is increased in the devaluing country is determined by the rise in exports stimulated by the devaluation and by the multiplier relationship. The constraints upon a rise in output are: the value of the multiplier itself; the extent to which a rise in output can be achieved in the devaluing country without a rise in the price level; and the extent to which the rest of the world can absorb the increase in exports of the devaluing country. These effects are well known and must be considered apart from other changes to which Alexander draws attention. He points out that the increase in y which is important is not the total increase in income induced by devaluation, but rather that amount net of the induced increase in absorption. This difference 'between the real production or income and the real expenditure on goods and services' he calls 'real hoarding' and by equation (1), i.e. $b = y - a$, real hoarding is the change in the foreign balance. The income-induced change in the foreign balance b

is then equal to the income-induced change in real hoarding, i.e. $y(1 - c)$ where $(1 - c)$ is the propensity to hoard. If c is greater than unity — and Alexander points out that there are grounds for believing that, at least at certain phases of the business cycle, an increase in income may stimulate a still greater increment of absorption into consumption and investment — then the foreign balance will not improve as a result of the increased income.

In conditions of underemployment, it is, Alexander argues, undeniable that devaluation will boost income and employment; although he adds the cautionary rider that, if unemployment is world-wide, the devaluation of one country will only increase employment in that country at the expense of decreasing it in others. Moreover, one devaluation will probably spark off a series of other competitive devaluations. The maximum benefit from devaluation, therefore, occurs in a country which is underemployed and in which c is less than unity. If the country is fully employed, the only hope of improvement by a devaluation 'must depend on the more tenuous and less attractive direct effects on absorption'.[10]

Another income effect of devaluation which must be considered is that on the terms of trade. It may be argued that, since (for mature countries) exports are commonly more diverse than imports, there will be a decline of export prices in foreign currency greater than the decline of import prices in foreign currency. Some deterioration t in the terms of trade is likely to result. This t is also a measure of the reduction of the country's real income resulting from the deterioration of the terms of trade. If we apply the first term of equation (3), i.e. $(1 - c)y$, to this amount t in order to find the effect on the foreign balance, then, since y the change in income is in this case $-t$, it can be seen that $-t(1 - c)$ will result in a deterioration of the foreign balance as long as c is less than unity. Only if c is greater than one will the adverse terms of trade improve the foreign balance.

It may usually be assumed that devaluation of a country's currency will cause its import prices in *foreign currency* to decline. Since import prices in the home currency will have risen as a result of the devaluation, foreign suppliers may be expected to counter this by reducing prices in their own currency in an attempt to hold their markets. This influence may be expected to act powerfully in cases where the importing country is a monopsonist or near-monopsonist. For example, the foreign-currency price of certain staple primary products were reduced for Britain in 1949 and 1967 because Britain was the largest single buyer. In both of these devaluations, import prices for Britain have risen very slowly after the devaluation and initially have fallen in the foreign currency.

To sum up on income effects, $(1 - c)y$: the change in income will be compounded of the positive 'idle resources effect' coming from the increased production arising from devaluation, and the probably negative terms-of-trade effect. Clearly, since the analysis of the first term of $b = (1 - c)y + d$ leads to no firmer conclusion than this, the direct effects on absorption d must be carefully examined. If there is initially full employment or if c is unity or greater, any favourable influence of devaluation upon the trade balance can only come through d.

In examining the direct effect on absorption, assume the economy to be at full employment, so that money incomes and prices increase proportionately with any injection, while real income is constant. It is also assumed that the foreign supply of imports and the foreign demand for exports are perfectly elastic, so that there is no terms-of-trade effect. Thus, we assume away all income effects, $(1 - c)y$, whether from idle resources or from terms-of-trade effects. The direct absorption effect d can then be divided into: (1) a cash-balance effect, (2) an income-redistribution effect, (3) a money-illusion effect, and (4) miscellaneous direct-absorption effects.

1. The cash-balance effect is well known. If the money supply is fixed, and if individuals wish to hold constant real cash balances, then they must increase their cash balances as prices rise. This they can only do at the expense of their expenditures. For one individual, it might be possible to replenish his balance by selling assets, but for the economy as a whole this is not possible if the money supply is fixed. (It might be possible also to sell assets abroad. Repatriation of foreign-held capital is, however, ruled out by Alexander.) There is, therefore, a direct effect on absorption from the cash-balance effect. There is also an indirect effect in that by some sale of assets their price will have gone down, that is, the rate of interest will have risen. Such a rise in interest rates may have an indirect effect upon absorption (in the same direction as the direct effect) by reducing domestic investment and possibly government expenditures.

One feature of the cash-balance effect which is worth noting is that, insofar as the reduction in absorption takes the form of a reduction of consumption, it may reduce employment. Unless the factors engaged in the production of the now unsold consumer goods can be transferred quickly to the export trade, unemployment might result. If c were less than one, this adverse income effect would lead to a deterioration of the foreign balance which would, to some degree, offset the improvement stemming from the absorption effects.

2. Income redistribution may take place with devaluation. Prices will rise with the devaluation and wages follow with the customary lag that gives a shift of income to profit earners. Fixed income groups, rentiers, and others are losers, while, with a progressive tax system, the state takes

a larger share of income. If income is redistributed in favour of those with a high propensity to absorb, the foreign balance will worsen; if in favour of those with a low propensity, it will be improved by devaluation. It must be remembered, however, that the propensity to absorb is influenced both by consumption and investment so that it is difficult to say *a priori* what the actual effect of a shift to profit will be. On the one hand, it may diminish consumption; on the other, it may encourage investment. In any event, to the extent that the net effect is to reduce absorption, the foreign balance will benefit.

3. The effects of money illusion upon absorption are so problematic as to make it hardly worthwhile to speculate what their net effect may be. Already the cash-balance effect will, with rising prices, have drawn money from absorption to maintain habitual cash balances. If, in addition to this, at higher prices people consume less, then the effect on the foreign balance will be favourable. It is equally arguable that rising prices, even with rising money incomes, will erode the propensity to save, i.e. stimulate consumption; although empirical evidence of consumption–savings patterns in the postwar period does not give much support to this view.

4. Of the other direct-absorption effects, some may work towards a favourable and some towards an unfavourable foreign balance. For example, short-run expectations of further price rises may follow devaluation and cause a consumer spending spree, thus temporarily raising absorption with deleterious short-run effects on the balance. Or again, where investment goods come mainly from abroad and rise in price with the devaluation, absorption may fall, with beneficial effects on the foreign balance.

It is difficult to make any assessment of the net effect on d, the direct-absorption effects, of all these various factors, some favourable, some otherwise. Moreover, when we consider the time element, it is clear that some of these influences are likely to be very transitory in their effects, while some, such as those coming from income redistribution, are lagged in effect and gradual in influence. Alexander's own view appears to be that 'under conditions of full employment, the favourable direct absorption effects are likely to be weak',[11] and that it would be more effective 'to operate on absorption directly through monetary and credit policy'.[12]

The real contribution of Alexander's paper is not, however, the conclusions to which the paper leads. These are, as the author is the first to say, unoriginal and could have been reached by traditional methods using a supply-and-demand analysis. It is rather the change in method which is important. Not only does the paper direct the policy-maker, bent on improving the foreign balance and in particular on improving it by devaluation, to focus his attention on the income-absorption relationship, but it also arrays the main factors for examination. It directs the policy maker to ask: how can absorption be reduced relative to income, and what is to be the incidence of a cut in absorption made with foreign-balance improvement in view? Moreover, although devaluation is one policy designed to improve a trade balance, Alexander's examination of its power to reduce absorption invites examination of the 'disabsorption' effects of other well-known balance-of-payments policy weapons – weapons such as monetary policy, direct domestic controls on investment or consumption, or controls on imports. The whole approach to the foreign balance problem becomes policy-oriented around measures operating on the constituents of domestic absorption of national income.

One case in which disabsorption policies are not appropriate is that of the country which is underemployed. Such policies will only exacerbate the already existing unemployment. In this case, improvement of the foreign balance should be sought by other means, by devaluation or import restriction.

(iv) The Payments Approach

The absorption approach has found approval with many economists on the grounds that it views the balance of payments in terms of the aggregate receipts and expenditures of the economy, relates it to the policy tools, fiscal and monetary, which are considered to be applicable to control of outlay, and provides a far more practical and fruitful approach to balance of payments policy than did the old elasticities approach. A useful development of the absorption approach and a synthesis of the work done on its basis for balance-of-payments policy has been made by Harry G. Johnson[13] and is worthy of comment here.

Johnson begins by restating the basic balance-of-payments equation

$$B = R_f - P_f \qquad (1)$$

where the balance B is equal to the difference between receipts by residents from foreigners R_f and payments by residents to foreigners P_f. This can be restated by including in the basic equation receipts and payments between residents in the country. All payments by residents to residents are at the same time receipts by residents from residents; thus $R_r = P_r$. We may now write the balance-of-payments equation

$$B = R_f + R_r - P_f - P_r = R - P \qquad (2)$$

This equation shows what equation (1) did not, that the balance of payments is the difference between aggregate receipts and payments by residents, deficit implying an excess of P over R and an increase of R as a remedial measure, and the converse for a surplus. This restatement of the nature of a balance-of-payments deficit is the starting point for what Johnson calls the 'payments approach', directing attention to two key aspects of any deficit: its monetary significance, and its relation with the level of activity of the economy.

Look first at the implications of the excess of P over R. The first is that residents are reducing their cash balances as their payments, in domestic money, are transferred abroad. There is an end to this, for cash balances are soon reduced to the minimum that the community is prepared to hold. With this the disequilibrium cures itself through a rise in the rate of interest, tighter money conditions, and thus a reduction in aggregate expenditure. How far in this process the monetary authorities are prepared to let matters go depends upon the size of the country's monetary reserves. Most likely these form such a small part of the country's monetary supply that they would be exhausted long before the corrective forces of dis-hoarding had completed their work. The authorities would, in all likelihood, early reinforce the effects of dishoarding by direct policies to reduce demand and end the deficit. The larger the reserves are in relation to the domestic money supply 'the less (is) the probability that the profit or utility maximising decisions of individuals to move out of cash into commodities or securities will have to be frustrated by the monetary authorities for fear of a balance of payments crisis'.[14]

But there is an alternative to this process. As the cash balances of residents are depleted by excessive foreign payments, they are renewed by open-market operations by the monetary authority. Such open-market operations might be the vehicle of a deliberate policy to peg interest rates, or they might result from the foreign-exchange authority lending on the home market its surplus of the home currency obtained from the sale of foreign currencies to support the exchange rate. In any event, the correcting effect of the decline in cash balances described above would not be forthcoming, and the deficit in this case would go uncorrected as long as the foreign-exchange reserves lasted.

The corollary of the argument that a deficit, by depleting the money supply, will ultimately be self-correcting is that any prolonged deficit in a country's balance of payments will require domestic credit creation to keep it going. Further, it would appear that balance-of-payments disequilibria are monetary phenomena and spring from two causes: too low a level of international reserves in relation to the money supply, so that the authorities cannot wait and rely upon the self-correcting monetary forces induced by the deficit; or policies by which the monetary authorities sustain the deficit by credit creation.

By presenting the balance of payments as a monetary problem, Johnson does not imply that deficits spring only from monetary causes. A deficit may be, and usually is, due to real factors, such as a change in the trade balance, and the monetary aspects may be passive.

This conclusion that balance-of-payments problems can be viewed monetarily throws new light on methods of correcting a deficit. Moreover, it integrates balance-of-payments theory with monetary theory and monetary management of the economy.

Johnson then turns to the second aspect of the payments approach; its relation to the level of activity of the economy. Here he distinguishes between two sorts of decision (by residents in the aggregate) leading to a balance-of-payments deficit: a 'stock' decision, which is a decision to alter the composition of the community assets in so far as they are divided between goods, bonds, and domestic money; and a 'flow' decision, which involves a decision to spend more currently than is being received. The balance-of-payments deficit resulting from either type of decision may manifest itself in either current or capital account—since decisions to switch assets or to overspend may involve buying either goods or bonds. The main difference between stock and flow deficits in the balance of payments lies in the fact that a stock deficit is temporary and implies no worsening of the country's basic economic position, while a flow deficit may be of longer duration and may involve a deterioration of the country's economic position. For example, in the former case, a stock decision to move from money to stocks of goods means merely a deficit now as the additional goods are imported, and a surplus later as the stocks of goods are drawn down; it is 'a once-for-all change in the composition of a given aggregate of capital assets'.[15] A flow deficit may reflect sustained overspending abroad and may continue until offsetting action is taken. Only if the foreign-exchange reserves of the country are small will remedial policies have to be followed in the case of a stock deficit. A flow deficit, however, is almost certain to require remedial policies.

In analysing the policy problems involved in countering a flow deficit, Johnson assumes the deficit to be located in the current account. This means that the balance of payments can be expressed as the difference between the value of the country's national income and its total domestic expenditure, so that

$$B = Y - E$$

and a deficit consists of an excess of real expenditure over real income.

This formulation poses the external balance problem in the same terms as those used by Alexander. It concentrates attention on policies of two types for correcting current account deficits: policies which aim at increasing income and those which aim at reducing expenditure. This distinction centres on the 'effects' of the policies. Johnson is quick to point out this distinction applies to the initial policy step only. Since income and expenditure are interdependent, a decision to alter one will at a later stage have repercussions on the other. It can be shown that as long as an increment of income produces a smaller increment in aggregate expenditure, multiplier effects will not be sufficient to offset the effect of a change, and thus an increase in output will always improve the balance of trade.[16] Johnson prefers a policy which centres on the 'methods' by which the effects are achieved. Since output can only be changed by changing the level of expenditure which creates it, then with any given level of expenditure changes in output must involve switches of expenditure from foreign output to domestic output. We can therefore, by reference to method, distinguish between expenditure-switching policies and expenditure-reducing policies.

Expenditure-reducing policies are familiar. Monetary and fiscal policy and direct (factor) controls have all been used for the purpose. In general, the attitude towards such policies will depend on the current state of the economy with regard to employment. If the country is in a state of full employment and incipient inflation, expenditure-reducing policies will have the additional advantage of being counter-inflationary. If the country is underemployed or if the impact of expenditure reduction falls mainly on home produced goods, the deflationary effects of expenditure-reducing policy may be intolerable. Finally, any expenditure-reducing policy, if carried to great lengths, may by its deflationary effects reduce domestic prices within the country and, according to demand and supply elasticities, induce expenditure-switching effects.

Expenditure-switching policies are of two types; general and selective. Devaluation (or induced changes of domestic price level achieved by deflationary policies) is the prime example of the former. It aims at switching demand, both home and foreign, away from foreign goods and onto domestic output. Direct controls on trade is the latter. Such controls are usually imposed on imports and are aimed at switching domestic demand from foreign goods to domestic output. Since in all cases of expenditure-switching policies the aim is to switch demand away from foreign goods and onto domestic output, the ability of the economy to supply the additional output becomes crucial. Clearly only if the economy is underemployed can the switch be made without inflationary effects.

Suppose the economy to be underemployed; then the additional output generated by the switch can be obtained by bringing formerly unemployed factors into employment. This means that the switching policies achieve three desirable results at one stroke: they improve the foreign balance, they increase income, and they increase employment. It may be that the move to full employment may involve some increase in the price level and hence some slight offset to the foreign-balance effects of the switching policy, but these are not likely to be great. Theoretically up to the point at which the economy reaches full employment, the supply of goods should be elastic. In practice, however, immobility of factors and inflexibilities in production will reduce this elasticity before the point of full employment is reached.

If the economy is already fully employed no further output is available from increased production; it can only be made available if there is a reduction in the former level of real expenditure. Such a reduction can be made in two ways: by simultaneously implementing an expenditure-reducing policy side by side with the switching policy; or by allowing the inflationary effects of the switching policy to work themselves out. In the event of a switching policy and an expenditure-reducing policy being applied simultaneously, favourable results for the foreign balance will only accrue if there is a high degree of substitutability between the goods released by the expenditure reduction and the foreign output which must be displaced by exports. If the reduction in expenditure reduces demand only for non-traded goods, its effect on the foreign balance may be zero and it will merely create unemployment in the non-traded goods field. Only in a longer run, as factors move over to the hard pressed export goods field, will the foreign balance benefit.

If a switching policy only is employed, then the result will be an excess of aggregate demand in the economy over supply, and price increases will result. These in turn will tend to counteract the effect of the switch. It is likely, however, that the inflation will work to reduce the deficit, for it may impel a reduction in the level of real expenditure from the full-employment output. Progressive tax rates may increase the proportion of real income taken by the state as money incomes and prices rise. There may be a shift to profit with the price rise which may reduce the propensity to consume, and the Pigou effect may operate to increase savings. Neither the magnitude nor the incidence of these effects can be judged, however, and as offsets they must be regarded as windfall gains if all act in the required direction and with the required force. The sober and conservative conclusion must surely be that expenditure-switching policies are inappropriate to a country in a condition of full employment.

Johnson's analysis carries the absorption approach of Alexander to a higher level of sophistication and a wider range of applicability. His distinction between 'stock' and 'flow' deficits, springing from different causes and each calling for different policy treatments, gives a demonstration of the extensions possible to the original absorption approach. As Johnson points out, by this the way is opened for an extension of the analysis to deficits in both current and capital accounts. But the greatest merit of the analysis is its restatement of the problem of trade-balance deficit in terms which enable it to be discussed in monetary and macro-economic terms. By this, the whole problem of the foreign balance becomes integrated with national income analysis and divorced from the old elasticities approach, which was surely being stretched, in its application to such subjects as devaluation, to and beyond the limits of its usefulness.

(v) The Critics of Absorption

The original absorption approach to devaluation analysis and, in particular, the view that the older elasticity approach should be scrapped came in for criticism in the later fifties by a number of writers[17] and led Alexander to make some modifications in his original position. Although this controversy is too diverse for us to examine it closely — some of the issues are still *sub judice* — it is certainly worth glancing briefly at a few of the criticisms made of the original absorption approach. They centre around three aspects of the analysis.

The first difficulty lay in finding and assigning quantities to supplement the guidelines which were supplied for balance-of-payments policy. The main quantitative problem was to estimate values for the marginal propensity to absorb, which was the sum of the marginal propensities to consume and to invest. Or the same problem could be approached in another way by estimating the marginal propensity to hoard (i.e., not to absorb). These were important quantities, for it was necessary to link changes in output caused by a devaluation with changes in absorption. To derive the functional relationship between output and absorption, to know its slope and its probable movement as a result of devaluation, was a natural next step. But this presented a grim problem of statistical estimation. Difficult enough was it already to estimate acceptable marginal propensities to consume suggested by straightforward income analysis, but to add to this the difficulties of a marginal propensity to invest was a last straw to break the back of an already burdened camel. Neither consumption nor investment is a simple function of output. Moreover, apart from these difficulties there was the problem of relating the exchange rate to output. Here, exactness or precision were hopeless: only the most general assumptions could be made as to how output would react to upward or downward movements of the exchange rate. All in all the estimations required to bring the absorption approach up to 'operational' level were just as formidable as those involved in the old elasticities approach.[18] Moreover, they were just as necessary. In that case the elasticities had to be calculated in order to determine whether the stability condition was satisfied. In the case of the absorption approach the relevant propensities had to be known before it was possible to say whether a devaluation would be beneficial to the trade balance.

A second criticism of the absorption approach came from Machlup. He argued that certain elasticity considerations in the model had been ignored. One of the acknowledged uses of absorption analysis was to explore the trade-balance effects of devaluation in both fully employed and underemployed situations. Alexander had seen these situations in terms of different supply and demand conditions for commodities, which necessarily involved elasticities. Elasticities also appeared in Alexander's analysis of the impact of devaluation upon the level of absorption out of a given level of income. All this, it might be argued, gave the absorption approach a more hybrid appearance than Alexander, who had played down the role of elasticity in his model, might care to admit. He had been too anxious, perhaps, to make a clean break with the past.

Finally, it was necessary to embody within the model the fact that an improvement in the balance of trade of a devaluing country involved opposite changes in the trade balances of the rest of the world; or, in absorption terms, that the increase in domestic hoarding, which an improvement of the home-trade balance involved, implied an equal decrease in hoarding abroad. How was this to be achieved? Alexander had assumed that the rest of the world was passive to the devaluation and to the trade balance change in the adjusting country.

The result of these criticisms of the original absorption approach was a reformulation which included elasticity effects and was more nearly a synthesis of the elasticity and the income approaches than anything theretofore. In an article published in 1959,[19] Alexander presented a new version of the approach which examined the sequential reactions of the home country and foreign countries to a devaluation, taking account of both price and income changes. The first stage of the sequence was concerned with the initial effects of devaluation on the trade balance; these were determined by the supply and demand elasticities, assuming income to be constant. Since foreign demand and supply elasticities were of equal importance, as far as the initial impact of devaluation was concerned, to the elasticities in the home country, the assumption, in Alexander's earlier work, of passive adjustment abroad disappeared. Should devaluation improve the trade balance, income would rise in the devaluing country and fall abroad. These income changes in their turn would produce certain secondary income effects which would have a further impact on the trade balance, tending to reverse the initial improvement in the balance of the home country. The price and income effects in the foreign country that acted to reduce the initial impact of devaluation were referred to as 'reversal factors'.

Alexander is quick to point out that as an operational device a compensating monetary policy by which the increased demand on the home market is cancelled out by deflationary monetary restriction has much to recommend it. Aggregate money outlays within the country would be held constant and the initial effects of the devaluation would be its only effects. 'It does', he argues, 'represent an ideal line of policy: with one hand guide the money supply so as to maintain full employment without inflation, and with the other set the exchange rate for foreign balance.' While approving such compensatory income adjustment for policy, however, his theoretical aim in the paper is to examine the reactions of devaluation on the trade balance at home and abroad when 'there is no compensating monetary policy actually to keep money incomes constant'.[20]

The effects of these reversal factors are worth spelling out. In the devaluing country the devaluation may be assumed to generate a rise in income, due to the improvement in the trade balance. This rise in income will cause a rise in imports, which will tend to reverse the original improvement in the trade balance. Moreover, the rise in domestic incomes will generate an increase in the demand for goods at home, increase their price, and thus tend to reduce the price differentials which the devaluation originally set up. Both these factors from the home country's point of view are reversals, in direction but not in magnitude, of the original improvement in the trade balance. In the foreign country the reactions are in the opposite direction. Income falls with the decline in exports, and with the fall in income comes a fall in imports to set against the original increase. Pricewise, the fall in income abroad drops the demand for domestic goods abroad and thereby reduces their price. As for the home country, the secondary income and price effects are reversals of the original effects on the trade balance.

It is easy to evolve algebraically (assuming the pre-devaluation balance to be zero) the formal effect of the reversal factors that results when income changes in two countries follow an initial change in the foreign

The Economics of the Balance of Payments

balance between them. Thus, if E_h is the initial improvement in the foreign balance of the home country and E_f is the initial change in foreign balance of the foreign country and R_1 and R_2 are the initial reversal factors for these two countries, then the formulae for the final changes in the trade balance measured in foreign and domestic prices are

(a) $$\Delta B_f = \frac{R_1 R_2 E_f}{1 - (R_1 - 1)(R_2 - 1)}$$

(b) $$\Delta B_h = \frac{R_1 R_2 E_h}{1 - (R_1 - 1)(R_2 - 1)}$$

and the multiplier of the Es (the original trade balance changes at home and abroad) is

$$\frac{R_1 R_2}{1 - (R_1 - 1)(R_2 - 1)}$$

This term Alexander calls the 'final reversal factor' in contrast to R_1 and R_2 which were the initial reversal factors. If we take $R_1 R_2$ as the original first stage effect of the reversal then the term

$$\frac{1}{1 - (R_1 - 1)(R_2 - 1)}$$

is a multiplier applied to it and is the sum of an infinite series of subsequent adjustments and readjustments to the original reversals.

Consider more fully the economic content of the reversal factors. Assume for the purpose that the entire change in exports and imports at the initial stage produces corresponding changes in expenditure on domestic output. This implies that, if as a result of a given devaluation, exports in the devaluing country measured in home currency increase by $1 and total imports decline by $2, aggregate demand for goods and services in the country increases at the initial stage by $3 – this made up of $1 increase coming from abroad on exports and $2 additional demand for domestic goods which was switched from imports. As imports fall the demand for imports may switch (a) to domestic goods, or (b) to hoarding, or (c) to some domestic goods and some hoarding. For the present we assume (a). We are in other words assuming that, in the initial effect of devaluation, there is no change of hoarding. This comes only in subsequent effects through changes of money income.

If in the home country a $1 increase of money income per period leads to some induced hoarding h_1, and some money-income induced deterioration of the balance of payments f_1, we may regard h_1 and f_1 as money income induced factors. Thus in period 1, $h_1 + f_1$ will be drawn out of income and $(1 - h_1 - f_1)$ will go to the next period as additional domestic absorption of goods and services. This leads in period 2 to additional hoarding of $h_1(1 - h_1 - f_1)$ and a further trade balance deterioration of $f_1(1 - h_1 - f_1)$. This is, of course, the familiar series of leakages from the income stream which we encounter in multiplier analysis, where the multiplier k is equal to the reciprocal of the total of the leakages. In this case total money income in the country will finally have increased by $1/(h_1 + f_1)$. Aggregate-induced hoarding per dollar of the original increment in expenditure, H_1, will be h_1 times the increase in money income, so that

$$H_1 = h_1 \cdot \frac{1}{(h_1 + f_1)}$$

and the aggregate-induced deterioration of the foreign balance F_1 will be

$$F_1 = f_1 \cdot \frac{1}{(h_1 + f_1)}$$

and

$$F_1 + H_1 = 1$$

This last equation follows upon the principle that, at the completion of the multiplier process, total induced leakages — in this case hoarding and foreign balance — must equal the original increment of expenditure.

Given the initial impact of the devaluation in home currency E_h and the assumption made above that the whole of the initial change in the foreign-trade balance goes to increased expenditure in the home country, then money income in the home country will increase by $E_h \cdot [1/(h_1 + f_1)]$. An increase of income of this amount will induce a deterioration in the foreign balance such that

$$F_1 E_h = f_1 \left[E_h \cdot \frac{1}{(h_1 + f_1)} \right]$$

Therefore the foreign balance after the first reaction of the home country to the devaluation is

$$E_h - F_1 E_h = E_h(1 - F_1)$$

and since

$$(1 - F_1) = H_1$$

then

$$E_h - F_1 E_h = E_h(1 - F_1) = E_h H_1.$$

But as R_1 (the initial reversal factor) was defined, the foreign balance after the first reaction is also $R_1 E_h$: so that $R_1 E_h = E_h H_1$, and $R_1 = H_1$ and similarly $R_2 = H_2$. Moreover since $H_1 + F_1 = 1$ and $R_1 = H_1$ then $F_1 = 1 - R_1$.

If we now substitute $R_1 = H_1$ and $(1 - R_1) = F$, in equations (a) and (b) above, we get

(a) $$\Delta B_f = \frac{H_1 H_2 E_f}{1 - F_1 F_2}$$

(b) $$\Delta B_h = \frac{H_1 H_2 E_h}{1 - F_1 F_2}$$

We may sum up the economic content of the argument so far by the following generalisations. Firstly, the initial effect of the devaluation depends upon the four elasticities of demand and supply of imports and exports. Secondly, how much of the initial effect survives depends upon the relative strength in each of the two countries of (a) the influence of additional money income on money hoarding, and (b) the effect of additional money income on imports and exports, i.e. on the trade balance. If, in either country, an additional unit of money income causes a rise of imports or fall of exports which is large relative to the induced additional money hoarding, then the initial effects of the devaluation will tend to be offset by its impact upon domestic income. If the hoarding effect in both countries springing from an increase in money income is strong, relative to the foreign balance effects, there will only be a small reduction in the original impact of the devaluation as indicated by the elasticities. Limiting cases are those when h_1 or $h_2 = 0$, and f_1 or f_2 has some positive value, then $\Delta B_f = \Delta B_h = 0$. If f_1, f_2 are zero, and h_1, h_2 are not zero then $\Delta B_f = E_f$ and $\Delta B_h = E_h$. The final value of the reversal coefficient depends on the ratios of f to h.

The way is then open for a fuller investigation of f and h. This Alexander simplifies by distinguishing two cases: that of an increase in money income in an underemployed economy, and that of an increase in an economy at full employment. The former is simple. If an increase in money expenditure takes place, it results in an increase in output and real income. It does not raise prices, nor does it bid away goods from exports. In this simple case f is the familiar real propensity to import, the amount of increase in import demand for a given increase in income; h is the real propensity to hoard or $(1 - a)$, where a is real absorption, i.e. real consumption plus real investment induced by a given increase in real income. Thus every increment of income is divided into three parts: one part, f, goes to purchase imports and thereby worsens the foreign balance; one part, d, purchases additional domestic goods; one part, h, goes into money balances or hoarding.

The second case is more complex. Here, an increment of additional expenditure goes only to raise prices, and there is no increase in production or real income. It will still hold that the increment will be divided into three constituents d, f, and h, so that $d + f + h = 1$; but the values of these coefficients will be different when prices are rising than when prices are constant. For example, the ratio of f and h will differ: f is likely to be much larger under the second, full employment case, when the rise in domestic prices will tend to shift demand from dearer domestic goods to imports; h will probably be smaller under full employment. The price effects will ensure that h is almost equal to the average propensity to hoard, while, without price effects, it would be equal to the marginal propensity to hoard. On the assumption of a foreign balance of zero, hoarding is also zero. (This follows from the basic equation $B = y - a = h$.) In the absence of cash-balance effects, h is therefore likely to be close to zero in a fully employed economy. If cash-balance effects are present, h may, however, have some positive value. If, with a given money stock in the country, prices rise, the relation of money incomes to money stocks will be changed and this may result in an attempt to build up money stocks to conventional levels. In this way hoarding would be increased.

If increased hoarding is not forthcoming from the cash-balance effect, devaluation at full employment will bring no improvement of the foreign balance if this was initially zero, because net improvement in the foreign balance must equal the net increase in hoarding. It would appear, then, that for a country at full employment the main hope of a devaluation improving the foreign balance lies in an increase in hoarding from the cash-balance effect.

Subsequent sections of Alexander's article explore the effects of modifying some of his simplifying assumptions and provide a mathematical appendix clarifying the derivation of his formulae. But the main structure of his argument has now been described and may be summarised as follows in the author's own words:

Instead of saying, as does the literature up to 1950, that the effect of a devaluation on the foreign trade balance depends on the four elasticities, we must now say that it depends on these four elasticities subject to the income-induced readjustments in the countries concerned—readjustments which will tend to reverse the effects of the elasticities. These readjustments in turn depend on the relative strength of factors inducing hoarding and those inducing deterioration of the foreign balance in response to increased levels of money expenditures, as reflected in the h's and f's respectively. The h's and f's will have different values depending on the levels of domestic resource employment and the institutional circumstances which govern the extent to which an increase of expenditure will go either into increasing real incomes or raising prices.[21]

Alexander's second absorption model brought devaluation adjustment theory to a new point. The elasticities were back in the game as determin-

The Economics of the Balance of Payments

ants of the initial impact of devaluation; but in his analysis of the reversal factors, Alexander made possible a much more complete and realistic model of what is in practice an attenuated process. The model still had its critics[22] but the task now was to elaborate the absorption model, closing gaps and adding refinements. The basis remained intact.

(vi) Conclusion

We may close this section on devaluation analysis by reflecting upon the complexity of the practical policy decision of whether to devalue which faces any country in balance-of-payments disequilibrium. The complexity of this decision springs from the many parameters involved, the frequent lack of knowledge of the numerical values shown by theory to be strategic, and the uneasiness induced in the mind of the policy-maker by the simplifying assumptions of the model—in particular, the ubiquity of the two-country model which drives him to the lame counter-assumption that the 'other country' is 'the rest of the world'. In the end, it is perhaps not surprising that the policy-maker—rather than asking the economist: what does theory say?—is more likely to ask the economic historian, what happened last time?

Kindleberger tells us, pithily, that 'disequilibrium can be repressed, corrected or financed'. In Chapter 12 we lumped these 'repressings', 'corrections' and 'financing' together under the loose tag of balance-of-payments policies. Of these, adjustment, in the true sense of correction, is but a part, but it is the heartland. Quasi-adjustment policies such as direct controls on trade or payments, in order to contain imbalance or tolerance of imbalance because the means is available to correct it, do nothing to remove the source of instability.[23] They are ways whereby, for the time being, we may live with it.

We have now completed our discussion of what economic theory has to offer on the adjustment systems proper. The quasi-adjustments measures will be dealt with elsewhere in appropriate context. To complete our picture of adjustment, however, two topics require attention. These are not theories of adjustment, but they bear so closely upon such theories and are so inextricably bound up with them that it is necessary to consider them here. They are: the treatment of international investment in the adjustment process, and the consideration of equilibrium for the domestic economy in relation to equilibrium of the international system. To these topics in successive chapters we now proceed.

15
Adjustment and International Capital Movements

(i) Statement of the Problem

THE transfer of capital from one country to another is a common process of international trade. Nationals in a poor country may wish to borrow the savings of nationals in a richer country. Mature industrial countries supply grants-in-aid to developing countries. Defeated countries have, after war, been obliged to make reparations payments to the victors. Corporations in one country may wish to acquire capital assets or set up subsidiaries in another. All these are examples of capital transactions between countries. All these involve money capital in one currency being transferred via the exchange market to another; all involve the transfer of real resources as well as money.

Whatever the method, a country imports capital only when it gets goods (and/or services) in excess of the value it exports; a country exports capital only when it sends abroad goods in excess of the value it imports. In either case, the borrowing or lending country must experience changes in its balance of payments which are directly connected with the borrowing or lending. For example, when country A borrows from country B, residents of A have their purchasing power enhanced by the money transfer; but unless this leads to an exactly equal import surplus there will be no 'real transfer' of goods and services and the increased purchasing power will only press upon domestic goods, bidding up their prices if the country is already at full employment or raising income and output if it is not. It is the manipulation of these balance-of-payments changes and the causal relationship with the capital movement which is the topic of this chapter. The process of transferring the real wealth which is inherent in borrowing or lending is referred to as 'the transfer' problem. It has a long history in the literature of international trade.[1]

Inevitably, economic literature on the transfer problem grew up around the study of particular cases. The work of Taussig and a group of his Harvard students gave great impetus to the growth of capital transfer theory and the books containing these early studies have become well known.[2] This initial work was concerned mainly with the transfer problem as it appeared in a period of rapid economic development when capital in large quantities was moving from Britain and Western European countries to the quickly developing countries overseas. Much of this work was concerned with testing the classical theory of the price-specie-flow mechanism. A good example is Viner's well-known study of Canadian borrowing between 1900 and 1913. Viner showed how the inflow of capital to Canada from the London capital market and elsewhere was, through the price-specie-flow mechanism, allowed to raise domestic prices in Canada and create an import surplus comparable in magnitude to the borrowing.

A second phase in the literature came with discussion in the twenties, and in particular the controversy between Keynes and Ohlin, as to how the massive transfer of reparations payments required of Germany under the Treaty of Versailles could be made from that country to the main allied powers, Britain, France and the United States. Keynes argued that the transfer could not be made because Germany could not achieve the necessary export surplus. The elasticities of demand for her exports were too low for her to achieve the necessary export surplus by lowering prices. Ohlin was not concerned about prices or demand elasticities but argued that the transfer could be made through changes of income. It is interesting that Keynes, who later was to be the founder of modern income theory, argued the classical view against Ohlin, who preferred to discuss the problem in income terms.[3] But income theory was not yet developed to provide him with the prescription for the internal policies which Germany should pursue to facilitate the transfer. The controversy was overtaken by events. Throughout the twenties, Germany had borrowed long term from the United States to help her to pay reparations, but this source of relief dried up in 1928. There was a short period during which the country borrowed short term and had a small import surplus; but in 1930, the onset of depression reduced imports drastically while exports were well maintained. The export surplus of $230 million in 1930 rose to over $700 million in 1931 when the Hoover moratorium ended war-debt payments. The ability to transfer the reparations payments had been achieved here by domestic deflation, but it resulted in severe unemployment and had appalling political repercussions.

A question which is worth considering as a preliminary is the order of events in the capital-transfer process. Which is the first and autonomous factor, the capital movement or the trade deficit? The short answer is either. The classical case assumed a prior autonomous capital movement which took place for some clearly distinguished purpose, such as a development loan or reparations payments, and then induced by some process the trade deficit required. This was the form of the early case studies. But clearly a country may by expansionary domestic policies induce a high level of domestic investment which leads to inflation and an import surplus may then be met by foreign lending. Investors seeking money capital, for example, are likely to find that interest rates in the home country are higher than those abroad, and will therefore seek capital in foreign capital markets. In both of the above cases, whichever may be the prime mover, capital movement or import surplus, there is a clear causality between them, but a case where there is no causal relationship is quite conceivable. It is possible for a country to expand quickly because, for the moment, investment, induced by profitable investment opportunities, exceeds the propensity to save. This will result in inflation, an import surplus, and a tendency for the country to seek funds abroad, since savings are inadequate at home. Here there is no causal relationship, but the mutually dependent foreign borrowing and import surplus both arise because of the deficiency of domestic saving.

In discussing the transfer problem in this chapter we shall distinguish three topics of importance: the classical transfer theory; the modern theory; and the impact of transfer on the terms of trade.

(ii) The Classical Theory

The classical theory of the transfer process is in two parts: one is appropriate to gold standard conditions, the other to free rates of exchange and a paper currency. We shall deal with them in turn.

Let us suppose that Canada borrowed from England. The money which was borrowed on the London capital market would be exchanged in the foreign-exchange market for Canadian dollars. This sale of sterling would depress the sterling exchange rate and, once it passed the gold export point, gold would flow out of England and into Canada. Interest rates would probably be raised in England and this, combined with the loss of gold, would have a contractionary influence which would lower prices. Conversely in Canada prices would be raised as gold flowed in and interest rates would fall. This change in the price levels of the borrowing and lending countries would result in an export surplus in England, that is, in the lender country, and an import surplus in Canada, the borrower. Through this change in the balance of trade the real transfer would be effected.

The real transfer of goods then reverses the process. England's export surplus causes gold to flow into London; the Canadian import surplus

The Economics of the Balance of Payments

causes it to flow out of Canada. When the total capital has been transferred in goods the gold movement has been completely reversed. This, of course, ignores the interest on the loan payment, which will start during the latter part of this process, and also the productivity of the capital in Canada, which will have its own distinct effect on the Canadian price level. This entire process has been one in which the terms of trade have turned against the lender and in favour of the borrower during the process of transfer but the real transfer causes them to revert to their former level.

To this classical view of the transfer mechanism under the gold standard there are a number of criticisms. The first is that the classical model assumed that the marginal propensity of the borrowing country to import and the marginal propensity of the borrower to spend their loan abroad were the same. This was not a necessary assumption. To the extent that part of the loan was spent in Canada the increase in demand for Canadian goods would increase prices and divert demand to imports. The import surplus for the borrower would occur anyway. The simplest case would be when the borrowers spent part of the loan in Britain at once. In this case, that part which was so spent would not cross the exchanges and the transfer would occur immediately in real terms with no money transfer necessary.

The second criticism is that, as in all gold standard theory, the classical transfer process relied on acceptance of the quantity theory of money and its implicit assumption of full employment. In underemployed economies the quantity of money was not a determinant of the price level. Money might be held in idle balances. Even if it were not but were used immediately for spending, it would be output which would be increased and not prices.

Finally, the theory assumes tacitly, as with all classical adjustment theory, that demand and supply elasticities were in sum greater than unity — a topic on which enough has been said already.

A second classical version of the transfer mechanism deals with transfer under conditions of free exchange rates. In this case, the monetary transfer of the loan (in our example) from England to Canada would depreciate the exchange rate for sterling in the market as the loan was converted into dollars. This depreciation would increase in magnitude with the size of the transfer. With the depreciation British export prices would be lowered for Canadians (in terms of Canadian currency), and imports from Canada would be raised in price in terms of British currency. This would (still assuming high demand elasticities) increase the demand for British exports in Canada and diminish the demand for Canadian imports in Britain. In this way, the necessary export surplus for Britain would be created and real transfer take place. When all the funds borrowed by Canada had been transferred and the real transfer through the export surplus completed, the sterling exchange rate would appreciate to its former level.

It will be observed that the creation of the export surplus in the capital-exporting country is in its methods, whether under gold standard or under free exchange-rate conditions, the same mechanism under classical theory as is employed for adjusting a balance-of-payments disequilibrium. This is not surprising, for a capital transfer, in the last resort, is but a special case of a balance-of-payments disequilibrium. The former is a 'unilateral' payment, within the balance of payments; it involves an outflow of money only from the home country. If international transactions are initially in balance, the capital movement produces disequilibrium in independently motivated transactions. This is in contrast to the numerous 'bilateral' items, such as the exchange of commodities for cash. With all these two-sided items, value (money) flows out and money payment (or value) flows in. No adjustment is necessary. In the case of a loan transfer, money is exported and there is no matching inflow. That is why a unilateral payment of this type has to be transferred in real terms. The process is the same, in principle, as an adjustment for a deficit.[4]

As a special case of adjustment theory, consideration of the transfer process has had much influence and bearing on adjustment theory. The case studies of capital transfer already referred to did much to arouse speculation as to the working of the general balance-of-payments adjustment processes – their very smoothness suggesting forces more powerful than those of the classical model.

(iii) The Modern Theory

The transfer mechanism may be examined in income terms. Thus, the tools which we used in Chapter 13 can be brought to bear upon this special case of adjustment. Consider the transfer case in these terms. The money proceeds of the loan are transferred from A the lender to B the borrower. What is required for real transfer to take place is to raise income in B and lower it in A by amounts which will create the required change in the trade balance. Take first the simplest case, where the money transfer means an increment of investment equal to the loan in B and an increase in saving equal to the loan in A. If we use a simple diagram showing the relations of the foreign balance and the domestic saving-investment situation we can then see what happens.

The Economics of the Balance of Payments

In Fig. 13.8 we demonstrated the effects of either an increase in domestic investment I_d or an increase in exports X upon the level of national income. The equilibrium condition of such income was then expressed in the form

$$X + I_d = S + M$$

We can rearrange this expression in the form

$$X - M = S - I_d$$

which is more convenient for our present purpose. The new form tells us that the balance of trade is equal to the difference between saving and domestic investment, and it too can be shown diagrammatically as in Fig. 15.1 (a). Here the basic schedules $X - M$ and $S - I_d$ may be derived from earlier diagrams. To obtain $X - M$ we subtract the value of imports in Fig. 13.1 from the value of exports in Fig. 13.2 (a). The result is a downward-sloping $X - M$, since the upward-sloping M function is subtracted from a constant level of exports. The $S - I_d$ schedule is upward-sloping, since savings rise with income, whereas investment I is assumed to be constant at all income levels. The $X - M$ and $S - I_d$ schedules intersect at E, which is an equilibrium level of national income and in this case also an equilibrium for the balance of payments.

Now add to this the effect of increased investment in the borrowing country. It is assumed that there is a constant increase in investment and no foreign repercussions. $S - I_{d_1}$ shows the new level of investment, where I_d has been increased by the amount of the loan and has thus moved the $S - I_d$ curve downwards by that amount. Income has been increased and a balance-of-payments deficit of yz has been created. It is clear that, since yz is less than the total injection (xz) by xy the amount of saving, the balance-of-payments deficit cannot transfer the full injection represented by the loan. It would only do so if saving were zero or if we redrew $S - I_d$ in $S - I_{d_2}$ so as to allow for induced investment through an accelerator, relaxing our assumption that I_d is constant for all levels of income. $S - I_{d_2}$ now slopes upwards away from $S - I_d$ because investment increases with the accelerator and thus increases the intercept yz. yz would eventually become greater than the original loan and, in spite of positive saving (x_1, y_1), the loan would be fully transferred.

Fig. 15.1 (b) shows the situation in the lending country. $S' - I_{d_2}$ now rises with the increase in savings. At E_1, the intersection point with $X - M$ there is a fall in income of YY_1, and a balance-of-payments surplus of E_1Y_1. But this is short of the amount of the loan by Y_1F_1. The balance-of-payments surplus is insufficient for the transfer of the loan.

This diagrammatic illustration of the transfer process can take no

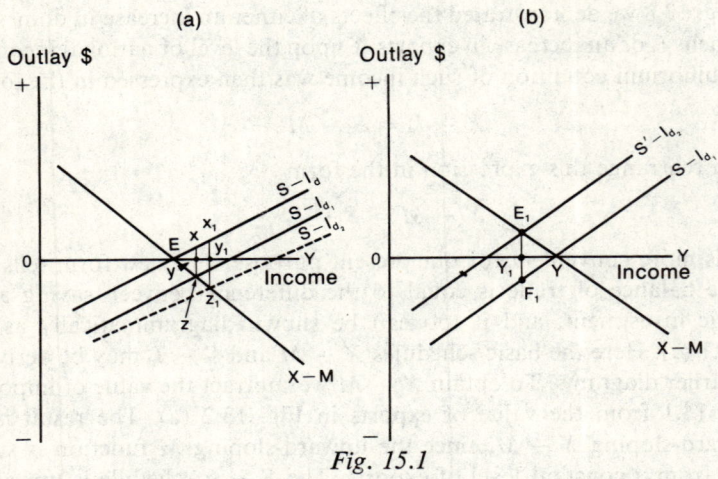

Fig. 15.1

account of the foreign repercussion. A numerical example clearly shows, however, that the inclusion of the repercussion makes little difference. We have added a leakage, but as long as there is a positive marginal propensity to save and no accelerator to boost investment full transfer will not take place.

If we take the case of country B, the borrower, then the change in income in that country will be shown by the formula

$$\Delta Y_b = L \cdot \frac{1}{S_b + M_b + {}^bR_a}$$

where L is the injection to B's income stream from the loan, S_b is the marginal propensity to save in B, M_b is the marginal propensity to import and ${}^bR_a$ is the foreign repercussion. If $L = 100$, $S_b = 0.1$, $M_b = 0.2$ and ${}^bR_a = 0.02$ then we have

$$\Delta Y_b = 100 \cdot \frac{1}{0.1 + 0.2 + 0.02} = 312.5$$

The rise in B's income with a multiplier of 3·125 is 312·5. The total leakages must be equal to the original injection of 100 and with the propensities given savings would be 31·25, increased imports 62·5, and reduction of exports to A, 6·25. With these leakages, full transfer would only be made if the savings of 31·25 made in B were lent to A, but since B is already borrowing from A this is extremely unlikely. Only $68·75 million of the original $100 is therefore transferred from A to B through income changes. The remaining $31·25 million, offset by the amount of new savings in *B*, will remain on the foreign exchange market as an excess supply of the currency of the lending country or an excess demand for the currency of the borrower. The real transfer of this residual will then require one or other of the processes of price change described above, according to whether a gold standard or free exchange rate is the current system between countries.

We assume in the above example that domestic investment in the borrowing and lending countries is altered by no more than the amount of the loan. There might well be induced changes in either or both countries.

The income effects are, it appears, insufficient to bring about the real transfer of the loan, unless the marginal propensity to save in the borrowing country is zero, or unless there is sufficient compensation from induced investment to boost income to that point where all the leakages other than saving are equal to the original injection.

This model of income reactions to the money transfer of a loan is a very simplified one.[5] Although we have shown that of themselves the main income forces are not sufficient to effect the whole of the real transfer we must realise that many other forces, including price changes, may enter the picture, and from the smoothness and swiftness with which all but the largest adjustments appear to be made in practice the aggregate force of these other influences must be great. Without attempting any exhaustive classification of the other factors involved, let us try to get a little nearer to reality by looking at conditions first in the lending and then in the borrowing country.

In the lending country the money must be raised before it is transferred. It may be raised in various ways. Some, such as increased taxation, an increase in savings, or a reduction of domestic investment, are deflationary, tending to reduce income and, by reducing imports and freeing goods for exports, aid the transfer. Some, on the other hand, are expansionary. Credit-creation to provide the capital will tend to raise income and perhaps prices as well, increasing imports, frustrating exports, and thus retarding the transfer. External lending is, however, only one type of capital export. The transfer may be one of a reparations payment or a grant of aid to a developing country. Each of these cases produces qualitative differences within the country. Reparations payments may, for example, be raised within the country partly by borrowing from abroad—as in the case of Germany in the 1920s—partly from taxation, partly from domestic borrowing, perhaps even by a domestic capital levy. Each method will have its own domestic effects which in turn will affect the efficacy of the required real transfer. In the case of a country making foreign aid grants it must raise these internally by savings and/or taxation. To the extent that it does not lower domestic income by so doing and achieve an export surplus, it may in the last resort finance them out of gold reserves very much as the United States has financed foreign aid, external direct investment, and military occupation and interventions in the sixties.

In the borrowing country one may usually assume that, since the borrowing is likely to have taken place for productive investment, both expenditure and money income will be rising. This will aid real transfer. If the capital inflow comes, however, from receipt of a reparations payment, the effects are more problematic. The country may conceivably lower taxes or use the proceeds for capital works. It may repay government debt, which may lower interest rates and so boost domestic investment. It may, if conservatively inclined, fear the possible inflationary effects of such a capital receipt and purposively offset them, thus throwing the burden of real transfer heavily onto the paying country. The case of a country in receipt of foreign aid is much simpler and more predictable. The borrowing or grant will be used for projects which will raise income and almost certainly create an import surplus or add to one already existing.

Apart from the influence upon the real transfer of the loan in the two countries, there is the simplest case of all which we must not overlook—that where a loan made to a developing country is 'tied'; that is, it must be used for purchases from the lending country only. In this case, the full real transfer of the loan is assured and is completed when the full loan has been spent. This case is worthy of mention not only because it provides the simplest possible case of real transfer but also because of the ubiquity of tied loans in current economic development operations.

Before concluding this section it is appropriate to say something about the multilateral aspect of adjustment to capital movements. The mechanisms of price and income adjustment have been discussed in terms of the traditional two-country model. What are the implications of moving from this to a many-country world? Briefly, we shall discuss two.

The first implication is that the adjustment changes become more diverse as they are distributed between lending country, borrowing country and third countries. Borrowers will now increase their imports not only from the lender but from third countries; lenders will reduce their imports from the borrowing country and from third countries. The condition after adjustment must still be that the amount of lending-country currency and borrowing-country currency offered on the exchange markets should be in equilibrium. If, for example, the compounded balances of payments of the third countries are in equilibrium but their deficits with the lender and their surpluses with the borrower do not match the flow of capital to be transferred, then there is an excess supply of lending-country currency and an

The Economics of the Balance of Payments 379

excess demand for borrowing-country currency which will promote, through gold flow or exchange-rate variation, a continued change in the external balances of the three so as to even up supply and demand. Another possibility might be that third countries be in overall balance-of-payments surplus, excess exports to the borrowing country more than offsetting excess imports from the lending country. In this case third country-currency would be in excess demand and the group as a whole would gain gold (or their currencies would strengthen) and experience expansion. But expansion for the third group would be greater relative to the lending country, which is already contracting in pursuit of its export surplus, than it would be relative to the expanding borrowing country. As a result, the trade balance adjustment effect on the third countries as a group would be greater relative to the lending country than to the borrowing country, and would cause imports from the lending country to rise while choking off exports to the borrowing country. Thus, the balance-of-payments surplus of the third countries would not only be adjusted but the 'distribution' of the adjustment between the two other groups would be appropriate to general equilibrium.

It would be tedious to follow further possible cases of multilateral adjustment. The principle is one of flows of gold along the gradients of the many cross-balances towards a condition in which the money quantity (or demand pressure) in each country is such that the original impact of the unilateral transfer is met.

The second implication of introducing a multilateral world lies outside the purely monetary aspects of transfer. It is the welfare effect that, in a multilateral world of free trade, the borrower and lender are free to maximise their real advantages while still being subject to the processes of monetary adjustment. It is not necessary for the lending country to achieve its export surplus by selling to the borrower only those goods which the borrower wants. It may now seek its export surplus by selling abroad those goods in the production of which it has a comparative advantage. The borrowing country need not obtain the goods (on which it wishes to spend the loan) in the lending country, nor need it even obtain them abroad at all. If the goods can be had more satisfactorily from a third country or at home there is a net transfer of real goods and services into the borrowing country. They are obtaining more real resources for their own projects without taking resources away from fellow countrymen. International transfers of real resources can take place freely on a multilateral basis. Although direct financial arrangements for a loan may take place bilaterally, trade need not be deprived of its multilateral character in order to make the necessary real transfers.

(iv) The Terms of Trade

During the transfer process the terms of trade between the borrowing and lending countries are likely to be altered. More specifically, the net barter terms of trade, that is the ratio of export prices to import prices, will be changed. This is distinct from the gross barter terms of trade which is the ratio of the total import quantity to the total export quantity. If export prices for either country rise relative to import prices, the buying power of exports is increased and the terms of trade are improved, and conversely when import prices rise relative to those of exports. What pattern of change may we expect the terms of trade to follow as a result of a real transfer?

This is a difficult question to answer. We have established that the real transfer following a unilateral money transfer is effected predominantly by income changes in the two countries; that whether the price mechanism is required to supplement income changes to bring about transfer is determined by such factors as the level of saving in each country, the impact upon spending in the lending country of raising the money capital, and the proportion of the loan which is spent by the borrowers in the lending country. We may assume either that the real transfer is made solely by income changes, or that it is made predominantly by income changes with marginal assistance from price changes. As far as price changes are concerned, the effect on the terms of trade is fairly predictable. The import surplus in the borrowing country and export surplus in the lending country reflect the price changes brought about by gold flow or exchange-rate change. The terms of trade will have moved in favour of the borrower and against the lender. Directly income changes in the two countries are considered there is no such certainty. In the simplest case, where savers in the lending country free goods which are bought entirely by the importers of the borrowing country using the loan proceeds, there is no change in prices anywhere in the two countries: the terms of trade are unchanged. Various switches of demand between import and export goods in the two countries can turn the terms of trade against the borrower; while the conditions under which the loan was raised in the lending country may influence the terms of trade also, probably in favour of the lending country if the loan proceeds were raised by inflationary methods.

This difference in the terms-of-trade effects as between price effects and income effects makes it virtually impossible to say anything significant about the ways in which the terms of trade will move when both price and income forces effect the real transfer. We must retreat and, since income effects are predominant, see if any pattern can be established for terms-of-trade changes when transfer is effected by income changes only.

Under income adjustment the effect on the terms of trade depends upon: the income changes in the two countries; the propensities to consume and to import in the two countries; and the elasticities of supply in the two countries. No elaborate model is possible here because of difficulties of methodology. Income changes, propensities and multiplier analysis assume linear relationships which depend on constant prices and under-employment. Terms-of-trade analysis is interested solely in price changes. Any approach to the problem of the terms-of-trade changes attendant upon income adjustment must be approximate and intuitive rather than rigorously analytical.

Kindleberger[6] using a method suggested by Meade[7] provides us with a picture which is of value, although, as he readily admits, it is far from satisfactory.

If income changes occur in one country only, the borrowing country — a situation which would arise if the loan were raised in the lending country by credit-creation, so that total expenditure was for the time being unchanged — total expenditure in the borrowing country would rise by $1/(\Delta S + \Delta M)$. If we assume a marginal propensity to save of 0·2 and to import of 0·3 and a loan of $100 million, then the total expenditure in the borrowing country would rise by $200 million, i.e. by the $100 million of the original loan plus $100 million of induced consumption. Imports would have increased by $60 million which would represent (in a two-country model) an export increase of $60 million to the lending country, the only increase in its expenditure. In this situation, with increased expenditure in the borrowing country more than three times that in the lending country prices will rise more in the borrowing than in the lending country — provided that elasticities of supply in the two countries are similar but not infinite. If they are infinite, the prices will not rise with a rise in demand. To the extent that the elasticity of supply in the lending country is greater than that in the borrowing country, the improvement in the borrowing country's terms of trade will be reduced.

We have now evolved the simple method of judging relative price-level changes in the two countries by the relative size of the changes that occur in each country's level of spending. From the simple case where all the initial change in income occurs in the borrowing country, we may move on to cases where income changes occur in both countries. In other words: what happens to the relative price levels (i.e. to the terms of trade) when total spending on the lender's goods changes as compared with the borrower's?

If we assume that there is no net change in the total money income of the two countries (the increment to income in the borrowing country being matched by the decline in income in the lending country), and if we assume also that there are no savings, then the distribution of total increased spending between the two countries is determined by the sum of the marginal propensities to import in the two countries. The spending and receipt of income can then be set out in the form of a matrix in which A and B are shown vertically as spenders and horizontally as receivers.

	Spenders		Spenders	
	A	B	A	B
Receivers A	MPC_a	MPM_b	0·6	−0·4
B	MPM_a	MPC_b	0·4	−0·6

Thus, reading vertically, A spends out of any increment of income an increased amount on consumption and an increased amount on imports. B does the same. As receivers of income, A receives the additional amount she spends out of income on consumption plus the additional imports taken by B; while B receives the additional consumption made by herself plus additional exports to A.

Suppose that, in this matrix, MPC_a and MPC_b are both 0·6 and MPM_a and MPM_b are also equal at 0·4. The sum of the MPM's is less than one. If income increases in A and diminishes by the same amount in B then (a) the increase in spending on A's goods by A ($0·6\Delta Y$) will exceed the decrease in spending on A's goods by B ($0·4\Delta Y$), and (b) the increase in spending on B's goods by A ($0·4\Delta Y$) will be less than the decrease in spending on B's goods by B ($0·6\Delta Y$). The net result is an increase in net spending on A's goods and a decrease in net spending on B's goods. A's price level will rise and B's will fall, the terms of trade turning in favour of A.

The case where the sum of the marginal propensities to import is one is neutral (assuming still that there are no savings). Net spending is unchanged, and the terms of trade do not change. If we take a value for the two MPM's of 0·6, making their sum greater than one we get a matrix as follows

	Spenders	
	A	B
Receivers A	0·4	−0·6
B	0·6	−0·4

The Economics of the Balance of Payments

In this case the increase in A's income produces an increase of $0.4 \Delta Y$ by A for A's goods, but also a decrease of $0.6\Delta Y$ in B's demand for A's goods; and for B's goods there is a decline of demand of $0.4\Delta Y$ in B and an increase of $0.6\Delta Y$ in A. There is an increase in net spending on B's goods, a decrease on A's goods and the terms of trade move in favour of B.

It appears from our three matrices that, assuming zero saving, equal marginal rates of spending in the two countries, and equal elasticities of supply, the terms of trade move in favour of the borrower when the marginal propensities to import in the two countries are together less than one; they move in favour of the lender when they are more than one; and they remain unchanged when they are equal to one.

If we take account of savings (and still with equal changes in spending), the following matrix reflects a situation in which the sum of the marginal propensities to import is less than one. The changes in spending in the two countries will be as follows

$$\text{Spending on } A\text{'s goods} = 0.3\Delta Y - 0.6\Delta Y$$
$$\text{Spending on } B\text{'s goods} = -0.2\Delta Y + 0.3\Delta Y$$

Thus there is a net decrease of spending on A's products and a net increase on B's, moving the terms of trade in favour of B. It would appear to be the criterion here for an improvement in the terms of trade of the lender that the marginal propensity to import in the borrower should be greater than the marginal propensity to consume in the lender, and that the marginal propensity to import in the lender should be greater than the marginal propensity to consume in the borrower. The sum of the marginal propensities to import is no longer relevant.

		Spenders	
		A	B
Receivers	A	$+0.3$	-0.6
	B	$+0.3$	-0.2
Savings		$+0.4$	-0.2

We will not set out the matrix for the case where spending in the two countries is unequal. Here, it is necessary to know the changes in income as well as the propensities before one can foretell terms-of-trade changes. The most likely case is probably that where income rises more in the borrowing country than in the lending, and if this is coupled with a higher propensity to consume than to import, then prices will rise in the borrowing country relative to the lending and turn the terms of trade in favour of the former.

The removal of the assumption of equal supply elasticities makes matters no simpler. Only in the case where there are equal increases in spending on the goods of both countries can we forecast the result. Here, if supply is inelastic in the lending country and elastic in the borrowing country, prices will, for any increase in demand, rise more in the lending country than in the borrowing and improve the lending country's terms of trade.

It is time to draw these very frayed and tangled threads together. What we have had to say about the transfer mechanism and the terms of trade has been adequate only to form some presumptive opinions about their interrelationship. No embracing generalisation, still less any formula for forecasting, has emerged. Perhaps the main *raison d'être* of this section has been to give practice in handling a few of the formative variables. As is so often the case in economic processes the final outcome is the result of a balance of forces, the magnitudes of which we do not know. Here, it is the mix of price changes and income changes; the differences of spending power and its distribution, which are in question. All we have been able to do is to marshal the forces and examine them a little more closely.

Perhaps the best way in which to close this section is to ask a determined (not to say despairing) question: which country, borrower or lender is likely to be favoured by a change in the terms of trade? Let us marshal the probabilities. Borrowing countries are usually borrowers for development, lenders are lenders for profit or duty, or both. It is likely that the income change in the borrower and lender will, in this most common situation, be sufficient to transfer all the real capital, that the changes will be mainly concentrated in the rise in income in the borrowing country, and that much of the rise in income will be spent. The terms of trade will then favour the country in which the bulk of the spending takes place or the country with the lower elasticity of supply for the demanded goods, or both. These effects are easy to assess where they coalesce, but imponderable where they are offset, and the net effect is important. How the borrowing country will 'place' its additional spending is problematic. If it is underdeveloped one is tempted to say that it will go in rising imports, particularly of capital goods. It may, however, spend predominantly at home. This question must remain open. On the elasticity of supply, it is likely that, if the borrower is a developing country, its supply will be less capable of swift expansion than would be the case in a mature country with a long-established productive system. Prices may rise sufficiently in the borrowing country even to offset any filip to prices in the lender caused by additional spending coming to it from the borrower.

On balance, it might appear that more factors favour a rise in borrowing-country prices than in lending-country prices; that the terms-of-trade change will favour the borrower and be adverse to the lender.

(v) Conclusion

The transfer problem may be viewed in two ways: as a special case of the theory of adjustment, where large unilateral payments within the capital section of the balance of payments must have their compensating adjustment in the current account; or as a series of special problems manifesting themselves in a particular context, each with its own peculiar circumstances, background and political trappings—as a reparations transfer facing an impoverished Germany in 1920; as the capital imports of Canada over a lifetime matched by the changing behaviour pattern of her current account; as the transfer of real wealth from mature industrial countries to poor and underdeveloped countries. The continuous supply of new case studies has kept the problem ever alive. Indeed, it is in terms of case studies that the literature of the transfer problem has mostly been written.

One reason for the unflagging interest in the problem is that, as manifested in the actual cases, it differs quite considerably. Rarely, if ever, does it appear in classic simplicity. A country with large unilateral payments to make—either a lending country or a country making reparations payments—will almost always be importing capital at the same time. If it is making a reparations transfer it may borrow from abroad in order to do this—as Germany did in the 1920s—thus spreading the transfer burden over a longer period. Even a large lending country will itself often borrow, so that it is the net transfer which is important. Again, political influences complicate the working of the economic forces. Countries making unilateral transfers should, in theory, have export surpluses, but not infrequently recipient countries do not want to be markets for their exports. This was the case in the 1920s, when France, Britain and the United States were, in varying degree, unwilling to receive exports of the German products which should have given Germany her export surplus.

Another semi-political influence comes from the almost universal drive for full employment in the mature countries. Such countries as lenders are unwilling to accept the conventional deflationary adjustment which capital transfer dictates. They are likely to meet deflationary influences by counter policies, monetary or fiscal, to promote growth and expansion. The full weight of the transfer falls in this case on the borrowing country. The drive for both internal and external stability tends some countries towards the dual aim of full employment and price stability at home and current-account balance with the external world. The inflexibility in the matter of balance-of-payments adjustment which we noted earlier appears again, and is inimical to the flexibility which is necessary for the real transfer of resources between lender and borrower. The movement towards discouragement of capital flows which manifested itself in measures such as the United States interest equalisation tax of 1963 can, when the choice between balance-of-trade equilibrium and full employment becomes acute, go one step further to direct control of long-term capital export. The lending role of the great industrial countries, however, has been and still is a function of great importance to economic development. Large capital transfers between countries are high politics. The foreign aid programmes and development loans of the post-war period have been a major factor in the international finance of the period, closely watched by both donors and recipients for their effects and implications.

It is likely that reparations payments as capital transfers will fade into historical obscurity. The great powers seemingly learned their lesson in the interwar period, and the Hoover Moratorium of 1931 closed the epoch which began with the French war indemnity of 1871. No such reparations or war-debts payments were mooted after 1945. In future if wars are small they will hopefully not involve reparations settlements: if they are large and involve the great powers, then financial reparations will be the least of worries to the survivors.

16
Internal and External Equilibrium

(i) The Conflicting Aims of Economic Policy

THE optimum condition for any country to enjoy is that in which prices are steady at a high level of employment and the balance of payments is in long- and short-run equilibrium. If heaven is divided into nation states that is the way it will be. On earth just now it is different.

Balances of payments for various reasons can go into deficit or surplus (see p. 286 above). The disequilibrium when it occurs can be repressed, as with direct controls on trade and payments; adjusted, by allowing price changes, income changes and capital flows to work out their correctionary effects; or financed, by allowing reserves to move from the deficit country to the surplus. Whatever course of action is adopted to deal with balance-of-payments disequilibrium must be judged not only for its effect on the balance of payments but for its effect on the policies, monetary and fiscal, which are being used to achieve domestic stability. Clearly there may be conflicts. In particular there is a central conflict between adjustments which may be made to the foreign balance via price and income changes, and domestic policies for price stability and full employment. Adjustment involves downward or upward movement of prices and incomes; domestic policy aims at pegging these at the unique level appropriate to full employment. Of the true adjustment measures, only capital movement appears to be feasible without this conflict. Moreover, avoidance of conflict may drive countries to adopt quasi-adjustment policies (which repress disequilibrium as opposed to 'basic-adjustment' policies which correct it),[1] in particular to bottle up a deficit by imposing controls on trade or payments, or by postponing basic adjustment by using reserves or borrowing to supplement these.

There is nothing new in the conflict of policies for internal and external stability. The gold standard presented this conflict in a direct form. The whole *modus operandi* of that adjustment system implied a sacrifice of domestic price (and employment) stability in the interests of maintaining a fixed gold parity value for the currency. In the heyday of the gold standard this was accepted. Because capital flows played a larger role in the adjustment process than is sometimes thought; because the great mature countries were liberal lenders; and because the late nineteenth century was predominantly a period of economic expansion the inherently deflationary attributes of that system did not assert themselves unduly before 1914; but in the interwar period the conflict of gold standard procedures with the price and employment policies of the great powers was a major reason for its abandonment. Free exchange rates were at first sight a vehicle of price adjustment with less potential conflict than the gold standard, but on closer inspection it is found that the conflict is still there in other forms. If the exchange rate is allowed complete freedom to move in response to monetary flows in the exchange market it may well produce such variations in export demand and in import prices as to vitiate domestic price stability. If it is strongly influenced or pegged to a narrow range of variation it comes so near to a fixed rate as to partake, to some extent at least, of the drawbacks of a near-gold standard. Moreover on the delicate balance of the price level of a fully employed country, a floating exchange rate may have dire effects. Through its upthrust on import prices it might set the whole domestic price level on an inflationary course. In the most extreme case, this might be seen as in turn raising export prices, worsening the trade balance and depreciating the rate still further. A country might be caught in a circle of depreciation and domestic price rise from which only subtle use of domestic monetary and/or fiscal policies might free it. Thus, the conflict and reconciliation of external and domestic policies arise in a new form.

But it has been in the period since the Second World War that the policy conflicts of domestic and external stability have become sharp and defined. Three factors have caused this. The first has been the determination, backed often by electoral commitments,* of government to preserve 'high and stable levels of employment'. The second has been the realisation that, in walking the razor's edge between underemployment and inflation it is better, politically, to err on the side of inflation; but not to err too much, so policies for price stability have been added to policies for full employ-

---

* To the British White Paper on Employment Policy of 1944 and the U.S. Employment Act of 1946 might be added many more. On the rising flood of Keynesianism and fear of a return to the stagnation of the thirties, full employment became a main policy aim of most post-war governments. Failure to preserve it was seen as the mark of Cain for any government.

The Economics of the Balance of Payments

ment. Third, has been the effect of the international monetary problems of the period, in particular the shortage and maldistribution of international liquidity and the thrust of international organisations like the IMF to induce countries to correct balance-of-payments deficits promptly and without resort to direct controls. All these have posed again and again in recent years problems, general and specific, about the counter-pulls of the home and international economies.

A small but significant theory of economic policy aimed at resolving these apparently paradoxical aims has grown up in recent years, and we must examine it briefly. Before doing so it may be useful to ask ourselves what are the significant questions to which in this matter we are in need of answers. They are:

1. What form of basic adjustment (as distinct from quasi-adjustment) is least likely to interfere with a country's policies for domestic stability?
2. In choosing weapons for controlling the domestic economy, e.g. monetary or fiscal policy, which are likely to interfere and which to mesh with policies for foreign balance adjustment?
3. If the conflict between domestic stability and basic adjustment policies is irreconcilable what other choices are open — e.g. is a country then entitled to resort to quasi-adjustment policies and, if so, to which ones?
4. Since the efficiency of the adjustment mechanism involves a burden on the adjusting countries, how should this burden be distributed between deficit and surplus countries?

We will not, except in the cases of (2) and (4), attack these problems frontally. Rather, we will briefly review the literature as it stands and glance back in conclusion to see what light, if any, seems to have been shed upon them.

(ii) Expenditure-Switching and Expenditure-Changing

Incomes and employment depend upon the level of spending. No automatic mechanisms ensure that spending attains or stays at the level appropriate to full employment. The balance of payments also depends upon spending and varies with it. This last fact should by this stage be basic to student's thinking. It is most easily recalled, for the forgetful, by the equation $Y - (C + I + G) = X - M$, where $X - M$ is the balance of trade. Our purpose in this section is to explore what forces, if any, lead to the coincidence of 'internal balance' (i.e., full employment) and 'external balance' (i.e. balance of trade equilibrium) levels of spending.

In the simplest case, where balance-of-trade disequilibria are temporary and minor, one may assume that spending policies will be aimed at internal balance, and external imbalance will be met by an outflow from the country's international reserves. It is arguable (though by no means proven or accepted by this writer or others) that balance-of-trade disequilibria of longer duration may be met by quantitative import restrictions allowing policies for internal balance to continue unimpeded. In neither of these cases should the deficit be due to overspending. If it is, then the obvious cure for it is to reduce spending. If, however, the external deficit is temporary, small and not due to fundamental and longer term forces such as an unfavourable movement of the terms of trade or a rise in real wages in the deficit country relative to its productivity, then it is permissible to reconcile internal and external balance by the use of quasi-adjustment policies.

This, however, is but the fringe of the problem. The danger is that quasi-adjustment policies may be used to meet the fundamental disequilibria in the external balance, which are caused by terms of trade or productivity/ wage level changes, and spending may be pushed to the full employment limit and beyond. This way lies the distortion of domestic inflation, controlled foreign trade, a permanent but suppressed balance-of-payments deficit, and warped patterns of investment and production. From this nightmare one may rightly turn and seek for some explanation of where the level of domestic spending, which determines both external and internal balance, should be set.

It is useful at this stage to recur to the dichotomy of policies basic to balance-of-payments adjustment which was first made by Harry Johnson[2] and was described on pp. 360–2 – the distinction between expenditure-switching and expenditure-changing policies. Switching policies are those which reallocate a given level of expenditure between the constituent items of demand, for example, between domestic expenditure and expenditure on imports; changing policies involve altering the aggregate of outlay, but with a constant distribution between constituent items. Let us follow through the effect of these two types of policies on the balance of payments and the level of employment, i.e. upon the two leading elements of external and internal balance respectively.

It is first necessary to formalise the relationships which exist between employment, the balance of payments and real expenditure. This Trevor Swan has done in a famous series of diagrams which we now consider.[3] Assume that productivity, the terms of trade, monetary transfers and capital

The Economics of the Balance of Payments

movements are given, then Fig. 16.1 shows how employment and the foreign balance both depend on the level of real expenditure. On the x axis is shown the real expenditure, that is total domestic consumption plus investment (private and public) at constant prices. This we call E. (Changes in E are therefore expenditure-changing policies). R on the y axis is a measure of the competitive position of the country shown by the ratio of international prices to an index of domestic wages. (Such an index would be weighted, the weights showing the response of supply and demand for different commodities to changes in relative costs.) The higher one moves on R the greater are exports, the smaller are imports. In a condition of fixed exchange rates, the exchange rate is progressively undervalued as we proceed north along the R axis. Changes in R also approximate to switching policies in the Johnson classification.

Consider first the A curves on the diagram. Each curve represents a given level of employment. The level of employment A can be sustained either by a very high value of R, i.e. by a very favourable ratio of external prices to domestic costs, so that much is exported and little is imported, or by a high level of expenditure E. Let us suppose that A_1 represents a level of employment less than full, that A_2 represents the 'mix' of cost ratios and levels of spending which will maintain full employment, and that A_3 represents some given amount of overemployment. The B curves show balances of payments each produced by a mix of cost ratio and spending. Their shape and position is important. Such curves must slope upward and to the right with progressive steepness. A low value of E will release resources for

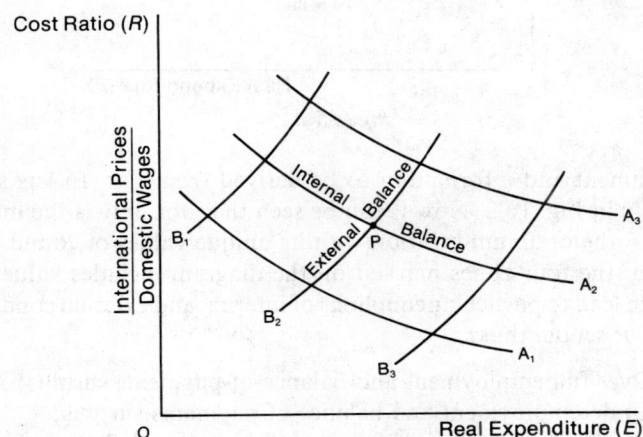

Fig. 16.1

export (and generate low imports); as E increases, a progressively large amount of expenditure will draw imports and frustrate exports, so that a greatly increased R will be required to maintain any given balance $(X-M)$. B_1 is a curve appropriate to a balance of payments which is in surplus, B_2 is for the case where $X-M=0$, and B_3 is a curve for a balance of payments which is in deficit.

For the curves with the subscript 2, any combination of spending and cost ratio on A_2 gives full employment and represents internal balance; any combination on B_2 gives external balance, since for B_2 there is equality of foreign receipts and payments. The intersection point P is the only point at which the economy depicted can enjoy both internal and external balance. It shows the unique value of spending and the unique cost ratio or competitive position which will achieve this optimum position.

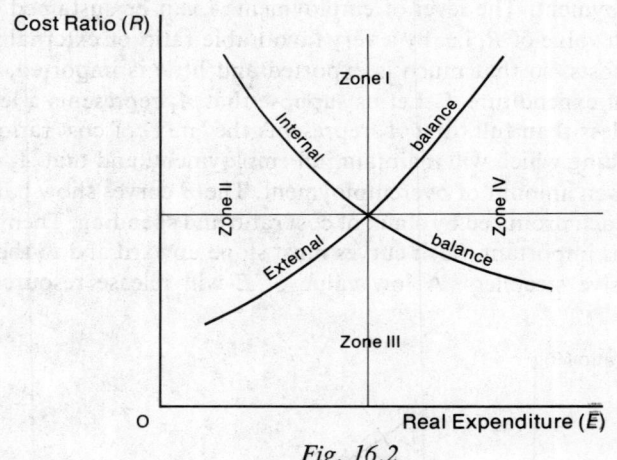

Fig. 16.2

The argument and information to be derived from Fig. 16.1 is set out more clearly in Fig. 16.2. Now it can be seen that not only is the intersection point P the optimum position with its unique values of R and E, but that each of the four zones marked on the diagram includes values of R and E which lead to particular couplings of internal and external conditions. These may be set out thus:

Zone I   Over-full employment and balance-of-payments surplus;
Zone II   Underemployment and balance-of-payments surplus;
Zone III Underemployment and balance-of-payments deficit; and
Zone IV Over-full employment and balance-of-payments deficit.

The Economics of the Balance of Payments

By finding which zone we are in, we define merely the facts of our situation. We know, for example, that in Zone II spending is too little while in Zone IV it is too much: we know that in Zones I and III costs are too low and too high respectively. But this is not enough for policy. We must know more than the mere location in a particular Zone tells us. For example, if we increase outlay in Zone II (which is apparent), we need to know also whether we need to increase or decrease R. If in Zone I we need to lower the cost ratio, we need to know also whether we must couple with this a raising or a lowering of expenditure. We can readily answer these questions by dividing the diagram through P into quadrants by means of the broken vertical and horizontal lines. Now it becomes possible to tell whether in any zone a given change in either E or R should be coupled with a rise or fall of the other variable. This can be seen from Fig. 16.3. Here we have two positions a and b both in Zone I, that is in the zone of over-full employment and balance-of-payments surplus. It is clear here that for both positions the cost ratio is unequivocally too high and should be reduced. Whether at the same time outlay should be reduced or expanded only becomes apparent when Zone I is divided by the vertical broken line. It is then evident that to get from a to P we need to reduce R and expand E, but to get from b to P we need to reduce R by the same amount and contract E. Thus, for policy action, we not only need to know what zone we are in, we need to know also what quadrant we are in. There is nothing in the economic facts, derived from location in a particular zone, which will tell us when we change one variable, what we should do with the other. That, we can only know by finding our location both within the zone and the quadrant.

The assumptions made at the outset should be borne in mind before too much is claimed for this formulation. The distinction between the long and short run is of the essence in making policy decisions, and it is that distinction which is blurred by the assumptions. For example, the terms of trade are likely to vary. If they are, for the moment, better than the long-run average, we may be temporarily in Zone I rather than in Zone III, the position appropriate to the long-run average. Changes in the factors taken as given at the beginning of this section shift the curves bodily. Improvement in the terms of trade or in capital-import shift all B curves rightward and downward. Equilibrium now occurs, with E higher and R lower. An improvement in productivity shifts all A curves rightward and upward and B curves rightward and downward so that equilibrium occurs with a higher E and probably a lower R. Another factor which must be taken into consideration is that both the A and B curves are flatter in the long run than in the short. This is because sensitivity of supplies and demands to changes in R are slight in the short run and take effect only

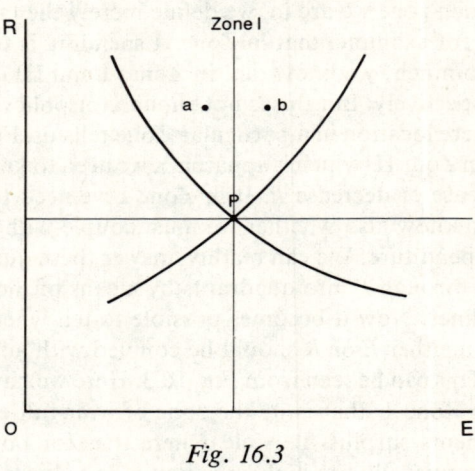

Fig. 16.3

over a long period, while the effect of changes in E is immediate. The lesson of this is that there should be no attempt to adjust short-run equilibria by changes in R, since these would probably involve instabilities and inflexibilities in the cost structure. It would appear desirable that R should at all times be adapting gradually, keeping in harmony with long-run trend movements while short-run fluctuations are met by the use of reserves. If it is necessary to work with a low level of reserves and it is necessary to extend the time for average cost adjustments to be made, then there may be some argument for the use of direct balance-of-payments controls. The desiderata of this argument must wait, however, until Chapter 19.

What can be said of the long-run cost adjustments which may be made in R? These are essentially adjustments of real wage rates and are notoriously hard to achieve. The formulating and implementing of incomes policy has so far eluded most governments – in particular, those which have most need of it. In the absence of adequate wage adjustment and with inadequate reserves there may be a tendency for countries placed in Zones III or IV to allow their 'temporary' import restrictions to drag on to permanency. Here, the trade-off for freedom from wage-planning for the workers is deprivation of certain restricted imports and/or a rise in the price of those imports which are quantitatively controlled. This rise in price may occur in several ways: by allowing the restricted volume of the goods to find their own price level through the ordinary forces of supply and demand; by auctioning import licences to dealers, who then pass the scarcity price on to the consumers; by the issuing government charging a fee for the import licence; or by foreign exporters raising their supply price. To the extent that the price rise is widespread and is transmitted from imports to the general price level, real wages are reduced. This is precisely what workers wished to avoid by non-acceptance of a wage policy.

This is not the place to set up a full discussion of a wage policy and its place in the running of the economy. Probably in no department of economics is there such a gap between what is economically desirable and what is politically feasible. There are in practice only two courses open. In limited circumstances — where the working population is small, where the country's stake in foreign trade is small, where labour union organisation is recent and forward-looking — it may be just possible to set up and work a wage policy. In default of these favourable conditions real wages must be regulated through the state of the labour market, and variations in expenditure (E) must be used to move the state of employment in the economy about the level of full employment. Fortunately there is reason to believe that full employment for most economies is not a precise level of employment of the labour force but a spectrum within which there is room for manoeuvre.

Finally, in connection with this diagram, there is the question of controlling E, the level of spending. Control of this variable is vital. If it does not exist or is only partial the choices between other policies — controls, wage policy, use of reserves — are meaningless. Four facets of control claim attention, but since discussion of them would carry us far into the subject of domestic budgeting and monetary planning we shall be content simply to draw attention to them and to such aspects of them as are relevant to our immediate problem of reconciling internal and external balance. The first is the efficiency of the various devices, fiscal and monetary, which control spending in the private sector. Here we include the frequency with which direct and indirect taxation may be changed, the sensitivity of the economy to changes in monetary conditions, and the efficiency of the banking system. Second, is the choice of monetary or fiscal policy to influence spending — a matter of importance to which we shall return in a later part of this chapter. Third, is the spending propensity of government, either on current projects of social and political importance such as social services or defence programmes, or on capital projects – roads, public works, fuel and power and the like – deemed no less important. Only a long-term phase programme with flexibility to enable cuts to be made and restored and switches to be achieved, can hope to reconcile the spendthrift propensities of government on the one hand and the need to avoid overspending on the other. The records of the major governments are not encouraging. Both Labour and Conservative parties have struggled in vain to reduce government outlay in the United Kingdom; the Republicans under Eisenhower were scarcely more successful than the Democrats under Truman in reducing budget deficits. Under Kennedy, Johnson and Nixon the cost of defence, aid and the war in Vietnam wrought havoc with the budget and the balance of payments alike. In large economies, it seems that public outlays have a life of their own, whose behaviour pattern governments can only partially control. Fourth, is the problem of timing desired changes in expenditure. Even if the necessary cut in outlay is made when it is required, its effects in terms of reduced outlays at the crucial time may be delayed by as much as a year.

We cannot hope for precision or rectitude in spending — neither on the record nor on the theory. Swan advocates that we should try to achieve a position as near as possible to the northwest border of Zone IV, where we would have minor adjustments to the balance of payments and spending on a scale which gives over-full employment. Such a prescription, if it is the best within the bounds of practical possibility, is depressing, for it has been the most common condition of many economies since the war — a condition of creeping inflation with recurrent balance-of-payments crises, checked when they occur either by domestic deflation, by import controls or occasionally by devaluation.

The Swan diagram, while it does not lead to any exciting conclusions or prescriptions for policy, has given us an ingenious marshalling of the factors involved in choosing and reconciling policies for internal and external equilibrium, in pointing out the conditions under which switching policies should be used by changing the exchange rate and using other devices to alter the cost ratio, and when expenditure-changing policies should be used as when we seek to alter E.

(iii) The Coupling of Monetary and Fiscal Policy

Expenditure-changing policies may be implemented by either monetary or fiscal policy. The choice between these must now be considered. Fiscal policy, implying movements in budget deficit and surplus, has effects on both internal and external balance, acting through changes in spending by both the public and private sectors. Monetary policy, through the interest rate and credit availability, has an influence also upon the level of outlay; but its influence on the external balance is mainly made via the interest rate and through short-term capital movements. Any country anxious to maintain its exchange rate for long periods and to avoid direct monetary and trade controls will, unless its foreign exchange reserves are great, have to make continual choices between fiscal and monetary policies as instruments to attain external and internal balances. The elements of this choice have been well arrayed by Robert Mundell.[4] What follows leans heavily upon his analysis.

The conditions of equilibrium are similarly defined to those in section (ii). Internal balance implies full employment, where aggregate demand for domestic output is equal to the aggregate supply produced with all factors in use. Excess demand implies inflationary pressure; deficiency of demand, underemployment of resources. Transitory inequalities between aggregate demand and output capacity at full employment can, however, be met by the accumulation or running down of inventories.

External balance implies that the balance of trade equals the net capital flow at the existing exchange rate with no net change in the central bank's reserve holdings. It is assumed that all export demands and foreign economic policies are given, and that capital flows are sensitive to interest-rate changes. In these circumstances, domestic outlay depends upon either fiscal policy or monetary policy.

It is possible with these two policy variables to show on a diagram the variations of external and internal balance. In Fig. 16.4 the x-axis measures monetary policy applied through the rate of interest, and the y-axis measures fiscal policy in the budget variations from deficit through balance to surplus. For pairings of fiscal and monetary policy at any level of employment, an internal balance curve, sloping downward and to the right, may be drawn. We show only the internal balance curve applicable to full employment AA. This shows, by reference to the axes, all possible mixes of fiscal and monetary policy which will produce full employment. The curve slopes downward and to the right because expenditure must be consistent all along the schedule in order to maintain full employment. The expenditure may come from a 'low-interest-rate induced' monetary demand at the top of the curve with demand throttled back through the budget surplus to compensate; or, at the bottom of the curve, high demand from the budget deficit requires a cut-back of monetary demand from a high interest rate. Curves for internal balance between AA and the origin will depict levels of over-full employment, because they are coupling lower rates of interest with a growing level of budgetary spending; curves further from the origin than AA are for conditions of depression.

The BB line shows the external balance schedule. It is, as Mundell puts it, 'the locus of pairs of interest rates and budget surpluses (at the level of income compatible with full employment) along which the balance of payments is in equilibrium'.[5] The curve is negatively sloped because high rates of interest lower capital exports, increase capital imports, and reduce domestic expenditure, all of which improve the balance of payments. The constant level of spending is ensured, because at low rates of interest there is a high budget surplus which, by curtailing domestic demand and reducing imports, still maintains the balance of payments in equilibrium even with low interest rates. All points to the right of *BB* show balance-of-payments surpluses; all points to the left show deficits.

Since both *AA* and *BB* slope downward and to the right, it is essential to know which of the curves is the steeper. In fact *BB*, the external balance curve, will be more steeply sloped if there is any mobility of capital in response to interest rates. The slope of the internal balance curve *AA* is the ratio of the sensitivity of domestic spending to the rate of interest and the response of domestic spending to the budget surplus. If we may assume, for this purpose only, that capital export is constant, then the balance of payments depends solely on spending because exports are assumed constant and the only change to the external balance can come from spending-induced changes in imports. This is another way of saying that, if capital exports are constant, the slope of *BB*, the external balance curve, is equal to the ratio of the sensitivity of spending to the rate of interest as compared with the response of spending to the budget surplus. Thus, if capital exports are assumed away, the slopes of the curves are the same. If one admits capital exports to *BB*, the responsiveness of capital exports to the rate of interest, however small, makes *BB* steeper than *AA*.*

This can be illustrated on Fig. 16.4. *P* is the unique situation of overall equilibrium for the policy variables. Suppose that the equilibrium is disturbed by an increase in the rate of interest of *PQ*. This higher rate of interest exerts deflationary pressure and at *Q* there is a balance-of-payments surplus. The deflationary pressure can now be eliminated by lowering the budget surplus (or increasing the deficit) until the point *R* on the internal balance schedule is reached. At *R* spending is the same as at *P*. Therefore, imports and the balance of trade are the same as at *P*. But at *R* there is a balance-of-payments surplus of *RS*. This means that the balance-of-payments surplus must be accounted for by the capital imports drawn by the higher rate of interest. There must be, at this rate of interest, a further reduction of budget surplus (increase in deficit) in order to get rid of the

---

* This argument depends upon a form of fiscal policy that is neutral between home and foreign spending. Mundell uses the example of income tax changes. To the extent that the fiscal policy is biased towards or against domestic goods, the argument is strengthened or weakened. The more the change in the budget surplus comes from a change in spending on domestic goods, the more the slopes of *BB* and *AA* differ.

The Economics of the Balance of Payments

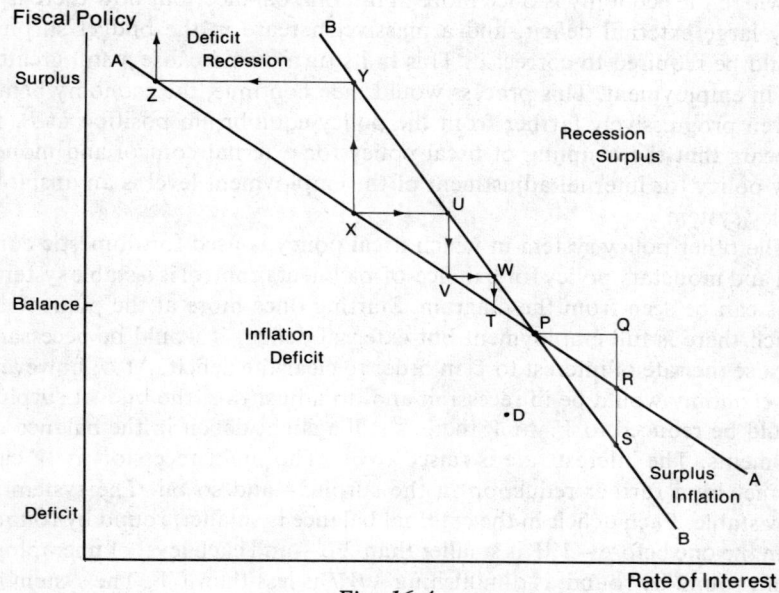

Fig. 16.4

balance of payments surplus. In the diagram, the more sensitive capital imports are to interest-rate changes the further S is below R and the more the economy will require to be pushed into inflation in order to bring the balance of payments to equilibrium.

Consider now the policy systems which may be used when we are at some point on the diagram other than P, that is, when external and internal balance have not been simultaneously achieved. There are two possible systems if both monetary and fiscal policy are to be used. The government may use monetary policy for policies aimed at internal stability and fiscal policy for external; or it may use fiscal policy for internal stabilisation and monetary policy for external control. Consider first the coupling of interest-rate policy for internal stability and fiscal policy for external control.

We start from a position of full employment combined with an external deficit. Such a point on the diagram would be X. In order to correct the deficit by means of fiscal policy, we must raise the budget surplus from X to Y, at which point the balance of payments will be in equilibrium. But the increase in the budget surplus will have pushed the economy out of internal balance and into recession. If monetary policy is used to attack the recession, the rate of interest must be lowered so that we now move to

Z, where the economy is once more in internal balance; but now there is a very large external deficit, and a massive increase in the budget surplus would be required to correct it. This in its turn would cause a still greater fall in employment. This process would then continue, the economy being driven progressively farther from the policy-equilibrium position at P. It appears that the coupling of fiscal policy for external control and monetary policy for internal adjustment of the employment level is an unstable policy system.

The other policy system in which fiscal policy is used for domestic control and monetary policy for balance-of-payments control is a stable system. This can be seen from the diagram. Starting once more at the point X at which there is full employment but external deficit, it would be necessary to raise the rate of interest to U in order to clear the deficit. At U, however, the economy would be in recession and, to adjust this, the budget surplus would be reduced to V. At V there is still a slight deficit in the balance of payments. The interest rate is raised to W. The slight recession at W can be met by a further reduction in the surplus — and so on. The system is now stable. Each deficit in the external balance is smaller, round by round, than the one before — VW is smaller than XU — and each level of unemployment, round by round, is diminishing — WT is less than UV. The system in this case is stable, converging on equilibrium at P.

The thrust of the diagrammatic argument may be summed up by noting that at X or anywhere in the quadrant of *Deficit* and *Recession*, the budget surplus is higher and the interest rate lower than at P the point of equilibrium. To use fiscal policy for external balance and interest rate reductions for internal balance simply drives the variables further and further from their equilibrium level. The second and alternative system moves them towards equilibrium.

We may now move round the other quadrants. In the opposite quadrant — *Surplus* and *Inflation* — restoration of equilibrium, i.e. movement towards P, requires a reduction of interest rate and contractionary fiscal policy. Monetary policy must be used for the external purpose, fiscal policy for the internal if there is to be convergence on P.

In the remaining two quadrants — *Inflation* and *Deficit* and *Recession* and *Surplus* — both monetary policy and fiscal policy will move in the same direction whatever the coupling of the policies. This is because interest rates and budget surplus will both rise either to correct an external deficit or to check inflation; both fall to amend a recession or an external surplus. It would appear from this that it is not important in these two large quadrants (which reflect the two most commonly experienced couplings of internal and external imbalance) whether we couple monetary policy with domestic or external balance policies. Closer scrutiny of the diagram will, however, show that the importance of the former coupling remains. If the economy were located at D we would be indifferent as to the coupling of policies only if we could locate P exactly, increasing both the budget surplus and the rate of interest by the precise amount required to locate us there. If D is in the northwest sector of the Inflation–Deficit zone the movement from D to P becomes more problematic, because now the surplus has to be reduced while the rate of interest still requires to be increased. This change of direction of the variables according to the position of D is because as in the Swan diagram (see p. 392) we must know our location, not only within the zone but within the quadrant. This is a complication which we ignore here. Suffice it to say that, wherever D is, it is likely that the search for P will begin with a move onto AA or BB.

That we could locate P exactly is very unlikely. Almost certainly we shall move from D by increasing either interest rate or budget surplus until we arrive on either AA or BB. Once there, we can converge on P and move towards equilibrium—but only if we couple monetary policy with external policy and fiscal policy with domestic employment policy. If the coupling is converse, we invoke instability and move away from equilibrium.

It would appear from this diagrammatic analysis that monetary policy in the form of interest-rate changes is the appropriate weapon to use for influencing the balance of payments; fiscal policy, changes in the size of the budget surplus, is the tool appropriate to adjustment of the internal level of employment.

(iv) The Distribution Between Countries of the Burden of Adjustment

Adjustment of its balance of payments is an inescapable process for a country in disequilibrium unless it has huge international reserves, or unless it is prepared to make use of direct controls to repress the disequilibrium — a course of action which has costs as well as advantages. But, as we have seen, adjustment involves a sacrifice for the adjusting country. If it is in a condition of external deficit and full employment it will, in order to eliminate the deficit, require to reduce domestic income below the full employment level. How far it will require to do this depends not only on the size of the deficit but on the strength of the adjustment forces bearing on the balance-of-payments disequilibrium from the size of the surplus country or countries. The onus of the adjustment can be thrown, theoretically, on the deficit or surplus country. In practice, both will probably share the adjustment burden. We must, however, seek to investigate the distribution of the adjustment burden. How far must the surplus country expand: how far must the deficit country contract? Moreover, what effect, if any, does the distribution of the burden have upon the efficiency of the adjustment mechanism?

It is conventional to distinguish a number of criteria according to which the burden of adjustment should be distributed. The examination of a number of these should take us near to an answer to the above questions.

The first criterion is that of internal stability and emphasises the extent to which there is internal balance in the deficit and surplus countries. Adjustment in each case should improve the internal balance as well as the external. If the deficit country is in a state of overemployment and the surplus country in recession, the same adjustment serves both internal and external equilibrium. The deficit country must contract and purge its inflation while adjusting its deficit; the surplus country must expand out of recession to dissipate its surplus. This at first seems the simplest case and constitutes no more than a 'rolling' adjustment for each country in a desired direction. But it is perhaps not so simple. It may not be easy where the full employment is not precisely defined to say where a country should stabilise. Some countries are prone to run their economies at very high levels of employment which to other countries appear inflationary. Britain, whose balance of payments since the Second World War has been in frequent deficit, has often been blamed for not adjusting by adopting a lower level of employment, say 4 per cent unemployment rather than 2 per cent. Germany, whose fear of price inflation is, in view of her history, understandably great, was under continual pressure to expand her economy during the fifties in order to reduce her external surplus and accumulation of gold. In practice, countries will regulate their policies according to their own subjective ideas of internal balance.

A qualification to this idea of a rolling adjustment is that where all countries in the world are in a state of depression. Here the surplus countries should expand and bear the brunt of the adjustment. Any deflation by the deficit countries will only intensify the depression. In the opposite case, in a condition of world inflation, both surplus and deficit countries should deflate; but the deflation should be led by the deficit countries for whom deflation leads to both internal and external balance. If the surplus countries lead the deflation, they will greatly intensify their external imbalance.

If we view the situation in a more dynamic sense, in a world in which economies are all growing but growing at different rates, deficit countries whose rates of growth are in excess of other countries can achieve external balance by checking back their rates of growth to accord with those of other countries. Surplus countries can often achieve external balance by speeding up their growth rate, provided that this does not produce for them a state of inflation at home.

In all the cases so far mentioned, application of the internal stability criterion produces harmony of interest. When, however, we go to the perhaps less common cases of deficit countries which are depressed and surplus countries which are in inflation, clashes of interest appear. If deficit countries which are depressed deflate, they will improve the external balance, but at the cost of intensified depression; while expansion in the surplus countries might bring balance-of-payments equilibrium, but at the cost of intensified inflation. In these cases the internal stability criterion breaks down and other solutions must be sought. In the clash of interest which occurs, it is likely under modern conditions that countries caught in this dilemma will do everything in their power to give primacy to domestic stability. If reserves are insufficient to sustain external imbalance, resort may be made to controls.

Mundell considers at this point the feasibility of applying a 'relative cost criterion' to the cases in which the internal stability criterion breaks down.[6] If we consider the case where surplus countries are already in a condition of inflation and deficit countries in recession, then there is a cost incurred in intensifying the inflation in the former and the recession in the latter – a cost which is certainly conceptual if hardly measurable. What, to use Mundell's example,[7] is the cost to Europe of a continuing rate of inflation of 4 per cent per annum compared to the cost to the United States of an excessive unemployment rate* of, say, 3 per cent? If the cost of inflation in the surplus countries is less than the waste from unemployment in the deficit countries, then adjustment should take place by expansion in the surplus countries. Such a criterion, however, is useless in practice. In the first place, the comparison probably becomes much more difficult as the rates of inflation and unemployment get larger. Within or near the full employment spectrum adjustments either way are small compared to large increases outside the spectrum. Almost certainly the costs of inflation and the wastes of unemployment increase sharply as both are increased. This would then suggest that for large adjustments the burden should be shared between the deficit and surplus countries. Secondly, the measuring of the

---

* Excessive unemployment rate is here defined to be a rate in excess of the unemployment rate for frictional unemployment; e.g. if the United States regards a frictional unemployment rate of 4 per cent as allowable at full employment, then a rate of 6 per cent represents excess unemployment of 2 per cent.

costs of inflation and the wastes of unemployment would fall far below the precision necessary to make such measurement useful. The costs of inflation — indeed, the very definition of inflation — would differ as between the inflation-tolerant British and the price-stability-loving Germans. The whole calculus of comparison would in all cases collapse into a cloudy impressionism which would be useless for policy guidance.

Baulked once more of a solution to the problem of assigning the burden of international adjustment in what we may call, for simplicity, the difficult case (i.e. between surplus countries in inflation and deficit countries in depression) it is tempting to apparently opt out of the difficulty by abrogating income and price adjustment as a method and resorting to exchange-rate changes. By changing the method of adjustment can we really opt out of the distribution problem? The short answer is that we cannot; and moreover, we may introduce some new difficulties as well. It is worth looking at the question briefly.

We will waive at the outset the practical and political difficulties involved in frequent exchange-rate changes. We will waive also the fact that once exchange-rate changes are used for adjustment, we come to live in an exchange-conscious world in which the politics of change and counter-change leap to importance. But one aspect of this politics we cannot ignore, for it is the nub of our problem: the question of whether, in a given situation of imbalance between two countries, the surplus country should appreciate or the deficit country depreciate. This is a very real and practical question. Western Germany, a country perennially in surplus since 1951, has frequently countered the demands of other West European countries that she should appreciate her currency by a curt suggestion that they should depreciate theirs.

When we come to marshal the considerations attached to exchange-rate changes relative to the burden of adjustment the following emerge.

Firstly, the problem of reconciling external and internal balance cannot be solved by an exchange-rate change alone. One single policy action will not produce the dual balance. Even if the exchange-rate change eliminates the external imbalance, it will be necessary in both countries to use other policies such as fiscal policy to deal with domestic imbalance. The burden of these remains undecided.

Secondly, the exchange-rate adjustment must also be distributed. In its simplest form, the question here is, should the deficit country devalue or the surplus country revalue? In the last resort, one may add, does it make any difference?

We may answer this question by looking at what happens when two countries both change their currency rates in the same direction and the

The Economics of the Balance of Payments

same proportion. If an identical revaluation (devaluation) in both countries leaves real and money values unchanged, then it is a matter of indifference whether the deficit country devalues or the surplus country revalues. Consider an example. Let us suppose that in a two-currency world Germany revalues the mark against the pound by 10 per cent of an initial rate of 10 DM = £1, so that the Bundesbank is prepared to support a new rate of 10 DM = £1·1. Suppose also that the United Kingdom simultaneously revalues the pound against the mark by 10 per cent of the initial rate, so that now the Bank of England is prepared to support a new rate of £1 = 11 DM. But these equal and opposite changes of exchange rate would produce an untenable situation. The Bank of England in supporting the new rate would be buying and selling marks at 9·09 pence each, while the Bundesbank would be buying and selling marks at 11 pence each. Dealers would not need to be very smart to make arbitrage profits by buying pounds at the Bundesbank where they are cheap and using them at the Bank of England to buy back marks with pounds. The incompatible rates would result in each central bank being swamped with its own currency and losing its reserves of the other currency. This loss of reserves would have deflationary effects on both countries. We certainly cannot say that equal revaluation of both currencies has no significant economic effects.

Consider the case of a deficit in the United Kingdom balance of payments with the United States. This, it might be argued, could be eliminated equally by a devaluation of the pound of, say, 10 per cent or alternatively a revaluation of the dollar by 10 per cent. Suppose, for the purposes of this example, that the par values of currencies under IMF are defined in terms of gold, a devaluation of the pound would increase the price of gold in terms of pounds by 10 per cent. The value of the gold reserves in pound terms held by both the United States and the United Kingdom would rise by 10 per cent with the devaluation, while their dollar value would be unchanged. Thus the purchasing power of both the gold stocks (in terms of British goods) rises. In American goods terms they remain unchanged. World liquidity has been increased. If the United States revalues the dollar by 10 per cent, the dollar price of gold falls by 10 per cent with the revaluation. In this case, however, the dollar value of both the American and the British gold reserves has fallen by 10 per cent and the pound value of gold reserves is unchanged. World liquidity in this instance has decreased. Again the choice between revaluation of the surplus country and devaluation of the debtor country is a real choice with different economic effects for each alternative.

It is possible, then, to summarise our conclusions on the burden of adjustment when exchange rates rather than income levels are altered to make the adjustment. They are these. Devaluation in the deficit country is not the same as revaluation in the surplus country. There are different economic effects according to which way relative to each country the exchange rate is changed. The problem of the distribution of the burden of the exchange-rate change remains. We simply re-pose the distribution question in a different form: how far should deficit countries devalue and surplus countries revalue? We have no answer to this problem. It awaits solution.

Finally, in our search for a criterion of the distribution of the burden of adjustment we come, perhaps inevitably, to size. This criterion is stressed by Mundell who demonstrates not only that adjustment should be divided 'in inverse proportion to the sizes of the countries', but that such a division is optimal for world price stability.[8] Let us start with a simple model of two countries operating on a gold standard and each with a quantity of money proportionate to its size. Suppose one country has a deficit and loses gold to the other; then the price level in each country will change in proportion to the change in its money stock – prices rising in the surplus country with the gold inflow and falling in the deficit with the gold outflow. The *percentage* change in the price level in either country will equal the percentage change in the money stock – the percentage change being equal to the gold flow divided by the initial stocks of gold. But the surplus in one country is the same as the absolute amount of gold lost by the deficit country; therefore, since the stocks of money in the countries reflect their sizes, the ratio of the price changes will be inversely proportionate to the size of the countries. An example makes the argument obvious. If Germany develops a balance-of-payments deficit with Luxembourg as a result of a capital movement from Germany to Luxembourg which is not at once transferred in real terms, then the monetary effects of the surplus in Luxembourg will be very great compared to those arising from the deficit in Germany. Luxembourg prices will rise sharply while German prices will be affected hardly at all. The adjustment burden falls predominantly on the small country.

It makes no difference whether the disequilibrium is a surplus to the small country or a deficit. If, in our example, the capital flow were in the opposite direction, creating a deficit in Luxembourg and a surplus in Germany, the monetary effects of contraction in Luxembourg would be relatively far greater than the monetary effects of the surplus in Germany. The small country bears the greatest weight of adjustment of the disequilibrium, whether it be a surplus or a deficit.

The argument does not depend for its validity on the simple classical terms in which it has been expounded. The same argument holds for income changes and interest rate effects. Where the surplus country is large as compared to the deficit country, gold flows will have little effect on interest rates in the large country but a considerable effect in the small. The percentage change in money income will be great in the small country and slight in the large country.

It is easy to see how this unevenness of distribution of the adjustment burden between large and small countries makes for greater stability in the world economy, whether we think of adjustment by price or by income changes. If we think in price terms, the relatively large variations in price in the small country are lost in an index of world prices in which the price levels of the leviathans are the determining factors. If we think in income terms changes in income and employment levels in small countries have neither the inflation- nor depression-propagating effects which similar changes in the large countries would have. It seems that, as far as adjustment of balances of payments is concerned, it is tough to be small but for the world as a whole it is better like that.

(v) Conclusion

It is appropriate at this stage to look back to the questions which in section (i) of this chapter we had the temerity to ask (see p. 389 above). Several aspects of the problem of how far countries in an international system can hope to reconcile external and internal equilibrium have come under scrutiny. We have drawn widely on the recent literature. Are we now able to answer these questions?

Briefly, we are not. A complete answer to these questions would require a general theory of balance-of-payments policy. This we do not have. We have, however, made significant progress merely by arraying the various situations in which national states may find themselves and by identifying some weapons to deal with particular couplings of the external balance and the domestic state of employment. Specifically, question (1) on the appropriate form of basic adjustment most likely to reconcile domestic and external stability is still unanswerable and must remain so until we have examined the various ways in which exchange rates may be used in the adjustment process. Question (2) has, with the aid of Mundell, been answered. Monetary policy, it has been shown, is the 'handmaid' of external manipulation; fiscal policy, of domestic income and employment control. On question (3) it has been shown that in several cases conflicts between external and internal equilibrium may drive countries to concentrate upon the former and to seek the latter by resort to balance-of-payments controls or other quasi-adjustment devices. To question (4), the division of the burden of international adjustment, Mundell has given at least a partial answer. By showing that the internal stability criterion fails to establish the distribution of adjustment between surplus and deficit countries in the important case where surplus countries are inflating and deficit countries are depressed; that the relative-cost criterion is of no practical use because of the measurement problem; that resort to exchange-rate manipulation does not sidestep the question of how to allocate the burden, but rather poses it in another form – by disclosing the facts, Mundell has demonstrated the limitations of these approaches and the wide gaps in the literature which remain to be filled. In his 'relative size criterion' he has provided a simple and practical yardstick which serves partially to measure the gap left by his demolition of the other criteria.

III Some Current Account Problems

17
Trade and National Currencies: The Foreign Exchange Market

(i) The Foreign Exchange Market

FOREIGN trade consists of the sale of goods and services across national boundaries. The transactions of foreign trade are different from those of domestic trade, not only because they cross frontiers, but because in so doing they involve the exchange of one national currency for another. This exchange of currencies arises so that the debts incurred in foreign trade transactions may be settled in a form and currency agreeable to the parties to the transactions. It is not only goods transactions which involve a foreign exchange transaction but all transactions which are reflected in a country's balance of payments—a transfer of capital resulting from a long- or short-term loan, a unilateral transfer, a dividend or interest transfer, or government transactions of various kinds. Accommodating transactions by central banks for the purpose of influencing the state of the foreign exchange market themselves involve transactions in that market.

The foreign exchange market is, therefore, a market not only in money but in forms of money and (at one time) near-money. Tourists wishing to visit a foreign country will require cash, i.e. notes and coins, and money forms near to cash such as travellers cheques. Exporters and importers who fifty years ago settled debts mainly by bills of exchange now do so in demand deposits. There is, however, little necessity to differentiate the forms of money bought and sold in the foreign exchange market. Demand deposits and cash, both money rather than near-money, are now the dominant forms and foreign exchange markets exist for the pound, the dollar, the lira, the franc and a large number of other currencies frequently used in international trade. Such markets exist in a number of financial centres throughout the world in each of which dealing in currencies takes place, so that the market for, say, dollars consists of the offer of and demand for dollar currency in all of these centres. Similarly with pounds, marks and other currencies. The foreign exchange market is really a horizontally stratified market for many currencies available for buying and selling throughout the world, surplus balances in, say, New York being available in London, Milan, or Frankfurt and vice versa. It is wrong to imagine that the market for pounds is in London or the market for francs in Paris. Each currency has a world market in which the various financial centres are in close touch, by cable, telephone and teleprinter. The market, although world-wide, conforms well to the basic criteria by which all markets are judged: that there should be all the time complete knowledge of prices, demand and supply in all parts of the market.

For a large bank operating in the inter-bank market and directly with banks and dealers in foreign centres, the nerve centre is the dealing desk in the trading room. Each dealer at the desk is in direct contact by many modern aids with correspondent banks at home and abroad. The desk is presided over by a master dealer who watches trends in main exchange rates, checks deals and keeps a running check on the bank's holdings of main currencies, on its long and short positions and on the relation between spot and forward rates. Key information is flashed to dealers from the head of the table. The day's dealing begins with the working through of the overnight accumulation of cable and mail orders. Traders deal by telephone with traders in other banks at home and abroad. Quickly they learn the market trends in rates for currencies in markets already open in other parts of the world and closing rates in those already closed. Time differences ensure an almost continuous world market in main currencies. By the time the London market is closing at 3 p.m. the New York market is opening. San Francisco opens four hours behind New York and Tokyo completes the world market. The traders, from their knowledge of their bank's long and short position in each currency, know how to react when quoting rates and responding to quotations from others. Rates are quoted as a narrow spread, the lower rate being the buying price and the higher the selling price. When a trader asks for a quotation he does not say whether he wishes to buy or sell. Profit for the bank from dealing depends on quickness and turnover. The spread between buying and selling is of the order of one-eighth or one-tenth of 1 per cent. Apart from meeting orders for clients and adjusting the bank's position in the various currencies, traders are alert for the chance of arbitrage profits which may arise from slight differences in currency rates as between centres, and from cross rates via which it may be possible to make profitable deals. In all this much depends upon the traders. They must have a keen appreciation of moving trends and influences in the market, an alert eye for the quick and profitable deal, a swift head for mental arithmetic and the ability to deal in several languages.

We have spoken thus far of a world market for currencies in which the buyers and sellers are banks and near-banking institutions. We must expand this and make our picture more realistic. To do this, we must look at two aspects more closely: the currencies dealt in and the relations of the buyers and sellers in the world market. First, the currencies. Although in a remote literal sense all of the scores of national currencies which exist are dealt in somewhere at some time, only a few currencies, perhaps twenty in number, are dealt in in any volume. Many countries finance their foreign trade not in their own currencies but in major currencies such as the U.S. dollar, the pound, or in some set of major currencies in which they hold working balances. They expect payment for their exports in these currencies or in a currency convertible into them. They pay for their imports also in these currencies. In such circumstances, the sale of their own currency is limited to a 'tourist' sale to persons wishing to travel in the country. The surprising leading example of such a 'non-traded currency' is that of the U.S.S.R. rouble. Since the Russians trade on a bilateral basis, settling deficits in trade, when they arise, in gold, the rouble has only a high tourist rate which bears little relation to what the true rate would be if the U.S.S.R. financed its trade in the British or American fashion. In the main, however, the non-traded currencies are those of the small countries. The quoted currencies on the world exchange market are those of the great trading and banking countries and the rate quoted is the price for each currency in the financial centres dealing in those currencies. The operators in these dozen or so centres—London, New York, Frankfurt, Zürich, to name a few—trade the currencies in and between the centres. Each traded currency will have a price in terms of every other.

We turn next to the second aspect of the foreign exchange market, its participants. Within the market for each currency, buyers and sellers fall into fairly clearly defined groups. Firstly, there are customers, that is, persons or institutions wishing to obtain a currency other than their own for purposes of trade, finance or travel. Secondly, there are the commercial banks operating in the inter-bank market mainly through their foreign exchange dealing departments at head office. The banking networks, for their dealing with their own customers, hold working balances of the main currencies, which they replenish or diminish by buying or selling in the market. More precisely the banking participation is 'pyramidal'. Banks which have limited foreign exchange business with their customers tend to replenish their balances from a central office (in the case of a banking chain) or from another bank which transacts large foreign exchange business. In the New York foreign exchange market about twenty-five American banks maintain working foreign exchange balances abroad. Fewer than half of these do most of the business. The New York market also includes some branches of foreign banks.[1] There is also, apart from the commercial banks, the large group of merchant banks and international banks whose business is much concerned with international trade in goods, capital transfers and international investment. Third is the central bank of the country whose currency we are discussing. The central bank is not only the custodian of the national foreign exchange reserves of the country but, under existing exchange rate practices, is responsible for maintaining the exchange rate, stabilising it at the required level within the range of 2·25 per cent above and below the defined IMF parity if it is fixed, or influencing its fluctuations if it is floating. Such operations involve the central bank in intervention in the foreign exchange market for its own currency, buying it with foreign currencies drawn from the national reserves when it is oversold and selling it for foreign currencies, to be added to the reserves, when it is overbought. The management of foreign exchange reserves and the maintenance of the official exchange rate by the central bank is in the hands of a special department which is usually called the Exchange Fund. In the United States the title is the United States Stabilisation Fund, in the United Kingdom, the United Kingdom Exchange Equalisation Account, in Canada, the Canadian Exchange Fund. This intervention in the market by the Exchange Fund of the country ensures that the central bank is often the largest single operator in the foreign exchange market for a currency.

These three groups, operating in a multi-centred world market form the foreign exchange market within which all transactions in foreign exchange are finally cleared. Within the total, market transactions take place between these groups at a number of different levels:

1. there are transactions between banks and their customers, e.g. John Jones buys Swiss francs from the Midland Bank in Rochdale to finance a skiing holiday in Switzerland;
2. there are transactions between banks in the same part of the market, e.g. the Midland Bank in Rochdale, finding its Swiss franc working balances depleted by Jones and other would-be skiers, replenishes the balance by a Swiss franc purchase either from another bank or more likely from the Midland Bank in Manchester or some large centre where large foreign currency balances are held;
3. there are transactions between bank head offices in different centres, e.g. the Midland Bank foreign exchange head office in London buys

Swiss francs from a dealer or bank in Zürich, Frankfurt or some other centre;
4. there are transactions between banks and central banks, as when central banks provide foreign exchange to banks in order to influence the rate for their own currency; and
5. there are transactions between central banks in different centres by 'swap' facilities which by-pass the market, i.e. central bank A allows central bank B to overdraw its currency in return for reciprocal privileges.

This five-tier structure of the foreign exchange market imparts to it a pyramidal structure through which the multifarious transactions at all levels are cleared ultimately through intracentre transactions made by the largest bank operators or by the central banks themselves.

The prices at which currencies are traded in the foreign exchange market are referred to as foreign exchange rates. Such a rate is the price of one currency in terms of another and can be expressed in two ways. In some countries it is customary to express the exchange rate as the price in terms of a foreign currency of one unit of the home currency. Thus the British habitually list the sterling exchange rate as £1 = 2.4 U.S. dollars or £1 = 10 DM. It would be equally informative to give the same information in the form $1 U.S. = 41·6 pence or 0·416 pounds. By contrast the United States usually lists the price in home currency of a unit of foreign currency, using the form $0.24 = 1 DM. It is immaterial which form is used, particularly if both currencies are metric currencies. It is, however, essential to remember which way one is going. If the British, quoting their sterling rate at £1 = $2.8, devalue the pound by say 14 per cent the new rate is £1 = $2.4. If the rate were quoted as $1 = £0·357 then a 14 per cent devaluation would make the new rate $1 = £0·416.

Primarily an exchange rate is a price, but, more fundamentally, it is a bridge between prices and costs in one country and those in another. It enables intracountry comparisons of relative prices and costs to be made. Without an exchange rate it would be impossible to compare the price of a coat which costs $50 in the United States with a similar coat costing £20 in Britain. Once the exchange rate is known, however, a reasonably meaningful comparison may be made, not only of the prices of the coats, but of the prices of coats with other goods and with incomes. These factors become important at a later stage when we come to consider the forces which determine exchange rates. For the moment it is sufficient to notice the linkage which exchange rates give between the domestic prices of goods within different countries.

Since an exchange rate is the price of a foreign currency in terms of the home currency, it follows not only that each country has as many foreign exchange rates as there are other currencies but that all these exchange rates infer cross rates between the other currencies. For example, if £1 = $2.4 U.S. = $2.6 Canadian = 10 DM = 13·5 fr., and so on, then it is also true that $1 U.S. = $1·08 Canadian; that $1 U.S. = 0·4 DM; that 1 DM = 1·35 fr. and so on. In short, although exchange rates are most usually quoted as units of a few great currencies in terms of units of a few other great currencies there exist by inference great numbers of cross rates (if there are twenty major currencies quoted habitually in the foreign exchange market there are, by implication, 190 cross rates) all of which must be consistent with one another. If they are not consistent it becomes possible for, say, an American purchaser of pounds to find that two different prices for pounds relative to U.S. dollars exist simultaneously: one by buying pounds direct with U.S. dollars and one by buying some other currency with which in turn he can buy pounds at a different price. If this latter price is cheaper he and others will embrace this option and by doing so bid up the dollar price of pounds. We will recur (see p. 423 below) to the role of arbitrage as a means of removing inconsistencies and of unifying the market for a given currency. For the moment, it is sufficient to note that, despite the bewildering tangle of cross-rates, the markets for given currencies are single markets in which one price exists but in which that price may be quoted directly in terms of any other currency or indirectly through the cross-rates.

It is convenient to discuss the foreign exchange market in terms of three important functions which it performs: its clearing function, through which it makes transfers of purchasing power; its ability to provide credit for foreign trade; and its mechanisms for dealing with the special risks of foreign exchange. We shall deal with each of these in turn.

A simple model of the process by which the foreign exchange market makes transfers of purchasing power can be devised. Let us confine ourselves for simplicity to intra-country transactions involving the purchase and sale of goods, and assume that payment does not take place in some third-country currency. Take the case of two-country trade between Canada and Britain. Exporters in Canada acquire money claims abroad; importers have payments to make abroad. Goods move between Canada and Britain but, by means of the clearing mechanism, payment takes place within each country, save for the settlement of residual balances. Suppose that trade takes place between Canada and Britain, Canada exporting goods to an importer in Britain and an importer in Canada buying from an exporter in Britain. Goods pass between the two countries. Net money claims do not

The Economics of the Balance of Payments

flow along the same paths but in opposite directions. The Canadian exporter is paid by a money claim on the British importer and the British exporter by a claim on the Canadian importer. Each country ends with claims against the other. The foreign exchange market ensures that such claims are offset. In the extreme case where the import and export transactions between the two countries are equal in value, no residual balance remains and all claims are fully cleared. The Canadian importer pays the Canadian exporter and in Britain the importer pays the exporter. In the more likely event that imports and exports are not equal in value, only the balance or difference between their values remains to be cleared. How does this happen? Probably the British importer buys Canadian dollars in the London foreign exchange market to meet the claim against him in Canada. The Canadian dollars in the London market have been obtained from the proceeds of the British exports to Canada for dollars. The dollars earned by the British exporter are bought for sterling by the British importer and paid to the Canadian exporter. In this case, the transaction has been financed in dollars through the London foreign exchange market. Equally it could be completed in sterling through the Montreal exchange market. The Canadian exporter in this case might draw a bill in sterling on the British buyer and, on acceptance, discount this bill in a Montreal bank. This bank sends the bill to a London discount house for rediscount and sells the sterling proceeds to a Canadian importer for settlement of sterling claims against him in favour of a British exporter.

In the real world this example would be complicated by the fact that in both Britain and Canada habitual importers and exporters would each hold working balances of the other's currency and working balances would be held also by banks and foreign exchange dealers. Nevertheless the plan shown in Fig. 17.1 would hold in principle for the transactions.[2] The

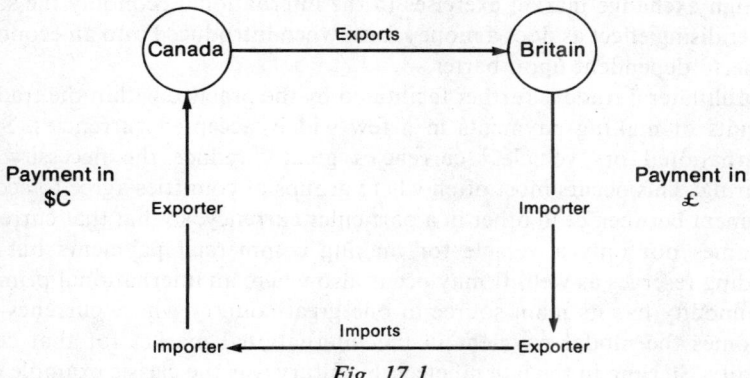

Fig. 17.1

fact that the channels shown hold reservoirs at certain points does not vitiate the directional flow of the circuit.

It is now possible to list the various ways in which for this example the market can be cleared. The following table summarises them:

Foreign exchange deal	Market	Currency of payment by British importer	Currency of payment by Canadian importer
1. Canadian exporter sells £ to Canadian importer	Montreal	£	£
2. British exporter sells $ to British importer	London	$	$
3. Canadian exporter sells £ to (buys $ from) British exporter	London or Montreal	£	$
4. Canadian importer buys £ (sells $ to) from British importer	London or Montreal	$	£

This circuit diagram of the clearing process applies even when we enlarge the example to cover the clearing of many transactions occurring through many types of financial instruments. Large sums will still cancel out and leave only residual net balances for settlement. The model may be applied also to clearing on a multilateral basis. Britain may earn Canadian dollars from exports to Canada paying these to the United States for imports of cotton. The United States in turn may use these in payment for imports of aluminum from Canada, thus closing the circuit.

Clearly the foreign exchange market enables complex patterns of multilateral payments to be made which would never be possible in its absence. Without it international trade would be reduced to a bilateral basis or to such simply contrived trilateral arrangements as could be made. The foreign exchange market exercises in the international economy the same generalising effect as does a money form when introduced into an economy hitherto dependent upon barter.

Multilateral trade is further facilitated by the practice within the trading circuits of making payments in a few widely accepted currencies. Such international or 'vehicle'[3] currencies greatly reduce the necessity for clearing. This occurs most often where groups of countries agree to accept payment between each other in a particular currency, so that that currency becomes not only a vehicle for making commercial payments but for holding reserves as well. It may occur also where an international primary commodity has its main source in one great country whose currency bebecomes the modal payment in the international market for that commodity. Sterling in the late nineteenth century was the classic example of a great international currency. In the interwar period it shared that role with the United States dollar to which since the Second World War it has yielded precedence.

The second function of the foreign exchange market is that credit is available for the conduct of foreign trade. While credit and its provision are features of all trade, domestic or foreign, they are especially necessary in the case of foreign trade, where goods are in transit for long periods of time and where weeks may elapse between the sale of goods by an exporter and their resale in a foreign country. During this 'waiting' period someone must carry the financial burden of holding an asset which is doing nothing more productive than lying in the hold of a ship. Who is to finance this burden is determined by the form of credit covering the transaction. Take an example. A consignment of British cars valued at £50,000 has been purchased by a dealer in British Columbia. Their transportation from Birmingham via Liverpool and the Panama Canal to Vancouver takes six weeks. In Britain the seller of the cars wants payment at once. In British Columbia the dealer must wait six weeks and more before, by selling the cars, he can hope to be reimbursed for his outlay. The transaction can be financed in several ways, but in principle they are similar. They enable the seller to get his money at the time of sale, the buyer to postpone payment until the goods are in his hands and become a working asset again. The simplest form of payment is for the Canadian dealer to borrow the money from his bank in Canada on security of title to the shipment. He then pays the British exporter by a sterling (or dollar) draft and repays the loan to his bank, either when the cars are received or, more likely, at a later stage when they have been sold. In this case, the credit for the shipment is provided by a simple bank loan. An alternative is to finance the transaction by a three month bill of exchange drawn by the British exporter on the Canadian dealer. This bill, accepted for payment ninety-one days hence, is then in the hands of the exporter who will discount it either with his own bank or with a London discount house, receiving £49,250 (assuming the going rate on trade bills to be 6 per cent). At the end of three months the discount house (or whoever then holds the bill) collects £50,000 from the Canadian importer. By this method all parties to the transaction have been convenienced. The Canadian importer has not been required to make payment until the consignment of cars is in his hands and their sale has begun. The British exporter has received payment for his shipment on dispatch, with no more deduction by the discount house for discounting them than the seller would have himself made in trade discount for prompt payment on a cash transaction. In this example the bill was drawn by the British exporter in sterling and its acceptance in this form meant that the

Canadian acceptor had to purchase £50,000 in the foreign exchange market, giving Canadian dollars in exchange. The credit was provided by the discount market in Britain and paid for by the exporter. It is worth noting also, in passing, the balance-of-payments effect of this transaction when financed by a bill. The British export, recorded as a credit in the merchandise trade account, has its corresponding debit item in the capital section of the account in the form of a short-term loan from Britain to Canada. When the bill is paid on maturity the payment is recorded as an incoming unilateral transfer on the credit side of the current account and repayment of short-term credit on the debit side of the capital account.

The third function of the foreign exchange market is to provide mechanisms for guarding against the special risks involved in foreign exchange transactions, specifically for hedging against changes in the price of a currency between the time when a debt in that currency is incurred and when it must be liquidated. A Canadian importer who has to discharge a debt in Deutschmark currency in, say, three months' time and who has accepted a ninety-one-day bill payable on maturity in Deutschmarks, is exposed to the risk that if the exchange rate for Deutschmarks in terms of Canadian dollars rises during that period the dollar equivalent of his debt will rise by the extent of the Deutschmark appreciation. A bill of 10,000 DM when the exchange rate is \$1 = 4 DM will cost the Canadian \$2500 to pay on maturity. If, however, the dollar/Deutschmark rate is revalued during the period of the bill so that it becomes \$1 = 3 DM, liquidation of the debt will cost the Canadian \$3333. In the opposite direction, an exporter expecting payments in foreign exchange may have the domestic currency value of his claims cut if before settlement his own currency is devalued. To cover such risks as these a market exists in forward exchange. In this market a foreign exchange risk can be 'hedged' without recourse to the forward exchange market. Fearing the depreciation of the domestic value of his foreign exchange receipts one month ahead, the exporter may borrow now to the value of his debt in the foreign country, repatriate the loan at the current exchange rate and use his export proceeds to pay off the loan in one month's time. The hedge will still cost him money—in this case one month's interest on the loan. *Ex-post* his hedge has only been worthwhile if the exchange rate of his own currency relative to the foreign currency has so depreciated by the end of one month that the exchange loss would have exceeded the month's interest on the loan. In order to understand the nature of the processes known as 'covering' and 'hedging' it is necessary to examine the forward exchange market more closely.

So far in this chapter we have assumed that foreign exchange bought and sold is for immediate delivery. In fact, foreign currencies so bought are

The Economics of the Balance of Payments

described as 'spot exchange'. They are purchased in the 'spot market' and at the 'spot rate'. But foreign currencies can also be bought for specified future delivery. In this case they are referred to as 'forward exchange' purchased in the 'forward market' at the 'forward rate'. Usual forward exchange contracts are for delivery of currencies in 30, 60, 90 or 180 days. Longer contracts than six months are rare. The forward rates of exchange are expressed as a premium over or discount from the spot rate.

Let us suppose that a Canadian exporter has been paid for exports to Britain by a promise of pounds ninety days hence. He wishes not only to know now the value of his export sale in Canadian currency but to ensure that it will not change by maturity of the claim at the end of ninety days. Accordingly he sells the pounds to his bank now for future delivery in exchange for dollars at an agreed price. In other words, the Canadian has bought dollars by the forward sale of pounds to his bank. He has, as the saying goes, hedged his exchange risk. Hedging is the sale of foreign exchange balanced by a purchase, so that there is no 'open' position in the market. The term hedging is of course applied widely to markets other than the foreign exchange market, for example to primary commodity futures markets. It is also used to cover the acquisition of assets whose value rises *pari passu* with the general level of prices. Thus, we speak of buying equities or house property as being a hedge against general price inflation, since the goods value of these assets tends to remain stable for changes in the general price level. If a foreign exchange liability is exactly matched by a claim of like amount we describe the position as 'covered'. If the risk is accepted and no claim matches the liability at the maturity date, the position is described as 'open'.

From the bank's point of view, how is the forward price of these pounds in Canadian dollars determined? The bank has, by making the forward contract, now assumed the exchange risk. It has to produce dollars ninety days hence at the agreed rate. It covers itself by a process known as a 'swap'. Simultaneous with buying the forward pounds it sells an equal amount of pounds spot thereby reducing its holding of pounds and increasing its holding of dollars. But this switch of assets may involve a change of interest rate to the extent that the Canadian bank may have to hold its dollars at a lower or higher interest income than it held its pounds. To the extent that interest rates in Canada are lower than those in Britain the bank incurs a loss of interest by the switch. This loss it passes on to the Canadian by adjusting the price at which it buys the pounds forward from him. It will lower the price of the pounds commensurately with the spot rate so that the forward rate is at a discount relative to the spot rate. To the extent that interest rates are higher in the foreign country than in the home country, the forward rate will be at a discount relative to the spot; to the extent that interest rates at home are higher than those abroad, the forward rate will be at a premium relative to the spot.

It would appear then that the spread of exchange rates between spot and forward depends mainly upon differences between national rates of interest in the two countries to which the exchange rate applies. It depends also upon speculation in the forward exchange markets. With stable exchange markets and no speculation, the forward spread is determined solely by interest arbitrage, that is, by the movement of funds from one country to another in search of higher interest rates. Such funds when moved are hedged in the forward market. Let us suppose a Canadian, observing that the rate on British Treasury bills is higher than the rate on Treasury bills in Canada, moves his money to British bills — although here we should state that there is no reason to confine the interest rate comparison to Treasury bill rates. Treasury bills are common media in which to hold assets in another country. They are low in risk and highly liquid. Other asset forms are, however, frequently used. It has been common in recent years for sterling funds in London to be held in the form of short loans in the local authority market or in the inter-bank loan market. Funds may also be held as time deposits. However, to return to our Canadian. When he buys the pounds to purchase the bills he also sells pounds (buys dollars) ninety days forward to cover his position — the amount of the sale being equal to the amount he will receive from the maturing British Treasury bills in ninety days' time. Because the interest rate abroad is higher than in Canada, there will be a discount on the forward rate for pounds against dollars, so that there will be a loss on the forward exchange sale of pounds. For the ninety-day investment to have been worth while the Treasury bill rate in Britain must exceed that in Canada by more than the discount on the forward cover. In these circumstances the movement of funds into Britain will continue until the interest-rate differential and the cost of forward cover are equal. The interest arbitrage will ensure that this takes place altering all the variables to achieve this. Present demand for British pounds will force up the spot rate; forward sales of pounds will increase the discount on forward pounds, depressing the forward rate; while the flow of funds to Britain will tend to lower interest rates in that country. In ultimate equilibrium the forward discount will equal the interest-rate differential, making further movements of funds pointless. The relation between the forward and spot exchange rates when interest arbitrage is the main determinant may be summarised in the equation

$$R_f/R_s = \frac{1 + i_d}{1 + i_f},$$

where R_f is the forward rate, R_s the spot rate and i_d and i_f home and foreign interest rates respectively.

An arithmetical example may be useful. The spot exchange rate between Canadian dollars and pounds is £1 = \$2.6. Suppose that the forward discount is 2 per cent per annum, or 0·5 per cent for ninety days. With this the Canadian investor pays \$2.6 for one pound spot and sells it three months forward for £2.587. The situation might then be like this:

	Yield %
U.K. Treasury bills	$5\frac{1}{2}$
Canadian Treasury bills	3
Interest-rate differential	$2\frac{1}{2}$
Forward exchange cover	2
Net yield	$\frac{1}{2}$

It should be borne in mind that the assumption that movements of funds between countries is a function only of interest-rate differentials is a considerable one. In fact, relative interest rates are only one factor among several which impel such movements. Speculation and freedom from political risk are others. To the extent that other factors operate, the forward spread and the interest-rate differential may differ widely at particular periods. Speculation in the exchange market can also cause the rate spread to differ considerably from that appropriate to the interest-rate differential. A common form of such speculation occurs when foreign exchange speculators, anticipating the imminent devaluation of a currency, sell the currency forward leaving an open position, i.e. not closing the position with a spot purchase. Were the currency to be devalued they can close the position at or before delivery by buying at the devalued rate. In doing this they run little risk. If the currency devalues (or depreciates) during the period they will gain when they close the position and deliver. Presumably if the currency is in the popular view in danger of devaluation it will hardly appreciate. This is a pleasant position for speculators – a very small chance of loss and a good chance of gain. There is, however, a chance of loss to speculative 'bears'. The monetary authority may enter the exchange market, buy its own currency, bid up its price and 'catch bears'. To the extent that currency speculators take up open positions, in the forward market, the rate can diverge widely from the interest parity, and the process of hedging for genuine commercial purposes can become an expensive one.

It is necessary before closing this section on the foreign exchange market to deal more fully with the process of arbitrage. Interest arbitrage, the process of moving funds between assets and countries in pursuit of higher interest rates, has already been discussed, but arbitrage has wider connotations than that of the short-term market for international funds. Indeed it is a general term applicable to any multi-centred market in which a uniform price is secured by simultaneous buying and selling and mobility of the traded commodity between the various centres. Here, however, we confine ourselves to the foreign exchange market in which we find three forms of arbitrage: space arbitrage, time arbitrage and interest arbitrage. Since examination of the forward exchange market led us to discuss the last of these we must now deal with the other two.

The foreign exchange market is multi-centred. That is, currencies may be sold against each other in several centres simultaneously – dollars against pounds in London, New York, Amsterdam and Paris. It is essential to a unified market for sterling and dollars that the sterling/dollar exchange rate should be the same in all of these centres. The same applies to markets for all other currencies. At the same time, it is necessary, if the market is to be wholly unified and international, that rates established through the cross-rates should be uniform. Let us deal with these two aspects of the foreign exchange market in turn.

The maintenance of a uniform rate for a currency in a number of centres is ensured by space arbitrage. Suppose that in Montreal the rate for pounds in Canadian dollar terms is \$2.56 = £1 but that in London some temporary local spurt in the demand for pounds has made the rate \$2.6 = £1. Assuming that all rates are cable rates, an exchange trader can purchase pounds in Montreal at \$2.56 and instantly sell them in London for \$2.6 = £1, thereby making 4 cents profit on each pound. This simultaneous purchase and sale of two monetary units in two market centres is the simplest form of space arbitrage. It is referred to as 'two-point' or bilateral arbitrage. As long as the price differential exists in the two centres, arbitrageurs will be induced by it to buy the currency in the centre where it is cheap and sell it in the centre where it is dear, thereby evening up the price in the two centres. In order to make the point clear we have made the price difference in the example ridiculously high. In practice fractional differences will reveal themselves to the eagle eye of a trader, who will quickly act upon them.

Space arbitrage can be more complicated, however, when we come to the case of operating through the cross-rates, probably in three or more currencies and markets simultaneously. An example of 'three point' arbitrage would be as follows. The rate for sterling is £1 = \$2.6 Canadian in Montreal, while in the same centre the rate between Canadian dollars and Swiss francs is \$1 = 4 frs. Therefore the cross-rate between pounds and francs in Montreal is £1 = 10·4 frs. Suppose that at the same moment in Zürich it is possible to buy pounds at a rate of 10 frs., the dollar price of francs in Zürich and the dollar price of sterling in Paris are the same as their price in Montreal. An arbitrageur can profit from this situation by making the following transactions:

(a) buying 100,000 francs in Montreal for $25,000;
(b) selling 100,000 francs in Zürich for £10,000; and
(c) selling £10,000 in Montreal for $26,000.

The profit from these transactions is $1000 less the cost of the various cables. Arbitrage here has been possible because of the different cross-rates between the franc and sterling in Montreal and Zürich, £1 = 10·4 fr. and £1 = 10 fr. respectively. It is possible, then, to purchase francs through dollars in the cheaper market and, selling them for pounds in the dearer market, return to dollars at a profit by selling the pounds. The purchase of the francs in the Montreal market will raise their dollar price; the sale of francs in Zürich will raise the price of sterling in terms of francs; and the sale of sterling in Montreal will lower its dollar price. When eventually the franc/sterling cross-rate in Montreal comes to equal the franc/sterling rate in Zürich, arbitrage will no longer be profitable and will end.

Arbitrage operations are carried on by professional dealers in the market. They are not speculation but are a necessary part of the market process. They are made possible: (a) by the discrepancies in quotations for currency rates which arise in different centres and through the cross-rates; (b) by the almost perfect knowledge of the market prices in the different centres made possible by modern communications; and (c) by freedom in the market, i.e. the existence of free movement of currencies throughout the world system. The first two conditions are inherent in the exchange market itself, but the third condition is not. The maintenance of a free market has since the Second World War been frequently impaired by exchange control and restrictions on payments by certain countries. Given freedom from government interference, the foreign exchange market is a very delicate and sensitive mechanism and the best, perhaps the only, example of a perfect market. To the extent that mobility of currencies is impaired by state interference and currency regulations, it is apt to become sectionalised and the unity of its price structure disappears.

We turn now briefly to 'time arbitrage'. This process is a feature of the forward market only and consists of dealers taking advantage of the differences which exist between forward margins for different maturities. Theoretically, the premium or discount on a forward rate for a currency relative to its spot rate is directly proportional to the length of maturity of the deal. (This is readily apparent from the formula on p. 422.) It should be twice as great for two months as it is for one. In practice, however, considerable discrepancies exist between the forward margins[4] and it is possible for dealers to take advantage of these by accumulating those forward positions which are advantageous and going short on those which are less so. To the extent that this happens the discrepancies which gave rise to the advantages might be expected to be eroded and to tend to narrow or disappear. In practice, however, this does not necessarily happen, since the views of dealers may differ widely on the prospects of the longer maturities and biases may appear in their behaviour which tend to accentuate rather than reduce the original discrepancies.

It should be noted that time arbitrage is a much less purposive process than its simpler space counterpart. The latter is an active procedure arising from an observed difference in rates in different parts of the market or through the cross-rates; the former may indeed be active when banks deliberately embark on operations designed to redistribute their long and short positions in order to take advantage of discrepancies between maturities, but it may also occur passively as a result of banks, in the process of business, building up positions which do not have evenly graded maturities and leaving these positions uncovered. If banks decide to adjust these fortuitous positions they are not necessarily doing so for arbitrage reasons and in anticipation of changes in forward rates, but more likely in anticipation of their future currency needs and to achieve a better balance in maturities.

Before leaving the topic of arbitrage, it is important to emphasise that arbitrage and arbitrageurs are distinct and different from speculation and speculators. Arbitrage is carried on by foreign exchange dealers who exploit the market as they find it, taking advantage of daily trading discrepancies in the ways which we have described. Their functions are useful and essential to an orderly and efficient market. Speculators attempt to make profit (and often they incur losses) by differences in the prices of currencies over time and by taking up a position as to the direction in which they will change.

(ii) The *Modus Operandi* of International Payments

The methods and procedures of transferring funds between currencies and of providing credit for the carrying on of international trade are many and various. Their full description belongs to a book on practical business procedures rather than to one on international economics. However, a brief description in general terms of some of the salient features is useful for economists.

There are two elements which are common to all methods and procedures for money transfer: the existence of banking facilities in each of the countries between which transfer takes place; and, the use of credit instruments. The most common instruments are the telegraphic transfer and the bill of exchange.

The telegraphic transfer is a cabled order by a bank in one country to a correspondent bank in another to pay a specified amount in the currency of that country to a specified person or account. The only difference in principle between a telegraphic transfer and a draft lies in greater speed, the latter being mailed, the former being cabled. A commercial bill is an unconditional order sent by one person to another requiring the person to whom it is addressed to pay after a specified period a sum of money either to the sender, to some specified person, or to bearer. The recipient of the bill is the debtor and once he accepts the bill by signing it, it becomes a negotiable instrument. It may be discounted with a bank or a discount house, or used as a means of payment of further debts by the holder on endorsement. A more sophisticated variant of the simple bill procedure is that of the accepting house and the reimbursement credit. In this case, large importers with many and frequent payments to make abroad arrange for bills to a total stipulated value to be accepted on their behalf by an accepting house of high financial standing. The bills so accepted thus bear the signature of an accredited finance house, rank for the most favourable rates of discount and are acceptable as means of payment in further transactions. On maturity of a bill it is paid by the accepting house, which is reimbursed and paid a commission by its client. One of the main advantages of this method is that the importer need not be known to the exporter. His credit-worthiness is implied by the standing of the Accepting House which accepts his bill. It, in its turn, has satisfied itself through bank references of its client's credit standing. The use of London accepted bills as media of payment in international trade was very widespread from the late nineteenth century until the 1920s. The 'bill on London' was almost a standard form of payment, even for foreign trade transactions in respect of goods which did not touch British shores or for goods in the large British entrepôt trade. In recent years, the relative decline of sterling as an international currency, the interruption and dislocation of international payments by the Second World War and by the long interlude of British exchange control which followed it, have served to reduce greatly the use of such bills.[5]

With a telegraphic transfer, bank draft or bill of exchange, the value may be denominated in the currency of either the exporter or the importer. Let us suppose a Canadian exports goods to Britain and is paid by a sight draft in pounds, i.e. a bill of exchange, payable at sight, due when the goods are received in Liverpool. The Canadian, when he receives the accepted draft, has no immediate use for pounds and sells it to the Bank of Montreal for Canadian dollars in accordance with the current sterling/Canadian dollar exchange rate. The Bank of Montreal in turn may do two things: it may resell the draft to some Canadian wanting pounds, or it may send it to the Bank of Montreal (London branch) for collection. It takes the latter option. The draft is presented to the British importer who pays it (in pounds) to the London office of the Bank of Montreal, whose working balance of sterling is thereby augmented. Such working balances of sterling are held by each of the one hundred or so overseas banks in London. When the British trade balance is favourable, such balances increase; when it is unfavourable they fall. They are used by such banks to receive and make foreign payments, usually between clients of their own banking chain (or correspondent banks) abroad and nationals of the country in which they themselves are located. The existence in main financial centres of such a group of overseas banks enables the working balances of foreign and home currency used in international trade to be concentrated, thus greatly facilitating clearing. While goods cross frontiers, payment is made predominantly by switching between these balances, only residual clearing taking place between financial centres.

(iii) The Determination of the Foreign Exchange rate

In this section we revert to theory in an attempt to achieve some generality in assessing the forces which determine exchange rates between currencies. We examine two market situations: one where rates in the foreign exchange market are free to move without interference reflecting the full force of supply and demand for the currencies; and one where exchange rates are pegged at upper and lower levels, as under a gold standard. We deal with these in turn.

A country's trade position involves the exchange of home for foreign money — a demand for foreign money to be bought with home money. This constitutes a supply of home money to be used in buying foreign money. Whether goods traded are priced in home or foreign money is not

The Economics of the Balance of Payments

important. A Canadian importer from Britain may pay in Canadian dollars or in sterling. If he pays in dollars, it is the British exporter who demands sterling in exchange for the dollars he has earned. If the Canadian pays in sterling, the initiative for the foreign exchange transaction rests with him. The only difference is that in the first case the exchange takes place in the sterling/dollar exchange market in London; in the second case it occurs in the sterling/dollar exchange market in Montreal or Toronto. Since these constitute but two parts of a single international market in which home money demands foreign money and vice versa, we may regard supply and demand as being two forces operating in a single international currency market. In what segment of the market the exchanges of currency are made merely locates the pressure points. We are concerned with total pressures.

Examine the foreign exchange market for pounds and Deutschmarks. British imports and other transactions which involve a payment to Germany create a demand for Deutschmarks to be bought with pounds – in other words they create a supply of pounds to be offered for Deutschmarks. British exports and transactions which earn a receipt from Germany create a supply of Deutschmarks to be sold for pounds – in other words, a demand for pounds to be purchased with Deutschmarks. There are two ways of looking at the rate of exchange which clears the market; we can see the rate of exchange between pounds and Deutschmarks as determined by supply and demand for Deutschmarks, with the price of Deutschmarks in pounds, or we can see the rate as determined by supply and demand for pounds, with the price of pounds in Deutschmarks. Two diagrams can be constructed showing the two market situations. These are shown in Fig. 17.2.

Fig. 17.2 (a) shows the result of plotting the demand and supply of Deutschmarks against various levels of their price in pounds. The demand curve reflects the fact that the lower the price of Deutschmarks in terms of pounds, the cheaper German goods and services appear to the British, the larger the amount of imports from Germany the more Deutschmarks the British demand in order to pay for them. The supply curve reflects the fact that the higher the sterling price of Deutschmarks, the more are supplied. This follows because a high sterling price of Deutschmarks is also a low Deutschmark price of sterling so that British goods are cheap to Germans and attract a higher Deutschmark demand than would be the case if the purchasing power of the Deutschmark over British goods were less high. The intersection point of the demand and supply curves shows the exchange rate in the form £0·1 = 1 DM. Fig. 17.2 (b) shows the same price quantity relations, this time for prices expressed in the form of how many Deutschmarks will buy £1. Again we derive a demand and supply curve, this time for pounds. The demand curve slopes downward and to the right, expressing the increasing demand for pounds as their price falls and as the price of goods expressed in pounds falls. The supply curve falls from right to left because, with the cheapening of the Deutschmark (i.e. rise in price of £1 in DM), there is an increasing offer of pounds to buy cheaper German goods. Once more, the exchange rate is shown by the intersection of the demand and supply curves—this time in the form of 10 DM = £1. The exchange rate in both (a) and (b) in Fig. 17.2 is the same

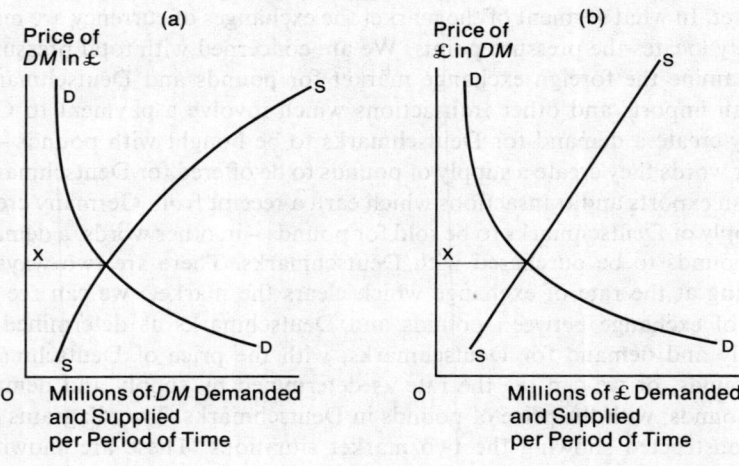

Fig. 17.2

but is expressed in different ways. In the diagrams, however it may be expressed, it is an equilibrium exchange rate. At any rate in excess of OX the Deutschmark would be over-valued in pound terms and some suppliers of Deutschmarks would be unable to sell them and get their pounds without forcing the rate downwards; at a rate lower than OX the Deutschmark would be under-valued in pound terms (over-valuing the pound) and some demanders of Deutschmarks (suppliers of pounds) would be unable to obtain them save at a higher price. In a free market the rate is always bid towards its equilibrium level at OX.

Some writers show the two sets of curves (a) and (b) as prevailing simultaneously in two different centres for the world market in the two currencies. Thus, (a) might represent the demand for Deutschmarks and their supply in London, while (b) would represent the same data in

The Economics of the Balance of Payments

Frankfurt, pounds there being priced in Deutschmarks. The same rate would still be achieved, however, in both since any divergence between the pound price of Deutschmarks and the Deutschmark price of the pound in the two markets would be evened out by swift space arbitrage movements. If we take the two-centre view, we can also combine the two diagrams by the use of offer curves. We can derive a total offer curve, for both centres, of pounds against marks and a total offer curve of marks for pounds. These can be seen in Fig. 17.3 where OX shows the offer of pounds

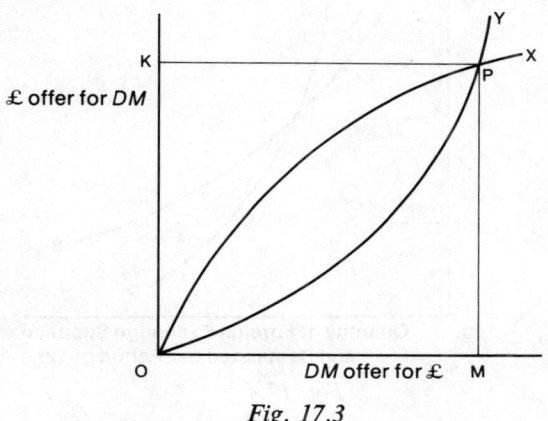

Fig. 17.3

for Deutschmarks by those wanting the latter currency. The curve slopes sharply upwards initially as buyers at first give high pound offers to build Deutschmark balances but later flattens as Deutschmark users find they have adequate supplies. OY is the Deutschmark offer for pounds and again follows the same form, this time inverted. The intersection point P indicates equality of the pound and Deutschmark offers at the equilibrium exchange rate, which is PM/PK or the slope of the line joining P to the origin.

We have assumed a refreshing normality in the shapes of the supply and demand curves in our example. Such curves ensure a stable equilibrium. We must be a little more critical, however. As we have seen, forms for these curves are conceivable which would give odd results (see p. 309 above). For example, the demand for and supply of foreign exchange might be very inelastic. The demand curve might slope downward steeply, while the supply curve, reflecting a low elasticity of demand for the country's exports and hence a low elasticity of supply of foreign currency, might slope even more steeply, thus providing an intersection point implying unstable equilibrium as shown in Fig. 17.4. In this case, at an exchange rate in excess of OX the quantity of foreign exchange demanded would exceed the amount supplied and the rate would be bid up still higher; at exchange rates less than OX, there would be excess supply and the rate would be driven down still further. The forces in this diagram are such that any

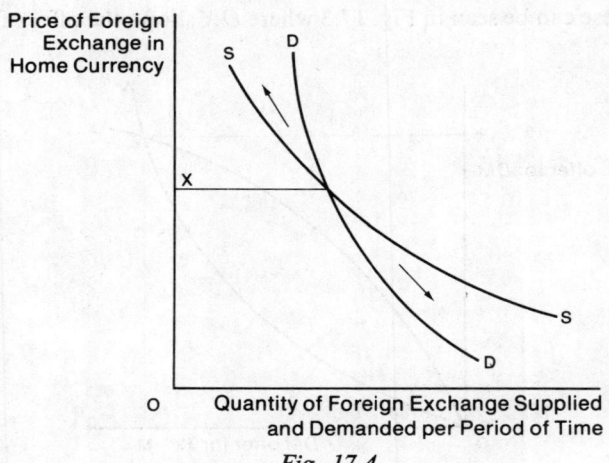

Fig. 17.4

movement away from OX tends to accentuate itself. The reason for this is of course the strong backward slope of the supply curve of foreign exchange, though this in itself would not be sufficient to cause instability if the demand curve were elastic enough to cut the supply curve as in Fig. 17.5. It is fairly clear that the demand curve will be downward-sloping to the right. A rise in the price of foreign exchange and thus in the home currency price of foreign goods would not make buyers increase their purchases of foreign goods and of the foreign exchange to buy them. In short D, while it may be steeply or slightly sloped according to the elasticity, will always slope downward and to the right. To do otherwise would be to contravene the basic law of demand. The question of stability in the market must therefore depend on the slope of the demand and supply curves of foreign exchange, predominantly of the latter.

We do no more at this stage than to point to this case of instability and remind readers of its existence. We have already explored in Chapter 12 its implications fairly fully.

Thus far we have examined the determination of the exchange rate in a

The Economics of the Balance of Payments

free market. We have now to examine the case where the exchange rate is free to vary only between fixed limits. The most common case, and that which we shall examine first, is that of the gold standard where the gold import and export points set the limits of exchange rate variation. The most immediate historical case, in that it applies to the exchange market of our own period, is that where the exchange rate is allowed to vary between limits defined by the central bank and at which the rate is supported by the intervention of the authorities in the market. This case we shall examine in its turn.

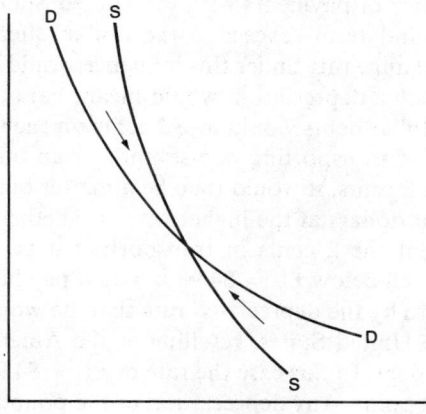

Fig. 17.5

The classic case of the pegged, or restricted, exchange rate is that of the international gold standard which, from about 1870 to 1914 and from 1925 to 1931 (in the case of the Gold Bloc countries until 1936) was regarded as the desirable norm in accordance with which countries should order their exchange rates and their balance-of-payments policies. It is not perhaps correct to describe the international gold standard as a system. It was rather a set of practices which, during the last years of the nineteenth century, developed from conventions to have almost the sanctity of law. From practice to usage and by much analysis and commentary by economists, the structure became definable enough to warrant its description as a system. Under this system, nation states defined the value of their currency units in terms of a certain weight of gold, so many grains of gold to the pound, the dollar or the franc. Institutionally, this was reflected by the readiness of the central bank to buy and sell gold at a specified price. Thus, using values which simplify the arithmetic, if the official United States price of gold were set at $35 per ounce and the official British price at £7, by these gold parities the exchange rate between pounds and dollars would be £1 = $5. In general terms, under a gold standard, the exchange rate for any two currencies was equal to the ratio of their mint par values. For any country, the mint par value of its currency market was the centre of a limited range of exchange rate fluctuation, the extremities of which were set by the cost of shipping gold from one country to another. (If one wished to be perversely complicated one might say that the range defined the limits of commodity arbitrage in gold terms.)

To illustrate this let us suppose that Britain for the time being had a deficit on its balance of payments with the United States, so that demand for dollars in pound terms exceeded the dollar offer for pounds. The sterling/dollar exchange rate under this influence would depreciate perhaps to £1 = $4.98. Such a depreciation would mean that any British importer wishing to settle dollar debts would lose 2 cents on each £1 by the depreciation. If the cost of transporting one-seventh of an ounce of gold to the United States was 2 cents, it would then be a matter of indifference to him whether he bought dollars at the higher rate or whether he bought gold at mint par and spent the 2 cents in transporting it to the United States. Clearly if the rate fell below £1 = $4.98 it would pay him to ship gold, for he would lose more by the depreciated rate than he would by buying gold, shipping it to the United States, reselling at the American mint par and settling his dollar debt. In this case the rate of £1 = $4.98 would be the so-called gold export point. Any depreciation of the pound beyond this point would induce British importers to ship gold in settlement of American debts without changing currencies in the exchange market. In the opposite case, where Britain had a favourable balance of payments with the United States and the pound appreciated to $5.02, the American would now be on the point of paying his sterling debts in gold. The purchase of £1 would now have risen on the exchange market by 2 cents, i.e. by the exact cost of shipping £1 worth of gold to Britain. An appreciation beyond £1 = $5·02 would be prevented by Americans resorting to gold payments rather than to exchange purchases. Thus £1 = $5.02 would be to Britain the gold import point, and to the United States the gold export point. The range of £1 = $4.98 to $5.02 would thus be defined by gold import and export points located above and below mint par by the cost of shipping gold between Britain and the United States. In general, the cost of shipping gold could be said to vary according to distance, the cost of insurance cover and loss of interest for the period in which gold is held. Narrower gold points would clearly obtain for the DM and French franc than for the DM and the U.S. dollar. It should be noted that the mint parity has no significance other than to define by inference the gold import and export points.

Fig. 17.6 illustrates the determination of the exchange rate under a gold standard. The exchange rate E can, with given demand and supply conditions, be located at any value between the gold points. There is no special reason for it to be at mint parity.

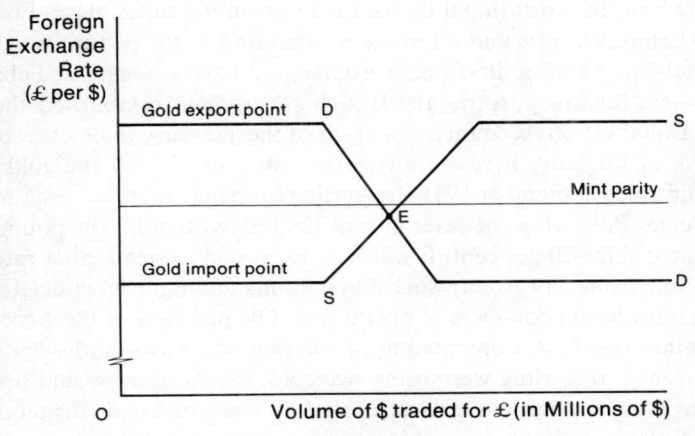

Fig. 17.6

It is interesting to note that the spread of the gold points could be widened at any time by the administrative device of the central bank's having two prices for gold, a buying and a selling price. These would have the effect of widening the frontiers for gold arbitrageurs. The wider the spread between the two prices, the wider would be the addition to the spread of the gold points, and the more the country would rely on movements of the exchange rate rather than gold movements to balance its international payments. Directly we come to consider devices such as this we move away from the pure international gold standard into the spectrum of influenced and controlled exchange rate systems. We are here concerned with principles, rather than with the description of past or existing systems. We shall therefore, be content to point out that the introduction of any feature which increases the cost of sending gold abroad — either an increase in its supply price at the central bank, an export tax, a handling charge — has the effect of broadening the gold points, increasing the range of exchange rate variation, and reducing reliance on gold movements for settlement of balance-of-payments deficits and surpluses.

We turn now to exchange rate determination in a market where exchange rates have only a limited freedom. Official interference in the market takes the form of two main constraints operating to set upper and lower limits to the movements of the exchange rate and operating within this limit for certain limited purposes – to iron out excessive day-to-day fluctuations in the rate and to discourage undue currency speculation. Such official intervention in the market must be understood specifically. We must know precisely how, in institutional terms, the intervention takes place. For this, we must digress a little and fill in the background to the picture.

Official intervention in foreign exchange markets began in February 1932, when, for this purpose, the British government established the Exchange Equalisation Account as an agent of the Treasury to be operated by the Bank of England. Five months earlier, Britain had left the gold standard, and since September 1931 the sterling exchange rate had been free to to fluctuate. Following the severance of the link with gold, the pound had depreciated some 10 per cent. It was now proposed to steady that rate and to iron out from day to day such fluctuations as might have deleterious effects on trade and commercial operations. The principle of the Account's intervention was that it operated in the market as a buyer and seller of its own currency. If sterling were being oversold, the Account would become a buyer, using foreign currencies; if sterling were in excess demand, the Account would sell sterling, taking foreign currencies in exchange. Very simply the Account operated against the trend of the market in order to reduce exchange rate variation. For this purpose, it required large balances both of sterling and of leading foreign currencies. The former could, of course, be supplied more or less *ad lib.* by the British government, the money being raised by domestic borrowing, but the latter had to be earned by balance of payments surpluses, or bought by the sale of gold. Initially, the Account was equipped with a substantial balance of sterling Treasury bills and, as in the first period of its operation its main function was to hold down the sterling rate to the level to which it had depreciated after the departure from gold, it took in large amounts of foreign currency for the reserves. At a later stage, in 1939, it became the repository of the main sterling area reserves of gold and foreign currencies so that a direct link between the sterling exchange rate and the official reserves was forged from that time.

In 1934, when Roosevelt devalued the dollar, the proceeds available from the increase in the value of the United States gold stock were concentrated in an American Exchange Stabilisation Fund, which was charged with functions somewhat similar to those of the British Account. At the time, there seemed little point in this action save to provide an American engine which could circumvent such actions in the exchange market as the United States regarded as hostile to its immediate monetary interests. The activities of the two exchange funds between 1934 and 1936 showed indeed an extreme rivalry, and mark a low tide mark in the Anglo-American economic relations of the period. In 1936 the Gold Bloc came to an end. The group of six European countries—France, Holland, Italy, Belgium, Luxembourg and Switzerland—were no longer able to sustain the overvaluation of their currencies relative to the rest of the world, and each was proposing to adopt a free exchange rate and to set up an exchange account to regulate its fluctuation. The world now faced the prospect of not two rival exchange regulators but eight. Moreover, the disappearance of the Gold Bloc brought technical difficulties for the British and American accounts which had hitherto held their foreign currency balances in French francs, which, as a gold currency, was not subject to market fluctuation outside a narrow range. Now all was to be in flux. To avoid anarchy in the exchange market a conference was called which produced an agreement by which Britain, France and the United States agreed to observe certain principles in operating their accounts. These set the tone for countries operating exchange accounts and represented a significant step in the development of co-operation in the exchange rate field. The Tripartite Monetary Agreement of 1936 was a beginning to a process of thought on international monetary co-operation which was re-invoked in 1944 in the Bretton Woods Agreement.

The exchange fund has now become the modal method of official intervention of a country in the exchange market. In principle, such intervention means that whatever exchange rate, or spread of rates about a mint parity, is to be preserved can only be preserved by the purchase and sale of the country's currency in the exchange market. If the rate, under the influence of ordinary market forces, depreciates below the lower support point, then the fund must buy its own currency, meeting all offers of it for foreign currencies at that rate. If the currency is strong, the fund must supply its own currency without limit at the upper support point. In this way the official reserves of the country are augmented in times of exchange-rate strength, depleted in times of weakness. Between 1947 and 1971 the countries party to the Bretton Woods Agreement of 1944 and members of the International Monetary Fund defined the parities of their currency units in terms of the United States dollar (which was tied to gold by the willingness of the United States to buy monetary gold at $35 per ounce—this obligation was terminated in August 1971), and agreed to preserve the resulting exchange rates with a permissible variation of 1 per cent above or below parity. This gave a very narrow range of fluctuation and meant in effect that fluctuations in the balances of payments of countries fell on the reserves rather than on the exchange rate. During 1970 and 1971, a growing number of countries abandoned their Bretton Woods parities and allowed the rates for their currencies to float in a virtually free market. It is still too early to assess whether new parities with wider limits will ultimately be established, or whether a system of floating exchange rates is now (late 1973) establishing itself. In either event, some degree of official intervention in exchange markets is inevitable, and it obeys the principles which we are here describing.

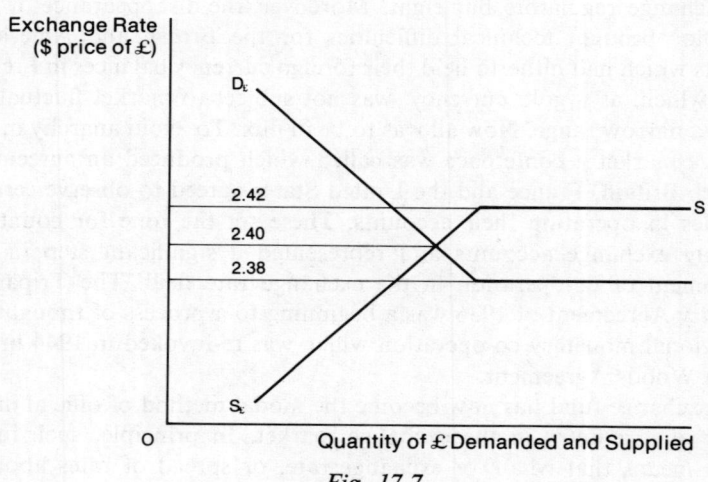

Fig. 17.7

After this necessary digression we may return to the main theme. A typical exchange-rate situation between pounds and dollars can be shown in Fig. 17.7. Here, the authorities are shown as ready to supply unlimited quantities of pounds at the rate $2.42 = £1, so that, whatever the demand for pounds, the rate cannot rise above this level. In the opposite direction they are prepared to buy all pounds offered at $2.38. Under these conditions the Exchange Equalisation Account operations, beyond whatever point in terms of quantity the Account begins operations, turn the supply and demand curves for the currency into horizontal lines. Between these lines the rate may fluctuate under the influence of short-term commercial and speculative forces.

A more sophisticated diagrammatic picture of the process of official support for an exchange rate between narrow (i.e. IMF type) limits has been given by Robert Mundell.[6] Since it gives a more complete picture of the intervention process in the exchange market we will make use of it.

The Economics of the Balance of Payments

Fig. 17.8 shows the demand and supply of dollars in exchange for Deutschmarks. The situation is simplified by taking dollars to encompass all foreign exchange and all transactions involving it. DD is the demand curve for dollars by German nationals ($D_d = f(P_d)$), assuming that the Deutschmark price of German goods and the dollar prices of foreign

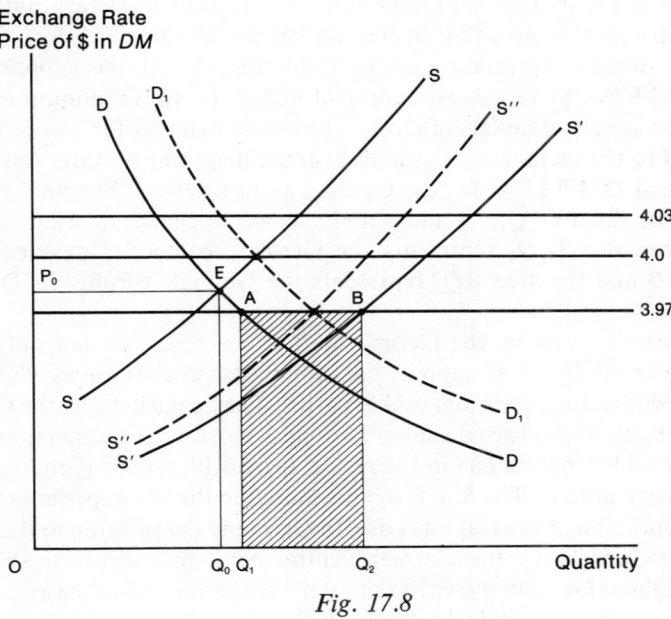

Fig. 17.8

goods are constant. For any given price the area enclosed by the ordinate from the y-axis and the price represents the total sum in Deutschmarks that Germans are prepared to pay for the quantity of dollars represented by that price and the curve on the x-axis. Thus the demand for dollars by Germans represents also the supply of Deutschmarks offered by Germans in exchange for dollars.

The curve SS shows the supply of dollars offered by the rest of the world for Deutschmarks at various exchange rates. SS is, therefore, the supply of dollars and the demand for Deutschmarks, this latter being described by the area at any price/quantity coupling on the supply schedule.

If the market were free from intervention the price would be P_0 determined by the intersection at E of DD and SS. At this price Q_0 of dollars is exchanged for the rectangle P_0Q_0 of Deutschmarks. The price P_0 of dollars in terms of Deutschmarks is within the range Deutschmarks 3·97–4·03 centred on a parity of 4·0.

Suppose that there is an autonomous increase in the demand for German goods, so that the supply of dollars is increased at any given price. SS now shifts to the right to some position such as that of $S'S'$. In a free market this would mean that the price of the dollar would fall below the lower support point of DM 3·97, but this the German monetary authorities would prevent, intervening in the market at the rate DM 3·97 = $1 to prevent further appreciation of the Deutschmark. At the support point of DM 3·97 = $1 the excess supply of dollars is AB an amount equal to an excess supply of dollars of Q_1Q_2. The excess demand for Deutschmarks is equal to the rectangle AQ_2 shaded on the diagram. In order to stabilise the rate at DM 3·97 = $1, the German authorities will buy up the excess supply of dollars (Q_1Q_2) and supply to the exchange markets AQ_2 of Deutschmarks. Q_1Q_2 represents the German balance-of-payments surplus in $ and the area AQ_2 represents the German surplus in Deutschmarks.

The intervention by the German authorities described not only raises the rate to the DM 3·97 support point, but also invokes forces which tend to correct the disequilibrium in the market. The acquisition by the German central bank of the excess supply of dollars must, in the absence of a creation of additional dollars in the rest of the world, reduce spending in the world using dollars. The $S'S'$ is by this shifted to the left as prices in the rest of the world fall or interest rates rise. In Germany the addition to the supply of Deutschmarks by the German central bank will serve to shift DD to the right as German prices rise or interest rates fall. After the adjustment, a new equilibrium would be established at the interrection of D_1D_1 and $S''S''$.

The last phase of this diagrammatic process may be omitted in practice. It is most likely that the German authorities (as would those of any other country) will be anxious to prevent the working of automatic adjustment forces on their domestic price level. It is likely nowadays that adjustment would be prevented by counter actions by the central bank and that in the absence of the adjustment phase in the diagram there will be a change in the level of reserves held by the two countries.

One final word is necessary on the foreign exchange market of the Bretton Woods type. We may have variants of this system. There is nothing sacred about the limits of fluctuation prescribed by the IMF. They come as near to a fixed rate system as it is practically possible to come. A completely fixed rate system is impossible in an international exchange market. Demands and supplies of currencies, however they may be in equilibrium in the longer run, are bound to differ from hour to hour and from day to day with mere bunching of transactions. Once these divergences are recognised as inevitable prices must vary and, to perfect the market, arbitrage and speculation must occur. It is to define the limits of this speculation and short-term price variation that limits are set even with a so-called fixed rate. It would, however, be quite possible to extend the limits to encompass a band of 5 per cent above and below parity. Such a 'band' system, when the band is wide, comes near to flexible rates. Variations within it might be expected to take care of quite considerable movements in the balance of payments without inducing the authorities to support the rate. A band system of various amplitudes has often been advocated as an alternative to the present system. We shall be hearing more of it in Chapter 18.

(iv) The Euro-dollar Market

This chapter on the foreign exchange market will be concluded with a brief description of what was perhaps the most important institutional development on the international payments scene in the sixties — the foreign markets which have developed outside their own country for dollars and, to a lesser extent, sterling and the major Western European currencies, the group of markets which we have loosely come to call the Euro-dollar market.[7]

The Euro-dollar is a dollar balance in the books of a bank outside the United States. The balance may be held by a client of any nationality, including Americans. This definition may be broadened to include many short-term deposits held with British or Western European banks and expressed in some currency other than the domestic currency of the bank in which the deposit is held. Thus, deposits denominated in dollars have been placed as deposits with banks in Canada, Japan and Western Europe, and deposits in sterling, Deutschmarks, lire, Swiss francs and guilders have been and are accepted by banks in countries other than that in which the particular currency circulates. The dominant currency of the Euro-dollar market is, however, the U.S. dollar, and we will disregard the other currencies with similar characteristics. Euro-dollar — sometimes Euro-currency — is the usual term for deposits of this sort. Their basic characteristics are two: they are short-term assets, and they are liabilities of banks outside the United States. A Euro-dollar balance is typically re-lent by the depositor in the Euro-dollar market in London or one of the other centres in which the market operates.

This market arose after 1958, when convertibility of Western European currencies was restored and when London was able, as a result of the dismantling of British exchange control, to resume its role as a leading financial market for international funds. The main factor which encouraged the market and stimulated its location in London rather than in New York, was the so-called Regulation Q of the Federal Reserve System. By this regulation interest paid by U.S. banks on time deposits was fixed, while dollar deposits in foreign banks were not subject to any interest ceiling. Returns on such deposits rose in 1959 one-quarter per cent above the Regulation Q level. As a result, London banks came to bid for dollar deposits which in turn they re-lent to New York. Some depositors of dollars found it convenient to hold deposits outside the United States free from the jurisdiction of the Federal Reserve. Thus a group of lenders and borrowers in dollars grew up in London where lenders were prepared to lend to large borrowers at more flexible rates than those available in New York. Another contributory cause of the market's location in London was that there Europeans could deal within a common time zone. New York's 'five hours back' was a disadvantage, since there would then be a very limited time during which Western European centres and New York would be open together. The deficit of the United States in the early sixties ensured that dollar balances were plentiful in Europe to form a basis for the growth of the market. Most of the lenders in the market are banks, and 'transactions can be regarded as wholesale dealing in dollars outside the bounds of the officially regulated United States monetary system'.[8] The banks dealing in dollar balances are both numerous and varied, including British clearing and overseas banks, European and foreign banks (both with and without branches in London), London branches of American and Canadian banks and Japanese banks. The market, which has grown rapidly since 1958, has been greatly encouraged by the British overseas and merchant banks, whose foreign exchange departments have acted as intermediaries. Although London is the main centre for the market other centres than London and other currencies than dollars have come to be traded outside their domestic markets. In 1967 there were eight European countries whose bank liabilities in Euro-currencies were $14.7 billion in dollars and the equivalent of $3.6 million in other Euro-currencies.

The supply side of the market may typically be a European bank holding a dollar balance earned in the ordinary process of trade, for example by collecting the proceeds of an export sale to the United States. The European bank offers the dollar balance through a broker in the Euro-dollar market in London: the broker matches supply and demand by making the dollar balance available to some borrower requiring the use of a dollar balance. This borrower may be another European bank or it may be an international trading organisation. Perhaps it may be a large American business firm which is able to secure better terms in the Euro-dollar market than elsewhere. Transactions in the market are large and are modally in units of a million dollars. The period of the loan may vary from a few days to three months. Repayment is by cheque drawn on a bank in the U.S.A.

A further development of the market in the 1960s has been the issuing by American banks in London of Euro-dollar certificates of deposit for amounts of $25,000, to run from one to six months.

A difficulty exists for British residents in that, under the British foreign exchange regulations, they are not permitted to enter into an agreement to repay a loan in dollars. To borrow Euro-dollars would infringe this regulation. A way round this difficulty, however, exists through the forward exchange market, and serves to make foreign funds available to British borrowers. If an operator wishes to lend at favourable rates in, say, the British local authority loan market, he may borrow Euro-dollars. With these he buys sterling but hedges by buying forward dollars against the future repayment of his Euro-dollar loan. If the interest proceeds from his local authority loan in sterling exceed the cost of hedging in the forward market for repayment in Euro-dollars, the transaction is worthwhile. Thus the Euro-dollar market can be made a channel through which funds may flow into the British short-term money market. The flow in this channel depends, however, upon the relative rates of interest in the Euro-dollar and British short-loan markets. The latter must exceed the former by more than the cost of the swap in the forward market.

The markets in Euro-currencies are now highly developed and have become a large source of short-term credit. They provide an alternative to domestic money markets and impel countries to regard their interest-rate policies in their international setting. There are signs, too, that the Euro-dollar market is acquiring a life of its own nurtured by the concurrent post-war movement for central bank co-operation. In 1966 there were signs that leading central banks were taking the market in hand. A potential shortage of dollars in the market and an increase in rates was forestalled by a number of central banks, including the Swiss National Bank and the Federal Reserve Bank of New York, who temporarily supplied more dollar deposits to the market. This looked much like an embryonic open-market operation to adjust rates and credit supply.

Clearly a market such as this—which has grown swiftly and almost spontaneously with no official support from governments during a mere decade—must meet some deep-felt need in the international monetary system. Behind the very complex façade what are the real needs to which this market caters? Firstly, it represents a form of borrowing and lending outside the regulations and limitations of national monetary systems. Secondly, the market supplies in many cases higher yields on mobile short-term international capital than the old asset forms such as U.S. or U.K. bank deposits or Treasury bills. Even some central banks may now hold part of their foreign exchange reserves in dollar-deposit claims in this market. Thirdly, the advantages not only in yield profits but in the fostering of business contacts which the inter-bank Euro-dollar market gives to large banks in main financial centres have led such banks to foster, refine and perfect the market, until it has become in the international field a refined instrument of matching lender and borrower, often separated at either end of a long chain of bank intermediation. Finally, as an unsought-for incidental, the market has enlarged to an unknown but comparatively small amount the stock of international liquidity. Dollar balances earned by exporters to the United States and not exchanged for their own currencies have been a welcome cushion to the dollar in the early sixties.

18
Exchange Rate Policy

(i) Introduction

WE move in this chapter from theory to practice, from principle to policy – a transition perhaps welcome to those who prefer the world of reality to the realm of abstraction. For those, however, who imagine that with practical issues comes simplicity there is no comfort in this or the succeeding chapter. Escape from the partial equilibrium analysis of exchange rate levels to the fog of exchange rate policy, from the simple models of adjustment to the enunciation of balance-of-payments policies in differing and rapidly changing circumstances, from the absorption models to the practical choices of finance ministers and central bankers in the ordering of monetary and fiscal policy – these changes are no escape, but a new and daunting ridge on a climb that apparently has a limitlessly receding horizon and no summit in sight. The meagre equipment which the foregoing chapters have offered is and will long remain inadequate to solve the problems of the policy-makers.

We have set out in previous chapters what theory has to offer as general guidance in balance-of-payments adjustment and exchange rate matters. In the present chapter we shall be concerned with the practical problems of adjustment and exchange rate policies. First, we shall examine some of the practical aspects of the concept of the equilibrium exchange rate, then we shall scrutinise in turn the nature of the choice between systems of adjustment.

(ii) The Equilibrium Exchange Rate

The role of the exchange rate within a system of balance-of-payments adjustment has undergone several changes during the past century. Under the international gold standard, the rate of exchange was regarded as immutable save between the narrow limits of the gold points. Certainly the exchange rate was never regarded as a vehicle of adjustment. Such words as devaluation, revaluation and depreciation were not to be found in the literature of comment and policy criticism. The idea of the Bank of England deliberately varying its buying price for gold in the interests of its balance-of-payments policy — indeed the idea that the Bank should have a balance-of-payments policy — would have seemed novel to Bagehot and his successors down to 1914.

With the short interlude of floating exchange rates in the early twenties the gold standard view of the exchange rate persisted until the demise of that system in the thirties. The departure of Britain and other countries from gold in September 1931, and the recognition by the setting up of the Exchange Equalisation Account in February 1932 that the gold standard had gone for good, changed the view hitherto held of the exchange rate. The many efforts to vary domestic prices in the interests of the balance of payments and the effects of such efforts on national levels of employment had driven policy-making opinion to regard internal stability of prices and employment as best sought through domestic policy, while the exchange rate would be left to determine the relationship of internal and external value of the currency. With some variations this view of the exchange rate still survives. It is, however, the variations that are important. In the immediate post-war years, it was thought by many that the system established at Bretton Woods whereby exchange rates would be altered only at long intervals, to adjust the structural changes which are at all times at work in the international economy, would be an efficient compromise between the extremes of gold standard inflexibility and the uncertainties of floating exchange rates. In the shorter period balance of payments disequilibria could be met by inter-country reserve flows for the lubrication of which the IMF had been set up. By the mid-fifties, the conventional wisdom of the IMF and controlling opinion in many countries had moved to the view that changes of exchange rates, particularly those involving key currencies, should be of such infrequency as to approach the condition of the gold standard itself and abandon the exchange rate as an adjustment device. Parallel to this official view, but never meeting it, was a growing body of academic opinion which favoured a return to floating exchange rates in some form or other, either tempered by the operations of exchange funds, confined within a band of varying width, or changing from year to year in accordance with some mutually agreed formula.

In moving towards an evaluation of these viewpoints it is convenient to start by concentrating upon a common attribute: the belief that the international monetary system is one which is held in equilibrium by a series of equilibrium rates of exchange. To the gold standard theorist, the equilibrium rate was, hopefully, that at which the external value of the currency was pegged by its mint parity. To the advocate of moving exchange rates, whether continuously or at intervals, the equilibrium rate was the sought-for level towards which the actual rate should always be adjusting itself. To appreciate this view, it is necessary to examine the attributes of the equilibrium exchange rate qualitatively. It would also contribute to our judgement were we able in given circumstances to attempt a calculation of the actual value of such a rate.

We start with a definition. For any country, the equilibrium exchange rate is 'that rate which, over a certain period of time, keeps the balance of payments in equilibrium'.[1] This definition stresses two features: a time period, and the balance-of-payments condition associated with the exchange rate. It is necessary to examine these features separately.

In examining the time element we move along a spectrum from daily movements to influences on the rate which manifest themselves only over months and years. It is clear that no stable exchange rate can reflect the equilibrium of day-to-day changes brought about by speculation, arbitrage, bunched settlements for commercial transactions and the like. In this very short period the rate will vary about an equilibrium but that equilibrium will be nowhere identifiable. Moreover as days lengthen to weeks, longer-term influences will manifest themselves. From weeks on into months seasonal influences will bear upon the rate. Even beyond one year the fluctuations of the business cycle may be at work and the equilibrium rate of the trough will not be that of the boom. We must clearly lengthen our time focus, selecting a period long enough for the rate to preserve a balance-of-payments equilibrium – that is, for short-term deficits and surpluses to cancel out and ensure that outflows of monetary reserves are balanced by inflows, leaving the country's reserve holding unchanged. It is apparent that the period chosen must be long enough to include at least one complete set of recurrent influences on the balance. Thus short-period and seasonal influences should certainly be included, placing a minimum of at least a year upon the standard period. Whether we should expect a rate to maintain the balance of payments (and reserves) as we move progressively to longer and longer periods is highly debatable. To lengthen it to the ten to twelve years necessary to encompass the whole business cycle is not desirable. In a period as long as this, it would probably be possible to eliminate influences causing recurrent fluctuation of the balance of payments but it would also allow the interplay between countries of all sorts of influences which bear upon the exchange rate, and which are assumed away in the partial equilibrium analysis by which in theory we derive the exchange rate—relative rates of growth of investment and population, major and permanent swings of consumer taste and demand, changes in technology and changes in income distribution. In the modern world, the short period becomes shorter and the long period soon becomes history. We are looking in our definition for a period which encompasses the short-run but is not too intruded upon by the changes of the long. A period of two or three years seems appropriate. This permits adequate time for adjustments attendant upon an initial alteration of the exchange rate to be absorbed by the economy.[2]

Changes in the balance of payments within the standard period of three years are met by transfers of gold, international currencies or international borrowing facilities; in other words, by changes in international liquidity. If the rate is an equilibrium one, the end of the standard period will find the reserves of the country unchanged in quantity as compared with those at the beginning of the period. In the light of this we can refine our definition which now becomes: that an equilibrium exchange rate is such that over a standard period of three years, 'there would be no net change in a country's reserves of international means of payment'.[3] The longer we make our standard period, the larger the amount of international liquidity the country requires for adjustment purposes. Conversely the larger 'the stock of international liquidity held by any country and by countries in the aggregate the less will be the need for changes in exchange rates'.[4] A larger world stock of international liquidity is necessary to maintain stable rates of exchange over the whole business cycle than to meet only seasonal or short-term fluctuations. The significance of this for exchange rate policy is evident. If it is desired to establish an international payments system with stable exchange rates, there must be an adequate and appropriately distributed stock of international liquidity.

Turn now to the second feature stressed in the original definition of the equilibrium exchange rate, namely, what is included in the balance of payments. It is clear that gold and currency reserve transfers must be excluded. If they are included, continuous balance in the account is automatic. Movements of short-term funds should also be excluded, whatever their type. If they are movements made in response to interest rate differentials and are used by a country to conceal a deficit, the effect is the same, as far as balancing is concerned, as with a gold outflow. Such funds are liable to quick withdrawal. They are a liability and should be regarded as a negative gold reserve and thus an offset to the country's international liquidity. All other items of the balance of payments should be included.

Two general qualifications must be made before we complete our description of the equilibrium exchange rate. Both have to do with means other

The Economics of the Balance of Payments

than the exchange rate which may preserve consistency of reserves and give a spurious appearance of equilibrium. The first way of sustaining a spurious balance is by direct controls. These suppress the trade imbalance, which would, in their absence, prevail as a result of several factors, possibly of the level of the exchange rate itself. We are anxious to establish the conditions of equilibrium exchange under free movement of goods and currencies. Our examination can allow the existence of only such minor restrictions and frictions as are generally accepted as desirable. Some interference with international trade is inevitable. Countries will always wish to exclude certain goods. With the growing complexity of international economic relationships, even the allowable minimum of such intervention must be considerable. What is, of course, necessary for our definition of equilibrium is that, over the standard period of three years, the background of trade and currency control should not be changed. It is when some basic change in the balance of payments is promptly countered by some direct measure of control that the rate which is thus maintained is not a true equilibrium one.

The second means of sustaining spurious balance is by tolerating in the country such a degree of underemployment as will reduce the demand for imports to a level appropriate to an accounting balance. This means of achieving equilibrium in the balance must be excluded. A high and stable level of employment is now such a widely accepted policy goal of the leading economies that we can regard it as certain that underemployment would not be tolerated today in the interest of balance-of-payments stability. The classic historical example of this was that of Britain between 1925 and 1931. During this period the sterling exchange rate, it is now agreed, was overvalued by about 10 per cent, yet because of heavy unemployment in the basic industries the British balance of payments did not go into deficit and there was no gold outflow until confidence factors precipitated one in 1931.

We may now give a final form to our definition to take account of the foregoing conditions. An equilibrium rate is such a rate as will, over a standard period, during which full employment is maintained and with no change in the amount of restrictions on trade or payments, cause no net change in the holdings of gold and currency reserves of the country concerned. We may also extend this definition to the wider focus of a world system and 'define an ideal system of equilibrium rates as one that maintains the external accounts of all countries simultaneously in equilibrium when all countries are free from mass unemployment on the one hand and inflation on the other'.[5]

While these definitions may seem cumbrous, they are still of use for the forming of policy judgements and for examining particular exchange rate situations. The role and, in particular, the importance of the quantity of international liquidity become apparent, while the level of employment and the direct control of foreign trade are brought into perspective in their relation to international equilibrium.

What we may call the 'balance-of-payments definition' of the equilibrium exchange rate is useful for the making of qualitative judgements. It enables symptoms of over- and under-valuation to be recognised and cases to be made for changes in exchange rates. It has bearing on the fixed versus flexible exchange rate argument. Beyond the problem of describing the attributes of the equilibrium rate there is, however, a further question: what in given circumstances is its numerical value? What should be the rate between currencies A and B?

It might appear at first sight that this is a vain quest. After all, it is the qualitative aspects of the rate which are important. Actual values are, it is arguable, the result of cumulative error from the past. Who can conceive of making a clean start by calculating all the rates and cross-rates and setting to work afresh with what hopefully was an equilibrium system? Yet this argument does have validity. We must have a calculation by which to check existing rates, and on at least two historical occasions the setting up of a new complex of calculated rates was at least seriously advocated. The first of these occasions was after the First World War when different rates of price inflation during the war period raised sharply the question of whether the exchange rates implicit in the pre-war mint parities of currencies with gold were appropriate to a renewed gold standard. In most cases, they clearly were not. What then were the mint parities appropriate to a new gold standard? The second occasion occurred in 1946 when the newly established IMF called upon its member governments, once more after a major war and attendant inflations, to notify their currency par values to the Fund. The choice lay between accepting the pre-war values or a new set of calculated post-war estimates. The former was done.

The purchasing-power-parity theory which provides the only method of calculating an exchange rate is not new. It is not held in high esteem but like a poor relation is allowed to stay around in case it might be useful. It was first put forward by Gustav Cassel in 1920[6] during the controversy on the parities which currencies should have in the new post-war gold standard. Basing his ideas on some of the writings of Ricardo and Wheatley, Cassel gave a simple formula for calculating the exchange rate from the relationship between relative price levels. Originally put forward as an *ad hoc* theoretical contribution to the devaluation-versus-deflation contro-

The Economics of the Balance of Payments

versy of the immediate post-war period, the purchasing-power-parity doctrine came to be much used in the discussions of exchange rate policy which took place in the later twenties and in the thirties, and was often applied to situations for the analysis of which it was totally unsuited.

The theory is based upon the statement that the equilibrium exchange rate between two currencies is such as gives equality in their purchasing power. The demand for a foreign currency is a derived demand, derived from the wish for purchasing power over its goods. If the rate of exchange is such that a given amount of money converted into the foreign currency will buy a larger basket of goods in the foreign country than it will buy at home, then the rate of exchange at which the foreign currency sells is too low. There will be pressure to obtain the currency in order to buy the foreign goods, which are, because of the undervaluation of the foreign currency, relatively cheaper abroad. This pressure will force the rate upward. Conversely, if with a given amount converted into the foreign currency only a smaller basket of goods can be bought than can be bought with the same sum at home, then the foreign transaction is not worthwhile. The rate is overvalued in terms of the foreign currency. The equilibrium rate will then be located at such a level as will provide no incentive to the nationals of either country to exchange their currencies and import goods from the other rather than obtain an exactly similar basket of goods at home. Trade will be limited to goods in which one country or the other has a cost advantage. The argument may be put in another way. Converted at the equilibrium rate, the prices of identical goods are equal in all countries. A shirt costing £3 in London and $7.80 in Montreal indicates an exchange rate of $2.6 = £1, if we ignore transport and additional selling costs. Under such conditions, import of shirts into either country would not take place. If the price of a shirt in Montreal were lower in dollar terms than in London at the existing rate, it would still not be imported if the price differential were equal to or less than transport costs plus tariffs.

The theory has two forms, an absolute and a comparative. The former deals with the determination of a rate of exchange at any given point of time, the latter, with movements of the rate caused by movements of price levels relative to some earlier date. Because one cannot define the value of a currency save in a relative sense, it is only the comparative form which is significant. One cannot satisfactorily measure the value of money at a given moment of time. One can say only that a unit of currency buys x units of this or y units of that. To say, however, that today a currency buys x units of bread and last year it bought $x + y$ units of bread, is meaningful. We know from this that, in terms of bread, the value of the currency has fallen and the price of bread has risen. We can calculate the amount by which prices have risen relative to some given point in the past. Thus we calculate the equilibrium exchange rate by multiplying a chosen previous equilibrium rate by the relative change which has taken place in the price levels since that equilibrium rate ruled. Since price level changes are statistically expressed in index numbers, the formula for the calculation of the new equilibrium rate is

$$R_t = R_{t-1} \cdot \frac{P_1}{P_2}$$

where R_t is the new equilibrium rate, R_{t-1} is the rate one period ago, P_1 is the index number change for the currency in terms of which the exchange is expressed and P_2 the index number change for the other currency.

It is unnecessary to give anything but brief discussion to this theorem. In its absolute form it is a truism as long as one assumes a costless flow of commodities from country to country. As soon as one recognises the existence of numerous frictions to such a flow and the existence of a large category of goods which do not (and some which cannot) enter into international trade, the theory breaks down completely. Moreover, it is the whole structure of supply and demand for the currency implicit in the balance of payments which determines the rate: purchasing power parity takes account only of commodity trade. In its comparative form the theory is somewhat more meaningful but still has serious defects. The use of index numbers in calculation introduces all the defects to which these are subject. It presents the difficult decision of choosing indices appropriate to the task in their coverage, base year and method of calculation. Consequently there has been much controversy. It is tempting to take indices of internationally traded goods for which transport costs are unimportant. Such goods, however, are traded in a single world market in which there can be but one price — which makes the doctrine a tautology. Consumer price indices which contain some non-traded goods are preferable. Yet these also contain prices which are extraneous to the purpose. What is required is an index of prices which impinge directly on the balance of payments, an index number which is conceptual but rarely, if ever, actual. We must assume not only that the balance of payments was in equilibrium in the base period, but also that there have been in the interim no structural changes in the underlying factors — in technology, resources, tastes and the like. Metzler gives as an example of a change which would distort purchasing power parity, a change in capital movements traceable to a reduction in the propensity to save. With this higher rate of consumption capital exports may decline. The most serious defect of all, however, lies in the difficulty of choosing a past year when the rate was in equilibrium. We have already argued that it takes a period longer than one year in which to assess qualitatively the equilibrium characteristic of a rate. To say that the rate of exchange between sterling and the Canadian dollar in any year — indeed, at a particular time in a year — is an equilibrium rate would be a dangerous assessment to make and could be little but a guess. If the base rate is not an equilibrium one, then its divergence from it is carried as a continuing error into the new and all subsequent calculations based on that date. Finally, the purchasing-power-parity formula applies most to a country whose balance of payments is determined by the merchandise trade account. It is inappropriate to countries which, like Switzerland or Canada, have the key to their exchange rate in the capital account.

The purchasing-power-parity doctrine, whose claim to fame, if any, must lie in the practical field, invites empirical verification. Here it has not done well. Bela Balassa, in a reassessment of the doctrine,[7] found that not only were the consumer price indices which have been most often used unsuitable for the purpose but wide discrepancies occurred in the purchasing power parity and therefore in the implicit exchange rates for different types of goods. An OECD report[8] which compared real incomes between countries with money incomes converted at the exchange rate found many anomalies. The exchange rates of the more advanced countries seemed to be increasingly over-valued as one moved from commodities to services. It was evidently misleading to compare real per capita incomes between countries through conversion of money incomes at going rates of exchange.

Such a case built up against the spurious exactness of the purchasing-power-parity theory almost robs it of any credence. It is clearly only a crude means of calculating the exchange rate between two currencies. Yet, imperfect as it is, it is still the only way in which we can calculate an actual figure for the rate of exchange. Knowing its traps and difficulties, we must, in default of better, make occasional cautious use of it. Used in conjunction with the qualitative criteria which have been discussed, the theory may be a useful check either upon an existing rate or upon one which is contemplated. The serious defect that the formula deals in relative terms which carry forward into the new calculation the defects of the base period can, to some extent at least, be offset by careful scrutiny of the exchange rate in the base year. Certainly only a fool would be dogmatic in an argument based on parity calculations. They may serve as rough guides only, since no other is to hand.

If the correct inferences had been drawn from purchasing power parity in 1918 disastrous errors in establishing post-war rates of exchange would have been avoided. Metzler argues that much of the discredit under which the theory has fallen stems from its improper use. For general price level movements due to inflation the theory has use. During periods of slower price change, however, balance-of-payments disequilibrium arises often from relative price changes with which it is beyond the power of index numbers to deal. While useful in the argument as to whether exchange rates should or should not be devalued after the 1914–18 war the doctrine, Metzler argues, was completely unfitted for the more complex international monetary problems of the thirties.[9]

In what has preceded, we have attempted to show the recognisable attributes of the equilibrium exchange rate. These attributes should enable us at this stage to set down some broad principles which may be useful in approaching the problem of exchange adjustment. To be brief, we shall set these principles out seriatim.

1. In selecting a rate of exchange between two currencies the aim should be to select a rate which, in the light of probable future conditions (government policies and programmes, trade trends, overseas capital commitments), promises long-term equilibrium in the country's balance of payments and which will provide price/cost and income relationships consistent with high levels of trade at full employment.

2. The rate chosen must be such as may prevail unsupported by exchange control or direct controls on imports.

3. A precise rate must be decided upon and it must be considered how far reliance can be placed upon purchasing power parity calculations. The parity formula may be used, provided that any proposed rate is subjected to searching scrutiny and qualitative criticism.

4. Particular care must be taken to decide whether, with a given capital flow, a rate is really an equilibrium rate. If the capital flow is steady and predictable in quantity then it is not destabilising and may be taken into account when settling the rate, but if it is fitful and erratic, the rate should be settled in order to balance the current account and there should be no reliance on capital flow.

5. In considering the circumstances in which a country should change its exchange rate, the criteria should be applied that devaluation should only take place (a) to meet a passive balance of payments, (b) to enable a country whose balance of payments is in equilibrium only by reason of underemployment to expand to full employment, or (c) to enable the removal of direct controls by the aid of which a spurious balance-of-payments equilibrium has hitherto been preserved.

The final conditions should be taken by inference to preclude the use of devaluation to cure unemployment within a country which has a balance-of-payments surplus. Under such circumstances, it is appropriate to eradicate simultaneously the underemployment and correct the surplus by domestic monetary and fiscal expansion. Devaluation in this case, while it might raise the employment level, would only serve to increase the surplus and attempt to snatch from neighbouring countries an inordinately large share of the world demand for output. Nor should a deficit in the balance of payments be regarded as an infallible permit to undertake devaluation. In the case where a deficit is accompanied by domestic inflation, it may well be that the existing exchange rate is an equilibrium rate and that removal of the inflation by domestic policies would adjust the balance of payments.

(iii) The Systems of Adjustment

In the broad spectrum of balance-of-payments policies, by which countries may seek to order the surpluses and deficits of their balance of payments, we have already distinguished between adjustment policies which make use of certain inherent characteristics of economic systems, working through the exchange rate or the demand forces within economies, to discipline the balance; and quasi-adjustment policies, such as direct controls on the balance of payments which suppress imbalance but do not necessarily correct it. Direct controls will be considered in the next chapter. Here it is our purpose to isolate and discuss separately the pure adjustment policies and to examine in some detail those which rely on changes in the exchange rate. What form should such changes take? How, if at all, may the adjustment system be linked with the exchange market to provide a built-in stabiliser for the balance of payments?

One link between the domestic and the external position of a country is strategic and enables us to classify our adjustment exchange rate policy system. It is the link inherent in the fact that the equilibrium exchange rate for a country's currency is a reflection of its domestic price level. If we accept this, it follows that the pattern of exchange rates ruling in the international economy in equilibrium is a reflection of the domestic price levels of the participant countries. Since four cases limit the description of the behaviour of national price levels, it follows that this limits also the number of exchange rate conditions. We may tabulate the possibilities as follows: (see table* page 456).

From this it seems that, if we want a world of fixed exchange rates, we must have some means of co-ordinating the movements of national price

---

*This table is based on one used by F. D. Graham in his *Fundamentals of International Monetary Policy*, Essays in International Finance No 2, Princeton, 1943, p. 7.

Domestic price levels may:

(1) Move independently in every country.
(2) Move in unison, both as to direction and rate of change.
(3) Move in some countries and remain stable in others.
(4) Remain stable in all countries.

And to each of these cases the appropriate exchange condition is:

(1) Proportionately fluctuating rates.
(2) Fixed rates.
(3) Proportionately fluctuating rates.
(4) Fixed rates.

levels or of ensuring their collective stability. Alternatively if we are to allow price levels to move freely relative to one another, then we must accept the corollary of exchange rates which vary freely, or at least freely enough, to reflect these price-level movements. If we choose the latter option, we must also determine what degree of rate variation we regard as tolerable. Will the rate be allowed to vary with all the influences of the market, or will it be varied discretely from time to time to reflect, by lagged response, earlier movements of the price levels; or will it be allowed to vary continuously within some stipulated range of fluctuation? In a word we must decide which is more tolerable: domestic price variations or exchange rate variation. If we decide for the latter, we have contingent questions of scope and method of variation.

A threefold choice of adjustment mechanism is before us: fixed rates of exchange with the balance of payments being adjusted by domestic price and income changes; free and fluctuating exchange rates and their modifications; and the method of so-called 'managed flexibility', under which exchange rates are changed only at long intervals on the decision of the monetary authorities. These three possible systems have all obtained in the world economy following each other approximately in the order in which we have set them down. As any critical discussion of the working of the international monetary mechanism must include consideration of these alternatives, we shall consider each of them in turn. We shall compare them, however, only as balance-of-payments adjustment media. They have many important aspects apart from this. They influence world income and its distribution; they have non-economic and political implications. Only the most general of these implications will be noted.

(iv) Adjustments in Domestic Income and Prices

The world has ample experience of the process of external balance adjustment through changes in domestic prices and income. During the classic gold standard period from 1870 to 1914, during the agonised pursuit of a stable gold exchange standard in the twenties and thirties; and during the many nervous and shifting adjustments of the 'stop-go' policy in Britain in the 1950s and 1960s, a large 'economic pathology' has grown around this system.

This method of adjustment is based both upon Hume's law and classical adjustment and upon the more recent income theory. Both theories envisage a more or less automatic process for the restoration of equilibrium. They differ only in the causal factors — price changes and income changes — which they stress. From the large theoretical and critical literature and from the long record of experience, we are probably better informed upon this than upon any of the alternative methods of adjustment.

If we are better informed, we are also more prejudiced. The international gold standard reveals its advantages and subtleties only under the closest scrutiny: they are lost upon those who associate this system with the currency confusion of the interwar years, with overvaluation and sagging basic industries in Britain; with the slow attrition of the Gold Bloc in the thirties and with American unemployment under the Hoover administration. Whether a full gold standard could once more provide a viable adjustment system for the international economy is a problem hardly worth investigation, for it is politically unacceptable in almost every major country. The undertakings of major governments to maintain full employment, the popular Keynesianism that pervades much economic discussion, the belief that domestic stability and economic growth should have primacy over balance-of-payments policy — all these set the tone for modern attitudes towards the gold standard and classical adjustment.

But this rejection of domestic price and income adjustment has not been clean and irrevocable. Thrown out by the front door, it has subsequently eased in again through the back window. The failure to evict it completely is a striking illustration of the fact that the international economy must have an adjustment system or its malfunction becomes intolerable. This point is worth developing. Since the setting up of the Bretton Woods system in 1947 the adjustment element in that system has been progressively weakened. (The Bretton Woods Agreement of 1944 established the system. The IMF did not, however, begin to function officially until March 1947.) It was at first thought that exchange rate changes would be sanctioned by the IMF and would take place frequently enough (a) for the exchange rate structure to approximate at any time to an equilibrium one, and (b) for existing national holdings of international liquidity supplemented by the resources of the IMF to be adequate for the maintenance of the system. But this conception has not been fulfilled in practice. The policy of the IMF has been to discourage either floating rates or frequent changes of the pegged rates so that in effect the system has become one of fixed exchange rates. In the twenty-five years since 1947 there have been three major revisions of exchange rates, in September 1949 when devaluation of the pound caused several other countries to change their rates; in November 1967 when sterling was again devalued and in 1971 when a number of the most important countries relinquished their fixed IMF parities and allowed their currencies to float. Apart from these group changes individual countries have devalued on a number of occasions. France devalued in 1948 and 1958; Germany revalued in 1961 and 1969. Canada adopted a floating rate from 1951 to 1960 and returned to a floating rate in May, 1970. Because of the IMF's policy of fixed exchange rates and because countries themselves have been opposed to rate changes, the existing holdings and distribution of international liquidity have been inadequate. Deficit countries, anxious to live by the rules and to maintain their exchange rates, yet having insufficient reserves to do so indefinitely, have thus been driven back upon the price and income adjustment method. They have attempted to adjust by making miniscule changes in their level of domestic activity while still striving to honour their full employment obligation. Britain has been the prime example of this method. Beset with structural balance-of-payments difficulties since the Second World War, with a capital account loaded with quick liabilities making sterling highly susceptible to speculative attack, and with the responsibility of administering a major international currency, her economic policy has demonstrated a continual battle between the aims of full employment and economic growth on the one hand and balance of payments surplus and the need to foster currency reserves on the other. Since 1955 her record has been one of fitful expansion inducing external deficit followed by deflation, external balance and renewed expansion – a cycle from which she has been woefully unable to escape despite the sterling devaluation of 1967. The malaise of the British economy during this period requires careful analysis and many factors have undoubtedly contributed,[10] but the belief of the British Treasury and of key groups within the financial establishment that the balance of payments would adjust to small variations in the level of domestic activity has been the main cause of this depressing cycle.

For a time analysts of the British problem argued that minor changes in income were sufficient to make the necessary adjustment, and that as far as price levels were concerned it was necessary only to ensure that the British price level should rise less quickly than those of its main competitors. It was hard to sustain this view in face of the facts. The repeated checks to British income growth did no more than impose a passing check to imports, while the price level rose even during the periods of deflation and the British competitive position worsened relative to her leading competitors in the export field. It became clear that, to achieve a major check to price inflation, still more to reduce prices, would require a sharp deflation generating such a level of unemployment as would be politically disastrous for the government which initiated it. The phenomenon of deflation and unemployment of resources concurrently with rising prices was a new feature, first observed during the stop-go period of the sixties. Later this same phenomenon appeared in Canada and the United States. In 1971 Britain experienced a price inflation running at 10 per cent per annum concurrent with the highest unemployment rate she had experienced since the war.

How may we summarise the record and view of price and income adjustment as we now find it? There is only one occasion when, by general agreement, this method is still applicable. This is when a country has pushed expansion too far and domestic inflation creates a deficit in its external balance. The approved remedy for such a domestic and external imbalance is to reduce domestic income by fiscal policy.

Three arguments may be used against price and income adjustment. Firstly, domestic prices, costs and incomes are, under modern conditions, highly inflexible. To attack them with fiscal or monetary methods results, not in that smooth reduction which theory envisages, but in a dispersed and uneven series of price checks, long delayed and with many distortions; in price falls in some sectors, and in heavy unemployment in others. For example, it has been argued by some critics of British 'stop-go' policies that they could never adjust the balance of payments by changing prices. To change prices, it was alleged, would require a degree of deflation which would create 5–6 per cent unemployment. Since any increase of unemployment even to 3 per cent is hotly resisted in Britain, neither political party is willing to incur the risk of such a policy. Adjustment would be attained, if at all, not by a smooth series of demand switches resulting from changes in relative prices but by a clumsy mass reduction of demand for foreign goods through a fall in real incomes.

Secondly, frequent adjustments to prices and incomes in the interest of the balance of payments impair the whole long-run stability of the economy. They adversely affect investment and development programmes and a series of such checks, if persevered in, malform the whole pattern of economic growth of the economy. Thirdly, the political peril to governments of creating any marked increase in unemployment ensures that this policy is clumsily used by governments. It is seldom pressed to a conclusion and hastily retracted if it leads to any significant increase in unemployment.

One feature of deflation as a vehicle of adjustment is its malignant effect on regional policies of the deflating country. The richer regions with new and adaptable industries may suffer hardly at all. Fringe areas with existing high unemployment rates may bear the brunt of the deflation and be reduced by it to a crisis condition.

(v) Free Rates of Exchange

We turn now to consider the merits of flexible exchange rates as an adjustment device, and find ourselves involved in one of the hottest economic controversies of the past half-century. While the architects of Bretton Woods turned their backs on flexible rates in 1944 and the financial establishment for a quarter-century hardened in its opposition to them, they have always had some support from academic economists and from those watchdogs of economic policy, the financial journalists. From 1969 onward, the pendulum began to swing in their favour. Germany adopted a floating rate for the DM in that year and Canada, who had already the experience of her ten-year float in the fifties, followed in May 1970. In the summer of 1971, Britain, Holland, Switzerland and several other countries floated their rates, and a floating rate even for the U.S. dollar formed part of an economic package deal introduced by President Nixon in August 1971 to deal with the weak American balance of payments. Clearly a great conversion to belief in the merits of free rates has taken place. The IMF, however, remains staunch in its support of the Bretton Woods fixed parity system. To assess the merit of flexible exchanges in the midst of this whirl of controversy is by now next to impossible. We can go no further in this controversy without practical experience, that is, by a major group of countries adopting and practising the method for a considerable period. At this stage we can only marshal arguments for and against and temper our reaction by whatever teaching experience has to give.

The first claim which may be made for flexible rates is that of simplicity. It is the rawest form of the doctrine of equilibrium price in the exchange

The Economics of the Balance of Payments

market. Whatever may be the supply and demand for the currency emanating from the complex of items in the balance of payments, there must be some exchange rate which will equate the demand for and supply of the home currency. Changes in this exchange rate will be induced by changes in supply and demand, and in turn will restore equilibrium by inducing shifts in exports and imports or short-term speculative capital movements, or both. If a deficit or surplus appears in the balance of payments, the exchange rate will at once be affected, a deficit reducing its value as excessive offers of the home currency for foreign currency are made; a surplus causing it to rise as foreigners seek the home currency to settle payments.

It is worth examining fairly carefully the ways in which changes of the exchange rate are expected to accomplish adjustment of the trade balance. Consider the case of a deficit which has caused the exchange rate to depreciate. The depreciation causes the prices of exports of the depreciating country to fall in terms of foreign currencies and will cause foreign demand for them to rise. The expansion of demand for exports, because of the fall in the foreign currency price, will cause the supply price of export goods to rise in the supplying country, checking domestic demand for export goods and increasing the amount available for export. The less elastic the supply curve for such goods the more the home currency price will rise with the expansion of demand. The revenue (in foreign currency) from exports will rise if the elasticity of demand for exports is greater than unity. On the import side the price of imports will rise in domestic currency, and if the demand is elastic the import bill will fall. The price will probably fall in foreign currency. As the rise in the domestic currency price reduces the demand for imports, the price will fall, the extent of the fall depending on the elasticity of the foreign supply curve of import goods. The more inelastic this supply curve the more the price will fall. Provided that the elasticities of demand for imports and exports are high, the balance of trade of the depreciating country will be improved and adjustment will tend to take place.

How great the immediate adjustment effect is will depend on the many factors which condition the elasticities of demand and supply of imports and exports, in particular, the readiness of customers and suppliers to make switches quickly and in response to small changes in price. The view was expressed on p. 315 that long-run elasticities are greater than short-run elasticities. This view is still held, and we may expect that substitutions will take time and that small changes in price relationships may be ignored by buyers and sellers. To the extent that this is so, the rate may depreciate considerably in the short period but as time passes and switches of demand are made, it will tend to appreciate again. Of itself, the adjustment of trade flows through changes in the rate of exchange might require and induce sharp downward and upward movements of the rate. A force is invoked, however, to dampen such swings: a force provided by the movement of short-term speculative funds. Conditioned by the known behaviour pattern of exchange rates in a free market, speculators will know that an exchange rate normally falls under such influences as we have described and then partially at least, recovers. They will, therefore, begin to buy the depreciating currency at what they consider to be the limit of its depreciation for later sale when it recovers. For this purpose they will use funds withdrawn from an appreciating currency, the peak of whose rise is anticipated. Both movements have a smoothing effect. The depreciation of the deficit country's currency is cushioned, while the appreciation of the surplus country's currency is checked. In this way, speculators perform the useful task of checking the movements of the exchange rate by financing a temporary deficit until the new exchange rate exerts its full influence to restore the balance of payments to equilibrium.

There is a second aspect of the simplicity argument. It is this: of all the variables in the balance-of-payments model, the exchange rate is the easiest to alter, and the easiest way to alter it is by the processes of the market. To allow the rate to depreciate by, say, 5 per cent in terms of another currency is a great deal easier than to reduce prices and costs in the home country by 5 per cent relative to the other; a great deal easier than reducing income in the deficit country by an amount which would adjust the trade balance; and a great deal easier than holding onto a fixed rate (at great cost to the exchange reserves) until the rate is no longer tenable and then reducing it by 5 per cent at one fell swoop.

The second claim made for flexible exchange rates is that it is a smoother and more painless way of making balance-of-payments adjustments than the available alternatives; that, for a deficit country whose exchange rate depreciates, the corrective forces begin to work through the market, spreading from there into the economy, from the moment that imbalance occurs. That trade-induced movements of rates are smoother than periodic crisis-invoked alterations of a fixed rate is certainly true but the qualification made above concerning the elasticities of demand for imports and exports must be remembered. Elasticities are bound to be low in the short run and the supposition that even a slight depreciation will progressively invoke correcting influences in the goods flows of the trade balance is almost certainly false. Yet the depreciation will begin to invoke such correction at some stage and whether early or late can be left to the market. There is with the free rate an escape from the contingent choices which go with every devaluation or revaluation: namely, when and how much? With free rates the market exerts its influence at the appropriate point, and the magnitude of the rate change is determined by the market.

The third advantage claimed for a free rate system is that it enables adjustment of the balance of payments to take place with the minimum of interference with the domestic stability of the economy; that in a world of full employment a free exchange rate system is the appropriate method of adjustment. If this claim is justified, it is a powerful one in support of the system; but we must examine it a little more closely. Adjustment to the balance of payments must be effected through movements either in the exchange rate or in the prices and incomes of the adjusting country, or by direct control of transactions in foreign exchange. Since in the modern world of full employment-seeking economies adjustment through income deflation or inflation is denied us, we are driven back upon exchange-rate changes and direct controls as the alternatives. If we refuse to accept the first of these then it is certain that direct control of foreign trade will be widely practised and will become a major technique of adjustment. This happened for more than a decade after the Second World War. The coexistence of policies of full employment with fear of the possible dire results of flexible rates of exchange produced a thicket of controls and a division of the world economy into regional groups which international organisations were for long powerless to remove. As long as the nature of the choice of adjustment weapons is not understood the danger of a reversion to controlled trade and a breakdown of multilateral trade and payments will continue. Removed in a period of easement in the late fifties, the difficulties of working a fixed exchange rate system and the refusal to adopt free rates may yet drive governments with persistent liquidity and balance-of-payments problems to resort once more to control and bilateralism. In this sense, free rates may indeed be the only viable alternative to such control.

Even if it is admitted that balance-of-payments adjustment by the free-rate mechanism requires no initial purposive interference with the domestic level of prices and incomes, even if it is possible that small 'rolling' adjustments can be thrown on the exchange rate, it is still not possible to claim that by this mechanism the external problem of balance-of-payments equilibrium and the domestic problem of high employment without inflation can be sealed off from one another. They never can be: whatever method of adjustment is used, the trade flows and the domestic economic situation are linked. That is after all what adjustment is about.

One immediate difficulty arises from the fact that, once a floating exchange rate is adopted as an adjustment mechanism, then the rate method must be used whatever the cause of the balance-of-payments disequilibrium. Whether the country is in a condition of external surplus and domestic recession or external deficit and domestic inflation, whether the external disequilibrium is one likely to be short-lived or is the first manifestation of prolonged structural change, the same forces are brought to bear upon the balance of trade to effect its improvement. This is contrary to earlier arguments. The whole burden of the argument in Chapter 16 was that internal and external equilibria were interrelated and that the choice of which was acted upon to achieve equilibrium, domestic or external, was a matter conditioned by the nature of the disequilibrium itself and was a policy choice of some delicacy and discernment. It would seem, therefore, that flexible rates, by providing a blanket remedy for external deficit, leave the domestic situation, whatever it may be, to accommodate itself to the changes in the rate. Let us take some specific cases. The case of external deficit coupled with domestic underemployment is simple. The external deficit will cause the rate to depreciate and, assuming favourable elasticities, the balance of trade will improve. This improvement will have a stimulating effect on the domestic economy and remove some part at least of the underemployment. In this case, depreciation of a floating rate has had the effect of bringing the economy to external balance and at least nearer to domestic balance. The case of external deficit coupled with domestic inflation is less satisfactory. Here the depreciation of the rate due to the external deficit may correct the deficit, but it is not at all certain that this will be the case. If there is domestic inflation it is likely that export goods in the deficit economy are in short supply and none or few will be available for export. The X term of the expression $X - M$ cannot be improved without a reduction in domestic absorption. However, the more that the rate is depreciated due to the external deficit the more it will add to the inflationary pressure at home. If it completely corrects the external imbalance, it does so only at the expense of intensifying the domestic imbalance. In the extreme case, it may not even correct the adverse trade balance. By increasing demand for exports the depreciation may do little or nothing to increase export revenues; for if the economy is already at full employment there is little slack in the productive system to produce the additional export goods. The price of factors in the export industries may be bid up sharply. At the same time, the price of imports, having been increased by the depreciation, will extend its influence to the domestic price level which will rise. All influences tend to increase the inflation. If the foreign balance does not improve, the rate will depreciate still further and extend these influences. Thus, at the worst, a self-perpetuating cycle of deficit, depreciation, rising domestic price level, worsening deficit and further depreciation may be created. Only drastic intervention with deflationary domestic policies will serve to break this cycle. Such policies, possibly less drastic, would have been the applicable solution to the original condition in which the deficit was caused by the domestic inflation.

It would appear then, that while we might concede that flexible rates are the adjustment system most appropriate to a full employment situation, in that direct and immediate interference by domestic policies with the level of income, prices or employment is not required, we must make serious qualifications. The first is that domestic adjustments to prices and income by fiscal policy may be necessary at a later stage to steady and complete the adjustment. If, for example, the correction of the balance of payments over-stimulates the economy into a condition of inflation. The second is that for certain types of deficit—in particular for that which is caused by domestic inflation—any attempt to adjust the deficit by exchange depreciation will only worsen the inflation. The entire adjustment in this case lies with domestic policies to damp the inflation.

It is arguable, as Mundell claims, that the truth of the assertion that flexible rates are the system most appropriate to a full employment situation rests on money illusion; that 'the community is unwilling to accept variations in real income through changes in money prices, but it will accept the same changes in real income through adjustment in the rate of exchange'.[11]

The fourth claim for flexible rates is that such an adjustment system reduces the need of the economy and of the world system for international reserves—in modern jargon, that it alleviates the international liquidity problem. When the rate of exchange is held at a given level, it can only be so held by the intervention of the monetary authorities who support it, when necessary, by buying their own currency in the exchange market with internationally acceptable currencies or with gold. Countries with balance-of-payments deficits must have large reserves of such media if they are to avoid devaluation. Moreover, the longer countries wish to stabilise their exchange rates the more they must be prepared to hold large reserve balances and, for the world economy as a whole, a stable exchange rate system can only be preserved if large and well-distributed reserves exist to support it. At the other extreme, if the rate is free to move without support no reserves will be required. In practice, even under a free-rate system, however, some minimal intervention by the authorities will take place to steady the rate and to limit day-to-day fluctuations. Such intervention, however, requires smaller reserves. The quantity of reserves required increases with the scope of intervention and the degree of stability of the rate which is required.

Finally, it is argued by some proponents of the free-rate system that, whatever risks may be involved in its adoption, it is at least superior to its alternatives; that domestic price and income adjustment is undesirable and politically non-feasible, that direct controls on payments abrogate the advantages of multilateral trade and that the system of periodic exchange rate adjustments has proved unworkable in practice. Only free exchange rates remain. The *a priori* case for such a system is strong. Moreover it is the one system of adjustment which has never truly been tested. The strength of such arguments is questionable. We shall leave this aspect of free exchange rates aside until we have looked more closely at the present system of so-called managed flexibility.

The case against flexible rates is fivefold. Firstly—and, patient reader, we shall be brief—there is the elasticity condition which broods menacing and imponderable over any adjustment system which relies on exchange rate variations. Even in the absence of reliable data on the magnitude of import-demand elasticities, it is certain that the foreign trade structure of some countries is less amenable to exchange rate adjustment than that of others. The adjustment qualities of a fluctuating rate are therefore likely to vary from country to country. The inelasticity of demand for imports and exports in the short run has already been referred to. Only for considerable rate changes which the commercial world deems likely to be of long duration will established trade links be severed and demand be switched from one country to another. For this reason the depreciation which influences the trade balance may have to be considerable and long-lasting, and the process of adjustment is likely to be a longer one than at first appears.

Secondly, it is alleged that rates of exchange that are free to vary from day to day have a deterrent effect on international trade. Profit margins are generally lower in international than in domestic trade. There is a danger that they may be eliminated entirely through a sudden change in the exchange rate which changes a price to be paid or received in respect of a foreign transaction. The additional trouble which is involved in selling abroad rather than at home is, it is argued, always considerable. To add an additional risk is to heap Pelion upon Ossa. These criticisms may be answered by three counter-claims. Firstly, are we sure that exporting and importing are so lightly motivated as to succumb so easily? Three types of firms engage in foreign trade: firms producing for an international market whose main or entire interest is in foreign trade; firms which, by the nature of their product or for other reasons, never engage in international trade; and firms which market their products both at home and abroad, and are in a position to make switches. This threefold classification applies to the export sector in foreign trade but it has its parallel on the import side.

The Economics of the Balance of Payments

Importers may be roughly divided into: habitual and committed importers who buy abroad because it is the only source of supply; traders who have no connection with foreign trade at all; and a larger group who move in and out of the import trade according to opportunities, price differentials and profit. Once more it is only upon the third group in each case that free rates will impose a choice of action. The deterrent effect of free rates, if it exists, will only bear upon the last group and it is doubtful if it will alter their decision to trade abroad one way or the other. It must not be assumed that free rates will necessarily be so unstable as to impair dealers' profit margins seriously. Day-to-day variations are likely to be slight and to impose negligible risk. Insofar as variations in the exchange rate occur, traders are as likely to gain as to lose by the variations. Moreover, risks can be hedged in the forward exchange market, although it must also be remembered that the coverage given by forward exchange transactions involves additional cost. All in all, it seems to the writer that the deterrent effect of free rates upon ordinary day-to-day import and export trade may be inconsiderable.

In Chapter 12 of his *International Monetary Relations*, Yeager reviews the whole question of exchange risk and how far it may act as a deterrent to international trade and investment. On exchange risk as a barrier to trade he reviews the empirical evidence and finds it inconclusive. As he points out, it is virtually impossible to compare trade for a given country in periods of fixed rates with trade in periods of floating rates since so many influences other than the exchange rate bear upon trade levels. From an excellent general discussion no firm conclusions emerge.

The third objection to free rates is that frequent variations in the value of a currency impede international investment. There is, under such a system, no fixed monetary relationship upon which international borrowing and lending contracts may be based. The prospect of a constantly fluctuating money value for a loan may certainly be discouraging either to borrower or lender, and the possibility of a varying burden for servicing and repayments may also be daunting. Nor can the risk be entirely avoided. The lender may shift the risk to the borrower by insisting that the loan be repaid and serviced in his own currency or some currency of his choice, but the risk and a possible deterrent effect remains. Yet is this risk sufficient to deter any but marginal borrowers from accepting foreign loans? It is arguable that borrowers and lenders are much more sensitive to price level prospects in their two countries than they are to changes in the exchange rate and that stability in the real domestic value of currencies is the true basis for international investment. Moreover, unless exchange rates are to be held steady forever, the effect of uncertainty as to their future value must always exist. Where loans are made for periods of five years or more the element of uncertainty as to what the rate may be at repayment will hardly be greater under flexible than under fixed rates. Uncertainty as to prospective rates of exchange, may, even with forward exchange markets, diminish slightly the volume of short-term lending which is dependent upon narrow interest rate differentials and cannot sustain even small exchange risks. But short-term funds movements more often than not are destabilising in their effects, and any tendency for them to diminish is not a matter for grief.

Fourthly, certain market aspects of free exchange rates are highlighted by critics as having potentially damaging features. Two such aspects stand out: the possibility of manipulation by government exchange funds to force a rate other than an equilibrium rate upon its neighbours; and the possibility of harmful speculation in the foreign exchange market. Let us look at these in turn.

There is little doubt that, in the absence of any co-ordinating international authority or agreed formula of foreign exchange manipulation, the system might lapse into anarchy as countries sought, not merely to iron out day-to-day fluctuations, but to establish unilaterally favourable exchange rates of their choice. Who can doubt, having read the currency history of the thirties or of the middle sixties, that the exchange rate is regarded by governments (and by some governments more than others) as a legitimate weapon of economic warfare. There is every reason to fear the effects of an undisciplined market of competitively manipulated rates. In the thirties, with the unemployment problem to solve and with the great trading countries hungry to hold and expand their markets in a world of stagnant international trade, competitive depreciation quickly emerged. The danger of its recurrence has been much in the minds of critics of flexible rates since the Second World War. But in the present age of full employment and near inflation competitive depreciation is a less likely problem than it was in the thirties. Some countries determined to improve their trade balances might incline towards it but most countries are now less eager to seize export markets than to import cheaply in order to ease the inflationary pressure in their economies. This might indicate a possibility of competitive appreciation but this is unlikely, for shortages of gold and foreign exchange reserves usually preclude deliberate attempts to force up currency values in an effort to improve the terms of trade. In present circumstances, there is little cause for anxiety that currency manipulation would be any more of a problem under flexible rates than it has been during the period of managed flexibility. Moreover, it is realistic to assume that any flexible rate system of the future would not be so entirely free as to permit unilateral manipulation, but would be under the supervision of an international organisation or be governed by specified working principles through which this danger might be avoided.

Another alleged danger of a free exchange market is that of harmful speculation. Here, there is considerable difference of opinion; and before assessing the weight of this criticism we must decide just what speculation has to do to be 'harmful'. Speculation is, after all, a part, an indispensable part, of any foreign exchange market. The role which it plays in subjecting rates and cross-rates in the market to continuous scrutiny, and in settling the relation between the spot and forward markets, has already been described. In general, speculation may be described as harmful if it causes a rate to fluctuate more frequently or in greater amplitude than it would in the absence of speculation; if it causes a rate to be held for a prolonged period at a level other than the equilibrium level, or if it places strain on a country's reserves in order to preserve the equilibrium level, and finally, if speculators are able to earn abnormal profits at the expense of traders. Opponents of flexible rates who argue that adverse effects come from speculation claim empirical support[12] and invoke one of the minor ghosts of the thirties to appear to the deluded proponents in dreadful warning.

It is hard to see much unanimity, one way or the other, in the empirical evidence. Tsiang examined the record for three European countries for the period 1919–26[13] and concluded that, on balance, speculation had not been destabilising. An examination of Peru's experience with flexible rates from 1950–1954 brought the opinion that speculation did not increase the instability of the rate. Two other writers,[14] however, examining the cases of Europe in the early twenties and Canada in the 1950s, found no evidence to suggest that speculation destabilised exchange rates. Whatever the opinions and interpretations, it seems likely that conditions have so changed since the early twenties that experience in that period probably has little relevance to the present day. In the case of the Canadian experiment in the fifties, the balance of opinion appears to be that short-money movements played a stabilising role. Kindleberger argues, however, that this may have been the result of the monetary and fiscal policies pursued by the Canadian authorities during the free-rate period rather than of the behaviour pattern of the rate itself.[15]

There has been some theoretical attack on speculation. The argument of the critics is that, as a currency depreciates, speculators will anticipate a further depreciation by selling the currency short. This will drive the rate lower than ordinary trade forces might be expected to send it. It will go lower and recover later under the influence of speculation. Baumol in a well-known article,[16] develops a model according to which speculators buy on a rising market for a currency and sell on a falling market. If, as Baumol assumes, a foreign exchange rate will follow a cyclical path in the absence of speculation, then the intervention of speculators, who buy on the upswing and sell on the downswing, will cause an increase in the speed and amplitude of the cycle.

Milton Friedman leads the case for defence of speculation. To him, speculation is stabilising when it moves a rate nearer to its equilibrium level. Much of the linking of speculation with exchange rate movements is not, he argues, concerned with flexible rates, but with the very different case of a fixed rate under suspicion of alteration. Here there is no risk to the speculator. The rate may change or not change: if it changes, it will change only in one expected direction. Not only can speculation force the change by anticipating it, but it can be indulged in without fear of loss. The case against speculation, Friedman argues, is confused: 'many of the capital movements regarded as demonstrating that foreign exchange speculation is destabilising were stimulated by the existence of rigid rates subject to change by government action and are to be attributed primarily to the absence of flexibility of rates and hence of any incentive to avoid the capital movements'.[17] Turning then to speculation under flexible rates, Friedman argues that, since speculation takes place, speculators must, on balance, make money from the practice. At the same time to argue that speculation is destabilising 'is largely equivalent to saying that speculators lose money, since speculation can be destabilising in general only if speculators on the average sell when the currency is low in price and buy when it is high'.[18] If speculation were always destabilising then government foreign exchange operations, like the British Exchange Equalisation Account, could consistently make money at the expense of the speculators and could eliminate the destabilising speculation. This is equivalent to arguing that monetary authorities using public money are better speculators than private speculators using their own – a point which Friedman, but not, one suspects, everybody, is unwilling to admit. To argue that profitable speculation is stabilising and that unprofitable speculation is destabilising and that, for the most part, we can therefore trust the speculators to make interventions in the market which are in the general interest has a certain naïveté which invokes suspicion. In reviewing the literature on the effects of speculation under flexible exchange rates it seems to this writer inescapable that we do not know either from *a priori* reasoning or from the record whether its influence would be baneful or beneficial. All that can be said is that at least it would be true speculation, with a chance for the speculator either of loss or gain. This is more than can be said of the one-way option which speculation becomes under the system of managed flexibility.

One may also say that under managed flexibility many persons and groups other than professional speculators take part in speculation. In the great speculative attacks on sterling from 1964 to 1967, the so-called leads-and-lags effect was of great importance and in this ordinary exporters and importers are the villains of the piece. Moreover the movement of balances out of sterling by large international companies played its part. Under free exchange rates, it may be argued, speculation would be largely confined to the professionals.

The fifth danger to which a free exchange market would be subject has already been mentioned; but to complete the catalogue of counter-arguments and because the writer believes it to be the greatest counter-argument and the one which, most of all, influences the financial establishment, we shall mention it again briefly. It is the possibility of 'feedback of depreciation upon the domestic price level of a country to produce inflation and therefore the need for further depreciation'.[19] This danger appears daunting to a country like Britain with a large unavoidable import of food and raw materials and an economy ever within the zone of inflation. It is arguable, however, as Lutz claims[20] that for most trading countries imports do not bulk large enough in the cost-of-living index to raise wages enough to nullify the depreciation. In any event, the time lag between a depreciation, a rise in the cost of living, and a rise in the wage level is likely to be so long that in the interim the depreciation might improve the trade balance considerably. Again, no one knows. It would be a courageous analyst who would be dogmatic as to what effect a floating rate for sterling would, if imposed in 1955, have had upon British economic fortunes in the later fifties and early sixties. To ponder this is to be quickly convinced that free rates require skilful domestic management, monetary, fiscal and wages policies to supplement them and to check and counter-check their effects. It is arguable, and the Canadian case gives some support, that a floating rate experiment is most likely to succeed in a country which is already in a strong economic position and which uses its floating exchange rate to consolidate that position by discouraging a large inflow of capital.

One device which might, if added to a system of flexible exchange rates, allow exchange rate changes to be used as the method of foreign-balance adjustment, while ensuring that depreciation proceeded neither so fast nor so far as to cause dire inflationary consequences, is that of the 'band' system. Under such an arrangement countries would define a range over which their exchange rates might vary but beyond which any depreciation would be checked by the use of foreign exchange reserves. Simultaneously domestic policies of disinflation could be pursued to nullify the inflationary effects of the depreciation. The band could be widened as experience and confidence grew. As long as free rates are not allowed to operate in a purely automatic fashion, there should be little danger that the inflationary influence will become uncontrollable.

Such is the argument for and against free exchange rates. As one writer says: 'There are clearly arguments on both sides. There is no absolute truth in this matter.'[21] The case is finely balanced. No system of international equilibrium can be perfect and the best that we can do is to decide wherein the balance of advantage lies. There are but four alternatives by which changes in a balance of payments can be met: by transferring reserves; by changing domestic income and prices; by varying the exchange rate; or by directly controlling flows of trade and payments. If we are driven to reject adjustment by variation of domestic income and prices then we must accept the only viable alternative within a liberal trade system, exchange rate variation. The implications of this choice have been sensed rather than understood. Prejudiced against flexible exchange rates by a questionable interpretation of limited historical evidence there was in 1944 an attempt to compromise and to dodge the issue by the adoption of a system which it was thought would make use of exchange rate changes when they were needed, but for the rest would allow for the use of reserve transfers. It is on the record of this system that the writer believes the acceptance or non-acceptance of flexible rates must hang. The case for and against them reviewed above is inconclusive, but if to that is added a strong argument, backed by twenty years' experience, that exchange rate variation of the Bretton Woods type is unsuccessful then, the writer believes, the balance of advantage must point to flexible rates as the sole untried alternative which can preserve the international economy from lapsing into a new era of rigidly controlled trade and protectionism.

Before leaving our examination of free exchanges, it is necessary to be more precise about the term itself. In presenting the case for and against free rates, the writer has envisaged a foreign exchange market in which rates would be free to follow market forces, but in which there would be some intervention by exchange funds to counter any adverse effects of speculation. This is the free-rate system implicit in much of the academic discussion of free rates over the past twenty years. Recently, however, and as the possibility of modifying the Bretton Woods system has become stronger, writers have been more specific and a recognisable set of variations to that system, all falling within the free-rate spectrum, have emerged. We shall do no more here than categorise the term. It would be impossible in short compass to discuss the many special problems of each sub-set of the system.

A free-rate system — defined as a movement towards greater freedom of rates than exists at present under the IMF — may be seen as dividing into the following alternatives:

1. Amendments to the present system, either
   (a) by more frequent changes of IMF parities, or
   (b) by a wider band between the upper and lower limits on either side of parities;
2. Floating rates, either
   (a) completely free rates settled in a market free from any intervention, or
   (b) flexible rates settled in a market stabilised by the monetary authority;
3. Mixed systems, either
   (a) 'crawling peg' systems whereby rates are subject to periodic small changes of, say, 2 or 3 per cent per annum, or
   (b) fixed exchange rates adjusted at stated intervals by a period of floating in order to find a new equilibrium rate.

(vi) Managed Flexibility

We come now to the third alternative system of international adjustment, that which has obtained since the Second World War — the so-called system of 'managed flexibility' or the method of the 'adjustable peg'. In examining this system we must distinguish between its theoretical model as envisaged by its founders and what it has become in practice.

Managed flexibility can only be understood in the light of its historical beginnings. The economists and financial experts who planned the post-war monetary system in the years 1942–4[22] were influenced by two features of the interwar period payments system and sought to avoid them: the disadvantages of the old gold standard, which required countries to subjugate domestic policy objectives to control of the balance of payments; and the apparent disadvantages of fluctuating rates, in particular, competitive depreciation. They tried to embody in the new system the advantages of both previous systems without incurring the disadvantages of either. The result was a compromise system referred to as one of managed flexibility since both the elements of control and flexibility were supposed to have been taken from the older systems. As time passed and the system proved anything but flexible the name adjustable peg became more common — though how frequently the peg (exchange rate) could be adjusted was open to question.

The system called for individual countries to stabilise their domestic economies at full employment and to seek adjustment of their balances of payments through infrequent changes in otherwise fixed exchange rates. From an institutional standpoint the system may be achieved by country A defining the value of its currency unit in terms of gold and, if countries B, C, and D do likewise, then indirectly the exchange rates between all four currencies are also determined. (In the case of the Bretton Woods system, parities were defined in terms of the U.S. dollar, which was in turn defined in gold terms.) The parity of a currency with gold may be defined at a single level, which gives a single value for the exchange rate, or different buying and selling prices for gold in terms of currency may be declared, thus giving the exchange rate a range of fluctuation commensurate with the spread between the two prices. When a country wishes to alter its exchange rate, it alters the parity of its currency unit with gold. Thus, under conditions of managed flexibility the change of rate is made on the decision of the monetary authority, is a deliberate policy action to achieve adjustment and is of such magnitude as will in its judgement serve to restore equilibrium. With this system, there are no short-term fluctuations of rate and for purposes of day-to-day business the rate may be taken as fixed and given.

The system of managed flexibility resembles in important aspects the method of free rates. Both envisage disequilibria in the external balance as correctable by exchange rate changes, both reject the method of domestic income adjustment, and both are subject to the same condition (i.e. the condition of high elasticity of demand for imports and exports) if they are to be effective. But the adjustable peg carries additional consequences and the choice between it and flexible rates is a very significant one. It raises, for example, the whole question of the management of exchange rates. Who is to manage? With whom lie the vital decisions of co-ordinating rate changes; of deciding when they shall take place and how big they are to be? The IMF as the sovereign authority was somewhat mistily seen to share responsibility with individual governments, but the division of authority was left to be worked out in practice. The question of the frequency of exchange rate changes also arises as does the size and distribution of stocks of international liquidity, whose world optimum level is conditioned by the role which exchange rates are expected to play in the system.

It is important in forming a judgement on the adjustable peg system first to see just how, in a given balance-of-payments disequilibrium, the system works and in particular what set of adjustment forces comes into operation in a situation of imbalance. Suppose that a country within the IMF system suffers a deficit in its balance of payments. The exchange rate

The Economics of the Balance of Payments

for the currency of that country will depreciate to the lower limit of the allowable range of 2·25 per cent above and below parity. At the lower point, it will be supported as the exchange fund of the deficit country buys, with its foreign exchange reserves, all excess offers of its own currency. If the deficit is brief and self-correcting, for example, if it were due to a crop failure, a sudden and brief failure of demand in a foreign market, or a temporary burst of inflation, the country may incur nothing worse than a fall in its reserves, but if the deficit is of longer duration, the drain on the reserves may be large and to avoid their depletion the deficit country will be obliged to seek some means of reinforcing them, either by borrowing from a surplus country or by borrowing from the IMF. If the deficit and the outflow of reserves persist to an extent in which even this reinforcement proves insufficient to support the rate, then we may suppose that it will be devalued. The time during which these events take place will, of course, differ according to the size of the deficit, the rate of outflow of the reserves, and the amount of reinforcement to them which is made available, but it is likely to extend over some months and even in some cases to exceed a year. We must ask ourselves: in the absence of domestic policies to correct the deficit, what adjustment forces within the adjustable peg system are invoked to correct the deficit? The short answer is, only very inadequate forces. The original deficit in the trade balance causes income to fall in the deficit country. This in turn causes imports to fall, thus partially correcting the original import surplus. If the deficit causes the country to lose gold and if the authorities allow the gold loss to reduce the money supply, interest rates will rise and by checking investment cause a further decline in income. This in turn will cause imports to decline still further. It is also possible that the rise in interest rates may attract short-term capital to the deficit country thus improving the balance of payments on capital account. It may be questioned whether this should be included as a movement of adjustment. Such short-term capital may move out again with the next change in interest rates, leaving the trade gap still open. It is also questionable whether the fall in imports stemming from the fall in income will be sufficient to fully adjust the deficit in the balance of payments. The likely situation is that, prices being inflexible, the fall in imports (and perhaps increase in exports) resulting from income changes in themselves will not be sufficient to completely adjust the balance of payments. Moreover, adjustment, to whatever extent it takes place, is likely to be a protracted affair. The longer it is delayed the greater the call which will be made upon the reserves of the deficit country.

The adjustable peg system does not present us with the same difficulties in assessment as does flexible rates. We have had over twenty years of experience of the system. Even with the pull which the known has over the unknown, the tried over the inexperienced, there are surprisingly few informed people who wish to retain the system. Those who do wish to retain it seem to do so not for its own sake but for what the system has become—a near approximation to the gold exchange standard. Whatever may be the aversion to fixed exchange rates and the gold standard in academic circles, it is still a much-loved old flame of central bankers and the financial establishment. The system's worth can now be assessed predominantly on the record, but it is worth adding to that, if only for the sake of completeness, a review of some of the advantages and disadvantages of the system.

The system has some theoretical backing. If, as is generally agreed, import and export demand are sensitive to price changes only in the fairly long run, why should we accept the disadvantages of continuously fluctuating exchange rates? Why not meet short-run movements of the balance of payments by drawing upon national exchange reserves and changing the rate only in response to changes in the long-run equilibrium position? If the ruling rate of exchange is an equilibrium one, then, in the long-run, the distribution of the existing stock of international liquidity will not be altered. This, however, and the fact that some of the irritant effects of free rates are avoided, seems to exhaust the case for the defence of the adjustable peg system. The case for the prosecution is more lengthy.

The greatest defect of the system of managed flexibility is that it lacks an adjustment mechanism and throws inordinate strain on the reserves of participant countries. Unless exchange rate parities are to be changed frequently there is no variable through which adjustment can be effected. With the gold standard the price/cost structure is the strategic variable. Under flexible rates, it is the rate of exchange. With the mixed system both domestic incomes and the exchange rate are stable, so that there is no means whereby in the short and medium term the foreign balance can be adjusted. It is arguable, and defenders of the adjustable peg have argued, that there is in any case no available means of adjustment and that deficit countries must live by their reserves but that, in the long period the exchange rate must be the adjuster. This is true, but if the adjustable peg is to have its claimed advantage over the freely varying rate system, changes in parities must be only at long intervals—presumably of years. Frequent discrete alterations of rate would be worse than a rate which moved with the market. The fact is that, by attempting to reap the best of both the pure systems of adjustment, managed flexibility is not a true adjustment system at all. Ideally an adjustment system should invoke restorative forces immediately a disequilibrium develops. This takes place under a gold

The Economics of the Balance of Payments

standard where short-term capital movements serve towards correction of the deficit as soon as the central banks involved react to the gold flow by appropriate changes in interest rates. Similarly under a system of flexible rates, the exchange rate will depreciate immediately there is any discrepancy between the demand for and the supply of the deficit country's currency. Under the system of the adjustable peg, however, correction of the deficit cannot begin until the deficit country's rate has been altered, and if the alteration is itself obliged to wait upon proof of the existence of disequilibrium, then by the time remedial measures are taken, the disequilibrium may be great. It is indeed hard to see how a movement of the adjustable peg can ever be anything save a crisis measure taken under the duress of a deteriorating situation.

The second defect of the system of managed flexibility lies in who is to manage and how. First, there is a problem of division of authority between individual national governments and whatever international authority may exist to oversee the system. If power is to be left with the individual national governments, how are their aims (even if similar in principle) to be co-ordinated so as to achieve the necessary parallel movements of prices and incomes. If management is to be by an international authority, how is that authority to establish power over member nations and how make it effective? This problem has never been met in the institutional arrangements which have governed world payments since 1945. The IMF has never been a sovereign authority, never possessed more than the power to persuade, cajole and nag. It has possessed few sanctions to apply to recalcitrant member states save, since 1956, the denial of its help to members. The main realignments of exchange rates, in 1949 and in 1967, were decided upon by states themselves and the IMF has often had to yield primacy of influence to other powers – for example, to the committee of central bankers comprising the so-called Basle Club or, in the fifties, to regional currency groupings such as the European Payments Union. The IMF has certainly provided a forum for discussion of international monetary problems; it has, by provision of currencies to deficit countries, augmented the world's stock of international liquidity and it has often influenced national policies. But the strategic decisions of a 'managed' adjustment system have been taken elsewhere, and it has not provided the control centre of an international payments and adjustment system. The fact that such a system has in fact endured for more than twenty years has not been due to the merits of the system itself but to various mitigating factors: to the fact that it was liberally bolstered up by direct controls over balances of payments until 1959; to the fact that in the days of dollar shortage the United States was prepared to supply its currency to deficit countries in liberal amount; and to the fact that central bankers favouring fixed exchange rates were, again and again in the sixties, prepared to make stabilisation loans available for the support of a key exchange rate.

The difficulties of management by national monetary authorities are two in number. First, it must be decided in what circumstances a change of rate should be made. Should a change be discretionary or according to a defined formula? If discretionary then countries may be tempted into unilaterally advantageous manipulations of rate; if according to formula, the change may be anticipated and be the occasion for one-way speculation. Moreover if change is to be by formula, what is the formula to be?

The difficulty of establishing a criterion according to which a country may devalue is extreme. It is well-nigh impossible to anticipate all of the conditions in which devaluation may be appropriate. One solution might be that a country with a chronic balance-of-payments deficit (chronic in the sense of size and longevity) should be allowed to devalue. But the cure cannot be divorced from the cause. If the balance-of-payments deficit is due to over-full employment in the domestic economy its cure lies, not in devaluation, but in domestic measures to reduce the level of activity in the economy. Conversely a country which is in external balance but is also underemployed is one whose problem might well be solved by devaluation which through expansion in the export industries would relieve domestic unemployment and still preserve foreign balance. Yet if we insist on balance-of-payments disequilibrium as our ruling criterion, the solution of devaluation would be denied to such a country.

There exists also the difficulty that, even if a country's balance of payments is in deficit, even if it is losing reserves, even if there is unemployment, it still does not follow that devaluation is the measure appropriate to deal with the disequilibrium. Balance-of-payments disequilibrium may spring from many causes, not all of which are amenable to this treatment. Such causes may be cyclical disturbances, changes in relative prices, or structural changes in demand and supply conditions. If the external deficit is due to cyclical causes the disturbance is likely to be world-wide, all countries suffering decline in incomes, prices and employment. Devaluation here would serve no useful purpose but would merely create a series of competitive devaluations. If the deficit is due to a change in relative prices (to a rise in domestic prices or a fall in prices abroad), then devaluation is an appropriate means of restoring an equilibrium price level relationship; and if the deficit is due to a structural shift of demand, the effects of devaluation will depend upon a number of contingent factors — upon the size of the country concerned, upon the nature of the products which it exports, and upon their relative importance in its balance of payments.

The difficulty of defining a suitable criterion for devaluation or of operating one once established has been met by the IMF with its vague condition that devaluation is only permissible in face of a 'fundamental disequilibrium'. This term remains undefined: there is an implication, however, that no definition is necessary but that the condition is clearly recognisable when it arises. It foredooms each case to be considered exhaustively on its merits making it inevitable that public as well as private debate shall pervade each balance-of-payments problem creating a crisis atmosphere and making devaluation a matter for speculation – in the most literal sense.

The second difficulty of national management under managed flexibility is that of choosing a value for the new rate once a change is decided upon. The difficulties of actually calculating a value for the equilibrium rate have already been referred to (see pp. 450–4 above) and it was seen that the alternatives were two: either to free the rate and allow it to find its own level before stabilising it, or to estimate it with the aid of the purchasing-power-parity formula. The former method is in itself a departure from managed flexibility, so that we are driven to the second. Apart from the difficulty of reliable estimation, there exists the likelihood that a country may devalue its rate by more than necessary. The fact that devaluation should not be made frequently may well tempt the deficit country's monetary authorities to make a sharp reduction, the preference being to err on the side of undervaluation. The consequences of error may be considerable. If the reduction has been too great, other countries may devalue also to protect their competitive position; if it has been too small, even the new rate may be quickly under suspicion of being too high. The brute fact is that a country faced with devaluation will choose the new rate in accordance with the crude practical politics of the situation and with scant regard for the concept of an equilibrium rate.

The third and possibly the greatest drawback of the system of the adjustable peg is the role which speculation assumes under that system. Once a currency falls under suspicion of impending devaluation speculators have a strong incentive to move funds from the weak currency to one which is strong. Without fear of loss and with the growing chance of handsome profit, the movement away from the threatened currency will continue either until it is devalued and the currency is bought back at a profit, or until the monetary authorities in the deficit country can convince speculators that devaluation will not take place. This speculation has special features which make it qualitatively different and more damaging to the whole payments system than any speculation likely under a free rate. In the first place it is extremely widespread. Not only professional speculators but all who carry on ordinary trade or who habitually hold working balances in foreign currencies may participate.[23] Traders speculate against the deficit country by delaying payments of their debts to it; importers at home pay their debts promptly in case the rate is devalued. Working balances are shifted out for safety. Professional speculators sell the currency forward, hoping for devaluation before delivery and the closing of the position. A second aspect of such speculation is that it may imperil more than one currency. If currency A falls under suspicion of devaluation, not only will it be under speculative pressure but other currencies may become questioned as well either because they are accustomed to preserve a parity with the threatened currency and would devalue with it or because a devaluation of A would cause a general realignment of currency values and B and C are likely to be devalued. It is even possible for a country whose balance of payments is in equilibrium to be threatened by speculation because another country is in strong surplus and its currency is suspected of being revalued. A speculative movement into such a strong currency must necessarily be to the detriment of the currencies which are sold.

It is not difficult to imagine that, in extreme circumstances, a country might be driven to devalue its currency by pressure of speculation alone. The long series of speculative attacks on sterling in the late fifties and in the sixties comes immediately to mind. As a reserve currency sterling is vulnerable to speculation. In 1957, it was brought near to devaluation by the strength of the Deutschmark and anticipation of its revaluation. This drained funds swiftly out of sterling until weakness of that currency caused speculators to turn their attention to it and to speculate on its devaluation. One of the fiercest speculative attacks ever made on sterling was in 1964, when it was expected that the Labour government would devalue. Only a hastily organised loan of \$3 billion by the central banks of the Basle Club saved sterling on this occasion. Such speculation as occurs with the adjustable peg serves no useful purpose. Indeed, being a one-way option it is hardly speculation at all, but a profit made at the expense of the monetary authorities in the deficit country. The monetary authority in A, the deficit country, will, in order to maintain the peg, have to buy its own currency as long as speculators are selling it, and later, when devaluation has taken place, they will have to sell it at the lower rate in order to maintain the peg. This form of speculation against the currency of the deficit country has been one of the most destabilising features of the foreign exchange market during the period of the adjustable peg.

Finally, in the case against the adjustable peg, there is the lesson of the record of the past twenty years. There is no intention here of examining this record in detail,[24] but it is worthwhile setting out what seem to the writer to be its main features. Four points seem to be significant.

First, although the adjustable peg system has been in operation since the IMF began currency operations in March 1947, it was for twelve years a hybrid system in which exchange rates were supported by large stabilisation loans and by the European Recovery Programme, while all major countries save the United States operated systems of control over trade and payments. Not until 1959, when Western European currencies were made freely convertible and the main structure of exchange controls was dismantled, was the so-called Bretton Woods system called upon to function in the way its architects had intended. Judgements upon its efficiency and durability must be based on a narrower range of experience than first appears. Since the Smithsonian Agreement of December 1971 brought the first major change in the Bretton Woods system we must regard the sixties as the period in which its performance must be judged.

The second feature of interest has been that, as might have been expected on theoretical grounds, the need for large and well-distributed international reserves manifested itself from the first. Not only was this need born of the fact that a system of fixed exchange rates needs higher reserves, but also that reserves had come in the sixties to mean key currencies, the United States dollar and the pound, and that each of these currencies had its own special problems which inhibited its efficiency as a key currency. The IMF with its limited currency resources and, in particular, its limited supply of key currencies, proved woefully inadequate in its original role as supplier of international liquidity. The slowness of governments and monetary authorities to accept the principle of an international credit unit and to proceed with the technical task of providing one left a basically simple dilemma: that there was not sufficient international liquidity to maintain the sort of fixed rate system which the IMF and the main monetary authorities of the world appeared to want. Something had to give. Either there had to be a large creation of international liquidity, or, with existing liquidity there had to be more frequent variations of exchange rates.

The third feature which must emerge from any close scrutiny of the adjustable peg system in action is the way in which over its life its image has changed. Seen originally by its founders as a system in which exchange rates were to be varied from time to time, it became in the sixties and seventies virtually a system of fixed rates. All behaviour, all utterances and public pronouncements either by the pundits of the IMF or the inmates of central banks and treasuries in member countries indicated a collective view that an exchange rate should be almost immutable, that only in the last of many last ditches should it be changed and that all other policies for dealing with balance-of-payments disequilibria should have priority over devaluation. The opposing view, that the exchange rate, although an important price, is still only a price, and as such subject to change; that it is in fact of all prices the one whose changes are most effective in changing the relative price structures of countries, and that variations in this strategic price as a key control in economic policy are too important to forego – this view has been and is held by academic economists and some of the more enlightened financial journalists. It is a vocal group. It has commented often on the driving, but unfortunately it does not sit at the wheel.

Finally, from the record comes one overwhelming fact. It is that speculation plays a unique and destabilising role in the adjustable peg system. The record of the system over the past ten years gives ample demonstration of speculation's deleterious effects.

(vii) The Choice of an Adjustment System

The choice between the available adjustment policies is now before us. In essence, it is a choice between how much we shall use manipulation of the domestic economy and how much we shall use exchange rates and, if the latter, which of two possible systems will we employ.

It is the opinion of the writer that manipulation of the domestic income and price level must now be regarded as subsidiary to changes in exchange rates. The firm commitment of governments to full-employment policies and the unimpressive record of stop-go policies in dealing with balance-of-payments deficits have, we believe, relegated domestic policies to limited use in two particular situations: as back-up policies to exchange rate changes; and as means of dealing with external imbalance which is the result of the domestic level of income, that is to say, where a deficit is the result of domestic inflation or a surplus of domestic underemployment. With the relegation of domestic adjustment to this subsidiary role, we must turn to exchange rate changes as the main vehicle of adjustment. We are faced with the choice of two systems, fixed or flexible. Which shall it be?

The case for and against both exchange rate systems has been reviewed and the balance of advantage may be variously interpreted. A choice has to be made and the writer believes that it should be for flexible exchange rates. The reason for this choice is twofold: firstly, because it seems that, even on *a priori* reasoning the balance of advantage lies narrowly on that side; secondly, because the record of the adjustable peg system has demonstrated its faults abundantly – in particular, the vulnerability of key exchange rates to speculation and the inadequacy under present conditions of international reserves to underpin a fixed exchange rate system.

If we choose flexible exchange rates, how flexible should they be? This is a wide choice ranging from free rates, free to vary with every market influence to flexible rates, influenced in their daily variations by exchange funds and perhaps limited in their fluctuation by a specified range. This latter system has much to commend it. If the exchange fund interventions are skilful, the day-to-day fluctuations of the rate will be minimal; speculation and all the normal operations of an orderly exchange market, spot and forward, will be able to function. If this market is defined by the monetary authority as operating within a range ± 5 per cent from the notified parity of the currency, we then have a permissible depreciation and appreciation which is large enough to influence goods flows and relative prices, but not so large even at its maximum amplitude as to allow uncontrollable swings in domestic prices. Moreover the degree of major intervention by exchange funds will be lessened. Smoothing operations within the range will largely iron themselves out over a period of months. Only when the rate depreciates to the lower end of the range will continued large-scale support operations be necessary. It will be necessary, however, to provide means whereby the range may be widened in the longer run. Where a structural change in a country's trade takes place, the rate may well depreciate to the lower limit and remain there, supported by a continuous outflow of the national reserves. A choice will then have to be made between widening the range, say from 5 per cent to 10 per cent, or of keeping the range at ± 5 per cent and reducing the median parity. In general it appears preferable to do the latter and to write into the IMF rules a procedure for the altering of parities at long intervals to meet structural changes in countries' trade. There is nothing sacrosanct about 5 per cent and that figure is chosen merely as an example. A very wide range would, however, approximate to a full free rate system. Whatever the range may be it would be well for its limits to be regarded as inviolable and not as points to be changed arbitrarily from time to time.

There would be little difficulty in adapting such a mechanism as this to fit into and preserve the Bretton Woods System. Section (iv) of the articles of Agreement of the IMF could be amended to allow a wider range than 2·25 per cent above and below parity. The rules for changing a parity should remain and be applied, as now, to deal with the case of a fundamental disequilibrium.

In the discussion of alternative adjustment systems in this chapter and by our advocacy, at the eleventh hour, of a method of adjustment chosen from those already discussed, we have to some extent implied a rejection of a balance-of-payments policy which is often loosely regarded as a form of adjustment, namely the method of direct controls of either goods flows or payments. That this method is not a true adjustment policy but a policy of suppression of balance-of-payments disequilibrium we have already argued. That it has uses as a balance of payments policy is, however, undeniable. To the uses and limitations of such controls we turn in the next chapter.

19
Direct Controls on Trade and Payments

(i) Introduction

CONTROLS on trade and payments do not constitute a method of adjustment of the balance of payments; rather they are intended to suppress imbalance and neutralise its effects. Yet, in practical situations this somewhat academic distinction is often blurred, and to the policy-maker the choice between direct controls and true adjustment methods appears simpler than to the economist. Logic and completeness demand consideration of all aspects. Moreover, in a world where economic policies, including the processes of balance-of-payments adjustment, express the authoritarian and neo-mercantilist spirit of the age, controls become economic tools in the hands of politicians, to be used partly for economic and partly for political ends. They take unto themselves a rather sinister aura and the motivation of those who employ them is clouded.

In the matter of choice of direct controls or of true adjustment methods we stand now in a critical position, and the historical aspects of the choice are worth brief consideration. The high tide of free trade and belief in the merits of a multilateral world economy, which had flowed in the late nineteenth century, ebbed in the twentieth, as the old international economy disintegrated under the impact of the First World War and governments sought not only new external policies but also defence mechanisms whereby they might be protected from the effects of the breakdown of *laissez-faire* and the impact of the business cycle. In Britain, first the McKenna duties in 1915 and later the Ottawa Agreements of 1932 marked the reversion from free trade of the only major power which had gone to the limit in her nineteenth-century open-door policies. In the United States, a series of protective measures sought to mitigate the effects of cheap imports upon the American economy. In Canada, the progressive lowering of the tariff which had gone on between 1900 and 1930 was interrupted by drastic increases aimed forlornly at insulating the Canadian economy from the effects of world recession. In the monetary sector the break down of the gold standard in 1931 marked a watershed between the old multilateral world and the new encroachments of neo-mercantilism. The innocent announcement by the British government in February 1932 that an Exchange Equalisation Account was to be set up to eliminate the effects of minor fluctuations in the sterling exchange rate marked the beginning of control by the British monetary authorities, which quietly in the thirties and spectacularly in the forties was to develop into the most grandiose and complete structure of exchange control ever seen. In Central Europe, the thirties saw the development, particularly in Nazi Germany, of elaborate exchange control systems. By the end of the Second World War the processes of control over payments and discrimination and protection of trade had become world-wide and included every major power. When the IMF began operations in 1947 only five members – El Salvador, Guatemala, Mexico, Panama and the United States – were reported as not applying direct restrictions on their trade and payments.

Yet this resurgence of control over world trade produced its own reaction. The United States, itself a protectionist country, while tolerant of tariffs, was in the late thirties and in the forties hostile to payments controls and discrimination in trade. The views of Cordell Hull and the group who had worked for American acceptance of the most-favoured-nation principle in the 1920s were formative in American post-war foreign economic policy. The Americans emerged in the negotiations which preceded Bretton Woods (1942–4), in the Fund itself and in all their overseas trade policies in the forties and fifties, as the leaders of a new drive to establish and maintain multilateral trade and payments. The Bretton Woods system and the IMF, conceived by the British primarily as a supplier of international liquidity and a framework for the ordering of exchange rates and only secondarily for the removal of restrictions on trade and payments, was seen by the Americans as having the inverse order of priorities. Urged by the Fund, liberally assisted by American programmes of aid and stabilisation loans, the international economy moved haltingly towards the liberation of trade and payments. Not until 1959, when the main Western European countries declared their currencies convertible into dollars and dismantled their systems of exchange control, was the Bretton Woods system fully established.

The Bretton Woods system has been in full operation for little more than a decade – a period in which two forces have emerged which threaten its continuance and, in particular, the multilateral trade which it established. These two forces are (a) the lack within the IMF system of any built-in system of adjustment and (b) a shortage and maldistribution of inter-

The Economics of the Balance of Payments

national liquidity. Changes in exchange rates on the Fund pattern are, as we have argued above, an ineffectual adjustment device while the large reserves which would be needed to underpin a system of almost unchanging exchange rates are lacking in the present world economy. In this situation and with the major powers anxious to avoid deviations from full employment, it is an ever-present danger that they will fall back upon 'imbalance repression' rather than 'imbalance adjustment', that is upon direct controls on trade or payments. There are straws in the wind. The 15 per cent import surcharge imposed by the British government in 1964 in response to the considerable lobby in that country calling for direct controls; the resort by France to import controls in the fall of 1968; the various fiscal devices imposed by countries to influence imports (an example of such a device would be the import-deposit scheme imposed by the British government late in 1968) and exports; the two-tier currency markets introduced by France and other countries in the early seventies — all these are signs that we might quickly revert to direct controls to seek solutions to our balance-of-payments-problems. To these have been added in the late sixties the growing realisation that the United States, once the powerful opponent of direct interference in trade and the balance of payments, has become an increasing exponent of quota restrictions and direct monetary controls in order to deal with her prolonged and growing external deficit. As the difficulty of adjusting her massive balance of payments in order to preserve the gold value of the dollar has become chronic, and as the instability of her currency has involved confidence problems, she has retreated progressively into a new protectionism which already has taken, and may continue to take, many restricting forms, of which the 10 per cent surcharge on imports imposed by Nixon in August 1971 was but one example. American acceptance of suppression methods and retaliation by other countries could well lead us into a new jungle of trade restrictions from which it would be difficult to free ourselves.

An emotive note creeps into discussion of direct controls on trade and payments. Their evaluation, although an economic task, still lies too near to politics for the balanced view and the sober judgement to prevail. In this chapter we shall try to stand back a little and see the outline of the whole picture. We shall attempt to answer a simple question: how can direct controls and import restrictions be of use in balance-of-payments policy?

(ii) The Mechanism of Control

The devices of control on trade and payments are many and various. A complete catalogue cannot be attempted. We can, however, attempt a classification and try to identify the main principles upon which the functioning of control devices relies.

Three main groups of controls exist. There are financial controls, which include all the systems and devices of exchange control, of multiple currency practices and of fiscal policies designed to influence specific items of the balance of payments. The second group is that of commercial controls, including quantitative restrictions, embargoes, tariff quotas and the buying policy of state-trading monopolies. Finally, there is control of capital movements, which although relevant to the class of financial controls, is important enough to be worth separate attention.[1] Within each group there is much diversification. On the whole, however, controls are all variations on these three main themes.

Central among financial controls is exchange control, which aims at equilibrating receipts and payments in the foreign balance. The main distinguishing feature of any system of exchange control is that all incoming payments to the country, representing a receipt of foreign currencies, are surrendered to a central, government-imposed authority, which in turn allocates and must sanction all payments to foreigners. Thus the available foreign currency is pooled and rationed to users according to government-established criteria of priority. The chosen official exchange rate may be maintained by always holding the foreign currencies supplied to those wishing to make payments abroad to the amount becoming available from foreign currency earnings. Typically and in more practical terms, all foreign currencies earned by home nationals must be surrendered to the central bank: all payments to foreign nationals must be sanctioned by the central bank. The central bank seeks to regulate demand and supply so as to maintain the official exchange rate. Throughout the Second World War (earlier in Germany and some central European countries) and for some years thereafter, the right of citizens of the large economies (except the United States and Canada) to acquire and dispose of foreign currencies for purposes of trade, travel, investment and speculation was restricted. Foreign currencies could only be acquired by licence or allocation and disposed of in ways approved by the monetary authority.

The vesting of a monopoly of exchange dealing in the central monetary authority confers upon that authority formidable powers to manipulate its monopoly in a variety of ways. It can determine scales of priorities

The Economics of the Balance of Payments

according to which currencies will or will not be supplied to importers, it can enlist the aid of customs authorities to enforce its rules, it can act as a discriminating monopolist charging low rates of exchange for foreign currencies purchasing essential imports and high rates for those purchasing luxury imports, and it can subsidise exports to certain countries by extending advantageous rates or facilities to those of its nationals earning especially desirable foreign currencies,

It also involves a cost in terms of the elaborate bureaucratic machinery which it necessitates. Even with such machinery, it is doubtful if the monopoly of the monetary authorities can ever be made absolute. Leakages may occur. For example, currency notes may be imported and exported through the post or in the pockets of travellers. The exchange of such notes may then take place in a 'black' currency market, usually at a depreciated rate. Moreover nationals of the controlling country find ways of avoiding the surrender of all their foreign currency earnings to the control. They may hold such earnings abroad as a contingency balance. More likely they will sell them for their own currency at a rate of exchange lower than the official rate. Foreigners who acquire the currency may also sell it in 'free' markets outside the country. Thus, despite the efforts of the controlling country to monopolise dealings in its currency, free markets for it inevitably develop abroad in which the rate is lower than the official rate. If the rate were not lower but climbed to parity with the control's official rate this would reflect a balance of payments for the country which would, at least for that time, be in equilibrium even without the control.

Once monopoly of dealing in the currency is established by the monetary authority numerous variants of exchange control are possible. These arise because, since the balance of payments would, without exchange control, be in deficit, the amount of foreign currency earned is less than the unrationed demand for it by home nationals to make payments abroad. It is in the means chosen by the central monetary authority to allocate the scarce currency that variation in the type of exchange control occurs. We will look briefly at three methods of allocation: allocation according to priorities, multiple exchange rates and bilateral payments agreements.

The first method is the simplest. Given that £x million* is available in

---

* One uses a £ sign naturally when discussing exchange control. The exchange control which protected sterling from the outbreak of war in 1939 until the declaration of its convertibility into other currencies in 1959 was probably the most efficient and elaborate which ever existed. The German system which began in the early thirties and was perfected by Hjalmar Schacht was impressive. But Keynes was probably right when in the tough negotiations with the Americans in 1945, he painted a grim picture of Britain's expected post-war balance of payments and said: 'Britain, before we are through, will be forced to teach Dr Schacht his business.'

foreign currency earnings the central monetary authority will make allocations in this amount to finance imports and to make other foreign payments. In doing so, they will observe agreed principles in establishing priorities. Essential food and raw materials will presumably stand at one end of the spectrum; imports of caviar and mink and holidays in Miami will stand at the other. This was the method of the Bank of England in administering the British exchange control. Within a framework of principles precedent piled upon precedent until there were few forms of external payment uncovered. Inevitably while fairness of application was perhaps attainable between extremes of the spectrum, within it inequities were inevitable. In the last resort, one may say that any system of priorities for allocation is bound to be arbitrary, that its application inevitably leads to inequities, and that the processing of the myriad applications made for foreign exchange imposes formidable administrative costs.

The method of multiple exchange rates is capable of almost endless elaboration. By offering different rates for foreign currency according to the way it has been earned, and by charging different rates for foreign currency according to the way in which it is to be used, the central authority can, in effect, impose concealed tariffs and pay export subsidies, encouraging the export of this or that commodity and determining rates of exchange according to priority in import commodities and according to its estimate of the elasticity of demand for them. Clearly such a system implies a great discriminatory power in the hands of a skilful control. Indeed, operated in such a way as to cause a decrease in the foreign currency value of imports and an increase in the foreign currency value of exports, it may achieve balance-of-payments equilibrium for the country without the use of direct import and export controls. The use of a simple multiple exchange-rate system can be illustrated by the following example.

Assume that the British exchange control authorities impose a system of several official rates of exchange, purchasing and supplying all foreign currencies at these rates. Suppose that, between each currency and sterling there is one official rate of exchange of $4x = £1$ and that, at this rate, all exporters are required to surrender their foreign currency earnings while importers of specified essential commodities are sold foreign exchange at the same rate. If $4x = £1$ is a rate which is pitched rather high by the authorities, then not all of the available foreign currency will be taken up by importers, who will restrict their needs to the minimum. The Bank of England may offer the remaining foreign exchange at a higher rate which it judges would clear the market, or it may auction it in a free market to importers of luxuries, allowing the rate to be settled by relative supply and demand. Such a rate may be $3x = £1$. Thus will be established an official buying rate for foreign currency for the import of high priority commodities and a much higher free market rate for the import of luxuries. The effect of this will be not to debar the import of luxuries, but to subject them to an imposition—in this case to a concealed tariff of $33\frac{1}{3}$ per cent—the extent of the imposition being determined by the extent to which the free rate is higher than the official. If the tariff effect is high enough, the country may be able to suppress imbalance by the multiple exchange rate alone, dispensing with the use of quantitative import controls.

Another aspect of multiple exchange rates is that they cut down costs of control as compared with the priority allocation method. By dividing the import sector into a few broad categories, each with a different exchange rate for its payments, the machinery of the market and of elasticity of demand are harnessed in place of costly licensing and the scrutiny of thousands of individual applications. During the forties and fifties, many Latin American countries made ingenious use of multiple exchange rates. Although a free and an official market for sterling coexisted in the last years of British exchange control, the British did not make purposive use of multiple rates for import control. The free-market rates for sterling in Zürich and New York were used merely as a barometer by which to read the strength of sterling—the extent of the discount in the free markets being an indication of sterling's readiness or otherwise for full convertibility.

To describe the rationale of bilateral payments agreements we must come to the matter by a rather circuitous route. Central to the explanation is an understanding of the term 'convertibility' when it is applied to a currency. In a condition of multilateral trade the individual balances of payments of country X with countries A, B and C are not of direct consequence. They matter only insofar as they constitute a part of X's general balance of payments with the rest of the world. As long as this balance is in equilibrium, X's surplus with A will enable it to settle its deficits with B and C. In, for example, a triangular system of trade, if X has a deficit with A but a surplus with B, which in turn has a surplus with A, the excess of B's currency available to X can be used by X to pay A. As long as the overall demand for and supply of X's currency are equal, the exchange market takes care of the settlements of residual balances—however many-sided the trade system may be. But suppose that X has a deficit with A, while B and C also have deficits with A. There is now a shortage of A's currency with X and with B and C. There will be a tendency as long as X, B and C all share a shortage of A's currency, i.e. as long as they are collectively in deficit with A, to economise in the use of A's currency. They might meet this situation by devaluing their three currencies relative to A's currency, or they might induce A to revalue (i.e. to raise the value of) its currency.

But if they choose to meet the situation by the use of direct controls, they will make their currencies inconvertible into A's currency. That is, they will each impose control in their exchange markets over the sale and purchase of A's currency, restricting its sale, hoarding its balances and rationing its use. Restrictions on the use of a currency for foreign trade mean that this currency is to some degree inconvertible. In the above example, X, B, and C's currencies are inconvertible into A's currency. They remain convertible each into the other. As soon as exchange control comes to be widely applied by a number of countries, several currencies will become inconvertible. Multilateral trade is progressively restricted and ultimately breaks down. In the new condition, individual balances of payments become important, each country buying from the other only to the extent that it can earn the other's currency by selling to it. Trade will now flow only in bilateral channels, each country balancing its trade and payments with other countries individually, ultimately limiting purchases from each by its earning power in each. A bilateral payments agreement is then a means by which X buys goods from Y to a certain value in Y's currency, Y using these earnings to purchase an agreed amount from X.

The constricting effect of such agreements is great. They tend to ramify, stipulating not only amounts of goods in currency terms to be exchanged, but types of goods and commodity classes as well. If the amount of 'the swing' for a given year is exhausted in six months, trade between the two countries may cease for the remaining period of the agreement. (The term 'swing' was applied to the stipulated amount of a bilateral deal between two countries in the late forties, when there were hundreds of such agreements between non-dollar countries.)

It remains to mention very briefly some of the forms of machinery through which payments are regulated. Three forms claim attention: bilateral clearing agreements, payments agreements, and private compensation schemes.

Bilateral clearing agreements were common in the foreign trade of Nazi Germany in the period 1934–9 but had their most dramatic flowering in post-war Europe during the period of disequilibrium in world payments. At the end of 1947, there were over two hundred such agreements among European countries, and by 1950 this number had nearly doubled. Such agreements were concluded by governments according to a fairly uniform pattern. The central banks, as technical agents, supplied their own currency at a fixed rate of exchange against that of their partner, up to a certain limit, which was referred to as the 'swing'. This was intended to afford room for minor fluctuations in commercial deliveries between the two countries, since over the period of the agreement A might at times be

The Economics of the Balance of Payments

in surplus with *B* and at times in deficit. Beyond the limit thus fixed, settlements had generally to be made in gold or a convertible currency.

Bilateral agreements usually include a clause on exchange rates. The rates of exchange fixed in the agreement may be (and in the post-war European cases were) consistent and yield a uniform pattern of cross-rates, but if the agreements form only a part of a wide and tight system of exchange control, they may be arbitrary and reflect the relative bargaining strengths of the countries party to the agreement.

One interesting feature of such bilateral agreements is the consequence of the size of the swing for the domestic economies of the countries concerned. If the exports of one country exceed that of the other and go to the limit of the swing, then exporters in that country will have their incomes augmented by the central bank's advance of the swing and the monetary supply of the export surplus country will be increased by this amount. Since the extra demand pressure so generated cannot, because of the bilateral agreement, spill over into additional imports, it must inevitably increase domestic demand pressure. This, in the likely event that the economy is already at full employment, will generate inflationary pressure. For the deficit country, the payments by importers in local currency over the local currency proceeds of exports will cause a depletion of the domestic monetary supply by this amount. Unless this is offset by a domestic credit expansion, a deflationary influence will be generated. This direct gearing of swings in trade to the domestic money supply can, if not offset, produce destabilising influences on the domestic economies of both countries. At least, however, the amount of the swing limits these influences, which in its absence could be considerable with inconvertible currencies. Care needs to be taken in deciding the size of the swing. If too small, its limit may quickly be reached and trade may cease between the two countries—as happened in 1947, when for many agreements margins of credit reached the limit of the swing and further trade (if any) had to be financed in gold; if too large, or if no swing is defined, large unusable balances may accumulate to the credit of the surplus country.

The bilateral trade agreement represents perhaps the extreme measure in the pathology of international payments. The best that can be said of it is that the limited trade for which it caters is better than no trade at all. It belongs to the most extreme conditions of the international economy: to the determined rush of Nazi Germany to full employment under the stimulus of rearmament in the thirties and her determination to preserve minimal trade with her underemployed neighbours; to the European payments system in disintegration after the Second World War; and to recent Latin America, where roaring inflation, economic nationalism and the thirst for economic growth produced economic conditions in which normal payments usages were impossible.

Payments agreements, the second form of payments regulation, are wider in scope than the bilateral agreement. Where bilateral agreements are confined to current trade, payments agreements often cover past as well as present transactions and may cover a wide range of a country's foreign trade dealings, reflected in many items of the balance of payments. It is, therefore, not possible to find in them the uniformity which characterises bilateral agreements, and it is possible only to give examples rather than precise definitions. A good example of a payments agreement is afforded by the series of agreements made between Britain and a number of sterling balance holders – India, Ceylon, Egypt, Argentine, Brazil, Uruguay and others – in late 1947 for the ordering and running down of these balances. The agreements provided for the temporary blocking of the balances of some countries and for restrained use by others. For those whose balances were blocked, two accounts were created for their central banks at the Bank of England. The No. 2 Account was blocked and was to hold previously accumulated sterling. From this, amounts were released to the No. 1 Account by mutual agreement, while in the No. 1 Account were accumulated, in addition to such releases, balances accruing after the date of the agreement. All No. 1 Account balances were to be freely available for current use.

Probably the most grandiose payments agreements ever concluded, and the best known, were the three agreements which governed Western European payments between 1947 and 1950 and which paved the way for the European Payments Union of 1950. These three agreements – the Multilateral Monetary Compensation Agreement of November 1947, and the First and Second Intra-European Payments Agreements of October 1948 and September 1949 respectively, were extremely complex and cannot be described here.[4] They bridged the gap in the recovery of European payments between the clumsy bilateralism of the immediate postwar period and the sophisticated European multilateralism of the European Payments Union, which in its turn was superseded by complete convertibility of the European currencies in 1959.

The third and final form of payments machinery paradoxically eliminates payments altogether by substituting direct barter deals for money transactions. The simplest example of such 'private compensation schemes' is the case where a firm in one country undertakes to make an export shipment of some commodity (or commodities) in exchange for an agreed export shipment of a specified commodity from the other country. The transaction is usually approved by the governments of both countries.

The Economics of the Balance of Payments

Value for value in the two currencies, the shipments are equal at the official exchange rate and each of the firms operates as both exporter and importer.

In this last fact lies the main disadvantage of such schemes. What is a firm which exports steel plates to do with the contra-import shipment of perishable citrus fruits? All the classic disadvantages attributed to the barter economy in the elementary textbook are inherent in such a transaction. Not surprisingly, therefore, the typical private compensation scheme is quadrilateral rather than bilateral. Such a scheme is illustrated in Fig. 19.1.

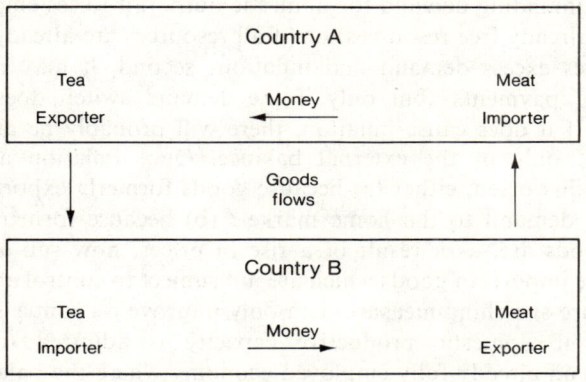

Fig. 19.1

If country A is a larger exporter of tea and an importer of meat; and country B is a large exporter of meat and also imports tea, it is possible for trade to be carried on in both commodities without use of inter-country money payments. Only goods pass between the two countries. In A the tea exporters are paid by the meat importers; in B the meat exporters are paid by the tea importers. In the simplest case, if there are only four firms then it is easy for these firms to coordinate the value of the shipments in order to balance the deals both between firms and between the two countries. If several or many firms are involved on both sides, then matters are more complicated. Firms have to find one another in order to start dealing and it is easier to have a single agency to keep the accounting in order. For this purpose so-called 'barter brokers' arise whose purpose it is to fulfil these functions. Frequent in the 1930s, private compensation schemes appeared again in the sixties; although understandably their scope was limited.[5]

We come now to the second of three main groups of controls, namely, commercial controls. These include quantitative restrictions on imports, import embargoes, tariff quotas and the buying policy of state-trading monopolies. All involve the limitation of imports, either by deterrent, restraint or veto. Here lie some of the most familiar devices which have been used in recent years by governments to influence the balance of payments.

Before embarking upon an examination of each type of import control it is necessary to examine the nature of the breed in general. Import restrictions, of whatever form, are, in Johnsonian terms (see p. 360 above) 'expenditure switching' policies. They serve to switch domestic demand from foreign goods to home-produced goods. This switch has two main effects: first, by stimulating demand for domestic output, it raises employment (if there are already free resources) or (if all resources are already employed) it generates excess demand and inflation; second, it may improve the balance of payments — but only if the demand switch does not cause inflation. If it does cause inflation, there will probably be an *initial* improvement only of the external balance. Once inflation appears, the balance will worsen, either (a) because goods formerly exported are now drawn by demand to the home market; (b) because formerly marginal export goods are, as a result of a rise in prices, now sub-marginal; or (c) because imports of goods which are not subject to control are increased. Expenditure-switching measures can only improve a country's balance of payments if domestic productive capacity is adjusted to meet the switch. In an already fully employed economy where the balance of payments deficit is due to the existence of a measure of inflation, import controls will only intensify the inflation. The obvious solution to the external imbalance is to purge the inflation in the first place.

It might appear, then, that the solution lies in expenditure-reducing policies, but this oversimplifies the issue. Expenditure-reducing policies would, in fact, be the solution only if inflation were the prime cause of the deficit or if, in its absence, prices and factor costs were flexible enough for a reduction of outlay to reduce prices and restore international balance without, at the same time, creating an intolerable amount of underemployment. In practice such flexibility of costs does not exist, and in its absence two things tend to happen. Either there is a resort, willy nilly, to expenditure-reducing policies which do not reduce prices, do not improve competitiveness and which are abandoned or curtailed when the inevitable unemployment appears, leaving the external deficit uncorrected; or there is a rush to use import controls directly, with the destabilising secondary effects we have described. Either alternative is unfortunate. The first is typified in the stop-go policies of the British economy in the fifties and sixties, the second in the inflationary restrictionism of the Latin American countries during the same period.

Another argument used to support the imposition of import controls is that they may be used temporarily to supplement another form of switching policy, namely, devaluation. It is usually argued that, whatever the values of import and export elasticities may be, the effects of a devaluation upon imports and exports will be slight *in the short run*. Why not, therefore, impose import controls as a temporary measure, until the devaluation begins to take effect? Such a plan seems superficially plausible, but on closer inspection is almost certainly defective. In the first place, what is the length of this interim period required for devaluation of itself to achieve the necessary switching? If the looked-for improvement in the external balances is delayed the import restrictions will probably 'build themselves in' to the economy. If the devaluation works beneficially on the trade balance, there will still be a temptation to keep the controls in order to reap an additional bonus of advantage – provided that other countries will tolerate without retaliatory action both a devaluation and import controls. In any event, there is a strong chance that the imposition of the import controls and the devaluation at the same time will cancel each other out, that the protectionist and easy home market conditions engendered by protection will nullify the thirst for export sales and opening of foreign markets which should accompany devaluation. The discussion of import controls so far has been unfavourable to their use in certain short-run situations. What, if any, is the case against using them as a long-run suppressive measure against a deficit? Here there are at least two economic counter arguments and one political.

The political argument at this moment of time (1973) is that the international economy has managed to emancipate itself in the fifties from most of the direct impediments to trade which had come with the Second World War and the authoritarian government which accompanied it, and any return to controls by major powers must be regarded as retrograde. Apart from the general abrogation of the advantages of free trade, most Western countries are bound under the rules of GATT and Article VIII of the IMF Articles of Agreement to resort to import controls only for balance-of-payments reasons. It is sometimes argued that there is less need to fear import restrictions nowadays than there was in the thirties, when such devices were used by countries to protect themselves from the import of mass unemployment. While this may be in part true, it would then be possible to extend this logic to justify the gradual erosion of the gains which have been made in establishing free and multilateral trade and the great expansion of world trade which this has facilitated.

The economic arguments are two in number. The first is the simple yet powerful one implied above: that free trade and the advantage of the theory of comparative costs are worth having. Import controls involve a reduction of this advantage. The advantages of a free-trade system have been discussed elsewhere. We will not repeat them here (see Chapter 7).

The second argument is that there is a built-in tendency for import restrictions to fail in their efforts to achieve balance-of-payments improvement. We have already thrown some doubt upon the expenditure-switching effect of import restrictions to achieve such an improvement. We must now be more precise in our assessment and cast it in more general terms. For this purpose we return to the simple equations which are basic to the so-called 'absorption approach' (see Chapter 14).

Starting with the basic equation $B = Y - E$, where B is the balance of payments, Y is total income from production and E is total domestic expenditure, we can derive another simple equation which enables us to make use of an alternative set of relationships. Given that E must be domestic expenditure either upon domestic consumption goods C or domestic investment goods I then $E = C + I$. Also Y total income can be distributed between consumption C and saving S.

We have now three equations:

$$B = Y - E \qquad (1)$$

$$E = C + I \qquad (2)$$

and

$$Y = C + S \qquad (3)$$

If we substitute in (1) the values of E and Y in equations (2) and (3) we get

$$B = S - I \qquad (4)$$

This equation expresses the balance of payments in different terms. From it we see that any improvement in B the balance of payments implies an increase in savings, a fall in investment, or some element of both. What effect do import restrictions have upon these two variables?

As far as saving is concerned, there can be no certainty. The short-run effect may well be for saving to increase as buyers are prevented from spending upon imports. There will be an expenditure switch, but will it be a switch between import goods and domestic goods or will it be a switch of expenditure to saving? In the longer run, it may well be that the switch will lead to a fall in real income and hence a fall in saving. Equally, in the short run, investment may fall as stocks of domestic goods are run down as a result of the switch in demand; while, in the long run, investment may fall with real income as a result of an accelerator effect. Two features emerge: in the short run it may well be that from a rise in saving and a fall in investment the balance of payments will improve. This is the supposed association which in the popular view seems to justify import restrictions as a policy. But in the long run, and in a more sophisticated analysis, the balance-of-payments effect is likely to be bound up with changes in real income. We are committed, in order to explore the long-run effects, to an examination of every variable which bears upon the variation of real income set up by the decline in imports.

There is a further complication. It is apparent that, even with no change in income (Y) any improvement in the balance of payments must be associated with a reduction in E the level of domestic absorption. If real income falls, the reduction in E has to be greater to achieve an improvement in B. We are faced with a second question: since it is apparent that import restrictions must be accompanied by a reduction in absorption, what is the size of such a reduction to be?

We are not in a position to answer these questions here.[6] Three significant facts emerge, however, from even this brief discussion. The first is that there is no theoretical evidence to support the popular view that import restrictions improve the balance of payments: they may do so in the short run; their ultimate effect is problematic. Second, it is apparent that any import restrictions, to have their desired effect on the balance of payments, need to be accompanied by simultaneous domestic policies for disinflation. Finally, since import restrictions affect the level of income, and since they must be accompanied by reductions in real income then it is at the ultimate effects of these income changes upon the balance of payments that we must look before we can form a judgement upon them as a policy weapon.

It remains in this section to review briefly the main forms of commercial controls. Commonest and simplest among these is the quantitative import control which restricts directly (either by quantity or value) the amount of a commodity which may be imported. Such a control is simple and is enforceable by customs authorities. It may be applied in many ways: either generally and without discrimination, seeking only to restrict the import bill for balance-of-payments purposes; or it may go further, encompassing industrial policies as well, discriminating in favour of this industry or that and having a detailed protective application. For example, it may be ruled (a) that no foreign cameras be imported into Britain, or (b) that only x foreign cameras may be imported, or (c) that foreign cameras, except those from Germany, may be imported, or (d) that only cameras in a certain price range may be imported, or (e) that an import licence is required by any person wishing to import a camera.

The main purpose of quantitative import control is to curtail the value of imports to a target amount according to chosen balance-of-payments objectives. Thus, a government decision as to the total quantity of imports has to be made. Further it must be decided of what the global total of imports is to be composed, and which products are to be given priority and which excluded. While general principles may govern these high-level decisions, their application to individual cases must necessarily be left to the bureaucracy and an elaborate system of licensing must result. The conventional method is to issue licences to individuals by which they may import specific quantities (or values) of a commodity, the aggregate of such licences being the total quantity to be allowed into the country.

Limitation of the amount of a good imported affects its demand price on the home market, which rises as the supply of the good is restricted. But the good's supply price (i.e. its selling price to the foreign exporter) is reckoned to be unaffected and although this is not certain it is the most reasonable assumption to make. Perhaps if the import control is by quantity the foreign supplier may raise his price if he judges the elasticity of demand for his product to be low. But if the restriction is by value, he may lower his price in order to still sell the same number of units and hold onto the market in the hope that the import control is temporary. If, as a result of a good's supply price remaining unaffected, a special profit accrues from the margin between the supply and demand prices, who is to receive this profit margin? There are several possibilities. It may (1) go to the foreign exporters who raise their supply price, (2) go to importers who raise their selling price, (3) be taken by the government of the importing country in the form of an import licence fee, (4) go to a consumer in the importing country who, if the price of the imported commodity is controlled, buys at the controlled price and resells at the market demand price, or (5) go in part to the importer and in part to the officials of the importing country as a bribe for the granting of the import licence. Whether the margin goes to the exporters or the importers is important for the terms of trade. A chaotic and undesirable system is that of the 'open quota', where a limited time is allotted for free import. Here, there is inevitably a rush to import before the quota time is exhausted. The successful importers are then able to unload their imports on the home market at an abnormal profit.

More elaborate than the quantitative quota is the 'tariff quota' by which a specified amount of a commodity may be imported duty-free, while imports above that amount are subject to an import tariff. Scarcity of the commodity in the importing country results in the raising of the demand price of the imported good within that country beyond the supply price at which, at least initially, the importer may obtain the good. How far import continues above the amount of the free quota depends upon the relation between the import tariff and the margin between the importer's supply price and the domestic demand price. If, even after the imposition of the tariff, there is such a margin, then additional units of the good will be imported until, with the decline of its scarcity, the demand price falls to the point where it is equal to the supply price plus the import tariff. This method has certain manipulative advantages. For example, the tariff may be raised or lowered according to whether the government wishes to import more or less of the good beyond the quota. It is sometimes argued that a tariff quota 'may actually be thought of as a device for trade liberalisation, making possible at least some reduction in import restrictions'.[7] Whether, however, it is easier to negotiate an increase in a quota or a reduction in a tariff is open to question. The decline in use of the device in recent years is more probably due to its lack of precision in controlling imports than to its potential for disappearance with trade liberalisation. The straightforward quantitative quota is a far more precise and certain way to control imports than the tariff, whose degree of restriction depends on the market conditions for the product in the supplying and importing countries.

A further refinement of quantitative import control is the state-trading monopoly. Under this method, all import of the chosen commodity by the private sector is forbidden, and importing is done only by a state-operated organisation. The genus is familiar in the Soviet bloc countries but is by no means confined to Socialist countries. During the Second World War the British regulated a great part of their import trade in food and staple commodities through bulk purchase agreements negotiated by the Ministry of Food and by various boards appointed to regulate specific sectors of trade and industry. Western European countries have used a similar method at various times and a number of developing countries have more recently resorted to it. Given such control, the state organisation is able to regulate the amount of the commodity which is imported to accord with national balance-of-payments policies. Here again, a margin appears between the importer's supply price and the public's demand price under conditions of scarcity. The margin in this case accrues to the state organisation in the form of abnormal profit.

A method of 'import deterrent' rather than control is that of 'advance deposit requirements',[8] a method introduced somewhat tentatively by the United Kingdom in late 1968 in an effort to curtail the country's seemingly irreducible import bill even after the devaluation of sterling in November 1967. This system demands that the importer should deposit an amount at a commercial bank equal to a specified percentage of the value of the import. The percentage may be either a uniform one or it may vary with the nature of the good, the gradient rising between essential and luxury imports. The deposits are usually transferred from commercial banks to a special account at the central bank and are repaid to the importer only after a stated period, which once more is variable at the discretion of the authorities. By such an arrangement two aims are sought: first, since the importer must bear the cost of forgoing use of his own funds for the period, imports will become unprofitable for the marginal importer and thus be reduced; and second, by reducing for the time being the liquidity of the banking system by forcing the commercial banks to transfer deposits to the central bank, it is hoped to exert a disinflationary pressure upon the economy. The scheme at first sight looks ingenious but it has serious drawbacks. The administration of the whole system is bound to be costly and serves to make cumbrous one of the normal transactions of foreign trade. While it may employ monetary forces in a direction which is often appropriate to a deficit country, such forces can be applied, if that is the policy-maker's choice, by more direct and conventional weapons. There will inevitably be a tendency for the authorities to accumulate these deposits if only because having withdrawn liquidity they find it hard to choose a time to release it. Finally, the scheme bears most hard on the small and the new business and least on the large corporation flush in liquid funds.

One type of balance-of-payments weapon requires attention to complete our description of the armoury: control of capital movements. An initial problem here lies in deciding the types of capital movement which must be controlled: a contingent problem is how to make the control effective. Let us start with short-term capital movements.

In the pursuit of balance-of-payments adjustment, from the classic gold standard to the manipulative interest-rate policies of an anxious Britain in the sixties, short-term money movements have played both a constructive and a destructive role. Equalising short-term capital movements have a useful part to play in a price-adjustment (or an income-adjustment) system. They are essential to the smooth achievement of adjustment by those means or to the accommodating of balances of payments to major capital transfers. At the same time, it is evident historically that there is a genus of short-term capital movements which is as inimical to balance-of-payments stability as the equalising type is necessary. How, for purposes of control are we to distinguish between these two types? The fact is that it is impossible for purposes of control to distinguish between stabilising and destabilising short-term capital, and this difficulty of segregation makes it inevitable that both (or neither) should be controlled. It is possible, of course, to proceed piecemeal and to legislate against particular imports of short-term capital (and thus against their subsequent export) by closing the channels through which they enter. The British in 1971 sought reduc-

The Economics of the Balance of Payments

tion of inward short-money flows by restricting the rights of foreigners to invest in the short-term money markets in London (e.g., the local authorities' short-loan market) which had hitherto been the temporary resting place of foreign short money.

When we turn to long-term capital movements, it is easier to distinguish between the desirable and undesirable in the light of balance-of-payments policy. Moreover, it is easier to justify control. A country with a recurrent unfavourable balance on current account cannot be an extensive long-term lender abroad. It is possible that control may be desirable for political and non-economic reasons in order to coordinate monetary and political policies. A simple control of long-term overseas investment can be imposed by the monetary authority requiring that all schemes of overseas direct investment and all applications to raise money in its own capital markets should be subject to its approval, and that all earnings attributable to foreign investment should be repatriated to the investing country. Measures of this type were taken by the United States in January 1968 to protect the American balance of payments from the erosion of the very high rate of American overseas investment.[9] It may come as a surprise to some readers that the United States, which was so opposed to balance-of-payments controls in the forties and fifties should in the sixties have had recourse to them. Since 1959 a series of restrictions on current-account transactions has been imposed, notably measures taken in 1959 and later designed to reduce the foreign-exchange cost of foreign aid, of which the tying of aid to purchases in the United States is the most notorious, measures regulating the use abroad of military expenditures and, from 1961, the regulation of imports by tourists. Over the same period extensive, complex and largely unsuccessful measures were taken to curb capital outflow. But while measures such as these would impose control on a high proportion of overseas capital investment, they would not be a complete control. Indeed complete control of capital movements, even if desirable, is elusive. In the first place it is not possible to impose it in isolation. To have any chance of success it must involve a control and qualitative examination of all foreign payments, capital and current. Often apparently routine transactions can conceal a capital transfer. For example, capital sums may be exported by mutual agreement between exporters and foreign buyers whereby shipments are under-invoiced — a British shipment worth $10,000 being invoiced at $7000, paid for by a normal bill for that amount plus a covert payment of $3000 to an account in New York. Sometimes perfectly legal procedures can take on the role of a capital movement and defy control. The so-called leads and lags effects in payments for imports and exports is an obvious example. Here immediate payment for imports by home buyers and delayed payments for exports by foreigners is equivalent to a speculative capital outflow in its effect on the country concerned. To a large trading country suspected of impending devaluation, such a speculative attack, in however innocent a guise, can be fatal. Leads and lags have played a consistent role in the speculative attacks on sterling from 1949 to 1967. Even if we abandon the idea of imposing and administering a completely 'capital tight' exchange control we must still decide whether some form of control on capital movement is desirable. The answer to this depends on how the balance of advantage is deemed to lie. On the one hand, experience of 'hot money' movements in the interwar period and to some extent since 1945 would lead to advocacy of control. On the other hand, if, in order to control capital movements, it is necessary to set up the whole constricting paraphernalia of exchange control on current payments, then that is too high a price to pay and we must accommodate ourselves to capital movements as best we can.

(iii) Uses and Abuses

This brief description of the main types of controls which may be used by a country to suppress imbalance in its external trade serves to show the wide range of mechanisms which are available. They have been widely used, and a high degree of expertise in their use has been acquired.[10] They are, for better or worse, part of the battery of balance-of-payments policy weapons. It is difficult to achieve a balanced view of their utility as such. The clear view is necessarily clouded by value judgements, by the predilection for free trade or protection, by the preference for economic freedom or authoritarian planning, by the preference for quickness and certainty over reliance on the built-in processes of the system. Two approaches are possible in evaluating controls: an evaluation which must rest upon the comparison of controls with the various systems which we have already described as adjusters of the balance of payments, together with what we may call the 'welfare considerations', namely, how each system influences the magnitude and distribution between nations of world income.[11] This is, in the long run, the most important aspect; but it is beyond our present scope, and we must confine ourselves here to one simple aspect, that of efficiency. We will attempt a practical appraisal of controls in workaday terms, examining their usefulness and range of applicability.

First, we must invoke again an old 'friend', the elasticity condition. If this condition is amply fulfilled and elasticities of demand for imports are high, then adjustment through price changes will be possible without too great a movement of the terms of trade; if the elasticities are low then resort to direct controls is likely, if not inevitable, if both stable domestic incomes and external balance are to be maintained. As one writer puts it, 'controls can keep balances of payments in order when other methods of adjustment would work painfully, if at all'.[12] Something like this argument is used by opponents of the post-war system of IMF fixed exchanges to show the inevitability of controls. They argue that, robbed of exchange rate variation as an adjustment device, deprived of income and price variation by the determination of governments to preserve full employment and growth, governments fall back upon the only method left to deal with balance-of-payments imbalance, direct controls. From arguing that controls are a last resort to arguing that they are a convenience is only a step.

A second argument for controls is that they are swift and sure in application. A country whose foreign balance is subjected to a sudden and unexpected external influence — for example, depression in an export market, a sudden sharp rise in imports, a domestic harvest failure, or the like — may by their use counteract such shocks effectively and quickly. The form of control may be varied to suit the circumstances. In such conditions, market adjusters such as the exchange rate may work, but they will not work as quickly.

A third supporting argument is more problematical. It is conceivable that when a balance-of-payments deficit is threatened the choice between controls and exchange depreciation must be conditioned by which of these has the least impact on the correcting country's terms of trade. While both methods will make imported goods more expensive, controls can be used to minimise the terms-of-trade effect. It is, at least theoretically, possible for the authorities to choose the form of control and apply it discriminately so as to obtain the optimum effects on the terms of trade and on the balance of trade. Formidable theoretical choices clearly arise here. How much trade, in volume, must be sacrificed in order to get better terms of trade? What is the 'optimum' degree of trade restriction, and how is it influenced by long-run demand and supply elasticities? What strategies should be used so as to invoke only the minimum of counter manipulation?[13]

Fourthly, direct controls can reduce imports selectively, preventing scarce foreign exchange from being wasted on non-essential imports. The ordinary forces of the market can exercise no such discrimination. One such justifiable case for the use of import controls is that of the developing country whose domestic investment and development programmes combined with a wide divergence in the level of personal income can generate a large demand for luxury imports for rich residents. If it is agreed that gold-plated Cadillacs and even colour television sets are unjustifiable luxuries, and if there is a government courageous enough to enforce common standards of asceticism, import control is the most efficient way of achieving it.

Once more, we point out that any classification of import goods on an 'essential' and 'non-essential' basis must in the last resort be arbitrary and the controlling authority can make some odd evaluations, probably based on the personal preference scale of some official far back in the government chain of command. Apart from distinguishing between imports which are 'necessary' and imports which are 'frivolous', there are economic implications. Will exclusion of some forms of imports cause a switch of factors of production at home to the manufacture of substitutes to the detriment perhaps of more necessary lines of production? Once the ordinary working of the market is baulked, some odd distortions may appear. In the Britain of the seventies which is more detrimental to the balance of payments: a holiday in Italy costing £200 (which must be reduced to £100 under existing controls) or the purchase of a £6000 Mercedes, which is permissible?

This, then, is the pragmatic case for the use of controls in certain limited circumstances — quickness and certainty in operation over a defined range of goods, but with many uncertainties in secondary effects and some qualms even as to the claimed efficiency. We have already discussed some general criticisms of controls on balance-of-payments grounds (see p. 498 above). Let us close this chapter by listing some further defects which are less general.

First, the use of controls tends to create vested interests for the continuance of the controls. Although most often thought of as balance-of-payments devices, they may be used protectively for industries just as tariffs may be. To admit the 'infant industry' case as a warrantable exception to free trade is tacitly to do likewise for the use of controls for industrial protection. The commonest situation is one in which controls are imposed primarily for balance-of-payments reasons but are used discriminately as well to protect particular industries. To attempt removal of the controls when balance-of-payments conditions no longer warrant them is then to evoke howls of protest from these industries. Another group with an interest in the continuance of controls is that which has been receiving the scarcity profits resultant upon the restriction. These are joined in turn by the administrators and organisers of the control system. A large lobby builds up for retention.

Second, it is argued[14] that controls produce inequities far beyond what is justified by their effectiveness as a balance-of-payments policy. Examples of such inequities occur frequently in the literature:[15] the special profits of the importer who is favoured above him whose trading is curtailed by arbitrary choice, the trader who is allowed foreign currency for some favoured project as compared with him who is denied it. In the complex web of regulations, in the multiplicity of arbitrary decisions made by a growing bureaucracy of controllers, the potentiality for injustice is great. Whether the moral issues invoked are greater than under a free market system, who can say? Moreover, morality in economics is an elusive criterion which often accelerates judgements and sometimes makes them impossible.

We will make no effort to sum up the case for and against balance-of-payments controls. We have described them, we have discerned a few advantages and powerful defects in their use. We have inferred that, in the last resort, the choice between direct controls and market processes depends more on events and the political currents of the times than on whether the alternative market processes can work more satisfactorily. Controls are as political as they are economic. The mere fact that imbalance suppression through direct controls carries with it the potentiality of political as well as economic motive is sure to recommend it to some, as much as it makes it repugnant to others.

20
Adjustment and International Liquidity

(i) Introduction

This chapter and its successor deal with the institutions which serve policies for adjustment of the balance of payments; with the systems through which they function, and with the economic pathology of those systems. This is a large subject matter and, in order not to lose our way, it is necessary to map out our line of advance.

First, it is necessary to define the nature of international liquidity, the international media of exchange through which final balances are settled and in which reserves are held. We must not only examine its nature, but form opinions on its optimum quantity and distribution in a world of expanding trade. We must remind ourselves from the subject matter of earlier chapters of how that optimum quantity will alter according to the particular system of adjustment which obtains in the international economy.

The second task is to examine the role which gold has played in the world payments system — first with a quick look at the international gold standard to which we have often referred but of which there has not yet been any formal discussion, and then at gold's present and future monetary role.

In the following chapter the so-called Bretton Woods system, which defines the parameters of our present international monetary system, and its central institution, the International Monetary Fund will be examined.[1] We conclude with a brief glance at some of the plans for the amendment and improvement of that system.

(ii) The Nature and Need of International Liquidity

International liquidity is the name given to the generally acceptable money media in which international residual balances are settled and in which countries hold international reserves. Such media, under the gold exchange standard of the post-Second World War period, are three in number: gold; international, or so-called key currencies; and the at present small, but potentially larger, category of the liabilities of international organisations, in particular the IMF.

These three categories comprise what we may describe as 'first-line international liquidity'. They constitute the three forms in which the international reserves of individual countries are held and which are reproduced as such in the main statistical returns.[2] Behind them, however, is a much broader band of what we may call 'second-line international liquidity', which exists for or which may be created by countries to supplement the first line categories. Examples of second-line international liquidity would be working balances of foreign currencies held by traders and commercial banks, international trade credit, short-term foreign assets held by domestic nationals, long-term but realisable foreign bonds held by home nationals, and stabilisation loans and accumulation facilities negotiable with other countries to support a deficit in the balance of payments. While it strains terminology somewhat to refer to some of these as liquidity, it is clear that, if we accept the economist's view of international liquidity as the means of sustaining a balance of payments deficit without a change of exchange rate or the help of direct controls, there is a broad spectrum of assets shading from gold (as a commodity money), through currencies to intangible assets such as trade credit, all of which may be mobilised by a country in order to obtain liquidity to clear residual balances. The published figures of national gold and exchange reserves are but the immediately usable international money; they bear a similar relation to a nation's ultimate supporting resources as do a private person's cash and demand deposits to his total potential purchasing power derived from his total assets. It will be observed here that there is also the question of ownership. For example, foreign currency balances in the Exchange Fund at the central bank are international liquidity pure and simple; working currency balances of traders are only second-line liquidity because they are only available for settlement of residual balance-of-payments transfers through a switch of ownership. Similarly, realisable foreign bond holdings of the government are in a different category to those of private persons for the same reason.

This distinction between first- and second-line international liquidity is not as academic as may at first appear. It is made here to focus attention upon a problem which is constantly with us in discussing international liquidity—the problem of quantifying it. If we discuss its relationship without the rigour of quantification, there is a danger that our attempted analysis may derogate to mere 'social conversation';[3] if we attempt to attach numbers to categories we approach progressively variables which are without statistical coverage, and we imply relationships which can only be embodied in an abstract model with assumptions which take us too far from the world of policy, where any consideration of international liquidity necessarily belongs. We shall return to this problem of quantification later. For the present we shall include under the term 'international liquidity' only international cash money and not the various credit facilities which may certainly supplement it but whose magnitude is variable and dependent upon many non-economic factors. The analogy with the domestic money supply is clear. International liquidity is to the world economy what the money supply—coin, notes and immediately usable bank deposits—is to the domestic. Just as the domestic money supply may be augmented by credit creation, so may the international. As we shall later argue, it is by the creation of international credit to augment international money that the problem of providing adequate international liquidity for a growing world economy may be solved.

The mechanism of final balance settlement between nations has been described elsewhere (see p. 437 above) and it is not necessary to do more than remind the reader of it here. National reserves are held by the monetary authority usually in exchange stabilisation funds operated by the central bank. With fixed exchange rates between currencies a deficit in the balance of payments of a country, representing as it does an excess demand by the home country (that is, an excess supply of the home currency) for foreign currencies, would cause the exchange rate of the home currency to depreciate.* This depreciation is prevented by the exchange fund of the deficit country, which enters the foreign exchange market and, using its foreign currency reserves, purchases its own currency to support the rate. The amount of support required is conditioned by two factors, one major and one minor. The major factor is, of course, the size of the deficit itself which determines directly the oversupply (and hence the depreciation) of the home currency; the minor factor is the range of fluctuation of the exchange rate which is regarded as allowable. Under present (1973) IMF arrangements, where currencies may fluctuate through a range which is $\pm 2\cdot 25$ per cent from the defined IMF parity, the depreciation would be limited to 2·25 per cent, although the exchange fund might for its own purposes and strategy of the moment wish to halt the depreciation before that

---

* For example, if Britain were the deficit country the sterling–dollar exchange rate might depreciate from $2·4 = £1 to $2.395 = £1. The home currency has depreciated, the foreign currency has appreciated. The movement of the two currencies advantages the surplus country as a buyer and disadvantages the deficit country.

limit was reached. Obviously, a prolonged balance-of-payments deficit depletes the exchange fund of the deficit country and enriches the exchange funds of those countries which are in surplus, thus redistributing the stock of international liquidity.

The mechanism described above applies also in principle to the outward and inward flows of gold which take place with movements of the balance of payments under a full gold standard. In this case, the rate is initially fixed at the defined mint parity of the home currency with gold as compared to the mint parities of other currencies. When a deficit occurs, an excess demand for foreign currencies occurs as before and the rate of exchange begins to depreciate. With this, the cost of foreign currency rises for residents. As soon as it has risen to that point at which it becomes as cheap for residents to settle debts by buying gold from the central bank and exporting it as by purchasing foreign exchange, the former method will be adopted and gold will flow out of the central bank as it is purchased for export. This places a limit to depreciation of the currency at the gold export point. In a surplus country, appreciation of the currency is, by a similar process, limited at the gold import point. Thus, outside the so-called gold points, there is no fluctuation of exchange rates and international balances are settled by flows of gold between countries, even without the intervention of exchange funds or of the monetary authorities. All that is required is that the central bank should be prepared to buy and sell gold at (or near) the mint parity and that nationals of the country should be permitted to import and export gold. As has been explained elsewhere (see p. 435) the central bank may in practice widen the gold points by setting different buying and selling prices for gold, or even by imposing some sort of concealed tax in the form of a handling charge.

Under a condition of freely flexible rates of exchange, flows of international liquidity would be reduced and theoretically should cease if the market is free and perfect. In fact small transfers would probably still take place. The exchange funds of participant countries would probably wish to iron out the more violent and trade-deterring daily and weekly fluctuations of the rates and would intervene in the market for this purpose. The amount of transfer of international liquidity would in this case be conditioned directly by the amount of exchange fund intervention. In any event it would be small compared with the intervention required to support fixed rate systems.

We have now established the nature of international liquidity, its repositories and the mechanism of its movement from country to country. We have established also that the need for reserves individually and in the aggregate grows with the determination to preserve fixed rates of exchange, the minimum being required under a condition of freely moving exchange rates. Implicit also in our description is the fact that distribution of the world stock of international liquidity between countries is determined by the long-run trend of the balances of payments of major countries. Persistent surplus countries accumulate international liquidity; persistent deficit countries find that their stocks are depleted and are driven to pursue policies for the swift correction of their deficits.

Let us summarise the argument so far in somewhat different language to that already used. We can set up our international liquidity analysis as a grandiose demand and supply model. Seen from the level of the international economy demand is motivated by:

1. the necessity of countries to meet short-term fluctuations in current account receipts and payments;
2. the necessity to 'buy time in a current account disequilibrium';[4]
3. the need to meet speculative attacks; and
4. the necessity to deal with short-term variations in capital account items.

To meet this demand the supply of international liquidity is dominated by:

(a) the net additions to the world's stock of monetary gold;
(b) the deficit in the balances of payments of countries whose currencies are key currencies; and
(c) the capacity to create international credit media to supplement (a) and (b).

While we may set out the categories of demand and supply we cannot marry the two variables as we do in market theory by an equilibrium price. We may only say that there is some optimum level of reserves which satisfies the system and argue in given circumstances a meeting of, or a shortfall from, that optimum level. There are two ways to approach this optimum level. We may approach it qualitatively and say that it is a level and distribution of reserves, sufficiently large that policies of control for the domestic economies, for preservation of employment and avoidance of inflation, are not prejudiced by the state and prospects of the balance of payments. Alternatively we may approach it quantitatively and seek some objective statistical measure of reserve adequacy or, more ambitiously, of reserve optimality.

To try to compute such measures is to seek an elusive accuracy. For individual countries, the desirable level of reserves might appear to be determined by four things: the measure of year-to-year fluctuation in the balance of payments; the method by which the balance of payments is adjusted — for example, by the use of free or fixed rates; the magnitude of 'quick' capital liabilities; and the susceptibility of the currency to speculative attack. These are general criteria. Efforts have been made, by the IMF and others, to give statistical measurement of reserve adequacy. Three reserve ratios are commonly used: the percentage ratio of reserves to imports; the ratio of reserves to money supply; and the ratio of reserves to quick liabilities. These indicators serve to underline the variability rather than the consistency of a country's reserve levels. They show too that even the general criteria listed above must fail to fit many actual cases. Each country's reserve requirement requires a study in itself. For example, a country may, by reason of its importance as a banking centre and by the widespread use of its currency in international trade, feel obliged to limit movements of its exchange rate. This self-denial of the use of a quickly adjusting mechanism forces it to regard a higher level of reserves as desirable than a country which lacks these responsibilities. Switzerland the 'capital entrepôt' country of the world, is a country which honours such requirement. Britain, with a combination of low reserves and high short liabilities, is embarrassed by her inability to do so. Table 20.1, compiled and extended from Table 2, page 13 of the *IMF Annual Report* for 1966, shows the reserve ratios carried by a number of countries in 1949, 1964 and 1970.

Table 20.1 Gross Monetary Reserves, Imports and Money Supply, 1949–70

	Percentage ratio of reserves to					
	Imports			Money supply		
	1949	1964	1970	1949	1964	1970
I World	77	43	31	—	—	—
II World except U.S.A.	38	37	31	—	—	—
III Reserve centres:						
U.S.A.	345	82	33	24	10	6
U.K.	21	15	10	8	7	7
IV Other countries:						
France	18	66	21	7	17	10
Germany	9	54	45	6	47	44
Switzerland	192	86	83	66	48	48
Canada	42	38	29	27	37	32
Japan	25	25	21	9	8	7

Source: International Financial Statistics, IMF.

Individual countries' needs for international liquidity are also tempered by the policies they follow with regard to the level of employment. A country prepared to deflate its economy even at the cost of some unemployment will thereby have a measure of adjustment at its disposal which will reduce its calls on reserves, as compared with a country determined to run its economy at full employment. The three determinants of a single country's demand for international liquidity are therefore approximate and do not make possible any precise measurement of a given country's demand. Robert Triffin puts the point well. After discussing the influence of exchange rate stability and domestic income and employment policies on the demand for reserves, he goes on:

These considerations do not lend themselves to any scientific determination of an 'ideal' level of reserves, either for an individual country or for the world at large. There is certainly a very wide range of actual reserve levels that might be regarded as satisfactory, or acceptable, by the monetary authorities and that would not induce them to modify their policies in such a way as to sacrifice other and more fundamental policy goals, such as desirable rates of employment and economic growth, price stability, and so on.[5]

The varying strength from country to country of the determinants of the demand for international liquidity make intra-country comparisons of statistical measures of reserve adequacy difficult, if not impossible. For a given country we may assume, however, that these determinants do not change in the short period so that over time-periods of a few years comparisons of a country's reserve strength may be made, albeit with caution.

The task of arriving at a quantitative measure of the optimum reserve level for a particular country is beyond the scope of our present discussion. Such attempts as have been made are tentative and are still the subject of methodological debate.[6] They attempt to combine into a single index the factors which bear upon the amount of international reserves which a country should hold. The very simple model which is used to isolate an external disequilibrium and its adjustment is so constrained by assumptions that its realistic application is restricted. We must leave it to the reader interested in the application of quantitative techniques to investigate these bold, but as yet not very helpful, exercises.

When we turn from single countries to the world economy as a whole, the problem of quantification becomes no easier. We must guard against saying that the desirable total of international liquidity is conditioned by the volume of world trade. It is not. International liquidity is required only to settle residual balances. It would be perfectly possible for a very large volume of international trade in a world of neutral balances of payments to generate only a small demand for international liquidity; conversely, for a much smaller volume of trade in a mercurial world to generate a large need for liquidity. The required amount of international liquidity is determined by the degree of imbalance in world trade, not primarily by the size of world trade.

It does not escape the writer that the maximum requirement for international liquidity would come with a large volume of international trade and a large degree of intra-country imbalance. He sees few if any reasons, however, to expect that such imbalance tends to increase with trade volume and some reasons to expect that shrinking trade and imbalance may go together.

To turn to the historical data concerning world totals of reserves and their relation to the volume of world trade does not help much either. Table 20.2 shows the ratio of reserves to world imports for selected years since 1913.

Table 20.2 Ratio of Reserves to Imports: All Countries Excluding the Communist Bloc, Selected Years, 1913–71

Year	Imports (billion dollars)	Countries		Countries and international organisations	
		Gold as per cent of imports	Gold and exchange as per cent of imports	Gold as per cent of imports	Gold and exchange as per cent of imports
1913	21·0	19	21	19	21
1928	30·6	32	42	32	42
1937	27·3	93	101	93	101
1938	23·6	110	117	110	117
1948	60·0	55	77	57	80
1950	59·3	57	80	60	82
1951	81·4	41	57	43	59
1952	80·2	42	58	44	61
1954	79·6	43	62	46	65
1955	89·0	39	57	42	59
1956	98·1	36	53	38	55
1957	107·0	35	49	35	51
1963	143·7	28	44	29	48
1965	175·3	24	37	25	41
1967	202·2	20	34	20	37
1969	256·6	15	28	16	31
1971	329·7	11	32	12	37*

* Includes SDRs.

Source: International Financial Statistics, IMF.

Certain interesting facts emerge from this table which demonstrate the relative nature of the supply of international liquidity. Notable is the very low ratio of reserves to trade in 1913 — a year not associated by economic historians with an international liquidity problem. The fact that such a large trade volume could be supported by such slender reserves was probably due to (a) the great basic stability of the international economy at that time, (b) the willingness of the authorities to apply stern corrective measures if imbalance occurred, and (c) the fact that the strain of imbalance, if it occurred, did not fall heavily on international reserves which were amply cushioned by the international credit system. Nevertheless the low ratio of gold to world imports in 1913 did much to generate the fear of gold shortage which dominated much of the immediate post-1918 thinking about rehabilitation of the international gold standard, and which impelled the Genoa Conference of 1921 to recommend the adoption of a gold exchange standard — a feeling which by 1928 had given way to mild optimism and the conviction that, with the gold standard, normality had been restored. During the later thirties, the world gold stock increased dramatically, stimulated by the increase in the American gold price in 1934 and the fall in mining costs in the thirties. The liquidity feature of the later thirties was not shortage but maldistribution, as much of the world's gold drained to the United States under the impulse of political tension and impending war in Europe.

During the post-Second World War period, international liquidity has been much lower relative to trade value than in the later thirties. By 1948 it had fallen by 32 per cent as compared with 1938, predominantly because of the great inflation in world prices. In the fifties the ratio declined further when an almost static level of gold and foreign exchange reserves (despite the modest supplement of IMF and EPU drawing rights) had to be related to a trade value growing now under the influence of rising prices and volume. In the sixties the large dollar supply resulting from the United States' deficit served as some supplement to reserves but, as Triffin rightly pointed out, the decline in United States' reserves, although to the benefit of the rest of the world, might also be taken as 'a sign of improper adjustment policies on the part of some, or all, of the countries concerned'.[7] The very low ratios of the late sixties clearly demonstrated that the whole process of reserve creation was inadequate.

Table 20.2 may be an interesting comment on the international monetary history of the past half century, but it leads us to no precise conclusion of what is the desirable level of world international liquidity. Frustrated in the task of defining any ideal absolute level for reserves, it is arguable (and some have argued)[8] that adequacy of monetary reserves is better definable in terms of rates of increase rather than in absolute terms. For this, the growth of a country's GNP or the average growth of its foreign trade may be suitable indicators, provided they start from a point at which reserves are at a satisfactory level. Unfortunately, reserves at any starting point (and particularly at present — 1973) are maldistributed, so that any rescue operation aimed at establishing a satisfactory world liquidity condition must be two-pronged. It must first establish a satisfactory reserve distribution between countries, taking into consideration for each its trade participation, economic maturity and capital position. Next, it must assure that, from this base, reserve growth in future be determined by some chosen indicator as those mentioned above. Since such a phased approach is clearly over-idealistic, a workable compromise would be for the rates of growth of reserves of individual countries to be adjusted according to the condition existing at the inauguration of the scheme; for countries starting with depleted reserves to have a quick rate of growth, and those with adequate reserves to accept a slower rate. In this way we must ensure that the world reserve stock both grows and redistributes, albeit slowly for the latter. Finally, as the percipient reader will have noted, all this subsumes the existence of a reserve medium variable at will. How such a medium is to be created is the great problem faced by all exponents of international monetary reform. Our consideration of it must wait until we have examined the present constituent elements of which international liquidity is composed — gold, key currencies and the credit of international organisations.*

Gold is the oldest form of international money. It holds this position by virtue of its long acceptance as a commodity-money form. However widely acceptable certain great national currencies — the dollar, the pound — may be, they are still national monies, usable as reserves in the world economy only by reason of their wide transactions use and acceptability. However widely acceptable they may be, we have learned to our cost that they are never so perfectly acceptable as to preclude an assets switch by holders, away from them and into gold. Gold, long since withdrawn from transactions use, has become the international unit of account. In terms of it all national currencies are defined. Its use springs from three motives: a limited transactions motive by certain banks, which results from its use in intra-central banks settlements; a precautionary motive, which induces certain groups to switch into gold if and when currencies, as reserve assets, fall under suspicion; and a speculative motive, which induces persons and groups to acquire and hold gold in the hope that the value of key currencies in terms of gold will be reduced.

* In May 1973 world reserves were divided in the following proportions: gold, 24 per cent, foreign exchange 66 per cent, and IMF positions and SDRs 10 per cent. For an explanation of SDRs, see p. 552 below.

In international payments, as in domestic monetary systems, a money form depends, among other things, predominantly upon its general acceptability. Apart from legal definition as the money form, acceptability is made complete if, as a commodity, the money form has the same value as it has when it acts as money. Originally, in the nineteenth century, gold had this identity of value, as coin or commodity. Should its value as a commodity rise above its value as a coin, coins would disappear from circulation, being melted down and sold as a commodity in the bullion market; should its value as coin rise above its commodity value (plus the cost of minting), then the commodity would become money and be minted into coin. In fact, the commodity value of gold depended upon its money value and in the pure gold standard these were identical. But quickly historical change destroyed the parallelism of domestic and international money. Within a single economy the need for money for the transactions of a growing exchange economy outgrows the gold supply. Representative money in the form of notes and ultimately bank deposits erects itself as an imposing edifice, at first on a gold base, later on a fractional reserve base, and ultimately upon a base of pure confidence and acceptability. For these later steps the international economy is only partially ready. Gold as a commodity stock cannot grow in pace with the development of trade. It is subject to the constraints of geology and mining techniques, and latterly to the competition of industrial demand. Left to the forces of the market it has risen in price. But as a money form its price in terms of representative money should, in the interests of the latter, be preserved. If switches between gold and representative money are to be avoided, then the price of gold in terms of representative money should be stable. But with this gold production is denied the stimulus of any advance in the market price, and growth of the world gold stock at anything like the rate of growth of world trade becomes impossible.

The international monetary history of the last half-century is in great part the story of our attempt to meet this dilemma. In the years which followed the First World War we banished gold from the shops and the market place to the vaults of central banks, even to a few central banks, and used in those currencies based upon gold a large addition of 'international representative money'. This measure met only qualified success. Confidence and acceptability are hard to transmit from the domestic to the international sphere. The belief in commodity money is still too strong and gold remains a preferred asset, for which the preference may at any time on trivial pretext provoke the assets switch by international liquidity holders which imperils the whole system. Meanwhile the gold stock, robbed of growth by gold's constant price in a price-inflationary world and depleted by hoarding, declines in relative magnitude to the key currencies.

The next stage of international liquidity development, following the domestic parallel, is intellectually clear: to build onto the international money supply, as we did years ago to the domestic cash supply, a flexible and variable addition of international credit units, similar in function to the world economy, as bank deposits are to persons in the domestic. This step, simple in theory, eludes us in practice. We remain with a gold exchange standard in which the limited gold supply seeks to burst through the price-ceiling artificially imposed by its parity with the key currencies. Moreover, a new force begins to manifest itself in that new industrial uses raise the commodity demand for gold yearly. Already the yearly industrial demand is near to the total yearly mined output, and there is, with hoarding, net depletion of the world monetary gold stock. Flows of gold into international liquidity have now become, not the first call upon new supplies, but the residuum, if any, after other demands are met.

The essential aspects of gold's legal monetary position may be quickly sketched. They are two: the defined monetary gold price, and the role of gold in the IMF under the Bretton Woods Agreement of 1944.

The monetary price of gold was fixed quite arbitrarily by President Roosevelt in January 1934, when it was raised from $20.50 to $35 per ounce. At the same time, the American Treasury undertook to buy gold from and sell it to foreign official holders 'for legitimate monetary purposes'. This commitment linked gold and the dollar as the main datum points of the international monetary system. It did more: it determined the value of the American dollar not only in terms of gold, but in terms of all other IMF gold-parity-defined currencies, so that any rise in the United States' gold price would constitute a *de facto* devaluation of the dollar — a course for long unacceptable to the American government for many reasons. Thus was precluded one obvious means of increasing the value of international liquidity — a rise in the gold price. A doubling of the gold price would automatically have increased international reserves by about 50 per cent, with gold rising to some 68 per cent of the new total.[9]

In December 1971 the United States, under the Smithsonian Agreement, increased the price of gold to $38 per ounce but ended the Federal Reserve's obligation to buy gold at that price. The dollar was, at one step, devalued by 8 per cent and made inconvertible into gold. Meanwhile, the price of gold on the free market rose to unprecedented heights under the influence of speculative demand.

Apart from the long-standing refusal of the Americans to devalue their currency there are arguments against increasing international liquidity in this way. The incidence of a rise in the gold price is uneven and increases the maldistribution of the gold stock. Large gold holders have their reserves handsomely written up; developing countries with minimal stocks barely benefit. Gold producers, South Africa and the Soviet Union, are enriched. It is argued that the whole effect of a large official price increase would be inflationary in an already inflationary world. 'Irresponsible' central banks might be unable (or unwilling) to neutralise the accretion of their gold reserve from the domestic money supply, a rise in which would generate internal inflation.

Trouble with the gold price began in the late forties when so-called premium gold sales incurred the disapproval of the IMF. In June 1947 the Fund circulated to all member countries a statement pointing to the danger to exchange stability of a growing volume of gold transactions at prices diverging from the official parities.[10] By 1951 the Fund found it impossible, in the face of the volume of such sales, to maintain its policy of trying to prevent them and reported that it was 'impracticable to expect all members to take uniform measures in order to achieve the objectives' of their premium gold policy. Immediately a number of countries, hitherto following the Fund's instructions, relaxed their restrictions on gold sales and movements; and with an increase in supplies to the free market, gold declined to about $37 per ounce. In March 1954 the London Gold Market was reopened, and from that time the Union of South Africa prohibited its gold producers from selling their output in free markets. All future sales were to be made through the South African Reserve Bank, which was to sell as much of its gold as possible on the London Market.

By 1961 the Americans were worried that the price in the London Market was running away from their $35 buying price and on their initiative a gold pool of the Federal Reserve and the leading European central banks was established. The pool augmented from official stocks the supplies of gold to the London Market in order to maintain the price within the narrow limits of 35.08\frac{3}{4}$ and $35.20 per ounce. This provided only temporary alleviation. From 1966 mounting private purchases took up all new supplies to the market and dug into the supplies of the gold pool. From November 1967 to March 1968 private buying of gold reached a feverish level, and on the latter date the non-American members of the pool withdrew their support. After hurried counsel among the central bankers and a two-week closure of the London Market, a two-tiered market emerged: a central bank market still exchanging gold for monetary purposes at the Federal Reserve price; and a free market. In the latter, located in London and Zürich, the price is free and gold is bought and sold by speculators and industrial users. In the London market, trading is conducted as before the crisis by the city's five licensed bullion dealers — Mocatta & Goldshmid (a subsidiary of Hambros), Samuel Montagu & Company, Sharpe, Pixley & Company, Rothschilds and Johnson Matthey. Now, however, the Bank of England no longer supplies gold to the market as agent for the South African Reserve Bank, nor does it supply bullion as agent for the now defunct gold pool.

The price in the free market rose gradually during 1968 and 1969 but fluctuated in the latter year around the $40 mark. As the series of dollar crises of 1971 and 1972 proceeded the price rose very sharply and in May 1973 went to well over $100. This represented an excess demand stemming from lack of confidence in the dollar and speculative demand for gold itself both for hedging against currency loss and for commodity arbitrage.

Let us consider the role and nature of key currencies more fully. Any currency which is to serve efficiently as a reserve or key currency must satisfy certain conditions. Firstly, it must be the currency of a great trading nation, one which may be earned easily by the normal processes of trade and one whose balances ensure that they may be exchanged for goods both desirable in themselves and for the world demand which exists for them. Secondly, the currency must be stable in value, both in goods terms and in terms of other currencies. At least, in a world where currencies are losing value, it must lose value no faster than other currencies. Thirdly, it must be a currency which is supported in its home country by a reliable and sophisticated banking system complete with all the paraphernalia of money markets and ancillary institutions. Finally, and most problematically, it must be a currency whose balance of payments must conform to certain principles. This aspect we must examine rather carefully and shall return to shortly.

There have been two major key currencies in the past century: the pound and the dollar. Sterling, as a result of Britain's great mercantile dominance after 1870, was first in the field. Britain's trading structure, the structure of her balance of payments and its reaction to the business cycle were all conducive to sterling's efficiency as a key currency. Although Britain ran a surplus on current account, there was no scarcity of sterling, since she lent widely and on long term. Moreover, in recession her exports tended to fall more than her imports and thus provide either a diminished surplus or a deficit. The currency did not tend to become chronically scarce in the recession phase of the cycle.

The dollar, a powerful world currency since the First World War, was slow to enter the field as a key currency (perhaps because of the late development of the American banking system and its late participation in international banking); but after the Second World War, when Britain's foreign trade declined relatively and when its banking system was sealed off from the rest of the world behind the barrier of exchange control, the dollar surged to the leading position as an international currency. Since 1959, when the pound became fully convertible, that currency has shared with the dollar, though in the minor position, the dual-key-currency system which has been a feature of the Bretton Woods period, which the writer would define as 1959 to the present. For although the IMF came into operation in February 1947, the so-called transition period during which the existence of widespread exchange controls held the Bretton Woods system in abeyance, was lengthened from five years to twelve. It was not until the full convertibility of the Western European countries was established in January 1959 that the system came into its own. During the Bretton Woods period, sterling has furnished 10 per cent of total world reserves. The dollar has risen in importance fairly steadily, from about 18 per cent in 1959 to nearly 30 per cent in 1969.

To return to general principles. Key currencies must serve in the world both as transactions currencies and as reserve currencies. In the first role, as with domestic money, their supply is important; in the second, stability in value is vital and confidence in their continuing value is a *sine qua non* of their efficiency and continuance as a key currency.

Supply of key currencies to the world at large must be through the balances of payments of the key currency countries. A key currency must be earnable through trade, or alternatively the country concerned, if it is earning a surplus on current account, must lend abroad so that it is freely available to other countries. To the extent that it becomes scarce it is ineffective as a key currency. Certain conditions are obviously advantageous. For example, a key currency country may run a large surplus but invest much of it abroad. Or such a country with large reserves of gold may tolerate a balance-of-payments deficit which supplies the rest of the world with its currency. From the supply angle, the key currencies have in the sixties been reasonably adequate. Sterling, with either bare balance or deficit in its balance of payments, has not been scarce. The United States, with a deficit born of its great investment abroad, its aid programme and its military commitments has, at great cost to its gold reserve, allowed dollars to move into international monetary use. It is not the supply aspect which is defective, it is another element, the confidence element, which detracts from the efficiency of these currencies in the international field.

It is clear that, to satisfy the confidence condition, any key currency has to walk a razor's edge. On the one hand it must never be a 'hard' currency, that is, it must never be in short supply, difficult to earn by reason of a very favourable balance of payments; on the other hand it must never be so 'soft' that its balance-of-payments deficit gives rise to lack of confidence that its external value (exchange rate) is maintainable. It might have appeared, say, in 1960, that the United States was admirably placed to provide, in the dollar, the services of a key currency. Its deficit was large enough to supply the world with dollar balances but not so large as to cause uneasiness about the strength of the dollar. Moreover with a gold reserve of $17.8 billion, the United States could tolerate deficits in its balance of payments for many years. It could, it might have appeared, regard its external deficit as a currency service, supplying international liquidity to the world at large. Alas, in 1969 it became apparent how many elements of doubt compounded to destroy that comfortable belief: French intransigence, sterling's prolonged weakness, a belief that the United States would eventually be forced to devalue and raise the price of gold, all threatened the dollar in its role as key currency. After two further uneasy years of makeshift and with a worsening balance of payments, the United States was forced in 1971 to place the whole Bretton Woods system in jeopardy by suspending gold convertibility of the dollar and using direct import controls to influence its balance of payments.

The fact is that, looking back over the Bretton Woods period, we have never been without a confidence problem. It has manifested itself in two forms. From 1959 to the middle sixties we feared that, in a dual-key-currency world, holders of international balances would shift uneasily from one currency to the other as estimates of their individual strengths and prospects ebbed and flowed; that there would be a see-sawing movement of confidence which would be particularly detrimental to sterling as the weaker of the two currencies. This confidence problem proved less difficult than it might, but it gave place in the later sixties to a more extreme problem: lack of confidence in both key currencies. The devaluation of sterling in November 1967 created a general lack of confidence in key currencies which came to include the dollar and to lead to a flight from currencies into gold, which precipitated the gold crisis of March 1968.

It might be argued that, in the light of its chequered record during the Bretton Woods period, the key-currency approach to the international liquidity problem has failed. That is not so. Key currencies, due to their transactions' value in use and their role as trading currencies, will always form part of the total stock of international liquidity. It is as impossible to stop their limited use for the holding of balances as it is to expand it to fill the gap left by the shrinking amount of gold. The confidence and stability aspects of such currencies, and the difficulties for the countries which operate them in reconciling their own domestic economic problems with those appropriate for maintaining confidence in the key currency, make it imperative that efforts to increase the supply of international liquidity should be switched to the purposive creation of a flexible form of international settlement unit.

This brings us to the third form of existing international liquidity: the claims of countries which are members of the IMF upon borrowing rights from that organisation. Since the working of the IMF will be described in the next chapter, we may be content here with a very brief account of the role which it plays in supplying supplementary international liquidity. Suffice it to say that for this function the Fund consists of a pool of currencies contributed by member nations according to a quota system. From this pool members may purchase foreign currencies (to supplement their reserves) in return for their own currency. However, such purchases (or, as we say, 'drawing rights') are strictly limited by the Fund's rules. Were they not so limited, the Fund's entire stock of a scarce currency might quickly be depleted if the surplus country took no action to correct the surplus and if it were large and prolonged. In fact, drawing rights on the Fund are progressively curtailed as each country draws upon it. Only the first 25 per cent of the quota, the so-called 'first tranche', may be drawn on by member countries automatically. For this reason we can only rightly include in our total of international liquidity the total of members' automatic drawing rights in the Fund.

The original conception of the IMF was that it would provide only short-term supplementation of its members' own gold and currency reserves. In the longer run, balance-of-payments deficits would be corrected by changes in members' exchange rates. That conception has not been fulfilled in practice. The desire of the Fund (and of its members) to maintain exchange rates for long periods, the small currency resources of the Fund itself, the growing shortage of international liquidity to serve in a world of swiftly growing trade and great payments instability, and latterly the confidence crises in respect of the key currencies — all these have demonstrated the need for expansion and reorientation of the world's stock of international liquidity. The Fund's currency resources have over the years been expanded (a) by revising on several occasions the quota subscriptions of members, and (b) by the right to borrow currencies from its ten largest members; but these came increasingly to be seen as palliatives, insufficient in scale and kind to deal with the problem. As the sixties passed, it became apparent that the international monetary system had to cross the chasm which the leading domestic systems had crossed nearly a century earlier; it had to devise means of moving beyond commodity and representative money to the creation of flexible credit units, optimally distributed and internationally controlled. The efforts of the Group of Ten and then of the IMF to devise such a system culminated in the Rio Agreement of 1967 and the creation of the Special Drawing Rights administered by the IMF. This system will be discussed in Chapter 21 when we deal with that organisation.

(iii) The Gold Standard and the Gold Exchange Standard

We now turn to examine briefly the salient features of what has been, on the record, the most successful international currency system, the international gold standard. For sixty years, from the 1870s to the 1930s with a brief intermission for the First World War, it was the accepted mechanism of world payments, looked back upon with nostalgia or with loathing according to whether the mind focused on its early heyday or its final disruption in the interwar period. Its structure and principles are vestigial in the system of the post-war period.

There are three possible gold standards and they have followed one another in historical sequence: the pure gold standard or gold specie standard; the gold bullion standard; and the gold exchange standard. We deal with these in turn.

Under a pure or gold specie standard the monetary authority undertakes to buy and sell gold without limit at fixed prices. The buying and selling prices may differ, but not widely, allowing a small margin to the central bank as a handling charge. Gold circulates domestically as coin and, if bank notes are in circulation, they are backed 100 per cent by gold and are convertible on demand at par by the banking system. Gold in any form and with stipulated fineness may be freely imported and exported.

With such conditions existing in a number of countries, all such countries would be on a full gold standard. That is, their currency units, each defined in gold terms, would be thus defined relatively through a series of fixed exchange rates, free to move only between the narrow band of the gold points. (For a description of the determination of this band and of the gold points see p. 434 above.) Since gold is acceptable within and between all countries and is also held as reserves, its flows between countries follow the variations of balances of payments.

The adjustment effect of these movements operates by its influence on relative price levels. Surplus countries accumulate gold, deficit countries lose gold. Prices rise in the surplus countries and fall in the deficit countries. Demand, assumed to be sensitive to price changes, is switched away from the goods of surplus countries to the goods of deficit countries, while within countries factors move smoothly in response to switches in demand for final products. Gold flows cease only when balances of payments are in equilibrium. For this theoretical process to be viable, individual countries are required to observe certain tacitly accepted rules of the gold standard game. There must be no artificial impediment to trade flows, such as tariffs or import quotas. Countries must accept the effects of gold inflows or outflows upon their price level without demur and without any policies of neutralisation.

The gold specie standard endured in forms approximating to the above model from the 1870s to the outbreak of the First World War. A fixed value for sterling in terms of gold had been in force since 1816. In 1850 the French franc became a gold-based unit. The German Empire made gold its standard in 1871. Switzerland and Belgium followed in 1878. The United States had a bimetallic standard and did not adopt monometallism based on gold until 1900. Yet withal, there was little uniformity in the application of the gold standard principle and there were variations in the legal and institutional practices. Britain, Germany and, belatedly, the United States had a full gold specie standard. France conformed only partially, since her monetary authorities could exchange notes either for gold or for full legal-tender silver coins. Numerous countries, including Russia and Japan, were only on a gold exchange standard, holding their exchange reserves in gold-backed currencies.

There were other more fundamental divergences of the nineteenth-century gold standard from the theoretical model so often presented. The first lies in the falsity of the picture of adjustment by varying price levels. In fact, the influence of gold movements on price levels was slight and, owing to the large cushion of international credit and the expansion of world trade during the period, there was but small movement of gold from country to country. Had large quantities of gold in fact flowed, and had prices varied in accordance with the quantity theory, the price history of the period would have been one of sharp deflation and inflation. In fact, the ubiquity of internationally traded commodities gave to domestic and international prices a strong backbone of stability and the whole apparatus of the reaction of trade flows to changes in relative national price levels was never really put to the test. In the later years of the century, the interest rate was being used to attract capital and gold flows, and it provided an adequate mechanism of adjustment via the capital account of the balance of payments under the prevailing conditions.

But by far the most interesting qualification to the traditional gold standard model is that, within the framework of the standard, sterling operated as an international currency on equal terms with gold. One writer on the subject hints that sterling was the stronger of the two and that gold derived its value as a monetary asset from its convertibility into sterling. Certainly the record of sterling as an international currency long after the collapse of the gold standard shows its great power to stand alone as such.[11] Sterling was, for many countries, the normal means of settling trading indebtedness, and gold was transferred only as a balancing item—for example, when a country's commercial banks were called upon to make more payments to foreigners than were compensated by receipts. In such a situation any tendency for banks to quote higher rates for foreign currencies would be checked by the purchase of gold from the central bank and its shipment abroad. (This shipment, in practice, would be undertaken by bullion merchants as an arbitrage transaction.) Apart from this trading use, sterling was used equally with gold as a means of settling international balances between countries, that is, for compensatory monetary movements. Overseas banks in many countries held working balances of sterling, in the form of London acceptances, loans to the London discount market or London bank deposits, and were prepared to use these balances for residual clearing. Moreover in some countries, central banks held part or all of their main reserve in sterling, preferring sterling to gold, partly for the interest which the sterling assets yielded and partly because the bulk of their trade lay with the United Kingdom. Sterling balances were a trading convenience. Thus, the picture of gold standard operation before 1914 is one of a close interchangeability of gold and sterling which gave to the Bank of England not only the role of regulator of the British monetary system but, in great part, that of regulator of the gold standard and the international payments system. This system was capable of enduring only as long as sterling, as the international currency operating with gold, was unimpeachably strong and was backed by financial institutions of strength and probity, and as long as its convertibility into gold was at all times assured. In the gold standard of the interwar period these conditions were not satisfied. Not only was sterling weak and incapable of assuming its prewar goal but other gold based currencies, of varying strength, operated with it as reserve currencies in a gold exchange system whose structure was inherently weak.

Three features strengthened the pre-1914 gold standard; features missing from its later reconstruction in the 1920s. First, was the trade structure of the period, based on free trade? For the standard to function smoothly there had to be no scarcity of sterling, while at the same time the British balance-of-payments structure had to be sound to ensure the unquestioned gold convertibility of the pound. Both conditions were satisfied. British loans to primary-producing countries allowed them to increase their purchases not only from Britain but from other countries. Debt service then in turn helped the British invisible account and prevented any significant loss of gold by Britain.[12] Meanwhile the ever-increasing British market benefited the primary producers, who were able by sales to Britain to finance not only their debt service but import of manufactures as well. Trade and capital flows moved easily in the relatively free trade and confident world of the nineteenth century.[13] The second feature which advantaged the gold standard in this period was that, as an international payments system, the standard functioned in an epoch of unparallelled commercial and industrial expansion and that the inherently deflationary tendencies, so strongly to be revealed in the dismal 1930s, did not manifest themselves in strength between 1880 and 1914.

Finally, the nineteenth century saw the steady growth of an international financial fraternity, which expressed itself through international banking and the co-operation of the great central banks of the leading countries. This gave to the system a loosely knit, flexible, institutional framework through which to function. Such central bank co-operation was very real, involving all the participant countries in some surrender of international sovereignty — a surrender partly to the objective gold standard rules of the game and partly to the discretionary authority of the London money market and the Bank of England, which virtually managed the gold supply. Although it is customary to regard the nineteenth century gold standard as an automatic system without formal organisation or specified modes of operation, it is arguable that the standard was in fact quasi-organisational, being operated by a coterie of central bankers co-operating under the leadership of the Bank of England on behalf of the world business community. The restored gold standard of the 1920s had no such institutional framework. The international financial fraternity had been shattered by the war, by rampant nationalism and by a collapse of confidence. The new standard was diversely operated mainly by national governments and politicians for national ends. There were exceptions to this. One thinks, for example, of the influence on monetary affairs of the friendship of Montagu Norman of the Bank of England and Benjamin Strong of the Federal Reserve. Such exceptions were few, however; and it is true that, after 1918, concerted monetary co-operation between central bankers had completely broken down. The old gold standard had been operated by monetary technicians, according to widely accepted technical criteria; the new was operated by 'monetary authorities' for diverse and often ill-understood objectives.

All that we have said indicates that the gold standard of the nineteenth century, both in its institutional arrangements and in its working, diverged far from the theoretical model. It worked well because of a concomitance of favourable circumstances not to be repeated in the interwar period. Its success was apparent, and the almost universal demand for its rehabilitation after 1918 was understandable. It was hardly realised at that time, however, that the pre-war gold standard had not really worked in accordance with the model. Unfortunately its successor of the twenties would neither work like the model nor was it favoured by circumstances to achieve its own *modus operandi*.

The gold bullion standard, advocated by Ricardo as early as 1816 in his *Proposals for an Economical and Secure Economy* as a means of economising the use of gold by concentrating it in national reserves, resembled its predecessor save that gold coins were not in circulation and, within countries, bank notes were not redeemable in gold and in most cases were backed only by fractional gold reserves. In 1918 the Cunliffe Committee[14] recommended that the link between the pound and gold should now be made by the Bank of England selling gold to all comers at £3 17s. 10½d. per ounce, but only in bars of 400 fine ounces. This, with free import and export of the metal, would retain the principle of convertibility, preclude the internal circulation of gold, and limit its use to monetary final settlements. To this was later to be added the common practice of exchanging gold 'by earmark', i.e. by allowing it to remain in one central bank although its ownership might be shifted to another. (This practice was facilitated by the establishment in 1929 of the Bank for International Settlements, which aided the practice by keeping earmark accounts.)

Internationally the international liquidity problem in the early interwar years was seen as one of gold shortage. The great price inflations wrought by the war, the loss of confidence in paper currencies, the inability of Britain and sterling to resume their role of the nineteenth century, all necessitated a great expansion of world reserves. To devalue currency units against gold, that is, to increase the price of gold, was an obvious solution; but a complete reorientation of the whole structure of the exchange rates of the world was a task beyond accomplishment in the confused conditions and *ad hoc* thinking of the immediate post-war years. The response of most countries was to increase their reserves by taking gold coin out of circulation, and between 1913 and 1925 $2.7 billion of gold was channelled to international reserves by this means.[15] The Genoa Conference of 1922 endorsed this procedure and advocated the return of the powers to a standard on the gold exchange principle as soon as possible. Germany, exhausted and depleted by her inflation, returned to gold in 1924 with American help from the Dawes Loan. Britain, doggedly following the

Cunliffe Committee's advice, returned in April 1925, France in 1928. The United States had already led the way for Europe in June 1919.

The effect of the new gold bullion standard was to rob gold of its function as a national commodity money and to set up paper currencies, albeit gold-backed, as international reserve money. For the first time in the history of international money gold coexisted with alternative forms of international liquidity, with all the potential for switching between the forms which that entailed. The key currency principle had been established.

It may be argued that in the nineteenth century sterling had been held with gold, but up to the First World War the main purpose in holding sterling was settlement of trading debts. It was held for the 'transactions' rather than the 'precautionary' motive.

The paradox of the key currency—that it is only available when the key currency country is in deficit and that when it is in deficit the currency is suspect and its acceptability impaired by a confidence problem—was not understood at this juncture. Britain had sensed rather than understood it when she decided to return to the gold standard in 1925 at the pre-war parity of gold with sterling, but by so doing she created in the resultant over-valuation of sterling the very circumstances which sapped foreign confidence in her currency and ultimately forced her retreat from gold in September 1931. Her relatively weak position in foreign trade due to the uncompetitiveness of her basic export industries and the sluggishness of her economy relative to those of other industrial countries, did much to reduce the status of sterling as a key currency between 1925 and 1931; but her relatively swift recovery from the depression (1929–33) and the formation of the sterling bloc after 1931[16] did much to repair this decline.

The breakdown of the interwar gold standard cannot be adequately described without tracing the monetary history of the Western world in the period.[17] Britain led the way off gold in 1931 and was accompanied by much of the British Commonwealth and such Western European countries as had a large volume of trade to finance in sterling. Germany and much of Eastern Europe left the standard soon after and retired behind trade and payments barriers which reflected increasingly autarkic economic policies. France, Belgium, Holland, Italy, Poland, Luxembourg and Switzerland remained on gold, with increasing evidence of overvaluation of their currencies until the breakup of the Gold Bloc in 1936.

To understand fully the pathology of the gold standard it would be necessary to examine its record country by country—a task impossible here. Some general comments upon the breakdown are, however, in order.

First, there was no acknowledged leader of the standard in this period. Britain, the arbiter of the nineteenth-century standard was now too economically weak to assume leadership. The United States, with her new and untried banking system and her volatile economy, was equally unqualified.

Second, it proved impossible to operate the new standard as an adjustment system. In the contractionary economic environment of the period, price adjustment by purposive expansions and contractions as gold flowed along the contour lines of balances of payments was impossible. Unemployment-plagued countries with deficits could not improve their trade by deflation. Surplus countries either would not expand or could not; their banking systems choked with excess reserves. It has been said that 'the gold standard failed largely because the deficit countries could not and the surplus countries would not observe the rules'.

Third, the international financial fraternity which had been the 'institutional' framework of the old gold standard had been shattered by the war and replaced by a fierce nationalism. International monetary policies were now made by politicians and not by central bankers. The whole period was punctuated by rivalries and antagonisms which were inimical to the working of any truly international system.

Fourth, interest rates and capital flows under the new standard operated in a destabilising fashion rather than according to gold standard theory. Long-term capital outflow from Britain was not, as it had been before 1914, equilibrating. Recipients of British capital now had a wide choice of industrial countries in which to shop for industrial goods, and capital outflow served rather to build British short-term liabilities. Moreover, British external lending had declined by 1929 to average over the previous five years 37 per cent of the pre-1914 flow.[18] Meanwhile Paris and New York were emerging as financial centres. With this multicentre world, interest-rate changes tended to be competitive rather than complementary, and as Brown, the leading analyst of the gold standard in this period says, co-operation between the centre creditor countries broke down and 'violated the first principle of any stable gold standard system . . . that there must be stable credit conditions at the centre'.[19]

Finally confidence, that elusive yet essential quality of any international system, was lacking. An essential of such a 'mixed' gold standard was that, in times of crisis, funds should flow towards the key currency countries with their short-term liabilities. Instead they, and particularly sterling, tended to lose capital, so that confidence in exchange rates and in the whole gold standard was impaired. The departure of funds from London to New York and Paris in the summer of 1931 drove Britain off gold in September of that year. Once Britain left the standard it was doomed. Thirty-five countries left gold between April 1929 and April 1933.

Only the United States with its satellite Canada and the tottering Gold Bloc remained.

The third stage in the international career of gold is still being enacted. It has been and still is described as a 'gold exchange standard', but its claim to such a description is vague, and the main aim of these concluding paragraphs is to examine its spurious nature. It partakes of three elements of a gold standard. First, gold is the international unit of account, in terms of which national currency units and therefore, by inference, exchange rates are defined. Second, gold is still held as a form of international reserve asset, side by side with key currencies. And third, balance-of-payments disequilibria and therefore flows of reserves between countries have to be met by marginal adjustment in income in the countries concerned. The first two of these elements require no comment. Let us concentrate on the third.

The Bretton Woods Agreement of 1944 established the present world monetary system. Exchange rates are fixed in accordance with the defined gold parity of currencies and are only variable by agreement with the IMF in circumstances described as 'fundamental disequilibrium'. A large literature grew up[20] aimed at clarifying the circumstances which this phrase might encompass, but we may take it to mean a condition of structural balance-of-payments deficit or surplus which cannot be adjusted by domestic policies without incurring domestic underemployment or inflation, and which is too prolonged to be met by drawing upon or accumulating reserves. Reserves are held predominantly by countries themselves in the form of gold and key currencies, but the world total is augmented by the currency pool of the IMF upon which member countries have stipulated drawing rights according to a quota system.

Suppression policies are also denied. It is a central tenet of the Bretton Woods system that 'the interests of political harmony and economic welfare are jointly served by a system of unfettered, multilateral trade and convertible currencies'.[21] The IMF was charged, therefore, with establishing, after a five-year transition period, a system of multilateral trade which precluded the use of trade or exchange controls for balance-of-payments purposes.

The model of the international economy which emerged from the agreement was inherently defective in that it lacked an adjustment mechanism. The aim in theory of limiting exchange-rate changes and in practice of preserving wellnigh rigid rates precluded the use of changes of exchange rates for adjustment purposes. Repression of deficits by exchange controls was also precluded. Two alternatives only remained: the financing of deficits by drawing upon reserves, and the engineering of such changes as might be regarded by countries as acceptable in their domestic levels of income, prices and costs. The first of these became progressively difficult for key currencies because of the inadequate amount of international liquidity and the meagre augmentation provided by the IMF. The second was haltingly adopted by some countries, in particular, by Britain, in spite of its costs in income and growth foregone. One of the key features of the gold standard thus reappeared: the linking of outflows of reserves with deflationary policies by reserve-losing countries. It was not now linked directly to the domestic price level, as it was under a gold specie standard; nor even through the fractional reserve systems of the central banks, as in the thirties. Changes in the reserves held by exchange stabilisation funds are not linked directly to the domestic money or credit supply. There is no automatic element. But the reaction of the monetary authorities of a reserve losing country has, by a reflex action, been to raise interest rates and deflate, usually by monetary policy, the level of their economic activity. It is arguable that, because of full-employment commitments and the expansionary conditions of the postwar period, deflations have not been pressed to damaging extent. None the less, the conscious use of deflation to cure external deficit, the choice between policies for domestic or external stability, have reappeared. Deflationary policies for the deficit country have been favoured by the Fund and the financial establishment as in the traditional gold standard model. Germany, the only consistent surplus country of the period, has been pressed (particularly in OEEC confrontations in the late fifties) to expand her economy in order to dissipate her surplus. While it is inevitable that adjustments of domestic income must play a part in correcting balance-of-payments deficits, the part assigned to them since the war has been purely that of old gold standard theory.

The Bretton Woods system undoubtedly partakes of most of the elements of a gold exchange standard. It was not, however, regarded as a return to the gold standard during the period of its planning. The British in particular were deeply hostile to the gold standard in the forties, and would never have agreed at Bretton Woods to any return to it. The Keynes and White Plans both steered a middle course between the gold standard, which would have been unacceptable to several of the leading countries, and the demonetising of gold, which would have been opposed both by the gold producers and by the United States. In 1943 there were some critics who opposed the new currency world because it was, they said, a return to the gold standard. Others were critical because it was not a return to gold. It has, however, been the case that the working of the system by the main powers and by the IMF has destroyed this compromise and produced conditions which approximate to a gold exchange standard. Whatever the system was intended to be, that is what it has become.

(iv) Conclusion

It is but a hundred years since the old gold standard established itself. Through just one century of search for a stable international monetary system, a number of facets of the whole wide problem run and interweave like continuous threads. They are revealed alike by what theory has to tell us of the behaviour of international systems and by the facts of economic history. We will end this chapter by cataloguing them.

The first, perhaps the most challenging, problem which is posed is that of the conflict between the policy aims (often mutually exclusive) of domestic price and income stability at full employment and stability of the balance of payments. This was the quandary basic in the gold standard: solvable in the nineteenth century by a concomitance of favourable circumstances which allowed marginal adjustment in the centre country to condition the whole system; disastrous in the twentieth century, when the system required adjustments in the surplus and the deficit countries which they were not prepared to make.

The second problem is that of the role in the system which the exchange rate is expected to play. Away from the fixed exchange rates of the gold standard, the agony of not knowing what to do about exchange rates seizes us. Apart from a general acceptance of the fact that completely free rates in an unfettered market are destabilising and undesirable, there is no agreement as to where in the spectrum between totally free and rigidly fixed rates an optimum system should be located.

Thirdly, any international system should contain within itself forces which make for the adjustment of balances of payments of member countries. Much of the theoretical argument of recent chapters has been concerned with how such forces may operate, where they will bring pressure to bear and how they may be reconciled with other forces in the system. It has been argued with persistence that the Bretton Woods system under which we now operate is defective in its lack of an adequate adjustment mechanism.

Fourthly, the development of the international monetary system demands an adequate and well-distributed stock of international money to act as settlement of final balances and to be held by countries as reserves. In the evolution of such international money, we seem unable even in a technically sophisticated age to progress beyond a point which in the evolution of domestic money we had reached in the late nineteenth century. To pass from gold and key currencies, with their size limitation and involuntary supply variations, to a flexible system of internationally created money increasing *pro rata* with the growth of world trade is at the moment the greatest practical operation demanded of us.

Finally, there is the ubiquitous problem of confidence. To operate an international monetary system which, in the jet age, is as compact as was the English monetary system of 1900, we require a vastly greater measure of confidence than we now have. Much of the instability of the Bretton Woods system is born of lack of confidence in a currency, in a price of gold, in the ability of a government to manage its economic affairs, or in the authority of the IMF to discipline governments. To make further progress we must be capable not only of confidence in these things, but also in the new and novel creation of an international monetary unit and in the international body which orders its affairs.

21
The Bretton Woods System and the International Monetary Fund

(i) Introduction

THE IMF is the institution which symbolises, interprets and has given continuity to the Bretton Woods system. This chapter will describe its nature, growth and functions and, very briefly, comment on its usefulness. No more is necessary here. The literature on the Fund is now large and grows continually.[1] To this specialist literature the reader must go for the minutiae. Here we concern ourselves, hopefully, with principles.

(ii) The Model and Operation of the Fund

The Bretton Woods system was conceived as a whole. The wartime discussions between the United States and British governments which culminated in the Bretton Woods Conference of 1944 created two international institutions, the IMF and the International Bank for Reconstruction and Development – now called the World Bank. The IMF was to have jurisdiction over currencies, exchange rates and the balance-of-payments policies of member countries; the World Bank was to raise and lend capital for development purposes. In the original conception[2] a third body, the International Trade Organisation was later to be set up to regulate and harmonise commercial policies and lead a drive for free trade, and there was a vague declaration of intent to promote international policies for full employment and stabilisation of primary commodity prices. The Havana Charter, proclaiming ITO, was never ratified by the main governments concerned, and ITO as an organisation died still-born, although much of its intended work later passed to GATT. The declaration of intent on international full employment and primary product price

The Economics of the Balance of Payments

stabilisation bore some fruit in a series of reports prepared by *ad hoc* committees of the United Nations in the late forties and early fifties. But, in general, the great integrated conception of international economic co-operation in the post-war world faded as the idealism of the immediate post-war period gave way to hard-headed politics. The Fund and the Bank became so-called specialised agencies of the United Nations and later, in 1948, GATT appeared to deal with tariff reduction and codes of commercial policy. For practical purposes, each of these organisations goes its separate way and operates in its own functional area. In effect the IMF and the Bank operate without interference from the United Nations. Eastern bloc countries are not members, and this has prevented the organisations from becoming a forum for cold war political debate, like the United Nations Regional Economic Commissions. The only formal requirement is that 'their annual reports are placed before the Economic and Social Council'. This, however, is a mere formality.

In July 1944, after two years of intensive thought and planning by the British and American governments, the Bretton Woods Agreement established the Fund and Bank. After a delay for ratification of the Agreement by governments, the Fund was established with a membership of thirty on 27 December 1945, and held its first meeting at Savannah, Georgia, in March 1946. It opened for currency operations on 1 March 1947. These events are now only of historical importance. What is important, in retrospect, was the establishment by the Agreement of certain basic principles in international finance, which have only recently been abrogated and which progressively moulded the international economy to the shape it now has. First, is the principle of international economic co-operation itself; for, daunting though international monetary affairs have been since 1944, they have not shown the naked self-interest or unconcern for the consequences of national action that was evident in the interwar years. Second, the principle that responsibility for balance-of-payments disequilibrium rests both on surplus and deficit countries has been, in the main, accepted — by the United States between 1945 and 1953 and by West Germany during the fifties. Finally, the principle that multilateral trade maximises the welfare derived from international commerce restored, albeit somewhat belatedly, a world of convertible currencies and freedom from direct control in December 1958. It might have appeared at first as though the establishment of these principles was to be more important than the establishment of the Fund itself, which seemed at first unequal to the task of administering them. Later (from the mid-fifties), the Fund took on new life, and faith in its mission and future was renewed.

The Fund consists of a pool of currencies and of gold contributed by member states according to a quota system which has been revised several times during the life of the Fund. The largest quotas are those of the United States and Great Britain. Upon this pool, members have specified drawing rights, being permitted to buy a currency which is, for the time being, scarce to them in exchange for their own. Thus, the Fund acts as a buffer between deficits in members' balances of payments and their own gold and currency reserves. In its articles are laid down conditions and limits for the supply of currencies, for ensuring that it holds an adequate amount of each currency, and for the repayment by members of their drawings on the Fund. The pool is, in essence, a supplement to international liquidity.

The pool, originally $8.8 billion in 1944, has been augmented during the twenty-seven years of the Fund's life: (a) by the addition of the quotas of new members—the membership has risen from thirty-five at the end of 1945 to seventy-one at 31 January 1961, and to 125 at 1 July 1973; (b) by revisions of quotas in 1959, 1965 and 1970; and (c) by the Fund's right, under an agreement of 1961, to borrow up to a limit of $6 billion from the so-called Group of Ten which consists of Belgium, Britain, Canada, France, West Germany, Italy, Japan, Sweden, the Netherlands and U S A. This group—the ten richest industrial nations in the IMF—soon acquired great influence and power and in the sixties became the negotiating body concerned with plans for the reform of the Fund and the creation of SDRs. In July 1973 the total of Fund quota subscriptions had grown to $29,169.4 million.

Drawing rights are limited by the following conditions. First, drawings of foreign currencies by any member must not, within any yearly period, cause the Fund's holdings of that member's currency to rise by more than 25 per cent of its quota. Second, a member's accumulated drawings must not cause the Fund's holdings of its currency to be more than 200 per cent of its quota although, on the basis of precedent, a waiver may be granted to countries to exceed the 200 per cent of quota limit. Third, within these limits the right to draw the first 25 per cent of quota is virtually automatic. Beyond this 'gold tranche' the successive 'credit tranches' up to 100 per cent of quota are subjected to increasing Fund scrutiny and growing Fund advice on how the country may eliminate its deficit.

The theory underlying the virtually automatic access of members to the gold tranche is that, since as a rule a country's quota payments to the Fund are made 25 per cent in gold and 75 per cent in the member's currency, the first drawing of 25 per cent will only serve to increase the Fund's holding of the member currency to 100 per cent of the quota. In this sense,

The Economics of the Balance of Payments

the member is simply borrowing back the gold originally contributed as part of the quota.

Since drawings upon the Fund are supposed to cover temporary balance-of-payments deficits, members are expected to repay the Fund within a short period – in practice, three to five years. By the close of each financial year of the Fund, a member must repurchase with gold or convertible currencies one-half of any increase during the year in the Fund's holdings of its currency in excess of 75 per cent of its quota. There are waivers of this condition if the member's national currency reserves are inadequate. However, the conditions ensure that a member (a) will not ordinarily finance more than half of a balance-of-payments deficit by drawing on the Fund, or (b) will not increase its own reserves by drawing from the Fund and adding to these reserves.

Repayments to the Fund must be made with either gold or convertible currencies; but, of the latter, repayment must not be made in a currency of which the Fund holds more than 75 per cent of the quota. From early 1964 Fund holdings of United States dollars rose above this datum and the dollar was no longer the modal currency of repayment. However, the United States facilitated countries which normally hold their reserves in dollars by drawing convertible currencies (certain European currencies and Canadian dollars) from the Fund and selling them for dollars to countries wishing to make Fund repayments.

To avoid a tedious and lengthy examination of the Fund's constitution, we shall rest our discussion of its activities upon three ideas which are basic to the operational plan:

1. A satisfactory structure of world trade can only be built upon an ordered pattern of stable exchange rates.
2. Disequilibria in balances of payments are of short duration and are often self-correcting. To meet these, deficit countries may draw upon the resources of the Fund. Only when disequilibrium is prolonged and would entail a heavy drain upon these resources is the Fund prepared to sanction a change in the member's exchange rate. Short-term disequilibria are met by drawings; 'fundamental disequilibria' by change of the member's exchange rate.
3. Only under conditions of multilateral trade, absence of exchange control and freedom from discrimination, can full benefit be derived from international trade. A period of five years from the date of commencement of Fund operations (1 March 1947) was appointed as a transition period during which restrictions and discrimination were deemed tolerable. Member states were to be progressively under pressure to make their

currencies convertible and were in any case to end all restrictions on payments by March 1952.

These ideas have motivated the Fund in the three most important fields of its activity:

    I. exchange-rate policy;
   II. its work in the establishment of a system of multilateral payments; and
  III. the provision of currencies.

These fields and the Fund's record in respect of them, we shall deal with in turn.

I. The Fund's exchange rate policy rests upon the principle of managed flexibility which has already been discussed (see p. 473 above). There is no necessity to redefine it here or to harp upon its importance in shaping Fund policies. It is necessary, however, to note certain events and attitudes which have shaped the Fund's exchange policy. A determining event at the outset was its attitude towards the fixing of initial parities in 1946. Wartime inflations had re-aligned national price levels and rendered obsolete the exchange rates which had obtained in 1939. The task of establishing a structure of initial exchange parities to govern the international trade of the post-war world was a difficult one. Moreover, the chaotic condition of world trade and finance in 1946 was such that exchange rates could have little meaning or influence. Any system of rates, even if successfully established for a short period, would soon have been superseded. It was clear that, for some time, need and not cost (and therefore not exchange rates) would dictate the pattern of world trade. For this reason, the Fund accepted in December 1946 the rates notified by its members, more than half of which were the same as or higher than they were in September 1939. This cautious and, in the circumstances, perhaps unavoidable action had two unfortunate effects: it made the Fund's attitude towards exchange rates appear passive, if not negative, from the outset; but it also implied that at some later stage an attempt would be made to establish a more appropriate structure of rates appropriate to general payments equilibrium. This was never attempted. The initial exchange-rate structure hardened and became the structure of the post-transition as well as of the transition period.

Four major exchange-rate crises have taken place during the Fund's reign: the devaluations of September 1949; the devaluations of November 1967; the Canadian experiments with free rates from 1950 to 1962 and from 1970, and the reversion to floating rates of many of the Fund's leading members since 1971. The first two were crisis adjustments, both triggered by the devaluation of sterling and bringing devaluation by those countries wishing to align their currencies with sterling, both carried out with the passive approval of the Fund but without its aid; the Canadian eleven-year experiment in floating rates from 1950 to 1961 and reversion to that system in May 1970, represented unilateral action by a member country to use its existing rate as a weapon of economic policy. The final crisis was a more fundamental one, in which the durability of the whole adjustable-peg system and of the Bretton Woods arrangements was called in question.

Little can be said of the Fund's role in the two major exchange-rate reorientations of the period. Neither were systematic exchange-rate adjustments carried out in accordance with a Fund pursuit of an orderly exchange-rate policy. There were signs before the 1949 devaluation that the Fund hankered after such a policy. The *Annual Report* of 1948 noted the restraints which exchange rates were having upon trade expansion but went no further. This was a time at which, if the Fund had pursued a positive policy and suggested to members a planned revision of parities, it would probably have been supported by its leading members. In the events leading up to the 1967 sterling devaluation the Fund's role was simplified by the fact that both it and the British government wished to preserve the existing sterling parity. When the British could clearly no longer sustain the parity, the Fund bowed to the inevitable and approved the change. The fact is that, once its failure to give a lead on exchange-rate policy in the immediate post-war years was apparent, the Fund, in default of a policy, seems to have fallen back upon a series of maxims for good exchange behaviour by members. Of these, the two most important have been its belief in an exact and unswerving application of the exchange-rate rules of Bretton Woods, and its abhorrence of fluctuating rates, multiple rates or any divergence from the system of managed flexibility.

Dangerous to the Fund's position and authority have been two major divergences from the rules and one 'near miss'. The first divergence occurred early in the Fund's career, when in January 1948, France devalued the franc by 44 per cent and created a free market for gold and dollars. Part of the proceeds of French exports to the United States were sold at the new official rate to those requiring foreign exchange for essential imports; part was sold in the free market at a rate which constituted a *de facto* devaluation of over 60 per cent against the dollar. This practice offended in two ways: firstly, the French had devalued without Fund approval, and secondly they had created a dual exchange rate for the franc. The Fund refused to approve the plan which the French government submitted to it. When the plan was implemented they denied France access to the Fund's resources, an exclusion which lasted until October 1954.

A further rebellion against the Fund's rule of managed flexibility was that of Canada, who, in September 1950, abandoned (it is said on notice of only twenty-four hours to the Fund by the Canadian government) official support of its fixed par value and reverted, for the time being, to a flexible rate. This step was taken to adjust the Canadian balance of payments—strong for the moment, and its strength giving rise to a belief that the Canadian dollar was undervalued relative to its United States counterpart. Speculative inflow of capital in anticipation of revaluation was increasing the domestic Canadian monetary supply, lowering interest rates and contributing to inflation. The Canadian authorities were convinced of the need for revaluation of their currency and were determined to implement it but they baulked at the question of 'how much'? The rate between the Canadian and United States dollar is of great importance to Canada—too important to risk setting it at the wrong level. It was decided to let the market settle the rate.

This is not the place to recount the history of the Canadian first free rate experiment.[3] The eleven and a half years of its duration (from September 1950 to May 1962) form an interesting phase of Canadian monetary history. From the external point of view, perhaps its most interesting features were the way in which the desired objective was attained, the narrow range of fluctuation of the currency despite the sensitivity of the rate to trade balance changes and the fact that capital movements did not play a disturbing role. The Canadian case demonstrated a difficulty inherent in the Fund mechanism, that of deciding upon a new rate once a change of rate becomes necessary.

The whole episode was a serious breach of the Fund's system. Although the flexible-rate system was initially excused as 'temporary' and to be terminated by the finding of a new par value, it quickly became clear that the Canadian authorities found the system highly workable. It wove itself into the fabric of Canadian policy and was given much informed support.

The Fund mishandled this incident. Indeed, its whole policy towards flexible rates, woefully weak in its basis, dates from precipitate action at this time. Instead of inviting a full high-level enquiry by chosen experts into the implications of free rates within the Bretton Woods system, it rushed to present its own case in the 1951 *Annual Report*. This was clearly done in fear that others might follow Canada's lead, but it was repeated in the 1962 *Annual Report* and formed a hard, but intellectually insecure doctrine supporting the existing exchange-rate system. This was tersely summed up in the 1951 Report:

The essence of this whole analysis may be very simply expressed. The par value system is based on lessons learned from experience. There is ample evidence that it continues to be supported by the members of the Fund. Exceptions to it can be justified only under special circumstances and for temporary periods. The economic and financial judgement of the Fund in such cases must be tempered by recognition of its responsibilities in the wider field of international relations.

A decade of experience, some increase in empirical knowledge, and a growing body of exchange-rate theory still did not enable the Fund in 1962 to advance beyond the doctrine of 1951. The 1962 report saw the events of the intervening years merely as corroborative evidence for its earlier findings and declaration.

The report of the Fund on the role of exchange rates in the adjustment of international payments which was presented to the 1970 Meeting of the Fund in Copenhagen gave no sign of conversion. Taking advantage of the prevailing doubts as to the wisdom of introducing a free system of exchange rates which had been created by the quickening rate of inflation in the industrial countries, and anxious to preserve intact as much of the original Bretton Woods system as possible, the report rejected three proposals for change in the exchange rate system.

To the proposal for a complete elimination of the parity system and a flexible market in currencies, the Fund gave an emphatic 'no'. Such a system, it was argued, would exacerbate the already alarming rate of price inflation and, in the present international monetary system, it would not be possible to establish a workable system of reasonably stable market rates. The most probable outcome of such a flexible market would be cumulative declines in the parities of countries with high rates of inflation and serious interference with the flows of international investment.

The second proposal, for a widening of the then 1 per cent margins of fluctuation about the parity, fared no better, although it had the support of some governments—in contrast to the 'complete freedom' proposal, which relied for its support mainly on academic economists. The 'wider margins' proposal the Fund condemned as being tantamount to adopting a floating exchange system. The wider margins could act cumulatively so that a 2 per cent margin between currencies A and B could result in allowable variations of much more, perhaps as high as 8 per cent between currencies C and D through the cross-rates. The Fund was hostile to any substantial broadening of margins and though it did not define its terms, it was clear that almost any change worth making would be opposed.

The third proposal, for frequent adjustment of parities according to some agreed formula, was rejected on similar grounds to the other two. In this case, however, it was felt that additional disadvantages would make the proposal unworkable. The anticipatable character of the parity changes would induce large and destabilising capital movements, while the anti-inflationary domestic policies of governments would be prejudiced by the regularly recurring changes of parity under the scheme.

But the Fund's Copenhagen Report came almost on the threshold of sweeping changes which made all of its earlier objectives obsolete. By May 1971 it was apparent that the continuing and intensifying American deficit and the confidence problem which it had invoked, the exchange-rate adjustments which had already taken place with the revaluation of the Deutschmark in October 1969 and the floating of the Canadian dollar in May 1970, and the growing predilection, particularly by West Germany, for free-rate systems, were all bustling the international monetary system towards a break with the Bretton Woods parity system. On 9 May West Germany and Holland floated their currencies; Austria and Switzerland revalued their currencies by 5·05 and 7·07 per cent respectively. After an uneasy summer on the exchange markets, the 'package deal' of measures introduced by President Nixon in August to defend the dollar set off further currency changes which completed the breakup of the Bretton Woods system of fixed exchange rates. The U.S. dollar was freed from its gold convertibility, the pound was partially freed (the British freed the pound from the upper limit of its old parity, allowing it to float upward, but kept the lower support point), and the French franc came to be traded in a two-tier exchange market. Events had achieved what persuasion and academic discussion could not—a condition of floating exchange rates in which individual countries managed their rates through their exchange funds in an otherwise free market. The Fund, its authority, its place in the international system, indeed what sort of international system—all this was in the melting pot.

It is impossible to examine at any length the implications of the Fund's long-standing faith in managed flexibility. We shall be content with two comments. Firstly, it was almost inevitable that such a method, under which exchange-rate changes were only made at long intervals to correct fundamental disequilibria in balances of payments, should lead to conditions in which rates became virtually fixed, except in extreme crisis, when a rate could no longer be maintained, or for a country so small or financially unimportant as to have the luxury of independent action. Secondly, as time has passed, it has become all too clear that rates can never be altered by negotiation. Devaluation is, of all national actions, one which must be taken unilaterally, without prior notice or leakage and without consultation. To avoid speculation against their currencies countries have avoided using rate changes, while the Fund has shown clearly that it regards exchange-rate variation as undesirable and as something to be avoided at almost any cost — a view which until recently was shared by many leading governments. The uneasy duality of the key currencies of pound and dollar, each with satellites, has meant that a rate change must have wide repercussions. The events of the years 1964 to 1967 showed how far governments, central bankers and the Fund were prepared to go to prevent the devaluation of a major currency; events since 1969 have shown how quickly all but the Fund can be converted to a new doctrine.

Two other aspects of the Fund's exchange-rate policy must be mentioned briefly: its efforts in the early post-war period to get rid of disorderly cross-rates between currencies; and its unrelenting war on multiple currency rates. Disorderly cross-rates occurred frequently during the immediate post-war period under exchange control and were used by some countries to achieve a concealed devaluation of their currency. Multiple currency rates, often used by countries unable or unwilling to institute an orderly or systematic exchange control and common for a period in Latin America, were the object of relentless Fund opposition. Since many schemes of multiple rates were used as protective devices for balances of payments, as well as for less worthy ends, the Fund had to tread warily and act with discernment. By formulating certain principles whereby countries might progressively dismantle systems of multiple rates, it succeeded over a period of years in reducing these practices to an unimportant level.

II. The Fund's task of fostering multilateral trade, of ending direct restrictions on trade and payments and of discouraging discriminatory practices was a twofold one: to induce member nations to remove progressively restrictions imposed on the transfer of their currencies and for the protection of their balances of payments, which were the result of the war and its aftermath; and to induce member nations to discard the use of direct controls in their balance-of-payments policies and in the normal usages of international trade.

The first of these tasks was a formidable one, and once more early events were inauspicious for the success of the Fund's policy. Within the first six months of the Fund's operational life (i.e. from 1 March 1947) Britain had, under the impulse of the Anglo-American Loan Agreement, made her attempt to re-establish sterling as a currency convertible for current external transactions, had failed and by August 1947 had regrouped and re-established the formidable protective screen of exchange control which was to endure for eleven years. Of the key currencies, only the United States dollar remained free of restrictions, but the scarcity of that currency, resulting from the overwhelming post-war surplus on the American balance of payments, forced all the leading trading countries to apply not only controls as between one another but strong discriminatory controls over their trade with the United States. The prevailing conditions of most of the Fund's member countries in the later forties was one of acute external imbalance, with inability to export until industrial reconstruction had taken place, coupled with an immediate necessity to import on a large scale. Under such conditions it was useless to seek balance-of-payments equilibrium by exchange adjustment. There was no use in stimulating demand for exports which did not exist. A very great measure of depreciation would have been required to limit imports and the fillip given to domestic inflation would, in many cases, have been great. It was far preferable to control imports selectively and quantitatively by direct controls and rely on foreign credits to meet the deficit of the balance of payments. In Western Europe the necessity to conserve foreign exchange resulted in the extension, and indeed often the elaboration, of wartime restrictions. In Eastern Europe exchange restrictions supplemented direct and comprehensive state intervention through state trading and barter arrangements. In Latin America multiple currency rates were widespread.

In March 1952, when the five-year transition period ended, during which, under the Fund Agreement, member countries might employ direct controls and payments restrictions, there was some sign of an easement of the problems which justified their use. The dollar problem was less acute, the Western European economies were stronger. But in fact, the initiative in the drive to end controls had passed from the Fund and was now reflected in intra-governmental arrangements. Typical of this was the movement towards convertibility of sterling known as the Collective Approach: launched by the British and American governments in 1954. The progressive dismantling of direct import controls among the Western European countries went forward during the fifties under the stimulus of OEEC.

As the fifties wore on, hopes of general currency convertibility rose and fell with the changing fortunes of the British balance of payments. In the last few days of 1958, sterling and ten other European currencies shed their restrictions, and general non-resident convertibility of these currencies was secured. For the first time since 1939 the way was open for multilateral trade throughout the non-Communist world. The Bretton Woods system had weathered its prolonged transition phase and was now to operate at last in a world approximating to the original conception of 1944. This had a twofold significance: first, it came at a time when the Fund was, in other fields of its activity, quitting its ten-year role of docile detachment. It was able to advance now on a broad front. Second, the scrapping of direct controls brought virtually to an end a side of the Fund's activities which had earned it no love and scant respect. It enabled it to become, not a hectoring and didactic preacher of the merits of multilateralism, but a predominantly financial organisation.

III. Table 21.1 gives a summarised account of the Fund's currency transactions from the beginning of its operations on 1 March 1947 to 31 December 1972.

The Fund's currency transactions fall into four phases. The first phase, from the beginning of operations until 30 April 1949, was marked by a heavy demand for the United States dollar—then a scarce currency. Between 1 July 1947 and 30 April 1948, that is, in the period immediately preceding the European Recovery Programme, the demand for dollars, at a rate of $600 million per annum, was such as, had it continued, would have quickly depleted the Fund's holdings of that currency. It is noteworthy that the Fund did not at this time, or at any time, declare the United States dollar a 'scarce currency'. Nevertheless, discriminatory controls against United States goods and payments were in force in many other countries and were at this time allowable under the 'transition period' provision. From the operational beginning of the European Recovery Programme in 1949, the Fund was relieved of the demand for dollars from countries in receipt of Marshall Aid since the Fund ruled that these countries should not be eligible to use its resources.

The second phase, from 1949 to late 1956, may be described as the phase of stagnation. During these years the Fund purposely curtailed the use of its resources. It was recognised that, during the years of post-war reconstruction, many claims might be made upon the Fund's resources and that the Fund must not become the underwriter of relief and rehabilitation, still less of grandiose schemes of economic development. On the other hand, it was realised that total withdrawal from the international monetary scene would entail a grave risk that the Fund would be regarded as devoid of use or initiative. It sought, therefore, a compromise, by regarding applications for assistance on their merits. Its decision that the European Recovery Programme was the appropriate source of dollar relief and that countries receiving dollars from that source were not entitled to call upon its resources, was no doubt a wise one in terms of the arithmetic of the size of the potential calls and the relatively meagre state of its own dollar resources but tactically it was an error. By this edict it removed itself from the centre of the great exchange problems of the immediate post-war period and yielded authority and influence to other international organisations administering Marshall Aid—OEEC, ECA and others. This virtual retirement from the monetary side of the international economy and its

Table 21.1 Summary of Fund Transactions 1 March 1947 to 31 December 1972

Year	Total gross drawings ($ million)	No. of currencies drawn
1947–9	777·3	3
1950	0	–
1951	34·6	2
1952	85·1	1
1953	229·5	3
1954	62·5	1
1955	27·5	1
1956	692·6	2
1957	977·1	1
1958	337·9	4
1959	179·8	4
1960	279·8	6
1961	2,478·5	11
1962	583·8	8
1963	333·2	10
1964	1,949·8	12
1965	2,433·5	16
1966	1,448·2	15
1967	834·7	22
1968	3,692·3	19
1969	3,081·2	36
1970	2,089·3	41
1971	1,900·3	35
1972	1,484·3	27

Source: International Financial Statistics, IMF.

carping attitude towards its members on the issue of controls and commercial policy, brought it to a point where its influence over its members was slight and where some of the most important would have left it without much regret. In the spring of 1952 Britain considered implementing a free exchange rate. If this plan had been effected it would have taken the whole sterling area out of the Fund and might well have crippled it irreparably. The fact was that, in this phase of retirement, the Fund yielded no advantage and little service to its members who for that reason saw no advantage in retaining it. At times it even seemed as though the Fund wished to antagonise its members. In 1951, as the end of the stipulated transition period approached, it became more militant in its efforts to persuade members to remove restrictions on trade and payments and it informed its members that its resources would in future be available only on certain conditions, e.g. that countries should adopt anti-inflation programmes and should progressively relax trade restrictions. This heavy insistence on 'conditional assistance' was resented, and since the Fund's policy declarations were contemporary with and identical to United States demands for anti-inflationary policies, it was regarded as further evidence of the Fund's pro-American proclivities.

In 1952 there was an important innovation with the inauguration of 'stand-by arrangements'.[4] These assured a member of the right to drawings upon Fund resources up to specified limits and within an agreed period. Such stand-by arrangements were to be negotiable between the Fund and the individual members, but in the negotiations similar tests were to be applied as to requests for ordinary immediate drawings. The Fund seemed determined that, at least for the transition period, there should be no automatic recourse to its resources.

The Fund's third phase, one of activity, began in 1956. Its beginnings coincided with the arrival of a new director, Per Jacobson, an economist and monetary technician who came to the Fund after a successful career as Research Director of the Bank for International Settlements. The phase began with the granting of large stand-by facilities to France and the United Kingdom in December 1956 to meet balance-of-payments difficulties caused by the Suez crisis. From that time onward a steady flow of transactions began. 1961 brought the largest volume of transactions in the Fund's history. Although 1959 and 1960 were quiet years, this was due primarily to greater stability in international finance and not to any tendency for the Fund to return to its former policies of reticence.

In 1963 the Fund introduced a so-called 'compensatory financing facility' to assist primary producing countries experiencing a balance-of-payments deficit through a temporary and unavoidable shortfall in their export earnings. This facility allowed members special drawings of up to 25 per cent of their quota (increased to 50 per cent in 1966 – with the limitation of not more than a 25 per cent increase in any twelve-month period) even if this brought total drawings beyond the normal limit of 200 per cent of the quota. This measure was designed to meet the need of the oft-quoted case of the single-crop developing country temporarily robbed of earning power by crop failure or natural disaster.

The new activity put strain on the Fund's resources. As early as 1958, it had become clear that the growth in the Fund's currency transactions was outrunning its resources and that its gold and currency holdings required to be expanded. At the annual meeting in 1959 it was agreed: (a) that there should be a general increase in quotas of 50 per cent; (b) that there should be special increases for Canada, West Germany and Japan because of their relatively high economic growth; and (c) that certain countries with small quotas should be allowed to increase their quotas by more than the general rise of 50 per cent. These increases more than doubled the currencies available for transactions and allowed the more open-handed policy to continue into the sixties.

The sixties marked the fourth phase of the Fund's currency transactions. They were years of sharp crises and strain, and a growing realisation not only of the inadequate supply of world liquidity but of the meagre augmentation which the Fund provided. The decade was dominated by the impact upon the Fund of the problem generated by progressive loss of confidence in the key currencies and, in particular, by the link between the United States dollar and gold. Sterling was under continuous suspicion and speculative pressure made necessary one reduction in its parity under duress in 1967. The fact is that, despite the increases in the quotas, the Fund is still pitifully short of the key currencies. The increases in quotas did not even compensate for the rise in prices which had taken place since 1948, much less for the increase in the volume of trade. It was progressively realised that its resources were far too small to deal adequately with the balance-of-payments problems of the period. That part of the total quota increase which was granted in 1959 to countries other than the five or six leading members served only to increase the potential (and automatic first tranche) demand of all those countries for the much-wanted key currencies, while the currencies of most of the Fund's 118 members were not demanded at all and were of little value to the Fund. Despite a further increase of quotas by 25 per cent in 1965, its shortage of wanted currencies became chronic. Realisation of its dilemma generated numerous suggestions for reform, ranging from minor adjustments in the Fund itself to complete reorientation of the Bretton Woods system.

(iii) Reform of the Fund

Discussion of reform began in the late fifties. The revision of the quotas in 1959 and the agreement of December 1961, whereby the Fund might borrow from the Group of Ten up to a limit of $6 billion, were the first practical results of that discussion. But even the earlier simplistic approach by which the Fund's resources would be augmented from time to time and adapted to a growing level of world trade by periodic increases of the quotas, gives rise to some awkward problems. True, the Fund's resources may grow by augmentation of quotas at a rate not very different from (although probably lagging somewhat behind) the rise in the volume of world trade, but anomalies as between the size of individual quotas are likely to remain.

The size of national quotas originally decided at Bretton Woods was based upon pre-war trade levels, and quota revisions such as those of 1959 and 1965 based on a general percentage increase, not only perpetuated the bias in the original quotas in favour of the large industrial powers but accentuated it. Any attempt to meet the shortage of key currencies by raising the appropriate quotas still further would exacerbate this anomaly and give a voting dominance in the Fund to a few powers. Even now, if we compare the share of countries in world trade and their share in the total of Fund quotas, we find Britain and the United States with very large quotas while countries whose post-war economic growth has been rapid, e.g. West Germany, Italy, France, Holland, Canada, Sweden and Japan have considerable quota 'deficiencies'. Moreover the quotas of many developing countries are woefully inadequate in view of their import surpluses and development programmes. The problem of adjusting quotas not only to general Fund needs, that is, to afford an adequate supply to the Fund of certain oft-demanded currencies, but to the needs of individual countries, provides delicate, perhaps intractable problems.

The simple international liquidity approach to reform of the Fund and the international monetary system was regarded in the mid-sixties as minimal. Unless the Fund could be adequately equipped with the needed currencies and provide a much greater augmentation to the country-held stocks of gold and key currencies, it would eventually break down and be discredited. But even in the late 1950s it had been open to question whether mere increase in Fund scale and resources was enough. The idea grew that it was not and that a more far-reaching reform of the entire international currency system was necessary.

Two distinct facets of the problem of reform of the international monetary system emerged: the question of imbalance and how this may be minimised and corrected; and the question of international liquidity, its nature and distribution. The optimum situation would be one in which countries were compelled to prevent or adjust balance-of-payments deficits, while at the same time machinery existed whereby the volume of international liquidity could be expanded quickly if need be. A number of plans to reform the international monetary system and to incorporate both of these desirable features were put forward and discussed in the late fifties and early sixties—the Triffin Plan of 1958 with various qualifications of later date, the Bernstein Plan of the same year, the Franks Plan, the Stamp Plan and others.[5] All of these plans have been discussed exhaustively elsewhere.[6] No useful purpose would be served by continuing the discussion here. It is wise to consider briefly, however, certain features which most of the plans had in common.

Firstly, the continuing utility and standing of the Fund are recognised in a majority of the plans. The arrangements advocated are adjustments or additions to the Fund's powers and functions. It is regarded as the established vehicle of international monetary co-operation and a natural starting point for further development.

Secondly, it has been suggested that the Fund's role of augmenting the existing stock of international liquidity would be greatly eased and its position vis-à-vis its members strengthened if some adequate adjustment mechanism could be included within the Bretton Woods system, as, for example, a wider range of exchange fluctuation.[7]

Thirdly, it has been suggested that the Fund should become the central repository of national gold and currency reserves. This would have the effect of placing with the Fund balances whose transfer would be the vehicle of final settlement and imparting to the Fund the role of an international central bank.

Fourthly, a number of plans seek to develop international monetary arrangements in the direction in which domestic monetary systems have gone long since, by adding to the existing international money stock by the purposive creation of some internationally accredited form of credit unit. At present international liquidity consists virtually of cash holdings, gold and accepted key currencies having a fixed relation with gold. This is, of course, augmented by a larger volume of 'secondary' international liquidity, but this is a variable whose amount or nature cannot be anticipated accurately and may not be counted as part of international liquidity proper. The essence of international liquidity is that its acceptability, quantity and nature are precisely known in advance. It is therefore limited at present to the known cash assets of countries. It is this failure to get beyond the cash nature of international liquidity which makes the Bretton Woods system and the activities of the Fund so inflexible. If, as with domestic banking systems, new liquidity can be created by international agreement, then we have progressed some way towards solving the problem of shortage of liquidity. Were the Fund to have powers of overdraft creation, then the international monetary system would have a more modern look.

An attempt to implement reform in the fourth of the above categories has been made. After four years of discussion both in the IMF and in the Group of Ten, a practical proposal has been implemented – a proposal for Special Drawing Rights (SDRs) to be allocated by the Fund to its members. First publicly outlined in September 1967 at the annual meeting of the IMF in Rio de Janeiro, a detailed scheme was submitted to the Board of Governors in April 1968 and was approved in May. The necessary amendments to the Fund's Articles of Agreement required acceptance by member governments, a process which for most countries required legislative action. By 1969, the amendments were accepted by 60 per cent of the member countries *and* by countries with 80 per cent of the total voting power, and once members with at least 75 per cent of aggregate quotas deposited instruments of participation, the new facility was established. The first allocation of the new reserve assets was made shortly after at the beginning of 1970.[8]

The SDR scheme provides for the creation by the Fund of a new supplement to world liquidity without any deposit (of gold or currencies) by member countries. SDRs, measured in units of account equivalent to the gold value of a U.S. dollar, once created, continue permanently in existence.

Every Fund member may participate and allocations of SDRs are made to members annually in proportion to their Fund quotas. Countries may use the new drawing rights unconditionally, transferring them in the books of the Fund to another participant (chosen by the Fund), who will be required to supply its own, or another, currency in exchange. To provide against a maldistribution of the new unit, such as would occur if units drained away from the deficit and to the surplus countries, members are required to hold on the average of a five-year period drawing rights to the amount of at least 30 per cent of the average of their net cumulative allocations over that period.

It is essential to realise that the Fund's contribution to international liquidity is now dichotomised. First, there is the General Account of the Fund through which all its business in national currencies is conducted. This reflects the currency holdings coming from its members' quota contributions and the purchase and sale of these currencies under the arrangements in force since the Fund's inception. Second, there is the Special Drawing Account through which all operations and transactions in SDRs are conducted. The SDR is essentially only an entry in this account at the Fund. Moreover it is an entry which may be held only by (a) national monetary authorities (who must be members of the Fund); and (b) by the General Account of the Fund to which participant countries are permitted to transfer SDRs for certain specified purposes, for example, to pay charges levied by the Fund or to repay drawings from the General Account. It is apparent, then, that the SDR is really a created deposit of the Fund — created, in the sense that it is an overdraft unit issued by the Fund deriving its credit standing from the fact that it confers on the holder the right to obtain its defined equivalent in foreign exchange from other Fund members, and that it discharges specified obligations of members towards the

Fund's General Account. Apart from the incentive which members have to hold and accumulate SDRs for the clearing of payments deficits, they have the further incentives that the new unit carries an absolute gold guarantee protecting national reserves held in SDR form from the effect of devaluation of a currency (or even in the event of devaluation of all currencies), and that interest at a low rate is paid on the excess of a member's SDR holdings over its cumulative allocation. (Interest is, however, charged at the same rate on a shortfall.)

Perhaps the most significant aspect of SDRs is that they are created by the Fund. For the first time in currency history an international organisation has been given power to create international fiat money. It is worth while glancing briefly at the nature and motivation of this power. The general directive is contained in Article XXIV, Section 1(a) of the Fund Agreement. It is worth quoting:

> In all its decisions with respect to the allocation and cancellation of special drawing rights the Fund shall seek to meet the long-term global need, as and when it arises, to supplement existing reserve assets in such manner as will promote the attainment of its purposes and will avoid economic stagnation and deflation as well as excess demand and inflation in the world.

With these general principles in mind, a decision to allocate may come from a proposal by the Managing Director, supported by the Executive Directors. It has to be voted upon by the Governors of the Fund and must receive an 85 per cent majority of the total voting power. It will be observed that the Fund in creating SDRs must cater to a 'global' need and not the need of particular countries, that the purpose of such creation is to supplement existing reserve assets, that the need for such supplementation must be a long-term need, and that the overall purpose of such a creation is to avoid either inflation or deflation in the world and further the Fund's aims of expanding trade, securing exchange stability and promoting orderly exchange adjustments.

We have already had two years' experience of SDRs. Of the Fund's 125 members only 10 have remained aloof from the scheme. The first allocation was for a period of three years. Approximately $3·4 billion of SDRs was distributed at the beginning of 1970; $3 billion at the beginning of 1971 and a similar amount at the beginning of 1972. The new asset is being used both for designated purchases of currencies and for repayment of drawings from the General Account. It is as yet too early to draw any general conclusions as to ways and circumstances in which they are being used, still less as to what changes may be made to the whole SDR system as a result of the new movement for international monetary reform.

It is appropriate to end this brief account of the SDR scheme by an

The Economics of the Balance of Payments 555

example showing how the unit is used. Suppose that Britain needs to use half its drawing rights and wishes to convert $58 million into usable currencies, it would approach the Fund, who would determine to which other participating country, or countries, it should transfer the SDRs in order to obtain the equivalent in convertible currency. The Fund would choose a country, or countries, with a strong balance of payments and reserve position. Assume that Germany and Italy are chosen for equal amounts. Both of these countries would be told by the Fund that they were to be credited with $29 million in the Special Drawing Account and that they in turn should credit the Bank of England with the Deutschmark and lire equivalent. Britain would be debited in the Special Drawing Account with $58 million. The result of this transaction would be that $58 million of SDRs of the United Kingdom would have been transferred to Germany and Italy and the United Kingdom would have acquired $58 million of convertible currencies for the support of her balance of payments. The United Kingdom would be charged a rate of interest — now $1\frac{1}{2}$ per cent — on its use of drawing rights. Germany and Italy would be paid interest at the same rate. As long as the United Kingdom used on average, over a period of five years or over, no more than 70 per cent of the SDRs allocated to it by the Fund, the United Kingdom would have no reconstitution obligation. Germany and Italy, on the other hand, or any other participant, would only be obliged to accept drawing rights beyond their allocation and provide currency in return, up to the point where they had accepted drawing rights equal in value to twice the amount allocated to them by the Fund.

The SDR scheme provides a useful automatic augmentation of international liquidity, more flexible than the older system of currency provision. It will be a fairly meagre supplement in the initial years of the scheme, but provided that the Fund is generous and consistent in its creation of new SDRs, the contribution will be a growing one.

(iv) The Present Position

It is not in order here to attempt a judgement of the Fund. Such a task would require a lengthy assessment of its controlling forces, its political influence and its adaptability to change, in addition to a deeper analysis of its economic activities over twenty-seven years than we have attempted here. Let us close this chapter with these reflections.

First, the Fund is firmly established. It is the first international monetary organisation — other than the much less important Bank for International

Settlements—to endure for so long. Not only is it still in business, but it shows strength and some adaptability. It is widely recognised as the venue through which international monetary reform must be made to work. Second, there is almost full realisation among the instructed and knowledgeable that the gold exchange standard over which the Fund presides is unstable, outmoded and ripe for replacement. Third, there has been a steady weakening of national sovereignty in matters pertaining to international monetary affairs. The jet age has shrunk the world. We are approaching in monetary affairs an international monetary system, an international capital and money market, where London, New York, Amsterdam and Zürich offer comparable venues for investment, albeit at different times of day. Portfolios are now diversified in an international market for wealth titles in which governments, banks and international corporations move smoothly between centre and centre. With the SDR scheme, there has been a significant move forward which will make the Fund increasingly a technical organisation and take it out of politics. Its achievements thus far have been considerable. Its most productive and useful work may still lie ahead.

Notes

Chapter 1

1. For example, in works such as Thomas Mun's *England's Treasure by Forraign Trade* (1664).
2. For a historical account of the growth of international organisations, see C. H. Alexandrowicz, *International Economic Organisations* (London: Stevens, 1952).
3. Such a book is H. R. Heller's *International Trade* (Englewood Cliffs, N.J.: Prentice-Hall, 1968).
4. Meade's two volumes are exceptions: both are fundamental works in their field. See *The Theory of International Economic Policy*, Vol. I: *The Balance of Payments* (1951); Vol. II: *Trade and Welfare* (London: Oxford University Press, 1955).

Chapter 2

1. J. Tinbergen, *International Economic Integration* (Amsterdam: Elsevier Publishing Co., 1965), p. 157.
2. For example, see J. Bhagwati, 'The Pure Theory of International Trade: A Survey', *EJ* (March 1964), pp. 1–84; R. E. Caves, *Trade and Economic Structure* (Cambridge, Mass.: Harvard University Press, 1960); and J. Chipman, 'A Survey of the Theory of International Trade', Parts I–III, *Econometrica* (July 1965, October 1965, and January 1966), pp. 477–519, pp. 685–760, and pp. 18–76.
3. For an example of this approach, see Murray C. Kemp, *The Pure Theory of International Trade* (Englewood Cliffs, N.J.: Prentice-Hall, 1964).
4. For a useful survey of international trade elementary geometry, see I. Walter, *International Economics* (New York: Ronald Press, 1968), Chapter 2.
5. J. Viner, *Studies in the Theory of International Trade* (New York: Harper & Bros, 1937; Kelley's Reprint Edition, 1965), p. 437. This book is an invaluable source of information on the history of international trade theory.
6. It is believed that Robert Torrens in his pamphlet *Essay on the External Corn Trade* (1815) gave the first exposition of comparative advantage. It is, however, with David Ricardo that the theory is usually linked and Chapter 7 of his *Principles of Political Economy* (1817) gives the most famous exposition. John Stuart Mill's *Principles of Political Economy* (1848) developed Ricardo's model.
7. Our exposition leans heavily on Haberler's discussion *Theory of International Trade* (London: William Hodge & Co., 1936; New York: Kelley's Reprint Edition), pp. 136–44, and on that of B. Södersten, *International Economics* (New York: Harper & Row, 1970), pp. 19–22.
8. See Taussig, *International Trade*, p. 45, quoted in Haberler, *Theory of International Trade*, p. 133.
9. The relation between the terms of trade and the balance of payments in this context are explored more fully by Haberler, *International Trade*, pp. 138–40.

Chapter 3

1. Haberler, *International Trade* (Kelley's Reprint Edition), pp. 175–8.
2. Ibid., pp. 171–3.
3. For an empirical study of these changing trade patterns see Alfred Maizels, *Growth and Trade* (Cambridge: Cambridge University Press, 1970).
4. See *Principles of Political Economy*, 7th ed. (London, 1871), Book 3, Chapter xviii. All quotations here are from the edition with preface by Sir W. J. Ashley, published in London in 1909.
5. A. Marshall, *Money, Credit and Commerce*, Book 3, Chapter vi and Appendix J. For a good brief exposition of the Marshallian ideas see Haberler, *International Trade*, pp. 150–9.
6. Students should read Wassily Leontief's great article 'The Use of Indifference Curves in the Analysis of Foreign Trade', *QJE* (May 1933), pp. 493–503.
7. See Marshall, *Money, Credit and Commerce*, Book 3, Chapter vi and Appendix J.
8. J. E. Meade, *Geometry of International Trade* (London: Oxford University Press, 1952), Chapters 2 and 3.

Chapter 4

1. A useful and critical account of the two approaches is contained in Romney Robinson, 'Factor Proportions and Comparative Advantage', *QJE* (May 1956), pp. 169–92, and also in Chapter 1 of R. Caves and H. G. Johnson, *Readings in International Economics* (Homewood, Ill.: Richard D. Irwin, 1968), pp. 3–23.
2. Bertil Ohlin, *Interregional and International Trade*, rev. ed. (Cambridge, Mass.: Harvard University Press, 1967).
3. P. T. Ellsworth, *The International Economy*, 4th ed. (Toronto: Collier-Macmillan of Canada, 1969), p. 80.
4. See Eli Heckscher, *Ekonomisk Tidskrift* Vol. XXI (1919), pp. 497–512. This article, originally in Swedish, is reproduced in abridged form and in English in H. S. Ellis and L. M. Metzler, eds., *Readings in the Theory of International Trade* (Homewood, Ill.: Richard D. Irwin, 1949), Chapter 13, pp. 272–300.
5. See Södersten, *International Economics*, p. 48.
6. A. P. Lerner, 'Factor Prices and International Trade', *Eca* (February 1952); also P. T. Ellsworth, *International Economy*, p. 91.
7. Ellsworth, *International Economy*, p. 135.
8. For example R. H. Leftwich, *The Price System and Resource Allocation*, 3rd ed. (New York: Holt, Rinehart & Winston, 1966), especially Chapter 7.
9. A more general diagrammatic treatment can be found in K. Savosnick, 'The Box Diagram and the Production Possibility Curve', *Ekonomisk Tidskrift* (September 1958).
10. These two basic propositions are highlighted by H. G. Johnson in his article 'Factor Endowments, International Trade, and Factor Prices', *MS* (September 1957), pp. 270–83, reprinted in Caves and Johnson, *International Economics*, Chapter 5.
11. For an examination of the factor-price equalisation theorem and factor reversal see Johnson, *MS* (September 1957).

12. See J. E. Meade, 'The Equalisation of Factor Prices: the Two-Country, Two Factor, Three Product Case', *Metroeconomica* (December 1950); and G. H. Land, 'Factor Endowments and Factor Prices', *Eca* (May 1959).
13. See Meade, *International Economic Policy*, Vol. II: *Trade and Welfare*.
14. For a good, brief account of this literature see Clement, Pfister, and Rothwell, *Theoretical Issues in International Economics* (Boston: Houghton Mifflin, 1967), pp. 56–60; and Bhagwati, *EJ* (March 1964), pp. 17–26.
15. Note, for example, the moderate language and qualified assertions made by Samuelson in his 'International Factor-Price Equalisation Once Again', *EJ* (June, 1949), reprinted in Caves and Johnson, *International Economics*, Chapter 3.

Chapter 5

1. I. F. Pearce, *International Trade*, Book II (London: Macmillan, 1970), p. 616.
2. For a simple graphical demonstration see Södersten, *International Economics*, pp. 66–7. Our discussion of trade and factor endowment owes something to the account given in Södersten, pp. 68–72.
3. The proposition was first examined in a famous article by W. F. Stolper and Paul Samuelson, 'Protection and Real Wages', *RES* (November 1941), reprinted in Ellis and Metzler, eds., *Readings in the Theory of International Trade*, pp. 333–57.
4. See Stolper and Samuelson, *RES* (November 1941), pp. 349–51.
5. See Bhagwati, *EJ* (March 1964). Bhagwati argues that Ricardo saw his theory as a demonstration of the advantages of free trade.
6. 'British and American Exports: A Study Suggested by the Theory of Comparative Costs': Part I in *EJ* (December 1951); Part II in *EJ* (September 1952).
7. L. Rostas, *Comparative Productivity in British and American Industry*.
8. MacDougall, *EJ* (December 1951), p. 697.
9. Ibid., pp. 708–9.
10. Caves, *Trade and Economic Structure*, p. 269.
11. See I. B. Kravis, 'Wages and Foreign Trade', *Review of Economics and Statistics* (February 1956) and '"Availability" and Other Influences on the Commodity Composition of Trade', *JPE* (April 1956); Karl Forcheimer, 'The Role of Relative Wage Differences in International Trade', *QJE* (November 1947); and Bela Balassa, 'An Empirical Demonstration of Classical Comparative Cost Theory', *Review of Economics and Statistics* (August 1963); R. Stern, 'British and American Productivity and Comparative Costs in International Trade', *OEP* (October 1962).
12. Bhagwati, *EJ* (March 1964), pp. 4–17.
13. MacDougall modestly attributed this failure to the possibility that horsepower was perhaps a dubious index of capital intensity. MacDougall, *EJ* (December 1951), pp. 707–8.
14. Wassily Leontief, 'Domestic Production and Foreign Trade: the American Capital Position Re-examined', *Proceedings of the American Philosophical Society*, September 1953, reprinted in *Economica Internazionale*, Vol. VII, No. 1 (1954), and in Caves and Johnson, *Readings in International Economics*, Chapter 30, pp. 503–27; also 'Factor Proportions and the Structure of American Trade: Further Theoretical and Empirical Analysis', *Review of Economics and Statistics* (November 1956).

15. Caves and Johnson, *Readings in International Economics*, p. 505.
16. Ibid., p. 509.
17. Ibid., p. 523.
18. These are pointed to by Caves, *Trade and Economic Structure*, pp. 274–5.
19. Caves and Johnson, *Readings in International Economics*, p. 523. The italics are Leontief's.
20. R. Bharadwaj, 'Factor Proportions and the Structure of India–United States Trade', *Indian Economic Journal* (October 1962).
21. Fairly full attempts to list and classify the comments on the Leontief paradox have been made by M. A. Diab and J. Cedras, 'Paradoxe de Leontief et Spécialisation Internationale', *Revue Économique* (July 1958). Short summaries are to be found in Caves, *Trade and Economic Structure*, pp. 275–81, and Clement, Pfister, and Rothwell, *Theoretical Issues in International Economics*, pp. 101–4. Prominent among the comments have been the following: A. J. Brown, 'Professor Leontief and the Pattern of World Trade', *Yorkshire Bulletin of Economic and Social Research* (November 1957); P. T. Ellsworth, 'The Structure of American Foreign Trade: A New View Examined', *Review of Economics and Statistics* (August 1954); J. L. Ford, 'The Ohlin–Heckscher Theory of the Basis of Commodity Trade', *EJ* (September 1963); R. W. Jones, 'Factor Proportions and the Heckscher–Ohlin Theorem', *RES*, No. 1 (1956); I. B. Kravis, '"Availability" and Other Influences on the Commodity Composition of Trade', *JPE* (April 1956); Romney Robinson, 'Factor Proportions and Comparative Advantage', *QJE*, Part I (May 1956) (reprinted in Caves and Johnson, *Readings in International Economics*, pp. 3–23); Part II (August 1956); B. C. Swerling, 'Capital Shortage and Labour Surplus in the United States', *Review of Economics and Statistics* (August 1954); and S. Valavanis-Vail, 'Leontief's Scarce Factor Paradox', *JPE* (December 1954).
22. See Robinson in Caves and Johnson, pp. 17–19.
23. See Brown, *Yorkshire Bulletin of Economic and Social Research* (November 1957).
24. J. Vanek, 'The Natural Resource Content of United States Foreign Trade, 1870–1955', *Harvard Economic Studies*, 1963.
25. Diab and Cedras, *Revue Économique* (July 1958).
26. Ellsworth, *Review of Economics and Statistics* (August 1954).
27. Caves, *Trade and Economic Structure*, p. 278.
28. W. P. Travis, *The Theory of Trade and Protection* (Cambridge, Mass.: Harvard University Press, 1964).
29. See W. Leontief, 'Factor Proportions and the Structure of American Trade: Further Theoretical and Empirical Analysis', *Review of Economics and Statistics* (November 1956).
30. Mill, *Principles of Political Economy* (London, 1848).
31. Mill, *Principles* (Ashley Edition), p. 587.
32. J. Viner, *Studies in the Theory of International Trade* (London: Allen & Unwin, 1938), p. 558.
33. F. W. Taussig, *International Trade* (New York, 1927), p. 113, and 'The Change in Great Britain's Trade Terms After 1900', *EJ*, Vol. 35, 1925.
34. Haberler, *International Trade* (Kelley's Reprint Edition, 1968), pp. 161–6, and Viner, *Studies in the Theory of International Trade*, pp. 562–4.
35. Ely Devons in his 'Statistics of the United Kingdom Terms of Trade', *MS*

(September 1954) presented estimates of the United Kingdom single factoral terms of trade for the years 1948–53.

36. The income terms of trade was first developed by G. S. Dorrance, 'The Income Terms of Trade', *RES*, 1948–9. The index was also used by A. H. Imlac, who called it the 'Export Gain From Trade Index', 'Terms of Trade of the United Kingdom', *Journal of Economic History* (November 1950).

Chapter 6

1. See Constitution of the United States, Article 1, Section 8.
2. Jacob Viner in his *Customs Union Issue* (New York: Carnegie Endowment for International Peace, 1950), pp. 66–7, argues that 'there is no way in which the "height" of a tariff as an index of its restrictive effect can be even approximately measured'.
3. A review of the problems of inter-country tariff comparisons and of the nominal and effective levels of protection is contained in Bela Belassa's 'Tariff Protection in Industrial Countries: An Evaluation', *JPE* (December 1965), pp. 573–94; also in Caves and Johnson, *International Economics*, Chapter 33.
4. This calculation and its implications may be further explored in H. G. Johnson's 'The Theory of Tariff Structure with Special Reference to World Trade and Development' in H. G. Johnson and P. B. Kenen, eds., *Trade and Development* (Geneva: UN, 1965). See also W. M. Corden, 'The Structure of a Tariff System and the Effective Protective Rate', *JPE* (June 1966), and *The Theory of Protection* (Oxford: Oxford University Press, 1971).
5. C. P. Kindleberger, *International Economics*, 4th ed. (Homewood, Ill.: Richard D. Irwin, 1968), p. 105.
6. This case is demonstrated by Kindleberger, ibid., p. 106.
7. See Heller, *International Trade*, pp. 67–8 and pp. 146–7.
8. The infant industry argument was developed in 1790 by Alexander Hamilton (see *Report on Manufacturers*, pp. 29 et seq.) and became popular in America. Friedrich List, the Tübingen economist and one of the intellectual architects of the German Zollverein of 1833, was much influenced by Hamilton while in America between 1825 and 1831, and after his return to Germany he expounded the argument in his *National System of Political Economy* (1841) when, according to Haberler, he expounded his ideas 'with wearisome verbosity and a vast display of historical illustrations'. John Stuart Mill, who took his ideas from Hamilton, gave a more precise and elegant expression to the argument in his *Principles of Political Economy*, Book 5, Chapter x, i (1848), and Marshall in his *Money, Credit and Commerce* made approving references. The argument became widely accepted among free trade economists. For a good brief account of the argument's derivations, see Haberler, *Theory of International Trade* (Kelley Reprint Edition), pp. 278–85. The argument is demonstrated diagrammatically in Södersten, *International Economics*, p. 377, and there is an interesting article by Murray Kemp, 'The Mill–Bastable Infant Industry Dogma', *JPE* (February 1960).
9. Mill, *Principles* (Ashley Edition), p. 922.
10. M. Manoilesco, *The Theory of Protection and International Trade* (London: King, 1931). The Manoilesco argument was developed by W. A. Lewis in 'Economic Development with Unlimited Supplies of Labour', *MS* (May 1954),

pp. 139–91; E. E. Hagen, 'An Economic Justification of Protectionism', *QJE* (November 1958), pp. 496–514; H. Myint, 'Protection and Economic Development', in R. Harrod and D. C. Hague, eds., *International Trade Theory in a Developing World* (London: Macmillan, 1963). The argument is reviewed by W. M. Corden in *Recent Developments in the Theory of International Trade, Special Papers in International Economics*, No. 7 (Princeton, March 1965).
11. See Corden, *Recent Developments*, p. 60.
12. H. G. Johnson, 'Optimal Trade Intervention in the Presence of Domestic Distortions', unpublished paper quoted in Corden, *Recent Developments*, pp. 60 and 72.
13. The important article in the field is H. G. Johnson's 'The Cost of Protection and the Scientific Tariff', *JPE* (August 1966). This synthesises some fragmentary early work and submits the problem to rigorous analysis. Early attempts to measure the economic effects of a country's commercial policy were those made by a committee of inquiry into the Australian tariff in 1927–9 and much later by J. H. Young in *Canadian Commercial Policy*, a study prepared for the Royal Commission on Canada's Economic Prospects in 1957. An article by W. M. Corden, 'The Calculation of the Cost of Protection', *Economic Record* (May 1957), is an interesting predecessor to Johnson's work. Readers anxious to explore this topic should begin their reading with the Johnson article – from which we have drawn extensively for our discussion.
14. See, for example, Beatrice Vaccara, *Employment and Output in Protected Manufacturing Industries* (Washington, D.C.: Brookings Institution, 1960).
15. Johnson, *JPE* (August 1966), p. 329.
16. Corden, *Recent Developments*, p. 37.
17. Johnson, *JPE* (August 1966), pp. 330–1.

Chapter 7

1. The phrase derives from the title of an excellent historical chapter in Wexler's *Fundamentals of International Economics* (New York: Random House, 1968), pp. 275–86.
2. Haberler, *Theory of International Trade* (Kelley Reprint Edition), p. 237.
3. Those who wish for a review of these secondary arguments for free trade should consult Haberler, *Theory of International Trade*, pp. 222–6.
4. For a good account of these arguments see Walter, *International Economics*, pp. 160–9.
5. See Kindleberger, *International Economics*, p. 203.
6. For this he should read Meade's *The Theory of International Economic Policy*, Vol. II: *Trade and Welfare*, Part I.
7. Ibid., p. 10.
8. Ibid., p. 51.
9. For a consideration of these other optima, see Meade, *International Economic Policy*, Vol. II: *Trade and Welfare*, Part I, Chapters v, vi and vii.
10. Ibid., p. 102.
11. H. G. Johnson, 'The Economic Theory of Customs Union', Chapter III in *Money, Trade and Economic Growth* (London: Allen & Unwin, 1962); also *Pakistan Economic Journal*, X, No. 1 (March 1960), pp. 14–32.
12. The following is a list of the important references: Jacob Viner, *The Customs*

Union Issue (New York: Carnegie Endowment for International Peace, 1950), pp. 41–78; J. M. Fleming, 'On Making the Best Balance of Payments Restrictions on Imports', *EJ* (March 1951), pp. 48–71; Meade, *International Economic Policy*, Parts I and II; R. G. Lipsey and K. Lancaster, 'The General Theory of Second Best', *RES* (1956–7), pp. 11–33; H. G. Johnson, 'The Economic Theory of Customs Unions', in *Money, Trade and Economic Growth*, Chapter III, pp. 46–52.
13. Meade, *International Economic Policy*, p. 201.
14. Ibid., p. 225.

Chapter 8

1. The literature of customs union theory is not large. The seminal book is Viner's *The Customs Union Issue*. Important contributions are Meade's *The Theory of Customs Unions* (Amsterdam: North-Holland Publishing Co., 1955); R. G. Lipsey, 'The Theory of Customs Unions: Trade Diversion and Welfare', *Eca* (N.S.) (February 1957), pp. 40–6, and 'The Theory of Customs Unions: A General Survey', *EJ* (September 1960), pp. 498–513. Johnson's 'The Economic Theory of Customs Unions', *Pakistan Economic Journal* (March 1960), pp. 14–32, and *Money Trade and Economic Growth*, Chapter III, is a useful survey of the basic literature. A more recent book on customs union theory is Bela Balassa's *Theory of Economic Integration* (Homewood, Ill.: Richard D. Irwin, 1962). A good survey chapter is 'The Theory of Customs Unions', in Clement, Pfister, and Rothwell, *Theoretical Issues in International Economics*, Chapter 4.
2. Lipsey, *EJ* (September 1960).
3. See *Customs Unions, U.N. Department of Economic Affairs* (New York, 1947).
4. J. Viner, 'The Most Favoured Nations Clause', *International Economics* (Glencoe, Ill.: The Free Press, 1951), p. 102.
5. G. Haberler, 'The Political Economy of Regional or Continental Blocs', in Seymour Harris, ed., *Postwar Economic Problems* (New York, 1943), p. 344.
6. Viner, *Customs Union Issues*.
7. Ibid., Chapter 4.
8. Lipsey, *EJ* (September 1960), p. 499.
9. Clement, Pfister, and Rothwell, *Theoretical Issues in International Economics*, p. 179.
10. See Johnson, *Money, Trade and Economic Growth*, Appendix.
11. See Meade, *Theory of Customs Union*, pp. 35–6.
12. Ibid., pp. 44–52.
13. In particular see F. Gehrels, 'Customs Unions From a Single Country Viewpoint', *RES*, No. 63 (1956–7), p. 61.
14. Lipsey, *EJ* (September 1960), p. 504.
15. C. A. Cooper and B. F. Massell, 'A New Look at Customs Union Theory', *EJ* (December 1965).
16. This breakdown of the general equilibrium analysis has been used by Clement, Pfister, and Rothwell in their excellent summary of this literature, *Theoretical Issues in International Economics*, pp. 190–9.
17. Lipsey, *EJ* (September 1960), pp. 500–3.
18. Lipsey says that the importance of the substitution effect seems to have been realised independently by a number of people: Meade, *The Theory of Customs Unions*; Gehrels, 'Customs Unions From a Single Country Viewpoint'; and

Lipsey himself, 'The Theory of Customs Unions: Trade Diversion and Welfare'. Our exposition follows Gehrels presentation.
19. Lipsey, *Eca* (February 1957), pp. 43–4.
20. Gehrels, *RES*, No. 63, p. 61.
21. Lipsey, 'Mr Gehrels on Customs Unions', *RES* (1956–7), pp. 211–14.
22. Lipsey, *EJ* (September 1960), p. 504.
23. J. Vanek, *International Trade: Theory and Economic Policy* (Homewood, Ill.: Richard D. Irwin, 1962), pp. 346–59.
24. See Clement, Pfister, and Rothwell, *Theoretical Issues in International Economics*, p. 199.
25. The following works are of interest: Balassa, *Theory of Economic Integration*, Chapters 5–8; T. Scitovsky, *Economic Theory and Western European Integration* (Stanford: University of California Press, 1958); and by the same writer, 'International Trade and Economic Integration as a Means of Overcoming the Disadvantages of a Small Nation', in E. A. G. Robinson, ed., *Economic Consequences of the Size of Nations* (London: Macmillan, 1960).
26. Scitovsky, *Western European Integration*, pp. 19–48.
27. Balassa, *Economic Integration*, pp. 101–16.
28. On the problem of definition see Balassa, ibid., pp. 29–33; H. Makower and G. Morton, 'A Contribution Towards a Theory of Customs Unions', *EJ* (March 1953).
29. A. Lamfalussy, 'Europe's Progress: Due to Common Market', *Lloyds Bank Review*, October 1961.
30. Scitovsky, *Western European Integration*, pp. 32–4.
31. Balassa, *Economic Integration*, pp. 49–53.
32. Viner, *The Customs Union Issue*, p. 51.
33. Ibid., Chapter 7.
34. Balassa, *Economic Integration*, pp. 42–3.

Chapter 9

1. See C. R. Whittlesley, *National Interests and International Cartels* (New York, 1946); E. Hexner, *International Cartels* (Chapel Hill: University of North Carolina Press, 1945); E. S. Mason, *Controlling World Trade* (New York: McGraw-Hill, 1946); D. Patinkin, 'Multiple Plant Firms, Cartels and Imperfect Competition', *QJE* (February 1945); and *Restrictive Business Practices* (Geneva: GATT, 1959).
2. See Walter, *International Economics*, p. 201.
3. Kindleberger, *International Economics*, 4th ed., p. 150.
4. See J. Viner, *Dumping: A Problem in International Trade* (Chicago: University of Chicago Press, 1923; reprinted in Kelley's Reprint Series, 1967). An excellent discussion of dumping is to be found in Haberler's *International Trade*, pp. 296–317. The problem is cast in a more modern setting in Robert E. Baldwin's *Nontariff Distortions of International Trade* (Washington, D.C.: Brookings Institution, 1970), pp. 139–43.
5. Haberler, *International Trade*, p. 300.
6. Ibid., p. 314.
7. Ibid., p. 172.
8. Ibid., p. 320.

Notes

Chapter 10

1. See R. Mundell, *International Economics* (New York: The Macmillan Co., 1968), p. 143.
2. W. M. Scammell, *International Monetary Policy*, 2nd ed. (London: Macmillan, 1961), p. 14.
3. H. G. Johnson, *The World Economy at the Crossroads* (Oxford: Oxford University Press, 1965), p. 2.

Chapter 11

1. Adapted, with slight amendment, from the definition given in the IMF *Balance of Payments Manual*, 2nd ed. (January 1950), p. 1.
2. See Leland B. Yeager, *International Monetary Relations* (New York: Harper & Row, 1966), p. 36.
3. See Meade, *International Economic Policy*, Vol. I: *The Balance of Payments*, p. 11.
4. See Mundell, *International Economics*, p. 141.
5. Meade, *International Economic Policy*, Vol. I, p. 7.
6. Ibid.; see also Yeager, *International Monetary Relations*, p. 452.
7. Meade, *International Economic Policy*, Vol. I, p. 11.
8. Scammell, *International Monetary Policy*, 2nd ed., p. 25.
9. For this view see Ingvar Svennilson, *Growth and Stagnation in the European Economy* (Geneva: United Nations Economic Commission for Europe, 1954).

Chapter 12

1. Johnson, *The World Economy at the Crossroads*, p. 27.
2. See Ricardo, *Principles of Political Economy and Taxation* (Everyman Edition), pp. 90–3. The argument referred to assumed a fixed world monetary supply. This was a tolerable assumption in Ricardo's day when money supply was equated to gold supply.
3. See Yeager, *International Monetary Relations*, p. 150. Yeager's Chapter 8 is an excellent discussion of the stability conditions and our discussion relies heavily upon it.
4. Guy Orcutt, 'Measurement of Price Elasticities in International Trade', *Review of Economics and Statistics*, Vol. 32, No. 2 (May 1950). This article contains a comprehensive bibliography of estimates of elasticities made up to that time.
5. Kindleberger, *International Economics*, 4th ed., p. 268.

Chapter 13

1. Notably those of J. H. Williams, Jacob Viner, F. W. Taussig, and Harry D. White. For an excellent review of this literature and its impact see L. A. Metzler's chapter 'The Theory of International Trade', in H. S. Ellis, ed., *A Survey of Contemporary Economics*, Vol. I (Philadelphia: Blakiston Co., 1948), pp. 212–14.
2. See in particular Mrs Robinson, *Essays in the Theory of Employment*, 2nd ed. (Oxford: Oxford University Press, 1947), the essay entitled 'The Foreign Exchanges'; R. F. Harrod, *International Economics* (Cambridge: Cambridge

University Press, 1933), Chapter 5; Fritz Machlup, *Foreign Trade and the National Income Multiplier* (Philadelphia: Blakiston Co., 1943). A longer list of references is given by Metzler in his survey. See note 1 (above).
3. Readers who are interested in exploring inter-temporal income relationships should consult Fritz Machlup's 'Period Analysis and the Multiplier Theory', *QJE* (November 1939). Machlup's *International Trade and the National Income Multiplier* uses a period analysis.
4. The diagrams used in this section are drawn from Romney Robinson, 'A Graphical Analysis of the Foreign Trade Multiplier', *EJ* (September 1952), pp. 546–64; and Kindleberger, *International Economics*, 4th ed., pp. 276–93. Other graphical presentations of income balance-of-payments relations are to be found in J. W. Black, 'A Geometrical Analysis of the Foreign Trade Multiplier', *EJ* (June 1957), pp. 240–3; and H. G. Johnson, 'A Diagrammatic Analysis of Income Variations and the Balance of Payments', *QJE* (November 1953).
5. Kindleberger, *International Economics*, pp. 281 and 292; Meade, *International Economic Policy*, Vol. I: *The Balance of Payments*; Oscar Lange, 'On the Theory of the Multiplier', *Econometrica*, Vol. II (1943), pp. 227–45; L. A. Metzler, 'A Multiple-Region Theory of Income and Trade', *Econometrica*, Vol. 18 (1950), pp. 329–54.
6. L. A. Metzler, 'The Theory of International Trade', in H. S. Ellis, *A Survey of Contemporary Economics*, pp. 219–20.
7. T. Scitovsky, 'A Study of Capital and Interest', *Eca*, Vol. VII (1940), pp. 293–317.
8. See also *Economic Theory and Western European Integration* (Stanford, Calif.: Stanford University Press, 1958), by the same author.
9. Scitovsky, *Economic Theory and Western European Integration*, p. 88.

Chapter 14

1. As an example of such a synthesis at a high level of abstraction, see J. Vanek, *The Balance of Payments, Level of Economic Activity and the Value of the Currency* (1962).
2. The main formative contributors to this approach were J. E. Meade, in *The Theory of International Economic Policy:* Vol. I, *The Balance of Payments*; J. Tinbergen, *On The Theory of Economic Policy* (Amsterdam: North Holland Publishing Co., 1952); and S. Alexander, 'The Effects of a Devaluation on a Trade Balance', *IMF Staff Papers*, Vol. II, No. 2, pp. 263–78 (reproduced in Caves and Johnson, *Readings in International Economics*, Chapter 22, pp. 359–73; subsequent references are to this chapter). Many other writers have contributed to the literature. For a useful list see H. G. Johnson's 'Towards a General Theory of the Balance of Payments' in *International Trade and Economic Growth* (London: Allen & Unwin, 1958), p. 154.
3. E. Sohmen, 'The Effect of Devaluation on the Price Level', *QJE* (May 1958).
4. J. Tinbergen, 'Unstable and Indifferent Equilibria in Economic Systems', *Revue de l'Institut International de Statistique* (1941); A. J. Brown, 'Trade Balances and Exchange Stability', *OEP* (1942).
5. G. Stuvel, *The Exchange Stability Problem* (Leiden: Stenfert Kruese, 1950).

Notes

6. A. C. Harberger, 'Currency Depreciation, Income and the Balance of Trade', *JPE* (February 1950) and 'Some Evidence on the International Price Mechanism', *JPE* (December 1957).
7. Ibid., *JPE* (December 1957).
8. Ibid., p. 521.
9. Alexander, *IMF Staff Papers*, Vol. II, No. 2, p. 359.
10. Ibid., p. 364.
11. Ibid., p. 369.
12. Ibid.
13. H. G. Johnson, 'Towards a General Theory of the Balance of Payments', from *International Trade and Economic Growth: Studies in Pure Theory*, pp. 153–68. Also reprinted in Caves and Johnson, *Readings in International Economics*, pp. 374–88.
14. Johnson in Caves and Johnson, p. 377.
15. Ibid., p. 379.
16. Ibid., p. 382n.
17. For example: F. Machlup, 'Relative Prices and Aggregate Spending in the Analysis of Devaluation', *AER* (June 1955); S. C. Tsiang, 'The Role of Money in Trade Balance Stability: Synthesis of the Elasticity and Absorption Approaches', *AER* (December 1961).
18. Machlup, *AER* (June 1955), p. 44.
19. See Alexander, 'Effects of a Devaluation: A Simplified Synthesis of Elasticities and Absorption Approaches', *AER* (March 1959).
20. Ibid., pp. 25–6.
21. Ibid., p. 34.
22. See S. C. Tsiang, *AER* (December 1961). Tsiang adapted an earlier devaluation model of Meade to help explain the impact of monetary conditions on the devaluation process.
23. Kindleberger, *International Economics*, 4th ed., p. 495.

Chapter 15

1. For surveys of the literature on the transfer problem see J. Viner, *Studies in the Theory of International Trade* (New York: Harper & Bros., 1937), Chapter vi; Paul Samuelson, 'The Transfer Problem and Transport Costs', *EJ* (June 1952), pp. 278–304 and (June 1954), pp. 264–89. Perhaps the most interesting single article, and one with which the student should start his more detailed reading is H. G. Johnson's 'The Transfer Problem and Exchange Stability', *JPE* (June 1956), pp. 212–25.
2. See J. H. Williams, *Argentine International Trade Under Inconvertible Paper Money, 1880–1900* (1920); J. H. Viner, *Canada's Balance of International Indebtedness, 1900–1913* (1924); H. D. White, *The French International Accounts, 1880–1913* (1933) (all published at Cambridge, Mass.: Harvard University Press); R. Wilson, *Capital Imports and the Terms of Trade* (Melbourne, 1931).
3. For a good brief account of this controversy see Haberler's *Theory of International Trade* (Kelley Reprint Edition, 1968), pp. 67–76. See also J. M. Keynes, 'The German Transfer Problem', *EJ*, Vol. 39 (1929); B. Ohlin, 'Transfer Difficulties Real and Imagined', *EJ* (June 1929).
4. For a discussion of this point, an exposition of the transfer process as a

special case of adjustment of the balance of payments and definitions and examples of bilateral and unilateral transfers, see Haberler, *Theory of International Trade*, pp. 63–4.
5. Readers interested in a more complex model with lagged reactions should consult Lloyd Metzler's 'The Transfer Problem Reconsidered', *JPE* (June 1942).
6. Kindleberger, *International Economics*, 4th ed., pp. 320–1.
7. Meade, *International Economic Policy*, Vol. I: *The Balance of Payments*, Parts II and III.

Chapter 16

1. J. Williamson, 'The Crawling Peg', *EIF*, No. 50 (1965).
2. See H. G. Johnson, 'Towards a General Theory of the Balance of Payments', Caves and Johnson, *Readings in International Economics*, Vol. XI, p. 382.
3. See 'Longer-Run Problems of the Balance of Payments', ibid., Chapter 27.
4. Mundell, *International Economics*, Chapter 16; also 'The Appropriate Use of Monetary and Fiscal Policy under Fixed Exchange Rates', *IMF Staff Papers* (March 1962).
5. Mundell, *International Economics*, p. 234.
6. Mundell, 'The Proper Division of the Burden of International Adjustment', *National Banking Review* (September 1965). See also *International Economics*, Chapter 13.
7. Mundell, *International Economics*, p. 189.
8. Ibid., pp. 192–5.

Chapter 17

1. See A. R. Holmes, *The New York Foreign Exchange Market* (New York: Federal Reserve Bank of New York, 1959), p. 18.
2. Figure 17.1 is adapted from a diagram by Kindleberger. See *International Economics*, 4th ed., p. 439.
3. The term is Kindleberger's. See his *International Economics*, 4th ed., p. 440.
4. For an examination of how such discrepancies arise see Paul Einzig, *A Textbook on Foreign Exchange* (London: Macmillan, 1966), pp. 76–7.
5. For a description of the bill thus used see *The Bill on London*, 2nd ed. (London: Gilletts Discount Company, 1959).
6. Mundell, *International Economics*, pp. 147–9.
7. There is a large and growing literature on Euro-dollars. The first source is in a much-quoted article 'The Market for Dollar Deposits in Europe' by Holmes and Klopstock in *Monthly Review* (Federal Reserve Bank of New York, November 1960). Oscar Altman's 'Foreign Markets for Dollars, Sterling and Other Currencies', *IMF Staff Papers* (December 1961), is a good survey. The best book on the subject is Paul Einzig's *The Euro-Dollar System* 5th ed. (London: Macmillan, 1973). Good recent surveys are A. K. Swoboda's *The Euro-Dollar Market: An Interpretation*, Essays in International Finance, No. 64 (Princeton, 1968), and Milton Friedman's 'The Euro-Dollar Market: Some First Principles', *Review of the Federal Reserve Bank of St. Louis* (July 1971), pp. 16–25.
8. R. S. Sayers, *Modern Banking*, 7th ed. (Oxford: Oxford University Press, (1967), p. 320.

Chapter 18

1. Ragnar Nurkse, 'International Monetary Equilibrium', *Essays in International Finance*, No. 4 (Princeton University, 1945). This paper is reprinted in *Readings in the Theory of International Trade* (Philadelphia: Blakiston Co., 1949).
2. Nurkse chose, after some discussion, a period of five to ten years in order to take account of the business cycle. For reasons, other than those above, for shortening the period, see my *International Monetary Policy*, 2nd ed. (London: Macmillan, 1961), pp. 54–5.
3. Nurkse, *Essays in International Finance*, p. 7.
4. Ibid.
5. Keynes, *Lloyds Bank Review* (October 1935), p. 528.
6. Gustav Cassel, *Memorandum on the World's Monetary Problems*, International Financial Conference (Brussels, 1920). For a résumé of the evolution of the purchasing-power-parity doctrine see Viner's *Studies in the Theory of International Trade*, pp. 379–87.
7. Bela Balassa, 'The Purchasing Power Parity Doctrine: A Reappraisal', *JPE* (December 1964).
8. *The Balance of Payments Adjustment Process*, Working Party No. 3, Economic Policy Committee (Paris: OECD, August 1966).
9. See L. Metzler, 'Exchange Rates and the IMF', in *International Monetary Policy*, Board of Governors of the Federal Reserve System, Post-war Economic Studies, No. 7 (September 1947).
10. A good analysis is Richard Caves and associates, *Britain's Economic Prospects* (London and Washington: Brookings Institution, 1968), particularly Part II.
11. See R. A. Mundell, 'The Monetary Dynamics of International Adjustment Under Fixed and Flexible Exchange Rates', Chapter 11 of *International Economics* (New York, 1968), p. 152.
12. See Nurkse's *International Currency Experience*, pp. 117–22.
13. See S. C. Tsiang, 'The Fluctuating Exchange Rates in Countries With Relatively Stable Economies, Some European Experiences After World War I', *IMF Staff Papers* (October 1959) and 'An Experiment With a Flexible Exchange Rate System: The Case of Peru, 1950–1954', *IMF Staff Papers* (February 1957).
14. See H. C. Eastman, 'Aspects of Speculation in the Canadian Market for Foreign Exchanges', *Canadian Journal of Economics and Political Science* (August 1958), and R. Z. Aliber, 'Speculation in the Foreign Exchanges: the European Experience, 1919–1926', *Yale Economic Essays* (Spring 1962).
15. See Kindleberger, 'Flexible Exchange Rates', *Monetary Management*, prepared for the Commission on Money and Credit, 1963.
16. W. J. Baumol, 'Speculation, Profitability and Stability', *Review of Economics and Statistics* (August 1957).
17. Milton Friedman, 'The Case for Flexible Exchange Rates', *Essays in Positive Economics* (Chicago: University of Chicago Press, 1953), pp. 157–203; also in Caves and Johnson, Chapter 25.
18. Friedman, in Caves and Johnson, p. 426.
19. 'Exchange Rates: Fixed or Flexible' in Clement, Pfister, and Rothwell, *Theoretical Issues in International Economics*, p. 269.

20. See F. Lutz, 'The Case for Flexible Exchange Rates', *Banca Nazionale del Lavoro Quarterly Review* (December 1954).

21. See Sir Donald MacDougall, 'Flexible Exchange Rates', *Westminster Bank Review* (August 1954). This is perhaps the place to name some of the academic economists who have been engaged in the controversy. A good case was made by Milton Friedman in *Essays in Positive Economics* (Chicago: University of Chicago Press, 1953), while the case against was put by Lionel Robbins in *The Economist in the Twentieth Century* (London: Macmillan, 1954), Chapter 5. The present writer made an early plea for flexible rates in 'What Sort of Exchange Rates', *Westminster Bank Review* (May 1954). (The article by MacDougall listed above was a reply to this.) Meade was an early and consistent exponent of free rates. His 'Case for Variable Exchange Rates', *Three Banks Review* (September 1955), was a notable contribution. The most notable book on the subject is Egon Sohmen's *Flexible Exchange Rates, Theory and Controversy* (Chicago: University of Chicago Press, 1961). An excellent review of the controversy and a very useful bibliography is 'Exchange Rates: Fixed or Flexible', Chapter 6 of Clement, Pfister, and Rothwell, *Theoretical Issues in International Economics*. Recent books at the policy level have been Samuel Brittan's *The Price of Economic Freedom: A Guide to Flexible Rates* (London: Macmillan, 1970) and Paul Einzig's *The Case Against Floating Exchange Rates* (London: Macmillan, 1970).

22. For an account of the planning which preceded the Bretton Woods Conference see the writer's *International Monetary Policy*, Chapters 5 and 6.

23. For an interesting study of the speculative role of traders who defer payment for the deficit country's exports and, at home, accelerate payments for imports, thereby creating the so-called leads-and-lags effect, see 'Leads and Lags in Overseas Trade', *Bank of England Quarterly Bulletin* (March 1961), pp. 18–23.

24. Readers wishing for factual information on the monetary history of the international economy since 1945 must read widely. There is no definitive text covering the period but many books have dealt with particular periods and problems. Leland Yeager's *International Monetary Relations*, pp. 347–493, is a good starting-point. The writer's *International Monetary Policy*, Chapters 7, 11, 12 and 15, deals with certain specific aspects of post-war monetary history. Robert Triffin's *Europe and the Money Muddle* (New Haven: Yale University Press, 1957) and his *Our International Monetary System – Yesterday, Today and Tomorrow* (New York: Random House, 1968), Chapters 1 and 2 are useful. R. F. Mikesell's *Foreign Exchange in the Postwar World* (New York: Twentieth Century Fund, 1954), deals well with the problems of the immediate post-war years. There is a huge literature of articles in the learned journals and bank reviews.

Chapter 19

1. This is James Meade's classification. See *The Theory of International Economic Policy*, Vol. I: *The Balance of Payments*, p. 263.

2. For a fuller account of sterling area exchange control and the efforts to establish full convertibility of sterling in the post-war years see Scammell, *International Monetary Policy*, 2nd ed., pp. 248–56.

3. See *Financial Agreement between the Governments of the United States and the United Kingdom*, 6 December 1945, Cmd. 6708 of 1945, Clause 8 (ii).

Notes

4. For a full description see Scammell, *International Monetary Policy*, pp. 275–311, and G. L. Rees, *Britain and the Postwar European Payments Systems* (Cardiff: University of Wales Press, 1963).
5. For an account of this mild resurgence of barter see an article in *The Economist*, 'Barter is Respectable' (29 January 1966), pp. 428–9.
6. Such questions are explored in M. F. W. Hemming and W. M. Corden, 'Import Restriction as an Instrument of Balance of Payments Policy', *EJ* (September 1958).
7. Wexler, *Fundamentals of International Economics*, p. 253.
8. E. A. Birnbaum and Moeen A. Qureshi, 'Advance Deposit Requirements for Imports', *IMF Staff Papers* (November 1960), pp. 115–25.
9. For an analysis of these measures, see G. Haberler and Thomas Willett, *Presidential Measures on Balance of Payments Controls* (American Enterprise Institute for Public Policy Research, 1968).
10. Those who seek detailed knowledge of the use of restrictive controls since the Second World War should consult the IMF's *Annual Reports* on Exchange Restrictions.
11. Readers seeking such an evaluation will find it in James Meade's *Trade and Welfare*, Vol. II of his *Theory of International Economic Policy*, Parts II and IV.
12. See Yeager, *International Monetary Relations*, p. 122.
13. See Sydney S. Alexander, 'Devaluation Versus Import Restrictions as an Instrument for Improving the Foreign Trade Balance', *IMF Staff Papers* (April 1951).
14. Yeager, *International Monetary Relations*, pp. 129–30.
15. G. Winder, *The Free Convertibility of Sterling* (London: Batchworth Press, 1955), pp. 58–9.

Chapter 20

1. For a fairly full description of the evolution and history to 1960, of the Bretton Woods system, see Scammell, *International Monetary Policy*, 2nd ed., pp. 117–225.
2. As, for example, in *International Financial Statistics*, a monthly statistical bulletin published by the IMF.
3. The phrase is that of R. G. Lipsey and R. Clower and is used in an interesting article 'The Present State of International Liquidity Theory', *AER* Papers and Proceedings, Vol. 63, No. 2 (May 1968).
4. Lipsey and Clower, *AER* Papers and Proceedings, Vol. 63, No. 2 (May 1968).
5. Triffin, *Our International Monetary System; Yesterday, Today and Tomorrow*, p. 89.
6. The most notable attempt has been that of H. R. Heller, 'Optimal International Reserves', *EJ* (June 1968).
7. Triffin, *Our International Monetary System*, p. 92.
8. See Triffin, *Our International Monetary System*, pp. 92–3, and F. Machlup, 'The Need for Monetary Reserves', *Banca Nazionale del Lavoro Quarterly Review* (September 1966).
9. An estimate made by *The Economist* (20 July 1968), p. 56.
10. *IMF Annual Report* (1948), p. 41.

11. See Brian Tew, 'Sterling as an International Currency', *Economic Record* (June 1948).
12. A. G. Ford, *The Gold Standard, 1880–1914: Britain and Argentina* (Oxford: Oxford University Press, 1962), p. 28.
13. For an interesting brief account of the pre-1914 gold standard see Ian Shannon, *International Liquidity* (Chicago: Henry Regnery Company, 1966), pp. 1–16.
14. *Report of the Committee on Currency and Foreign Exchanges after the War*, Cmd. 464, December 1919.
15. See Ragnar Nurkse, *International Currency Experience* (League of Nations, 1944), p. 7.
16. See Scammell, *International Monetary Policy*, 2nd ed., pp. 242–65.
17. The reader who wishes to examine this period should consult Nurkse, *International Currency Experience*; W. A. Lewis, *Economic Survey, 1919–1939* (London: Allen & Unwin, 1949); and Yeager, *International Monetary Relations*, pp. 266–332.
18. See R. F. Mikesell, *United States Private and Government Investment Abroad* (Oregon University, 1962), p. 26. Quoted in Shannon, *International Liquidity*, p. 23.
19. W. A. Brown Jr, *The International Gold Standard Reinterpreted, 1914–34*, 2 vols (New York: National Bureau of Economic Research, 1940), p. 823.
20. The vagueness surrounding the term 'fundamental disequilibrium' is probably intentional. R. F. Mikesell, who, we are told, 'had access to the unpublished minutes of the pre-Bretton Woods meetings', tells us that 'the principal criterion for rate alterations in the minds of the authors of the text of the Fund Agreement was the existence of a disequilibrium in the current international accounts of the members requesting a change'. See R. F. Mikesell, 'The Role of the International Monetary Agreements in a World of Planned Economics', *JPE* (December 1947); also Alvin Hansen, 'Fundamental Disequilibrium', *Review of Economic Statistics* (1946), and G. Haberler, 'Currency Depreciation and the International Monetary Fund', *Review of Economic Statistics* (1946).
21. Scammell, *International Monetary Policy*, 2nd ed., p. 155.

Chapter 21

1. On the embryonic stages of post-war monetary planning readers might consult the following works whose references will lead them still deeper into the literature: Richard N. Gardner, *Sterling–Dollar Diplomacy*, 2nd ed. (Oxford: Oxford University Press, 1968); R. F. Harrod, *Life of John Maynard Keynes* (London: Macmillan, 1951), Chapter XIII; Scammell, *International Monetary Policy*, 2nd ed., Chapters 5 and 6. On the operations and record of the IMF the best single book is S. Horie, *The International Monetary Fund* (London, 1964). See also Scammell, *International Monetary Policy*, Chapter 7, and 'The International Monetary Fund', Chapter 9 of *The Evolution of International Organizations*, edited by Evan Luard (London: Thames & Hudson, 1966). The *IMF Staff Papers* publishes from time to time an ongoing bibliography of books and articles on the Fund and its work. The first twenty years of the Fund was marked by the publication of a large three-volume work, *The International Monetary Fund, 1945–1965* (Washington: IMF, 1969). This contains a history of the Fund's evolution, an

Notes

analysis of the main problems which it has encountered and copies of the founding and all other relevant documents.

2. See Article I of the *Final Act*. United Nations, Monetary and Financial Conference, *Final Act* (London: H.M.S.O., Cmd. 6546 of 1944).

3. Readers interested in this case study in the working of free rates should consult: P. Wonnacott, *The Canadian Dollar, 1948–58* (Toronto, 1960); H. C. Eastman and S. Stykolt, 'Exchange Stabilisation in Canada, 1950–54', *Canadian Journal of Economics and Political Science* (May 1956) and ibid. (May 1958); T. L. Powrie, 'Short-Term Capital Movements and the Flexible Canadian Exchange Rate', ibid. (February 1964); Samuel I. Katz, 'The Canadian Dollar: A Fluctuating Currency', *Review of Economics and Statistics* (August 1953).

4. For a complete examination of the Fund's stand-by arrangements see Joseph Gold, *The Stand-By Arrangements of the International Monetary Fund* (Washington: IMF, 1970).

5. The original sources for these international currency plans are as follows: Triffin Plan: Robert Triffin, *Banca Nazionale del Lavoro Quarterly Review* (March and June 1958); *Gold and the Dollar Crisis* (New Haven: Yale University Press, 1960). Stamp Plan: Maxwell Stamp, 'The Fund and the Future', *Lloyds Bank Review* (October 1958). Franks's Plan: Oliver Franks, *Lloyds Bank Annual Statement* (1958). Bernstein Plan: E. Bernstein, *International Effects of United States' Economic Policy*, Study Paper, No. 16 (January 1960), presented to joint committee of United States Congress. T. Balogh: 'International Reserves and Liquidity', *EJ* (June 1960). Alan Day: Evidence to Radcliffe Committee, *Committee on the Working of the Monetary System*. Minutes of Evidence, Questions 9891–9977.

6. For an interesting survey see K. V. Gowda, *International Currency Plans and Expansion of World Trade* (New York: Asia Publishing House, 1964).

7. See Scammell, *International Monetary Policy*, 2nd ed., p. 416.

8. The best accounts of the SDR scheme at the time of writing (1972) are: Fritz Machlup, *Remaking the International Monetary System – The Rio Agreement and Beyond* (Baltimore: Johns Hopkins Press, 1968); and 'The SDR: Some Problems and Possibilities', *IMF Staff Papers* (March 1971).

Bibliographical Note

THE literature of international trade is large. It would be pretentious to describe what follows as a bibliography. It is rather a basic list of readings which will help the student both to widen and deepen his knowledge and establish a position from which he can go on alone to explore the literature according to his bent. The list, after an introductory general section, is categorised according to the basic divisions of the table of contents of the book. Where books or articles are listed in the introductory section their relevance, in varying degree, to the later sections is taken for granted and they are not listed again.

I Treatises, Monographs and General Texts

(a) Treatises

CAVES, RICHARD E., *Trade and Economic Structure* (Cambridge, Mass.: Harvard University Press, 1960).

GRAHAM, FRANK D., *The Theory of International Values* (Princeton: Princeton University Press, 1948).

HABERLER, GOTTFRIED, *The Theory of International Trade* (London: William Hodge, 1950).

MARSH, DONALD B., *World Trade and Investment: The Economics of Interdependence* (New York: Harcourt Brace, 1951).

MARSHALL, ALFRED, *Money, Credit and Commerce* (London: Macmillan, 1923).

— *The Pure Theory of Foreign Trade* (Reprints of Scarce Tracts on Political Economy, London: London School of Economics, 1930).

MEADE, J. E., *A Geometry of International Trade* (London: Allen & Unwin, 1952).

— *Theory of International Economic Policy*, Vol. I, *The Balance of Payments* (New York: Oxford University Press, 1951).

— *Theory of International Economic Policy*, Vol. II, *Trade and Welfare* (New York: Oxford University Press, 1955).

OHLIN, BERTIL, *Interregional and International Trade* (Cambridge, Mass.: Harvard University Press, 1933).

TAUSSIG, FRANK W., *International Trade* (New York: Macmillan, 1927).

VINER, JACOB, *Studies in the Theory of International Trade* (1937); Reprints of Economic Classics, New York: Augustus Kelley, 1965).

(b) Texts

ELLSWORTH, PAUL T., *The International Economy*, 4th ed. (Toronto: Collier-Macmillan Canada, 1968).
HARROD, R. F., *International Economics* (Chicago: University of Chicago Press, 1958).
KINDLEBERGER, C. P., *International Economics*, 4th ed. (Homewood, Ill.: Irwin, 1968).
MUNDELL, ROBERT A., *International Economics* (New York: The Macmillan Co., 1968).
PEARCE, I. F., *International Trade*, Books I and II (London: Macmillan, 1970).
SCHELLING, THOMAS, *International Economics* (Boston: Allyn & Bacon, 1958).
SNIDER, DELBERT A., *Introduction to International Economics*, 5th ed. (Homewood, Ill.: Irwin, 1971).
SÖDERSTEN, BO, *International Economics* (New York: Harper & Row, 1970).
TARSHIS, LORIE, *Introduction to International Trade and Finance* (New York: Wiley, 1955).
VANEK, JAROSLAV, *International Trade: Theory and Economic Policy* (Homewood, Ill.: Irwin, 1962).
WALTER, INGO, *International Economics* (New York: Ronald Press, 1968).
WELLS, SIDNEY J., *International Economics* (New York: Atherton Press, 1969).
WEXLER, IMANUEL, *Fundamentals of International Economics*, 2nd ed. (New York: Random House, 1972).
YOUNG, JOHN PARKE, *The International Economy*, 4th ed. (New York: Ronald Press, 1963).

(c) Readings and Surveys

(i)

BALASSA, BELA (ed.), *Changing Patterns in Foreign Trade and Payments* (New York: Norton, 1964).
BHAGWATI, J. (ed.), *International Trade — Selected Readings* (Harmondsworth: Penguin Books, 1969).
CAVES, R., and JOHNSON, H. G. (eds.), *Readings in International Economics* (Homewood, Ill.: Richard Irwin for The American Economic Association, 1968).
CLEMENT, M. O., PFISTER, F. L., and ROTHWELL, K. J., *Theoretical Issues in International Economics* (New York: Houghton Mifflin, 1967).

ELLIS, H. S., and METZLER, L. A. (eds.), *Readings in the Theory of International Trade* (Philadelphia: The Blakiston Company for the American Economic Association, 1949).
JENSEN, F. B., and WALTER, INGO (eds.), *Readings in International Economic Relations* (New York: Ronald Press, 1966).

(ii)

CHIPMAN, J. S., 'A Survey of the Theory of International Trade': Part I, *Econometrica* (July 1965); Part II, *Econometrica* (October 1965); Part III, *Econometrica* (January 1966).
CORDEN, W. M., 'Recent Developments in the Theory of International Trade', *Princeton Special Papers in International Economics*, No. 7 (March 1965).
HABERLER, GOTTFRIED, 'A Survey of International Trade Theory', *Princeton Special Papers in International Economics*, revised ed. (1961).
METZLER, LLOYD A., 'The Theory of International Trade', in Howard S. Ellis (ed.), *A Survey of Contemporary Economics*, Chapter 6 (Philadelphia: Blakiston for The American Economic Association, 1948).

(d) *Miscellaneous*

ASHWORTH, WILLIAM, *A Short History of the International Economy, 1850–1950* (London: Longmans, 1952).
HEILPERIN, MICHAEL A., *The Trade of Nations* (New York: Knopf, 1947).
INGRAM, JAMES C., *International Economic Problems*, 2nd ed. (New York: Wiley & Sons, 1970).
JOHNSON, H. G., *The World Economy at the Crossroads* (London: Oxford University Press, 1965).
KENWOOD, A. G., and LOUGHEED, A. L., *The Growth of the International Economy, 1820–1960* (London: Allen & Unwin, 1971).
KINDLEBERGER, C. P., *Foreign Trade and the National Economy* (London: Yale University Press, 1962).
PENN, JAN, *A Primer on International Trade* (New York: Random House, 1967).
PERKINS, J. O. N., *International Policy for the World Economy* (London: Allen & Unwin, 1969).
STERN, ROBERT M. and LEAMER, E. E., *Qualitative International Economics* (Boston: Allyn & Bacon, 1970).
TINBERGEN, J., *International Economic Integration*, 2nd ed. (Amsterdam: Elsevier, 1954).

II The Pure Theory of International Trade

ALLEN, W. (ed.), *International Trade Theory: Hume to Ohlin* (New York: Random House, 1965).

BALASSA, B., 'An Empirical Demonstration of Classical Comparative Cost Theory', *Review of Economics and Statistics* (August 1963).

BALDWIN, R. E., 'Equilibrium in International Trade: A Diagrammatic Analysis', *QJE* (November 1948).

— 'The New Welfare Economics and Gains in International Trade', *QJE* (February 1952).

— 'The Role of Capital–Goods Trade in the Theory of International Trade', *AER* (September 1966).

BHAGWATI, J., 'Growth, Terms of Trade and Comparative Advantage', *Economia Internazionale* (August 1959).

— 'The Gains from Trade Once Again', *OEP* (July 1968).

— 'The Pure Theory of International Trade: A Survey', *EJ* (March 1964).

BLACK, JOHN, 'Economic Expansion and International Trade: A Marshallian Approach', *RES*, No. 3 (1956).

EDGEWORTH, F. Y., 'The Theory of International Values', *EJ* (March, September and December, 1894).

ELLSWORTH, P. T., 'A Comparison of International Trade Theories', *AER* (June 1940).

— 'The Structure of American Foreign Trade: A New View Examined', *Review of Economics and Statistics* (August 1954).

HABERLER, GOTTFRIED, 'Real Cost, Money Cost and Comparative Advantage', *International Social Science Bulletin* (Spring 1950).

— 'Some Problems in the Pure Theory of International Trade', *EJ* (June 1950).

— 'The Relevance of Classical Theory under Modern Conditions', *AER, Papers and Proceedings* (May 1954).

— 'The Theory of Comparative Costs Once More', *QJE* (February 1929).

HARROD, R. F., 'Factor-Price Relations under Free Trade', *EJ* (June 1950).

HELLER, H. R., *International Trade: Theory and Empirical Evidence* (Englewood Cliffs, N.J.: Prentice Hall, 1968).

JOHNSON, H. G., 'Factor Endowments, International Trade and Factor Prices', *MS* (September 1957).

JONES, R. W., 'Factor Proportions and the Heckscher–Ohlin Model', *RES* (October 1956).

KEMP, MURRAY C., 'The Relation Between Changes in International Demand and the Terms of Trade', *Econometrica* (January 1956).

KEMP, MURRAY C., 'Gains and Losses from Trade', *Canadian Journal of Economics and Political Science* (August 1961).
— 'Gains from International Trade and Investment', *AER* (September 1966).
— 'Some Issues in the Analysis of Trade Gains', *OEP* (July 1968).
— 'The Gains from International Trade', *EJ* (December 1962).
— *The Pure Theory of International Trade* (Englewood Cliffs, N.J.: Prentice Hall, 1964).
— 'The Relation Between Changes in International Demand and the Terms of Trade', *Econometrica* (January 1956).
KENEN, P. B., 'Distribution, Demand and Equilibrium in International Trade', *Kyklos* (1959).
LANCASTER, K., 'The Heckscher–Ohlin Trade Model: A Geometric Treatment', *Eca* (February 1957).
LAND, A., 'Factor Endowments and Factor Prices', *Eca* (May 1959).
LAURSEN, SVEND, 'Production Functions and the Theory of International Trade', *AER* (September 1952).
LEONTIEF, WASSILY, 'An International Comparison of Factor Costs and Factor Use', *AER* (June 1964).
— 'Domestic Production and Foreign Trade: The American Capital Position Re-examined', *Economia Internazionale* (February 1954).
— 'Factor Proportions and the Structure of American Trade: Further Theoretical and Empirical Analysis', *Review of Economics and Statistics* (November 1956).
— 'The Use of Indifference Curves in the Analysis of Foreign Trade', *QJE* (May 1933).
LERNER, ABBA P., 'Factor Prices and International Trade', *Eca* (February 1952).
— 'The Diagrammatic Representation of Cost Conditions in International Trade', *Eca* (August 1932).
— 'The Diagrammatic Representation of Demand Conditions in International Trade', *Eca* (August 1934).
LINNEMANN, H., *An Econometric Study of International Trade Flows* (Amsterdam: North-Holland, 1966).
LOVASY, G., 'International Trade Under Imperfect Competition', *QJE* (August 1941).
MACDOUGALL, G. D. A., 'British and American Exports: A Study Suggested by the Theory of Comparative Costs': Part I, *EJ* (December 1951); Part II, *EJ* (September 1952).
MCKENZIE, LIONEL W., 'Equality of Factor Prices in World Trade', *Econometrica* (July 1955).

MEADE, JAMES E., 'The Equalization of Factor Prices: The Two-Country Two-Factor Three-Product-Case', *Metroeconomica* (December 1950).
MICHAELY, M., *Concentration in World Trade*, Contributions to Economic Analysis, No. 28 (Amsterdam: North-Holland, 1962).
— 'Factor Proportions in International Trade: Current State of the Theory', *Kyklos* (1964).
MINHAS, B. S., *An International Comparison of Factor Costs and Factor Use*, Contributions to Economic Analysis, No. 31 (Amsterdam: North-Holland, 1963).
MISHAN, E. J., 'International Factor Price Determination with Neutral Technical Progress', *Eca* (August 1966).
MOOKERJEE, S., *Factor Endowments and International Trade: A Study and Appraisal of the Heckscher–Ohlin Theory* (Bombay: Asia Publishing House, 1958).
MORGAN, E. V., and REES, G. L., 'Non-traded Goods and International Factor Price Equalisation', *Eca* (November 1954).
MUNDELL, ROBERT, 'International Trade and Factor Mobility', *AER* (June 1957).
— 'The Pure Theory of International Trade', *AER* (March 1960).
OLIVERA, J. H. G., 'Is Free Trade a Perfect Substitute for Factor Mobility?', *EJ* (March 1967).
PEARCE, I. F. and JAMES, S. F., 'The Factor–Price Equalisation Myth', *RES* (1952).
—, MCKENZIE, L. W. and SAMUELSON, P. A., 'Symposium on Factor–Price Equalisation', *International Economic Review* (October 1967).
— 'A Note on Mr Lerner's Paper', *Eca* (February 1952).
— 'A Further Note on Factor–Commodity Price Relationships', *EJ* (December 1959).
REITER, STANLEY, 'Efficient International Trade and Equalisation of Factor Prices', *International Economic Review* (January 1961).
ROBINSON, J., 'Factor Prices not Equalised', *QJE* (May 1966).
ROBINSON, R., 'Factor Proportions and Comparative Advantage': Part I, *QJE* (May 1956); Part II, *QJE* (August 1956).
— 'Factor Proportions and the Structure of American Trade: Further Theoretical and Empirical Analysis. Comment', *Review of Economics and Statistics* (February 1968).
RYBCZYNSKI, T. N., 'Factor Endowments and Relative Commodity Prices', *Eca* (November 1955).
SAMUELSON, PAUL A., 'International Price Equalisation Once Again', *EJ* (June 1949).

SAMUELSON, PAUL A., 'International Trade and the Equalisation of Factor Prices', *EJ* (June 1948).
— 'Prices of Factors and Goods in General Equilibrium', *RES* (October 1953).
— 'Summary on Factor–Price Equalisation', *International Economic Review* (October 1967).
— 'The Gains from International Trade', *Canadian Journal of Economics and Political Science* (May 1939).
— 'The Gains from International Trade Once Again', *EJ* (December 1962).
— 'Theoretical Notes on Trade Problems', *Review of Economics and Statistics* (May 1964).
— 'Welfare Economics and International Trade', *AER* (June 1938).
SAVOSNIK, K. M., 'The Box Diagram and the Production–Possibility Curve', *Ekonomisk Tidskrift* (September 1958).
STOLPER, W., and SAMUELSON, PAUL A., 'Protection and Real Wages', *RES* (November 1941).
TINBERGEN, J. 'The Equalisation of Factor Prices between Free Trade Areas', *Metroeconomica* (April 1949).
UZAWA, HIROFUMI, 'Prices of the Factors of Production in International Trade', *Econometrica* (July 1959).
VANEK, J., 'An Alternative Proof of the Factor–Price Equalisation Theorem', *QJE* (November 1960).
— 'Variable Factor Proportions and Inter-Industry Flows in the Theory of International Trade', *QJE* (February 1963).
WILLIAMS, J. H., 'The Theory of International Trade Reconsidered', *EJ* (June 1929).

III Commercial Policy

ANDERSON, J., and NAZA., S., 'Substitution and Two Concepts of Effective Rate of Protection', *AER* (September 1969).
BALASSA, BELA (ed.), *Studies in Trade Liberalisation* (Baltimore: Johns Hopkins Press, 1967).
— 'Tariff Protection in Industrial Nations and its Effects on the Exports of Processed Goods from Developing Countries', *Canadian Journal of Economics* (August 1968).
— 'Tariff Reductions and Trade in Manufactures among the Industrial Countries', *AER* (June 1966).
— *Trade Liberalisation among Industrial Countries* (New York: McGraw-Hill for the Council on Foreign Relations, 1967).

BALDWIN, R., *Non-tariff Distortions of International Trade* (London: Allen & Unwin, 1970).
— 'The Case Against Infant Industry Tariff Protection', *JPE* (May 1969).
— 'The Effects of Tariffs on International and Domestic Prices', *QJE* (February 1960).
BARBER, C. L., 'Canadian Tariff Policy', *Canadian Journal of Economics and Political Science* (November 1955).
BASEVI, G., 'The Restrictive Effect of the United States Tariff and Its Welfare Value', *AER* (September 1968).
BENTICK, B. L., 'Estimating Trade Creation and Trade Diversion', *EJ* (June 1963).
BHAGWATI, J., 'On the Equivalence of Tariffs and Quotas' in R. E. Baldwin *et al. Trade, Growth and the Balance of Payments: Essays in Honour of Gottfried Haberler* (Amsterdam: North-Holland, 1966).
— 'Protection, Real Wages and Real Incomes', *EJ* (December 1959).
—, and RAMASWAMI, V. K., 'Domestic Distortions, Tariffs and the Theory of Optimum Subsidy', *JPE* (February 1963).
BLACK, J., 'Arguments for Tariffs', *OEP* (June 1959).
CAMPS, M., *Britain and the European Community, 1955–63* (London: Oxford University Press, 1964).
COHEN, B. I., 'Measuring the Short-Run Impact of a Country's Import Restrictions on Its Exports', *QJE* (August 1966).
COOPER, C. A., and MASSELL, B. F., 'Towards a General Theory of Customs Unions for Developing Countries', *JPE* (October 1965).
— 'A New Look at Customs Union Theory', *EJ* (December 1965).
CORDEN, W. M., *The Theory of Protection* (London: Oxford University Press, 1971).
— 'The Calculation of the Cost of Protection', *Economic Record* (April 1957).
— 'Tariffs, Subsidies and the Terms of Trade', *Eca* (August 1957).
— 'The Structure of a Tariff System and the Effective Protective Rate', *JPE* (June 1966).
CURZON, G., *Multilateral Commercial Diplomacy* (London: Michael Joseph, 1965).
CURZON, G. and V., *Hidden Barriers to International Trade* (London: Trade Policy Research Centre, 1971).
DALES, J. H., 'The Cost of Protectionism with High International Mobility of Factors', *Canadian Journal of Economics and Political Science* (November 1964).
DE GRAAF, J., 'On Optimum Tariff Structures', *RES* (1949).

EASTMAN, H. C., and STYKOLT, S., *The Tariff and Competition in Canada* (Toronto: Macmillan, 1967).

EFTA SECRETARIAT, *The Effects of EFTA on the Economies of Member States* (Geneva: EFTA, 1969).

FLEMING, J. M., 'On Making the Best of Balance of Payments Restrictions on Imports', *EJ* (March 1951).

FLEMING, M., 'The Optimal Tariff from an International Standpoint', *Review of Economics and Statistics* (February 1946).

GEHRELS, F., 'Customs Unions from a Single-Country Viewpoint', *RES* (June 1958).

GORMAN, W. M., 'The Effect of Tariffs on the Level and Terms of Trade', *JPE* (June 1959).

GRUBEL, H. G., and JOHNSON, H. G., 'Nominal Tariffs, Indirect Taxes and Effective Rates of Protection: The Common Market Countries, 1959', *EJ* (December 1967).

GUISINGER, S., 'Negative Value Added and the Theory of Effective Protection', *QJE* (August 1969).

GUPTA, K. R., 'GATT and Quantitative Restrictions', *Asian Economic Review* (February 1967).

HABERLER, GOTTFRIED. et al., *Trends in International Trade* (Geneva: United Nations, 1958).

HAGEN, E. E., 'An Economic Justification of Protectionism', *QJE* (November 1958).

HEMMING, M. F. W. and CORDEN, W. M., 'Import Restriction as an Instrument of Balance of Payments Policy', *EJ* (September 1958).

HILGERDT, F., 'The Case for Multilateral Trade', *AER* (March 1943).

H.M.S.O., *Britain and the European Communities: An Economic Assessment*, Cmnd. 4289 (London: H.M.S.O. 1970).

HORWELL, D. J. and PEARCE, I. F., 'A Look at the Structure of Optimal Tariff Rates', *University of Southampton Discussion Papers*, No. 6704 (1967).

HUMPHREY, D. P., 'Measuring the Effective Rate of Protection: Direct and Indirect Effects', *JPE* (September 1969).

JENSEN, F. B., and WALTER, I., *The Common Market: Economic Integration in Europe* (Philadelphia: Lippincott, 1965).

JOHNSON, H. G., 'An Economic Theory of Protectionism, Tariff Bargaining and the Formation of Customs Unions', *JPE* (June 1965).

— *Aspects of the Theory of Tariffs* (London: Allen & Unwin, 1971).

— 'Discriminatory Tariff Reduction: A Marshallian Analysis', *Indian Journal of Economics* (July 1957).

— 'Optimal Trade Interventions in the Presence of Domestic Distortions', in R. E. Baldwin et al., *Trade, Growth and the Balance of Payments: Essays in Honour of G. Haberler* (Amsterdam: North-Holland, 1966).

JOHNSON, H. G., 'Optimum Tariffs and Retaliation', *RES* (1953–4).

— 'Optimum Welfare and Maximum Revenue Tariffs', *RES* (1951–2).

— 'The Cost of Protection and the Scientific Tariff', *JPE* (August 1960).

— 'The Standard Theory of Tariffs', *Canadian Journal of Economics* (August 1969).

JONES, R. W., 'Comparative Advantage and the Theory of Tariffs: A Multi-Country, Multi-Commodity Model', *RES* (June 1961).

KAHN, R. F., 'Tariffs and the Terms of Trade', *RES* (1947–8).

KEMP, M. C., 'Tariffs, Income and Distribution', *QJE* (February 1956).

KRAUSE, LAWRENCE B. (ed.), *The Common Market: Progress and Controversy* (Englewood Cliffs, N.J.: Prentice Hall, 1964).

— *European Integration and the United States* (Washington, D.C.: Brookings Institution, 1968).

LAMBERT, J., *Britain in a Federal Europe* (London: Chatto & Windus, 1968).

LERNER, A., 'The Symmetry Between Import and Export Taxes', *Eca* (August 1936).

LIPSEY, R. G., *The Theory of Customs Unions: A General Equilibrium Analysis* (London: Weidenfeld & Nicolson, 1970).

— 'The Theory of Customs Unions: A General Survey', *EJ* (September 1960).

— 'The Theory of Customs Unions: Trade Diversion and Welfare', *Eca* (February 1957).

— and LANCASTER, K. J., 'The General Theory of Second Best', *RES* (1956–7).

LITTLE, I. M. D., 'Welfare and Tariffs', *RES* (1949–50).

MCDIARMID, O. J., *Commercial Policy in the Canadian Economy* (Cambridge, Mass.: Harvard University Press, 1946).

MAKOWER, H., and MORTON, G., 'A Contribution Towards a Theory of Customs Unions', *EJ* (March 1953).

MANOILESCO, MICHAEL, *The Theory of Protection and International Trade* (London: King, 1931).

MASON, EDWARD S., *Controlling World Trade* (New York: McGraw-Hill, 1946).

MEADE, J. E., *The Theory of Customs Unions* (Amsterdam: North-Holland, 1955).

MELVIN, J., 'Comments on the Theory of Customs Unions', *MS* (June 1969).

METZLER, L., 'Tariffs, International Demand and Domestic Prices', *JPE* (August 1949).
— 'Tariffs, the Terms of Trade and the Distribution of National Income', *JPE* (February 1949).
MICHAELY, M., 'On Customs Unions and the Gain From Trade', *EJ* (September 1965).
MISHAN, E., 'A Note on the Costs of Tariffs, Monopolies and Thefts', *Western Economic Journal* (September 1969).
MUNDELL, R. A., 'Tariff Preferences and the Terms of Trade', *MS* (January 1964).
OPHIT, T., 'The Interaction of Tariffs and Quotas', *AER* (December 1969).
PREEG, E., *Leaders and Diplomats: An Analysis of the Kennedy Round of Negotiations under the General Agreement on Tariffs and Trade* (Washington, D.C.: The Brookings Institution, 1970).
SCITOVSKY, TIBOR, 'A Reconsideration of the Theory of Tariffs', *RES* (1941).
— *Economic Theory and Western European Integration* (London: Allen & Unwin, 1958).
SHOUP, CARL, *Fiscal Harmonisation in Common Markets*, 2 Vols (New York: Columbia University Press, 1966).
SPRAOS, J., 'The Condition for a Trade-Creating Customs Union', *EJ* (March 1964).
SWANN, D., *The Economics of the Common Market*, Penguin Modern Economic Texts (Harmondsworth: Penguin Books, 1970).
TAUSSIG, FRANK, *Some Aspects of the Tariff Question*, 3rd ed. (Cambridge, Mass.: Harvard University Press, 1931).
VANEK, J., *General Equilibrium of International Discrimination: The Case of Customs Unions* (Cambridge, Mass.: Harvard University Press, 1965).
VINER, J., *Dumping: A Problem in International Trade* (Chicago: Chicago University Press, 1923).
— *The Customs Union Issue* (New York: Carnegie Endowment for International Peace, 1950).
WALKER, F. V., 'The Restrictive Effect of the U.S. Tariff', *AER* (December 1969).
WERSTATE, C., 'The Economic and Political Implications of a Customs Union', *QJE* (May 1948).
WEXLER, I., 'Trade Creation and Trade Diversion: A Geometrical Note', *Southern Economic Journal* (April 1960).
WILCZYNSKI, J., *The Economics and Politics of East–West Trade* (New York: Praeger, 1969).

YEAGER, L. B., 'The Size of Gain from an Optimum Tariff', *Southern Economic Journal* (October 1964).
—, and TUERCH, D., *Trade Policy and the Price System* (Scranton Pa.: International Textbook Company, 1966).

IV The Economics of the Balance of Payments

ALEJANDRO, C. F. D., 'A Note on the Impact of Devaluation and the Redistributive Effect', *JPE* (December 1963).
ALEXANDER, S., 'Devaluation versus Import Restriction as an Instrument for Improving Foreign Trade Balance', *IMF Staff Papers* (April 1951).
— 'Effects of a Devaluation: A Simplified Synthesis of Elasticities and Absorption Approaches', *AER* (March 1959).
— 'Effects of a Devaluation on a Trade Balance', *IMF Staff Papers* (April 1952).
ALIBER, R. Z., 'Counter Speculation and the Forward Exchange Market: A Comment', *JPE* (December 1962).
— 'Gresham's Law, Asset Preference and the Demand for International Reserves', *QJE* (November 1967).
— 'More About Counter Speculation in the Forward Exchange Market', *JPE* (1963).
— 'The U.S. Role as a Reserve Currency Country', *QJE* (August 1964).
ALLEN, W. R., 'The International Monetary Fund', *OEP* (June 1961).
ALTMAN, O. L., 'The Management of International Liquidity', *IMF Staff Papers* (July 1964).
AUBREY, H. G., *The Dollar in World Affairs* (New York: Praeger, 1964).
AUFRICHT, H., *The International Monetary Fund* (New York: Praeger, 1964).
AUTEN, J. H., 'Counter-Speculation and the Forward Exchange Market', *JPE* (February 1961).
— 'Forward Exchange Rates and Interest Rate Differentials', *Journal of Finance* (March 1963).
— 'Monetary Policy and the Forward Exchange Market', *Journal of Finance* (December 1961).
BALOGH, T., 'International Reserves and Liquidity', *EJ* (June 1960).
BEHRMAN, J. H., *Direct Manufacturing Investment, Exports and the Balance of Payments* (Washington, D.C.: National Foreign Trade Council, 1968).
BELL, G. L., 'The Euro-Dollar Market', *Federal Reserve Bank of St Louis Review* (December 1963).
'Bernstein Report', *The Balance of Payments Statistics of the U.S.: A Review and Appraisal*, Report of the Review Committee for Balance of

Payments Statistics to the Bureau of the Budget (Washington, D.C.: 1965).

BICKERDIKE, C. F., 'The Instability of Foreign Exchange', *EJ* (March 1920).

BLACK, J., 'A Savings and Investment Approach to Devaluation', *EJ* (June 1959).

BLOOMFIELD, ARTHUR, *Capital Imports and the American Balance of Payments, 1934–9: A Study in Abnormal International Capital Transfers* (Chicago: Chicago University Press, 1950).

— 'Foreign Exchange Rate Theory and Policy', in Seymour E. Harris (ed.) *The New Economics: Keynes' Influence on Theory and Public Policy* (London: Dennis Dobson, 1947).

— *Monetary Policy Under the International Gold Standard, 1880–1914* (New York: Federal Reserve Bank of New York, 1959).

— *Short-Term Capital Movements under the Pre-1914 Gold Standard* (Princeton: International Finance Section, Princeton University, 1963).

BRITTAN, SAMUEL, *The Price of Economic Freedom: A Guide to Flexible Rates* (London: Macmillan, 1970).

BRONFENBRENNER, M., 'Exchange Rates and Exchange Stability', *Review of Economics and Statistics* (February 1950).

BROWN, A. J., 'The Rate of Exchange' in T. Wilson and P. W. S. Andrews (eds) *Oxford Studies in the Price Mechanism* (London: Oxford University Press, 1951).

CAVES, RICHARD E., 'Flexible Exchange Rates', *AER* (May 1963).

— 'International Liquidity: Towards a Home Repair Manual', *Review of Economics and Statistics* (May 1964).

CLARK, P. B., 'Optimum International Reserves and the Speed of Adjustments', *JPE* (March 1970).

CLARKE, W. M. and PULAY, GEORGE, *The World's Money* (London: Allen & Unwin, 1970).

COHEN, B. J., *Balance of Payments Policy*, Penguin Modern Economics Texts (Harmondsworth: Penguin Books, 1969).

COOPER, RICHARD N., 'The Balance of Payments', in Richard Caves (ed.) *Britain's Economic Prospects* (London: Allen & Unwin, 1968).

COPPOCK, J., *International Economic Instability* (New York: McGraw-Hill, 1962).

DEVRIES, M., 'Multiple Exchange Rates: Expectations and Experiences', *IMF Staff Papers* (July 1965).

EINZIG, PAUL, *A Dynamic Theory of Forward Exchange* (London: Macmillan, 1961).

EINZIG, PAUL, *A Textbook on Foreign Exchange* (London: Macmillan, 1966).
— *Foreign Dollar Loans in Europe* (London: Macmillan, 1965).
— *Parallel Money Markets*, Volume One: *The New Markets in London*; Volume Two: *Overseas Markets* (London: Macmillan, 1971).
— *The Case Against Floating Exchanges* (London: Macmillan, 1970).
— *The Euro-Dollar System*, 2nd eds. (London: Macmillan, 1973).
— *The History of Foreign Exchange* (London: Macmillan, 1970).
ELLSWORTH, P. T., 'Exchange Rates and Exchange Stability', *Review of Economics and Statistics* (February 1950).
FLANDERS, M. J., 'International Liquidity is always Inadequate', *Kyklos* (1969).
FLEMING, J. M., 'Guidelines for Balance of Payments Adjustment under the Par Value System', *Princeton Essays in International Finance*, No. 67 (Princeton: 1968).
— 'Towards Assessing the Need for International Reserves', *Princeton Essays in International Finance*, No. 58 (Princeton: 1967).
FLOYD, J. E., 'International Capital Movements and Monetary Equilibrium', *AER* (September 1969).
FRIEDMAN, M., *Dollars and Deficits* (Englewood Cliffs, N.J.: Prentice Hall, 1968).
— 'The Case for Flexible Exchange Rates', in *Essays in Positive Economics* (Chicago: University of Chicago Press, 1953).
— 'The Euro-Dollar Market: Some First-Principles', *Federal Reserve Bank of St Louis Review* (July 1971).
FRISCH, R., 'On the Need for Forecasting a Multilateral Balance of Payments', *AER* (September 1947).
FURTH, J. H., 'International Monetary Reform and the "Crawling Peg"', *Federal Reserve Bank of St Louis Review* (July 1969).
GARDNER, RICHARD, *Sterling–Dollar Diplomacy*, 2nd ed. (New York: McGraw-Hill, 1969).
GILBERT, MILTON, *Problems of the International Monetary System* (Princeton: International Finance Section, Princeton University, 1966).
— *The Gold-Dollar System: Conditions of Equilibrium and the Price of Gold* (Princeton: International Finance Section, Princeton University, 1968).
GOWDA, K. V., *International Currency Plans and Expansion of World Trade* (New York: Asia Publishing House, 1964).
GRUBEL, HERBERT G., *Forward Exchange, Speculation and the International Flow of Capital* (Stanford: Stanford University Press, 1966).
— *The International Monetary System*, Penguin Modern Economics Texts (Harmondsworth: Penguin Books, 1969).

GRUBEL, HERBERT G., (ed.), *World Monetary Reform* (London: Oxford University Press, 1964).
HABERLER, GOTTFRIED, 'The Choice of Exchange Rates After the War', *AER* (June 1945).
— 'The Market for Foreign Exchange and the Stability of the Balance of Payments', *Kyklos*, III (1949).
HAGEMANN, H. A., 'Reserve Policies of Central Banks and their Implications for U.S. Balance of Payments Policy', *AER* (March 1969).
HAHN, F. H., 'The Balance of Payments in a Monetary Economy', *RES* (February 1959).
HALM, GEORGE N., *The 'Band' Proposal: The Limits of Permissible Exchange Rate Variations* (Princeton: International Finance Section, Princeton University, 1965).
HANSEN, ALVIN, *The Dollar and the International Monetary System* (New York: McGraw-Hill, 1965).
HARBERGER, A. C., 'Currency Depreciation, Income and the Balance of Trade', *JPE* (December 1957).
— 'Some Evidence of the International Price Mechanism', *JPE* (December 1957).
HARROD, R. F., 'A Plan for Increasing Liquidity: A Critique', *Eca* (May 1961).
— *Reforming the World's Money* (London: Macmillan, 1965).
HELLER, H. R., 'Optimal International Reserves', *EJ* (June 1966).
— 'The Transaction Demand for International Means of Payments', *JPE* (January 1968).
HICKS, J. R., 'The Long-Run Dollar Problem: An Inaugural Lecture', *OEP* (June 1953).
HINSHAW, R. (ed.), *Monetary Reform and the Price of Gold* (Baltimore: Johns Hopkins Press, 1967).
— (ed.), *The Economics of International Adjustment* (Baltimore: Johns Hopkins Press, 1971).
— *Towards European Convertibility* (Princeton: International Finance Section, Princeton University, 1958).
HIRSCH, F., 'Influences on Gold Production', *IMF Staff Papers* (November 1968).
— *Money International* (Harmondsworth: Penguin Books, 1967).
HOLMES, ALAN R., *The New York Foreign Exchange Market* (New York: Federal Reserve Bank of New York, 1959).
HORIE, S., *The International Monetary Fund* (London: Macmillan, 1964).
HORSEFIELD, J. K. (ed.), *The International Monetary Fund, 1945–65:*

Vol. I *Chronicle*; Vol. II *Analysis*; Vol. III *Documents* (Washington, D.C.: IMF, 1969).
HOUTHAKKER, H. S. and MAGEE, S. P., 'Income and Price Elasticities in World Trade', *Review of Economics and Statistics* (May 1969).
IVERSON, CARL, *Some Aspects of the Theory of International Capital Movements* (Copenhagen: Levin & Munksgaard, 1936).
JOHNSON, H. G., 'International Liquidity—Problems and Plans', *Malayan Economic Review* (April 1962).
— *International Trade and Economic Growth: Studies in Pure Theory* (Cambridge, Mass.: Harvard University Press, 1961).
— *Money, Trade and Economic Growth* (London: Allen & Unwin, 1962).
— 'The Case for Flexible Exchange Rates 1969', *Federal Reserve Bank of St Louis Review* (June 1969).
— 'The Future of Gold: The Gold Rush of 1968 in Retrospect and Prospect', *AER* (May 1969).
— 'Theoretical Problems of the International Monetary System', *Pakistan Development Review* (1967).
— 'The Transfer Problem and Exchange Stability', *JPE* (June 1956).
JONES, R. W., 'Depreciation and the Dampening Effects of Income Changes', *Review of Economics and Statistics* (February 1960).
— 'Stability Conditions in International Trade: A General Equilibrium Analysis', *International Economic Review* (May 1961).
KALDOR, N., 'The Problem of International Liquidity', *Oxford University Institute of Statistics Bulletin* (August 1964).
KEMP, M. C., 'The Rate of Exchange, the Terms of Trade and the Balance of Payments in Fully Employed Economies', *International Economic Review* (September 1962).
KENEN, P. B., 'International Liquidity and the Balance of Payments of a Reserve Currency Country', *QJE* (November 1960).
— 'Reserve Asset Preferences of Central Banks and Stability of the Gold Exchange Standard', *Princeton Studies in International Finance*, No. 10 (Princeton: 1963).
—, and YUDIN, E. B., 'The Demand for International Reserves', *Review of Economics and Statistics* (August 1965).
KEYNES, J. M., 'The German Transfer Problem', *EJ* (March 1929).
KINDLEBERGER, C. P., *Balance of Payments Deficits and the International Market for Liquidity* (Princeton: International Finance Section, Princeton University, 1963).
— *Europe and the Dollar* (Cambridge, Mass.: M.I.T. Press, 1966).

KINDLEBERGER, C. P., *International Short-Term Capital Movements* (New York: Kelley, 1965).
— 'Measuring Equilibrium in the Balance of Payments', *JPE* (November 1969).
— 'The Foreign Trade Multiplier, the Propensity to Import and Balance of Payments Equilibrium', *AER* (March 1949).
KLOPSTOCK, F. H., 'The International Money Market: Structure, Scope and Instruments', *Journal of Finance* (May 1966).
LARY, HAL B., *Problems of the United States as World Trader and Banker* (Princeton: Princeton University Press, 1962).
LAURSEN, S. and METZLER, L., 'Flexible Exchange Rates and the Theory of Employment', *Review of Economics and Statistics* (November 1950).
LEDERER, WALTHER, *The Balance on Foreign Transactions: Problems of Definition and Measurement* (Princeton: International Finance Section, Princeton University, 1963).
LERNER, ABBA. P., *The Economics of Control* (New York: The Macmillan Co., 1944).
LUTZ, FRIEDRICH, *The Problem of International Liquidity and the Multiple Currency Standard* (Princeton: International Finance Section, Princeton University, 1963).
MACDOUGALL, DONALD, *The Dollar Problem: A Reappraisal* (Princeton: International Finance Section, Princeton University, 1960).
— *The World Dollar Problem* (London: Macmillan, 1957).
MACHLUP, FRITZ, *International Payments, Debts and Gold* (New York: Scribner, 1964).
— *International Trade and the National Income Multiplier* (Philadelphia: Blakiston, 1943).
— 'Relative Prices and Aggregate Expenditure in the Analysis of Devaluation', *AER* (June 1955).
— *Remaking the International Monetary System* (Baltimore: Johns Hopkins University Press, 1968).
— 'The Cloakroom Rule of International Reserves', *QJE* (August 1965).
— 'The Terms of Trade Effects of Devaluation upon Real Income and the Balance of Trade', *Kyklos* (1956).
MCKINNON, RONALD I., *Private and Official International Money: The Case for the Dollar* (Princeton: International Finance Section, Princeton University, 1969).
— 'Optimum Currency Areas', *AER* (1963).
—, and OATES, WALLACE, *The Implications of International Economic Integration for Monetary, Fiscal and Exchange Rate Policy* (Princeton: International Finance Section, Princeton University, 1966).

MEADE, JAMES E., 'The Case for Variable Exchange Rates', *Three Banks Review* (September 1955).
METZLER, L., 'Exchange Rates and the International Monetary Fund', in *Postwar Studies*, No. 8 (Washington: Board of Governors of the Federal Reserve System, 1947).
— 'The Transfer Problem Reconsidered', *JPE* (June 1942).
MICHAELY, M., *Balance of Payments Adjustment Policies: Japan, Germany and the Netherlands*, Occasional Paper 106 (New York: National Bureau of Economic Research, 1968).
— 'Multilateral Balancing in International Trade', *AER* (September 1962).
MIKESELL, R., *Foreign Exchange in the Postwar World* (New York: Twentieth Century Fund, 1954).
— 'Negotiating at Bretton Woods 1944', in R. Dennett and J. E. Johnson (eds) *Negotiating with the Russians* (1953).
— 'The Role of International Monetary Agreements', *JPE* (December 1947).
MORGAN, E. V., 'The Theory of Flexible Exchange Rates', *AER* (June 1955).
MUNDELL, R. A., 'A Theory of Optimum Currency Areas', *AER* (September 1961).
— *Monetary Theory: Inflation, Interest and Growth in the World Economy* (Pacific Palisades, Cal.: Goodyear Publishing Company, 1971).
— 'The Appropriate Use of Monetary and Fiscal Policy for Internal and External Stability', *IMF Staff Papers* (March 1962).
— 'The Monetary Dynamics of International Adjustment under Fixed and Flexible Exchange Rates', *QJE* (May 1960).
—, and SWOBODA, A. K. (eds.), *Monetary Problems of the International Economy* (Chicago: University of Chicago Press, 1969).
NURKSE, RAGNAR, *Conditions of International Monetary Equilibrium*, (Princeton: International Finance Section, Princeton University, 1945).
— 'Domestic and International Equilibrium' in S. Harris (ed.) *The New Economics: Keynes' Influence on Theory and Public Policy* (London: Dennis Dobson, 1947).
— *International Currency Experience* (Geneva: League of Nations, 1944).
OFFICER, LAWRENCE H. and WILLETT, THOMAS D. (eds), *The International Monetary System: Problems and Proposals* (Englewood Cliffs, N.J.: Prentice Hall, 1969).
OHLIN, B., 'The Reparation Problem: A Discussion', *EJ* (June 1929).
ORCUTT, G., 'Exchange Rate Adjustment and Relative Size of the Depreciating Bloc', *Review of Economics and Statistics* (February 1955).

ORCUTT, G., 'Measurement of Price Elasticities in International Trade', *Review of Economics and Statistics* (May 1950).
PEARCE, I. F., 'The Problem of the Balance of Payments', *International Economic Review* (January 1961).
REDDAWAY, W. B., *Effects of U.K. Direct Investment Overseas* (Cambridge: Cambridge University Press, 1967).
ROBINSON, JOAN, 'The Foreign Exchanges' in *Essays on the Theory of Employment* (London: Macmillan, 1937).
ROBINSON, R., 'A Graphical Analysis of the Foreign Trade Multiplier', *EJ* (September 1952).
ROLF, S. E., *Gold and World Power* (New York: Harper & Row, 1966).
ROOSA, ROBERT V., *Monetary Reform and the World Economy* (New York: Harper & Row, 1965).
— *The Dollar and World Liquidity* (New York: Random House, 1967).
SALANT, WALTER, et al., *The U.S. Balance of Payments in 1968*. (Washington, D.C.: The Brookings Institution, 1962).
SCAMMELL, W. M., *International Monetary Policy*, 2nd ed. (London: Macmillan, 1961).
— 'The Working of the Gold Standard', *Yorkshire Bulletin of Economic and Social Research* (May 1965).
— 'What Sort of Exchange Rates?', *Westminster Bank Review* (May 1954).
SCHLESINGER, EUGENE, *Multiple Exchange Rates and Economic Development* (Princeton: International Finance Section, Princeton University, 1952).
SCITOVSKY, T., *Money and the Balance of Payments* (London: Allen & Unwin, 1969).
— *Requirements of an International Reserve System* (Princeton: International Finance Section, Princeton University, 1965).
SHANNON, IAN, *International Liquidity: A Study in the Economic Functions of Gold* (Chicago: Regnery, 1966).
SNIDER, DELBERT, *International Monetary Relations* (New York: Random House, 1966).
SOHMEN, EGON, *Flexible Exchange Rates: Theory and Controversy* (Chicago: University of Chicago Press, 1961).
— *International Monetary Problems and the Foreign Exchange* (Princeton: International Finance Section, Princeton University, 1963).
— *The Theory of Forward Exchange* (Princeton: International Finance Section, Princeton University, 1966).
SPRAOS, JOHN, 'Consumers' Behaviour and the Conditions for Exchange Stability', *Eca* (May 1955).

SPRAOS, JOHN, 'Speculation, Arbitrage and Sterling', *EJ* (March 1959).
— 'Stability in a Closed Economy and in the Foreign Exchange Market and the Redistributive Effect of Price Changes', *RES* (June 1957).
— 'The Theory of Forward Exchange and Recent Practices', *MS* (May 1953).
STEIN, J., 'International Short-Term Capital Movements', *AER* (March 1965).
STOLPER, W., 'The Multiplier, Flexible Exchange Rates and International Equilibrium', *QJE* (November 1950).
STRANGE, SUSAN, *Sterling and British Policy* (London: Oxford University Press for the Royal Institute of International Affairs, 1971).
STUVEL, G., *The Exchange Stability Problem* (Leiden: H. E. Stenfert Kruese, 1950).
TRIFFIN, ROBERT, *Gold and the Dollar Crisis* (New Haven, Connecticut: Yale University Press, 1960).
— *Our International Monetary System: Yesterday, Today and Tomorrow* (New York: Random House, 1968).
— *The Balance of Payments and Foreign Investment Position of the United States* (Princeton: International Finance Section, Princeton University, 1964).
— 'The Dollar and International Liquidity Problem Reconsidered', *Kyklos* (1958).
— *The Evolution of the International Monetary System: Historical Reappraisal and Future Perspectives* (Princeton: International Finance Section, Princeton University, 1964).
TSIANG, S. C., 'The Role of Money in Trade Balance Stability', *AER* (December 1961).
VINER, J., *Canada's Balance of International Indebtedness, 1900–13* (Cambridge, Mass.: Harvard University Press, 1924).
WALSHE, G., *International Monetary Reform*, Macmillan Studies in Economics (London: Macmillan, 1971).
WILLIAMS, J. H., *Postwar Monetary Plans and Other Essays* (New York: Knopf, 1947).
YEAGER, LELAND B., 'Absorption and Elasticity: A Fuller Reconciliation', *Eca* (February 1970).
— *International Monetary Relations* (New York: Harper & Row 1966).
— *The International Monetary Mechanism* (New York: Holt, Rinehart & Winston, 1968).

V International Economics and Growth

ATKINSON, A. B., 'Import Strategy and Growth under Conditions of Stagnant Export Earnings', *OEP* (November 1969).

BALASSA, BELA, 'Tariff Protection in Industrial Nations and its Effects on the Exports of Processed Goods from Developing Countries', *Canadian Journal of Economics* (August 1968).

BALDWIN, R. E., 'Secular Movements in the Terms of Trade', *AER* (May 1955).

— 'The Effects of Tariffs on International and Domestic Prices', *QJE* (February 1960).

BALOGH, T., and STREETEN, P. P., 'Domestic versus Foreign Investment', *Bulletin of the Oxford University Institute of Statistics* (August 1960).

— 'The Inappropriateness of Simple "Elasticity" Concepts in the Analysis of International Trade', *Bulletin of the Oxford University Institute of Statistics* (March 1951).

BAUER, P. T., and PAISH, F. W., 'The Reduction of Fluctuations in the Incomes of Primary Producers', *EJ* (December 1952).

BHAGWATI, J., 'International Trade and Economic Expansion', *AER* (December 1958).

— 'Optimal Policies and Immiserising Growth', *AER* (December 1969).

— 'Immiserising Growth: A Geometrical Note', *RES* (June 1958).

— 'Growth, Terms of Trade and Comparative Advantage', *Economia Internazionale* (August 1959).

CAIRNCROSS, ALEC K., 'International Trade and Economic Development', *Eca* (August 1961).

CHENERY, H. B., 'Comparative Advantage and Development Policy', *AER* (March 1961).

CORDEN, W. M., 'Economic Expansion and International Trade: A Geometrical Approach', *OEP* (June 1956).

ECKAUS, R. S., 'The Factor Proportions Problem in Underdeveloped Areas', *AER* (September 1955).

HABERLER, GOTTFRIED, 'Terms of Trade and Economic Development', in H. S. Ellis (ed.) *Economic Development for Latin America* (New York: Macmillan, 1961).

— 'Integration and Growth of the World Economy in Historical Perspective', *AER* (March 1964).

HARROD, R. F., and HAGUE, D. C. (eds.), *International Trade Theory in a Developing World* (London: Macmillan, 1963).

HICKS, U. K., *Development Finance: Planning and Control* (New York and Oxford: Oxford University Press, 1965).

JOHNSON, H. G., 'Economic Expansion and International Trade', *MS* (May 1955).
— *Economic Policies Toward Less Developed Countries* (New York: Praeger for the Brookings Institution, 1967).
— 'Effects of Changes in Comparative Costs as Influenced by Technical Change' in R. F. Harrod and D. C. Hague (eds.), *International Trade Theory in a Developing World* (London: Macmillan, 1963).
— (ed.), *Trade Strategy for Rich and Poor Nations* (Toronto: University of Toronto Press, 1971).
KEMP, M. C., 'International Trade and Investment in a Context of Growth', *Economic Record* (June 1968).
— 'Technological Change, the Terms of Trade and Welfare', *EJ* (September 1955).
KENEN, P. B., *Giant Among Nations: Problems in United States Foreign Economic Policy* (Chicago: Rand McNally, 1963).
KINDLEBERGER, C. P., *Economic Development*, 2nd ed. (New York: McGraw-Hill, 1965).
— *Power and Money: The Politics of International Economics and the Economics of International Politics* (New York: Basic Books, 1970).
KOMIZA, R., 'Economic Growth and the Balance of Payments, a Monetary Approach', *JPE* (January 1969).
MEIER, GERALD M., *International Trade and Development* (New York: Harper & Row, 1963).
— *Leading Issues in Economic Development*, 2nd ed. (New York: Oxford University Press, 1970).
— *The International Economics of Development* (New York: Harper & Row, 1968).
MELVIN, J., 'Demand Conditions and Immiserising Growth', *AER* (September 1969).
MIKESELL, RAYMOND F., *Public International Lending for Development* (New York: Random House, 1966).
— *The Economics of Foreign Aid* (Chicago: Aldine Publishing Co., 1968).
MYINT, H., 'Protection and Economic Development', in R. F. Harrod and D. C. Hague (eds) *International Trade Theory in a Developing World* (London: Macmillan, 1963).
— 'The "Classical Theory" of International Trade and the Underdeveloped Countries', *EJ* (June 1958).
— 'The Gains from International Trade and the Backward Countries', *RES* (1954).
NURKSE, RAGNAR, *Problems of Capital Formation in Underdeveloped Countries* (Oxford: Blackwell, 1953).

PEARSON, LESTER B., *Partners in Development: Report of the Commission on International Development* (New York: Praeger, 1969).

PINCUS, J. A., 'The Cost of Foreign Aid', *Review of Economics and Statistics* (November, 1963).

PREBISCH, R., 'Commercial Policy in Underdeveloped Countries', *American Economic Association, Papers and Proceedings* (May 1959).

PRYOR, F., 'Economic Growth and the Terms of Trade', *EJ* (March 1966).

ROSENSTEIN-RODAN, P. N., 'International Aid for Underdeveloped Countries', *Review of Economics and Statistics* (May 1961).

ROWE, J. W. F., *Primary Commodities in International Trade* (Cambridge: Cambridge University Press, 1965).

SINGER, H. W., 'The Distribution of Gains between Investing and Borrowing Countries', *American Economic Association, Papers and Proceedings* (May 1950).

STERN, ROBERT M., *Policies for Trade and Development* (New York: Carnegie Endowment for International Peace, 1964).

SWERLING, BORIS C., *Current Issues in International Commodity Policy*. (Princeton: International Finance Section, Princeton University, 1962).

VINER, JACOB, *International Trade and Economic Development* (Oxford: Oxford University Press, 1953).

YANG, S. C., 'Foreign Trade Problems in Economic Development', *Scottish Journal of Political Economy* (June 1964).

Index

Absorption approach 352–7, 362–9
Adjustment process. Need for 253–7; balance-of-payments disequilibrium, correction a necessity 291–2; five options for a country with a deficit 293–7; imbalance defined 298; the classical approach 299–301; adjustment by price changes summarised 317–18; elasticities approach 350; absorption approach 352–7; criticism of 362–9; payments approach 357–62; adjustment burden, distribution of 402–7; adjustments in domestic income and prices 457–9; and arguments against 459–60; advantages claimed for flexible exchange rates: simplicity 460–2; painless way of making balance-of-payments adjustments 462–3; provides minimum interference with domestic stability of economy 463–5; alleviates international liquidity problem 465; only system never truly tested 466; case against flexible rates: the elasticity condition 466; deterrent effect on international trade 466–7; frequent variations impede international investment 467–8; potentially damaging aspects — international anarchy 468–9, and harmful speculation in foreign exchange market 469–71; inflation produced by depreciation 471–2; balance-of-payments changes, met by: transfer of reserves, changing domestic income and prices, varying exchange rate, controlling flows of trade and payments 472; free-rate system defined 473; managed flexibility ('adjustable peg' method): historical beginnings 473–4; resembles free rates 474; the system at work 474–5; lacks adjustment mechanism 476–7; problem of management 477–9; speculation's role 479–80; record of twenty years 480–2; adjustment policies, choice between use of domestic economy manipulation and the two systems of exchange rates 482–4; controls on trade and payments: not a true adjustment policy 485–7; part played by Bretton Woods system and IMF 486–7; the three groups of controls — *financial* and exchange systems 488–94; *commercial* including embargoes and restrictions on imports, tariff quotas and buying policies of state-trading monopolies 495–502; *capital movements* 502–4; evaluation of controls 504–6; defects of controls 506–7

Alexander, S., the absorption approach 352–7, 362–9
American Exchange Stabilisation Fund, establishment and principles of 436–7

Balance of payments. Important statistical statement 266; record of 'flows', not 'payments' 266; quantitative explanation of a country's external transactions during given period 267; identifies main elements in foreign transactions 267; intra-country comparisons of flows 267; 'balance' defined 267–9; transactions not all money transfers 268; distinguishing credit and debit items 269–70; classification into sections 270–1; Trade Items section 271–2; Transfer Items 272–4; volume and direction of external transaction flows exemplified 274–8; surplus and deficit, implications examined 279–81; disequilibrium an international problem 279; the aspect of duration 281–2; seasonal fluctuations 282; short-term capital movements 282–5; imbalance, the nature of 285; methods of adjustment 286; disequilibrium, main causes of: 'acts of God', government policy changes 286–7; cyclical fluctuations in domestic economy 287; long-period 'structural' changes 287–8. *See also* Adjustment process; Income analysis

Balassa, Bela, classical theory of trade sustained by statistical work 122; purchasing-power-parity theory 453

Bank for International Settlements 4

Banking system, its place in the international monetary system 251–3, 260

Barter deals 494–5

Basle Club 5

Baumol, W. J., speculation in foreign exchange market 469–70

Bhagwati, J., classical theory of trade, doubts on statistical work 122

Bickerdike, C. F., foreign exchange stability 307

Bilateral agreements. 'Convertibility', the term explained 491; constricting effect of agreements 492; trade agreements 492–3; the 'pathology' of them 493

Bretton Woods system. The Agreement as part of movement for trade freedom 170; continuance of the role of gold 249; system threatened by confidence crises 288; the Agreement as example of international monetary co-operation 437; whereby exchange rates altered at long intervals 446; adjustment element weakened 457; flexible exchange rates 460, 472; currency parity 474, 483; 'adjustable peg' system 481; American part in its formation 486; continuance threatened 486–7; dual-key-currency system 522–3; established present world monetary system 532–3; lack of adequate adjustment mechanism 534; established IMF and World

Index

Bank 536–7; basic principles of Agreement 537
Brigden Committee on Australian tariff cost 162–5
Brown, A. J., the elasticities approach 351

Capital movements, means of control 502; short-term 502–3; long-term 503–4
Cartels, forms and purpose of 225–6
Cassel, Gustav, purchasing-power-parity theory 450–1
Caves, Richard, parity between productivity and export performance 121; productivity of American workers 127
Commodity prices, reasons for differences 76; influence of factor price on 76–7
Comparative advantage. Theory of 16, 19–27; relation between quantities demanded and supplied 52–3; the theory's paradox 64; comparison with Heckscher–Ohlin theory of factor endowments 73; result of differing factor endowments 99; Ricardian and Heckscher–Ohlin theories compared 114–17; factor abundance the basis of comparative advantage 115
Comparative costs, theory of 13; relative prices 73, 75; causes of price differences 75; Heckscher–Ohlin approach 76; main cause of trade 77; empirical test of theory 120
Competition, perfect, the elementary facts of 220–1; imperfect: main feature of, influencing price by varying amount of product offered for sale 221–2; seller's price discrimination 223–6; buyer's price discrimination 226–8; dumping 228–32; export subsidies 232–4; state trading 234–40
Cooper, C. A., customs union theory 200
Corden, W. M., infant industry protection 158; cost effects of tariffs 163, 165, 167
Costs, constant and increasing 38–40; decreasing opportunity costs 40–1; transport costs 44–8; determinants of comparative 73
Council for Mutual Economic Aid (COMECON) 239
Currencies, three classes of: national bought and sold for purposes of travel within country, as used in international trade, held also for speculation and used as reserves by individual countries 250–1; free market for currencies replaced gold standard 256–7; currency transactions of the IMF 547–50, summary 548. *See also* Gold; International liquidity
Customs union theory. Wider significance than new European groupings 189; theory deals with problems of country discrimination 189; types of discriminatory groupings: the free-trade area, customs union, common market, and economic union 190; production effects 191; trade creation and diversion, examples of 192–7; consumption effects 197–9; unilateral tariff

Customs union theory—*continued*
reduction 200–2; union member, effects on when consumption is fixed 203–4; when pattern of consumption is variable 204–5; when consumption and production vary in two union countries and one non-union country 206–10; dynamic effects outside formal analysis: competition within a customs union, acceleration of technological change, investment stimulus, economies of scale 210–13; practical aspects of customs unions — European Community, EFTA, Latin American Free Trade Association, Central American Common Market 213–18

Devaluation, analysis 349–69; when it should take place 454–5. *See also* Absorption approach

Direct controls, as adjustment mechanism in balance of payments 257

Dumping — its practice as case of international price discrimination — the word defined 228; conditions to be satisfied 229; sporadic 229; intermittent 229; long-period 229; attitudes to dumping 230; adverse effects of 231; implications of for exporting country 231; frowned upon by governments 231–2

Economics, 'international' and 'general', distinction between 1, 2
Edgeworth–Bowley box diagram 78
Edgeworth, F. Y., offer curve as analytical device 66

Elasticities in foreign trade 303, 307–8, 347, 349–52. *See also* Marshall–Lerner condition

Ellsworth, P. T., criticism of 'Leontief paradox' 126–7

Employment and balance-of-trade equilibrium 389–96

Euro-dollar market 5, 441–4

Exchange Equalisation Account, establishment and principle of 436–7; end of gold standard recognised 446; marked beginning of control by British monetary authorities 486

Exchange rate. Effects of changes on exports and imports 25, 302–12; equilibrium exchange rate defined and examined 447–54; principles stated 454; purchasing-power-parity theory 450–4; flexible rates as adjustment device 460; it use as a control mechanism 488–91; exchange-rate policy of IMF 540–4

Expenditure-changing policies 389–96; monetary or fiscal policy, the choice between 396–401

Expenditure-switching 160

Export subsidies 232

Exports. Government subsidised 232–4; affected by changes in exchange rate 302–12; relations with income in balance-of-payments adjustment 321–4

Factor-endowments. Examination of the phrase 73, 75; country-to-country variation as basis of trade 76–7; factor intensity illustrated by isoquants 86–92; construction of a two-factor/two-

Index

commodity model box diagram 93; the Heckscher–Ohlin theorem 100, 117

Factor-price equalisation theorem 73; influence on commodity price 76–7; theorem reduced to a statement of tendency 111; phenomenon of factor reversal 111

Forcheimer, Karl, investigation of importance of relative wage differences on composition of foreign trade 121–2

Foreign exchange market. A world market in demand deposits 251, 256–7; essential knowledge of prices, demand and supply 412; currencies dealt in 413; buyers and sellers, relations of 413–15; the exchange rate, what it is 415–16; functions performed: clearing function 416–19; credit for foreign trade 419–20; provision for guarding against special risks 420; 'covering' and 'hedging' 420–1; forward exchange market and interest arbitrage 420–3; space arbitrage 424–5; time arbitrage 425–6; determination of exchange rate: in a free market 428–32; where rates are pegged 433–5; where rates have limited freedom 435–41; Euro-dollar market described 441–4

Foreign trade, a major role in economics 2, 3

Foreign trade multiplier, diagrammatic analysis of open economy 332–9

Free trade. Versus protection, elements of the argument examined 169; an unattainable condition 170–1; international division of labour 172; mobile factors 172–3; efficiency and output v. social welfare a weakening factor 173; self-interest 174; factor mobility 175; the arguments for tariffs: sustain socially important industries 175–6; protect domestic workers from low-paid foreign competition 176; reduce imports 176; diversify industrial structure of a country 177; bargaining power in trade negotiations 177; counter discriminatory practices by foreign suppliers 177; improve country's terms of trade 178; Pareto optimality 179; the three facts which cause free trade to be a qualified case 179–80; trade liberalisation 179–84; free trade in a two-country tariff-protected world; the case examined 180–4; free and multilateral trade 184; welfare situation in the move to free trade 184–8

Friedman, Milton, speculation in foreign exchange market defended 470

Gehrels, F., customs union theory 206

General Agreement on Tariffs and Trade (GATT), qualified success 170; unsatisfactory institution to poor countries 264; rules concerning import controls 497; its appearance in 1948 537

Gold. As international money 248–9; development of gold standard 254–6; control of gold standard

Gold—*continued*
258–9; international gold standard as the institutional approach to adjustment problem 300; foreign exchange rate determination under gold standard 433–5; system of external balance adjustment through changes in domestic prices and income 457; the international unit of account 517–18; monetary price fixed in 1934, increased in 1971 under Smithsonian Agreement 519; price fluctuations 521; pure or gold specie standard 525–9; gold bullion standard 529–30; breakdown of gold standard 530–2; gold exchange standard 532 — unstable and outmoded 556

Goods. Trade process examined 28; production possibilities curve (linear) of U.S.A. and Britain illustrated 28–35; marginal rate of transformation ratio 31–5; 'terms of trade' explained 34–5; production possibilities curve (concave) 35–41; curve affected by technological advance 49–51; the offer curve approach in analysis of trade demand 53–5; and the indifference curve analysis 55–7; community indifference curve — its advantages 57–8; derivation of offer curve 66–70; its usefulness and applications 70–2; the optimum tariff problem and the offer curve 152–6

Graham, F. D., national price levels, behaviour and exchange rates 455

Group of Ten 5, 524, 538, 552

Haberler, G., on dumping 230; export subsidies 232; power of price mechanism 351

Hagen, E. E., infant industry protection 158

Heckscher–Ohlin theorem of factor-endowments, comparison with theory of comparative advantage 73; difference from Ricardian theory 75–6; relative factor abundance and intensities the basic variables of the theorem 78; analysis of theorem 99–110; compared with Ricardian theory 114–15, 117; enhancement of value of trade theory, three claims 117; empirical investigation of theorem 120, 122, by Leontief 123–7

Hull, Cordell, and American postwar foreign economic policy 486

Hume, David, classical approach to adjustment problem 299, 457

Imports. Affected by changes in exchange rate 302–12; relations with income in balance-of-payments adjustment 321–4; embargoes and restrictions of as means of control 495–501; 'advance deposit requirement' as a method of import deterrent 501–2

Income analysis. Foreign balance and the Keynesian approach 319–20; import and export functions 321–4; income-creation process and multiplier analysis: in closed economy 324–8; in open economy 328–31; diagrammatic analysis of open economy 332–9; national income

adjustment 339–40; monetary factors 340–6; interest rate changes, their adjustment influence on balance of payments 342–6
International capital transfer. Classical theory — in gold standard conditions 372–3; under conditions of free exchange rates 373–4; modern theory — income reactions 374–7; conditions in lending and borrowing countries 377–8; multilateral adjustment 378–9; pattern of change on terms of trade 380–5; reparations payments 385–6
International economics, growing power of international organisations 4; multinational corporations 5; theoretical content constantly changing 8; unification of world banking and finance 5
International Labour Organisation 4
International liquidity. Nature of 508–11; demand and supply 512; optimum level of reserves 512–17; money media, 'first line' and supplementary categories, distinction between 509; gold 517–21, 525–32; key currencies, conditions to be satisfied 521–2; serve both as transactions' and reserve currencies 522; sterling and the dollar 521–2; borrowing rights of IMF members 524; reform of the IMF 550–5
International Monetary Fund. Birth and history 536–7; currency units, parities defined in terms of U.S. dollar 437; currency transactions, the four phases of 547–50; devaluation, effects on trade balance 349; permissible only in face of 'fundamental disequilibrium' 479; exchange rate as adjustment device 446; management 474; policy 540–4; fixed parity, Bretton Woods system supported 460; floating rates and frequent changes of pegged rates discouraged 458; gold, role of 519–20; international liquidity, supplier of 481, 486, 524; managed flexibility, implications of faith in 544–5; multilateral payments, establishment of a system of 545–7; multilateral trade, system established 532; operation 537–40; parity, rules for changing 483; power and influence 4, 5, 260, 262, 477; present position 555–6; reform 550–5; reserve ratios in 1949, 1964, 1970 513; summary of transactions 548. *See also* Bretton Woods system
International monetary system. Integral part of international economy 246; its four elements: international money 247–9; institutional arrangements 250–3; 'adjustment mechanism' to minimise balance-of-payments movements 253–7; control and co-operation 258–63; conditions of control: loss of national sovereignty 261; sanctions 262; recognised as part of problem of international economic planning 263; developing countries, their

International monetary system—*continued*
    discontent 264; essential condition for economic growth 265; agreements of co-operation 437; search for a stable system, the interweaving problems 534–5
International payments, methods: telegraphic transfer 427–8; bills of exchange 427–8

Johnson, H. G., infant industry argument 158; 'expenditure switching' in absorption theory 160; cost of protection 162; cost effects of tariffs 163, 167; absorption and payments approach 357–62, 390–1

Kennedy Round, qualified success 170
Keynes, J. M., German reparations, controversy with Ohlin 319, 371; *General Theory of Employment, Interest and Money* 319; monetary theorising 341
Kindleberger, C. P., tariff effects distinguished 143, 156; allocation of demand 226; demand elasticities 308; exchange rate 316; disequilibrium repression 369; speculation in foreign exchange market 469
Kravis, I. B., classical theory of trade sustained by statistical work 122; empirical investigation of the Heckscher–Ohlin theorem 123

Labour, costs of, and their influence on supply and demand 17, 19, 20–6; classical value, theory of 74; international division of labour, benefits of, basis of free-trade argument 172
Land, G. H., factor–price equalisation 112
Leontief, Wassily, summary of work on capital structure and trade of U.S.A. 123–7; empirical work on factor–price equalisation theorem 123–7
Lerner, Abba, diagram of factor intensity 86; foreign exchange stability 307
Lewis, W. A., infant industry protection 158
Lipsey, R. G., customs union theory 189, 193, 199, 203–7
Lutz, F., the case for flexible exchange rates 471

MacDougall, G. D. A., study of comparative costs and Anglo–U.S. model of labour productivity and exports 120–3
Machlup, F., criticism of the absorption approach to devaluation analysis 363
Manoilesco argument 158
Marshall, Alfred, theory of comparative advantage developed by 53; reciprocal demand, or offer, curve 66; classical approach to adjustment problem 299
Marshall–Lerner condition of depreciation in balance of trade 307–8, 313–16, 319, 351
Massell, B. F., customs union theory 200
Meade, James, employed geometric device to construct offer curve

66; factor–price equalisation 112; the free-price system 185; maximum and optimum production and effort, conditions 186–7; discusses whether reduction of a tariff is beneficial to welfare 188; customs union theory 189, 196–9; balance of payments 270, 272, 277

Metzler, L., income adjustment in balance of payments 341; purchasing-power-parity theory 452–4

Mill, John Stuart, theory of comparative costs, development 13; comparative advantage, new principle contributed 16, 20; attempted to extend theory of comparative advantage 53; 'Equation of International Demand' 128; protecting duties defended 157

Mundell, Robert, international money 248; balance of payments 270; fiscal and monetary policies to attain external and internal balances 397–8, 403, 406–8; flexible exchange rates 465

Myint, H., infant industry protection 158

National product, criterion to measure effect of trade 172

Offer curve 66–72

Ohlin, B., treatment of interregional and international trade 74; controversy with Keynes on German reparations 319, 371

Orcutt, G., estimates of elasticities 314, 351

Payments agreements, compared with bilateral agreements 494

Production factors, as a cause of price differences 75; nations' different endowments the reasons for trade 77

Production function, defines relation between factor inputs and final output 78; demonstrated by isoquants 79–82; marginal productivities of production factors 83

Pure theory of international trade. Introduction 6; concerned with barter exchange between countries 13; seeks answers to questions of positive and of welfare economics 13; a 'vast body of theorems' 14; algebraic and geometric analyses of concepts 15; gains for participant countries 15; as seen by classical economists 16–19; comparison with autarky 21. *See also* Comparative advantage; Labour, costs of

Ricardo, theory of foreign trade 3; theory of comparative costs 13; theory of comparative advantage 16, 20, 22, 23, 29, 64, 66; comparison with Heckscher–Ohlin theorem 75, 114–15, 117; Bhagwati's criticism 122; comparative cost ratios 127–9; balance-of-payments equilibrium 300; advocated gold bullion standard 529

Robinson, Joan, foreign exchange stability 307

Robinson, Romney, factor proportions account of comparative advantage 73

Scitovsky, T., competitive effect in European Community 211; and scope for trade creation 214; liquidity preference theory of interest rates 343; equilibrating capital flows 344

Second best, theory of 184–8

Smith, Adam, theory of foreign trade 3; theory of comparative costs 13; theory of comparative advantage 16, 20; division of labour 19

Sohmen, E., elasticities approach 351

Special Drawing Rights of IMF, as an international money 249; creation and operation 538–9; allocation scheme 552–6

State trading. Monopoly of country's import and export trade 235; bulk purchase and bilateral agreements 235; state agencies in mixed economies 236; governments as major purchasers 236–7; trading between private enterprise economies and collectivist states 237–8; between two fully collectivist states 238–9; pricing in Eastern bloc a major problem 239–40; state-trading monopoly as a means of control 501

Stern, R. M., labour productivity and comparative advantage 121–2

Stolper–Samuelson theorem 118–19, 124, 161, 176

Swan, Trevor, diagrams of relationships between employment, balance of payments and expenditure 390–6

Swerling, B. C., criticism of Leontief 127

Tariffs. Definition 137, *ad valorem* 137, specific 137, compound 137; tariff schedule — 'single column', 'multi-column' — 138; European Community, border checks still used 138; methods of comparison 138–9; protective effect 139; algebraically demonstrated 140–1; reducing imports 141–3; revenue tariffs 143; other effects distinguished: consumption, revenue, redistribution 144–7; terms of trade 147–56; competitive 156–9; national income 159–61; balance of payments 162; cost 162–8; free trade as opposed to protection 169; conventional arguments for tariffs 175–8; free trade in a two-country, tariff-protected world 180–4; welfare situation when tariffs reduced 184–8; 'quota' system 500–1. *See also* Customs union theory

Taussig, F. W., example of national wage rates for two countries 23; advocates index of time change in export/import quantities ratio 131; capital transfer theory 370–1

Technological change 49–52; three types distinguished 49

Terms of trade 127–33

Tinbergen, J., description of international trade 14; elasticities approach 351

Torrens, R., trade in comparative advantage theory 20

Trade. Domestic and foreign, difference as seen by classical economists 17–19; Ohlin's theory of international trade 74, 76; relative costs' and prices' differences

Index

Trade—*continued*
  disappear as result of trade 77; international trade as a factor proportions theory 78, 99; scarce and abundant factors, proposition examined 118–19; terms of trade defined in price terms 128–30, barter terms 130–1, factoral 132–3, income 133; effects of tariff on 147–56; liberalisation 179; multilateral, IMF's fostering of 545–7
Transport costs 26, 44–9; customs unions influenced by 216–17
Travis, W. P., distortion of trade by tariffs 127
Triffin, R., 'ideal' level of reserves 514
Tripartite Monetary Agreement 437
Tsiang, S. C., speculation in foreign exchange market examined 469

United States dollar, as an international money 248–9

Valavanis-Vail, S., criticism of input–output models in foreign trade examination 127

Vanek, Jaroslav, natural resources factor in U.S. production 125; equilibrium analysis 207
Viner, J., classical theory of international trade, reason for formulation 16; export and import price ratios 130; use of term 'net' 131; 'theory of the second best' 187; customs union theory 189, 191–2, 196–200, 203–4, 216; dumping 228–9; study of price-specie-flow mechanism in Canada 371

Wages, effects of changes in rates on exports and imports 25; in export industries 122; regulated through state of labour market 395
World Bank, formerly International Bank for Reconstruction and Development, establishment of 536–7

Yeager, Leland B., balance-of-payments terminology 266–7; exchange risk as a deterrent to international trade and investment 467
Young, J., definition of cost of Canadian tariff 163–5